THE LIFE AND COMPLETE WORK OF FRANCISCO GOYA

The burial of the sardine   [III.970] c.1812-19. 82·5×52 cm. Royal Academy of San Fernando, Madrid

THE LIFE AND COMPLETE WORK OF

FRANCISCO GOYA

*with 2148 illustrations including
48 colour plates*

HARRISON HOUSE – NEW YORK

The chapters on Goya's life and work, with the exception
of those on the prints, have been translated from French
by Christine Hauch and Juliet Wilson

Original French edition 1970

Text revised for English edition 1971

English edition published in Great Britain under the title
Goya: His Life and Work

Second English edition 1981

This edition is published by Harrison House,
distributed by Crown Publishers, Inc.,
by arrangement with William Morrow & Co., Inc.
h g f e d c b a
HARRISON HOUSE 1981 EDITION

Printed in Hong Kong
by South China Printing Co.

TABLE OF CONTENTS

LIST OF ILLUSTRATIONS

ACKNOWLEDGMENTS

We wish to thank here all those who have assisted us in our undertaking and first of all, in Madrid, Professor Enrique Lafuente Ferrari, eminent art historian and incomparable connoisseur of Goya's œuvre, who has honoured us with a preface to this book and has been most generous with his advice; F. J. Sánchez Cantón, who was Director of the Prado Museum when we first started on our project and whose publications on Goya are essential to any study of his life and work; Diego Angulo Iñíguez, his successor in the Prado and the Director of the Instituto Diego Velázquez whose library and photographic archives he put at our disposal; Xavier de Salas, the present Director of the Prado, author of many penetrating studies on Goya, who assisted us at every stage of our work; A. E. Pérez Sánchez, now Sub-Director of the Prado, who as its librarian and expert documentalist assisted us in many ways. We also wish to thank Elena Paez, Curator of the Department of Prints in the Biblioteca Nacional, who was always ready to help us with the most difficult problems, and Georges Demerson, Conseiller Culturel to the French Embassy in Spain, on whose friendly co-operation we could always count. We are bound to recall here the name of the late Valentín de Sambricio, the tireless researcher to whom students of Goya owe so great a debt. Our book is in large part based on the innumerable documents which he published in connection with the tapestry cartoons and with Goya's life in general. In Barcelona, we were particularly fortunate in the assistance we received from José Gudiol who made available to us not only the archives of the Instituto Amatller but also the manuscript of his catalogue raisonné of Goya's paintings.

In France we appreciated the friendly collaboration of Xavière Desparmet Fitz-Gerald who generously gave us much new information to add to her father's monumental catalogue, one of our principal sources of reference. Among the Goya specialists in France, we wish to thank Jeannine Baticle, Curator in the Department of Paintings at the Musée du Louvre; she kindly communicated to us the results of her own research, in particular that undertaken for the preparation, with A. B. de Vries, former Director of the 'Mauritshuis', of the 1970 Goya exhibition in The Hague and in Paris.

The compilation and illustration of the catalogue owe much to Enriqueta Frankfort Harris, of the Warburg Institute in London; we wish to express a particular debt of gratitude for the kindness and readiness with which she answered questions and gave her advice; she also made available many rare documents in her photographic collection. We must also acknowledge our debt to her brother, the late Tomás Harris, author of the catalogue raisonné of Goya's engravings and lithographs on which our own catalogue is based. The research and checking of the catalogue were mainly carried out in the libraries of the Warburg Institute and of the Victoria and Albert Museum where the staff were tirelessly helpful.

In the United States of America we profited from our personal contacts with Eleanor Sayre, Curator of the Department of Prints and Drawings in the Boston Museum of Fine Arts, whose publications on Goya's drawings and miniatures were indispensable to our work. In New York, Theodore Rousseau, Curator in Chief and Vice-Director of the Metropolitan Museum of Art, gave us valuable assistance. We recall with gratitude the warm welcome which we received in the Frick Art Reference Library and in the Hispanic Society of America.

Throughout the world we experienced kindness and co-operation from museum directors and curators and from private collectors, who provided us with the information essential to the catalogue and gave us permission to reproduce the works in their collections. We must also express our thanks to the many art historians and the historical and literary experts who assisted us in our task, as well as the usually unsung but immensely helpful body of art dealers and auctioneers through whose hands pass so many works of art.

Throughout the years of preparation of this book, we were able to rely on the advice and assistance of our friend Jean Fribourg, and we take this opportunity of expressing all our gratitude for his constant and invaluable support.

Finally, we wish to thank those who collaborated in the production of this book: Marie-José Treichler who organized the documentary material and co-ordinated communications with the authors, Simone Joly who was responsible for the preparation and correction of the texts in the different languages, and Franz Stadelmann who was in charge of technical production. We must add a special word of appreciation for the printers at the Presses Centrales in Lausanne, who overcame the very considerable difficulties posed by the setting and correction of the texts and catalogue in the different languages. The design and lay-out of the book, based on a project by François Lachenal, was entrusted to André Rosselet, Director of 'Ides et Calendes', who handled the extensive and complex material submitted to him in a masterly way.

This book is the result of a common effort and it is dedicated to all Goya's admirers in the hope that reading and consulting it will lead to increased understanding and admiration for the master's work.

PREFACE BY ENRIQUE LAFUENTE FERRARI

When I received a friendly invitation to write some introductory lines to this book I could not refuse since I share with Pierre Gassier and his colleagues, Juliet Wilson and François Lachenal, a common enthusiasm for the inspired and astonishing art of Goya. I have every admiration for their achievement and for their determination to give us a comprehensive account of the work of this great artist to whom, since 1928, I have devoted so much of my time in teaching and research. My own passion for Goya has nothing to do with the fact that he is my compatriot and much to do with the fact that he is a great and universal artist, an investigator of mankind, an intrepid explorer of inner worlds, one of the artists whose creative activity reaches out towards the widest horizons. He is not only a great painter, engraver and draughtsman but also, like his contemporary Beethoven, one of the men who revealed new worlds to mankind through the aesthetic power of his creations. These two artists, living at a time of crisis for Europe, have been able to pass on to us a message, a *frisson nouveau,* which has extended our conception of man to the limits of human understanding.

Goya's message had to wait many years before making itself heard. His fame and works were to some extent confined within Spain, *finis terrae* at the Western edge of Europe, cut off from close communication with the other peoples of our common civilization for historical reasons and because of mistaken national policies, and they were only gradually discovered during the nineteenth century. The *Caprichos* engravings revealed to the French romantics one of the artists whom Baudelaire likened to 'lighthouses' who from time to time illuminate humanity's intuitive understanding of itself; and the influence of Goya's painting on the development of modern art began with Manet and the impressionists and made itself ever more widely felt. But Goya is really many Goyas. There are so many hidden depths which must be explored before his complex œuvre, at once too vast and too obscure, can be grasped and understood. While his *Caprichos* were soon known in France, where they determined the romantics' notion of the artist, his other series of engravings, his paintings and his drawings were only discovered and appreciated more gradually, later on.

Goya is not a limited artist whose work maintains a level of absolute perfection within a small compass; on the contrary, he is a prolific but very unequal artist, capable of scaling the loftiest heights and also of falling headlong into the most dangerous pitfalls. This accounts for the numerous works which are not by his hand but which have been, and still are, attributed to him on the basis of superficial similarities (not to speak of more dishonest motives). Goya is like El Greco and other artists of genius; they have no real disciples but are painters inevitably subject to imitation, and even falsification, by reason of the Dionysiac character of their temperament. 'The Dionysiac artist,' as I have written elsewhere, 'usually fathers only natural children which are consequently the children of his sins rather than of his genius. As in life, these Don Juans of art pay the price of their sins, that is of their carelessness, with the shadow which the bastard productions of their imitators and counterfeiters casts over their œuvre.'

In order to write on Goya it is necessary to be a shrewd and careful connoisseur. This Pierre Gassier and Juliet Wilson certainly are, and they also show proof of their courage in the decision to produce an up-to-date catalogue of his œuvre. This is a difficult task; those that had previously ventured to undertake it had been daring but the time was not ripe. The difficulty is accentuated by the fact that Goya was a most prolific artist (Mayer's catalogue of 1923-25, for example, listed some 900 paintings, more than 700 drawings and nearly 350 engravings and lithographs). Moreover, since the studies by Von Loga (1903) and Mayer our knowledge of the artist has advanced significantly. A considerable number of works, particularly paintings, have had to be eliminated from Mayer's catalogue – and from Calvert's illustrated corpus (1908) – since their attribution is now inadmissible while, although false and doubtful paintings continue to appear in the art market, other unquestionably authentic and documented works have come to light. The same is true of the drawings, and the list of engravings has also been increased by a few examples discovered in recent years. For these reasons it was high time for a successor to Mayer's catalogue and all students of Goya will be grateful to the present authors for fulfilling this need with scholarship and exactitude.

The long years which Pierre Gassier has spent in Spain familiarized him with the large number of Goya's works still preserved in the artist's native country and whose study is still of fundamental importance for any serious understanding of his œuvre. The solid basis which this provided was enriched and complemented by study in the museums and private collections of other countries. It must also be said to his merit that Gassier had already been engaged on the book for a number of years when a disastrous fire destroyed a considerable part of his work. He had to start again, with the help of Juliet Wilson, with a courage of which few would have been capable and which we can only admire.

The catalogue was prepared by Juliet Wilson, with assistance from Pierre Gassier, she herself having worked in close collaboration with the late, lamented Tomás Harris.

The significance of our interest in Goya's art is at once complex and exceptional. For Goya, the great precursor of modern art, is really an example of *art vivant*. As has often, and rightly, been said, all great artists are modern since the major achievements of their aesthetic creation remain permanently valid and are not restricted to the context of the art of their time, even though they belong within it. However, Goya himself constitutes a case apart, for it is only in a few artists that one finds the aesthetic language of the future already formulated. This explains the surprise, the astonishment which he provoked when he became known outside Spain.

It is paradoxical that although Goya was at times criticized by the supporters of the academic art of his day, because they were well aware of the disturbingly nonconformist element in his work, he was nevertheless applauded by contemporary Spanish society. A court painter, fêted by the Spanish aristocracy of his period, always managing to survive the difficult situations created by a nonconformism which was not only aesthetic but also ideological and social, he was in no sense a *peintre maudit*, like so many of the great, misunderstood figures of the nineteenth century. Born in a period of crisis, straddling two centuries and two different societies, Goya was not an artist in an ivory tower, turning his back on the world. He was involved in the pleasures and passions of his time and knew how to express them. However, from a purely pictorial point of view, Goya used his great gifts to interpret his time – as Ortega y Gasset has pointed out – in opposition to the prevailing ideas of the day, which can be summed up in a single word: neoclassicism. We should not forget that Goya was the contemporary of David, the painter of the Revolution and the Empire which he elected to interpret with the cold correctness of his sculptural drawing style. Nothing could be more unlike Goya. On the other hand, we should not be misled into seeing in Goya a romantic *avant la lettre*. Goya cannot be classified and that is where his genius lies; he paves the way for modern art with his freedom of interpretation, his violent technique and his use of distortion. In the face of so revolutionary a genius critics are bound to take sides, and the often-cited points of view of Berenson and Malraux are an instance of this. Berenson judged Goya with admiring indignation: 'Modern anarchy begins with him'. Malraux, committed in favour of contemporary art, said the same thing, but the other way round: 'Goya prefigures the whole of modern art because modern art begins with this liberty.'

Goya also has the same attraction as a summit from which one can look out over two different landscapes. With him we greet the new century, with its accompanying aesthetic and social upheavals, and say a nostalgic farewell to the charms of the *ancien régime*. A double-faced Janus, his backward glance reaches as far as the limits of the baroque, sometimes lingering fondly over sweet rococo delights, but the autumnal glow of this twilight already illuminates the prophetic forebodings of the future. Everyone can find in him the attractions of his preferred aesthetic creed, whatever it may be, and he thus becomes a focus of general admiration. Goya is not only the countryman but also the great precursor of Picasso.

With Goya, as later with Picasso, excess becomes an integral part of modern art. Something profoundly Spanish unites them and it is well known that the Spanish temperament attains real universality only through excess. It was this which led to El Greco's admission to the Spanish *hortus conclusus*, and, although it is true that Velázquez seems to us to be the supreme master of restraint, we should not forget how human, how all too human, his art can be. Spain, a country of sharply defined frontiers set between the Atlantic and the Mediterranean, appears in art as in other fields to mark the ultimate limits of a historical situation: *finis terrae*. The Pyrenees constituted not so much a frontier as an isolating wall, which all great Spaniards in their turn have attempted to break down in search of liberty. Literature easily breaks out of such confinement and crosses the barriers without too much difficulty, but art has only been able to cross them in our own day when Spanish artists went to settle in Paris, the heart of Europe. Goya took a long time to get over the wall, but today there are no longer any obstacles in the way of a universal understanding of his art. This is because art has now abandoned the prejudices in favour of restraint, self-discipline and nobility, maintained for so many centuries, in order to seek expression by way of extremes. Verlaine described the Middle Ages as 'énorme et délicat' and one could say much the same of Goya because, as I have written elsewhere, he is at once rough and exquisitely polished, barbarous and infinitely human. In this he is just like Spain itself, a country of contradictions and paradoxes, the home – to take a contemporary example – both of Unamuno and of Juan Ramón Jiménez.

Goya began as a clumsy heir of the baroque and went on, in his first Madrid period (that of the tapestry cartoons) to acquire a rococo delicacy and a richly coloured palette with which to sing the dying graces of the eighteenth century. But behind the refined charms of European society the distant thunder of revolution was rumbling. The storm which finally broke in a sense found its poetic expression in Goya's denunciation of the sins of a tottering society in *Los Caprichos*. But when the storm reached Spain and it was time for abuses to be purged the country did not cut off its leaders' heads. On the contrary, it sought to defend them because they faced a foreigner, Napoleon, who was attempting to unite Europe by fire and sword. Goya, a son of the people, who believed in the enlightenment and in fraternity among men, poured forth his contempt in the terrible plates of *The Disasters of War*. The portraitist of the fragile beauties of the Bourbon court was capable of developing his art in a completely different direction in keeping with the historical circumstances.

Goya's life is marked by violent crises, some personal (his illnesses, his disappointments), some social (wars and revolutions), and each crisis gave rise to a new Goya, unforeseen and astonishingly different. This has led to the free use of a term from modern physics in describing him as a 'quantic' artist:

one who advances by sudden creative leaps rather than through the steady evolution of his artistic gifts. From 1794, after the illness which left him deaf, distortion triumphs in Goya's painting, beginning with the cabinet pictures in which he was first able to give rein to his 'fantasy and invention'. The period in which he lived afforded him an opportunity to delve into human cruelty and stupidity, which appear in all their nakedness at the time of great historical disasters. As I have written elsewhere, Goya points the finger of accusation at man and this is where his greatness lies, for he had dreamed of a better world. Man, as Goya knew him, could not be interpreted through the elegant, rythmical outlines of a Greek statue (for him neoclassicism was a farce) and he now felt the need to transpose his vision of the world on to canvas with strong, energetic brush-strokes laden with colour, which to some extent – but to some extent only – foreshadow the freedom of the impressionists. However, the brutal vigour of his technique tended to express rather than to describe and here Goya is also in a sense the precursor of the expressionists – one has only to think of the paintings of *The second of May* and *The third of May*.

When the war was over Goya was faced with a new society and the painter of the beribboned young ladies and the gentlemen with dress-swords of the end of the *ancien régime* was confronted by a new figure: the materialistic, concerned, liberal bourgeois of the nineteenth century (the *Session of the Philippines Company, Ramón Satue*). And he had yet to go on to explore the madness and the hallucinations of man's innermost soul in the *Disparates* – with a prophetic intuition of surrealism – and to give life to the most horrifying dreams in the visions of the Quinta del Sordo. Nevertheless, although Goya, like Picasso, proposes innumerable variations on the theme of man, he does not embark on a journey of no return. Both painters can offer us on the one hand havens of peace, on the other the deepest abysses of horror; both can pass from the most furious *allegro* to a *scherzo* full of charm. Goya sees in man the angel and the beast, beauty and horror, and his art can pass abruptly from blasphemy to a smile. His works may express a violent denunciation of the world or radiate a confidence which is full of hope, because the artist knows that there is room for everything in the human condition and that man, in spite of all adversities, can always take a hand in the shaping of his own destiny. Rarely has art expressed such different worlds.

What is important is that Goya is capable of creating such a rich and wide range of expression through purely pictorial means. He is neither a sociologist nor an illustrator; he is an artist who, with his brush, his engraver's tools or his crayons, always manages to find the language to convey what he feels. There is never in his work any internal contradiction between what he wants to say and the means he uses to express it, for Goya knows how to adapt his pictorial or graphic language to the new worlds which he discovers and reveals: the rich impasto and generous use of black found in the naturalists; the fine, separate brush-strokes characteristic of the impressionists; a violent use of the brush or palette-knife which would delight the boldest expressionists; his strange visions of fantastic worlds, where the secret desires of the unconscious are released and which bring him close to the surrealists in the hidden erotic regions which he was one of the first to illuminate. For this reason Goya's painted œuvre, even in its most advanced and prophetic form, must, to be fully understood, be studied in conjunction with the drawings – in particular with those from the last periods of his life – for this frank and intimate part of his work reveals the extraordinary complexity of his inner world.

Goya caresses beauty, denounces horror or mocks with a sarcastic laugh all that is absurd and grotesque in the world in which man lives. His accusing finger points out the good and the evil, the reason and the absurdity which, because human existence is woven from these same threads, are sometimes confused. His major contribution to modern art is a determined affirmation of freedom of expression; he shows the way to an intoxicated acceptance of the absurd – the absurdity which has come to influence modern man and the artistic creations of today. However, Goya avoided breaking those fine links of communicability, without which the work of art has now come to sail – and is sometimes shipwrecked – on the seas of an arbitrary and hermetic subjectivism. Although Goya, who loved liberty so much, succeeded in glimpsing the most distant horizons, he never crossed the line beyond which art becomes dehumanized; from the summits of his art we see the abyss, but we never plunge into it. His art, like life itself, offers us enjoyment or anguish, and contact with Goya's work is therefore not just an exercise in connoisseurship but a deep and unforgettable experience. I hope that this book will serve as a valuable guide to the complex and absorbing world of Goya.

General introduction   1746-1828

CHRONOLOGICAL TABLE 1746-1828

Dates	Life of Goya	Spanish History	History outside Spain	The Arts	Literature and Science
1746	Birth at Fuendetodos	Ferdinand VI king of Spain		Luis Paret; Ramón Bayeu	Pestalozzi († 1827)
1759		Charles III king of Spain		British Museum opened	Voltaire: *Candide*
1763	First visit to Madrid		The Peace of Paris	Reynolds: *Nelly O'Brien*	
1766	Second visit to Madrid	The Esquilache riots	Bougainville's voyage begins	La Tour: *Belle de Zuylen*	Mme de Staël († 1817)
1770	Stay in Italy	Death of Tiepolo in Madrid	Dauphin m. Marie-Antoinette	Beethoven (†1827)	Hölderlin († 1843) Hegel († 1831)
1771	Parma Academy competition Fresco in El Pilar, Saragossa			Houdon: *Diderot*	Walter Scott († 1832)
1773	Marriage with Josefa Bayeu	The fall of Aranda	Jesuit Order suppressed		Gœthe: *Gœtz von Berlichingen*
1774	Paintings for the Aula Dei Goya settles in Madrid		Death of Louis XV Louis XVI king of France		Gœthe: *The Sorrows of Werther*
1775	First tapestry cartoons			Turner (†1851)	Beaumarchais: *Barber of Seville*
1778	Etchings after Velázquez		Death of Pitt	Death of Piranesi (aged 58)	Death of Voltaire (aged 84)
1780	Goya made academician		Death of Maria Theresa	Ingres († 1867)	Nodier († 1844)
1781	Second fresco in El Pilar *The Queen of Martyrs*			Mozart: *Il Seraglio*	Rousseau: *Confessions* Kant: *Critique of Pure Reason*
1784	Birth of his son Francisco Javier († 1854)	Ferdinand VII († 1833) Godoy joins life-guards		Reynolds: *Mrs Siddons* François Rude († 1855)	Stendhal († 1842)
1786	Goya Painter to the King		Death of Frederick II		Mont Blanc climbed
1789	Goya made Court Painter	Coronation of Charles IV and María Luisa	French Revolution The Rights of Man	David: *The Tennis Court Oath*	Lavoisier: *Traité de chimie* Fenimore Cooper († 1851)
1792	Serious illness in Andalusia	Godoy Captain-General	The Convention	Rossini († 1868)	Shelley († 1822)
1796	Second stay in Andalusia Seville, Cadiz, Sanlúcar	Spain at war with England	Napoleon's Italian campaign Death of Catherine II	Corot († 1875)	Gœthe: *Wilhelm Meister* Senefelder invents lithography
1797	*The Madrid album*	Jovellanos Minister of Justice	Treaty of Campo-Formio	Schubert († 1823)	Alfred de Vigny († 1863)
1798	Frescoes in San Antonio de la Florida	Godoy replaced as prime minister by Urquijo	Egyptian expedition	Delacroix († 1863) Haydn: *The Creation*	A. Comte († 1857) Michelet († 1874)
1799	Publication of the *Caprichos* Goya First Court Painter		Death of Washington Coup d'Etat of 18 Brumaire	Beethoven: *Pathétique Sonata*	Pushkin († 1837) Balzac († 1850)
1800	*The Family of Charles IV* *The Countess of Chinchón*	Urquijo dismissed Godoy in power again	Murat takes Milan The Battle of Marengo	Ceán Bermúdez: *Dictionary of artists*	Volta produces electricity Cuvier: *Leçons d'anatomie*
1802	Death of the Duchess of Alba		Bonaparte Consul for life	Gérard: *Mme Récamier*	Victor Hugo († 1885)
1805	Marriage of Javier with Gumersinda Goicoechea	Battle of Trafalgar	Napoleon, king of Italy, dethrones Bourbons of Naples	Beethoven: *Fidelio*	Châteaubriand: *René* Death of Schiller
1806	Birth of Mariano Goya († 1874)		Berlin and Warsaw taken by Napoleon	Death of Fragonard (aged 74)	Hegel: *Phenomenology of Spirit*
1808	The *Majas* inventoried in Godoy's collection From 1810 Goya etches the *Disasters of War*	Abdication of Charles IV Riots in Madrid (2 May) Joseph made king of Spain War of Independence begins		Beethoven: *Pastoral Symphony* Daumier († 1879)	Gérard de Nerval († 1855) Barbey d'Aurevilly († 1889)
1812	Death of Josefa Bayeu Inventory of the property	Wellington in Madrid Constitution of Cadiz	Napoleon's Russian campaign	Turner: *Hannibal crossing the Alps*	Byron: *Childe Harold* Dickens († 1870)
1814	Goya paints the *Second of May* and *Third of May 1808*	Return of Ferdinand VII	Napoleon abdicates Return of Louis XVIII	Ingres: *The Grande Odalisque*	Stephenson invents the steam locomotive
1816	Publication of *La Tauromaquia*				
1819	Buys the 'Quinta del Sordo' First lithographs *St Joseph of Calasanz* Serious illness	Death of Charles IV and María Luisa in Rome Opening of the Prado Museum	The United States buys Florida from Spain	Géricault: *Raft of the Medusa* Chassériau († 1856) Offenbach († 1880)	First Atlantic crossing by steamship Walt Whitman († 1892) Ruskin († 1900)
1820	Works on 'black paintings' and *Disparates* prints (1820-23)	Revolt of Riego Liberal period (1820-23)	Napoleon on Saint Helena since 1815 (†1821)		Walter Scott: *Kenilworth* Engels († 1895)
1823	Donation of the 'Quinta del Sordo' to Mariano	France sends the 'Cent Mille Fils de Saint Louis' to Spain	Monroe doctrine enunciated	Beethoven: *Ninth Symphony*	E. Renan († 1892)
1824	Departure for France. Paris. Settles in Bordeaux	Absolutist régime until Ferdinand VII's death (1833)	Death of Louis XVIII Charles X king of France	Paris Salon (Delacroix, Ingres, Constable, Bonington)	Death of Byron
1825	*The Bulls of Bordeaux* (lithographs)		Death of Alexander I Nicholas I emperor of Russia	Death of David	Pushkin: *Boris Godunov*
1826	Visit to Madrid				Heine: *Reisebilder*
1828	Death of Goya in Bordeaux	Goya paintings in the Prado	Wellington and Peel in office	Berlioz: *Symphonie fantastique*	Tolstoy († 1910)

When we consider Goya's work as a whole, from the first academic competition in 1763 until his death in 1828, two things strike us: on the one hand, the span of this artistic career which began in the eighteenth century baroque period and ended, sixty-five years later, in the feverish intensity of European romanticism; on the other hand, the slow maturing of a creative force which only achieved its full expression when the artist was in his fifties.

The crockery vendor   [1.125] 1778. 259×220 cm. Prado Museum, Madrid

As a sturdy son of Aragon, of Basque descent, the time and place of Goya's birth and the length of his life exposed him firstly to the pleasures and aspirations of an enlightened Spain under Charles III, then to the corruption of the reign of Charles IV, which led to the martyrdom of his country under the Napoleonic occupation, and finally to the chaotic years of the confrontation between liberalism and the tyranny of Ferdinand VII, which forced him to end his life in exile. Yet although these extreme changes in the course of history made an impression on his art and were often a direct source of inspiration, they do not suffice to explain it. Goya was a contemporary of David, and he might well have become the David of Spain. His stay in Italy and the lessons of Mengs could have disposed him better than anyone for such a rôle. But the great current of neo-classicism which flowed from Winckelmann's theories failed to move him. He was too deeply rooted in the Spanish tradition to be swept along by alien fashions. This does not mean that he remained apart from the aesthetic influences and movements of his time. No one could have been more interested than he in new ideas nor experimented more boldly with different styles and techniques, with painting in oils or in fresco, with miniature painting, with drawing, etching and lithography. Despite the sometimes bewildering diversity of his enormous œuvre, he was able, even though not until fairly late in life, to give it a coherence and a striking individuality which is profoundly Spanish and at the same time universal in its appeal. Goya has become totally identified with Spain – or at least with the image of Spain which most of us cherish and for which he may well have been responsible – and at the same time with humanity in general, since his portrayal of the human predicament is so deeply felt.

It has become a commonplace to say that if Goya had died at the age of forty-five – which would have made him much older than Raphael, Watteau, Caravaggio, Géricault, Van Gogh or Seurat – his name would have been lost among the hordes of dull, second-rate artists. The terrible illness which almost killed him in 1792-1793, and whose exact nature is still uncertain, marked a decisive turning point in both his life and his art. So *See p. 105* radical was the change that it has sometimes led to the notion of two antithetical Goyas: the first, a gay young man leading a highly colourful life, handling the dagger as skilfully as the *muleta* (the matador's sword), a seducer of nuns and aristocratic ladies, the painter of the tapestry cartoons; then, hard on his heels, the second, his dark twin, the creative genius at the mercy of his passions, taking refuge in the lofty rôle of philosopher-painter, denouncing the vices of his times and the horrors of war and finally sinking into the esoteric obscurity of the 'black paintings', having assured himself a place in the calendar of popular saints as a martyr to Liberty. Even when stripped of the myth and legend surrounding his *Bibl. 102, pp. 330-332* life, Goya appears as a kind of two-headed giant, looking nostalgically back towards the eighteenth century and at the same time prophetically contemplating the new paths which he had opened to the art of the future.

In direct contrast to this essentially romantic conception of Goya's art, we now have *Part one 1746-1792* the much more reasoned and subtle conclusions of present-day scholarly research. Very detailed studies have shown the first period of Goya's life, from 1746 to 1792, to be considerably richer than was previously thought. The painter of the tapestry cartoons was also a sought-after religious painter, a portraitist of merit and a practised fresco painter; in short, an artist already experienced in a wide diversity of techniques and styles. Indeed, the paintings executed before 1792 now include more than a third of all the paintings catalogued. This is not surprising when we consider that Goya must have spent these early years working extremely hard in order to establish a position for himself at court.

However, although there is now far more information available, it has become more difficult to form a balanced opinion concerning Goya's early work, since increased knowledge has inevitably modified any general view. There is a danger that excessive specialisation may prove as distorting as extreme romanticism and could as easily succeed in falsifying the critic's judgments. It is therefore necessary to resist the enthusiasms justified

'Fine advice' Caprichos pl. *15* [II.481] 1797-98. Etching and aquatint

by research and still more by 'discoveries', and to base our judgment on those works whose quality and indisputable authenticity provide a standard for the artist's work as a whole.

We then realize that the importance which may be accorded to this or that religious or mythological subject of the early period, or even to a portrait as enchanting as that of *Ill. p. 59* the Countess of Chinchón as a little girl [1.210], is only justified by the existence of the great works for which they are the preparation and which they contain perhaps in embryo.

17

In themselves, most of the works which Goya painted before reaching maturity have little more value than those of his contemporaries, but any consideration of them is automatically affected by the knowledge that they were created by an artist who became a great master. Even a work as important in many respects as the huge fresco of the *Queen of Martyrs* [1.177], in the basilica of El Pilar at Saragossa, acquires an extra dimension because it cannot be separated from the marvellous frescoes of San Antonio de la Florida [11.717-735]. Every effort is thus made to discover traces of genius in the early work whereas, if Goya had succumbed to his illness in 1793, the same work would arouse no more than documentary interest.

Ill. pp. 52-54

We could go further and point out that many of Goya's fellow artists have only acquired a reputation because of his existence and because their names and their works have taken on some of the lustre which he shed over his period. Without him, the fine arts in Spain in the eighteenth and even in the nineteenth century would arouse little interest. Without the titanic figure who made them known to later generations, the Bayeu brothers, Maella, Paret, del Castillo, Esteve, Juliá and others would be no more than obscure names, kept alive by the curiosity of scholars. To understand why it took Goya thirty years to find himself, we must recall the extremely low level to which painting had fallen in Spain after 1750. Charles III realized this when he arrived from Naples in 1759 and lost no time in summoning Mengs and Tiepolo from Italy in the hope of injecting new blood into Spanish art.

It was within this virtual wasteland that Goya's artistic talent developed. In Saragossa, as later in Madrid, he was surrounded by academic routine, the polishing and repolishing of a soulless craft, under the strict guidance of Luzán and then of Mengs and Bayeu, the impassive guardians of what they sincerely believed to be an Ideal Beauty. There was no work to be seen which might have aroused his youthful enthusiasm. The great set pieces of Giaquinto, of González Velázquez or of Giordano can only have moved him to polite admiration. The one exceptional figure was Tiepolo who was in Madrid with his sons at the time of the two Academy competitions in which Goya took part; the young artist would have been struck by his virtuosity and by the warmth of his palette which contrasted with the cold tones sanctioned by Mengs. At the age of twenty-five, Goya also had the advantage of a stay in Italy. Little is known about the journey but it must have given him his first major experience of the world of painting and made him feel all the more keenly the artistic void in Saragossa and Madrid. Nevertheless, he did not immediately find the self-assurance to fight alone against the established order through which lay the only path to success.

See pp. 36-37

Goya's long career began, therefore, in the context of a prevailing mediocrity which he did not think to challenge. Madrid at that time was a small capital where a painter could have no hope of success outside the court. There were no great patrons, no Crozat, no Pompadour, only the all-powerful Mengs and the Academy. Goya's marriage to the sister of Francisco Bayeu, whose pupil he had been, confirmed his position within this artistic circle and he became one of its most promising members. All the more ambitious for having failed to achieve official success until then, Goya had but one aim: to equal or even perhaps to surpass his brother-in-law, already an academician at the age of thirty-one, Court Painter at thirty-three and soon, after Mengs' final departure, recognized as the first painter in Spain. Given these circumstances, one might well wonder how it was possible that, twenty-five years later, the same man could have engraved the *Caprichos* [11.451-613], executed the frescoes in San Antonio de la Florida [11.717-735], and painted the portraits of the *Countess of Chinchón* and the *Family of Charles IV* [11.783, 793]. The reason why it took him so long to find himself was no doubt that he had to sustain a long battle both against his environment and against himself.

Ill. pp. 42, 246

If it is true that the strongest personalities have almost always had to make their way against the prevailing taste of their period, it is also true that there have been few periods

The Countess of Chinchón   [II.793] 1800. 174·2 × 144 cm. Duke of Sueca, Madrid

The third of May 1808   [III.984] 1814. 266×345 cm. Prado Museum, Madrid

as uninspiring as Goya's. Everything that he was later to bring to modern art was directly opposed to the academic and neo-classic current of his day. As has been said, under the guidance of Mengs and Bayeu he might well have become the David of Spain. In fact, he became the anti-David *par excellence* and, as Malraux so aptly expressed it, 'an anti-Italian, an artist for whom art and beauty are distinct concepts'. But to break with the cult of an Ideal Beauty which Mengs and his disciples wished to enthrone at the court of Madrid meant a hard struggle, all the harder because he was alone. Delacroix at least had an opponent in Ingres, and Seurat his own impressionist friends whom he could disown. Goya did not even have an adversary of his own stature, hence perhaps the often repeated image of the solitary colossus or a giant assailed by dwarfs [III.946, 985, IV.1611].

Ill. p. 215

Goya also fought a battle against his own nature, for until the age of forty he appears to have been a vigorous, full-blooded, even violent man, inclined towards tangible pleasures like chocolate-drinking and partridge shooting. Although there is no reliable evidence to show that he was in fact the adventurer that has been described, he nevertheless remains the contrary of what today would be called an 'intellectual'. His general culture was virtually non-existent; everything he learned was self-taught. He had a great deal of good sense and intuition, was a lively and intelligent observer of everything around him, but cared little about the new ideas which, in Spain as elsewhere, provided the intellectual nourishment of his times. For Goya, painting itself was no more than a profession. If he applied himself to it with zeal he might win fame and fortune but it involved no deep creative urge and even less a sense of lofty purpose. His letters to Zapater show that he considered hunting a much more delightful pastime.

The culture which he acquired, and which was much more extensive than has often been thought, was linked to a new need for a deeper understanding of human problems. The fruits of his reflection were all the richer and their effect all the more powerful because the ground which nourished them retained its rude vigour to the end. Goya's spiritual and intellectual development, which was to have such an important effect on his work, owed its first impulse to the new circles in which he moved after 1780 and above all to the

Ill. p. 133 inspiration of his friendship with Jovellanos whom he met as early as 1780 in the Academy. He was also introduced to the enlightened society of the great families, with their cosmo-

Ill. pp. 64, 65 politan culture – the Medinacelis, the Benavente-Osunas, the Altamiras. Even so, friend-ship and environment do not explain everything. There were deeper causes which have been called the crises of Goya's life. These crises nearly always occurred at the time of more or less serious illnesses which, as they limited the physical capacities of the *bon vivant*, seem to have brought him to a consideration of more serious things than the simple pleas-ures of life. These periods of withdrawal within himself are always characterized by a renewed interest in more private forms of expression, in particular in drawings and prints.

'Useful work' Album E.*37*   [III.1406] Private coll., Paris

Goya's life is marked by a series of such crises which indicate the different stages in his spiritual evolution and the corresponding deepening and maturing of his artistic powers. Two of these crises, the illnesses of 1793 and 1819, were so serious and he escaped death by such a hair's breadth, that he himself and his subsequent work were profoundly affected. The first illness, which left him stone deaf, led not only to the series of small pictures shown to the Academy [II.317-330], in which fantasy and invention are first given free rein, but also to the two albums of drawings, known as the Sanlúcar and Madrid albums, from which emerged Goya's first work of universal significance, the *Caprichos* etchings [II.356-613]. The second illness, from which his friend Dr Arrieta just succeeded in saving him [IV.1629], corresponds to the period of the *Disparates* etchings and of the 'black paintings' [IV.1571-1627a] and probably also of a considerable part of the later albums of drawings [III.1244-1518]. We shall see later to what extent this illness influenced the mysterious 'black paintings' and what interpretation can be deduced as a result.

See pp. 313-318

Apart from these two great confrontations with death, other less violent crises marked the course of his life and work. The first of these, which is rarely discussed because Goya was only thirty-one at the time and less deeply affected by it, is nonetheless significant. In a letter of April 1777 to his friend Zapater, he wrote that he had 'only just escaped alive'; by July 1778 he had partially completed his series of etchings after paintings by Velázquez. These are not very accomplished works and their artistic value is slight, but they record a decisive encounter in his life. Velázquez, the incomparable magician of the *Meninas*, was Goya's first real master and beside him all the painter-theorists of his day were suddenly reduced to dwarfs. In fact it was Mengs himself who had advised young painters to copy and imitate Velázquez as the master of the 'natural style', who had so perfectly understood 'the effect of air circulating between different objects, making them appear at a distance from each other'. Mengs, however, did not follow his own excellent advice.

Ill. pp. 49, 50

See pp. 48-50

For Goya this was the first ray of light in the darkness, the first lesson from which he really benefited and which he was to remember all his life. Its immediate effects can be seen in the tapestry cartoons which occupied him at this time. The pleasant scenes which he was painting in company with the Bayeu brothers, Maella, del Castillo and others, gradually became distinguishable from those of his rivals by a 'natural' quality which he had learnt from Velázquez and began to apply to these purely decorative works. Even before he painted the great series of cartoons in 1786-1788, of which the sketch for the *Meadow of San Isidro* is the most advanced and perfect achievement [I.272], the influence is already apparent in the *Fair at Madrid* and the *Crockery Vendor* of 1778-1779 [I.124, 125]. The pupil of Bayeu has already become a disciple of Velázquez.

Ill. pp. 15, 67

There can be no doubt that the very serious illness to which he succumbed in 1792-1793, in the house of his friend Sebastián Martínez in Cadiz, marked the great turning point in his life and work. But the change had already been prepared by his age and by his frame of mind some time before his illness. The last years of the reign of Charles III, from 1783 to 1788, had been for Goya a time of carefree happiness and rapturous success; he was in constant demand with the great families for whom he painted portraits [I.206-214, 219-221, 231-233], religious pictures [I.234, 240-245] and decorative works [I.248-254], and after his nomination as Painter to the King, in 1786, he must have thought that he was well set to enjoy a long period of ease and comfort in his new rôle as court artist. But by 1790, the deep rumblings of the French Revolution could be heard even in Madrid and friends like Cabarrús, Jovellanos and Ceán Bermúdez were troubled. Goya himself fell ill in the autumn, after a stay in Saragossa, and wrote to Zapater, 'I have taken it into my head that I ought to maintain a firm line and preserve a certain dignity which a man ought to possess . . .' At the age of forty-four, Goya seems to have become a different man, capable of sacrificing the pleasures of his youth to his new 'line'. He does not specify what that means but it is of no importance; the essential point is that he was already feeling the

Part two 1792-1808

See p. 68

Asmodea or The witches' sabbath   [IV.1620] 1820-23. 123×265 cm. Prado Museum, Madrid

need for something else in his life. The thought of continuing to paint endless tapestry cartoons rankled and in April 1790 he categorically refused to do so. It seemed to him that the compromises and restraints entailed in painting commissioned works were hindering his development. Appointed Court Painter in 1789, he began to dream of liberty at the very moment when liberty itself became suspect.

Given his attitude at the time, it is hardly surprising that his illness should have had such a decisive effect on his mental and physical balance. The first consequence was his awareness of something which he had probably suspected for some time, namely that the hour of liberty had struck not only for nations but for Art. He was learning to live in a confused world of pain and silence, where his feelings were far more intense than his reasoning, and where only one word seemed capable of expressing this great idea: *capricho*. This word, which is widely known as the title of his great series of etchings, was applied by Goya and his contemporaries to all those works which represented the free expression of his genius, whether in prints or drawings or small paintings. But for a Court Painter in the service of the kings of Spain the realization of such an ideal appeared virtually impossible, since an artist could only survive by submitting to the demands of official or private commissions. Goya's extraordinary achievement, which may be unique in the history of painting, lies not in the fact that he engraved and published the *Caprichos* prints, which were the fruit of new ideas and a new aesthetic, but in that he imposed a boldly anti-academic, modern art upon the academic conventions of his time, even in the most official commissions, such as the frescoes of San Antonio de la Florida of 1798, and the portraits

Ill. pp. 19, 141-145, 149   of the *Family of Charles IV* and the *Countess of Chinchón*, both of 1800. Having submitted for some thirty years to the yoke of commissions, though not always with a good grace, Goya now subjected them to the newly unleashed creative power which was to impel him onwards for the remaining thirty years of his career. During this long period until his death, his *capricho* played an ever more important rôle in his work, although this rôle inevitably became an increasingly secret one because of the events which affected Spain so cruelly.

Part three 1808-1819   2 May 1808 is a date which is engraved on the heart of every Spaniard, for it symbolizes the unconquerable courage of his race and the thirst for liberty of an entire nation.

23

For Goya's art it meant another great crisis, though this time a collective one: the bloody ordeal which produced a whole series of works on the themes of liberty and violence. Publicly, these were dominated by the two paintings of the *Second of May* and the *Third of May* [III.982, 984], and in secret by the apocalyptic series of etchings of the *Disasters of War* [III.993-1139]. As a painting which no longer looks towards an Ideal Beauty but seeks to express what another great Spaniard, Miguel de Unamuno, has called 'the tragic sense of life', the *Executions of the Third of May* represents in many ways the birth of the art of our time. With this picture Goya gave to history painting, the old war horse of classical art, a completely new significance which only Delacroix after him was able to uphold. He put an end to the noble and edifying portrayal of the death of historical heroes whose names are carved in memory's marble halls. For the first time he showed the death of a hero as an ignoble event. Moreover, his hero had no name, he stood as a symbol of the People: not the people who had amused themselves so agreeably in the tapestry cartoons and the *sainetes* (comic sketches) of Ramón de la Cruz, but the people who had shed their blood in the guerilla war and who, conscious of their new-found strength, were surging forward to take their place in history. With a remarkable intuition of the major rôle which this new symbolic figure was to play, Goya gave him a predominant place in his work after 1808, whether as isolated figures who affirm the dignity of manual work, or in groups or even crowds which he knew how to combine with an astonishing economy of means. One thinks of a whole series of pictures which are among his most powerful works: the *Burial of the sardine*, the *Flagellants*, the *Bullfight* and the *Inquisition scene*, all in the Academy of San Fernando in Madrid [III.966-970], the *Water-carrier*, the *Knife-grinder*, the *Forge* [III.963-965], the *Making of gunpowder* and the *Making of shot* [III.980, 981], and the *Colossus* [III.946], not to mention the numerous small paintings of bandits, prisoners, plague victims and scenes of execution, robbery, rape and murder, all born of the war [III.914-945]. Similar or identical figures and scenes occur throughout his graphic work of this period, in the *Disasters of War* and *Tauromaquia* prints and drawings and in the three hundred odd drawings which make up four distinct albums [III.993-1518]. With this vast realist fresco Goya claimed his place both as one of the great artists of the nineteenth century and as the equal of his masters, Velázquez and Rembrandt.

Ill. pp. 20, 206

Ill. pp. 2, 211-215, 240, 244, 245

See pp. 216-239

It is difficult to believe that having reached a degree of maturity in his art which was already sufficient to make him outstanding, Goya should nevertheless have continued to surpass himself. At the age of seventy-three, he was to add an almost supernatural dimension to his vision of the world. It was the last and very serious 'crisis' of 1819 which produced this new change. The illness, which was almost responsible for his death once again, must have been so critical and death so close that he dedicated to Dr Arrieta a moving picture in which he shows himself half-dying in the arms of the man who saved him.

Part four 1819-1824

Ill. p. 307

At an interval of twenty years the same relationship was established between his illness and his work in its dual aspect of painting and engraving. In 1798-1799 he had worked on the frescoes in San Antonio de la Florida [II.717-735] and the *Caprichos* prints [II.451-613]; after 1819 came the 'black paintings' and part of the *Disparates* prints [IV.1571-1627a]. The first two are the works of an eighteenth-century artist who has just discovered a new artistic language; the last two – also a combination of mural paintings and etchings – show the extent to which he has succeeded in freeing himself from all restraint and in transcending the tragedies and delusions of his time. In the mysterious ambiguity of the 'black paintings' and the *Disparates* prints, we each recognize our own dreams and also the monsters we hide within us. Until now no one has been able to explain the significance of the 'black paintings' or to suggest why Goya should have wished to make these disturbing visions the setting of his daily life in the Quinta del Sordo. Perhaps Goya himself would have been unable to reply to such questions. Various learned theories have been put forward but they tend to attribute to the artist the erudition of their authors and succeed in establishing between these paintings relationships of such subtlety that they

See pp. 308-320

The milkmaid of Bordeaux   [v.1667] 1825-27. 74×68 cm. Prado Museum, Madrid

seem quite incompatible with the artist's temperament. Goya was undoubtedly a much more cultivated man than has often been supposed, but we should beware of falling into the opposite excess of crediting him with a degree of knowledge and learning which his known character and behaviour do not confirm. Such attempts make no allowance for the spontaneous nature of the creative act through which the artist expresses in plastic form the most deeply rooted and fundamentally individual aspects of his emotional life. These forms are all the more difficult for the artist to explain since, as in the case of the 'black paintings', they lie outside the sphere of logical reasoning.

The term 'crisis' is perhaps more appropriate to this period of Goya's life than to any other, since it seems to have been a time of extreme mental and emotional stress following his close encounter with death. The last works, executed in France after he had given the Quinta to his grandson, Mariano, are noticeably more serene, as if he had exorcized the demons which tormented him by transposing them onto the walls of his house. This greater tranquillity was due not only to his improved health but also to the quiet life which he finally came to lead in Bordeaux, far from dangerous political disturbances, and with Leocadia Weiss and above all her little daughter Rosario beside him. Part five 1824-1828

The daily presence of this child, whom he loved with all the blind affection of a father, seems to have communicated a certain tenderness and calm to his last works and in particular to the ravishing *Milkmaid of Bordeaux* [v.1667] which represents his final artistic state-ment, the last lesson of an old master close to death. As he never tired of repeating to the few faithful friends who remained with him, it is only Nature, the supreme mistress, who counts, and in a picture everything remains to be done if one has not succeeded in capturing that 'magic of the atmosphere' which Velázquez had taught him fifty years before. Ill. p. 25

Part one

1746-1792

Dates	Life of Goya	Spanish History	History outside Spain	The Arts	Literature and Science
1746	Birth at Fuendetodos Ramón Bayeu (†1793) Martín Zapater (†18..?)	Ferdinand VI King of Spain (†1759)		Luis Paret (†1799)	Pestalozzi (†1827) Monge (†1818)
1748		Birth of Charles IV (†1819)	Treaty of Aix-la-Chapelle	Louis David (†1825) Discovery of Pompeii	Montesquieu: *L'Esprit des Lois* Volume I of *L'Encyclopédie*
1751		Birth of María Luisa of Parma (†1819)			
1756	José Alvárez de Toledo, future Duke of Alba (†1796)		Pitt is British Prime Minister	Piranesi: *Antichita Romane* Mozart (†1791)	Voltaire: *Essai sur les Mœurs*
1759		Charles III King of Spain (†1788)		Opening of the British Museum	Voltaire: *Candide* Schiller (†1805)
1760	Goya in the studio of Luzán in Saragossa Leandro de Moratín (†1828)			Gainsborough: *Admiral Hawkins*	Rousseau: *La Nouvelle Héloïse* Macpherson: *Ossian*
1761	Mengs (33) arrives in Madrid	Family Compact with France		Greuze: *The Village Bride* Glück: *Orpheus and Eurydice*	
1762	María Teresa Cayetana, Duchess of Alba (†1802) Tiepolos arrive in Madrid	Anglo-Spanish war	The trial of Calas at Toulouse	Gabriel builds Petit Trianon at Versailles (1762-68)	Rousseau: *Emile*; *The Social Contract* André Chénier (†1794)
1763	Competition of the Academy of San Fernando in Madrid Fr. Bayeu settles in Madrid		The Peace of Paris	Reynolds: *Nelly O'Brien*	Voltaire: *Treatise on Tolerance*
1766	Competition of the Academy of San Fernando in Madrid	The Esquilache riots Manuel Godoy (†1851)	Bougainville circumnavigates the world (1766-69)	La Tour: *Belle de Zuylen*	Mme de Staël (†1817)
1768		Mariano de Urquijo (†1817)	Cook's voyage (1768-71)	Winckelmann murdered	Chateaubriand (†1848)
1769	Mengs returns to Rome		Napoleon Bonaparte (†1821)	Lawrence (†1830)	Cuvier (†1832)
1770	Death of G. B. Tiepolo. His son Domenico returns to Italy Goya in Italy		The Dauphin marries Marie-Antoinette	Death of Boucher (aged 67) Gérard (†1837) Beethoven (†1827)	Hölderlin (†1843) Hegel (†1831) Wordsworth (†1850)
1771	Parma Academy competition Goya back in Saragossa Fresco for the *coreto* in El Pilar			Houdon: *Diderot*	Walter Scott (†1832)
1773	Goya marries Josefa Bayeu in Madrid	Aranda out of office	Clement XIV suppresses the Jesuit Order		Gœthe: *Gœtz von Berlichingen*
1774	Paintings for the Aula Dei near Saragossa Mengs calls Goya to Madrid		Louis XVI succeeds Louis XV		Gœthe: *The Sorrows of Werther*
1775	First tapestry cartoons			Turner (†1851)	Beaumarchais: *The Barber of Seville*
1777	Mengs returns to Rome	Floridablanca Prime Minister			
1778	Etchings after Velázquez		Death of Pitt	Death of Piranesi (aged 58)	Buffon: *Epoques de la nature*
1780	Goya and Jovellanos made academicians Frescoes for El Pilar cupola in Saragossa (1780-82)		Death of Maria Theresa	Ingres (†1867) Houdon: *Voltaire*	Nodier (†1844) Wieland: *Oberon*
1781	Royal commission for San Francisco el Grande			Mozart: *Il Seraglio*	Rousseau: *Confessions* Kant: *Critique of Pure Reason*
1783	*Portrait of Floridablanca* Stay with the Infante D. Luis		Great Britain recognizes the United States of America	Gainsborough: *The Bailey Family*	Montgolfier's flight in a gas balloon
1784	Birth of Francisco Javier Goya (†1854)	Ferdinand VII (†1833) Founding of the Spanish Company of the Philippines		Reynolds: *Mrs Siddons* F. Rude (†1855)	Stendhal (†1842)
1785	Commissions from the Osunas Goya made Deputy-director of Painting at the Academy	Death of the Infante D. Luis	The affair of the Diamond Necklace	Mozart: *Marriage of Figaro* David: *The Oath of the Horatii*	Manzoni (†1873)
1786	Goya Painter to the King Tapestry cartoons for El Pardo (1786-88)		Death of Frederick II		Mont Blanc first climbed Arago (†1853)
1787	Paintings for the convent of Santa Ana at Valladolid			Mozart: *Don Giovanni*	Bernardin de Saint-Pierre: *Paul et Virginie*
1788	Paintings for the cathedral at Valencia	Death of Charles III Charles IV King of Spain	French States General summoned	Death of La Tour (aged 84) Houdon: *Washington*	Founding of 'The Times' in London
1789	Goya made Court Painter Royal portraits	Coronation of Charles IV and María Luisa	Storming of the Bastille *Declaration of the Rights of Man*	David: *The Tennis Court Oath* Death of Joseph Vernet	Lavoisier: *Traité de la chimie élémentaire*
1791	Last tapestry cartoons		Death of Mirabeau	Mozart: *The Magic Flute*; *Requiem*	J. Boswell: *Life of Johnson*
1792	Goya ill in Cadiz	Aranda reinstated, then succeeded by Godoy	The Convention Trial of Louis XVI	Death of Reynolds (aged 69) Rossini (†1868)	Moratín: *La Comedia Nueva* Shelley (†1822)

SPAIN IN THE EIGHTEENTH CENTURY. ABSOLUTE MONARCHY CHARLES III, AN ENLIGHTENED DESPOT

1700-1800. Reigns of Philip V of Bourbon (1746), grandson of Louis XIV, of his sons Ferdinand VI (1759) and Charles III (1788), and of Charles IV. Centralization of the administration in Madrid under Charles III; expansion of industry and commerce. In 1787 Spain had ten million inhabitants.

Self-portrait (detail) [26] c.1771-75
Marchioness of Zurgena, Madrid

Charles III and his court

Spain has always been a land of extreme contrasts to which her inhabitants are subjected as to some inevitable destiny from which only the mightiest efforts can free them. In the eighteenth century these contrasts were even more marked because the peculiar geographical structure of the country was accentuated by inadequate means of communication between one province and another. The compartmentalization of the kingdom was noted by everyone who travelled within it, starting with those Spaniards – admittedly not very many – who, like Jovellanos, were interested in visiting their country and studying the way in which it worked. How much in common could there be between the regions of the *meseta* (the central plateau) with its barren soil and extreme climate – 'nine months winter, three months swelter', according to the saying – and the rich Basque or Catalan provinces which were highly cultivated and well-populated with hardworking people? Everyone considered himself first and foremost Navarrese, Catalan, Aragonese or Castilian rather than Spanish and though successive monarchs from Philip II onwards had attempted to set up a centralized administration in Madrid, this was far from being achieved.

But with the accession of Charles III in 1759 a new era dawned for the capital and for the whole country. This forty-three year old monarch had already reigned for twenty-five years in Naples and was to remain on the Spanish throne for nearly thirty (1759-1788). Though he was undisguisedly ugly and cut a far from brilliant figure, he governed wisely and took gradual steps to enrich and modernize Spain. Madrid, in particular, owes a great deal to him. He improved the roads, had street lighting installed and, to ensure that thieves and murderers should not escape the law, he banned the wearing of the cape and wide sombrero. This interference with such fundamentally Spanish habits of dress provoked the so-called Esquilache riots, which forced the king to flee the capital and then dismiss his minister. (Esquilache was a Sicilian who became Minister of both Finance and War and his unpopularity, which almost led to his death at the hands of the rioting mob in March 1766, was probably connected with the expulsion of the Jesuits from Spain shortly afterwards.) In another field, Charles III also continued and expanded the work of artistic renovation undertaken by his predecessors. He summoned to the court of Madrid two of the greatest painters in Europe, Mengs and Tiepolo, and gave them the task of completing the decoration of the new royal palace. He was also responsible for laying-out the Paseo del Prado, which became the most fashionable meeting-place in Madrid, and alongside it the magnificent Botanical Gardens. The church of San Francisco el Grande was completed and the best court painters, Goya among them, were commissioned to decorate its chapels. Throughout the kingdom the network of roads was extended or improved. Finally, Charles III and his ministers were responsible for encouraging the widespread creation of the Societies of Friends of the Country which contributed so much to the economic development of the kingdom through the impetus of exceptional men such as Campomanes, Jovellanos and Olávide.

Even so, there is no point in comparing the court of the king of Spain to that of his cousin at Versailles or even to that of Frederick of Prussia. The court of Madrid was characterized by austerity and monotony and had lain frozen since the sixteenth century in a rigid ceremonial. Charles III led a very simple life, indulging in no kind of extravagance. Mindful of the affairs of the kingdom, he held frequent consultations with his ministers and with foreign ambassadors whom he questioned about the political life of their respective countries. The rest of the day was devoted to hunting, to his family and to prayer.

During the year the court divided its time between the various royal residences: the winter months were spent at the royal palace in Madrid, except for a few weeks at the palace of El Pardo after Epiphany. When Holy Week was over the court moved to Aranjuez, an oasis of running waters and woodland thirty-six miles from the capital. Then in July it went to the palace of La Granja which perched on the slopes of the Sierra de Guadarrama and was surrounded by a park laid out by Philip V in the manner of Versailles. Finally, at the beginning of October, the court installed itself for the autumn at San Lorenzo del Escorial, in the vast palace still haunted by the spirit of Philip II. About 10 December it returned to Madrid to await the new year when the same royal progress would be repeated, on the same dates and with the same complicated ceremonial.

Beneath the king and the princes of the blood came the nobility. Eighteenth-century Spain had a surfeit of nobles: when a census was taken in 1787, of the ten million or so inhabitants of the kingdom, about five hundred thousand were members of the nobility. They ranged from mere hidalgos, who often possessed little more than their title, to the grandees of Spain, owners of vast estates which they rarely visited but which enabled them, through their sometimes quite fabulous revenues, to live in great style in Madrid. Many of them have been preserved for posterity by Goya's brushes: Alba, Fernán-Núñez, Altamira, Benavente-Osuna, San Adrián, Santa Cruz, Pontejos, Villafranca and many more. *The nobles*

Beside the nobility and often closely connected with them, the churchmen formed a body of about two hundred thousand, of which one hundred thousand were regular clergy. Still according to the 1787 census, there were more than three thousand convents in Spain. The annual income of the Church was fifty per cent higher than the receipts of the Royal Treasury. In this generally poor country where people were content to live very simply and where even the palaces were soberly furnished inside, churches and monasteries displayed an extraordinary luxury. Here too there was great inequality, for though certain communities and bishoprics enjoyed considerable incomes (the cardinal-archbishop of Toledo had an annual income of more than eight hundred million reales), a large number of convents eked out a miserable existence and the majority of small town and country priests lived on public charity. *The churchmen*

As for the other Spaniards, the common people, they lived as best they could and their lot varied widely according to whether they were in the towns or in the country, in the northern and eastern provinces or in other poorer regions. Those living in the low-class districts of Madrid were probably the most carefree in the entire kingdom, and the *majos* and *majas* were to establish an undying image of a Spain built on pride and elegance, on a youthful provocative insolence which set its *casticismo*, or purely Spanish traditions, against the French customs which were taking an increasing hold on society. The fashion of the majos, or *majismo*, was in its turn to attract some of the Spanish aristocrats who took to wearing their costume and joining in their amusements. Goya later made these Spanish types so famous outside Spain that they were wrongly regarded as typical of the whole country. Nevertheless, this vulgar, motley, boisterous group, for whom real life was a kind of theatre, made a marked impression on society in the Madrid of the second half of the eighteenth century. It was opposed to the small minority of *afrancesados*, the men who admired the new French ideas and dreamed of a modern Spain stripped of its tawdry finery and its endless *seguidillas*, and it was to play a major rôle in the bloody struggles soon to succeed the period of the *fêtes galantes*. *The common people*

Majos and *majas*

The son of Philip V and Elizabeth Farnese, the Infante Don Carlos, future Charles III of Spain, was born in Madrid on 20 January 1716. He was Duke of Parma until 1734 and then reigned for twenty-five years over Naples and Sicily as Charles VII (1734-1759). This first reign was already marked by his enlightened liberalism and his taste for reform. On the death of his half-brother, Ferdinand VI, in 1759, he succeeded to the throne of Spain, remaining there until his death in 1788. Charles III was a 'philosopher' king, wholly devoted to the good of his people and anxious above all to arouse from its economic and social paralysis the 'giant's skeleton' to which Cadalso refers in his *Cartas Marruecas*. Supported by enlightened ministers like Roda, Aranda, Campomanes and Floridablanca, he fought against the conservative habits of the masses and the clergy and was not afraid to make himself unpopular at times. Widowed in 1760, Charles III remained faithful to the memory of his queen, Maria Amelia of Saxony; he had no amorous adventures and according to Casanova and a number of historians his passion for hunting was prompted by his need to overcome the sensual urges which he no longer wished to indulge.

In the field of the arts, Charles III continued the traditions of the Bourbons of Spain; recognizing that the arts had fallen into a serious decline in Madrid, he summoned foreign artists to his court. But where his predecessors had turned towards France, he looked to Italy and called on Mengs and Tiepolo to decorate the new royal palace. This decision was to have a profound influence not only on the future course of Spanish painting but also on Goya's artistic development. Goya painted two major portraits of Charles III: the one in court dress commissioned by the Bank of San Carlos in 1787 [224] and this one in hunting dress, of which four replicas are known [230 note].

Charles III   [230] c.1786-88. 206×130 cm. Duchess of Fernán Núñez, Madrid

The burial of Christ [12] c.1770-72. 130×95 cm. Lázaro Galdiano Museum, Madrid

1746-1763. At the Escuelas Pías in Sara-
gossa with Zapater. Apprenticeship in the
studio of José Luzán. Reigns of Ferdinand VI
(1759) and of Charles III.

Francisco Goya came from the north of Spain and, while Aragonese by birth, he originated on his father's side from the heart of the Basque country. The very name Goya is Basque, and traces have been found of several families who have borne it since the seventeenth century within the provinces of Navarre and Guipúzcoa. Many of these families emigrated, following the natural fall of the land towards the lower valley of the Ebro and settling in Saragossa where Basque names are still common today. These origins were to have a continuing influence throughout the artist's life. His patrons, his friends and even his relations by marriage included the Azaras, Goicoecheas and Galarzas, his invaluable friend Martín Zapater and the tempestuous Leocadia Zorilla who married a Señor Weiss but became the companion of Goya's old age. Even more importantly, we can say that with Goya a completely new kind of temperament made itself felt in Spanish painting. Before him, and since the unification of the kingdom by the Catholic kings, all the great Spanish painters, with very few exceptions, had come from Andalusia, Valencia or Castile: Velázquez, Ribera, Zurbarán, Murillo, to name only the greatest. Goya brought with him the toughness, at times harsh and obstinate, of the *baturros*, the Aragonese; but it was probably his Basque blood which accounted for the fantastic elements in his work, the dreams peopled with strange visions and above all the interest in witchcraft which he mocked and denigrated but found irresistibly fascinating.

Birth in Fuendetodos

It was probably only by chance that on 30 March 1746 Goya happened to be born at Fuendetodos, since his parents were always referred to as *vecinos de Zaragoza* (inhabitants of Saragossa). His father was a master gilder there and he appears to have remained a poor man all his life since he died intestate in 1781, having nothing to leave his family. Goya's mother, Gracia Lucientes, who was married in 1736, belonged to the large numbers of petty aristocracy in Aragon who possessed more pride than wealth. Of their six known children the only one apart from Francisco to leave any mark was the youngest, Camilo, who became vicar of the parish church at Chinchón near Madrid (an *Assumption* painted by Goya in 1812 [III.1567] still hangs there) and died in the same year as his celebrated brother.

Very little is known about the artist's childhood, leaving aside the legends and anecdotes which were obviously embroidered at a later date. In any case, what is the point in trying to establish that one of the great masters of painting was already a genius at the age of five or even twenty? He was probably just an ordinary pupil at the Escuelas Pías in Saragossa, where he met his intimate friend and confidant, Martín Zapater, in the same class.* Apart from a very elementary education, this was probably the greatest benefit he received from the teaching fathers, and it led to a lengthy and valuable correspondence with his friend. In his letters to Zapater, carelessly phrased and colloquial, and spiced with amusing drawings and sketches, Goya speaks of his family life and of his art, of his struggle to get on in the world and of his interests and preoccupations. Unfortunately, the greater part of this correspondence has not yet been published, and even the published letters are often given in fragments, taken out of context. They nevertheless remain one of the most important and revealing sources for our knowledge and understanding of Goya's character and career.

* Bibl. 72, p. 39.　Ill. p. 35

The burial of Christ
This is the best-preserved of the three large paintings from the series of seven executed by Goya in the chapel of the palace of Sobradiel in Saragossa. It was probably the very first important commission given to Goya, just before or after his journey to Italy, at the beginning of his career in Aragon. For the three large paintings, Goya borrowed his compositions from prints, in this case a French engraving after a painting by Simon Vouet. Goya had acquired this method, which was in current use in studios at that time, when he was a pupil of José Luzán, and he made use of it for many of the religious paintings which were later commissioned from him.

At the age of fourteen, Goya entered the studio of the painter José Luzán. There is no doubt that he must have shown some precocious talent, and his parents may have asked the advice of a friend of the family, Don Juan Martín de Goicoechea or Francisco Bayeu

Ramón de Pignatelli [292] c.1790. 79·5×62 cm.
Duchess of Villahermosa, Madrid

Juan Martín de Goicoechea [277] 1789. 86×66 cm.
Count of Orgaz, Madrid

who had previously been a pupil of Luzán and had just spent two years in the studio of
Antonio González Velázquez in the capital, Madrid, where the Neapolitan artist, Corrado
Giaquinto, was completing the ceilings of the new royal palace. Charles III had recently
ascended the throne and everything seemed to favour the expansion of the fine arts in the
capital. Francisco Bayeu was actively preparing for this and was already pushing forward
his younger brother Ramón, born in the same year as Goya. The effective patronage of
the 'Aragonese faction' would do the rest: the Pignatellis, Azaras, Rodas and Arandas,
powerful families who stood at the centre of the complex network of local recommendations.
The future looked bright from every angle, providing one was prepared to adopt the taste
of the times and hold resolutely to the new academic creed which had been imported from
central Europe via Rome and Naples.

A rebel by temperament against such precepts, Goya himself described his four years
in Luzán's studio where he was taught the principles of drawing by being made to copy
from prints, and only began to paint in oils, according to 'his own invention', towards the
end of his apprenticeship. He was doubtless taught that art consisted in careful imitation
of the accepted (though this does not necessarily mean the greatest) masters. His youthful
works show the effect of this training and are often directly inspired by some French or
Italian engraving. Goya was to remember this particular lesson throughout his life; almost

Bibl. 1, pp. 67-68; cp. 34, p. 99

Ramón de Pignatelli (1734-1793)
A member of the great Aragonese family of the Counts of Fuentes who were lords, in particular, of Fuendetodos, Goya's native village. Pignatelli was a canon, then rector of the University of Saragossa and played an important rôle in the capital of Aragon where he was one of the founding members of the Royal Economic Society. His name is connected above all with the work of the Imperial Canal in Aragon, of which he took active charge in 1772. It has often been suggested that Goya was helped at the beginning of his career by the Pignatelli family who patronized the studio of Luzán.

Juan Martín de Goicoechea (1732-1804)
His family came originally from Guipúzcoa and like many Basques, including Goya's forbears, had left there to settle in Saragossa. He became a very wealthy merchant in the city and one of the most active members of the Economic Society. After a stay in Lyons where he studied the production and weaving of silk, he founded a spinning factory 'à la Vaucanson' in Saragossa. Later on he created with his own funds an Academy of Drawing, and the Economic Society commissioned a replica of the portrait reproduced here as a mark of gratitude [277 note]. He is shown wearing the cross of a knight of the Order of Charles III which was conferred on him on 12 November 1789.

Martín Zapater (1746-18..)
This Aragonese contemporary of Goya, of whom relatively little is known, occupied an important place in the artist's life, from his earliest childhood years when they apparently met in the same class at the Escuelas Pías in Saragossa until the beginning of the next century when we lose track of him. They were bosom friends and for more than twenty-five years kept up an abundant correspondence of which Goya's letters, still preserved, are an invaluable source for our knowledge of his life. This portrait was probably executed in the autumn of 1790 when Goya was in Saragossa for the feast of the Virgin 'del Pilar'. The gentle, dreamy quality in his friend's expression gives this portrait a depth and humanity which is not generally found until the following period.

Martín Zapater   [290] 1790. 83×65 cm. Cramer Gallery, The Hague

all the later religious paintings are based on prints after works by seventeenth and eighteenth-century artists to whom he turned for inspiration whenever he had to paint one of the commissions which fame laid at his door but which his growing independence found increasingly distasteful.

While Goya sat in Luzán's studio in Saragossa, copying the prints from his master's collection, the news from the court was becoming more and more promising. The celebrated Mengs arrived in Madrid on 7 October 1761, followed a few months later by Giambattista Tiepolo and his two sons Domenico and Lorenzo. The great Venetian master, sixty-five years old and at the height of his fame, represented a dying world; Mengs, at the age of thirty-three, belonged to the new generation which believed with Winckelmann in a revival of classicism worked out according to scientific principles. This aesthetic dictatorship, of Germanic inspiration, was so opposed to the Spanish temperament that it could only meet with one of two responses: either blind submission or revolt.

To get on in the world, however, one must first take the course of submission, and this is what Francisco Bayeu did when called to the service of the king by Mengs. He established himself in Madrid with his younger brother Ramón in the spring of 1763. Goya, who was also impatient to enter the privileged circle of those who gravitated around Mengs, hurried to Madrid not, according to the legend, after a brawl and in order to escape the law, but simply in order to take part in the triennial competition of the Royal Academy of Fine Arts of San Fernando. It was his first disappointment for he did not receive a single vote.

We do not know whether Goya returned to Saragossa after this first academic setback in January 1764 and there is no further documentary information about his activities until 1766. In that year he again took part in the Academy competition, together with Ramón Bayeu and Luis Paret; all three were twenty years old. Ramón Bayeu, doubtless with the support of his brother who was an academician and a member of the jury, received a gold medal and Paret a first prize; for Goya, not a vote, not a sign of recognition.

For the next five years, between the ages of twenty and twenty-five, there are no records of his activities and we are reduced to conjecture. He may have painted the two little pictures of *The Esquilache riot* and *Charles III promulgating the edict for the expulsion of the Jesuits* [17, 18], which would be his first representation of an actual event, experienced in Madrid in 1766. It is also possible that at this time he painted a series of religious scenes on the walls of a chapel in the palace of Sobradiel, the home of the Counts of Gabarda in Saragossa [10-16]. Most of these were based on seventeenth-century French or Italian compositions which Goya, always somewhat at a loss with subjects which had no particular appeal for him, often copied quite literally from prints.

But the great event of these early years was his journey to Italy. After his harsh setbacks in Madrid, Goya decided – probably on the advice of Bayeu whom he described as his teacher at the time of the Parma competition – to seek fresh instruction and possibly to gather laurels away from the court of Madrid. The Spanish ambassador in Rome, an Aragonese named Nicolás de Azara, was a close friend of Mengs who had returned to Rome at the end of 1769. Goya may even have travelled to Italy with Mengs. He later declared that he had made the journey at his own expense, though this does not mean that he travelled like a lone vagabond, as legend would have it. He found support and help, especially in Rome where he appears to have stayed for at least a year, since the jury of the Parma Academy described him as a 'Roman'. He must have worked there and several small mythological pictures, like the signed and dated *Sacrifice to Vesta* and the *Sacrifice to Pan* [22-24], can be attributed to this Italian period.

From Rome he carefully prepared his entry for the competition held by the Parma Academy. He again chanced his luck with a history painting, but once again an academic

1763-1771. Goya is 17 to 25 years old. Competitions at the Academy in Madrid. First paintings. Journey to Rome. Takes part in the competition at Parma. Reign of Charles III.

Academy competition 1763
Bibl. 154, p. 8

Academy competition 1766

Bibl. 154, p. 10

See p. 29

Palace of Sobradiel   *Ill. p. 32*

Journey to Italy

Appendix III; Bibl. 150

Bibl. 154, doc. 56

Appendix III
Bibl. 120.   Ill. p. 37

Competition of the Parma Academy

jury decided against him and awarded the prize to an Italian, Paolo Borroni. However, this time he received six votes and a special mention from the jury which 'noted with pleasure the fluent handling of the brush, a warmth of expression in the face and a fine grandeur in the stance of Hannibal'. Thus for the first time – and this text represents the earliest known criticism of a work by Goya – he received official praise from one of the most famous Italian academies. It was a half-success which preserved his honour and could be turned to good account in Spain. He hastened home, having decided that before conquering the capital he would have to win over the provinces, which for him meant Saragossa.

Appendix III

Sacrifice to Vesta
Mythological subjects are extremely rare in Goya's work and are only to be found in the very early period. This little picture and its pendant, the *Sacrifice to Pan* [23], were probably painted in Rome where Goya was staying at least until 20 April 1771. On that date he wrote a letter in Italian to Count Rezzonico, the perpetual secretary to the Academy of Fine Arts in Parma, announcing that he had posted the picture (now unknown) which he was submitting to the Academy competition. The present painting is signed and dated on the altar, as part of the design. Attention has been drawn to the resemblance between the heads of the pagan priest and the biblical one in the *Circumcision*, executed in 1774 at the Charterhouse of Aula Dei (ill. p. 41). The Marquis of Lozoya has suggested that the Egyptian-style pyramid in the background is the pyramid of Gaius Cestius near the Porta San Paolo in Rome.

Sacrifice to Vesta   [22] 1771. 33×24 cm. J. Gudiol Ricart, Barcelona

37

The journey home from Italy seems to have been rather hurried. Goya asked the Parma Academy to return his picture to him in Spain but he wanted it sent straight to Saragossa, where he was already settled by the end of June 1771, instead of to Valencia.* He may have acted on promises received in Rome from Nicolás de Azara or from Mengs himself, or he may have been advised by them to return to Spain where his Italian success would now give him a better chance.

One fact is certain: on 21 October 1771, the Building Committee of the basilica of Nuestra Señora del Pilar (Our Lady of the Pillar), in Saragossa, asked him to submit sketches for the vault of the *coreto* (little choir). This was his first important commission and was probably obtained through the influence of Don Juan Martín de Goicoechea who was a friend of Zapater and who probably recommended Goya to Ventura Rodríguez, the architect of the Pilar choir. The committee made one condition: the sketches had to be approved by the Royal Academy in Madrid. Goya at once executed a piece of fresco painting to prove that he had the necessary ability. This shows, incidentally, that he was not already known in Spain as a master of this technique which he must therefore have learnt in Italy, the cradle of the greatest fresco painters.

The modest sum asked by Goya (fifteen thousand reales for sixty square metres of fresco) and the quality of the final sketch, described as a 'skilful piece in particularly good taste', carried off the decision of the committee who decided it was unnecessary to ask the approval of the Academy. Work was completed on 1 June 1772. Ramón Stolz, who restored the frescoes in El Pilar and San Antonio de la Florida, has shown the importance of this neglected work painted when Goya was twenty-six. Despite some awkwardness due to his youthful inexperience, and the obvious and ill-assimilated reminiscences of the baroque masters, the great artist who was later to emerge is already foreshadowed in the *Adoration of the Name of God* [30]. Lafuente Ferrari declared that in ʤhe exuberance of this baroque composition and in the tonality of the whole, Goya revealed all his latent qualities and he found even more significant the 'sketch-like technique' which undoubtedly constitutes one of the essential elements of his style and makes him the true precursor of nineteenth-century painting, as opposed to the smooth workmanship, perfectly finished down to the last detail, practised by the adherents of neo-classicism.

This fresco in the *coreto* provided a major start to Goya's career. He had proved his skill, but above all he had won the honour of decorating one of Spain's most cherished sanctuaries, in direct competition with such an established artist as Antonio González Velázquez. At first his fame spread modestly within his native Aragon and he received a number of local commissions. Very few works of this period can be attributed to him with any certainty, although there has been no lack of 'discoveries', with which he is credited from time to time. Some attributions seem plausible, but in general their mediocrity deprives them of any real importance. Their presence or absence in the catalogue neither enhances nor diminishes Goya's art. This is true of the four works which are contemporary with the *coreto*, the *Doctors of the Church*, painted in fresco on the pendentives of the hermitage of the Virgin de la Fuente at Muel, in the province of Saragossa, and repeated on canvas in the church of Remolinos in Aragon [34-41]. These youthful works show a freedom of execution which probably passed for carelessness or lack of experience at the time, but which today appears as a sign of the ferment which was to shatter the whole classic tradition of painting.

1771-1773. Goya is 25 to 27 years old. Marries Josefa Bayeu. First commissions: fresco in the basilica of El Pilar and Aula Dei mural paintings. Reign of Charles III.

* Bibl. 154, p. 22; 160, p. 184

Bibl. 190, pp. 157-159

Bibl. 105, p. 136

Ill. p. 39

Bibl. 105, p. 121

The Adoration of the Name of God   [30] 1772. Fresco approx. 7×15 m. Basilica of El Pilar, Saragossa

The Adoration of the Name of God
Goya learnt his fresco technique during his stay in Italy. On his return to Saragossa he was commissioned by the Building Committee of El Pilar to decorate the vault of the *coreto* (little choir) in front of the shrine of the Virgin 'del Pilar'. The sketch which he presented on 27 January 1772 was considered so successful that it was decided not to seek the approval of the Academy in Madrid, as had been intended. Within four months Goya had completed this fresco whose baroque composition recalls the work of Tiepolo and above all that of Corrado Giaquinto which had such an influence on the Aragonese school.

The Aula Dei murals
* *Bibl. 83, p. 83*
** *Ill. pp. 40, 41*

Goya marries Josefa Bayeu

Ill. p. 246

Goya's activity in the field of church decoration was certainly important. Though unfortunately much damaged and restored, the paintings in the charterhouse of Aula Dei, near Saragossa, are a major example [42-48]. They were executed between the completion of the work in El Pilar and Goya's departure for Madrid in 1774, and in fact probably in that actual year, according to the evidence of the charterhouse accounts.* The style of these paintings differs greatly from that of all Goya's other youthful works. As far as one can judge after the extensive nineteenth-century restorations, the most striking qualities of these great mural paintings are their monumentality and the effect of vertical perspective obtained through the arrangement of the figures at different levels on wide flights of steps. Handled with great sobriety, the figures are impressive on account of their hieratical poses, the broad drapery of their clothing and, above all, the dramatic contrasts of light and shade (especially in the *Visitation* and the *Circumcision* [45, 46]**) which in a curious way anticipate certain etchings from the first part of the *Caprichos*.

These large decorative paintings, designed for walls rather than for a vault, afforded Goya a useful preparation for the great task which awaited him the following year at the Royal Tapestry Factory of Santa Bárbara in Madrid. Although passing from sacred to profane subjects, the problems of composition, of the simplification of masses and the grouping of figures within a given framework, remained the same. He was therefore able to tackle them with the experience he had acquired during these three years of work in the provinces, from 1771 to 1774.

Meanwhile, we know that Goya was married in Madrid, on 25 July 1773, to Josefa Bayeu, the sister of Francisco and Ramón. He was twenty-seven and she was twenty-six. The two families had known each other for many years in Saragossa and Goya and Josefa married as childhood friends so often do, without surprise and probably without passion, to judge by the almost total eclipse of 'la Pepa' in Goya's work (the portrait in the Prado [II.686] is almost certainly not of her and there is just one small drawing which shows us her features at the age of fifty-eight [II.840]) and in his letters to Zapater.

The Visitation   [45] 1774. Oil on plaster 306×790 cm. Charterhouse of Aula Dei, Saragossa

But there was still the important question of Goya's career. Mengs had returned to Rome in 1769 and Tiepolo died in Madrid in 1770, so by 1773 Francisco Bayeu seemed more than ever the likely successor of Mengs, with whom he had worked for ten years. For Goya this marriage amounted almost to an official recognition, the first step in the *cursus honorum* of painting. For Francisco Bayeu, who was already furthering his younger brother's career at court, Goya represented yet another pawn to range on the side of the Bayeu clan. This brings us again to the question of Goya's character. It is inconceivable

The Charterhouse of Aula Dei, Saragossa. Interior of the chapel

The Charterhouse of Aula Dei
The Visitation
The Circumcision
The decoration of the walls of the chapel in the Charterhouse of Aula Dei, near Saragossa, is the most important ensemble of oil paintings which Goya was ever commissioned to make. The *Libro de Gastos comunes* in the Charterhouse has entries between April and December 1774 concerning considerable expenses in connection with paintings, scaffolding and eleven gilded frames; these must certainly refer to the eleven scenes of the life of the Virgin, executed by Goya during the months before he finally settled in Madrid. Of the eleven paintings, seven only remain, some of them much altered by the abusive restoration carried out at the end of the nineteenth century by two French artists, Amédée and Paul Buffet. Nevertheless, their impressive size (some of them cover nearly thirty-five square yards) and the monumentality of the figures and of the architectural settings which are emphasized by the broad foreground steps give a unique character to the whole scheme.

The Circumcision (detail)   [46] 1774. Oil on plaster. Charterhouse of Aula Dei, Saragossa

that Francisco Bayeu, as head of his family since the death of his parents and as academician and Court Painter, would have given his sister's hand in marriage to the man described in so many fanciful biographies. How could he have tolerated her marriage to an adventurer, to a man alleged to have fled from justice in Saragossa after a bloody brawl, to an itinerant bullfighter, to a seducer of nuns who is said to have been condemned to death in Rome when at that very time he was in fact entering the competition organized by the Royal Academy of Fine Arts in Parma, where he was described as a *scolare del Signor*

Appendix III *Francesco Vajeu Pittore di Camera de S.M. Cattolica* (pupil of Signor Francesco Bayeu, Court Painter to His Catholic Majesty). It is difficult to believe that such legends are still repeated by some writers, when it is so logical that Bayeu should only have married his sister to a young artist of talent whose already considerable œuvre and whose progress under Bayeu's own direction promised a brilliant future. We do not know what dowry Josefa brought with her, but the best 'present' which Goya received from the Bayeu family was the part which Francisco no doubt played in the decision of Mengs who called Goya to the court, towards the end of 1774, to work in the service of the king. At the age of twenty-eight, Fortune was smiling on him for the first time.

Francisco Bayeu (detail)   [229] 1786.
Museum of Fine Arts, Valencia

St Isidore   [54] c.1775-78. Red chalk
23 × 19·2 cm. Private collection, Madrid

Francisco Bayeu (1734-1795)
Born in Saragossa, Francisco Bayeu was a pupil of José Luzán before Goya; he then worked for two years, from 1758 to 1760, in the studio of Antonio González Velázquez in Madrid. In 1763 Mengs called him to help with the decoration of the new royal palace. Made an academician and Painter to the King in 1765 and director of the Academy from 1788 until his death, Bayeu was a devotee of the neo-classical style imposed on Spain by Mengs and became the leader of the Madrid school of painting. Goya was Bayeu's pupil between 1766 and 1771 and in 1783 he married his sister, Josefa. This severe portrait was painted at the time of Goya's nomination as Painter to the King, for which Bayeu was largely responsible and which marked their reconciliation after the violent clashes in Saragossa in 1781.

St Isidore
A hitherto unpublished drawing for one of Goya's earliest etchings [53]. 'San Isidro' is the patron saint of Madrid where Goya was to spend most of his life, and one of his most famous pictures shows the *Meadow of San Isidro* on the saint's feast day (see p. 66).

Goya's autograph account for a tapestry cartoon [70] (detail)   1776. Royal palace, Madrid

Goya's autograph account
The account for a tapestry cartoon, dated 30 October 1776 and addressed to D. Francisco Sabatini. In presenting his account, Goya described the picture 'of my own invention' executed 'under the direction of Sr. D. Antonio Rafael Mengs'.
Text of the account (with modern spelling):
Representa una merienda que cinco jovenes han hecho en el campo y una naranjera que va a venderles naranjas, y cuatro figuras mas lejos paseando y el país poblado de arboles que con algun principio de caserias demuestra estar cerca de población.
 Su ancho 10 pies y 10 dedos. Alto 9 pies y 14 dedos. Su precio... 7000 reales vellon
Madrid 30 de Octubre de 1776
 Fran.co Goya
(It represents a picnic which five young people have made in the country, and an orange-seller who is going to sell them oranges, and four figures walking further off and the landscape full of trees where the presence of a few houses indicates that there is a town nearby. Its width 10 feet and 10 fingers. Height 9 feet and 14 fingers. Its price... 7 000 reales. Madrid 30 October 1776.   Francisco Goya)

42

1773-1780. Goya is 27 to 34 years old. Mengs commissions him to paint cartoons for the Royal Tapestry factory. Subjects: hunting (1775) and popular amusements. Reign of Charles III. Floridablanca is Secretary of State (1777).

Boy with a bird
[137] 1779-80. 264×40 cm. Prado, Madrid

La novillada

Between 1778 and 1780 Goya executed nineteen cartoons for tapestries to decorate the apartments of the prince and princess of Asturias (the future Charles IV and Queen María Luisa) in the palace of El Pardo just outside Madrid. These two scenes are from the group of twelve intended for the antechamber and they were delivered to the tapestry factory on 24 January 1780. They were described by Goya in his account as 'a boy who is seated at the foot of a tree playing with a little bird' and 'four youths amusing themselves with a *novillo* [young bull], one just about to fix a rosette on him, another finishing a play with his cape, the other two running away; farther off are seen various figures leaning over a wall to watch the sport'.

This is Goya's first representation of a bullfighting scene and as additional proof of his *afición* (passion) for the 'national sport' he seems to have portrayed himself in the young majo with his head turned towards the spectator, cape in hand. It has often been said that he belonged to a *cuadrilla* (professional company) in his youth, but in Spain young amateurs have always played at bullfighting with *novillos* or *becerros* (one or two year-old calves), without killing them.

Besides this cartoon, Goya's principal works devoted to bullfighting are the series of little cabinet pictures painted in 1793 [II.317-324], the prints of *La Tauromaquia*, drawn and engraved in 1815-16 [III.1149-1243], the celebrated painting in the Academy of San Fernando [III.969] and finally, in 1824-25, a group of lithographs including the *Bulls of Bordeaux* [v.1704-1710] and a number of related paintings [v.1672-1675] (see pages 110, 228-229, 240, 347).

Boy with bird [137]   La novillada   [133] 1779-80. 259×136 cm. Prado Museum, Madrid

Goya's final establishment in Madrid at the end of the year 1774 marks what is undoubtedly one of the most important moments in his life and in his career as a painter, and opens a new chapter in his biography. After twelve years of obscurity, pierced only by occasional glimmers of light, Goya's life becomes accessible through the documents recording his official relations with the court.

Goya was already familiar with life in Madrid. His official appointment as painter of cartoons for the royal tapestry factory came after years of working and waiting. It seems likely that between his first journey to Madrid in 1763 and his final settling there, Goya had been a pupil of Bayeu – probably for a longer period than has generally been supposed. He certainly worked under Bayeu between 1763 and 1771 since he declared as much to the Parma Academy; and after his return from Italy, when he had determined to make his way at court and was no doubt already engaged to Josefa Bayeu, he probably also worked in the studio of his future brother-in-law whose style is reflected in Goya's first cartoons. Moreover, as a young married man, Goya lived for several years in the house of his brothers-in-law (from the date of his marriage in 1773 at least until the birth of his first child on 15 December 1775 in the Bayeu home), presumably for economic reasons. Thus the beginnings of Goya's official relationship with the court were set in the context of very close family and artistic ties with Francisco and Ramón Bayeu.

Bibl. 154, p. 9
Bibl. 154, p. 289, n. 69

Thanks to the researches of Valentín de Sambricio, which are of fundamental importance for our knowledge of Goya's life and work, it is now known that he painted a total of sixty-three cartoons for tapestries to decorate two of the royal residences, San

Bibl. 154

The quail shoot   [63] 1775. 290×226 cm. Prado Museum, Madrid

The quail shoot
At the end of the year 1774 Goya was summoned to Madrid by Mengs to work in the service of the king as a painter of cartoons for the Royal Tapestry Factory of Santa Bárbara, which had been founded by Philip V in 1720. Goya had then been married to Francisco Bayeu's sister for more than a year and he settled in Madrid in his brother-in-law's house, executing his first cartoons under the latter's direction. During the year 1775 Goya painted nine cartoons for tapestries to decorate the dining-room of the prince and princess of Asturias in the palace of San Lorenzo del Escorial. They were delivered in two groups, five on 24 May and the remaining four on 30 October. *The quail shoot* belongs to the last group. Like all the other cartoons in this series with the exception of *The angler* [66], it is a hunting subject. Goya was passionately fond of this sport, to which he often refers in his letters, and must have felt quite at home with these scenes.

This cartoon and the eight others in the series were attributed during Goya's lifetime either to Francisco Bayeu or to his younger brother Ramón. The two drawings in the Biblioteca Nacional in Madrid [64, 65], for the two hunters standing together on the left, have also been attributed to Francisco Bayeu, which shows how closely Goya's style and technique resembled those of his brother-in-law at the beginning of his career. Although this cartoon is the most successful of the series, the colouring and especially the composition are still rather clumsy; the figures are not clearly related to one another and appear stuck onto the landscape. Even the representation of two different kinds of hunting – the shoot with gun dogs and the hunt with hounds – is somewhat artificial.

Lorenzo del Escorial and El Pardo. Of these sixty-three paintings, many of which are very large (the *Harvesting* [263] in the Prado is the largest canvas ever painted by Goya), thirty-nine were executed before 1780 and represent one of the most fruitful periods in Goya's life, not so much for the number of works, though that in itself is considerable, as for the impressive way in which his art evolved in so short a time.

When he was first appointed to work for the tapestry factory, Goya had had no previous experience of this kind of decorative painting. All his early work had been in the field of religious, historical or mythological subjects. It is therefore quite natural that his brother-in-law should have taught him the specific techniques required for tapestry cartoons. Indeed, the receipt for Goya's first five cartoons was made out to Francisco Bayeu and specified that the paintings had been executed 'under his direction by Don Francisco Goya', whereas all subsequent receipts were made out in Goya's name. This explains why for a long time the cartoons painted by Goya in 1775 were attributed to Francisco or to Ramón Bayeu. At the age of nearly thirty, Goya was just an unknown beginner under the orders of his famous brother-in-law; he had no style of his own and not even a name, since a document of the time christens him Ramón Goya.

Bibl. 154, doc. 10   Ill. p. 42

Bibl. 154, doc. 5
First tapestry cartoons: hunting scenes

The first series of cartoons was delivered in two lots, on 24 May and 30 October 1775, and consisted of eight hunting scenes and one fishing scene [57-69]. They were designed for tapestries to decorate the dining-room of the prince of Asturias (the heir to the throne) and his wife, in the palace of San Lorenzo del Escorial where the court always spent the autumn. In spite of some obvious clumsiness, the largest composition, the *Quail shoot* [63], shows that right from the start Goya could hold his own against his most experienced rivals.

Ill. p. 44

Second series of cartoons: popular amusements

The second series painted between 1776 and 1778 includes ten cartoons commissioned this time for tapestries for the palace of El Pardo [70-84]. They were again intended for the decoration of the dining-room of the prince of Asturias, the future Charles IV, and his wife María Luisa of Parma, who were probably responsible for choosing the subjects. In 1776, at the age of twenty-seven and twenty-five respectively, the prince and princess had already been married for eleven years, and the placid Charles bore without a murmur the whims and wild affairs of the headstrong María Luisa. He was fond of hunting, like his father, but she preferred open-air entertainments, young people and above all the majos and majas who typified the natural gaiety and elegance of the people of Madrid. While the aristocrats at Versailles played at shepherds and shepherdesses, sighing like Julie and Saint-Preux, many of those in Madrid were attracted by the fashion for *majismo*. Although some of them were captivated by everything French and followed all the latest fashions, the majority preferred to 'slum it' in the Lavapies district or on the banks of the river Manzanares with the noisy, riotous populace who sang and danced and drank with the carefree gaiety which characterizes the people of Madrid. The majos and majas were elegant in their traditional costume, and through them and their followers the common people of a colourful and passionate Spain stood firm against the invasion of foreign customs. The lively and insubstantial charm of the *sainetes* (dramatic sketches) of Ramón de la Cruz was the literary counterpart of this movement. Goya had already been living in Madrid for several years and he undoubtedly knew and loved the picturesque and entrancing world of the majos which he had first encountered at the time of the Esquilache riots in 1766. It was therefore a wonderful chance to be asked to portray it at the request of the court. He might well have been commissioned to paint mythological or historical scenes; if so, the whole course of his art would have been entirely different.

Doc. ill. p. 42   Ill. p. 46

In 1776 and 1777 he began the new series for the Pardo palace with two splendidly original cartoons: the *Picnic* [70] and the *Dance on the banks of the Manzanares* [74]. At once the whole charm of the Spanish way of life finds expression in his work and one feels that he was painting confidently and with pleasure. The figures are convincingly natural within their landscape setting, where the recently finished cupola of San Francisco el Grande appears in the distance. Each group is harmoniously linked to the others, the composition

Dance on the banks of the river Manzanares   [74] 1777. 272×295 cm. Prado Museum, Madrid

Dance on the banks of the river Manzanares
The series of nine hunting cartoons executed in 1775 gave Goya an opportunity to prove his skill in this type of secular decoration which he had never undertaken before. His first child was born at the end of that year and, conscious of his new responsibilities, he applied for a fixed annual salary. Mengs was consulted and gave his opinion, on 18 June 1776, to the effect that 'Don Francisco Goya has also worked for the Royal Tapestry Factory, he is a person of talent and intelligence, who is capable of making great progress in his Art, supported by the Royal munificence, and at the present time he is already proving himself useful in the service of the King'. He proposed that he should be granted eight thousand reales a year (Bayeu, as Court Painter, was then receiving thirty thousand).

After this favourable testimonial from the great Mengs, Goya was given a more important commission, this time for the dining-room of the prince of Asturias in the palace of El Pardo. The ten cartoons were completed between 30 October 1776 and 25 January 1778. Goya delivered the *Dance*, the second in the series, on 3 March 1777 and was paid eight thousand reales. It already shows a much greater ease and assurance in the handling. Majos and majas are harmoniously grouped and the landscape is one of the most topographically convincing that he ever painted: the river Manzanares with the cupola of the recently completed church of San Francisco el Grande and the green trees of the Casa del Campo. He was conscious of his rapid progress and in April of the same year wrote to Zapater that he was already painting 'in a more acceptable way'.

is spacious without lacking coherence, and the brilliance of Goya's palette suggests an unfeigned *joie de vivre*. He had finally found his own style and soon dominated the enormous production of the tapestry factory, showing himself to be the best, the only painter of his day.

Hardly had he finished this series than he began another, much larger one, consisting of twenty cartoons for the bedchamber and ante-chamber of the prince of Asturias at El Pardo [85, 124-142]. He continued with more scenes of popular amusements, which suggests that those he had already painted for the dining-room tapestries must have

Study for the 'Dance' (above)   [75] 1777.
Black chalk 28·9×22·5 cm. Prado Museum, Madrid

Study for the 'Dance'
This is a preparatory drawing for the majo who 'beats the rhythm with his hands' seated to the right of the picture. Like the three studies for the *Picnic* cartoon [71-73], it is a typical eighteenth-century drawing in black chalk, heightened with white, on blue paper. The line is assured and the figure vigorously posed, but there is little to distinguish the author of this sketch from the crowd of competent draughtsmen of the period, and still less to give a hint of the great artist who was to create the *Caprichos* prints and the albums of drawings in the second half of his life.

The parasol

Among the ten cartoons for tapestries for the dining-room of the prince and princess of Asturias in the palace of El Pardo, a group of four was delivered on 12 August 1777: *The fight at the New Inn, The promenade in Andalusia, The drinker* and *The parasol*. The price of eighteen thousand reales asked by Goya was reduced to seventeen thousand and the last two cartoons, which are over-doors of smaller dimensions, were valued at one thousand five hundred reales each. *The drinker* is a rather dull design but *The parasol* is one of Goya's most enchanting and successful works in which he expresses all the 'douceur de vivre' so typical of the Madrid of that period and which is also found in the *sainetes* of Ramón de la Cruz. This figure of a young woman, with its exceptionally fresh colouring and delicate half-tones in the shadow of the parasol, begins a long series of 'poetic' portraits which were to end, fifty years later, with the *Milkmaid of Bordeaux* (see p. 25).

The parasol [80] 1777. 104×152 cm. Prado Museum, Madrid

Ill. p. 15

Bibl. 72, p. 24; 154, p. 109

Ill. p. 43

pleased the young royal couple. The first seven cartoons which he delivered to the factory on 5 January 1779 include such marvellous pieces as the *Fair at Madrid* [124], the *Crockery vendor* [125] and the huge *Game of pelota* [130]. Goya had the honour of showing four of these cartoons to the king and the prince of Asturias. Bursting with pride and happiness, he wrote to Zapater on 9 January, 'If I had more time I would tell you how I have been honoured by the king and the prince and princess who by the grace of God allowed me to show them four pictures, and I kissed their hands which I had never had the good fortune to do before, and I assure you that I could not hope to have pleased them more with my works, judging from the pleasure they took in seeing them and the satisfaction expressed by the king and far more so even by their Highnesses', and he added, as proof of his budding success, '. . . I am beginning to have more important and more hostile enemies'.

The last cartoons of this series were delivered on 24 January 1780. In one of them, the *Novillada* [133], Goya shows himself cape in hand, his gesture and expression full of the joy of his first triumphs and the certainty that there would be many more.

1778. Goya is 32 years old. Mengs recommends artists to study Velázquez. Goya etches his first series of prints after paintings by Velázquez. Reign of Charles III.

The blind guitarist
The largest plate which Goya ever etched, it represents the original design of one of his tapestry cartoons [85]. The scene is the Plazuela de la Cebada in Madrid and Goya, in a document, described the various figures including the guitarist and his *lazarillo* (boy guide), a negro water-seller, a Murcian peasant with his cart and oxen. Light and movement are expressed by the delicate, Tiepolesque quality of the etched line. Very few proofs are known of this etching which Goya signed on the stone in the foreground.

The blind guitarist   [87] 1778. Etching 39·5×57 cm. Metropolitan Museum of Art, New York

As a young student of art, Goya was brought up on prints. In the autobiographical note included in the 1828 Prado catalogue, he said that he had studied the principles of drawing with José Luzán 'who made him copy the best prints he possessed'. The copying of engravings after the works of the old and contemporary masters approved by Luzán cannot have proved very stimulating, but Goya later found inspiration in the profound originality of the great painter-engravers – Rembrandt, Piranesi and Giambattista Tiepolo – and he devoted a considerable part of his artistic career to producing large series of original prints such as the *Caprichos* [II.451-621] and the *Disasters of War* [III.993-1148].

However, Goya's first serious essay in print-making was still in terms of copying. He seems to have fallen seriously ill in the spring of 1777, and temporarily abandoned the large series of tapestry cartoons on which he was engaged. On 28 July 1778 the *Gaceta de Madrid* announced the publication of 'nine prints drawn and etched by Don Francisco Goya' after paintings by Velázquez. These paintings, together with others from the royal collections, had recently been brought to Madrid and in 1776 Anton Rafael Mengs addressed an open letter to Don Antonio Ponz, the Secretary of the Royal Academy of Fine Arts, 'concerning the merits of the most outstanding paintings which are preserved in the Royal Palace in Madrid'. In it he praised above all the works of Velázquez, referring to his understanding of light and shade and aerial perspective, and urging all young artists to study and to copy such great masters in order not to imitate their style but to understand their methods. This enlightened advice may well have been the spark which led to Goya's study of Velázquez during his convalescence and then to his decision to

Bibl. 1, p. 68

Bibl. 72, p. 24

Bibl. 88, II, p. 448

Bibl. 140, (T.VI), pp. 565-582; 154, p. 94

See p. 22

Prince Baltasar Carlos
One of the series of copies which Goya made
after the portraits by Velázquez, painted for
Philip IV, which had recently been brought
to the royal palace in Madrid where Goya
was able to study them. A comparison with
the original paintings, now in the Prado
Museum, shows that Goya interpreted them
in his own way, and this equestrian portrait
is one of the most successful of the series.
Using the lively etching technique which is
characteristic of this early group of works, he
has translated Velázquez's painting into the
idiom of the print without giving the lifeless
impression of a copy. The charm and assurance of the little boy on his fiery pony are
rendered with a sympathy which was to
characterize all Goya's portraits of children.

D. BALTASAR CARLOS PRINCIPE DE ESPAÑA. HIJO DEL REY D. FELIPE IV.
Pintura de D. Diego Velazquez del tamaño natural, dibujada y grabada por D. Francisco Goya, Pintor. 1778.

Prince Baltasar Carlos   [95] 1778. Etching 35×23 cm.

The Infante Don Fernando

From his earliest etchings, Goya almost always used the same basic method of work. He made a drawing – in this case in red chalk – and then transferred the design to the copperplate which he was to etch. The drawing, when placed face down on the prepared surface of the plate and passed through the press, left a trace of its image which Goya then followed with his etching needle. He thus worked with the image reversed on the copperplate, so the proofs came out in the same sense at the drawing. All the drawings used in this way show (when they have not been cut down) the mark where the edges of the copperplate were pressed into the paper during the transfer.

The print was first etched, as lightly and delicately as that of *Baltasar Carlos* (see p. 49), and Goya then attempted to add an aquatint tone. He had considerable difficulty in handling this more complex technique, and was forced to rework the plate several times. As a result, the final state of the print (illustrated here) is very different from the preparatory drawing and of course from Velázquez's original painting. He was only able to publish two aquatinted plates in this, his first series of prints, but was later to become one of the greatest masters of the aquatint technique.

The Infante Don Fernando   [98]
Red chalk 27·2 × 15 cm. Kunsthalle, Hamburg

The Infante Don Fernando   [97] 1778-79
Etching and aquatint 28·5 × 17·5 cm.

publish engraved copies of the master's work. Perhaps Ponz himself helped to launch the project and find a patron for the young artist since he devoted a long passage in his *Viage de España* to Goya's 'very praiseworthy undertaking' in the same year in which the prints were advertised for sale.

Bibl. 140, (T.VIII), p. 666

Goya was still unfamiliar with the etching technique and he lost or discarded a number of plates in the course of making this series. In all he was able to publish thirteen prints after portraits and one subject picture by Velázquez [88-106]. Two of the prints make use of aquatint, a recently invented technique which Goya was later to make so completely his own. It has been said that these copies are a travesty of the originals, but Goya, following the advice of Mengs and his own independent genius, was above all concerned to capture the spirit of the paintings. Some of the more complex prints are undoubtedly marred by his lack of technical expertise, and it is above all in the preparatory drawings that Goya's understanding of the qualities of Velázquez's originals can best be appreciated: the proud stance of the princes, the extraordinary liveliness of the expressions, the feeling for light and atmosphere around the forms, and the emotional intensity of a work like the *Child of Vallecas* [112, 113] – all qualities which were to become more and more a part of his own painting and which find their first original expression in his prints in the impressive etching of the *Garrotted man* [122].

1780-1788. Goya is 34 to 42 years old. Election to the Royal Academy of San Fernando in 1780. Birth of his son Javier in 1784. Frescoes in the basilica of El Pilar in Saragossa. Religious paintings commissioned for San Francisco el Grande in Madrid, for a convent in Valladolid and for the cathedral in Valencia. Reign of Charles III.

Ill. p. 39

Frescoes in El Pilar at Saragossa

Bibl. 190, pp. 157-177   Ill. p. 54

Bibl. 73

Bibl. 72, pp. 45-48; 190, pp. 174-177

Bibl. 72, pp. 25, 28

Bibl. 102, pp. 77-81

Altarpiece for San Francisco el Grande

Religious painting occupies an important place in Goya's œuvre, though this has long been disregarded or misunderstood. Nineteenth-century French critics made him into a painter of majas, bullfights and scenes of witchcraft, and it was therefore inevitable that no attention should have been paid to the religious works of a philosopher-painter whom it was fashionable to describe as an atheist and a revolutionary. A number of well-intentioned Spanish writers who wished to correct this one-sided portrait of the great Aragonese artist then went to the opposite extreme by maintaining that so profoundly Spanish a genius could not help being a good catholic, a good father and an exemplary patriot.

Goya's first fresco of the *Adoration of the Name of God* [30] had left an excellent example of his youthful talent in Saragossa. At Francisco Bayeu's suggestion, an even more important commission had been allotted him in 1776 in the basilica of El Pilar: the decoration of a cupola and its four pendentives. After five years of continuous work for the tapestry factory, and as a newly made member of the Academy of San Fernando, Goya left for Saragossa late in 1780, accompanied by the two Bayeu brothers.

What might be called the 'Saragossa affair' marks Goya's first open act of rebellion against the academic tradition as personified by his brother-in-law. His great fresco of the *Queen of Martyrs* [177] apparently pleased neither the building committee nor the public. Goya vehemently refused to have his work corrected by Bayeu and in a long note to the committee he defended his honour as an artist and refused to submit himself to his brother-in-law; in the last resort he was prepared only to accept the arbitration of 'one of the most distinguished' of the academicians, such as Mariano Maella or Antonio González Velázquez. In the end, Brother Félix Salcedo, the prior of Aula Dei, interceded and persuaded Goya to mend his quarrel with the building committee, chiefly by appealing to his christian feelings. He made new sketches, submitted them to Bayeu and even agreed to the large fresco in the cupola being corrected. But Goya was not one to give in readily, and the shame of having had to bow to an artist of whose real worth he was already well aware led him to write soon after to Zapater: '. . . when I think of Saragossa and of painting, I feel as though I'm burning alive'. He determined to think only of hunting in order to forget 'those vile men who had so little faith in my merit'.

Without implying that the frescoes in El Pilar are in any way a revolutionary masterpiece or even one of Goya's major works, they are significant in that they reveal the scandalous independence which made the members of the building committee feel that they were not 'finished' paintings. For Goya they were, and this is why, after 1781, the correct academician of the *Christ on the Cross* [176] opened the way to a completely new kind of painting in which the spontaneity of the sketch, with its rapid impasto and its irregular brushwork, replaces the impeccable but lifeless execution which Mengs had imposed on his disciples. This style, which enlarges the sketch to the proportions of the finished painting, has been discussed in a masterly study by Lafuente Ferrari who gives it the very apt Spanish name of *bocetismo* (sketch-like style), in which he rightly sees one of the most characteristic features of Goya's art.

Hardly back in Madrid, Goya was offered an unexpected compensation – one might almost say an opportunity to avenge himself. He received a royal command to paint one of the seven large altarpieces for the church of San Francisco el Grande which was nearing completion under the architectural direction of Sabatini. The order was in itself an extraordinary mark of distinction and Goya owed it to the influence of his friend and patron

The Queen of Martyrs [178] Sketch for the cupola in El Pilar. 1780. 85×165 cm. Museum of La Seo, Saragossa

Don Juan Martín de Goicoechea with the Count of Floridablanca. Goya's six rivals naturally included Francisco Bayeu (whom he ironically refers to as 'the great Bayeu' in his letters). All the others held titles far superior to his own and represented the flower of academic painting in Madrid. Goya wrote to Zapater '. . . God seems to have remembered me'. Realizing that this important commission was in the nature of a competition between the best painters at the court, he gave up his thrush-shooting and devoted himself entirely to his picture. The subject he had chosen, *St Bernardino of Sienna preaching before Alphonse V of Aragon* (who replaced René of Anjou, the king of Sicily) [184], was to cost him two years' work. Having received the commission on 20 July 1781, he worked on his sketches during August and September and on the twenty-second of that month wrote to Floridablanca, giving a detailed description of the scene represented and mentioning the difficulty of setting it within the tall, narrow shape of the altarpiece. He subsequently modified the composition (having borrowed it in the first place from Michel-Ange Houasse) and finally produced a large and rather uninteresting 'set piece' in which he portrayed himself among the crowd witnessing the miracle. When the pictures were finally unveiled in November 1784, he claimed in his letters to have carried the day and triumphed over all his rivals: 'It is a fact that I have been fortunate in finding favour both with the intellectuals and with the general public . . . since they are all for me, without any dispute'. However, he added that 'up to now no one knows what may come out of it for the future', and in April 1785 he had to join with two of his rivals, Ferro and Castillo, in presenting a claim for the additional remuneration due to them after they had 'spent two years on the sketches, studies and execution' of the pictures. Floridablanca granted them a further four thousand reales each, noting drily that 'the pictures have not been much of a success, though those by these [artists] are the least bad'.

Two great families, the Medinacelis and the Osunas who accorded him their patronage and later their friendship, also commissioned religious paintings from him. The former, in 1785, ordered an *Annunciation* whose sketch is one of Goya's finest pieces of improvisation [234, 235]; the latter, in 1788, commissioned two large canvases for their chapel in the cathedral at Valencia, *St Francis Borgia taking leave of his family* and *St Francis Borgia at the*

Bibl. 102, pp. 318-321

Bibl. 72, p. 25

Ill. p. 55

Bibl. 102, p. 321

Bibl. 72, p. 31; 28, facsimile of the letter of 11 December 1784

Bibl. 190, pp. 179-181

Paintings at Valencia

The Queen of Martyrs

In 1780, eight years after having completed his first fresco in the basilica of El Pilar at Saragossa (see p. 39), to the general satisfaction both of the Building Committee and of the faithful, Goya was given an even more important task in the same sanctuary. The decoration of all the vaults, cupolas and pendentives in the church had been entrusted to Francisco Bayeu who was responsible for ensuring their unity of style and execution. In 1775-76 he left the court in Madrid, in response to much persuasion, in order to paint two of the vaults. The Building Committee was so pleased that it decided to fix in advance the price of the paintings for the two cupolas which still remained to be decorated and agreed that they should be painted under Francisco Bayeu's direction by his brother Ramón and brother-in-law Goya.

On 23 May 1780 an agreement was reached between Bayeu and the Pilar authorities; on 5 October the sketches were presented to the building committee which examined them 'with great attention and pleasure' and ordered that the work should begin at once. Goya was given the subject of 'The most Holy Virgin Mary Queen of Martyrs', and one of his two sketches together with a part of the fresco are shown here and on the following page. Having been made an academician in the previous month of May, he was now full of his new dignity and did not relish the idea of carrying out this important commission, in his native province, *under the direction* of a man whose equal he now considered himself.

By December the two brothers-in-law had clashed head on; Bayeu could not tolerate Goya's lack of preparation, his freedom of execution according to the inspiration of the moment, in other words his sketch-like style, as it is described today, and Goya for his part obstinately refused to alter his work according to his brother-in-law's instructions. On 10 March 1781 Goya presented to the building committee the sketches for the four pendentives, representing *Faith, Patience, Fortitude* and *Charity* [180-183]. Not only were they not accepted but the *Charity* was harshly criticized and the administrator was instructed to inform the artist that the cupola had failed to please the public and that in general his work lacked care and taste. The committee made Francisco Bayeu responsible for the revision of the sketches and insisted that Goya should do nothing in future without the written approval of his brother-in-law.

Goya replied with a long memorandum, justifying his attitude and asking for the arbitration of 'one of the most respected' academicians in Madrid. Only the intervention of Brother Felix Salcedo, a monk at the Charterhouse of Aula Dei, succeeded in persuading him to accept the conditions imposed by the committee. He made the necessary corrections and obtained the approval of Bayeu, but his pride was deeply wounded. Considering that 'he was only losing his good name' in Saragossa, he asked to be paid his fee, determined to return at once to Madrid.

The Queen of Martyrs. Detail of the sketch [178], see p. 52

death-bed of an impenitent, for which the sketches have also been preserved [240-244]. In the second composition (also borrowed from Houasse), the appearance of the 'monsters' behind the dying man foreshadows the famous *Dream of reason* in the *Caprichos* prints [II.536].

Finally, an important place must be given to the three large paintings of 1787 in the convent of Santa Ana at Valladolid [236-239], for which Goya adopted a zurbaranesque

The Queen of Martyrs (detail)   [177] 1780-81. Fresco. Basilica of El Pilar, Saragossa (see p. 53)

Self-portrait (detail of [184])

St Bernardino of Sienna
This very large altarpiece (480×300 cm.)
was the result of two years work, from 1781
to 1783, and Goya put more effort and more
hopes into it than into any other of his
works. He obtained this royal commission
for the decoration of the recently completed
church of San Francisco el Grande thanks
to the influence of his friend and protector
Don Juan Martín de Goicoechea (see p. 34)
with the Count of Floridablanca (see p. 58).
Taking a painting by Michel-Ange Houasse,
the *Preaching of St Francis of Regis*, as his
model, he chose the subject himself and took
great pains over the composition which he
described to Floridablanca in a letter as
'pyramidal' and having to 'wind its way
through from foreground to background to
achieve the best possible decorative effect'
because of the tall, narrow shape of the picture. The preparatory sketches show the
alterations which Goya made to the composition before it took its final form. Goya himself appears at the extreme right edge of the
picture, in a striking self-portrait which is
shown in detail above.

St Bernardino of Sienna   [184] 1782-83. San Francisco el Grande, Madrid

The death of St Joseph
At the suggestion of the architect Sabatini, Goya received from Charles III a commission for three large paintings to decorate the side altars of the chapel in the convent of Santa Ana at Valladolid. The paintings, representing *The death of St Joseph, St Bernard and St Robert* and *St Lutgarda*, were executed between June and October 1787 in an 'architectonic style', according to Goya's own expression. The little picture at Flint treats the death of St Joseph in a quite different way from the large painting at Valladolid and is a first version of the subject rather than a sketch for the final painting.

The death of St Joseph   [237] 1787. Sketch 54·5×40·5 cm. Institute of Arts, Flint (Michigan)

The death of St Joseph   [236] 1787. 220×160 cm. Santa Ana, Valladolid

style which does not recur in his work and which demonstrates his experiments with a wide variety of styles during these very active years.

In conclusion one can say that although they do not count among Goya's greatest works, all these religious paintings executed in the space of ten years do nevertheless represent an often surprisingly high level of artistic experiment and research and were later to contribute to some of his most splendid successes, notably the frescoes in San Antonio de la Florida [II.717-735] and even, on a completely different plane, the 'black paintings' in the Quinta del Sordo [IV.1615-1627a].

St Francis Borgia
Among Goya's many commissions for the Osunas were two large religious paintings for their chapel in the cathedral at Valencia. The sketch, illustrated at right, is of exceptional interest in Goya's work; a rather unexciting religious subject is transformed into a *capricho*-like vision where hideous monsters appear for the first time, evoking the titles on so many later prints and drawings: *sueño* (dream) or *pesadilla* (nightmare).

St Francis Borgia at the death-bed of an impenitent [244] 1788. 38×29 cm. Marquesa de Santa Cruz, Madrid

On 29 June 1779, Anton Rafael Mengs, First Court Painter to the King of Spain, died in Rome at the age of fifty-one. Without losing any time, Goya solicited the position of Court Painter which became vacant. It seemed to him that the success of his tapestry cartoons and the warm reception accorded him by the king and the prince and princess of Asturias a few months before must weigh the balance in his favour. There is a significant passage in the petition which he presented to the king on 24 July: 'having practised this Art in Saragossa his birthplace and in Rome whither he travelled and lived at his own expense, he was summoned by Don Antonio Rafael de Mengs to continue it in the service of Your Majesty'. This is the only document which affords any precise information about his stay in Italy; Goya referred to it in order to point out the difference between himself and Mariano Salvador Maella, his immediate rival, who had had the advantage of a pension during his eight years in Rome. Maella, who was ten years older than Goya, was granted the position.

1780-1792. Goya is 34 to 46 years old. Portraits of his first patrons: Floridablanca, the families of the Infante Don Luis and of the Osunas. Made Painter to the King in 1786. Death of Charles III (1788), succeeded by Charles IV. Goya made Court Painter in 1789. Royal commissions.

Bibl. 154, doc. 56

The Count of Floridablanca and Goya   [203] 1783

Self-portrait (detail of [203])

The Count of Floridablanca and Goya
262 × 166 cm. Banco Urquijo, Madrid

The first important official portrait painted by Goya. Born in 1728 in Murcia, Floridablanca was First Secretary of State to Charles III from 1777 until the death of the king in 1788. Under Charles IV he managed to keep his position at the head of public affairs but in 1792 he finally had to make way for Aranda, the leader of the Aragonese party. After his disgrace and imprisonment at Pamplona until 1795, Floridablanca did not reappear on the political scene until 1808, when he took control of the rebellion against Napoleon. He died on 30 October of the same year at Aranjuez.

María Teresa de Borbón y Vallabriga   [210] 1783. 132·3×116·7 cm. Mrs Mellon Bruce, Washington

The family of the Infante Don Luis
This large and ambitious work was painted in Madrid, after Goya's stay with the Infante at Arenas de San Pedro in August and September 1783. Fourteen figures are grouped on the canvas, including Goya himself, painting in front of his easel in the lower left corner of the picture. The composition centres on the Infante's wife, Doña María Teresa de Vallabriga, shown here attended by her hairdresser and surrounded by her three young children and the family servants.

Born on 25 July 1727 in Madrid, the Infante Don Luis Antonio de Borbón was the brother of Charles III; after having been cardinal-archbishop of Toledo and Seville, he gave up his ecclesiastical dignities as well as life at the court by making a morganatic marriage in 1776 and withdrawing to his estates at Arenas de San Pedro, in the foothills of the Sierra de Gredos. The death of the Infante in 1785 put an end to the hopes Goya had placed in this first royal patron. His son, Don Luis María de Borbón y Vallabriga (1777-1823), later became cardinal-archbishop of Toledo [II.794]; Doña María Teresa (1780-1828), whose portrait he had just painted at Arenas de San Pedro (see p. 59), was married to Godoy in 1797 and posed for Goya again in 1800 as Countess of Chinchón (see p. 19). Doña María Josefa, shown in her nurse's arms, later married the Duke of San Fernando.

The family of the Infante Don Luis   [208] 1783. 248×330 cm. Ruspoli heirs, Florence (copy)

On the advice of Bayeu, Goya then turned to the Academy, though probably without much enthusiasm for the institution which had already rejected him on two occasions. He was now thirty-four, his 'Pepa' was expecting her fourth child and all commissions for the royal tapestry factory had just been suspended for an indefinite period; to keep the Bayeu clan happy, he therefore had to get down to some 'serious' painting. His presentation piece, the irreproachable *Christ on the Cross* in the Prado [176], borrowed so much from Mengs and Bayeu that in May 1780 the Academy elected him on a unanimous vote, whereas his contemporary Luis Paret was elected at the same session only by a 'majority of the votes'. However, being a member of the Academy was only an honorific distinction which brought with it a number of duties, such as attending its sessions, but no substantial reward. Goya had to wait another six years before even achieving the position of Painter to the King which finally gave him a regular salary. Until then he had to be content with chance commissions from the king or private patrons.

A year later the 'Saragossa affair', which represented a violent break with academic art, temporarily deprived him of the support of his brother-in-law. Goya returned hurriedly to Madrid where he put all his hopes in the competition at San Francisco el Grande and began to look seriously for patrons. He thought he had secured one in the Count of Floridablanca to whom he had been recommended by his friend Goicoechea and who commissioned a portrait from him in 1783. Goya had little experience of the great; in the eyes of the all-powerful First Secretary of State he was merely a poor painter, and the laborious portrait with its complicated allusions intended to flatter the vanity of this stony politician brought him only a few condescending words.

But soon a fresh source of hope appeared. On a recommendation – perhaps even from Floridablanca – the ex-cardinal Infante Don Luis, brother of Charles III, commissioned him to paint his entire family. Since his morganatic marriage in 1776 with María Teresa de Vallabriga, of noble Aragonese descent, the Infante lived in semi-exile at Arenas de

Election to the Academy of San Fernando

See p. 51

Ill. p. 58
Bibl. 72, p. 31

The family of the Infante Don Luis

60

Between 1785 and 1788 Goya painted six official portraits for the Bank of San Carlos, founded in 1782 by Cabarrús who continued as director until 1789. This commission included the portraits of the Count of Altamira and of Cabarrús himself. The commission was probably obtained through the good offices of Ceán Bermúdez who held a post in the bank's secretariat from 1783, and it was an important one for the artist's future career. It brought him the patronage of the noble Altamira family, in spite of the awkward and uncomfortable pose of the count whose diminutive size is emphasized by the height of the table. Goya was subsequently to paint *The Countess of Altamira and her daughter* [232], the eldest son, *Vicente Osorio de Moscoso* [231], and above all the wonderful little portrait of *Manuel Osorio de Zuñiga* [233].

In Cabarrús, Goya encountered one of the most enthralling but at the same time most disturbing figures of his time. Born at Bayonne in 1752, he was naturalized Spanish in 1781, after a somewhat reckless youth. Experienced in business affairs, he had a brilliantly successful career as a result of his association with the Bank of San Carlos. Although he was disgraced in 1789, following the failure of his financial measures, he was able to make himself indispensable behind the Spanish political scenes and kept the confidence of Godoy. He was Minister of Finance under Joseph Bonaparte and died in Seville in 1810. His daughter Teresa became the celebrated Madame Tallien.

The Count of Altamira   [225] 1786-87.
177×108 cm. Bank of Spain, Madrid

The Count of Cabarrús   [228] 1788.
210×127 cm. Bank of Spain, Madrid

Stay at Arenas de San Pedro

San Pedro which lay at the foot of the Sierra de Gredos, nearly sixty-five miles from Madrid. He had three delightful children: a boy of six who later became cardinal-archbishop of Toledo [II.794], María Teresa, aged two years and nine months, the future Countess of Chinchón and unhappy wife of Godoy [II.793], and the little María Josefa who was only three or four months old.

Goya's stay in this enchanting place, where hunting parties with the Infante gave the artist a chance to demonstrate his rare talent as a marksman, remained one of his happiest memories. He spent four weeks painting portraits of the Infante, his wife and their two eldest children [209-212], as well as studies for the large family portrait which he may have sketched on the spot but probably finished in his studio in Madrid [206-208]. The warmth of his reception and the sympathy he was shown helped Goya to paint freely and so quickly that he was surprised himself and, like Fragonard, made a note of it on the back of the picture. Though the family portrait is not a great success, this remarkable series includes a masterpiece of childish grace, in pure rococo style. This is the portrait of the

Ill. p. 59

little María Teresa [210] who stands at the edge of a terrace in the park, against a background of the distant Sierra reminiscent of Velázquez, and accompanied by a toy griffon which balances the composition and adds a note of humour.

Goya left Arenas delighted by his hosts who, over and above the agreed reward, had showered him with expensive presents for himself and his wife. He was to continue working for the Infante in the following year, 1784, sketching him beside his architect Ventura Rodríguez [213], before painting a very lively portrait of the latter, which already shows a much more personal style [214]. The artist must have thought that the end of his worries was in sight, but by 1785 the Infante was seriously ill. Goya paid him a last visit in Madrid and wrote to Zapater: 'The poor Infante Don Luis ... is very ill; today I kissed his hand

The Marchioness of Pontejos

Goya probably painted this marvellous portrait of the Marquesa de Pontejos on the occasion of her marriage with Francisco Moñino, brother of the all-powerful Count of Floridablanca (see p. 58), and shortly after the artist's appointment as Painter to the King. Little is known of her life. In 1787 she was made an honorary member of the Royal Economic Society in Madrid, of which the Duchess of Osuna was the ladies' president. In 1824, Goya was to encounter her, married for the third time, in the salons frequented by the Spanish *émigrés* in Paris. She died in 1834.

In this portrait, Goya shows her in all the radiance of her youth and elegance. There is a striking contrast between the tapestry cartoons and country scenes which he was painting at the time in a purely *castizo* (traditionally Spanish) vein [248-271] and this image symbolizing those ladies of the Spanish aristocracy who affected the Marie-Antoinette style and were called in Madrid *petimetras*. The background of a park in the French style sets off the fragile figure of the young marchioness in her gorgeous finery of festoons and ribbons and lace. The palette is all lightness, in pearly greys and pale rose pinks.

If we compare this perfect example of rococo painting with the portrait of the Count of Altamira, we see at once how disconcerting Goya's art can be: at the same moment he can produce a dull, awkward work or a real masterpiece. Goya was an impulsive artist who was highly sensitive to the people around him, and his sitters could either inspire or paralyse him, according to his feelings for them. The young Marchioness of Pontejos, like the Countess-Duchess of Benavente (see p. 65) and the little Manuel Osorio [233], seems to have provided a poetic image of the happiness and fulfilment which Goya experienced during the years 1785 to 1790.

The Marchioness of Pontejos   [221] c.1786. 211 × 126 cm. National Gallery, Washington

Self-portrait in the studio
This little picture has very rarely been exhibited and has therefore not been studied with the attention it deserves. Everyone has acclaimed it as one of the most revealing of Goya's self-portraits but there is considerable disagreement concerning the date of its execution. Some critics believe it to be a portrait of the artist as a young man, painted about the period of his first tapestry cartoons; others consider it to be a much later work, dating from just before or even after the illness of 1793. The line of his face do indeed appear drawn and the eyes have a feverish, restless look which is a far cry from the youthful arrogance of the self-portraits of the years 1775 to 1785 (see p. 29 and 55). Whatever its date, the fascination of this little picture is that it shows us, for the first and last time, the artist at work in his studio. He is dressed in long hose and a little embroidered jacket and he wears a remarkable hat garnished in front with metal clips so that he could work by candle light, as described in the biography written by his son: 'the final touches which give a picture its whole effect were added at night by artificial light'. He holds a palette on which there are no more than a dozen colours. In the background a large, glazed window bathes the scene with the diffused back-lighting often employed by Goya.

Self-portrait in the studio   [II.331] c.1790-95. 42 × 28 cm. Countess of Villagonzalo, Madrid

Bibl. 72, p. 33

to bid him goodbye . . . and from what I have seen and observed these last few days, because he seemed to like seeing me often, he will not recover'. He was to die soon afterwards and with him went the first patron Goya thought he had at last found.

On 18 March 1785, however, he was made Deputy-director of Painting at the Academy and his name began to be more widely known at court. In a short space of time he had proved that he was not only the best cartoon painter of his day; he also became much sought after as a portraitist. He was approached by two great families, the Medinacelis and the *See p. 52* Benavente-Osunas: his *Annunciation* [234] for the Medinacelis, with its tiepolesque elegance, has already been mentioned; the Osunas commissioned their portraits from him The Osuna family [219, 220]. At thirty-three, the duchess was the most celebrated woman in Madrid together with the Duchess of Alba. She was renowned not for her beauty but for her intelligence and her refined elegance which was totally French in inspiration. Captivated by the charm of this great lady, Goya succeeded in creating one of his most splendid portraits *Ill. pp. 62, 65* which, like that of the Marchioness of Pontejos [221], represents what might be called the Marie-Antoinette style – in Madrid they would have been described as *petimetras* (from the French *petit maître*). But while Goya's *Pontejos* is a fragile piece of Sèvres porcelain, the Countess-Duchess of Benavente seems to have emerged straight from the salons of the encyclopedists. This ability to capture the character of his models so perfectly proves that by 1785 Goya was becoming a truly great portraitist. And yet at the same period, between 1785 and 1788 – and this is a typical example of that 'swing of the pendulum' which Sánchez Cantón found so striking in his work – Goya painted the gallery of insipid

The family of the Duke of Osuna
The Countess-Duchess of Benavente

The ninth Duke of Osuna and his wife, the Countess-Duchess of Benavente, were Goya's most generous patrons between the years 1785 and 1799. They commissioned or bought from him some thirty paintings including their own portraits and those of their children as well as pictures to decorate their home in Madrid, their country palace at La Alameda and their private chapel in the cathedral at Valencia.

Born in 1755, the duke was interested in all the latest ideas and was above all concerned with the problems of industry and agriculture. Like the king and a number of other grandees, he maintained 'pensioners' in France whom he sent there to perfect their skills or to complete their scientific studies. But his own personality was eclipsed by that of the duchess, who was three years older than he. Together with the Duchess of Alba, she was the most celebrated and most original woman of her time. Neither beautiful nor eccentric like her rival, she was remarkable for her intelligence and sharp wit and for her elegance which was entirely French in inspiration. She was president of the women's section of the Royal Economic Society in Madrid but was also the friend and patron of actors, bullfighters and artists, though she never gave way to the fashion for *majismo*. This portrait provides a dazzling evocation of her character and tastes: it is a brilliant piece of virtuosity which shows off the extravagance of her fashionable Parisian dress and at the same time a perfect expression of the intelligence and strength of character which transforms an otherwise plain face.

The family of the Duke of Osuna   [278] 1788. 225 × 174 cm.
Prado Museum, Madrid

portraits in the Bank of Spain, then the Bank of San Carlos [223-228]. From the sombre *Charles III* [224], whom he was painting for the first time, to the complacent *Cabarrús* [228] and the uncomfortable *Altamira* [225], they are altogether dull and boring, with their rigid poses and lifeless expressions, but the commission was no doubt a useful one.

Portraits for the Bank of San Carlos
Ill. p. 61

Fortune was soon to favour Goya again, in a quite unexpected way. The death in 1786 of Cornelio Vandergoten, the director of the royal tapestry factory (whose portrait Goya may have painted in 1782 [200]), led to a general reshuffle in the organization of the factory. At the suggestion of Bayeu and Maella, who were both Court Painters, Ramón Bayeu and Goya were appointed Painters to the King, each with a salary of fifteen thousand reales a year. Goya immediately wrote to Zapater to express his happiness: *Martín mio, ya soy Pintor del Rey con quince mil reales,* and he went on to say that he owed this to Bayeu who had arranged that Maella should nominate Goya while he naturally nominated his younger brother. So the storm over the Pilar frescoes seems to have been forgotten and the reconciliation is proved by Goya's very fine portrait of Francisco Bayeu in the museum at Valencia [229]. In Spain as elsewhere family quarrels may be violent, but in the end the interests of the family are more important.

Goya appointed Painter to the King

Bibl. 72, p. 35

Ill. p. 42

Goya's financial position was now secure. In his letters to Zapater he reckoned up his accounts: with the twelve of thirteen thousand reales he was already earning, not forgetting his shares in the Bank of San Carlos, he now found himself in possession of twenty-eight thousand reales a year. Conscious of his new social position, he succumbed to the extravagances of the *nouveau riche* and tried to play the dandy. No sooner made Painter

The Countess-Duchess of Benavente   [220] 1785. 104×80 cm. Bartolomé March Servera, Madrid

The meadow of San Isidro [272] 1788. 44×94 cm. Prado Museum, Madrid

This celebrated picture is in fact a sketch for one of the tapestry cartoons intended for the decoration of the bedchamber of the Infantas in the palace of El Pardo. Only one cartoon, the *Blind man's buff*, was completed (see p. 69) since all further work came to an end with the death of Charles III. Goya, who was overwhelmed with work in the spring of 1788, created here with brilliant impetuosity and as if at a single sitting one of the most luminous landscapes in the whole history of painting.

He has represented an aspect of the Madrid which he loved so well, the banks of the river Manzanares sparkling in the bright atmosphere of the month of May and animated by the gay crowd of little figures gathered to celebrate the feast of their patron saint. But what would have become of this sketch, which seems to us so perfectly complete, transposed onto the huge canvas which was already prepared in Goya's studio? Something quite different, which would never have anticipated with the force of the sketch the clear palette of the impressionists. The little picture was bought by the Duke of Osuna in 1799.

to the King on 25 June than he bought a *birlocho*, a two-wheeled chaise, of which there were only three like it in the whole of Madrid. Unfortunately, Don Francisco was not used to this style of living and on his first outing he came a cropper and limped home in mortification. All this was related to Zapater with any number of picturesque details, and the letter is now signed Francisco *de* Goya. Success is not accompanied by any notice-able modesty.

Bibl. 72, pp. 35-36

He resumed work for the tapestry factory which he supplied in 1786 with the wonderful series of cartoons depicting the *Seasons* [262-265]. At the same time and in the same vein he painted seven decorative pictures for the walls of the Osunas' country palace near Madrid [248-254]; the duchess called the palace *El Capricho* (the Caprice) and it was generally known as La Alameda de Osuna. With these justly famous paintings, Goya reached the heights of his period of good fortune. Everything was in his favour: finally, to his great joy, he had a child who survived, Francisco Javier, born on 2 December 1784; he was Painter to the King, and above all he had become in a very short space of time the favourite painter of the most illustrious families at court. The Osunas heaped him with commissions and the Count of Altamira ordered the portraits of his wife and of their two sons, Vicente and above all Manuel Osorio, one of the most exquisite child portraits ever painted [231-233]. Goya now experienced the luxury of making himself sought after and of only working for those he found agreeable.

Decorative paintings for the Osunas

Bibl. 72, p. 36

This period of real happiness was to be short-lived. At the end of 1788 Charles III died. Charles IV and María Luisa had already shown Goya their favour ten years before and as soon as they were on the throne they proved it again in the clearest way by appointing him Court Painter. For Goya, therefore, the new reign began under excellent auspices and promised well for him. But the great shadow of the French Revolution of 1789 was spreading over an unsuspecting Spain and within the country the *afrancesados*, the admirers of French philosophical ideas, were threatened with persecution. Some of Goya's friends were affected; Cabarrús, the founder of the Bank of San Carlos [228], then Jovellanos who was exiled from Madrid, as was his faithful admirer Ceán Bermúdez [222]. Jovellanos had been responsible for commissioning the royal portraits of 1789 for the Royal Academy of History [281, 282], and had proved a sure friend, a man above all admirable for his ideals, his honesty and his profound patriotism. So around 1790 Goya seems to have been caught in a dilemma: on one side was the king whom he was bound to love and serve; on the other, the circle of new friends whose ideas were also dear to him. The Spain of the majos and majas, of *seguidillas* and dancing in the open air, receded into the distance as his mind was beset by other preoccupations. Towards the end of 1790 he wrote a rather clumsily-phrased but nonetheless revealing letter about his new perplexities to Zapater, saying, with reference to some *seguidillas* he was sending: 'How much you will enjoy hearing them. I have not yet listened to them and it is most probable that I shall never hear them, since I no longer go to the places where I would be able to hear them, for I have taken it into my head that I ought to maintain a firm line and preserve a certain dignity which a man ought to possess, all of which as you can imagine doesn't make me very happy'. How changed he was! One feels that he had suddenly decided to adopt a new attitude to life, and it may well have been Jovellanos and his friends who influenced this change. At the age of forty-four, Goya was discovering the world of ideas and, although the serious illness which struck him to the roots of his being two years later marked a great turning point in his life, it should not be forgotten that before then, and when he was still in good health, Goya had acquired maturity and an awareness, however confused, of human problems. In a darkening world the nineteenth-century man was beginning to emerge.

1788 Charles IV succeeds Charles III

Ill. p. 61

Royal portraits of 1789

Bibl. 58, p. 155; 154, p. 85

1786-1792. Goya is 40 to 46 years old. Cartoons for Charles III (The Seasons, the 'Wounded mason', etc.) and for Charles IV and María Luisa. Last series of cartoons left unfinished in 1792.

Goya had only just delivered the last cartoons in the series intended for the bedchamber and ante-chamber of the prince of Asturias at El Pardo [132-142], when a royal decree, dated 15 March 1780, suspended the execution of any further tapestry cartoons (Bibl. 154, doc. 67). These restrictions were due to economic difficulties arising from Spain's commitment to an effective policy of support for the English colonies in America.

Blind man's buff   [276] 1788-89. 269×350 cm. Prado Museum, Madrid

The wounded mason
268×110 cm. Prado Museum, Madrid

The straw manikin
267×160 cm. Prado Museum, Madrid

Harvesting or Summer

After an interruption of six years, from the time of his election to the Academy in 1780 until his nomination as Painter to the King in 1786, Goya again took up his work for the tapestry factory of Santa Bárbara. He executed two separate series of cartoons for the royal residences, one in 1786-88 which was interrupted by the death of Charles III and the other in 1791-92 which was intended for the secretariat of the new king, Charles IV, in the palace at El Escorial, but was interrupted in its turn by Goya's serious illness.

The first series included representations of the Seasons [262-265], of which the sketch for *Summer* is reproduced here, and the *Wounded mason*. This latter scene, dramatic, even tragic in character, in fact derives from a sketch representing a *Drunken mason* [260] which was probably rejected by the king as being unsuitable for his dining-room.

The cartoon with the *pelele – The straw manikin* – belongs to the second series begun just before Goya's illness. The style and execution have the same freshness and gaiety as the earlier cartoons but there is a new note of humour in the subject which already prefigures some of the *Caprichos* prints and was to reappear with much greater dramatic force, many years later, in one of the *Disparates* prints, the *Feminine Folly* (see p. 309).

The wounded mason   [266] 1786-87   The straw manikin   [301] 1791-92

Harvesting or Summer   [257] 1786. Sketch 34×76 cm. Lázaro Galdiano Museum, Madrid

Bibl. 154, doc. 78

When faced with the risk that the tapestry factory would have to close down and that the workers would be reduced to begging in the streets, the order was revoked in 1783 and it was decided to continue with the decoration of the palace of El Pardo. However, neither Bayeu nor Maella, who were responsible for seeing that cartoons were painted, made any move to call in Goya. This may have been due to Bayeu's ill-feelings towards him after the quarrel over the Pilar frescoes; equally, Goya may have refused the task because he was too busy with commissions and realized that it was only this kind of work which would bring him certain success. Nothing definite is known, but it was not until he had been appointed Painter to the King, in 1786, that Goya again began working for the tapestry factory.

Ill. p. 70

In 1786-1787 he executed a series of cartoons for the dining-room at El Pardo [262-271]. It includes the famous four seasons, represented by the *Flower-girls, Harvesting, Grape-harvest* and *Snow-storm* [262-265], and the two cartoons on 'social' themes, the *Wounded mason* and the *Poor people by a fountain* [266, 267]. All these paintings show Goya's brilliant virtuosity – as do the pictures executed at the same period for the Alameda de Osuna [248-254] – but there is a feeling that Goya is nearing the end of a decisive phase. A second series for El Pardo was put in hand at the beginning of 1788 but the death of Charles III brought it to a halt and only one cartoon, the *Gallina ciega* (Blind man's buff) [276], was completed for the weavers. Among the sketches there remained a masterpiece, the *Meadow of San Isidro* [272], later acquired by the Duke of Osuna.

Ill. p. 69
Ill. pp. 66-67

Goya appointed Court Painter

Bibl. 154, docs 128-135

Ill. p. 70

Having been appointed Court Painter on the accession of Charles IV, Goya refused to paint any more cartoons since he considered this kind of work incompatible with his new dignity. Only the threat of being deprived of his salary and the intervention of his brother-in-law persuaded him once again to give way. He painted seven final compositions for the tapestry factory of Santa Bárbara [300-306], including the *Pelele* (Straw manikin) [301] which already hints at a satirical intention in the same vein as some of the *Caprichos* prints. But this was still 1792 and Goya's work was now interrupted by his departure for Andalusia and above all by the very serious illness which was to transform his life.

Bibl. 34, p. 100

Goya's cartoons were originally intended only to serve as patterns for the master weavers and certainly never to be shown to the public. The sixty-three recorded cartoons, most of them now in the Prado (they were not handed over to the museum until 1870), constituted a kind of 'laboratory' for Goya's painting. Beneath these charming scenes of eighteenth-century popular life, which were to become the unforgettable *Goyescas* of Granados, the greatest of Spanish painters laid the foundations of his style and technique: drawing, composition, colouring, the relationship between figures and background, the 'magic of the atmosphere' as his son later recorded. The tapestry cartoons lie at the source of a large part of Goya's art and provided a vast reservoir from which he was to draw, consciously or unconsciously, throughout the rest of his work.

INTRODUCTION TO THE FIVE PARTS OF THE CATALOGUE

With the catalogue of Goya's entire œuvre now drawn up, and even though it may be open to criticism, like all catalogues, on points of detail, an analysis of the figures involved suggests several interesting features. In spite of the fact that this analysis is based on numerical considerations, and does not take into account either the quality or the aesthetic importance of the works, it is nevertheless of value in that it enables us to find what we might call the centre of gravity of Goya's work and to follow the displacement of this centre of gravity throughout the sixty-five years of his creative activity.

The first conclusion is that the greatest concentration of works occurs between 1808 and 1819 (Part III), when Goya was between sixty-two and seventy-three years old: of the almost nineteen hundred works catalogued, nearly seven hundred belong to this period. But the second, highly significant conclusion is that of these seven hundred works almost four-fifths are prints and drawings. The importance of Goya's graphic work as a whole is indeed one of the most outstanding features since it accounts for more than two-thirds of the catalogue, with the drawings representing almost a half of his entire œuvre. One is therefore justified in maintaining that Goya is essentially a master of black and white.

The relationship – again, merely numerical – between the paintings and the graphic work varies considerably in the course of his artistic career. Until 1792 (Part I), up to the age of forty-six and his very serious illness, prints and drawings only occupy about a sixth of the catalogue, the major part being taken up by paintings. In the last years of his life at Bordeaux (Part V), the proportions are exactly reversed: the drawings and prints, above all the lithographs, form the essential part of his production. Between these two extremes, the paintings constantly decrease in number in favour of the graphic work which comes to occupy a preponderant place during the second period of his life (Part II, 1792-1808) with the Sanlúcar and Madrid albums, followed by the work undertaken in connection with the *Caprichos*; these three series represent a group of some three hundred drawings of very similar inspiration.

If we now consider the paintings on their own, we are struck by the fact that half the known portraits were painted between 1792 and 1808 (Part II), whereas during the last nine years of his life (Parts IV and V, 1819-1828) we only find a very few portraits of friends. This tendency is still clearer where religious paintings are concerned: almost all of them were executed before 1808 (Parts I and II).

In conclusion, we should emphasize that whereas the paintings decrease in number over the years, though with a corresponding gain in depth and intensity, the sudden emergence of drawings, followed by prints on original themes, beginning with the Sanlúcar and Madrid albums when he was already in his fifties, constitutes the most important aspect of Goya's personality and one of the essential keys to his work.

ARRANGEMENT OF THE CATALOGUE

The catalogue is divided according to the five parts of the book. For ease of reference, the paintings, drawings and prints within each part are grouped by categories (portraits, genre, prints, etc.) and divided, often fairly arbitrarily, into periods. The illustrated catalogue includes 1,891 works: 688 paintings, 904 drawings, 290 engravings and lithographs and 9 prints after lost works. In addition, 82 replicas of the paintings are catalogued in the notes where copies and about fifty other works which have disappeared or whose attribution to Goya is not accepted here are mentioned or discussed. The danger of a too hasty acceptance or rejection of doubtful works has led to the inclusion of many which are accompanied by an expression of our opinion or that of other critics.

The *texts* incorporated in the catalogue introduce each group of works and give the essential facts. The *legends* below the illustrations give the basic information concerning each work and refer the reader to the illustrations in the text and to the notes. The *notes* complete the brief catalogue legends (where titles may be incomplete or translations lacking) and provide additional information: inscriptions, relevant documents, bibliographical references, indication of replicas and copies. A number of documents referred to in the notes are transcribed in the *appendices*. A numbered *bibliography* of the works referred to in the marginal notes to the main text and in the notes to the catalogue follows the appendices.

CATALOGUE I c.1762-1792

INTRODUCTION

PAINTINGS It is generally accepted that Goya's creative activity began about 1762-63 with the decoration of the reliquary in the church of Fuendetodos [1-4] and his participation in the competition at the Academy of San Fernando in Madrid. Between this time and the end of 1774, when he finally settled in Madrid at the age of twenty-eight, he must have worked a great deal. Nevertheless, the catalogue only includes some fifty works for this early period. This means that apart from several well-known groups of works, such as the mural paintings for Sobradiel [10-16] and El Pilar in Saragossa [30], for Muel and Remolinos [34-41] and the charterhouse of Aula Dei [42-48], a considerable number of works executed during these thirteen years remain unknown, either because they have been lost or because they have not yet been identified among the mass of unattributed paintings of the period. We have been able, thanks to the generosity of José Gudiol, to reproduce a number of works whose publication was reserved for his catalogue raisonné of the paintings.

This first part of the catalogue covers some thirty years of Goya's life, before his serious illness in 1792-93. During this long period of development, paintings, as already pointed out, are far more numerous than drawings and engravings. Within the paintings, there are two main streams: religious subjects, particularly in the form of huge mural schemes, and tapestry cartoons. In other words, his activity as a painter was mainly concerned with decorative works.

The most important religious works were executed after his return from Italy in 1771; they include the decoration of the sanctuary of El Pilar in Saragossa [30, 177-183] and the charterhouse of Aula Dei [42-48]. This last work alone originally represented some three hundred square metres of oil painting.

In a quite different spirit, the tapestry cartoons represent a sort of painting laboratory where he worked out his colour and his draughtsmanship. This fundamental group of works, preserved almost intact in the Prado Museum, was executed during three periods in his life which are clearly defined by the invaluable documents published by Cruzada Villaamil and by Sambricio. First, from 1775 to 1780, thirty-nine cartoons [57-85, 124-142]; then from 1786 to 1788, until the death of Charles III, eleven cartoons [256-276]; finally, under Charles IV, in 1791-92, seven cartoons [295-306]. It should be noted that most of this enormous production dates from the reign of Charles III and that the final cartoons made for Charles IV were executed under constraint.

Portraits appear rather late in the catalogue of Goya's work. After a few mediocre essays, we have to wait until 1783, when he was thirty-seven, the decisive year for him in this field where everything depended on obtaining commissions. The portrait of the Prime Minister Floridablanca [203] and those of the family of the Infante Don Luis de Borbón [206-213], executed in that year, mark the real start of his astonishingly productive career as a portrait painter. This section includes the first series of royal portraits [279-288] commissioned for the coronation of Charles IV and María Luisa of Parma in 1789.

Finally, among the paintings of this period, the six little canvases devoted to children's games [154-159] are of considerable significance. Goya's liking for 'series' of pictures of small dimensions and on a similar theme was to be a constant feature of his work and the idea probably developed from the series of cartoons for tapestries. The catalogue regroups all such series of pictures wherever there are documents to provide the necessary evidence.

DRAWINGS Judging from the sheets which have survived, drawings occupied a very small place in the first thirty years of Goya's career. Until the age of fifty, he only used his pencil, chalk or pen as a means of preparation for a painting or a print: studies of a figure or a gesture, especially for the tapestry cartoons – see [62-86]; the working out of a composition [193, 196, 197, 242, 245, 247] or its transcription, with a rare sensitivity for the pictorial qualities of the originals, in his copies after Velázquez made for the etchings – see [89-117]. In this sphere, Goya does not represent an exception to the custom, which was well-established among Spanish painters, of executing only a very few drawings in preparation for their paintings. If a preliminary study seemed necessary, it was usually executed directly with the brush on a small canvas, where the main lines of the design and the general colour scheme were indicated. It was not until 1796 that Goya began to discover his exceptional talents as a draughtsman.

ENGRAVINGS Goya's fame as an engraver rests on his large series of prints of exceptional originality and technical brilliance. He was already in his early fifties when he published the Caprichos [II.451-613] and his previous experiments in the art of print-making date from some twenty years earlier.

Two of his earliest known prints [53, 55] show close similarities in style and technique with those of Giambattista Tiepolo and his sons Domenico and Lorenzo. All three worked in Madrid and their influence, direct or indirect, probably accounts for the manner which Goya first adopted. Although his engraving style developed and changed over the years, his basic method remained constant. A preparatory drawing was almost invariably made and Goya normally transferred the drawing to the copperplate and followed its imprint with his etching needle. The St Isidore [53, 54] offers an excellent example of this method. For the etching of St Francis of Paula, however, the drawing served as a model which he copied on the copperplate [55, 56]. The print in this case appears as a reverse image of the drawing. In the Copies after Velázquez [88-117], Goya used the first method throughout. In this first series of prints, he achieved technical mastery in the pure etching plates and began to discover the possibilities of aquatint.

The Copies after Velázquez, executed in 1778-79, represent Goya's first venture in the field of publishing. With the exception of the prophetic Garrotted man [122], no further prints are known between this date and the years 1797-98 when he was working on the Caprichos. Of the total of 290 known prints by Goya – engravings and lithographs – only 20 fall within this first period of his career.

NOTES TO CATALOGUE I [1-316]

1-4 Goya's earliest known work, first mentioned by Zapater (Bibl. 72, p. 21). It was destroyed in 1936. Milicua suggested the scheme was executed towards the end of his apprenticeship with Luzán, and that the designs were based on prints (Bibl. 133, pp. 10-13).

2 and 3 The 'Virgen del Carmen' and San Francisco de Paula' were painted on the inside of the reliquary doors. The *Saint Francis* has the inscription *CA/RI/TAS*.

4 Painted on the outside of the reliquary doors.

5 and 6 A pair of paintings identified and published by Gudiol.

7-9 Paintings identified and published by Gudiol.

10-16 Described *in situ* by Ricardo del Arco, 'Pinturas de Goya (inéditas) en el palacio de los Condes de Sobradiel de Zaragoza', *Boletín de la Sociedad Española de Excursiones*, XXIII, 1915, pp. 124-131. See also Milicua (Bibl. 133, pp. 21-23) and Sambricio, 'Les peintures de Goya dans la chapelle du Palais des Comtes de Sobradiel à Saragosse', *Revue des Arts*, 1954, pp. 215-222.

10 Painted on the left wall of the chapel. The composition is taken from an etching by Carlo Maratta after one of his own works. See the illustrations in Sambricio (*op. cit.* p. 217). Milicua described this painting as a replica (Bibl. 133, p. 23), but see Held (Bibl. 89, no. 3) for his revised opinion.

11 Painted on the right wall of the chapel. Milicua and Sambricio identified the source as an engraving by Dorigny after Vouet; see illustrations in Sambricio (*op. cit.* p. 221). The painting is in a very damaged condition.

12 Painted on the chapel ceiling. The source of the Vouet composition was identified by Milicua as an engraving by Daret and by Sambricio as an engraving by Dorigny (*op. cit.* ill. pp. 218, 219).

13-16 Two of these small figures were painted on each side of the niche containing a cult image. Arco specified that the last two were the outermost figures (*op. cit.* p. 127). Correggio's frescoes on the pendentives of Parma cathedral have been suggested as a source. The paintings are said to have left Spain after the 1928 Saragossa exhibition.

17 and 18 See Milicua (Bibl. 133, pp. 15-17). The lack of comparative material and of a secure chronology in Goya's early work makes the attribution of these pictures an open question. The subject of the first, which has always been described as the 'Carrying out of the edict', was identified by Pierre Gassier who was able to read the inscription correctly.

19 and 20 First identified and published by Xavière Desparmet Fitz-Gerald, 'Peintures exécutées par Francisco Goya en 1771 et restées ignorées', *Pantheon*, XXII, 1964, pp. 400-403.

21 Painting recently identified and kindly communicated by Xavière Desparmet Fitz-Gerald.

22 Signed and dated on the side of the altar, as part of the carved decoration. First published with its pair [23] by Milicua (Bibl. 133, pp. 19-21) and exhibited in 1963-64 (Bibl. 27, nos 42, 43).

24 A recently discovered, larger version of [23], which supports the theory that these classical subjects were painted to help support the artist in Rome. Painting kindly communicated by Xavière Desparmet Fitz-Gerald.

25 First published by Lozoya (Bibl. 120, pp. 63-66). The curious form of the signature (Goya did not use the en-

nobling 'de' until many years later) could be explained as an extravagance of the unknown but ambitious young student abroad.

26 Possibly painted on the occasion of Goya's marriage to Josefa Bayeu in 1773 (Sánchez Cantón, however, dated it some ten years later). First exhibited in 1961 (Bibl. 23, no. XXVI).
Replicas: 62×42 cm. Saint Louis, City Art Mus. (14.23) M.290 Mayer cited another replica in the gallery of Maria Cristina (M.291), echoing Viñaza (Bibl. 190, p. 254, no. LXIV).

27 Dimensions as given by museum; those in recent catalogues: 37×53 cm. Often considered a self-portrait by Goya, it has also been attributed to Francisco Bayeu. See Sambricio (Bibl. 155, p. 24) and Held (Bibl. 89, p. 190).

28 Inscribed *Sr. Conde/de Miranda/año/1774* on the knob of the stick. All critics have noted the Mengsian qualities in this portrait which is not now generally considered to be by Goya.

30-33 See Viñaza for a full account with documents (Bibl. 190, pp. 20-21, 157-159), also Lafuente and Stolz (Bibl. 105, pp. 120-121, 136). Sánchez Cantón affirmed that Goya received the final payment on July 31, 1772 (Bibl. 166, p. 14). The sketch [31] and two drawings were published by José Gudiol, 'La primera gran obra de Goya', *Coloquio*, 35, 1965, pp. 19-23.

31 Exhibited 1970 (Bibl. 30, no. 1).

32 and 33 Identified by Gudiol as studies for the two angels standing together towards the left.
Another drawing, apparently belonging to the same group of studies, was reproduced by Paul Lafond (Bibl. 97, p. 11) and is probably the drawing catalogued with the same title: 'Tête d'étude' s. *Fran.co Goya* at right Red chalk 45×33 cm. Formerly Paris, Paul Lafond Lafond (*op. cit.* p. 153, no. 30).

34-41 See Milicua (Bibl. 133, p. 8 and n. 1) and Sánchez Cantón (Bibl. 166, p. 14).

34-37 The sanctuary at Muel was apparently built in 1770, and the paintings are in oil applied directly to the plaster.

38-41 If, as Milicua indicates (see note [34-41]), the church at Remolinos was not built until 1782, these oil paintings on canvas were either copied at a later date from Goya's original mural paintings [34-37] or were transferred from another church.

42-48 Mentioned by Father Tomás López, one of the monks at the Aula Dei monastery (Bibl. 190, p. 462). Beruete gave a full description of the paintings which he saw before 1903 (Bibl. 36, II, pp. 8-11). Documents connected with this work were published by Gudiol (Bibl. 83).

42 The left part of the painting over the main door. The Saint Anne on the right was completely repainted and the angels in the centre are in very poor condition.

43 On the right wall on entering through the main door. The following paintings are listed in order, continuing towards the altar.

46 On the three walls of the shallow crossing.

48 On the crossing opposite [46]. The left wall has been repainted, and this is the only fragment of Goya's work to have survived on this side of the chapel.

52 This proof was listed by Harris as 'Formerly Madrid, Gerona'. Carderera suggested the print may have formed part of a series (Bibl. 45, [III], p. 239).

54 Mentioned in Bibl. 189, p. 7.

55 The inscription is an abbreviation of *Caritas* (Charity). The original copperplate is in the Calcografía Nacional, Madrid (Bibl. 5, *Goya*, no. 194; inventory no. 1646).

57-69 The descriptions of [57-61] are from Goya's account dated 24 May 1775 (Bibl. 154, doc. 8). For further contemporary descriptions of the cartoons, see Vandergoten's receipt of delivery (*op. cit.* doc. 10) and the inventories of 1780 (doc. 74, nos 85-92) and 1782 (doc. 77). On the relationship with the cartoons of Ramón Bayeu, see Sambricio (*op. cit.* pp. 67-68).

57 ...*un Jabalí acosado de quatro perros, tres agarrados â èl y uno por tierra vencido, y cuatro Cazadores q.e con las bayonetas ban à acabarlo, y su país correspondiente.*

58 Over-door, pair to [59]. ...*dos perros de caza atados; en el suelo dos escopetas, volsas frasco, y morral, y su país correspondiente.* Prado title: 'Perros y utiles de caza'. One of the cartoons stolen from the Royal Palace in 1870; see Bibl. 154 (doc. 280, no. ...40) and note to [129].

59 (Hunt with owl and net). Over-door, pair to [58]. ...*una Red colgada de un Arbol, y un perro q.e sale p.r debaxo de ella, en el suelo una Jaula con un mochuelo dentro, y â al lado otra Jaula con un gilguero, y tres paxaros q.e vienen bolando acia el mochuelo.* Prado title: 'Caza con reclamo'.

60 (Hunter loading his gun). ...*un cazador cargando su escopeta, y un perro descansando à primer termino, un poco mas atras dos Cazadores ablando...*

61 (The hunter and his dogs). ...*un Cazador q.e se bà, y lleba dos perros àtados, y otro mas apartado à caballo, y su país correspondiente...*

62 Exhibited in 1963-64 (Bibl. 27, no. 142).

63 (The quail shoot). Goya's account lost; description from Vandergoten's receipt for delivery (Bibl. 154, doc. 13): ...*varios Cazadores, uno en postura de prevenir la salida de Codorniz óbservando la muestra del Perro, otro ápuntando a un Pajaro que Buela, y su compañero óservando, a lo lejos dos a Cavallo en seguimiento de los galgos que corren detras de una Liebre.* Prado title: 'Partida de caza'. See Lafuente (Bibl. 102, p. 105) for sources in Houasse and de la Traverse (reprinted from *Goya (Cinco Estudios)*, Saragossa, 1949, where the Houasse painting is reproduced, pl. I).

64 Drawing attributed to Francisco Bayeu in Barcia's catalogue.

65 Drawing undescribed by Barcia or Sambricio.

66 Description as [63]: ...*un pescador sentado a la Orilla de un Lago de água con caña; en segundo término, dos hombres con escopetas conbersando mirando una anade muerta, que el uno tiene en la mano, y el otro la suspende.*

67 Signed *D. Fran.co Goya* at lower left.

68 (...with an owl). Description as [63]: ...*tres Jovenes cazando con Mochuelo, al que tienen puesto en una Muletilla, y ellos a lo lejos óbservando si se posan los pajaros en la liga que tienen puesta.* Probably among the cartoons stolen from the Royal Palace in 1870, but not listed in the Madrid newspapers since it was attributed to Ramón Bayeu. See Sambricio for a full account, and also the note to [129].

69 (Hunting still-life). Description as [63]: ...*varias piezas de Caza muerta, Liebres, Conejos, y Gangas, colgadas de un tronco, y Arneses de Cazador junto a ello.* The cartoon had apparently already been lost by 1834.

70-84 These and other cartoons by Goya's colleagues, representing *las diversiones y trajes del tiempo presente*, were referred to by Antonio Ponz in volume V of his *Viage de España*, published in 1776 (Bibl. 140, pp. 478-479). Goya's accounts specify that they were painted *de mi invencion*. For further contemporary descriptions of the cartoons, see the inventories of 1780 and 1782 (Bibl. 154, docs 73, 74 and 76). For sketches, see note to [143-153].

70 ...*huna merienda, q.ᵉ cinco Jobenes an echo en el canpo y huna Naranjera q.ᵉ ba â benderles naranjas, y cuatro figuras mas lejos paseando y el pais poblado de arboles q.ᵉ con algun principio de caserias demuestra estar cerca de poblacion* (Bibl. 154, doc. 22, and see Vandergoten's description in doc. 24). Prado title: 'La Merienda a orillas del Manzanares'.

73 Studies for the seated figure half-hidden by the two drinkers and for the cloaked men standing in the background at the right edge.

74 (Dance on the banks of the river Manzanares). ...*un bayle â orilla del Rio Manzanares; dos Majos y dos Majas que baylan seguidillas, y otros dos que hazen Musica uno de ellos canta con la guitarra, otro acompaña con una bandurria y otro en el mismo termino que con las manos lleva el Compas. Detras de estos hay otra Maja y otros dos que se ven por entre medio que estan en el mismo grupo: Mas cerca del Rio hay un Militar con una Maja en conversacion y otra que de el Bayle hà hido a ver al Rio: hay varios despojos de Capas y Sombreros a primer termino y a lo lexos se vè un poco de Madrid por S.ⁿ Fran.ᶜᵒ* (Bibl. 154, doc. 28, and see Vandergoten's description in doc. 31). Prado title: 'El baile de San Antonio de la Florida'.
The sketch for this cartoon was apparently sent by Goya to Zapater in December 1778. Collection unknown S.11c (and p. 93).
Reduction: 29·5×67·7 cm. Formerly Buenos Aires, Alexander E. Shaw Reproduced in *Cicerone*, XXII, 1930, p. 270.

76 (Fight at the New Inn). Inscribed *VENTA NUEBA* on the inn-sign. ...*huna venta q.ᵉ an llegado caleseros y arrieros de barias probincias de España, y despues de descansar se pusieron a jugar a los naipes y sobre el juego armaron una camorra, y un Murciano, lleba a dos a mal andar, otro por despartir le tira de la chupa y le a roto por la aldilla. Otro por el mismo fin les amenaza con una rama de leña en las manos. Este primer grupo tiene cinco figuras. Ay dos luchando en el suelo, cuasi en el mismo termino y otro q.ᵉ no tiene tanto espiritu q.ᵉ esta con una piedra en la mano en ademan de querer huir. A la puerta de la venta ay barios el ventero recoje el dinero y otro q.ᵉ ba â bajar de un caballo con una pistola. Toda la conposicion de este cuadro tiene trece figuras y algunas q.ᵉ asoman a lo lejos* (Bibl. 154, doc. 33, and see Vandergoten's description in doc. 36).

77 Inscribed *MESON/DEL GALLO* (Cock Inn) on the façade of the building.

78 (Promenade in Andalusia). ...*un paseo de Andalucia q.ᵉ lo forma una arbolada de Pinos, por donde ba un Jitano y huna Jitana paseando y un chusco q.ᵉ esta sentado con su capa y sombrero redondo su calzon de grana con chareteras y galones de oro, media y zapato corespondiente, parece aberle echado alguna flor a la Jitana, a lo q.ᵉ el aconpañante se esta â armar camorra y la Jitana le insta a q.ᵉ ande ay dos amigos del de el sonbrero redondo acechando aber en q.ᵉ para. Estas cinco figuras estan en primer termino y otras tres q.ᵉ estan mas lejos* (Bibl. 154, doc. 33, and see Vandergoten's description in doc. 36). Prado title: 'La maja y los embozados'. Exhibited 1970 (Bibl. 30, no. 2). For a possible preparatory study, see [148].
A 'study' for the seated *embozado* is known from a photograph: 80×64 cm. Paris, Demotte (1922) S.13a; M.567a, DF.139 (Dimensions given by Desparmet: 85·5×65 cm.).

79 ...*huno q.ᵉ esta bebiendo con una bota a la catalana y un muchacho a su lado (sentados anbos) comiendo un rabano y media libreta, de tras ay tres figuras como q.ᵉ ban por un camino* (Bibl. 154, doc. 33, and see Vandergoten's description in doc. 36).

80 ...*una muchacha sentada en un ribazo, con un perrito en el alda, a su lado un muchacho en pie aciendole sonbra con un quitasol* (Bibl. 154, doc. 33, and see Vandergoten's description in doc. 36).

81 ...*cinco Jobenes q.ᵉ an salido al canpo a hechar una cometa, a la cual le estan dando cuerda, huno de ellos esta con el cigarro en la boca observâdo, y acen observacion barias Jentes q.ᵉ se an agregado a ellos y entre ellos huna Señorita con hun petimetre. El numero de las figuras q.ᵉ se ben en este cuadro, lejos y cerca para formar su conposicion, es trece. En la conposicion del canpo ay hun hedificio, a lo lejos arboles y hun perro echado, a primer termino* (Bibl. 154, doc. 38, and see Vandergoten's description in doc. 41).

82 ...*cuatro honbres Juagando a naipes detras de ellos ay tres mirando y huno de ellos aciendo señas con los dedos de el punto q.ᵉ tiene su contrario, a su companñero q.ᵉ esta enfrente, ganandoles el dinero. Estas siete figuras acen un grupo q.ᵉ conponen el cuadro, ay hun arbol con una capa q.ᵉ les ace sonbra y su pais corespondiente* (Bibl. 154, doc. 38, and see Vandergoten's description in doc. 41). For a possible sketch see [143].

83 (Boys blowing up a bladder). ...*dos muchachos en pie huno de ellos soplando una bejiga, y el otro espera p.ª atarla, detras de estos ay dos labradores, y dos mujeres q.ᵉ demuestran esperar a los muchachos, con su pais y arboles poblados* (Bibl. 154, doc. 38, and see Vandergoten's description in doc. 41).

84 (Boys picking fruit). ...*quatro muchachos cojiendo fruta y p.ª alcanzar se a puesto uno encima de otro, y los otros dos la aparan en el sonbrero, a lo lejos huna arbolada y montañas* (Bibl. 154, doc. 38, and see Vandergoten's description in doc. 41).

85 (The blind guitarist). ...*un Ciego canttando con su guittarra y su Lazarillo y Cattorze figuras q.ᵉ le esttan escuchando, y de las Prinzipales son, dos Mujeres, un Esttranjero, y un Negro bendiendo Agua, un Panadero, los resttantes esttan embozados con sus Capas, delantte de todo dos Muchachos senttados oyendole tambien. Ay en ottro termino una Carretta con Bueyes, al ottro lado un Grupo con muchas jenttes y enttre ellas uno q.ᵉ esta comprando un Melon. hay una prespettiva de Calle con Casas y una Obra q.ᵉ se fabrica en ella, se be el Orizontte y Cielo poblado de Nubes* (Bibl. 154, doc. 44; see also Vandergoten's descriptions in docs 47 and 49 where he specified that the cartoon shows a view of the Plazuela de la Cebada). The cartoon was subsequently modified: the oxen were almost eliminated, and comparison with the etching [87] shows that the buildings in the street were made much more conventional, the number of figures in the right background was reduced, and conventional foliage, including a tree and foreground plants, was added. See Sambricio (Bibl. 154, pp. 105-106).

87 Signed *Goya* on the stone in the left foreground. Apparently etched from the original design of the tapestry cartoon – see note to [85]. The proof illustrated was not known to Harris.

88-117 For the text of the announcements in the *Gaceta*, see Harris (Bibl. 88, II, p. 448). Series referred to by Ponz in 1778 (Bibl. 140, [VIII], p. 666), and by Goya in December of that year in a letter to Zapater (Bibl. 72, p. 24 and 36, I, p. 10; III, p. 8). The preparatory drawings, which belonged to Ceán Bermúdez, are mentioned in his *Diccionario* (Bibl. 47, V, p. 178). The date of Goya's illness (see text p. 48) is not entirely clear; the letter as quoted in Bibl. 72, p. 24, seems to belong to 1777 and Sambricio so interpreted it (Bibl. 154, p. 98), pointing to the influence of Velázquez already apparent in the tapestry cartoons delivered between August 1777 and January 1778 [76-84], but Sánchez Cantón gave the date as 1778 and suggested that the series was an immediate outcome of Goya's study of Velázquez during his convalescence (Bibl. 166, p. 19). The inscriptions on the drawings are all written with the pen and sepia ink in a careful hand, as a guide for engraving.

88 Engraved title: ...*un BACO fingido coronando algunos borrachos*... (a pretense Bacchus crowning some drunken men). Ponz referred to Goya's copy of the 'Triunfo de Baco en ridículo' by Velázquez (Bibl. 140, p. 1587) which at this period was considered a comic genre scene.
A small etching of the head of Bacchus was excluded by Delteil and Harris from the catalogue of Goya's prints. See Beruete (Bibl. 36, III, pp. 10 and 12, no. 5), Mayer (Bibl. 128, p. 79) and Delteil (Bibl. 55, II, 'Planches douteuses', no. 1).

89 Inscription: *Dibuxado por D. Francisco Goya del quadro original de D. Diego Velazquez, que está en el Real Palacio de Madrid.*

90 Engraved title: *FELIPE III. REY DE ESPAÑA.*

91 Inscription: *Pintado por Velazquez.* left, *Felipe III.* centre, *Dibuxado por Goya.* right.

92 Engraved title: *D. MARGARITA DE AUSTRIA, REYNA DE ESPAÑA, MUGER DE PHELIPE III.*

93 Engraved title: *FELIPE IV. REY DE ESPAÑA.*

94 Engraved title: *D. ISABEL DE BORBON, REYNA DE ESPAÑA, MUGER DE FELIPE QUARTO.*

95 Engraved title: *D. BALTASAR CARLOS PRINCIPE DE ESPAÑA. HIJO DEL REY D. FELIPE IV.*

96 Engraved title: *D.ⁿ Gaspar de Guzman, Conde de Olivares, Duque de Sanlúcar, &.*

97 Engraved title: *UN INFANTE DE ESPAÑA.* One of the two undated, aquatinted plates which were not included in the announcements of July and December 1778, and were presumably issued later, in 1779. Cp. the letter to Zapater (Bibl. 72, p. 24; 36, I, p. 10). See also [99].

98 See Bibl. 29, no. 104.

99 The buffoon's real name was Cristobal de Castañeda y Pernia. One of the two undated, aquatinted plates. See note to [97].

100 Inscription: *Velazquez le pintó* and *Goya le dibuxó.* See Bibl. 29, no. 105.

101 Engraved title: ...*Esopo el Fabulador*... (Aesop the Fabulist).

102 Reproduced by Campbell Dodgson in *Old Master Drawings*, I, no. 2, 1926, p. 20, pl. 28.

103 Engraved title: ...*Menipo Filosofo*... (Mennipus the Philosopher).

104 Engraved title: ...*un Enano del S. Phelipe IV*... (a Dwarf of Philip IV).

105 Engraved title as [104].

107 (The Maids of honour). The familiar title given to the unconventional portrait of the family of Philip IV. Proofs are printed on the verso of three of the eight known sheets.

108 Inscription: *Dibuxado por Goya del quadro original de Velazquez, que esta en el R.ˡ Palacio de Madrid.* This drawing was mentioned by Ceán Bermúdez in his *Diccionario*, in discussing Velázquez's original (Bibl. 47, V, p. 172).

109 One of the buffoons at the court of Philip IV. He took the name of Don John of Austria, and his real name is unknown.

110 See Bibl. 29, no. 106.

111 For details of the painting by Velázquez, see the exhibition catalogue *Velázquez y lo Velazqueño*, Madrid, 1960, no. 106.
A drawing attributed to Goya was exhibited in 1900 (Bibl. 8, no. 153) and published in *Boletín de la Sociedad Española de Excursiones*, XXX, 1922, pp. 109-115.

112 Unique proof, described in the Gijón catalogues (Bibl. 139) and mentioned in Bibl. 69 (p. 429, n. 2) but hitherto unrecorded in Goya print catalogues. Inscribed in ink (by Jovellanos?) *Velazquez pinx.* and *Goya delin. et sculp.* Photograph kindly supplied by A. E. Pérez Sánchez of the Museo del Prado. The dwarf's real name was Francisco Lezcano.

113 See Bibl. 29, no. 110.

114 (The Water-carrier of Seville). Inscribed *Pint. por Velazquez.* left, *Dibux. por Goya.* right, *El Aguador de Sevilla.* centre. The platemark (which measures 21×16 cm.) proves that the drawing was transferred for etching. See Bibl. 29, no. 111.
The painting by Velázquez, which was seized from Joseph Bonaparte's carriage after the battle of Vitoria in 1813,

forms part of the Wellington Museum collection (WM 1600-1948).

115 See Bibl. 29, no. 108.

116 See Bibl. 29, no. 107.

117 Inscribed *Pintado por Velazquez.* and *Dibuxado por Goya.* See Bibl. 29, no. 109.

118-120 See Sánchez Cantón (Bibl. 166, p. 19) and the Prado catalogue note to no. 2553 (pp. 753-754) for [118] and [119], also Bibl. 57, I, pp. 273-274. Copies of these two works of Velázquez, painted by Ramón Bayeu, were listed among the paintings and drawings in Francisco Bayeu's collection (Bibl. 153, doc. 8, pp. 68-80, nos 146, 147).

120 Inscribed *INOCENCIO X. PINTADO POR VELAZ-QUEZ, Y COPIADO POR F GOYA.* Authenticity doubted by Mayer (Bibl. 10, no. 38). The attributed Velázquez original, seized from Joseph Bonaparte's carriage after the battle of Vitoria in 1813, forms part of the Wellington Museum collection (WM 1590-1948).

124-142 Sambricio emphasized the darkening of the colours, due to the fusion of the pigments with the deep red ground colour (Bibl. 154, pp. 106-107, 114).
For sketches, see the note to [143-159].
For further contemporary descriptions of the cartoons, see Vandergoten's receipts of delivery (Bibl. 154, docs 55, 65 and 71) and the inventories of 1870 (doc. 74, nos 236-273) and 1872 (doc. 76, nos 11-30).

124 *. . .pasaje de Ferias en el Tpô de ellas, q.e es una prenderia delante de ella, el prendero tratando de la ventta de una alaja con una Señora, à quien acompañan dos Caballeros, el uno con un Antiojo mirando Ziertos Quadros q.e ay de Benta, detras de estos se descubren ótros quatro, y a mas distanzia Varias jentes* (Bibl. 154, doc. 52).

125 *. . .un Balenziano bendiendo Bajilla, dos S.ras Sen-tadas élixiendo p.a comprar, una Bieja sentada al mismo fin, à un lado dos Caballeros sentados sobre unos Ruedos mirando a un Coche q.e pasa por delante en el se be una S.ra detras dos Lacayos y un Bolante, y un Cochero en su Pescante, a mas distanzia se ben barias jenttes, y edifizios* (Bibl. 154, doc. 52).

126 (The officer and the lady). *. . .un Militar acom-pañiando a una S.ra la q.e esta ablando con otras dos, y otro q.e estan en un Corredor de un Jardín, detras de dicha S.ra se be un Lacayo, a mas distanzia dos hombres com-bersando, y parte de Edifizios* (Bibl. 154, doc. 52).

127 *. . .una Muger q.e bende Azerolas tres ombres detras en ademan de comprarle a mas distanzia se be otra q.e bende y genttes al redor todo demuestra esttar en Poblazion* (Bibl. 154, doc. 52).

128 (Boys playing at soldiers). *. . .dos muchachos como Jugando à los Soldados con Gorras y Escopetas ôtro tocàndo un Tambor, y otro Jugando con un Campanario de Ferias* (Bibl. 154, doc. 52). For a possible sketch see [144].

129 (Children with a cart). *. . .quatro niños Jugando dos dentro de un Carro, y ôtro bestido à la olandesa tocando un Tambor, el quinto niño toca una trompetilla* (Bibl. 154, doc. 52). One of six cartoons by Goya stolen from the Royal Palace in 1870, and described in the *Gaceta de Madrid* on 19 January 1870 (Bibl. 154, doc. 280, no. . . .30). See also nos [59, (68), 140, 142, 304, 306].

130 (Game of pelota). *. . .un Juego de pelota, Jugando tres a otros tres, y à berles Jugar ay beinte y cinco figuras a los lados del juego, en barias actitudes las q.e conponen el grupo princi.l q.e uno ay fumando, otros ablando del partido y otro señalando donde va la chaza* (Bibl. 154, doc. 52). For a possible sketch see [145].

131 *. . .una familia q.e an salido al canpo a dibertirsen, quatro niños y tres criadas la una se esta colunpeando en una cuerda q.e esta asida a un arbol y otra tiene a el niño chiquito de los andadores, las tres con los niños forman el grupo principal del quadro. y a lo lejos un coche esperando con el cochero y hunos pastores con ganado bacuno* (Bibl. 154, doc. 62).

132 *. . .un descanso de Labanderas à la orilla del Rio una de ellas se quedo Dormida en el regazo de otra à la q.e*

ban azer se dispierte con un Cordero q. la arriman à la cara dos dellas, otra sentada q.e se rie de berlo, y otra con un lio en la cabeza amas distanzia por donde se descubre Ropa tendida de las dichas q.e descansan. El Pais se com-pone de un Celage alegre, mucha Arboleda â un costado del Rio el qual se be benir de mui lejos rodeando porciones de tierras y matorrales con montañas nebadas à lo lejos (Bibl. 154, doc. 68). For a possible sketch see [146].

133 *. . .quatro Jobenes dibirtiendose con un Nobillo el uno en ademan de ponerle un parche, otro en postura de aber écho suerte con la capa, los otros dos uiendo, amas distanzia se ben barias gentes asomadas por encima de una Tapia mirando la dibersion* (Bibl. 154, doc. 68).

134 *. . .dos Jobenes jugando con un Perro de aguas sacando le la pelota de la voca detras de estos dos empie en combersacion se be mucha arboleda* (Bibl. 154, doc. 68). The cartoon had already been lost by 1834.

135 (The fountain). *. . .tres hombres q.e fatigados de la sed bienen a beber â una fuente uno de ellos esta bebiendo en el caño, y los dos aguardan q.e acabe, dond ai barias Yerbas y matorrales q.e con la humedad de dicha fuente se an criado* (Bibl. 154, doc. 68). The cartoon had already been lost by 1834.

136 (The tobacco guard). *. . .cinco guardas de rentas de Tabaco dos sentados descansando y uno en pie dan-doles combersazion, amas distanzia reconoziendo el terreno se ben dos ala orilla de un Rio dos de ellos con todas las armas q.e regularm.te lleban* (Bibl. 154, doc. 68). Described in Vandergoten's receipt (doc. 71) as 'dos Jaques' (two ruffians). The subject was discussed by Helman (Bibl. 93, pp. 98-102). For a possible study see [147].

137 (Boy with a bird). *. . .un Muchacho q.e esta sentado al pie de un Arbol jugando con un pagarito* (Bibl. 154, doc. 68).

138 *. . .un Muchacho agarrado à una Rama de un Arbol en postura de saltar, y otro detras con una Cesta* (Bibl. 154, doc. 68).

139 *. . .tres hombres cortando leña dos con achas en la mano, y el otro recojiendola el Monte vestido de matorrales* (Bibl. 154, doc. 68).

140-142 Nordström suggested that these three cartoons were allegories involving the seasons and the temperaments, with meditation and melancholy as the central motifs (Bibl. 136, pp. 11-28).

140 (Majo with a guitar). *. . .un hombre sentado can-tando con su Guitarra, y dos detras q.e le están escuchando y otra figura a lo lejos* (Bibl. 154, doc. 68). One of the cartoons stolen from the Royal Palace in 1870 – see note to [129] and Bibl. 154 (doc. 280, no. . . .34).

141 *. . .una Muger sentada y recostada sobre un terrazo detras de ella ay dos mirando su tristeza al otro lado quatro figuras à lo lejos* (Bibl. 154, doc. 68).

142 *. . .un Medico sentado calentandose a un Brasero, en el suelo a su lado barios Libros, y dos Estudiantes detras* (Bibl. 154, doc. 68). One of the cartoons stolen from the Royal Palace in 1870 – see note to [129] and Bibl. 154 (doc. 280, no. . . .36).

143-153 Goya made sketches for all his cartoons (since they had to be submitted to the king for approval) and they remained his property (see note to [74]). Some later sketches were sold to the Duke of Osuna [256-261, 272-275], and in 1824 'sixteen small sketches for the tapestries' were listed among his property in Madrid (Bibl. 57, I, p. 53, n. 1; see Appendix II, no. 1). The sketches sold to the Osunas form a homogeneous group, but the same is not true of those listed here [143-146], whose authenticity remains doubtful pending further study. They are very close to the compositions of the cartoons, whereas the later, 'Osuna' sketches show marked variations which can be traced in the pentimenti in the cartoons themselves.

Two larger paintings [148, 153] may have been prepared for tapestries. A probable cartoon published by Sánchez Cantón (Instituto de Valencia de Don Juan, Madrid, *Catálogo de las Pinturas*, 1930, no. 102 'Jovenes bailando'; repr. Bibl. 159, pl. 2) is not included here as part of Goya's œuvre.

147 Replica of the centre portion of the cartoon. Ex-hibited in 1959-60 (Bibl. 22, no. 131) and mentioned in the Prado catalogue (no. 788n).

148 Cp. the cartoon [78]. Published by August L. Mayer, 'Ein Teppichkarton von Goya', *Pantheon*, 1928, I, p. 10, ill. p. 11.

149 Dated by Gudiol a decade later. Exhibited 1961-62 (Bibl. 24, no. 9).

150 Sometimes described as a sketch for [70] but not accepted as such by Sambricio (Bibl. 154, p. 92). It be-longed, with [151], to the Marqués de la Torrecilla and both were exhibited in 1900 (Bibl. 8, nos 50, 51).
Sambricio referred to (and catalogued as no. 10d) a possible sketch formerly in the Lafitte collection, but there is also a small variant on the *merienda* theme. (An Otero photograph is in the library of the Prado Museum.)

151 See Sambricio (Bibl. 154, p. 93) and note to [150].
Another version (referred to and catalogued by Sambricio as no. 11b) was in the Lafitte collection. (Otero photograph; see note to [150].)
In this case the original sketch for the *baile* cartoon was sent by Goya to Zapater – see note to [74].

152 Dimensions unknown. Exhibited 1961 (Bibl. 23, no. LXXVII).

153 Close in style and handling to the cartoons of 1778-80. Held compared it with *La Cita* of 1780 [141] (Bibl. 89, no. 179).

154-159 Sambricio suggested that these were sketches for a series of tapestry cartoons (Bibl. 154, p. 173). Dated by Gudiol c.1781-85. The 'Santa Marca' replicas, known from Moreno photographs, are apparently as fine as the Stirling collection versions [154-157]. It has not been possible to trace the existence of a Marqués de Santa Marca in Spain.

154 Replicas: Formerly Madrid, Larios   G.190
Formerly Madrid, Santa Marca   G.192

155 Replicas: Valencia, Mus. (581)   G.198
Formerly Madrid, Ródena   G.196
Formerly Madrid, Santa Marca   G.197

156 Replicas: Formerly Madrid, Larios   G.195
Formerly Madrid, Santa Marca   G.193

157 Replicas: Formerly Madrid, Larios   G.204
Formerly Madrid, Santa Marca   G.206

158 Replicas: Madrid, Arredondo   G.203
Formerly Madrid, Ródena   G.200
Formerly Madrid, Santa Marca   G.201

159 Replica: Formerly Madrid, Larios   (Mentioned by Trapier, Bibl. 186, p. 50, and attributed to Lucas)
Copy: Madrid, Fund. Lázaro   G.208
Compare the tapestry, from a cartoon by Francisco Bayeu, in the Escorial.

159a Known only from a Moreno photograph (no. 651). Described by Araujo (Bibl. 33, no. 121) as having belonged to a canon of the Colegiata at La Granja, and mentioned by Mayer (Bibl. 128, p. 43).

160-195 For many of the individual paintings in this section, which are unknown to the authors in the original, the order and classification of Gudiol's catalogue has been followed, and no discussion of their attribution and dating is possible.

161 Published by Milicua (Bibl. 133, p. 25; the illustration republished in *Archivo Español de Arte*, XXVII, 1954, (p. 361), pl. VI).

162 Exhibited 1932 (Bibl. 102, p. 355, no. 3 and pl. VII).

163 Exhibited 1932 (Bibl. 102, p. 355, no. 2 and colour pl. VI). Incorrectly identified by Mayer (no. 67a) as Saint Thomas. Discussed by Sánchez Cantón (Bibl. 163, p. 288).

164-167 Published by Gudiol from a print in the (un-dated) catalogue of the collection of the Duques de Aveyro, Madrid.
167 The subject, if correctly identified, would lead to

the grouping of this picture with [196-198]. Cp. the same subject in [169].

168 Incorrectly identified by Sánchez Cantón as 'Noah and his daughters' (Bibl. 166, p. 31; 159, pl. 7). This example of a subject extremely rare in Spanish painting is a forerunner of the painting within the painting of the *Family of Charles IV* [II.783], recently identified by Muller (without reference to this picture) – see note to [II.783].

169 Gudiol gives the dimensions as 97×72 cm., but this is presumably an error since the painting appears to be of similar format to [168]. See note to [167].

172 Exhibited with [173] in Saragossa in 1928 (Bibl. 11, nos 462, 463), and discussed by Milicua (Bibl. 133, p. 9 and n. 2).

173 See note to [172]. Subject identified by the museum as 'La invención del cuerpo de Santiago'.

175 Published by the Marqués de Lozoya, 'Dos Goyas inéditos de tema religioso', *Archivo Español de Arte*, XXIV, 1951, pp. 5-10.

176 Presented to the Royal Academy of San Fernando on 5 July 1780 with Goya's request to become a member of that body, and described as *un quadro original de su invención, en que expresa al Señor Crucificado* (see D. Narciso Sentenach in *Boletín de la Real Academia de Bellas Artes de San Fernando*, September 1921, and Sánchez Cantón, Bibl. 157, p. 14). The 'originality' of the painting was discussed by Sánchez Cantón with comparative illustrations (Bibl. 166, p. 21, figs 3-5).

Replica: 205×105 cm. (Gudiol) or 256×157 cm. (1961 exhibition) Toledo, Mus. de Santa Cruz G.327 First exhibited 1961 (Bibl. 23, no. LXV) Dated by Gudiol c.1790.

Copy by Felipe Abas: see Viñaza (Bibl. 190, p. 201, no. V).

177-183 Father Tomás López mentioned the fresco and Goya's differences with Francisco Bayeu (Bibl. 190, p. 465), and the whole affair was discussed and documented by Viñaza (Bibl. 190, pp. 35-40 and 163-167). See also Lafuente and Stolz (Bibl. 105, pp. 122-124, 137). Calvert gave an English translation of Goya's memorandum to the Pilar authorities (Bibl. 41, pp. 40-46), and Helman referred to and discussed a first draft in the Lázaro Foundation, Madrid (Bibl. 94, pp. 33-34). For a sketch plan of the various Pilar cupolas, see Tormo (Bibl. 183, p. 283).

178 and 179 Dimensions as given in the 1961-62 exhibition catalogue (Bibl. 24, nos 15, 16); Gudiol repeats Mayer: 57×149 cm.
Goya wrote that the sketches were painted in Madrid, before he and Francisco Bayeu went to Saragossa (Bibl. 190, pp. 169, 171). They were listed about 1805 among paintings in the Chopinot collection (see Pascual Galindo, 'Goya pintando en El Pilar', *Aragón*, 31, 1928, pp. 152-158, and Bibl. 151, p. 31). See also Tormo (Bibl. 183, p. 283).
179 The banner is inscribed *REGINA MARTYRUM*. Exhibited 1970 (Bibl. 30, no. 4/3).

180-183 The pendentives are shown in order, starting to the left of the Virgin and moving round to the right. The two sets of sketches painted by Goya are unknown.
181 Gudiol suggests a possible first sketch for this pendentive (G.121).

184-187 See Goya's letters to Zapater (Bibl. 72, pp. 25, 28 and 31) and the note by Ponz, published in 1776 (Bibl. 140, [V], p. 441, n. 1). Viñaza listed all the altarpieces and published documents in connection with the commission (Bibl. 190, pp. 42, n. 2, and 179-181). Beruete gave a full account (Bibl. 36, II, pp. 22-26), and Goya's development of the composition was discussed by Lafuente, 'Sobre el cuadro de San Francisco el Grande y las ideas estéticas de Goya', *Revista de Ideas Estéticas*, IV, 1946, pp. 307-337 (reprinted in Bibl. 102, pp. 318-330). Lafuente pointed out the source in a painting by Michel-Ange Houasse (illustrated in Bibl. 185, p. 226/227). See also Nordström (*op. cit.* in note to [203]).

184 . . . preaching before Alfonso V of Aragon. Goya originally chose to represent René, Duke of Anjou, king of Naples and of Sicily, and rival to Alfonso V – see Lafuente (Bibl. 102, p. 321, n. 2) and the note to [187]. Goya's self-portrait appears at the right edge and is very close to [201]. Catalogued (but not exhibited) in 1961 (Bibl. 23, no. LXXI).

185 The painting is very close to the final altarpiece [184], and Lafuente suggested that it may have been a reduction rather than a sketch, painted by Goya for Zapater (Bibl. 102, p. 322; 72, p. 33, n. 1).

187 Probably the original sketch described by Goya in his letter to Floridablanca of 22 September 1781: *hé pintado en el borroncito . . . el Milagro, de q.do predicando el S.to en una espaciosa llanura (á causa de no caber el concurso en Calles, ni Plazas) inmediata a la Ciu.d Aquilina en presencia de Renato Rey de Sicilia, y de numeroso concurso; encareciendo la coronación de la Reyna de los Angeles, se vió con el m.r asombro por aq.l admirable Auditorio, descender de el Cielo una lucidisima estrella la que fijandose sre Su Cabeza, le bañó de Resplandor Divino* (Bibl. 102, p. 321).

188-191 Mentioned by Ponz in 1783 (Bibl. 140, [XII], p. 1098, n. 1). Jovellanos' letter of appreciation, with payment, of 11 October 1784, was published by Beruete (Bibl. 36, II, p. 27), Sánchez Cantón (Bibl. 166, p. 30), and in Bibl. 72, p. 32.

Jovellanos owned a 'Conception' by Goya, possibly a sketch for or reduction of the Calatrava painting. See the reference in Bibl. 119, pp. 101-102. Another 'Conception' was listed in the inventory of 1812 (Bibl. 161, pp. 85-86 and 106; see Appendix I, no. 30).
The authors were unable to consult the article by the Marqués del Saltillo, 'Las pinturas de Goya en el Colegio de Calatrava, de Salamanca', *Seminario de Arte Aragonés*, VI, 1954, pp. 5-9.

A painting of 'Saint Ramondo de Penhaforte', 86·4×63·5 cm., was exhibited in 1941 (Bibl. 16, no. 11, not ill.). A painting of 'Saint Vincent Martyr', 85·7×61·6 cm., was sold at Sotheby's, London, on 16 November 1955 (lot 125) with the note: 'It is possible that this picture may be one of the same series as the San Raimondo de Penaforte which Goya is known to have painted for. . . Calatrava'.

192 Sánchez Cantón suggested that this was the unspecified painting for which the Duque de Hijar paid 3,000 reales in 1783, and pointed out a source for the composition in a painting by Poussin (Bibl. 163, pp. 288-289, and figs 3, 4, and Bibl. 166, pp. 29-30, figs 7-9). The face of the Virgin appears similar to the women's faces in [198], signed and dated 1784.

Ponz, in 1788, referred to another painting by Goya at Urrea de Gaén, representing 'Saint Blaise', one of three altarpieces in the circular church recently built by the architect Agustín Sanz (Bibl. 140, [XV], p. 1357). This lost painting was catalogued by Mayer (no. 39) and Desparmet (no. 51).

194 Oil sketch published by the Marqués de Lozoya, 'Dos Goyas inéditos de tema religioso', *Archivo Español de Arte*, XXIV, 1951, pp. 5-10. No dimensions given.

195 This painting, outside the main stream of Goya's development and generally regarded as one of his least successful works, is difficult to date. The curious facial types are reminiscent of those in [198], dated 1784.

196 On the verso of a drawing for the tapestry cartoon *La merienda* [70] of 1776. Mentioned by Sánchez Cantón (Bibl. 168, II, no. 445).

198 Inscribed on the blade of the sword *FRANCISCO DE GOYA AÑO 1784*. Exhibited in 1928 (Bibl. 10, no. 3) by the Duque de San Pedro de Galatino. Seen and catalogued in 1964 by Held (Bibl. 89, no. 6).

A copy, purporting to be the original, has recently appeared in the art market. See note to [V.1668, 1669].

199 Reproduced in Bibl. 72, pl. 51. Identified as a self-portrait by Francisco Bayeu, by Mayer and Sambricio (Bibl. 155, pp. 23-24, pl. 39 and n.). Gudiol attributes it to Goya. Cp. the two documented portraits [299] and [II.345].

200 The son of the first, Flemish director of the Royal tapestry factory, he received and listed all Goya's cartoons from 1775 until his death in 1786. The authenticity of the inscription, if not the attribution of the portrait itself, is now considered doubtful.

201 The date in the lower left corner is possibly apocryphal, but this study was no doubt connected with the self-portrait included in [184]. Probably the first of the two portraits listed in the Brugada inventory of 1828 (Bibl. 57, I, p. 53, n. 1; see Appendix II, no. 6), since it belonged to Federico de Madrazo who acquired several of the paintings listed in the Quinta del Sordo.

202 Exhibited in 1922 (Bibl. 9, no. 173A).

203 Inscribed *AL EXC.MO SEÑO[R]/FLORIDA BLANCA/ Año 1783* at the foot of the plan of the Canal of Aragon, *Senor/Fran.co Goya* on the paper at the artist's feet, and *PALO/PRAC/DE L/PINTU/2-3* (i.e. Palomina, *Practica de la Pintura*) on the book lying on the ground.
22 January 1783: the portrait had already been commissioned (Bibl. 72, p. 26).
26 April: Goya painted the head from the life.
Nordström suggested that Goya was presenting to Floridablanca the sketch for the painting in San Francisco el Grande [187], referred to in his letter to the minister, and he identified the figure in the background as Francisco Sabatini, the court architect (cp. [205]). See Folke Nordström, 'Goya's state portrait of the Count of Floridablanca', *Konsthistorisk Tidskrift*, XXXI, 1962, pp. 82-94.

204 Inscribed on paper *Memor. . . / la formacion / del Banco / nacional / de S.n Carlos*. Reproduced in *Hispania*, 31, 1900, p. 170, and described as a pair to the full-length version of [215], both from the collection of Pablo Mila y Fontanals, Barcelona. The attribution of this portrait is uncertain, as is that of the very feeble portrait formerly in the Cathedral of San Isidro, Madrid:

174×114 cm. M.265, DF.301, G.141. Both reproduced by Nordström (see note to [203]), and see the note on the second portrait by Mélida in *Boletín de la Sociedad Española de Excursiones*, XVII, 1909, pp. 6-8. See note to [223-228].

205 It is difficult to situate this portrait within Goya's œuvre. Gudiol says the sitter is the same man who appears behind Floridablanca in [203], identified by Nordström as Sabatini (see note to [203]).

206-212 See Goya's letter to Zapater dated 20 September (Bibl. 72, p. 26), also D. Angulo Iñiguez ('La Familia del Infante Don Luis pintada por Goya', *Archivo Español de Arte*, XLI, 1940, pp. 49-58), Beruete (Bibl. 36, I, p. 22) and Sánchez Cantón (Bibl. 166, p. 33).

Other portraits by Goya of the Infante and his wife were catalogued by Viñaza (Bibl. 190, p. 227) and recorded by Tormo (see below), but are otherwise unknown:

María Teresa de Vallabriga Panel 65×37 cm. Formerly Boadilla del Monte (89) V.XXXV, M.181, G.153.

Infante Don Luis de Borbón 79×60 cm. Formerly Boadilla del Monte (91) V.XXXVI, DF.295, G.154.

Desparmet described another portrait of the Infante Don Luis 90×70 cm. Florence, heirs of Prince Ruspoli DF.544s This portrait is also unreproduced and unknown.

An equestrian portrait of María Teresa de Vallabriga was referred to by Goya in a letter to Zapater, dated 2 July 1784: *. . . aun no he acabado el retrato á caballo de la S.a del Infante pero lo falta poco* (Bibl. 72, p. 31). It is unknown, and has been catalogued since Viñaza from this reference (M.183, DF.314, G.155).
The paintings inherited by the heirs of Godoy and the Condesa de Chinchón were listed in the undated catalogue (Bibl. 37) referred to by Viñaza. Tormo saw the sixteen paintings by Goya still hanging at Boadilla del Monte between 1900 and 1902 and mentioned them all, including the replicas of [206] and [207] (Bibl. 182 p. 206, n. 1).

206 Usually described as on panel but in fact on canvas applied to panel. Inscribed on a paper on the verso (not by Goya): *RETRATO DEL SERENISIMO SEÑOR INFANTE DON LUIS ANTONIO JAIME DE BORBÓN, QUE DE 9 Á 12 DE LA MAÑANA, DIA 11 DE SEPT.RE DEL AÑO DE 1783, HACIA DON FRANCISCO GOYA*. Boadilla no. 34. First exhibited 1961 (Bibl. 23, no. XXX).

Replica: 42×37 cm. Madrid, priv. coll. Boadilla no. 226 G.147.

Replica or copy: Madrid, Marquesa de Casa Pontejos.

207 A paper (probably removed from the verso when the panel was reinforced) is inscribed *RETRATO DE DA MARIA / TERESA DE VALLABRIGA / ESPOSA DEL SER.MO S.OR YNFANTE / DE ESPANA DN / LUIS ANTONO / JAYME DE BORBON / QUE DE 11 A 12 DE LA MAÑANA EL DIA / 27 DE AGOSTO EL AÑO DE 1783.*

HACIA / D.N FRANCISCO GOYA. Boadilla no. 44. First exhibited but incorrectly catalogued in 1961 (Bibl. 23, no. XLVI – cp. ill).
Replica: 42×37 cm. Madrid, priv. coll. Boadilla no. 50 G.147.
Replica or copy: Madrid, Duque de Sueca.

208 Boadilla no. 137. Listed by Carderera (Bibl. 148, no. 36). First reproduced (colour) in *The World of Goya* (Time-Life Library of Art), New York, 1968, pp. 62-63.
Reduction: 97×124 cm. Madrid, Duque de Sueca Exhibited 1963-64 (Bibl. 27, no. 52).

209 Inscribed on map of Europe at lower right *AL S.D. LUIS MARIA / HIXO DEL SER. S. INFANTE / D. LUIS / Y DE LA MUI ILUSTRE S. / D. MAR. TER. VALLABRIBA / A LOS SEIS AÑOS / Y TRES MESES DE EDAD.* Boadilla no. 18. He was born 22 May 1777, and later became a cardinal. Cp. [II.794, 795].

210 . . .y Vallabriga. Inscribed at lower left *LA. S. D. MARIA TERESA / HIXA DEL SER. INFANTE / DON LUIS / DE EDAD DE DOS AÑOS Y NUEVE MESES.* Boadilla no. 15. Painted at the same time as the portrait of her brother. She later took the title of Condesa de Chinchón and was married to Godoy in 1798. Cp. [II.793].

212 Boadilla no. 136. The attribution of this painting is doubted by Gudiol who admits it as a possible copy by Goya after Mengs. Both this portrait and its companion [211] have been heavily restored.

213 Dimensions given by the owner. Sketch for an unknown painting. The composition is a variant of the Floridablanca portrait [203]. See note to [214] on Ventura Rodríguez. Sambricio attributed this sketch to Francisco Bayeu (see *Goya*, 13, 1956, p. 37). Exhibited 1956 (Bibl. 21, no. 124) and 1959-60 (Bibl. 22, no. 132). See Gudiol (Bibl. 82, ill. p. 144).

214 Inscribed on plan: *Retrato Original de D.n Ventura Rodriguez/Arquitecto del Sereni.mo S.r Infante D[on]/ Luis y Maestro mayor de la Villa de/Madrid que de orden de la mui Ill.a/S.ra Esposa de S.A. pinx. D.n Fran[?] Goya año de 1784.* Ventura Rodríguez was the favourite architect of the Infante Don Luis, and Jovellanos referred to the history of the portrait (see reference in Bibl. 27, no. 53). According to the 1959-60 exhibition catalogue (Bibl. 22, no. 133), he is holding the plans of the chapel of the Virgin of the Pillar in the basilica of El Pilar at Saragossa. Desparmet identified the plans as those of the Infante's palace at Boadilla del Monte.) See also Gudiol (Bibl. 82, pp. 141-156 and 180, illustrating two copies).
Copy by Zacarías González Velázquez: inscribed and dated 1794 Madrid, R.A. San Fernando (539) Repr. by Gudiol (*op. cit.* p. 154).

215 Inscribed on the paper *Al Ex.mo S.r Cond[e]/de Gausa cava/llero gran cruz/de la . . . // Ex.mo Señor/ . . .* He was created Conde in 1783. This portrait was catalogued by Viñaza with reference only to the engraving after Goya, and the authenticity of both the known paintings (which have not been seen for many years) is uncertain. They may be original paintings or copies, or paintings based on the lost drawing [313].
Full-length version: 200×114 cm. Formerly Madrid, Marqués de Casa Torres M.275, DF.283, G.168 Reproduced in *Hispania*, 31, 1900, p. 180 (see note to [204]).

216 Dimensions given by museum; those in the 1961 exhibition catalogue: 85×64 cm. The portrait is apparently dated by a letter from Goya to Zapater on 20 September 1783 in which he says that Zapater would see in Valencia the portrait which he had made of Ferrer 'cuando el estubo aqui'. Viñaza had dated the portrait 1790, when Goya went to Valencia with his wife. Exhibited 1961 (Bibl. 23, no. XXVIII, with text of letter and discussion of possible dates).
Replica or copy: inscribed *D.n Mariano Ferrer P.r Goya 1786* Barcelona, priv. coll. M.262 Cited in the 1961 exhibition catalogue.

217 This portrait, which belonged to the Cienfuegos family (descendants of Jovellanos), was discussed by Lafuente (Bibl. 102, p. 118 and n. 6). He referred to an article which suggested as a possible source Reynolds' portrait of John Musters. Both writers held some doubts about the attribution of the portrait, and the pose is almost identical with that of the Conde de Fernán-Núñez in the family portrait which is not included in this catalogue (exhibited 1961, Bibl. 23, no. LXXVI; Gudiol no. 244). See also Lozoya (Bibl. 119, p. 98) where he quoted from a letter written by Jovellanos in 1799 about an engraving after his portrait by Goya. It seems more likely, however, that this would have referred to the portrait painted in 1798 [II.675]. Shown in the *Exposición de retratos ejemplares*, Museo Nacional de Arte Moderno, Madrid, 1946, no. 21, pl. XI.

218 Inscribed at lower right *Goya lo hizo*. Boadilla no. 97 (Bibl. 37).
Replica: 103×83 cm. Formerly Saragossa, Antonio Mazarredo M.342, DF.306n. See notes by Tormo in Bibl. 183 (p. 248, ill.) and *L'Exposition Rétrospective de Saragosse 1908*, Saragossa and Paris, 1910, pl. 29.
Bust study, previously attributed to Goya: 56×43 cm. New York, Hispanic Society (A.246) M.341.
An attributed portrait of a child, Juanita Moyna de Mazarredo, from the same collection as the replica described above, was mentioned by Tormo (*op. cit.* p. 285, n. 1) and catalogued by Mayer, no. 343. Formerly New York, Mr and Mrs J. Watson Webb. Reproduced in Bibl. 72, pl. 46.
A portrait of D.a Antonia Moyna de Mazarredo was also mentioned by Tormo (*op. cit.*).

219 and 220 The order for payment of *4800 Rs de Vn por los dos retratos que ha hecho de sus Ex.as*, dated 16 July 1785, was published by Loga (Bibl. 109, p. 160, n. 125; see Appendix V). Sentenach gave an account of the origin of the duchess's portrait (Bibl. 174, p. 197). Both portraits were included in the Osuna sale of 1896 (Bibl. 32, nos 63, 64). The portrait of the duke was very little known until recently, and the later portrait in the Frick Collection [II.674] was frequently identified as the pair to [220]. The portraits were exhibited together in 1959-60 (Bibl. 22, nos 134, 135), that of the duke in 1963-64 (Bibl. 27, no. 57) and that of the duchess in 1970 (Bibl. 30, no.5).
Cp. the family portrait [278]. See Folke Nordström, 'Goya and the Duke and Duchess of Osuna', *Spanska Mästare*, Stockholm, 1960, pp. 157-169, 181. For brief but informative notices on the Osuna family, see McVan (Bibl. 135) and *Bulletin of the Art Division – Los Angeles County Museum*, vol. 10, no. 1, 1958, pp. 9-11.

221 Married Francisco Moñino, brother of Floridablanca [203], in 1786. See Trapier (Bibl. 188, p. 4).
A pen sketch attributed to Goya was in the collection of José Lázaro and is reproduced in Bibl. 51, p. 152.

222 Dimensions as given by Gudiol; those of the 1961 exhibition catalogue (Bibl. 23, no. LXXIX) are 82×55 cm. See note to [223-228].

223-228 The six official portraits were probably commissioned on the advice of Ceán Bermúdez who was 'primer oficial de la secretaría' of the bank and who advised Goya on his purchase of shares. See L. G. de Valdeavellano, 'Las relaciones de Goya con el Banco de San Carlos', *Boletín de la Sociedad Española de Excursiones*, XXXVI, 1928, pp. 56-65. The bank was founded by Cabarrús [228] and created on 2 June 1782 under the ministry of Floridablanca – cp. [204].

223 The payment for this first portrait was made to Ceán Bermúdez: *Pagado a D.n Juan Agustín Ceán Bermúdez p.r el Coste y gastos del Retrato de D.n Josef del Toro . . . R.on 2.328.*

224-226 The three portraits were paid for together: *Al Pintor Goya p.r los retratos del Rey, del Conde de Altamira y del Marques de Tolosa . . . R.on 10.000.*

227 *R.on 2.200 pagados al Pintor Fran.co Goya como sigue: R.on 2.000 por el retrato que ha sacado de D. Fran.co Xabier de Larumbe . . .*

228 *R.on 4.500 pagados a Fran.co Goya por la pintura y dorado del marco del retrato de cuerpo entero del S.or Fran.co Cabarrus.* See note to [223-228].

229 Inscribed on the back of the canvas painted by Bayeu, at lower right: *D.n Frco/Bayeu/P.r de Ca/por Fr.co Goya./1786* (according to the R.A. de Bellas Artes de San Carlos who also communicated the dimensions).
Replica or copy: 96·4×74·2 cm. Banbury, Upton House (Bearsted Coll. N.T.253).

230 Inscribed *REY N. Señor* on the dog's collar. Exhibited 1970 (Bibl. 30, no. 11).

Several replicas or copies of varying quality are known:
210×127 cm. Madrid, Prado (737) M.101, DF. 287, G.264.
211×127 cm. Madrid, Banco Exterior de España DF.285, G.265 Exhibited 1961 (Bibl. 23, no. VIII) and 1961-62 (Bibl. 24, no. 17). Possibly from the Louis-Philippe collection (Bibl. 31, no. 445).
210×127 cm. Madrid, Ayuntamiento M.100, DF. 285n., G.262.
207×119·4 cm. Tisbury (Wilts.), Lord Margadale G.263 Exhibited 1963-64 (Bibl. 27, no. 54).

231 . . .de Moscoso. Inscribed *EL EX.mo S.r D.n VICENTE OSORIO CONDE DE TRASTAMARA DE EDAD DE DIEZ ANOS./Goya f.t* See Trapier (Bibl. 188, p. 5).

232 . . .her daughter María Agustina. Inscr. *LA EX.ma S.a D.a MARIA YGNACIA ALVAREZ DE TOLEDO MARQUESA DE ASTORGA CONDESA DE ALTAMIRA / Y LA S.D. MARIA AGVSTINA OSORIO ALVAREZ DE TOLEDO SV HIJA. NACIO EN 21 DE FEBRERO DE 1787.* Listed by Carderera (Bibl. 148, no. 28). See Trapier (Bibl. 188, p.6).

233 Signed on a card in the bird's beak *Dn Franco Goya.* Inscribed below *EL S.r D.n MANVEL OSORIO MANRRIQVE DE ZVNIGA S. DE GINES NACIO EN A[BRIL] A 11 DE 1784.* Listed by Carderera (Bibl. 148, no. 29). See Trapier (Bibl. 188, p. 8). Exhibited 1970 (Bibl. 30, no. 10).

234 Commissioned by the Duke of Medinaceli for the convent of San Antonio del Prado, Madrid. Chapel and painting consecrated 8 December 1785. See Julio Cavestany, 'La Anunciación (cuadro inédito de Goya)', *Arte Español*, IX, 1928, pp. 351-355. First exhibited 1961 (Bibl. 23, no. LXXIII); exhibited with the sketch [235] in 1963-64 (Bibl. 27, nos 55, 56) and 1970 (Bibl. 30, nos 6a, 6b).

236-239 Goya's letter of 6 June 1787 (Bibl. 72, p. 39 and 154, pp. 253-254) referred both to the three paintings which had to be finished and hanging by the feast of Saint Anne (26 July) and also, as Mayer noted (Bibl. 128, p. 48), to the prevailing fashion at court for the 'estilo arquitectónico', to which these paintings conform. Sambricio published a document, dated 12 April 1787, in connection with the royal commission for six pictures from Ramón Bayeu and Goya (Bibl. 23, no. LXVII) and another referring to the materials used (Bibl. 154, p. 154 and doc. 109). See Sánchez Cantón (Bibl. 163, pp. 291-293), also the 1961 exhibition catalogue for full bibliography (Bibl. 23, nos LXVI-LXVIII).

236 Sambricio, following a reference in Sánchez Cantón (Bibl. 166, pp. 36-37), identified the source of the composition as an engraving by Dorigny after a painting by Maratta (Bibl. 23, no. LXVII), but see note to [237]. Cantón identified the source of this painting as an altarpiece by Crespi (Bibl. 163, pp. 291-293, figs 5, 6).

237 Sánchez Cantón referred to the 'excessive differences' between the sketch and the final painting, and seemed to have some doubts about the authenticity of the former. He believed the sketch was based on a painting by Carlo Maratta (Bibl. 166, pp. 36-37). However, the illustrations in Bibl. 166 (figs 12-14) show how closely the sketch itself is related to the Crespi composition (which Goya may have known from a reversed engraving). It was exhibited in 1963-64 (Bibl. 27, no. 65).

240-245 Goya's account dated 16 October 1788, for 30,000 reales for the two paintings, was published by Beruete (Bibl. 36, II, p. 33), together with a note from the Osuna accounts that this sum was paid on 22 May 1789. Sentenach, however, declared that only part of this sum was paid at that time, the remaining 6,000 reales being paid to Goya on 18 September 1790 in Valencia where he was staying with his wife (Bibl. 174, p. 199). Cp. Appendix V. See Sánchez Cantón (Bibl. 163, pp. 293-294), González Martí (Bibl. 69, p. 431) and the detailed analysis in Nordström (Bibl. 136, pp. 59-75).

243 Sánchez Cantón identified the source in a painting by Houasse (Bibl. 163, figs 10, 11; 166, figs 17-19) and Nordström suggested the influence of David (Bibl. 136, p. 72, fig. 34).

245 Inscribed below (not by Goya) *El Condenado Primer pensamiento de Goya para el cuadro de la cat.l de Valencia.*

246 Ramón Bayeu and Goya executed the paintings on either side of the main altarpiece which was signed and dated in 1790 by Francisco Bayeu. See Xavier de Salas, 'El Goya de Valdemoro', *Archivo Español de Arte*, XXXVII, 1964, pp. 281-293.

248-255 Goya's account for 22,000 reales, for a lost portrait of the Osuna children and *siete cuadros todos de composicion, asuntos de campo*, was published by Sentenach (Bibl. 174, p. 198; 176, p. 209, n. 1) and Beruete (Bibl. 36, II, pp. 62-63). The two orders for payment, dated 7 June 1787 and 26 February 1788, with Goya's receipts on the verso, were published by Loga (Bibl. 109, n. 128, p. 161). Cp. Appendix V.
Ezquerra del Bayo believed that the scenes were related to actual incidents which occurred on the Osuna estate at La Alameda, two of them involving the Duchess of Alba who is known to have kept a mule there for excursions and picnics (Bibl. 58, pp. 150-153).
The paintings were all included in the 1896 Osuna sale (Bibl. 32, nos 67-73). Goya's descriptive titles, given in the notes, are taken from Beruete's text of the account.

248 *6.º ...un Mayo, como en la plaza de un lugar con unos muchachos que van subiendo por él, á ganar un premio de pollos y roscas, que está pendiente en la punta de él, y varias gentes que estan mirando, con su campo correspondiente... 2.000 rs.* Osuna no. 72.

249 *3.º ...unos jitanos divirtiendose, columpiando á una jitana y otras dos sentadas mirando y tocando una guitarra, con su pais correspondiente... 2.500 rs.* Osuna no. 73. Cp. the drawing of 1796-97 [II.391].

250 *5.º ...una romeria en tierra montuosa, y una muger desmayada, por haber caido de una borrica, que la estan socorriendo un Abate y otro que la sostiene en sus brazos, y otras dos que van en borricas, espresando el sentimiento con otro criado que forma el grupo principal, y otros que se atrasaron y se ven á lo lejos, y su pais correspondiente... 2.500 rs.* Osuna no. 70.

251 (The attack on the coach). *2.º ...unos ladrones que han asaltado á un coche y despues de haberse apoderado y muerto á los caleseros, y á un oficial de guerra, que se hicieron fuertes, estan en ademan de atar á una muger y á un hombre, con su pais correspondiente... 3.000 rs.* This was the most expensive of the four paintings of equal size, and second only to the large *Apartado de toros* [254]. Osuna no. 71. Cp. the small painting of 1793-94 [II.327].

252 (Transporting a stone). *7.º ...una obra grande, á la que conducen una piedra con dos pares de bueyes, y un pobre que se ha desgraciado, que llevan en una escalera, y tres carreteros que lo miran lastimados; con su pais correspondiente... 2.500 rs.* Osuna no. 69. Cp. the *Wounded mason* cartoon of the same period [266].

253 (Village procession). *4.º ...una procesion de una aldea, cuyas figuras principales ó de primer termino, son el Cura, Alcaldes, Regidores, Gaitero, etc. y demas acompañamiento, con su pais correspondiente... 2.500 rs.* Osuna no. 68.

254 (Sorting the bulls). *1.º ...un apartado de toros, con varias figuras, de á caballo, y de á pié, y los toros para formar su composicion, con su pais correspondiente... 4.000 rs.* Osuna no. 67. This painting, the largest of the seven, has not been seen since it was exhibited at the National Gallery, London, in 1938-39, together with [II.871] and [III.954]. Sánchez Cantón (Bibl. 166, English trans.) mentioned it as being in the U.S.A.

255 Surprisingly, this small sketch was already in the Prado by 1828 when it was catalogued and exhibited together with the equestrian portraits of Charles IV and María Luisa [II.776, 777] (Bibl. 1, p. 81, no. 320). It may be the sketch referred to in the 1812 inventory of the property transferred to Goya's son (see note to [II.344]), and it is possible that the latter gave it to the museum on his father's death. See Appendix I, no. 26.
Replica or copy: 39·4×31·8 cm. s. at lower right *F. Goya*; dated on verso 1797 Philadelphia, Johnson Coll. (820) M.655a.

256-276 From 1786, with his appointment as a salaried Painter to the King, Goya no longer sent in accounts for the individual cartoons but only claimed for his expenses. There are, therefore, no contemporary descriptions of the cartoons delivered to the tapestry factory, only descriptions of the tapestries themselves in the various lists and inventories referred to by Sambricio.

256-261 Goya's account, dated 1 May 1787, included 384 reales *por un coche en diligenz.ª al R.l Sitio del escorial para presentar à S.M. (que Dios gue) los Borradores de la Pieza de Comer del Pardo* (Bibl. 154, doc. 103). Yriarte described these and other cartoon sketches [272-275] hanging with the 'witchcraft' pictures [II.659-664] in the Duchess of Osuna's library at La Alameda (Bibl. 193, pp. 143-144). Sentenach quoted a document which shows that Goya presented his account for 10,000 reales for some of these and the later sketches (*varias pinturas que ha hecho para el gabinete de S.E.*) on 6 May 1798 (Bibl. 174, p. 199). This account was not settled until nearly a year later, on 26 April 1799, although the Osunas were paying Goya for his current commissions with very little delay (cp. [II.659-664, 679] and Appendix V). The order for payment referred to *siete Pinturas, que representan una la Pradera de S.n Ysidro; quatro de las Estaciones del año; y dos asuntos de Campo, que hizo para el Gabin.te de la Condesa Duquesa mi muger* (Bibl. 109, p. 167, n. 185; 36, II, p. 66; 154, doc. 192). From the sketches catalogued here came the 'four Seasons of the year' [256-259]; the other two [260, 261], which were also in the Osuna collection, were perhaps acquired later or presented by Goya to his patrons. Until Sambricio published the documents which proved that all these little pictures were sketches for tapestry cartoons, it was generally believed that they were painted for the Osunas (the phrase *que hizo para el Gabin.te...* in the document quoted above seemed to bear this out), and that those which were related to known tapestry cartoons were reductions made at a later date. The Osuna sale catalogue numbers (Bibl. 32) are given in the notes.

256 (The flower girls). Osuna no. 75.

257 (Harvesting). Osuna no. 76. Exhibited 1970 (Bibl. 30, no. 7).

258 (The grape harvest). Yriarte, in his description of these sketches at La Alameda, published in 1867, noted that the *Autumn* was lacking and suggested that the original might be a picture which MM. Goupil in Paris were then offering for sale: 'C'est l'*Automne*, représenté par une jeune femme élégante, offrant des fruits à un enfant. Derrière elle, un cavalier, costume Empire. Joli paysage d'automne. Sur le premier plan, une branche de pampre' (Bibl. 193, p. 143). This description does not entirely correspond with the design of the cartoon [264]. The attribution of the Williamstown sketch was doubted by Soria who ascribed it to Asensio Juliá (note in Frick Art Reference Library files). Its provenance does not connect it with the Goupil picture.

259 (The snow-storm). Osuna no. 74. Exhibited 1941 (Bibl. 16, no. 12) and 1970 (Bibl. 30, no. 8).

260 (The drunken mason). In the cartoon, he was transformed into the nobler *Wounded mason* – see note to [266]. Osuna no. 82.

261 (Poor people by a fountain). Osuna no. 81. Reproduced in *Colnaghi's 1760-1960*, London, 1960, pl. 49, and exhibited 1970 (Bibl. 30, no. 9).

262-271 Goya's account for his expenses in connection with these cartoons up to 30 April 1787 was presented on 1 May 1787 (Bibl. 154, doc. 103). The accompanying documents included the carpenter's account giving the sizes of the stretchers, which Sambricio related to the cartoons (*op. cit.* p. 141, doc. 106). For a detailed discussion, suggesting sources, see Nordström (Bibl. 136, pp. 29-58).

266 The sketch shows a *Drunken mason* [260] and examination of the cartoon may reveal whether the change took place before or after Goya started work. This cartoon forms a serious, even sad, pair with [267], and both are clearly related to *Winter* [265]. Helman suggested a source for the subject in a decree of Charles III ('Why did Goya paint The Injured Mason?', *10th Anniversary of the Simmons Review*, 1957, p. 2 ff., and Bibl. 93, pp. 31-32, with text of decree in Appendix I, pp. 217-218).

268 There is no record as to why this cartoon left the collection in the Royal tapestry factory, but it was catalogued by Viñaza in the collection of Don Livinio Stuyck, former director of the tapestry factory (Bibl. 190, p. 325, no. XLV).

269 Prado title: 'Dos niños con un mastín', but the document quoted by Sambricio describes *dos Muchachos que llevan cada uno un perro de presa*, and there are in fact eight dogs' legs. Gudiol records a reference to a sketch.

270 Prado title: 'Cazador al lado de una fuente'.

272-275 For the identification of these sketches for cartoons, see Sambricio (Bibl. 154, pp. 154-157). The *cinco Bastidores con sus Lienzos para los diseños de los tapices* were included in a list accompanying Goya's account for expenses (*op. cit.* doc. 112). Only one cartoon was painted [276]. Goya's letter to Zapater was quoted by Sambricio (*op. cit.* p. 155) and also appears in Bibl. 72, p. 39.
For the sale of the sketches to the Duke of Osuna, see note to [256-261]. They included *la Pradera de San Isidro* [272] and *dos asuntos de campo*, probably [273] and either [274] or [275]. The third sketch (since all three were in the Osuna collection) was possibly acquired later or presented by Goya as a gift.

272 (The meadow of San Isidro). *...la Pradera de S.n Isidro en el mismo dia del S.to con todo el bullicio q.e en esta Corte acostumbra haber* (Bibl. 72, p. 39; 154, p. 155). The feast day of the patron saint of Madrid falls on May 15, and Goya's letter dated May 31 implies that the sketch was virtually made 'from the life'. Osuna no. 66.
A drawing was exhibited in 1922 (Bibl. 9, no. 207) but has never been reproduced: black chalk 33·7×49·7 cm. Inscribed below in ink (not by Goya) *Vista de Madrid, desde la Ermita de San Isidro del Campo, por D. Francisco Goya, Pintor de Cámara de S.M.* Madrid, Marqués de Casa Torres S.53a.

273 (The hermitage of San Isidro). The Prado catalogue adds '...el día de la fiesta' (...on the saint's day). See note to [272]. Osuna no. 79.
A drawing was exhibited in 1922 (Bibl. 9, no. 206B) but has never been reproduced: black chalk 34·5×51 cm. Inscribed below in ink (not by Goya) *Vista de la ermita de San Isidro del Campo de Madrid, por D. Francisco Goya* Madrid, Marqués de Casa Torres S.54a.

274 Osuna no. 78.

275 (Blind man's buff). The only sketch in the series which was made into a cartoon. The design was considerably simplified. Osuna no. 80.

276 The stretcher for this cartoon was supplied on 10 April 1788 (Bibl. 154, doc. 112 – see note to [272-275]) and Sambricio has shown that the cartoon was probably painted in the first months of 1789 (*op. cit.* p. 156).

277 Replica: 82×60 cm. Inscribed *Al Sr. Juan Martín de Goicoechea, Caballero de la Real distinguida Orden Española de Carlos III por haber erigido y conservado a sus expensas esta escuela de Dibujo a Beneficia de la Patria, La Real Sociedad Aragonesa ofrece esta muestra de su agradecimiento. Año de 1789.* Saragossa, Real Sociedad Económica Aragonesa de Amigos del País M.285, DF. 472n, G.269.
It is not certain which of the two portraits is the original. Sánchez Cantón gave the Saragossa version (which was catalogued by Viñaza, Bibl. 190, p. 257, no. CI) as the original, but the Society has said that it may be a copy.

278 Previous writers appear to have overlooked a document published by Sentenach (Bibl. 174, p. 198) which gives the date of Goya's account for this painting as 16 October 1788 (mentioning two dated accounts for 16,000 reales for this and the portraits of Charles IV and María Luisa – see note to [279-288]). Sánchez Cantón published the order for payment and Goya's receipt dated 27 February 1790 (Bibl. 166, pp. 44-45 and 168). The portrait, valued at 12,000 reales, appears in the undated list of paintings for the Osunas published by Loga (Bibl. 109, p. 161). Cp. Appendix V. Listed by Carderera (Bibl. 148, no. 18) and included in the 1896 Osuna sale (Bibl. 32, no. 65). Cp. the portraits of the duke and duchess of 1785 and the note [219, 220]. Cp. also the 1816 portraits of two of the Osuna children [III.1557, 1560].

Notes continued on page 373

ABBREVIATIONS AND SIGNS

[ ]	Numbers within square brackets refer to the works listed in the catalogue. The number is preceded by a roman numeral (I-V) referring to the section of the book in which the work appears. (This is omitted if the reference is to a work within the same section.)

TITLE

Goya's autograph titles are given in *italics*. Where there is no room for the whole title or its translation in the catalogue legend, it is continued in the note.

DATE

Examples:	*1797*	dated by Goya
	1797	certain date
	1797?	probable date
	c.1797	about 1797
	1797-99	executed during the period indicated
d.	Dated	
Doc.	Date indicated by a document	

SIGNATURE

s.	Signed

INSCRIPTION

italics	Title or inscription by Goya
Inscr.	Inscription
/	Change of line in an inscription
MS.	Manuscript

TECHNIQUE

All works are in oil on canvas unless otherwise specified

Aq.	Aquatint
L.	Lithograph

DIMENSIONS

cm.	Centimetres
approx.	Approximately
vis.	Visible dimensions (e.g. where work is partly covered by a mount or frame)
diam.	Diameter

Dimensions of the drawings are those of the sheet of paper.
Dimensions of the engravings are those of the copperplate.

COLLECTION

A.I.	Art Institute
B.M.	British Museum, London
B.N.	Biblioteca Nacional / Bibliothèque Nationale
C.	Calcografía Nacional, Madrid (see Bibl. 5)
Fund. Lázaro	Fundación Lázaro Galdiano, Madrid (the indication M = Museum, B = Biblioteca)
Gal.	Galerie / Gallery
Inst.	Institut / Institute / Instituto
Hispanic Soc.	Hispanic Society of America, New York
K.K.	Kupferstichkabinett (Print room)
Min.	Ministère / Ministerio / Ministry
Mus.	Musée / Museo / Museum (of Fine Arts, unless otherwise indicated)
M.F.A.	Museum of Fine Arts, Boston
M.M.A.	Metropolitan Museum of Art, New York
N.G.	National Gallery
Patr. Nac.	Patrimonio Nacional, Madrid
R.A.	Real Academia / Royal Academy
P. Palais	Petit Palais (Musée des Beaux-Arts de la Ville de Paris)
Rhode Is. S. D. Mus.	Museum of the School of Design, Providence (Rhode Island)

V. and A.	Victoria and Albert Museum, London
coll.	Collection (a capital C indicates a public collection, e.g. Frick Coll., New York)
priv.	Private
destr.	Destroyed

Acquisition or inventory numbers are given in brackets after the name of the collection. See Index of Collections, page 394.

BIBLIOGRAPHICAL REFERENCES

Bibl.	See the numbered Bibliography, page 386. The most frequently used abbreviations are:
B.	Barcia, *Catálogo de la Colección de Dibujos Originales de la Biblioteca Nacional* (Bibl. 3)
D.	Delteil, 'Francisco Goya', *Le Peintre graveur illustré* (Bibl. 55)
DF.	Desparmet Fitz-Gerald, *L'Œuvre peint de Goya* (Bibl. 57)
G.	Gudiol, *Goya* (catalogue raisonné) (Bibl. 85)
H.	Harris, *Goya. Engravings and lithographs* (Bibl. 88)
M.	Mayer, *Francisco de Goya* (Bibl. 128)
S.	Sambricio, *Tapices de Goya* (Bibl. 154)
SC.	Sánchez Cantón, *Museo del Prado: Los dibujos de Goya* (Bibl. 168)

ILLUSTRATION

Ill. p. (or p.)	See the reproduction in the text at the page indicated.

NOTE

*	Reference to a note on the pages preceding the illustrated catalogue.

CATALOGUE I
c.1762-1792

[1-316]

**RELIGIOUS PAINTINGS
c.1762-1771**

FUENDETODOS (Saragossa)
c.1762

Decoration of the reliquary in the parish church of Goya's native village. The decoration - destroyed in 1936 - consisted of oil paintings on the outside and inside of the reliquary doors and a canopy above the reliquary, painted in fresco(?) on the wall.

[1-4]   *

1

Canopy held by angels   c.1762.
Fresco(?) c.300×300 cm.
Fuendetodos, church - destr.
M.30, DF.46[a], G.1   *

2   3

Virgin and Saint Francis
c.1762.   Panels c.180×65 cm.
Fuendetodos, church - destr.
M.30, DF.46[a], G.2 and 3 *

4

Apparition of the Virgin of the Pillar
c.1762.   Panel c.180×130 cm.
Fuendetodos, church - destr.
M.30, DF.46[a], G.4   *

Apparition of the Virgin of the
Pillar to Saint James   c.1768-69.
79×55 cm.   Saragossa, Pascual
de Quinto   G.5   *

6

Holy Family   c.1768-69.
79×55 cm.
Madrid, Conde de Orgaz
G.6   *

7

Rest on the flight into Egypt
c.1768-70.   31×20 cm.
Paris, priv. coll.
G.7   *

8

Lamentation over the dead Christ
c.1768-70.
Oil on paper 36×20 cm.
Paris, priv. coll.   G.8   *

9

Mary weeping over the dead
Christ   c.1768-70. s. *Goya*
Oil on alabaster 33×25 cm.
Barcelona, priv. coll.   G.9 *

SARAGOSSA
PALACE OF SOBRADIEL
.1770-1772

Paintings in oil on the walls of
the palace chapel (transferred to
canvas and now dispersed).
The three large subjects from
engravings after Simon Vouet
and Carlo Maratta; the four small
paintings of saints partly based
on frescoes by Correggio.
Goya's first important commission,
executed just before or just after
the Italian journey in 1770-71.

[10-16]   *

10

Saint Joseph's dream   c.1770-72.
130×95 cm.
Saragossa, Mus. (162)
M.4b, DF.48[a], G.17   *

11

The Visitation   c.1770-72.
130×80 cm.
Florence, Contini-Bonacossi
M.4a, DF.48[a], G.18   *

12

The Burial of Christ   c.1770-72.
130×95 cm.
Madrid, Fund. Lázaro (M.2003)
M.4c, DF.48[a], G.19N.   p. 32 *

13

Saint Joachim   c.1770-72.
37×30 cm.   Coll. unknown
M.4d, DF.48[a], G.20   *

4

Saint Ann   c.1770-72.
37×30 cm.   Coll. unknown
M.4e, DF.48[a], G.21   *

15

Saint Vincent Ferrer   c.1770-72.
37×30 cm.   Coll. unknown
M.4g, DF.48[a], G.22   *

16

Saint Gaetan   c.1770-72.
37×30 cm.   Bilbao, Olabarria
M.4[f], DF.48[a], G.23   *

**HISTORY - MYTHOLOGY
c.1768-1771**

Possibly Goya's first attempt at
capturing a real scene - which he
may have witnessed during his
second visit to Madrid - the
so-called Esquilache riot in March
1766, which led to the expulsion
of the Jesuits in April 1767.
The mythological scenes were
probably painted in Italy.

[17-24]

17

The Esquilache riot   c.1767-70.
Inscr. *Muera/Es/quilache*
46×60 cm.   Paris, priv. coll.   *

18

Charles III promulgating the edict for the expulsion of the Jesuits   c.1767-70.   46×60 cm. Paris, priv. coll.   *

19

The pardon of Aman   1771. 39×52 cm. Paris, priv. coll.   G.11   *

20

The feast of Esther and Ahasuerus s.d. *Goya 1771*.   39×52 cm. Paris, priv. coll.   G.12   *

21

Venus and Adonis   c.1771. s. *Goya*   23×12 cm. Zurich, priv. coll.   G.13   *

22

Sacrifice to Vesta s.d. *GOYA / 1771*.   33×24 cm. Barcelona, J. Gudiol Ricart G.14   III. p. 37   *

23

Sacrifice to Pan   1771. 33×24 cm. Barcelona, J. Gudiol Ricart G.15

24

Sacrifice to Pan   c.1771. 40×30 cm. Paris, priv. coll.   *

EARLY PORTRAITS 1771-c.1775 [25-28]

25

Manuel de Vargas Machuca s.d. *Francisco J. de Goya / 1771*. 77×62 cm. São Paulo, P.M. Bardi   G.10   *

26

Self-portrait   c.1771-75. 58×44 cm. Madrid, Marquesa de Zurgena M.292, G.36   III. p. 29   *

27

Portrait study   c.1773-75. 32×43 cm. Saragossa, Mus. (171) DF.284n, G.38   *

28

Conde de Miranda   d. *1774*. 91×69·5 cm. Madrid, Fund. Lázaro (M. 1993) M.352, G.47   *

RELIGIOUS PAINTINGS 1772-1775

SARAGOSSA BASILICA OF EL PILAR   1772

Fresco on the ceiling of the *coreto* (little choir) 21 October 1771: sketches commissioned by Pilar authorities. 11 November: Goya submitted a fresco painting (lost) to prove his ability. 27 January 1772: final sketch approved [31]. 1 June: fresco completed.

[30-33]   *

30

The Adoration of the Name of God 1772.   Fresco 7×15 m. approx. Saragossa, El Pilar M.1, DF.47, G.25   III. p. 39

31

Sketch for [30].   Doc. Jan. 1772.   s. *Goya* on verso 75×152 cm.   Barcelona, J. Gudiol Ricart   G.24   *

32

Drawing for angel's head in [30]. Red chalk 43·5×34 cm. Madrid, Prado (473)   SC.450   *

33

Drawing for angel's head in [30]. Red chalk   Madrid, Carderera   *

MUEL and REMOLINOS
(Saragossa) c.1772

Paintings representing four
Doctors of the Church on the
pendentives of two small country
churches

[34-41] *

 34

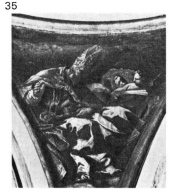 35

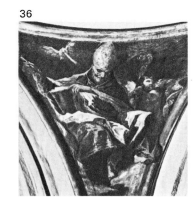 36

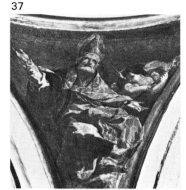 37

Saint Ambrose c.1772.
Oil on plaster c.250 cm. high.
Muel, Hermitage of the Virgen
de la Fuente G.33 *

Saint Augustine c.1772.
Oil on plaster c.250 cm. high.
Muel, Hermitage of the Virgen
de la Fuente G.32

Saint Gregory c.1772.
Oil on plaster c.250 cm. high.
Muel, Hermitage of the Virgen
de la Fuente G.30

Saint Jerome c.1772.
Oil on plaster c.250 cm. high.
Muel, Hermitage of the Virgen
de la Fuente G.31

 38

 39

 40

 41

Saint Ambrose c.1772? Inscr.
S.n Ambrosio c.180 cm. high.
Remolinos, parish church
M.5, DF.46[b], G.29 *

Saint Augustine c.1772? Inscr.
S.n Agustin c.180 cm. high.
Remolinos, parish church
M.5, DF.46[b], G.27

Saint Gregory c.1772? Inscr.
S.n Gregorio c.180 cm. high.
Remolinos, parish church
M.5, DF.46[b], G.26

Saint Jerome c.1772? Inscr.
S.n Geronimo c.180 cm. high.
Remolinos, parish church
M.5, DF.46[b], G.28

CARTUJA DE AULA DEI
(Saragossa) 1774

Paintings in oil on plaster in the
chapel of the Carthusian
monastery of Aula Dei.
Of Goya's original eleven
paintings illustrating the life of
the Virgin, seven remain - some
of them heavily restored.
The large, horizontal compositions
are remarkable for their sober
style and the gravity and monumentality of the figures.

[42-48] *

42

43

The Annunciation to Joachim
1774. Oil on plaster 306×844 cm.
Aula Dei (Saragossa)
M.3a, DF.48[b], G.40 *

The Birth of the Virgin 1774.
Oil on plaster 306×790 cm.
Aula Dei (Saragossa)
M.3b, DF.48[b], G.41 *

44

45

The Betrothal of the Virgin 1774.
Oil on plaster 306×790 cm.
Aula Dei (Saragossa)
M.3c, DF.48[b], G.42

The Visitation 1774.
Oil on plaster 306×790 cm.
Aula Dei (Saragossa)
M.3d, DF.48[b], G.43 Ill. p. 40

46

The Circumcision 1774.
Oil on plaster 306×1,025 cm.

Aula Dei (Saragossa)
M.3e, DF.48[b], G.44 p. 41 *

47

The Presentation in the Temple
1774. Oil on plaster 306×520 cm.

Aula Dei (Saragossa)
M.3g, DF.48[b], G.45

48

Adoration of the Magi 1774.
Oil on plaster 306×1,025 cm.

Aula Dei (Saragossa)
M.3k, DF.48[b], G.46 *

EARLY ETCHINGS
c.1771-1780

Goya's first attempts in the
medium which was to play so
important a part in his work.
The first plate may have been made
shortly before or after the journey
to Italy in 1771. The other two
suggest the influence of Giambattista and Domenico Tiepolo.

Abbreviations and signs, see p. 80
D = Delteil, Bibl. 55
H = Harris, Bibl. 88
If not a print from an edition:
1/1 = unique proof; 1/3 = one of
three proofs known.

[52-56]

52

The flight into Egypt c.1771.
s. *Goya inv.t et fecit*
Etching 13×9·5 cm. 1/7
Germany, priv. coll. D.1, H.1

53

Saint Isidore - patron of Madrid
c.1775-78. s. *Goya F.*
Etching 23×16·8 cm. 1/1
Madrid, B.N. (45606) D.3, H.2

54

Drawing for [53]. s. *F.co Goya fe*
Red chalk 23×19·2 cm.
Madrid, priv. coll. Ill. p. 42 *

55

Saint Francis of Paula
c.1775-80. Inscr. *CARI*
s. *Goya f.t* Etching and drypoint
13×9·5 cm. D.2, H.3 *

56

Drawing for [55]. Inscr. *CARI*
Pen and ink 13×11 cm.
Gijón, Inst. Jovellanos (318) -
destr.

TAPESTRY CARTOONS
1775-1778

Goya's first series of cartoons
made for the Royal Tapestry
Factory of Santa Bárbara

Abbreviations and signs: see p. 80
S = Sambricio, Bibl. 154
Doc. = document of delivery of
cartoon.
The titles given are those used by
Sambricio; alternative Prado titles
are given in the notes. The titles
from Goya's manuscript invoices
are also given in the notes.

[57-86]

TAPESTRY CARTOONS FOR
SAN LORENZO DEL ESCORIAL
1775

Nine cartoons of hunting scenes
for the *Pieza de Comer* (Dining-
room) of the Princes of Asturias.
The first five cartoons delivered
on 24 May 1775; the remaining
four on 30 October.
Goya was working under the
direction of Francisco Bayeu and
alongside his younger brother
Ramón. The traditional subjects
and a certain impersonality of
style make it difficult to distinguish the authorship of the cartoons without the evidence of
documents.

[57-69] *

57

La caza del jabalí (Wild boar
hunt) Doc. 24 May 1775.
249×173 cm. Madrid, Palacio
Real S.1; G.52 *

58

Perros en trailla (Dogs in leash)
Doc. 24 May 1775. 112×170 cm.
Madrid, Prado (753)
S.2; M.727, G.53 *

59

Caza con mochuelo y red
Doc. 24 May 1775. 111×176 cm.
Madrid, Min. de Hacienda (Prado
2856) S.3; G.51 *

60

Cazador cargando su escopeta
Doc. 24 May 1775. 292×51 cm.
Madrid, Min. de Educación
Nacional S.4; G.54

61

El cazador y los perros
Doc. 24 May 1775. 262×71 cm.
Madrid, Prado (805)
S.5; M.619, G.55   *

62

Drawing for [60] and [61].
Black chalk, heightened white,
blue paper 33·3×43·5 cm.
Boston, M.F.A.   *

63

La caza de la codorniz
Doc. 30 Oct. 1775. 290×226 cm.
Madrid, Prado (2857)
S.6; G.56   Ill. p. 44   *

64 recto of 65

Drawing for [63].
Black chalk, heightened white,
blue paper 32·2×20·6 cm.
Madrid, B.N. (B.820)   S.6a   *

65 verso of 64

Drawing for [63].
Black chalk, heightened white
See [64]. B.N. (B.820v.) *

66

El pescador de caña (The angler)
Doc. 30 Oct. 1775. 292×113 cm.
Madrid, Min. de Hacienda
(Prado 2897)   S.7; G.59   *

67 recto of 73

Drawing for [66]. s. Black
chalk, heightened white, blue
paper 32×24 cm.   Gijón, Inst.
Jovellanos (382) - destr.   S.7a *

68

Muchachos cazando con
mochuelo (Boys hunting ...)
Doc. 30 Oct. 1775. 171×51 cm.
Barcelona, Viñas   S.8; G.57   *

69

Caza muerta   Doc. 30 Oct. 1775.
Tapestry 170×100 cm.
Madrid, Patrimonio Nacional
S.9; G.58   *

**TAPESTRY CARTOONS FOR
THE PALACE OF EL PARDO
1776-1778**

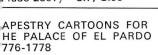

Ten cartoons for tapestries for
the *Pieza de Comer* (Dining-
room) of the Princes of Asturias.
Delivered at different dates
between 30 October 1776 and 25
January 1778.
Goya responds immediately to the
new choice of popular subjects
with brilliant colouring, lively
movement and a forceful charac-
terization of the figures among
whom the *majo* and *maja* make
their first appearance.

[70-84]   *

70

La merienda (The picnic)
Doc. 30 Oct. 1776. 272×295 cm.
Madrid, Prado (768)
S.10; M.561, DF.1, G.62   *

71 recto of 196

Drawing for [70]. Black chalk,
heightened white, blue paper
19·9×27·9 cm.
Madrid, Inst. de Valencia   S.10a

72

Drawing for [70]. Black chalk,
heightened white, blue paper
19×24·5 cm.
Madrid, Inst. de Valencia   S.10b

73 verso of 67

Drawing for [70]. Black chalk,
blue paper 24×32 cm.
Gijón, Inst. Jovellanos (382v.) -
destr. S.10c   *

74

El baile a orillas del rio Manzanares
Doc. 3 March 1777. 272×295 cm.
Madrid, Prado (769)   S.11;
M.583, DF.2, G.63   Ill. p. 46   *

75

Drawing for [74]. Black chalk,
heightened white, blue paper
28·9×22·5 cm.   Madrid, Prado (1)
SC.443, S.11a   Ill. p. 46

76

La riña en la Venta Nueva
Doc. 12 Aug. 1777. Inscr.
275×414 cm. Madrid, Prado (770)
S.12; M.701, DF.3, G.65   *

77

Fight at the Cock Inn - sketch
for [76]. Inscr. 41·9×67·3 cm.
Switzerland, priv. coll.
S.12a; M.702, DF.140, G.64   *

78

El paseo de Andalucía
Doc. 12 Aug. 1777. 275×190 cm.
Madrid, Prado (771)
S.13; M.567, DF.4, G.66   *

79

El bebedor (The drinker)
Doc. 12 Aug. 1777. 107×151 cm.
Madrid, Prado (772)
S.14; M.671, DF.5, G.68   *

80

El quitasol (The parasol)
Doc. 12 Aug. 1777. 104×152 cm.
Madrid, Prado (773)   S.15;
M.698, DF.6, G.67   Ill. p. 47   *

81

La cometa (The kite)
Doc. 25 Jan. 1778. 269×285 cm.
Madrid, Prado (774)
S.16; M.575, DF.7, G.69   *

82

Los jugadores de naipes (Card
players) Doc. 25 Jan. 1778.
270×167 cm. Madrid, Prado (775
S.17; M.571, DF.8, G.70

83

Niños inflando una vejiga
Doc. 25 Jan. 1778. 116×124 cm.
Madrid, Prado (776)
S.18; M.719, DF.9, G.72   *

84

Muchachos cogiendo fruta
Doc. 25 Jan. 1778. 119×122 cm.
Madrid, Prado (777)
S.19; M.714, DF.10, G.71   *

TAPESTRY CARTOON for the
Ante-Dormitorio (Ante-chamber)
of the Princes of Asturias in the
Palace of El Pardo.
Delivered 27 April 1778, but
returned to Goya for corrections
in October.
Its probable original form is known
from the etching [87].

85

El ciego de la guitarra
Doc. 27 April 1778. 260×311 cm.
Madrid, Prado (778)
S.20; M.623, DF.11, G.73   *

86

Head of a negro - studies for [85
Black chalk, blue paper 17×27 cr
Gijón, Inst. Jovellanos (718) -
destr. S.20a

ETCHINGS 1778

The real start of Goya's career as
an engraver. *The blind guitarist,*
copied from his own tapestry
cartoon [85], is the largest plate
he ever etched and less than a
dozen proofs are known. In the
Copies after Velázquez, Goya
made use of aquatint for the first
time.

Abbreviations and signs, see p. 80
aq. = aquatint
C = Calcografía, Bibl. 5
D = Delteil, Bibl. 55
H = Harris, Bibl. 88
If not a print from an edition:
1/1 = unique proof; 1/3 = one
of three proofs known.

[87-118]

87

The blind guitarist   1778. s.
Etching 39·5×57 cm.   1/10(?)
New York, M.M.A. (22.63.29)
S.20b; D.20, H.20   Ill. p. 48   *

COPIES AFTER VELÁZQUEZ
1778

Goya's first series of engravings,
after paintings by Velázquez in the
Royal Palace in Madrid (now in the
Prado - the Prado numbers are
given after the titles).
28 July 1778: announcement in
the *Gaceta de Madrid* of nine
prints [90, 92-94, 96, 101, 103-
105].
22 December: further announcement of two more prints [88, 95].
Altogether thirteen plates were
published and six preparatory
drawings in various techniques
are known for them [88-106].
Four editions of the equestrian
portraits and three of the other
subjects were printed from the
original copperplates between

1778 and about 1930. Modern
impressions are printed on
demand.
The copperplates are in the Calcografía Nacional, Madrid. Their
inventory numbers are given with
the prefix C (Bibl. 5, *Goya*).
All the plates are in etching, with
or without aquatint; drypoint and
burin retouches are not mentioned.
The engraved inscriptions below the
designs are not given, but where
they offer a title which differs
from that of the catalogue legend,
it is given in the notes.
Apart from the thirteen published
plates, four plates are known from
rare or unique proofs [107-113],
and four further drawings are
known [114-117].

[88-117]   *

88

Los borrachos (The drunkards)
(Prado 1170)   d.*1778.*
Etching 32×44 cm.
C.491; D.4, H.4   *

89

Drawing for [88].   Inscr.
Pencil 34×43·5 cm.
Madrid, Prado (474)   SC.442 *

90

Philip III   (Prado 1176)
d.*1778.* Etching 38×31 cm.
C.1532; D.6, H.5   *

91

Drawing for [90].   Inscr.
Pencil 37·5×32 cm.
Madrid, Fund. Lázaro
(M.I-11, 583)   *

92

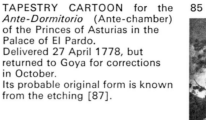

Margaret of Austria (Prado 1177)
d.*1778.* Etching 38×31 cm.
C.1533; D.7, H.6   *

93

Philip IV   (Prado 1178)
d.*1778.* Etching 38×31 cm.
C.1534; D.8, H.7   *

94

Isabel de Borbón (Prado 1179)
d.1778. Etching 38×31 cm.
C.1535; D.9, H.8   *

95

Prince Baltasar Carlos
(Prado 1180) d.1778.
Etching 35×23 cm.
C.1536; D.10, H.9   p. 49   *

96

Conde-Duque de Olivares
(Prado 1181) d.1778.
Etching 38×31 cm.
C.1537; D.11, H.10   *

97

Infante Don Fernando
(Prado 1186) 1778-79.
Etching and aq. 28·5×17·5 cm.
C.2860; D.12, H.11   p. 50 *

98

Drawing for [97].
Inscr. Velazquez and Goya
Red chalk 27·2×15 cm. Hamburg,
Kunsthalle (38538) Ill. p. 50 *

99

'Barbarroxa' (Prado 1199)
1778-79.
Etching and aq. 29×17 cm.
C.2859; D.13, H.12   *

100

Drawing for [99]. Inscr.
Red chalk 26·7×16·5 cm.
Hamburg, Kunsthalle (38548) *

101

Aesop (Prado 1206)
d.1778. Inscr. ÆSOPVS
Etching 30·5×22 cm.
C.2858; D.16, H.13   *

102

Drawing for [101].
Pen and sepia ink (the face in
Indian ink) 31·3×20·9 cm.
U.S.A., priv. coll.   *

103

Menippus (Prado 1207)
d.1778. Inscr. MOENIPPVS
Etching 30·5×22 cm.
C.2857; D.17, H.14   *

104

Sebastián de Morra
(Prado 1202) d.1778.
Etching 21·5×15 cm.
C.2862; D.18, H.15 *

105

Diego de Acedo 'El Primo'
(Prado 1201) d.1778.
Etching 22×16 cm.
C.2861; D.19, H.16   *

106

Drawing for [105]. Inscr. Pint.
por Velazquez. and Dibux. por
Goya. Black chalk 20×15·2 cm.
London, V. and A. (C.A.I.836)

UNPUBLISHED PLATES of
which only rare proofs are known.
Goya was only able to include
two aquatinted plates among the
published prints [97, 99]. The
others were technical failures,
and he must have regretted
that he was not able to publish
such masterpieces by Velázquez
as Las Meninas [107] and The
Water-carrier of Seville [114] of
which not even a proof is known.

[107-113]

107

Las Meninas (Prado 1174)
1778-79. Etching and aq.
40·5×32·5 cm. 1/11 London,
B.M.(1860.7.14.44) D.5, H.17 *

108

Drawing for [107]. Inscr.
Red chalk 40×32·8 cm.
Madrid, Carderera   *

109

'Don Juan de Austria' (Prado
1200) 1778-79. Etching and
aq. 28×17 cm. 1/4 Madrid,
B.N. (45580) D.14, H.18 *

110

Drawing for [109]. Inscr.
Velazquez. and Goya.
Red chalk 26·7×16·5 cm.
Hamburg, Kunsthalle (38539) *

111

The porter Ochoa 1778-79.
Etching and aq. 28×16·5 cm.
1/3 Berlin-Dahlem, K.K.(237.46)
D.15, H.19   *

112

'The Child of Vallecas' (Prado
1204) 1778-79. Etching and
aq. 21×16 cm. 1/1 Gijón,
Inst. Jovellanos (383) - destr. *

113

Drawing for [112].
Red chalk 20·2×15·7 cm.
Hamburg, Kunsthalle (38536)   *

ADDITIONAL DRAWINGS
after Velázquez

The first drawing shows the mark
of the copperplate, but no proof
is known.   The others are cut
rather close, but in any case do
not show the strong creases
which normally occur when the
drawings pass through the press.
These drawings, which are in
beautiful condition, give the
clearest evidence of Goya's
understanding of the original
paintings.

[114-117]

114

El Aguador de Sevilla.   (London,
Apsley House)   1778-79.
Inscr.   Red chalk 25·2×18·6 cm.
Hamburg, Kunsthalle (38537)   *

115

Philip IV   (Prado 1184)
1778-79.   Inscr. *Velazquez.* and
Goya.   Red chalk 27·7×18·9 cm.
Hamburg, Kunsthalle (38543)   *

116

Infante Don Carlos   (Prado 1188
1778-79.   Inscr. *Velazquez.* and
Goya.   Red chalk 27·3×17·2 cm.
Hamburg, Kunsthalle (38535)   *

117

Prince Baltasar Carlos
(Prado 1189)   1778-79.   Inscr.
Red chalk 26·9×15·8 cm.
Hamburg, Kunsthalle (38540)   *

PAINTINGS AFTER
VELÁZQUEZ

Traditionally attributed to Goya,
these paintings are difficult to
place within his œuvre and have
been grouped for convenience
near the etchings after Velázquez.
The fine portrait of *Innocent X* may
be of considerably later date.

[118-120]   *

118

Aesop   (Prado 1206)
180×93 cm.
Madrid, Prado (2553)

119

Mennipus   (Prado 1207)
179×93 cm.
Madrid, Prado (2554)

120

Innocent X   (London, Apsley
House)   Inscr.   55×45 cm.
Madrid, Conde de Villagonzalo
G.379   *

EL AGARROTADO   c.1778-80

The garrotted man is Goya's first
great original etching, and his
earliest essay in the grim realism
which is so characteristic of the
later work, cp. [II.498, III.1049,
1322-1328].
The first edition was issued on the
same paper as the *Copies after
Velázquez* and the plate was
probably etched shortly after the
completion of that series.   Four
editions were made from the
original copperplate between
c.1778-80 and 1928, and modern
impressions are made on demand.
The copperplate is in the Calcografía Nacional, Madrid (Bibl. 5,
Goya, 195, inv. no. 7).

122

The garrotted man   c.1778-80.
Etching 33×21·5 cm.
D.21, H.21

123

Drawing for [122].   Pen and
sepia ink over pencil 26·4×20 cm.
London, B.M. (1850.7.13.11)

TAPESTRY CARTOONS FOR
THE PALACE OF EL PARDO
1778-1780

Nineteen cartoons made for
tapestries to decorate the quarters
of the Princes of Asturias in the
Palace of El Pardo.
Another series representing the
'diversions and costumes of the
present time' - see the note to
[70-84]. Here the influence of
Velázquez is apparent: the
compositions are harmonious and
the emphasis is on the figures with
their lively, natural expressions.
The titles from Goya's
manuscript invoices are given
in the notes.

[124-142]   *

EL PARDO DORMITORIO
1778-1779

Seven cartoons for tapestries for
the *Dormitorio* (Bedchamber) of
the Princes of Asturias.
The first six delivered 5 January
1779 and the last on 20 July.

[124-130]

Abbreviations and signs, see p. 80
S = Sambricio, Bibl. 154
Doc. = document of delivery of
cartoon.

124

La feria de Madrid (Fair at Madrid)
Doc. 5 Jan. 1779   258×218 cm.
Madrid, Prado (779)
S.21; M.683, DF.12, G.74   *

125

El cacharrero (Crockery vendor)
Doc. 5 Jan. 1779.   259×220 cm.
Madrid, Prado (780)   S.22;
M.685, DF.13, G.75   III. p. 15   *

126

El militar y la señora
Doc. 5 Jan. 1779.   259×100 cm.
Madrid, Prado (781)
S.23; M.566, DF.14, G.77   *

127

La acerolera (Cherry vendor)
Doc. 5 Jan. 1779.   259×100 cm.
Madrid, Prado (782)
S.24; M.684, DF.15, G.76   *

128

Muchachos jugando a los soldados
Doc. 5 Jan. 1779.   146×94 cm
Madrid, Prado (783)
S.25; M.712, DF.16, G.79   *

129

130

EL PARDO ANTE-DORMITORIO
1779-80

Twelve cartoons for tapestries
for the *Ante-Dormitorio* (Ante-
Chamber) of the Princes of
Asturias. The first one delivered
on 20 July 1779 and the rest on
24 January 1780.

[131-142]

131

s niños del carretón
oc. 5 Jan. 1779. 145×94 cm.
bledo (Ohio), Mus. (59.14)
26; M.716, DF.17, G.80 *

El juego de pelota a pala
Doc. 20 July 1779. 261×470 cm.
Madrid, Prado (784)
S.27; M.572, DF.18, G.82 *

El columpio (The swing)
Doc. 20 July 1779. 260×165 cm.
Madrid, Prado (785)
S.28; M.576, DF.19, G.83 *

32

133

134

135

136

s lavanderas (Washerwomen)
oc. 24 Jan. 1780. 218×166 cm.
ladrid, Prado (786)
29; M.675, DF.20, G.87 *

La novillada (Amateur bullfight)
Doc. 24 Jan. 1780. 259×136 cm.
Madrid, Prado (787) S.30;
M.661, DF.21, G.88 p. 43 *

El perro (The dog) Doc. 24 Jan.
1780. Tapestry 267×75 cm.
Madrid, Patrimonio Nacional
S.31; M.728, DF.22, G.84 *

La fuente Doc. 24 Jan. 1780.
Tapestry 200×75 cm.
Madrid, Patrimonio Nacional
S.32; M.679, DF.23, G.85 *

El resguardo de tabacos
Doc. 24 Jan. 1780. 262×137 cm.
Madrid, Prado (788)
S.33; M.682, DF.24, G.91 *

37

138

139

140

141

muchacho del pájaro
oc. 24 Jan. 1780. 262×40 cm.
ladrid, Prado (790) S.34;
.720, DF.26, G.90 p. 43 *

El niño del árbol (Child with tree)
Doc. 24 Jan. 1780. 262×40 cm.
Madrid, Prado (789)
S.35; M.717, DF.25, G.89 *

Los leñadores (Woodcutters)
Doc. 24 Jan. 1780. 141×114 cm.
Madrid, Prado (791)
S.36; M.617, DF.27, G.95 *

El majo de la guitarra
Doc. 24 Jan. 1780. 135×110 cm.
Madrid, Prado (743)
S.37; M.622, DF.28, G.92 *

La cita (The rendezvous)
Doc. 24 Jan. 1780. 100×151 cm.
Madrid, Prado (792)
S.38; M.697, DF.29, G.94 *

42

**GENRE SUBJECTS
c.1775-1785**

A group of paintings which
includes some possible sketches
and studies for tapestry cartoons,
other compositions which are
close to the cartoons in style or
spirit, and finally the enchanting
group of small pictures of children
at play.

[143-159a] *

143

144

145

médico (The doctor)
oc. 24 Jan. 1780. 94×121 cm.
dinburgh, N.G. (1628)
.39; M.596, DF.30, G.93 *

Card players - possible sketch for
[82]. 87×58 cm.
Winterthur, Reinhart Coll. (75)

Boys playing at soldiers - possible
sketch for [128].
39×28 cm. Seville, Yandurri
DF.142, G.78

Game of pelota - possible
sketch for [130]. 35×50 cm.
Coll. unknown
S.27a; M.573, G.81

146

Washerwomen - possible sketch
for [132].   86·5×59 cm.
Winterthur, Reinhart Coll. (76)
G.86

147

Tobacco guards - possible study
for [136].   85×65 cm.
Göteborg, Börjessons Konsthandel
                                    *

148

Maja and two majos   c.1776-77?
183×100 cm.
Houston, Mus. (Kress 61.57)
G.49   *

149

The picnic   c.1776-78.
42×54·5 cm.   Paris, priv. coll.
DF.532s, G.272   *

150

The picnic   c.1776-78.
46×54 cm.   Madrid, priv. coll.
M.562, DF.124, G.60   *

151

The dance   c.1776-78.
46×54 cm.   Madrid, priv. coll.
M.585, DF.125, G.61   *

152

Bandits attacking a coach
c.1776-78.
Madrid, Barones de Lardies
M.602   *

153

Maja and celestina   c.1778-80
75×113 cm.
Madrid, Antonio MacCrohon
DF.533s, G.50   *

CHILDREN'S GAMES   c.1777-85

Series of six little pictures of
children playing. Between two
and four replicas are known of
each subject.   Similar in style to
the sketch for the *Riña* cartoon of
1777 [77], they recall the cartoons
with children of 1778 [128, 129],
but may have been painted rather
later.
Goya's first child was born in 1775
and all his life he was interested
in children and their games and
toys.
First example of a series of little
pictures on a common theme.
The replicas are listed in the notes.

[154-159]   *

154

Children playing at soldiers
c.1777-85.   29×42 cm.
Glasgow, Pollok House
G.191   *

155

Children playing with a see-saw
c.1777-85.   29×42 cm.
Glasgow, Pollok House
G.199   *

156

Children scrambling for chestnuts
c.1777-85.   30·5×43 cm.
Zurich, Mme Anda-Bührle
G.194   *

157

Children birds-nesting
c.1777-85.   30·5×43 cm.
Zurich, Mme Anda-Bührle
G.205   *

158

Children playing leap-frog
c.1777-85.   29×41 cm.
Valencia, Mus. (579)
G.202   *

159

Children playing at bullfighti
c.1777-85.   29×41 cm.
Formerly Madrid, Santa Marca
G.207

159a

The schoolmaster   c.1777-85
Coll. unknown   M.651, G.189 *

**RELIGIOUS PAINTINGS
1775-1785**

Three important moments in Goya's
career: his appointment as
Academician with the *Christ on
the Cross* [176]; the stormy
affirmation of his personality vis-
à-vis Bayeu with the frescoes in
El Pilar [177-183]; his official
triumph with the ambitious composition of *Saint Bernardino of
Sienna* [184].

[160-195]   *

160

Apparition of the Virgin of the
Pillar c.1775-80.   120×98 cm.
Barcelona, Julio Muñoz
G.100

161

The Visitation   c.1775-80.
Oil on paper 60×47 cm.
Madrid, Garcia
G.101   *

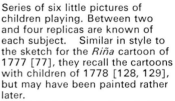

162

Saint Barbara   c.1775-80.
5×78 cm.
arcelona, Federico Torelló
.102   *

163

Saint Luke   c.1775-80.
76×61 cm.
Madrid, Ricardo Boguerín
G.103   *

164

Moses and the brazen serpent
c.1775-80.
Formerly Madrid, Duques de
Aveyro   G.104   *

165

Moses striking water from the rock
c.1775-80.
Formerly Madrid, Duques de
Aveyro   G.106   *

166

The sacrifice of Isaac   c.1775-80.
Formerly Madrid, Duques de
Aveyro   G.105

167

acrifice of Iphigenia(?)
.1775-80.
ormerly Madrid, Duques de
veyro   G.107   *

168

Lot and his daughters   c.1775-80.
90×125 cm.
Formerly Bilbao, Linker
M.14a, G.108   *

169

Sacrifice of Iphigenia(?)
c.1775-80.   97×120 cm.(?)
San Sebastián, José Várez
G.109   *

170

Saint Joachim and Saint Ann
c.1775-80.
Valencia, Cathedral - disappeared
1936   G.110

171

Vision of Saint Anthony
c.1775-80.
Valencia, Cathedral - disappeared
1936   G.111

172

irgin of the Pillar   c.1775-80.
8×52 cm.
aragossa, Mus. (169)   G.112 *

173

The death of Saint Francis Xavier
c.1775-80.   78×52 cm.
Saragossa, Mus. (167)   G.113 *

174

The baptism of Christ
c.1775-80.   45×39 cm.
Madrid, Condes de Orgaz
G.114

175

Apparition of the Virgin of the
Pillar to Saint James   c.1775-80.
Formerly Madrid, Rosillo
G.115   *

176

Christ on the Cross   1780.
255×153 cm.
Madrid, Prado (745)
M.23, DF.75, G.116   *

ARAGOSSA EL PILAR
780-1781

resco decoration of one of the
upolas and its pendentives.
3 May 1780: Goya commissioned
y Pilar authorities.
October: sketches presented.
1 Feb. 1781: cupola completed.
0 March: sketches for pendentives
ubmitted but not approved.
7 April: new sketches completed.
July: Goya back in Madrid.
n the catalogue, the whole cupola
s shown, followed by the two
alves of the fresco with corres-
onding details [177], the two
ketches [178, 179], and the
our frescoes on the pendentives
180-183].

177-183]   *

177

Regina Martyrum (The Queen
of Martyrs) 1780-81. Fresco
Saragossa, El Pilar - cupola
M.7a, DF.57, G.119 III. p. 54

View of half of the cupola showing
the Virgin - cp. sketch [178]

Details of the fresco

View of half of the cupola showing
the banner inscribed
REGINA MARTYRUM -
cp. sketch [179]

Details of the fresco

178

Sketch for half of cupola [177].
Doc. 5 Oct. 1780.   85×165 cm.
Saragossa, La Seo Mus.   M.9a,
DF.52, G.117   Ill. pp. 52, 53   *

179

Sketch for half of cupola [177].
Doc. 5 Oct. 1780.   85×165 cm.
Saragossa, La Seo Mus.
M.9b, DF.52, G.118   *

180

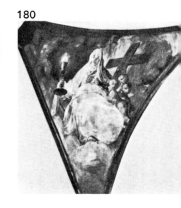

Faith   April-June 1781.   Fresco
Saragossa, El Pilar - pendentive
M.7b, DF.58, G.128   *

181

Patience   April-June 1781.
Fresco
Saragossa, El Pilar - pendentive
M.7e, DF.61, G.129   *

182

Fortitude   April-June 1781.
Fresco
Saragossa, El Pilar - pendentive
M.7d, DF.60, G.131

183

Charity   April-June 1781.
Fresco
Saragossa, El Pilar - pendentive
M.7c, DF.59, G.130

**MADRID SAN FRANCISCO
EL GRANDE   1781-1783**

Altarpiece for one of the chapels
in the newly completed church,
which Goya was invited to paint
by order of the king.
25 July 1781: Goya wrote to
Zapater about the 'competition'.
August-October: working on
sketches.
22 September: Goya's letter to
Floridablanca about the project.
31 October 1783: Goya gave
final touches to the picture.
November 1784: paintings
unveiled.
4 and 11 December: Goya wrote
to Zapater announcing the success
of his painting.

[184-187]   *

184

Saint Bernardino of Sienna...
1782-83.   480×300 cm.
Madrid, San Francisco el Grande
M.35, DF.65, G.138   Ill. p. 55

85

inal sketch for [184] or reduction?
.1782-83.   140×80 cm.
aragossa, Bergua Oliván
F.p.299, G.137   *

186

Sketch for [184].   c.1781-82.
62×33 cm.
Madrid, Condesa de Villagonzalo
M.36, DF.64, G.136

187

First sketch for [184].   1781.
62×31 cm.
Madrid, Condesa de Villagonzalo
M.37, DF.63, G.135   *

188-191

SALAMANCA COLLEGE OF
CALATRAVA 1784

Four life-size paintings
188 The Immaculate Conception
M.25, DF.68, G.159
189 Saint Benedict
M.32, DF.70, G.161
190 Saint Bernard
M.33, DF.69, G.160
191 Saint Raymond
M.67, DF.71, G.162

Commission obtained through the
influence of Jovellanos.
11 October 1784: paintings
completed.   Destroyed during the
French invasion 1810-1812.

[188-191]   *

192

Apparition of the Virgin of the
Pillar to Saint James   c.1780-85.
Urrea de Gaén (Teruel), parish
church - destr. 1936   G.281   *

93

Drawing for [192].   White chalk,
rey paper 26.8×21 cm.
Madrid, Prado (2)   SC.444

194

First sketch for [192]?
Valladolid, García Rodríguez
G.280   *

195

Holy Family with Saint John
c.1780-85.   200×148 cm.
Madrid, Prado (746)
M.26, DF.73, G.182   *

**HISTORY - MYTHOLOGY
c.1775-1785**

Two drawings recording an
unrealised project for a history
painting, and a mythological
subject which anticipates the
tapestry cartoons of 1791-92
[300-302] in its liveliness and
humour.
If the identification of their
subjects is correct, the two
Sacrifice of Iphigenia paintings
[167, 169] should also be included
in this section.

[196-198]

196   verso of 71

Surrender of Seville(?)
c.1776-86. White chalk, retouched
black, blue paper 27.5×19.9 cm.
Madrid, Inst. de Valencia   *

97

sketch for [196].   White chalk,
lue paper 24.3×19.7 cm.
Madrid, Inst. de Valencia

198

Hercules and Omphale   s.d.
1784.   81×64.5 cm.   Madrid,
heirs of Marquesa de Valdeolmos
M.70, DF.66, G.158   *

PORTRAITS 1780-1788

Apprenticeship in the art of
portraiture: from the naïve and
complicated rigidity of *Floridablanca* [203] - his first great
patron - to the sensitive simplicity
of *Manuel Osorio* [233].

[199-233]

199

Francisco Bayeu   c.1780.
49×35 cm.
Madrid, Marqués de Casa Torres
M.pl.311, G.97   *

200

Cornelio Vandergoten
s.d. *C. Vandergoten Goya 1782*
62×47 cm.   Madrid, Prado (2446)
M.288, DF.291, G.134   *

01

elf-portrait (age 37)
.(?)*1783.*   86×60 cm.
gen, Mus. (274 Ch.)
M.38/297a, DF.284, G.139 *

202

Self-portrait c.1783. s. *Goya*
Black chalk 10.9×8.1 cm.
U.S.A., priv. coll.   *

203

Conde de Floridablanca and Goya
s.d. *1783,* inscr.   262×166 cm.
Madrid, Banco Urquijo
M.263, DF.303, G.140   p. 58 *

204

Conde de Floridablanca   c.1783.
Inscr.   175×112 cm.
Madrid, Marqués de Casa Torres
M.264, DF.302, G.142   *

205

Man with a sabre   c.1783?
82.2×62.2 cm.
Dallas, Meadows Mus.
G.143   *

THE INFANTE DON LUIS
AND HIS FAMILY 1783

Sketches and perhaps the full-
length portraits executed during
Goya's stay at Arenas de San
Pedro (Avila). The great family
portrait was probably painted on
his return to Madrid - after
20 September 1783.

[206-212]   *

206

Infante Don Luis de Borbón
11 Sept. 1783.   42×37 cm.
Madrid, Duque de Sueca
M.170, DF.296, G.144   *

207

María Teresa de Vallabriga
27 Aug. 1783. Panel 48×39·5 cm.
Madrid, heirs of Mqs de Acapulco
M.180, DF.294, G.146   *

208

Family of the Infante Don Luis
1783.   248×330 cm.
Florence, heirs of Prince Ruspoli
M.169, DF.300, G.152   p. 60   *

209

Luis María de Borbón   Aug. 178
Inscr. 134×114 cm. approx.
Madrid, priv. coll.
M.174, DF.293, G.149

210

María Teresa de Borbón...
1783. Inscr. 132·3×116·7 cm.
Washington, Mellon Bruce
M.184, DF.292, G.150   p. 59   *

211

María Teresa de Vallabriga 1783.
151·2×97·8 cm.
Munich, Alte Pinakothek (HuW 2)
M.182, DF.307, G.148

212

Infante Don Luis de Borbón 1783.
152·7×100 cm.
Cleveland, Mus. (66.14)
M.172, DF.311, G.151   *

213

Infante Don Luis and Ventura
Rodríguez 1783-84. 25×20 cm.
Paris, priv. coll.
M.173, DF.544n., G.156   *

214

Ventura Rodríguez s.d. 1784
with inscr. 106×79 cm.
Stockholm, Nationalmus. (4574
M.401, DF.315, G.157   *

215

Conde de Gausa c.1784-85.
Inscr.   100×85 cm.
Formerly Madrid, Lázaro
M.276, DF. 282, G.169   *

216

Mariano Ferrer   1780-83.
s. . . . Fº Goya.   84×62·5 cm.
Valencia, Mus. (580)
M.261, DF.344, G.173   *

217

Gaspar Melchor de Jovellanos
c.1784-85.   185×110 cm.
Barcelona, Valls y Taberner
G.171   *

218

Admiral José de Mazarredo
c.1784-85. s. 105×84 cm.
Jacksonville, Cummer Gallery
M.340, DF.306, G.170   *

DUKE AND DUCHESS
OF OSUNA

Two of Goya's most important
patrons - he the ninth Duke of
Osuna and she the Countess-
Duchess of Benavente.   The
bluff, straightforward portrait of
the Duke is in the 'English
manner'; that of the Countess-
Duchess - one of the liveliest
and most intelligent leaders of
Madrid society and a *petimetra*
in the French fashion - is a chef-
d'œuvre of rococo colour and
delicacy of touch.   For other
portraits of the Osuna family see
[278] and [II.674].

219

IX Duque de Osuna   1785.
111·8×82·6 cm.
England, priv. coll.
M.367, G.164   *

220

Condesa-Duquesa de Benavente
1785.   104×80 cm.
Madrid, Bartolomé March Servera
M.369, DF.316, G.165   p. 65   *

221

Marquesa de Pontejos c.1786.
211×126 cm.
Washington, N.G. (Mellon 85)
M.388, DF.330, G.266   p. 62   *

222

Juan Agustín Ceán Bermúdez
c.1785. 100×70 cm.(?)
Madrid, Conde de Cienfuegos
Beruete 89, G.172   *

ADRID BANCO DE ESPAÑA

tween 1785 and 1788 Goya
ecuted six official portraits for
e Banco de San Carlos (now
e Bank of Spain) in which he
as a share-holder.
e first portrait was apparently
mmissioned on the advice of
án Bermúdez [222]. They are
rather formal and stiff. That
Altamira [225] is the most
portant both for its composition
d the fact that it led to further
mmissions [231-233].
e documents of payment are
eserved in the bank, and
tracts are given in the notes.

23-228]   *

223

José del Toro y Zambrano
Doc. 13 Apr. 1785. 113×68 cm.
Madrid, Banco de España
M.436, DF.317, G.163   *

224

Charles III   Doc. 30 Jan. 1787.
194×110 cm.
Madrid, Banco de España
M.102, G.213   *

225

Conde de Altamira
Doc. 30 Jan. 1787. 177×108 cm.
Madrid, Banco de España
M.200, DF.304, G.212   p. 61   *

226

Marqués de Tolosa
Doc. 30 Jan. 1787. 112×78 cm.
Madrid, Banco de España
M.435, DF.320, G.211   *

.7

ancisco Javier de Larrumbe
oc. 15 Oct. 1787. 113×77 cm.
adrid, Banco de España
.328, DF.325, G. 243   *

228

Conde de Cabarrús
Doc. 21 Apr. 1788. 210×127 cm.
Madrid, Banco de España
M.220, DF.326, G.249   p. 61   *

229

Francisco Bayeu   s.d. *1786* with
inscr. 109×82 cm.
Valencia, Mus. (582)
M.212, DF.328, G.209   p. 42 *

230

Charles III in hunting dress
c.1786-88. 206×130 cm.
Madrid, Duquesa de Fernán-Núñez
M.99, DF.286, G.261   *

231

Vicente Osorio . . . c.1786-87.
s. with inscr. 135×110 cm.
New York, Charles S. Payson
M.437, DF.323, G.210   *

32

ondesa de Altamira and . . .
1787-88. Inscr. 195×115 cm.
ew York, Lehman Coll.
M.201, DF.341, G.250   *

233

Manuel Osorio de Zuñiga
c.1788. Inscr. 127×101 cm.
New York, M.M.A. (Bache 49.7.41)
M.365, DF.332, G.251   *

RELIGIOUS PAINTINGS
1785-1788

The period of Goya's major
religious compositions,
commissioned after the success
of the altarpiece in San Francisco
el Grande [184].

[234-247]

234

The Annunciation   1785.
280×177 cm. Espejo (Córdoba),
Duquesa de Osuna
M.18a, DF.74, G.167   *

235

Sketch for [234].
42×26 cm.
London, priv. coll.
M.18, G.166

ALLADOLID CHURCH OF THE
ONVENT OF SANTA ANA
787

2 April 1787: three altarpieces
ommissioned by Charles III for
e neo-classical temple designed
y Sabatini.
June: Goya had not yet started
vork.
October: church and paintings
onsecrated.
mpressive but rather cold compo-
itions in a style expressly suited
o the architectural setting.

236-239]   *

236

The death of Saint Joseph   1787.
220×160 cm.
Valladolid, Santa Ana
M.51, DF.77, G.246   p. 56   *

237

Sketch for [236].   54·5×40·5 cm.
Flint (Michigan), Inst. of Arts
M.52, DF.76, G.245
Ill. p. 56   *

238

Saint Bernard and Saint Robert
1787. 220×160 cm.
Valladolid, Santa Ana
M.34, DF.78, G.248

239

Saint Lutgarda   1787.
220×160 cm.
Valladolid, Santa Ana
M.60, DF.79, G.247

VALENCIA CATHEDRAL
CHAPEL OF SAN FRANCISCO
DE BORJA 1788

Two paintings commissioned by
the Duke and Duchess of Osuna
in honour of their saintly
ancestor, Francisco de Borja.
16 October 1788: Goya presented
his account.
In the second painting, supernatural monsters make their first
appearance in Goya's work.

[240-245]   *

240

Saint Francis Borgia taking
leave of his family 1788.
350×300 cm. Valencia,
Cathedral M.43, DF.82, G.258

241

Sketch for [240]. 38×29 cm.
Madrid, Marquesa de Santa Cruz
M.44, DF.81, G.257

242

Drawing for [240]. s. *Goya*
White chalk, grey paper
29×21·5 cm.
Madrid, Prado (8) SC.445

243

Saint Francis Borgia at the
death-bed of an impenitent 178
350×300 cm. Valencia, Cathedr
M.45, DF.84, G.260

244

Sketch for [243]. 38×29 cm.
Madrid, Marquesa de Santa Cruz
M.46, DF.83, G.259 Ill. p. 57

245

Drawing for [243].
Black chalk 32×25 cm.
Madrid, Prado (475) SC.446 *

246

Apparition of the Virgin to Saint
Julian c.1790. 250×90 cm.
Valdemoro (Madrid), parish
church G.294   *

247

Drawing for [246]. White chalk,
grey paper 28·2×21·6 cm.
Madrid, Prado (9) SC.447

PAINTINGS FOR THE ALAMEDA DE OSUNA 1786-1787

Seven 'country pictures' painted
for the country residence of the
Osunas at La Alameda. The
paintings were delivered by April
22, 1787, and Goya sent in his
account with descriptions of the
paintings on May 12.
With this first important
commission for the Alameda
palace, Goya attained absolute
mastery in the art of decorative
genre painting. The paintings
are close to tapestry cartoons
of the same period [262-264],
and have long descriptive titles
which are given in the notes.

[248-255]   *

248

La cucaña (The greasy pole)
1786-87. 169×88 cm.
Madrid, Duque de Montellano
M.578, DF.150, G.236   *

249

El columpio (The swing)
1786-87. 169×100 cm.
Madrid, Duque de Montellano
M.577, DF.155, G.237   *

250

La caída (The fall)
1786-87. 169×100 cm.
Madrid, Duque de Montellano
M.703, DF.154, G.234   *

251

El asalto en el coche
1786-87. 169×127 cm.
Madrid, Duque de Montellano
M.598, DF.156, G.235   *

252

La conducción de una piedra
1786-87. 166×154 cm.
Madrid, Conde de Romanones
M.696, DF.162, G.238   *

253

Procesión de aldea
1786-87. 169×137 cm.
Madrid, Conde de Yebes
M.535, DF.161, G.239 *

254

Apartado de toros
1786-87. 165×285 cm.
Formerly Budapest, Baron Herzog
M.654, DF.160, G.240   *

255

A mounted picador - possible
study for [254]. c.1786-87?
56×47 cm. Madrid, Prado (744)
M.655, DF.167, G.242   *

TAPESTRY CARTOONS FOR THE PALACE OF EL PARDO 1786-1788

Series of cartoons, executed
between Goya's appointment
as Pintor del Rey (Painter to the
King) in July 1786 and the death
of Charles III in December 1788.

Abbreviations and signs: see p. 80
S = Sambricio, Bibl. 154

[256-276]   *

EL PARDO PIEZA DE COMER
(DINING-ROOM) 1786-1787

Autumn 1786: Goya went to the
Palace at El Escorial to present
the sketches for this series of
tapestry cartoons to Charles III.

From 23 October 1786 he was
supplied with materials, and he
presented his account up to
30 April 1787 on May 1.
The subjects of the cartoons are
the four seasons followed, for the
first time in Goya's œuvre, by
social themes: the *Wounded
mason* [266] and the *Poor
people by a fountain* [267],
which represent a new
contemporary concern.

SKETCHES for cartoons for the
Dining-room at El Pardo

Six sketches for the most importan
of the thirteen recorded cartoons
are known. They were later sold
by Goya to the Duke of Osuna.

[256-261]

256

Las floreras or Spring - for [262].
1786.   35×24 cm.
Madrid, Duque de Montellano
S.40a; M.93, DF.146, G.214   *

257

La era or Summer - for [263].
1786.   34×76 cm.   Madrid,
Fund. Lázaro (M.2510)   S.41a;
M.95, DF.147, G.216   p. 70 *

258

La vendimia or Autumn - for [264]?
1786 ?   34·4×24·3 cm.
Williamstown, Clark Art Inst.
S.42a; DF.148, G.218   *

259
La nevada or Winter - for [265].
1786.   31·7×33 cm.
Chicago, Mrs. Everett D. Graff
S.43a; M.98, DF.153, G.220   *

260

El albañil borracho - for [266].
1786.   35×15 cm.
Madrid, Prado (2782)
S.44a; M.705, DF.145, G.224   *

261

Los pobres en la fuente - for [267].
1786.   38×14 cm.
Hertfordshire (G.B.), priv. coll.
S.45a; M.681, DF.149, G222   *

CARTOONS for the Dining-room
at El Pardo

Ten cartoons are known: the six
from the sketches already listed
and four over-doors. Three further
small subjects have been identified by Sambricio from documents
(Bibl. 154, nos 50-52).

[262-271]   *

262

Las floreras (The flower-girls) or
Spring 1786-87.   277×192 cm.
Madrid, Prado (793)
S.40; M.92, DF.31, G.215

263

La era (Harvesting) or Summer
1786-87   276×641 cm.
Madrid, Prado (794)
S.41; M.94, DF.32, G.217

264

La vendimia (Grape harvest) or
Autumn 1786-87.   275×190 cm.
Madrid, Prado (795)
S.42; M.96, DF.33, G.219

265

La nevada (The snow-storm) or
Winter 1786-87.   275×293 cm.
Madrid, Prado (798)
S.43; M.97, DF.36, G.221

266

El albañil herido (The wounded
mason) 1786-87.   268×110 cm.
Madrid, Prado (796)   S.44;
M.704, DF.34, G.225 Ill. p. 70 *

267

Los pobres en la fuente (Poor
people by a fountain) 1786-87.
277×115 cm. Madrid, Prado (797)
S.45; M.680, DF.35, G.223

268

El niño del carnero (Boy on a ram)
1786-87.   124×110 cm.
Chicago, Chauncey McCormick
S.46; M.722, DF.45, G.226   *

269

Niños con mastines (Boys with
mastiffs) 1786-87. 112×145 cm.
Madrid, Prado (2524)
S.47; G.227   *

270

Cazador junto a una fuente
(Hunter by a spring) 1786-87.
131×130 cm.   Madrid,
Prado (2896)   S.48; G.228   *

271

Pastor tocando la dulzaina
(Shepherd blowing his horn)
1786-87.   131×130 cm.   Madrid,
Prado (2895)   S.49; G.229

EL PARDO   DORMITORIO DE
LAS INFANTAS 1788-1789

Series of tapestry cartoons for the
Bedchamber of the Infantas,
interrupted by the death of
Charles III and the decision to
abandon the palace of El Pardo
as one of the royal residences.

[272-276]

SKETCHES for the Bedchamber of the Infantas at El Pardo

12 February 1788: five canvases for the sketches were delivered.
31 May: Goya's letter to Zapater about the presentation of the sketches - which were still not ready - to the King and Princes, and mentioning the difficulty of representing the *Pradera de San Isidro* [272].
The sketches were later sold by Goya to the Duke of Osuna. Cp. [256-261]

[272-275]   *

272

La pradera de San Isidro
May-June 1788. 44×94 cm.
Madrid, Prado (750)   S.53;
M.581, DF.166, G.252 p. 66 *

273

La ermita de San Isidro
May-June 1788. 42×44 cm.
Madrid, Prado (2783)
S.54; M.582, DF.168, G.253 *

274

La merienda (The picnic)
May-June 1788. 41×25 cm.
London, N.G. (1471)
S.56; M.563, DF.163, G.254 *

275

La gallina ciega - sketch for [276]. May-June 1788.
41×44 cm. Madrid, Prado (2781)
S.55a; M.569, DF.157, G.255 *

CARTOON for the Bedchamber of the Infantas at El Pardo

The canvas and stretchers for four large cartoons and four over-doors were delivered in February and April 1788.
The sketches [272-275] were presented to Charles III during the summer, and Goya began work on the cartoon of *La gallina ciega*.
14 December: death of the king.
11 February 1789: Royal Order for the preparation of a new series of cartoons.

276

La gallina ciega (Blind man's buff) 1788-89. 269×350 cm.
Madrid, Prado (804)   S.55;
M.568, DF.44, G.256   p. 69   *

PORTRAITS 1789-1792

Series dominated by the numerous royal portraits painted after the accession of Charles IV and his queen María Luisa in January 1789.

[277-294]

277

Juan Martín de Goicoechea
Doc. 1789. 86×66 cm.
Madrid, Conde de Orgaz [M.285],
[DF.472n], G.270   Ill. p. 34   *

278

The family of the Duques de Osuna 1788. 225×174 cm.
Madrid, Prado (739)
M.366, DF.333, G.292 p. 64 *

279 pair to 280

Charles IV 1789. 220×140 cm.
Madrid, Min. de la Guerra
(Prado 2811)   M.124   *

280 pair to 279

Queen María Luisa 1789.
220×140 cm.
Madrid, Prado (2862)
M.136, DF.528s, G.288 *

281 pair to 282

Charles IV 1789.
137×110 cm.
Madrid, R.A. de la Historia
DF.335, G.286   *

282 pair to 281

Queen María Luisa 1789.
137×110 cm.
Madrid, R.A. de la Historia
M.137, DF.336, G.287   *

283 pair to 284

Charles IV 1789.
152×110 cm.
Madrid, Prado (740b)
M.119, DF.340   *

284 pair to 283

Queen María Luisa 1789.
152×110 cm.
Madrid, Prado (740c)
M.141, DF.334n   *

285 pair to 286

Charles IV 1789.
126×94 cm.
Córdoba, Mus. (Prado 740f)
M.125   *

286 pair to 285

Queen María Luisa 1789.
126×94 cm.
Córdoba, Mus. (Prado 740g)
M.142   *

287

Charles IV c.1789.
Madrid, Fund. Lázaro (M.3884) *

288

Queen María Luisa   c.1789.
Madrid, Fund. Lázaro (M.3889) *

289

Charles IV 1789-90. Inscr.
Drawing for frontispiece to the
Kalendario   Pencil 10·2×6·3 cm.
Madrid, Carderera   *

290

Martín Zapater   s.d. *1790* with
inscr. 83×65 cm. Priv. coll.
(loan to Gal. Cramer, The Hague)
M.454, DF.343, G.293   *

291

Ramón de Pignatelli c.1790.
Lost original - Copy 219×137 cm.
Saragossa, Canal Imperial de
Aragón M.385, DF.290, G.311 *

292

Study for [291]. 79·5×62 cm.
Madrid, Duquesa de Villahermosa
M.386, DF.289, G.312 p. 34 *

293

Luis María de Cistué   April-May
1791. Inscr. 125×90 cm. New
York, Mrs. John D. Rockefeller, Jr.
DF.554s, G.295   *

294

José Cistué, Barón de la Menglana
c.1789-92. 210×140 cm.
Saragossa, Pérez Cistué
G.314   *

**TAPESTRY CARTOONS FOR
THE DESPACHO DEL REY AT
EL ESCORIAL   1791-1792**

Goya's final series of cartoons,
for the King's Secretariat in the
Palace of San Lorenzo.   In spite
of his declared distaste for this
type of decorative work, they are
still an admirable success.
Goya fell seriously ill in the
winter of 1792-93, and the series
was never completed.

[295-306]

SKETCHES for cartoons for the
Despacho del Rey at El Escorial

At least six sketches were painted
for the principal cartoons.
20 April 1790: the King decided
that the themes should be 'rural
and humorous'.
Goya delayed work until May 1791.
3 June: he wrote that he had
almost completed the sketch for
La boda [298].

[295-299]   *

295

Las mozas de cántaro - sketch
for [300]. 1791. 34×21 cm.
Madrid, Antonio MacCrohon
S.57a; G.296   *

296

El pelele' (The straw manikin) -
sketch for [301]? 1791.
34×15 cm. Los Angeles, Dr. and
Mrs A. Hammer S.58a; G.300 *

297

El pelele - sketch for [301]?
1791. 44·5×25·4 cm.
New York, Mrs. Rush H. Kress
S.58b; M.57Oa, G.301   *

298

La boda (The wedding) - sketch
for [302]. 1791. 34·5×51 cm.
Buenos Aires, Jockey Club - destr.
S.59b; DF.158   *

299

La boda (The wedding) - sketch for
or reduction of [302]. 1791?
48·2×81·5 cm.
U.S.A., priv. coll. G.298   *

CARTOONS for the *Despacho
del Rey* at El Escorial

Seven cartoons are known for
this series for which twelve
stretchers were delivered to
Goya's studio.   His last account
was sent in on 30 June 1792.
In November-December he was in
Andalusia where he fell ill, and
the series remained incomplete.

[300-306]   *

300

Las mozas de cántaro
1791-92. 262×160 cm.
Madrid, Prado (800)
S.57; M.676, DF.38, G.297 *

301

El pelele (The straw manikin)
1791-92. 267×160 cm.
Madrid, Prado (802) S.58;
M.570, DF.42, G.302 Ill. p. 70

302

La boda (The wedding)
1791-92. 267×293 cm.
Madrid, Prado (799)
S.59; M.594, DF.37, G.299

303

Los zancos (The stilts)
1791-92. 268×320 cm.
Madrid, Prado (801)
S.60; M.574, DF.41, G.303

304

Las gigantillas (The little giants)
1791-92.   137×104 cm.
Madrid, Prado (800a)
S.63; M.715, DF.39, G.304   *

305

Muchachos trepando a un árbol
(Boys climbing a tree)   1791-92.
141×111cm. Madrid, Prado (803)
S.62; M.718, DF.43, G.305

306

El balancín   1791-92.
Tapestry 80×167 cm.
Madrid, Patrimonio Nacional
S.61; M.721, DF.40, G.306   *

**GENRE SUBJECTS
1780-1792**

[307-309]   *

307

Gossiping women   c.1792?
59×145·6 cm.   Hartford (Conn.)
Wadsworth Atheneum (1929.4)
M.631, DF.179, G.321   *

308

Young woman asleep   c.1792?
59×145 cm.
Madrid, Antonio MacCrohon
DF.538s, G.322   *

309

The wine vendor   1780-92.
Formerly Madrid, Marqués de
Chiloeches   M.679a, G.187   *

TWO DRAWINGS in the collection
of the Real Academia de Bellas
Artes de San Carlos in Valencia,
traditionally said to have been
made during Goya's visit there in
the summer of 1790.

310

Drawing from the male nude
1790?   Charcoal heightened
white, grey paper 60×45·5 cm.
Valencia, Mus. (589)   M.733   *

311

Study of a boy   1790?
Red chalk 38×24 cm.
Valencia, Mus. (590)   M.734
                              *

LOST WORKS
known from prints

312

Manuel de Villafañe   c.1775-85.
Engraving by F. Hubert, d.1791,
from a painting by Goya.   Inscr.
M.442, DF.281   *

313

Miguel de Muzquiz, Conde de
Gausa   c.1783-85.   Engraving
by Fernando Selma from a
drawing by Goya   M.684   *

314

Marqués de Bajamar   c.1785-91.
Engraving by J. Asensio from a
painting by Goya   *

315

Illustration to *Don Quixote,*
Book II, Chap. XXVII.   c.1778-80.
Engraving by J. Fabregat from
a drawing by Goya   *

316

Hommage to Charles Lemaur
c.1787-88.   Engraving by P.
Choffard from a design by Goya   *

Part two   1792-1808

Dates	Life of Goya	Spanish History	History outside Spain	The Arts	Literature and Science
1793	Death of Ramón Bayeu Moratín in Paris Cabinet pictures, sent to the Academy in 1794	France declares war on Spain Siege of Perpignan by the Spaniards	Execution of Louis XVI and Marie-Antoinette Assassination of Marat First Coalition	Death of Guardi (aged 81)	Metric system adopted in France
1795	Death of Francisco Bayeu Goya made Director of Painting at the Academy *Portraits of the Duke and Duchess of Alba*	Franco-Spanish treaty of Basle Jovellanos' report on agrarian reform Godoy, Prince of the Peace	White Terror Day of 13 Vendémiaire Directory established	Turner: *Tintern Abbey* Haydn: *Salomon Symphonies*	Keats († 1821) A. Thierry († 1856) Thomas Carlyle († 1881) Death of Ramón de la Cruz (aged 74)
1796	Goya in Andalusia Death of the Duke of Alba (aged 40) Stay with the Duchess of Alba Paintings for the Santa Cueva in Cadiz *The Sanlúcar album* *The Duchess of Alba* (in black)	Alliance of San Ildefonso Spain declares war on England	Italian campaign Death of Catherine II	Corot († 1875) Barye († 1875)	Gœthe: *Wilhelm Meister's Apprenticeship* Senefelder invents lithography
1797	Goya back in Madrid in April *The Madrid album* Goya works on the *Caprichos* *Bernardo de Iriarte* *Juan Antonio Meléndez Valdés*	Iriarte, Jovellanos and Saavedra are made ministers Marriage of Godoy and the Countess of Chinchón	Treaty of Campo-Formio	Schubert († 1823)	Gœthe: *Hermann and Dorothea* Schiller: *Ballads* Alfred de Vigny († 1863)
1798	Six witchcraft paintings for the Alameda de Osuna Frescoes in San Antonio de la Florida *Jovellanos, Saavedra, Guillemardet* *El Prendimiento*	Saavedra replaces Godoy Urquijo replaces Saavedra	The French take Rome Egyptian expedition Battle of Aboukir Second Coalition	Gros: *Bonaparte at Arcola* Haydn: *The Creation* Delacroix († 1863)	Schiller: *Wallenstein* Leopardi († 1837) A. Comte († 1857) Michelet († 1874)
1799	Publication of the *Caprichos* *La Tirana, Moratín* Goya is First Court Painter *Portraits of Charles IV and María Luisa*		Death of Washington Bonaparte abandons Egypt Coup d'Etat of 18 Brumaire Napoleon becomes First Consul	Death of Luis Paret (aged 53) Beethoven: *Pathétique Sonata*	Monge: *Traité de Géométrie descriptive* Pushkin († 1837) Balzac († 1850) Heinrich Heine († 1856)
1800	*The Family of Charles IV* *The Countess of Chinchón*	Second Alliance of San Ildefonso Urquijo dismissed Godoy in power again	Crossing of the Great St Bernard Pass Murat takes Milan The Battle of Marengo Act of Union between England and Ireland	Ceán Bermúdez: *Dictionary of artists*	Volta produces electricity from his cell Cuvier: *Leçons d'anatomie comparée* (1800-05) Macaulay († 1859)
1801	*Manuel Godoy*	War of the Oranges with Portugal. Godoy Generalissimo. Treaty of Aranjuez Jovellanos imprisoned at Bellver (1801-08). Urquijo imprisoned at Pamplona Ceán Bermúdez in Seville	English land in Egypt Pitt resigns Jefferson President of the U.S.A.	Gros: *The Battle of Nazareth* Turner: *Calais Pier*	Mme de Staël: *On Literature* Chateaubriand: *Atala*
1802	Death of the Duchess of Alba (aged 40)		Bonaparte Consul for life Peace of Amiens	Gérard: *Mme Récamier*	Chateaubriand: *Le Génie du Christianisme* Schiller: *Die Braut von Messina* Hugo († 1885)
1804	*Marqués de San Adrián* *Marquesa de Villafranca*	Anglo-Spanish War	Pitt takes power again Execution of the Duc d'Enghien Napoleon's coronation	Gros: *The Pesthouse at Jaffa* Beethoven: *Eroica Symphony*	Sénancour: *Obermann* Schiller: *William Tell* Sainte-Beuve († 1869) George Sand († 1876)
1805	Marriage of Javier Goya with Gumersinda Goicoechea Family portraits *Marquesa de Santa Cruz*	Trafalgar	Napoleon king of Italy Austerlitz Napoleon dethrones the Neapolitan Bourbons	Beethoven: *Fidelio* Prud'hon: *The Empress Josephine* Death of Greuze (aged 80)	Chateaubriand: *René* Death of Schiller
1806	Birth of Mariano Goya († 1874) Death of Juan Martín de Goicoechea (aged 74) *Tadeo Bravo de Rivero* Six *Maragato* pictures	Godoy founds a Pestalozzi Institute in Madrid	Joseph Bonaparte king of Naples Battles of Jena and Auerstedt Napoleon takes Berlin and Warsaw	Ingres: *La Belle Zélie* Beethoven: *Appassionata Sonata* Death of Fragonard (aged 74)	Hegel: *Phenomenology of Spirit* Moratín: *El sí de las niñas* Mrs Browing († 1861) Stuart Mill († 1873)
1807	Marriage of Leocadia Zorrilla y Galarza (aged 19) with Isidoro Weiss *Isidoro Máiquez*	Spain joins the Continental Blocade French troops enter Spain	Franco-Portuguese war Junot takes Lisbon	Gros: *The Battle of Eylau*	Mme de Staël: *Corinne* Longfellow († 1882)

THE POLITICAL SCENE. THE FRENCH REVOLUTION AND SPAIN. CHARLES IV, MARÍA LUISA AND GODOY

1792-1808. Goya is 46 to 62 years old. Serious illness in 1792-93. Marriage of his son Javier with Gumersinda Goicoechea in 1805. Engraves 'Los Caprichos'. Decorates the church of San Antonio de la Florida and paints the Duchess of Alba, the royal family, the 'Majas'. Reign of Charles IV, dominated by María Luisa and Godoy. Influence of the French Revolution. Joseph Bonaparte becomes king of Spain (1808).

The reign of Charles IV is undoubtedly one of the darkest in the history of Spain. At the age of forty, this spineless prince, so ill-prepared for power, had no sooner mounted the throne than he had to face the most explosive situation which Europe had experienced for centuries: the French Revolution. The situation was all the more difficult for the king of Spain since the two realms had been linked from the beginning of the century by bonds of blood and friendship. In the end, after twenty years of infamy and upheaval, his reign was to founder in 1808 in the farce of the Aranjuez plot and the blood of the second of May.

With the accession of Charles IV began the lamentable story of a reign dominated by Queen María Luisa and her favorite, Manuel Godoy. In 1784, when Charles III was still alive, this second scion of a family belonging to the petty nobility of Badajoz followed his elder brother and enlisted in the life-guards. He was eighteen years old and, to judge from a portrait of the period, was extremely attractive physically. He was immediately noticed by the future queen, then thirty-three years old and long past her first affair. For his part, the young guardsman, though not exceptionally intelligent, was what the Spaniards call *listo*, sharp. Realizing that the optimistically good-natured prince of Asturias was incapable of seeing harm even when it was staring him in the face, he cynically resolved to try his luck in any and every way.

After the death of Charles III, Godoy's rise to power was vertiginous. The old king was the only person capable of checking his ascent and he had not been able to prevent it in time. In less than four years Godoy rose from mere cadet to the rank of field-marshal, became a gentleman of the Privy Chamber, councillor of State and so on, until finally he was created Duque de la Alcudia, a Spanish grandee, and replaced Aranda as prime minister in 1792. At twenty-six, therefore, he was master of the political activities of Spain, and absolute master, since his decisions were imposed on the king himself by María Luisa in the conviction that she was acting only for the good of the country. The men of vision who, under Charles III, had seen their country prepare to shake off its lethargy and had felt its heart begin to beat in time with the rest of Europe, were well aware of the abyss into which it was now sinking. But all those who attempted to save an already gravely imperilled situation were eliminated one after another. Floridablanca and Aranda, who continued the policies of the old king, were ousted from power, and during the last years of the century, it was Goya's friends who were threatened: Saavedra, who replaced Godoy for a short time, Jovellanos, Urquijo, Ceán Bermúdez. All of them were dismissed from office, imprisoned or exiled. Jovellanos, the perfect example of a liberal Spaniard of the age of enlightenment, a man of great intellectual and moral honesty, who was constantly concerned with the advancement of his country, was imprisoned in the castle of Bellver at Palma, Majorca, until 1808. This one man stands as a symbol of the 'enlightened' Spain whose fresh forces might have been able to avert the catastrophe. Even if he had only been able to lessen its violence, the kingdom would at least have appeared to be governed by an honest man, whereas the unholy 'Trinity' (Charles IV - María Luisa - Godoy), of which the queen herself boasted, added a monstrous aspect to this decadent reign. These three figures were closely connected with Goya's life and work during these crucial years in Spain's history, and we shall soon see them transfixed by the merciless eye of the painter of the *Family of Charles IV* [783].

Fran.ᶜᵒ Goya y Lucientes, Pintor [451] 1797-98.
Caprichos plate 1

Ill. pp. 149-151

Equestrian portrait of Charles IV (detail) [776] 1800-01. Prado Museum, Madrid

Equestrian portrait of María Luisa (detail) [777] 1799. Prado Museum, Madrid

Charles IV   María Luisa   Godoy
Here, in Queen María Luisa's own words, is 'the Trinity on earth' which governed Spain for sixteen years, from 1792 to 1808, and at length foundered in the bloody *débâcle* which it had done so much to bring about. At the time when these portraits were painted, between the years 1799 and 1801, the king was fifty-two, María Luisa forty-eight and Godoy thirty-three.

Although Charles IV was the apparent head of state, it was Godoy who held the reins of power through the total hold which he had exercised for the last ten years over the depraved and infatuated queen. In 1784, at the age of eighteen, the future Prince of the Peace had joined the life-guards; heaped with favours and titles by the king, he experienced a scandalously rapid rise to fame in the political sphere, becoming the Count of Aranda's successor as prime minister in 1792, at the age of twenty-six, captain-general the following year, Prince of the Peace and a grandee of Spain after the Treaty of Basle in 1795. In spite of a brief eclipse for two years, from 1798 to 1800, he became more powerful than ever after the War of the Oranges in 1801, which earned him the title of Generalissimo of the Armies on Land and Sea.

It was on this occasion that Goya painted the pompous portrait in the Academy of San Fernando. Swollen with false pride and base ambitions, Godoy was pursued with ferocious hatred by the Crown prince, the future Ferdinand VII, and was almost massacred at Aranjuez in 1808. He was imprisoned, then freed by the French whom he had served so well to the detriment of his own country, and he followed the king and queen into exile. After their death in Naples in 1819, Godoy retired to Paris where he died in 1851.

Goya executed several allegorical paintings for Godoy's palace in Madrid (see pp. 136, 138) and painted the portrait of his wife, the Countess of Chinchón, in 1800 (see p. 19). Godoy also owned the two famous paintings of the naked and the clothed *Majas* (see p. 153), and in his memoirs he boasted that he had been responsible for the publication of Goya's *Caprichos* by the Madrid Calcografía in 1803.

Manuel Godoy   [796] 1801. 180×267 cm. Royal Academy of San Fernando, Madrid

Chapter 2

VISIT TO CADIZ. GOYA'S ILLNESS. DEVELOPMENT
OF HIS PRIVATE ART. THE NOTION OF 'CAPRICHO'
CABINET PICTURES 1793-1794

*1792-1794. Goya is 46 to 48 years old.
Journey to Andalusia. Serious illness leaves
him stone deaf. Eleven cabinet pictures sent to
the Academy of San Fernando. Reign of
Charles IV.*

All Goya's biographers have pointed to the decisive importance for his work of what is
referred to as the turning point of 1793, the terrible illness which undoubtedly brought
him face to face with death and, worse still, may have made him fear the possibility of
permanent physical or mental handicap. Everyone has referred to the resulting deafness
which affected him for the rest of his life and there have been innumerable and varied
commentaries, as well as medical diagnoses, concerning this illness and the bearing it is
thought to have had on the artist's work after 1793.

It is noticeable, however, that in most cases the essential factors are missing. What was
the nature of the illness? How was it caused and in what circumstances did it strike? The
various accounts are often contradictory, even as regards the dates, and leaving aside the
wildly romantic versions in which the Duchess of Alba, the Sierra Moreno, a freezing
night and a band of gunmen help to make up a fine Spanish adventure story.

Journey to Andalusia. Illness

The documents methodically published by Sambricio are once again invaluable and
are the only trustworthy records. The facts are as follows: on 2 September 1792 Goya
attended a session of the Academy of Fine Arts in Madrid; on 14 October he presented
Bibl. 74
Bibl. 154, doc. 159
an important report on the teaching of painting. Then we learn from a letter written by
the faithful Zapater in January 1793 to a mutual friend in Cadiz, Don Sebastián Martínez,
that Goya was very seriously ill at the latter's home and had already been there for some
time. These initial facts are confirmed by a marvellous work, the *Portrait of Sebastián
Martínez* [333] in the Metropolitan Museum at New York, signed and dated 1792. This
Ill. p. 107
implies that Goya was already in Cadiz and in good enough health to paint his host before
the end of the year 1792. However, matters are considerably complicated by the fact that
Goya had left Madrid, probably in the first half of November, without official permission
(as Court Painter he was in effect an appointed servant of the Crown and could not absent
himself from court at his pleasure). His illness was bound to force him to prolong his
absence which would then be discovered. After his difficulties with the palace officials
over the painting of the final tapestry cartoons on which he was working in 1791 and
See p. 71
1792 [I.295-306], he knew that they would not hesitate to stop his salary. Through his
friend Martínez, who was a wealthy merchant in Cadiz, Goya asked Bayeu in Madrid
to obtain two months official leave for him; this was granted in January 1793, 'so that he
Bibl. 154, doc. 157
may go to Andalusia in order to recover his health'. At the same time, probably because
he was short of money, he wrote to the Duke of Osuna's administrator; he pretended to
be in Madrid and asked for money to be made available in Seville, explaining that he had
Bibl. 154, doc. 158
been 'in bed for two months with colic pains and [was] going to Seville and Cadiz on leave'.
The Duke of Osuna arranged for him to be paid ten thousand reales in Seville. The most
remarkable thing is the obvious fear with which Goya took care to cover up the truth of
this unfortunate affair: the two months in bed with colic accounted for the lack of any
public appearance in Madrid, while the letter falsely dated from Madrid made it seem
that he had only left for Andalusia after obtaining the consent of the royal administration.
Bibl. 154, doc. 160
Another letter, written by Martínez on 19 March 1793 to the Lord Chamberlain's
secretary, points out that the two months' leave have expired, that Goya is still ill, and
that he is applying for a prolongation. Fresh details come to light in the letter: Goya left
Madrid to visit Cadiz and other towns on the way there; he fell ill in Seville and was
taken by a friend to Cadiz where he arrived at Martínez's house 'in a very bad state'.
Ten days later Martínez wrote again, this time to Zapater to give him news of the invalid:

'The noises in his head and the deafness have not improved, but his vision is much better and he is no longer suffering from the disorders which made him lose his balance. He can now go up and down stairs very well and in a word is doing things he was not able to before.' Finally, a letter from Zapater, written on 30 March to Francisco Bayeu, contains the mysterious phrase which has sparked off so many discussions: 'Goya, as I told you, has been brought to this by his own thoughtlessness.' What does this mean? To what event in his life does this discreet allusion refer? Bayeu certainly knew about it since the two friends understood each other without going into details. But we have nothing more to enlighten us on this point. Rather than conclude that it must have been a reference to youthful misbehaviour or to some more recent escapade, of which he was paying the consequences, we should simply take note of this fresh proof of Goya's impulsive and sometimes thoughtless nature.

Bibl. 154, doc. 161

Bibl. 154, doc. 162

The actual nature of his illness has often been discussed, and by highly competent medical experts. Unfortunately, since it is all too easy to make mistakes even with everyday diagnosis, this kind of diagnosis *a posteriori* is almost impossibly difficult and there is much contradiction between the published results. Some specialists have maintained that the illness was syphilis, claiming that the death in infancy of nineteen of his children was indisputable proof of this. However, no more than six children are in fact known to have been born and although only one, Francisco Javier, survived, this is not outside the norms of the infant mortality rate at that time. Moreover, several specialists have confirmed for us that it is impossible to envisage a case of syphilis, contracted in Goya's youth, which could have provoked major disorders at the ages of thirty-one (1777) and forty-four (1790), followed by the terrible illness of 1792-1793 and, twenty-six years later, another serious crisis at the age of seventy-three (1819), and which finally allowed him to die at the age of eighty-two, as solid as a rock until the end, and all the while continuing to produce his truly prodigious œuvre. It therefore seems wiser not to attempt a 'modern' diagnosis of Goya's illness but to establish one in the manner of Molière's doctors, by stating that the patient almost died, was temporarily paralysed and lost his sense of balance, but that his strong constitution and his sanguine temperament enabled him to win through, although he lost his hearing for ever.

Ill. p. 154

Finally, there is one last intriguing point, the question of what he was going to do in Cadiz and why he left Madrid without leave. We can only make conjectures. He may have wished to study the architectural setting of the paintings which had been commissioned from him for the oratory of the Santa Cueva, then under construction [708-712], and he perhaps decided to take the opportunity of visiting Seville, which he did not know, to see the churches and look at the works of art there, and to greet his friend Ceán Bermúdez who had been given the task of reorganizing the Archivo de Indias. He certainly did some painting in Andalusia before his illness; there is the superb portrait of Sebastián Martínez [333] and he may have painted at this time the three over-doors for his host's residence, mentioned by the Conde de Maule in 1813 and now tentatively identified as paintings of reclining or sleeping women [I.307, 308, II.746]. The fact that he did not ask for leave seems easier to explain; he probably intended to make only a short trip and was in any case afraid that he would be refused permission since he was engaged at the time in painting a series of cartoons which had been forced on him.

* *Bibl. 140, (T. XVIII), p. 1587*

Sebastián Martínez
He was chief treasurer of the Finance Committee of Cadiz. Goya stayed with Martínez during his serious illness in 1792-1793 and probably painted this portrait just before. It shows a refined and sensitive man of forty-five, elegantly dressed in the French fashion. Martínez's art collection was famous in his own day and included more than three hundred paintings and several thousand prints. In spite of his illness, Goya must have had an opportunity to study it and may have come across works which were as yet unknown to him, such as the Piranesi etchings owned by his friend. The portrait which he painted of Martínez is remarkable for the delicacy of its tones and the harmony of the composition which seem to express the whole character of the sitter.

Whatever the circumstances, and quite apart from his illness, this visit to Cadiz was of considerable importance. He stayed for about six months with Sebastián Martínez who was a great collector. According to Antonio Ponz, in his *Viage de España**, his home was renowned for the three hundred or so paintings and several thousand engravings which it contained. The list given by Ponz included prints by Piranesi and one can imagine Goya, still ill or semi-convalescent, racked by pain and a prey to the darkest thoughts, being deeply impressed by a series like the *Carceri* (Prisons), whose influence is clearly apparent in some of the *Caprichos* prints.

Sebastián Martínez   [333] 1792. 92·9×67·6 cm. Metropolitan Museum of Art, New York

There remains the problem of the three religious paintings in the Santa Cueva. When the dates and the real motives of his second journey to Andalusia in 1796-1797 were not so clear, it was thought that these three large paintings must have been executed partially if not entirely during his first stay in Cadiz in 1792-1793. But lack of time and above all his ill-health probably prevented him from undertaking such an important task at that time. The conception of the pictures and even the preparatory sketches [710, 712] may date from the winter of 1792-1793, but the actual execution of the paintings must have been postponed until the date of his second journey to Andalusia in 1796, which we now know to have been a working trip rather than an amorous excursion.

The three great canvases in the Santa Cueva were probably painted without constraint, in terms of religious or formal requirements, and they have the internal tension and rich orchestration of colour which distinguish Goya's greatest works. The *Miracle of the loaves and fishes* [709], possibly the finest of the three, is remarkable for the solid realism of the foreground figures, including the Christ, and the crowd flowing back in waves towards the distance and contained within the semi-circle of the canvas, painted with the vibrant little colour touches with which Goya knew how to bring them alive on canvas. These qualities set this painting quite outside the traditions of baroque art and even farther from the art of Mengs. We have reached the watershed and are already standing on the slopes of the nineteenth century.

Goya returned to Madrid but according to the documents of the tapestry factory was 'absolutely unable to paint'. This statement is belied by the superb portraits which he executed in 1793 and 1794: *General Ricardos* [337], *Doña Tadea Arias de Enríquez* [336] and above all *La Tirana* in the March collection [340], *Don Felix Colón de Larriategui* [339] and probably the *Condesa del Carpio, Marquesa de la Solana* [341]. The great *Tirana* in the Academy of San Fernando, painted in 1799 [684], evokes the extraordinary 'presence' of the actress

The Santa Cueva in Cadiz

Ill. p. 112

Return to Madrid.   Portraits
Bibl. 154, doc. 177

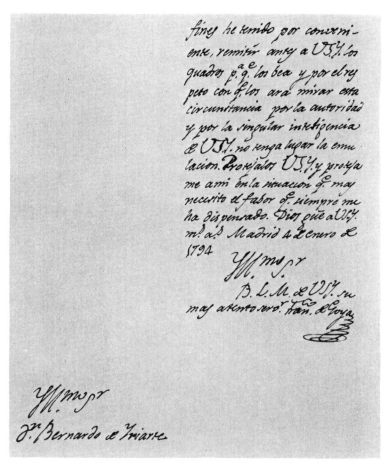

Autograph letter from Goya to Iriarte, dated 4 January 1794. British Museum, London

Letter from Goya to Iriarte
This celebrated letter was addressed to Don Bernardo de Iriarte, Vice-Protector of the Royal Academy of San Fernando and a friend of Goya. It refers to the little 'cabinet pictures' painted immediately after his illness: 'Most Excellent Sir, in order to occupy my imagination mortified by the contemplation of my sufferings, and in order to compensate in part for the considerable expense which they have caused me, I devoted myself to painting a set of cabinet pictures in which I have managed to make observations for which there is normally no opportunity in commissioned works which give no scope for fantasy and invention. I had thought of sending them to the Academy to the ends which your Excellency knows that I can expect in exposing this series to the judgment of the art professors; but in order to make sure of these ends, I have thought it fitting to send the pictures first to Your Excellency so that you might see them and that as a result of this there will be no occasion for jealous rivalry because of the respect with which they will be regarded by reason of Your Excellency's authority and singular understanding. May Your Excellency protect them and protect me too in the situation in which I need more than ever the favour which you have always accorded me. God keep Your Excellency many years. Madrid 4 January 1794. Your most faithful servant who kisses the hands of Your Excellency Francisco de Goya'   (See Appendix IV)

Bernardo de Iriarte

Iriarte was a member of the circle of *ilustrados* frequented by Goya, especially in the last ten years of the century. He was appointed Vice-Protector of the Academy of San Fernando in 1792 and in 1794 Goya sent him his set of little cabinet pictures. Bernardo de Iriarte and his brother Tomás, the poet, were collectors like Sebastián Martínez (see p. 106). Ceán Bermúdez mentioned their library and a large number of paintings including works by Velázquez, Murillo and Van Dyck. In 1797, the year in which this portrait was painted, Iriarte was Minister for Agriculture, Commerce and Overseas Relations in the 'liberal' cabinet to which Jovellanos and Saavedra also belonged.

This portrait is remarkable for the fine presence of the sitter and for its significant inscription: 'Don Bernardo Yriarte, Vice-protector of the Royal Academy of the three noble Arts, painted by Goya in testimony of mutual esteem and affection, in the year 1797.'

During the War of Independence, Iriarte, like many other *ilustrados*, supported Joseph Bonaparte who appointed him councillor of State and decorated him with the Royal Order of Spain. On the return of Ferdinand VII, he took refuge in Bordeaux where he died in 1814.

Bernardo de Iriarte [669] 1797. 108×84 cm. Musée des Beaux-Arts, Strasburg

on the stage, but the portrait dated 1794 is a symphony in grey, inspired perhaps by paintings he had seen in Cadiz, in the home of Sebastián Martínez. The same qualities appear to an even more marked degree in the *Solana* from the Beistegui collection which is now one of the treasures of the Louvre. More than any other portrait, it expresses 'the proud melancholy of the Spanish soul' with its harmonies of black and rose-pink and grey, and it dominates all the surrounding portraits in the collection.

Cabinet pictures sent to Iriarte

Doc. ill. p. 108

At the beginning of the year 1794 Goya wrote to Don Bernardo de Iriarte, Vice-Protector of the Academy, sending him 'a set of cabinet pictures in which I have managed to make observations for which there is normally no opportunity in commissioned works which give no scope for fantasy and invention'. In a second letter he described the final

Placing the banderillas [319] 1793. Tinplate 43×31 cm. Private collection, Madrid

Picador caught by the bull [322] 1793. Tinplate 43×32 cm. Cotnareanu coll., New York

Cabinet pictures *Letter of 7 January 1794*
Of the fourteen little pictures on tin, here catalogued together as the 'set of cabinet pictures' painted in 1793-94, only eleven were shown to the San Fernando academicians who referred to them by the general title of 'scenes of national diversions'. This could be explained by the predominance of the eight bullfighting scenes which form a series representing various phases of the corrida [317-324]. Five of them take place in a bullring which is probably the famous Maestranza in Seville, with its elegant colonnaded galleries, and would therefore be a direct souvenir of Goya's visit to Seville at the end of 1792, while another (far left) is set in a little village bullring or possibly on a breeding ranch. As for the remarkable *Yard with lunatics* (right), Goya described it in a letter to Iriarte dated 7 January 1794 and said that he would send it when finished because it completed the series, adding that it was a scene which he had witnessed in Saragossa (see Appendix IV).

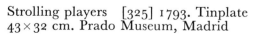

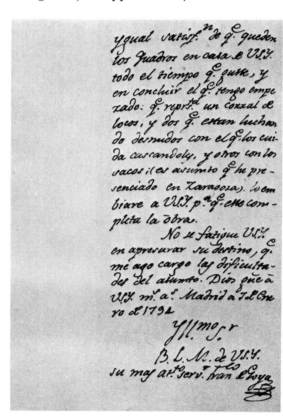

The marionette seller [326] 1793. Tinplate 42×32 cm. Private collection, Switzerland

Strolling players [325] 1793. Tinplate 43×32 cm. Prado Museum, Madrid

Letter from Goya to Iriarte, dated 7 January 1794 (last page). British Museum, London

picture in the series, which was still unfinished [330]: '... it represents a yard with lunatics and two of them fighting completely naked while their warder beats them, and others in sacks; (it is a scene which I saw in Saragossa)'. The eleven paintings sent with the first letter were shown to the academicians and described as representing 'various scenes of national diversions'. They were entrusted to Iriarte, together with the *Yard with lunatics*, and then taken away to be sent to a certain Marquis of Villaverde. For a long time it was

See Appendix IV

Corral de locos (Yard with lunatics)   [330] 1793-94. Tinplate 43·8×32·7 cm. Meadows Museum, Dallas

Miracle of the loaves and fishes   [709] c.1796-97. 146×340 cm. Santa Cueva, Cadiz

thought that the five wonderful panel paintings now in the Academy of San Fernando, the *Inquisition scene, Procession of flagellants, Madhouse, Bullfight in a village* and *Burial of the sardine* [III.966-970], were part of this group of pictures. There are two arguments against this view: firstly the fact that the *Madhouse* does not correspond with the description in Goya's letter, and secondly the style of the pictures which is much closer to that of the period 1808-1819. One could also add that the *Inquisition scene* and *Procession of flagellants* can hardly be described as 'national diversions'. *See p. 240.   Ill. frontispiece*

Recent opinion and above all the documentary material assembled and published by Xavier de Salas suggest that the pictures in question are a group of small paintings on tinplate, almost identical in size with the *Yard with lunatics* in the Meadows Museum at Dallas [330], which exactly fits the description given by Goya. Apart from the *Yard with lunatics*, the series would include on the one hand the *Strolling players*, the *Marionette seller*, the *Brigands attacking a coach*, the *Shipwreck* and the *Fire at night* [325-329], on the other hand the eight bullfight scenes from the Torrecilla collection [317-324] which, as a group, may have accounted for the description 'national diversions' in the minutes of the Academy. We would suggest that these small scenes of the *fiesta nacional* (national sport) are probably reminiscences of Goya's visit to Seville and portray famous monuments in the town. As to the other paintings, there is growing evidence to show that they may all be connected with events in Aragon which Goya either heard about or experienced directly during his visits to Saragossa, as he expressly noted in the case of the *Yard with lunatics*. He was anxious to sell the pictures – as he told Iriarte in his letter of 4 January – 'to compensate in part for the considerable expense which [my sufferings] have caused me', and it was for this reason that he took them away so soon after assuring Iriarte that 'the pictures may remain in Your Excellency's house for as long as you like'. By 1805 the group of fourteen pictures belonged to Chopinot, the court jeweller, and Manuel Godoy was apparently interested in acquiring them for his collection from Chopinot's widow. *Bibl. 149*
Ill. p. 111

Ill. p. 110

Ill. p. 108

See Appendix IV

Though some of these pictures are rather naïve and awkward, which would account for the lack of interest shown in them until recently, they are of the greatest significance in that they introduce a new and very important theme in Goya's work which he has described himself with a single word: *capricho*. What did he mean by this? The term is

Paintings in the Santa Cueva at Cadiz

The three great semi-circular religious paintings which Goya executed for the Santa Cueva in Cadiz have been very little studied until recently and are difficult to date. We know only that the oratory was consecrated on 31 March 1796 and that a painting in it which was commissioned from Camarón is dated 1795.

In normal circumstances, Goya should have delivered his pictures before the building was consecrated but his serious illness in 1793 suggests two hypotheses: either the paintings were executed in Madrid, after he had studied the positions they were to occupy and had made sketches on the spot at the end of 1792; or he returned to Andalusia in 1796 in order to paint the three canvases after the consecration of the oratory. He certainly could not have carried out such an important task in 1792-93 because his health would not have allowed it. It is therefore possible that he went to Cadiz at the end of 1792 in connection with this commission and that the conception of the whole work and possibly the sketches may date from that period, but the final execution was undoubtedly postponed until later.

The three subjects are taken from the New Testament. One of them is quite usual – the *Last Supper*, which Goya nevertheless treats in a rather unusual way – but the other two are rarely represented because of their lack of an iconographic tradition. In the *Miracle of the loaves and fishes* (St John, ch. 6, verses 5-15), Goya makes the crowd spreading out in successive waves the main subject of his picture, and with the extremely rare theme of the *Parable of the guest without a wedding garment* (St Matthew, ch. 22, verses 1-14), he creates a timeless group of figures whose expressive force has a validity far beyond the context of the subject; it looks forward to the theme of the prisoner which was to occur so often in Goya's later work.

Parable of the guest without a wedding garment (detail)   [708] c.1796-97. Santa Cueva, Cadiz

an old one; he may have borrowed it from Tiepolo, but he gave it a completely different meaning. For Goya, *capricho* is always synonymous with liberty, fantasy, and the private world of his thoughts and feelings, everything in which the painter and later the engraver and draughtsman could express directly what he felt and saw. He was at last making his own personal statements in painting, though it had taken him more than twenty years to fight through the forest of baroque and neo-classical styles which had hindered the growth of the new art developing within him.

In spite of the fact that Goya's first visit to Andalusia was darkened by illness, he must have been dazzled by this land of light and beauty. He may have gone there in order to paint the canvases for the Santa Cueva [708-712], but the principal object of that first journey was undoubtedly to search out the innumerable works of art which towns like Seville and Cadiz harboured then and still harbour today. Indeed this is confirmed in a letter written by his friend Sebastián Martínez: 'My friend don Francisco de Goya left the court as you know, with the desire to see this city [Cadiz] and those on the way . . .'

Although travelling was inconvenient and the inns were often very uncomfortable at that period, Goya knew that he could count on a hospitable welcome at the home of his learned friend, Juan Agustín Ceán Bermúdez, who was resident in Seville since 1790, and with the great collector Sebastián Martínez in Cadiz. His health was still not perfect and the winters in Madrid could be very hard. Moreover, if his illness in 1793 had prevented the execution of the paintings for the Santa Cueva, the dedication of the sanctuary on 31 March 1796 made it imperative that the three paintings should be installed. So for

1794-1797. Goya is 48 to 51 years old. Stay at Sanlúcar with the Duchess of Alba (1796-97). Album of drawings (A). Return to Madrid (1797). Album of drawings (B). Witchcraft paintings for the Osunas. Reign of Charles IV.

Bibl. 154, doc. 160

Ill. p. 136
Ill. p. 107

Bibl. 166, pp. 60-61

Self-portrait   [666] Metropolitan Museum, New York

Self-portrait
c.1795-1797
Indian ink brush and wash 23·3 × 14·4 cm.

The Duchess of Alba
Goya and the Duchess of Alba form one of the most celebrated – and over-exploited – couples in the history of art. They appear here in portraits made at the time of their stormy liaison which was broken off in 1797, the date on the Hispanic Society portrait.

Goya's self-portrait was later bound as the frontispiece to the album of drawings which was owned by Mariano Fortuny and acquired by the Metropolitan Museum in 1935. It is the most tragic of all the known self-portraits, evoking the images of his contemporary, Beethoven, and is close to the sketches which Goya made before etching the frontispiece to the *Caprichos* in 1797-98 [435].

The portrait of the Duchess of Alba dressed as a maja, in a black skirt and mantilla, appears to represent a clear avowal of Goya's feelings for her: she points out to the spectator the inscription *Solo Goya* traced in the sand at her feet, while the two rings on her fingers bear the names *Goya* and *Alba*. This avowal seems all the more significant when we consider that the word *Solo* was later carefully overpainted, possibly by the artist himself who kept this painting in his own home in Madrid where it appears listed in an inventory of his possessions in 1812. This elegant woman, set against a delicate Andalusian landscape, appears here as the dark angel who tormented the artist with her 'lying and inconstancy' and whom he later portrayed in two of the most bitterly satirical *Caprichos* [573, 619] (see p. 131).

The Duchess of Alba   [355] 1797. 210·2×149·3 cm. Hispanic Society of America, New York

the second time Goya left Madrid for Andalusia. This journey, like the previous one, has been the subject of much commentary which has not always clarified matters nor succeeded in establishing any certain dates for this key period in the artist's life.

However, when all the documents so far published are studied together, they reveal a number of indisputable facts. In the first place, any meeting with the Duchess of Alba in Andalusia in 1792-1793 was out of the question since the palace of Sanlúcar was let to the Archbishop of Seville from 1789 to 1795; Goya could therefore only have stayed there at the time of his second journey. We know from recently published letters that Goya left for Andalusia at the end of May 1796 and stayed with Ceán Bermúdez in Seville, leaving there at the beginning of the summer for a visit to Sanlúcar. He was still absent from Madrid in October, and on 24 January 1797 we learn from another exchange of letters that he was in Cadiz. By 1 April he was back in Madrid, where he tendered his resignation as Director of Painting at the Academy. Altogether, Goya seems to have stayed in Andalusia for nearly ten months, between May 1796 and March 1797, and this is confirmed by an official document which says that 'for the whole of the year 96 . . . he was absent in Seville'. Much later, in 1817, when the faithful Ceán Bermúdez was analysing the picture which his friend had just painted for the cathedral at Seville, *Saints Justa and Rufina* [III.1569], he recalled '. . . that he has stayed three times in that city and has seen and studied at great length all the works of art . . .'

So it was not in any way a question of the passionate lover rushing off to meet the Duchess of Alba in Andalusia, but rather of the great painter and well-known connoisseur, still not fully recovered from his serious illness, who was leaving to see the artistic treasures in the towns in the south of Spain and perhaps to do some private painting in the homes of his art-loving friends. Apart from the considerable work involved in the completion of the Santa Cueva paintings, Goya did not remain idle. The *Portrait of Judge Altamirano of Seville* [667] probably dates from this period as does the conception, and possibly the execution, of the four *Doctors of the Church*; two of them – *St Gregory* and *St Augustine* [714, 715] – were inspired by Murillo's *St Isidore* and *St Leander* in the cathedral at Seville, while the *St Jerome* [716] was the fruit of his long and attentive study of the sculpture by Torrigiano, in the company of Ceán Bermúdez, 'on two different occasions, remaining there each time for more than an hour and a quarter'.

But the course of what might be described as a studious holiday was suddenly altered by an unexpected event: on 9 June 1796 the Duke of Alba, who was alone on his estate at Seville, died suddenly at the early age of forty. Goya had known the Alba household since at least 1795, when he painted the dazzling portrait of the Duchess of Alba in a white dress [351] and the rather melancholy one of the Duke [350], as well as two little domestic scenes [352, 353]. Documentary evidence shows that by July Goya was at Sanlúcar, where the Albas had a summer residence, and the duchess must have gone at once to Andalusia although she had to return to Madrid for the funeral rites on 4 and 5 September 1796. They would therefore have spent the summer together at Sanlúcar, immediately after the duke's death. Goya, whose health was still poor, did not return to Madrid in September; his absence was noted by the Academy of San Fernando in the following month. As for the duchess, it is well known that she returned to spend her period of mourning in Andalusia. This is proved by the will which she signed at Sanlúcar on 16 February 1797, in which among other bequests she left a life annuity to Goya's son.

The famous encounter at Sanlúcar, which has been the subject of so much speculation, could therefore have occurred during two periods of time, the first extending from the end of June to the end of August 1796, and the second from 24 January 1797 (and in fact probably before then) until the end of March, by which time Goya was already back in Madrid. In 1796 the duchess was thirty-four and he, still much weakened by his illness, was fifty. Three years before, beneath that same Andalusian sky, he had thought that he was going to die. Now the enchanting Cayetana – of whom a French traveller wrote that

Bibl. 58, pp. 182-184

Bibl. 150
Bibl. 172, p. 21, n. 13
Bibl. 72, p. 59

Bibl. 154, doc. 188

Bibl. 70, p. 78

Stay with the Duchess of Alba at Sanlúcar

Bibl. 166, p. 61

Bibl. 47, V, p. 63; 114, pp. 63-64

Bibl. 150

Bibl. 154, doc. 160

Bibl. 58, pp. 202-203

Drawings from the Sanlúcar album (album A)

The Duchess of Alba
[356] Indian ink wash 17×9·7 cm.

The Duchess of Alba holding María de la Luz
[360] Indian ink wash 10·6×9·2 cm.

The small album of drawings known as the Sanlúcar album was executed in 1796-97, during Goya's stay with the Duchess of Alba on her estates at Sanlúcar de Barrameda near Cadiz. These little sketches from life represent Goya's first drawings made as a series and they contain the seeds of several of the *Caprichos* engravings, not so much in the actual subjects which Goya repeated [365, 369, 371] as in the latent eroticism which pervades them all.

The Duchess of Alba appears several times, as on these two pages from the album where she is instantly recognizable by her superb dark hair and by the little Negro child, María de la Luz, whom she had adopted sometime before 1795 – see [353]. There are also sketches of other young women, caught in intimate scenes and often in a state of undress.

The small format and still somewhat hesitant brush and wash technique mark the beginning of the new researches which were to develop through the Madrid album [377-450] and the *Caprichos* prints and drawings [451-647] and find their full expression in the albums of drawings executed during the last twenty-five years of the artist's life.

The Duchess of Alba. Album A [a]   [356]
1796-97. Biblioteca Nacional, Madrid

The Duchess of Alba holding María de la Luz
Album A [e]   [360] 1796-97. Prado, Madrid

Ill. p. 115

Sanlúcar album of drawings

every hair of her head excited desire – must have aroused in him one of those 'violent and anguished passions of a man's fiftieth year, the overwhelming love which one imagines will be the last' and which Balzac was later to experience, to the point of death, for Madame Hanska. Every one seems agreed on this. But did they in fact have an affair, however brief and stormy? Some would deny it. And yet the portrait of the duchess dressed as a maja [355], which is generally considered to have been painted at Sanlúcar, tends to prove this: the rings painted with the names *Goya* and *Alba* were already an indication, and the recent discovery of the complete inscription to which the proud duchess points imperiously at her feet – *Solo Goya* (Only Goya) – seems to leave no doubt as to the nature of their relationship. During that passionate summer of 1796, Don Francisco de Goya became the lover of the first lady of Spain after the queen. The estate at Sanlúcar afforded such total intimacy and freedom that Goya began a little sketchbook in which he captured scenes and figures in quite unconventional attitudes. Though several leaves have unfortunately been lost, this *Sanlúcar album*, also known as album A [356-376], shows us not only glimpses of the Duchess of Alba's private life but also unknown young women, sometimes almost naked and often in ambiguous poses. Summer and long siestas, bathing and dressing, the indiscretions of a roving eye, pleasures and little pains, all these are evoked with a light stroke of the brush, with no other thought than to capture these happy moments which might never return. But if passion can be violent and imperative in a man of fifty, for a man such as Goya his art was even more demanding and finally prevailed over everything else. At first slight and insignificant, these sketches gradually gave him a taste for drawing as a means of expressing something seen, figures caught in the reality of their everyday existence and free of any self-conscious mannerisms.

Another, larger sketchbook, originally entitled the 'large Sanlúcar album' by Sánchez Cantón, is now known by the probably more accurate name of the *Madrid album*, or album B [377-450]. It seems, however, quite possible that some of the drawings in it were in fact made at Sanlúcar at the same time as those of the first small album, or at any rate shortly afterwards. What is important is the change of intention from one album to the other. The first is a little pocket book of rather inaesthetic format, containing rapid sketches, made without any particular aim; in the second, larger book, the figures are grouped, the scenes are composed, and the autograph numbers, later accompanied by inscriptions, suggest a planned sequence and a satirical or moralizing intention which is underlined by the increasingly biting graphic style.

While some of the scenes at the beginning of album B could have been drawn from life, like those in album A, one soon has the feeling that Goya was composing his drawings

Madrid album of drawings
Bibl. 158

Bibl. 53, 115, 172

Album B.*65* [425] 1796-97. Private collection, Lille

Album B.*80* [438] 1796-97. William M. Roth, San Francisco

B.*65* *Cantan para el q.ᵉ lo hizo* (They are singing for the one who made it up) [425] Indian ink wash 23·3×14·6 cm.

B.*80* *Mascaras de semana santa del año de 94* (Masquerades of Holy Week in the year '94) [438] Indian ink wash 23·2×14·1 cm.

B.*55* *Mascaras crueles* (Masks, cruel ones) [415] Indian ink wash 23·7×15 cm.

The so-called Madrid album of drawings is closely linked to the Sanlúcar album and is at once a continuation and a development of the earlier album, both in theme and technique. Some of the pages at the beginning may indeed have been drawn at Sanlúcar or at Cadiz, before Goya's return to Madrid.

The album must originally have included at least forty-seven pages, with drawings on both sides as in the Sanlúcar album. Thirty-seven pages are known today and within them we can follow the radical change which occurs in Goya's art. The first nineteen pages take up the gallant themes which ultimately derive from the inexhaustible reserves of the tapestry cartoons and the light-hearted art of the eighteenth- century rococo tradition: majos and majas, scenes on the traditional Spanish *paseo*, lovers' quarrels, old bawds, *tertulias* and so on... Then the mood suddenly changes with the sheet with drawings numbered *55* and *56* (see pp. 119 and 120): masks, witches and caricatures appear with, for the first time, trenchant captions to underline their meaning. Goya's work is now invaded by the irrational world.

We see a striking example of this change in the theme of the concert, which appears twice in the album: near the beginning, on page *27*, there is a charming duo in the best eighteenth- century tradition between an elegant young woman and a *petimetre*; but on page *65* (far left) all the figures have become grotesque and the ensemble is a caricature, emphasized by the apparent seriousness of the title. Even Holy Week, with its processions of penitents and of blood-spattered flagellants, did not escape the indignant satire of the friend of Jovellanos and Moratín. The earlier, realistic figures bathed in an evenly diffused light give way, in the second half of the album, to scenes where strong contrasts of light and shade are set against a wash background applied in the manner of an aquatint, as in the plates of the *Caprichos* which owe so much to this album.

Album B.*55* [415] 1796-97. Private collection, Paris (see verso p. 120)

B.*56* *Brujas á bolar* (Witches, about to fly)
[416] Indian ink wash 23·7 × 15 cm.

B.*33* Young woman running up steps
[401] Indian ink wash 23·7 × 14·7 cm.

B.6o? *Parten la Vieja* (They are cutting the old woman in two) [420]
Indian ink wash 20·9 × 12·5 cm.

In this album, as in so many of Goya's prints and drawings, popular customs and sayings occupy an important place. The drawing in the Louvre (far right), unfortunately cut and lacking its autograph number, is a caricatural representation of Mid-Lent, symbolized by an old woman who is cut in half with a saw. It is difficult to tell whether the figures are wearing masks or are themselves of grotesque appearance, and this is the kind of ambiguity which Goya delighted in creating. Years later, in Bordeaux, he returned to the same theme in a drawing which he actually entitled *Mitad de cuaresma* (Mid-Lent) over a very similar title *Partir la vieja* (Cutting the old woman in two) [v.1722].

The drawings on pages *33* and *56* again illustrate the contrast between the two halves of the album: the first (right) is all lightness and grace with the scantily clad young woman rushing to the brilliantly lit doorway to watch the soldiers go by; the second (left) is a hideous and ludicrous caricature, the first witchcraft scene which appears in Goya's work and which he engraved for one of the *Caprichos* plates [591].

Album B.*56* [416] 1796-97. Private collection, Paris (see recto p. 119)

from memory and giving them a particular meaning. After a number of sheets where majos, majas, soldiers, young women and *petimetres* play the various parts in a comedy of love which is not without its acid moments, a new universe suddenly emerges with the inscriptions which appear for the first time on the drawing numbered *55* [415]. The *Ill. p. 119* same brush now traces strange words: *Mascaras* (masquerades), *Brujas* (witches), *Caricaturas* (caricatures). The figures, which have so far been agreeable to the eye, become grotesque or ridiculous, and their faces grow deformed, taking on a brutish or hideous appearance until what began as a mask becomes the actual face. It is the beginning of the 'monstrueux vraisemblable' (credible monstrosity) in Goya's work, so brilliantly defined by Baudelaire.

Ill. p. 131 On the evidence of some of the *Caprichos* plates and in particular that of the *Dream. Of lying and inconstancy* [619] which was never published, the affair between Goya and the Duchess of Alba came to an abrupt end. It seems that the second half of their stay at Sanlúcar, during the winter of 1796-1797, became more and more stormy and the happiness of the preceding summer months turned into an intolerable situation. If one accepts that

Album B.*33*   [401] 1796-97. Anton Schrafl, Zurich

Album B.60?   [420] 1796-97. Musée du Louvre, Paris

121

The witches' sabbath   [660] 1797-98. 44×31 cm. Lázaro Galdiano Museum, Madrid

Pedro Romero matando a toro parado.
(Pedro Romero killing the halted bull)
Tauromaquia 30 [III.1210] 1815-16.
Etching and aquatint (detail)

Pedro Romero (1754-1839)
Pedro Romero came from Ronda in the province of Málaga and was one of the most celebrated bullfighters of his day. With his brother José he created the modern form of bullfighting and is said to have killed nearly six thousand bulls in the course of his twenty-three year career, without ever being wounded. At the end of his life, in 1830, Ferdinand VII appointed him director of the Royal School of Bullfighting in Madrid. Both the portrait and the detail from one of the *Tauromaquia* etchings suggest the restrained and classic manner which characterized his style of fighting.

The witches' sabbath
This is one of six scenes of sorcery painted for the Osunas' country palace of La Alameda. Goya's account is dated 27 June 1798 and the pictures were therefore executed while he was working on the *Caprichos* and are very close in their black comedy to many of the prints (see plates *44, 45, 47* and *60*).

Witchcraft was a fashionable topic in 'enlightened' circles at the end of the eighteenth century and the interest in these monstrous customs born of ignorance and credulity led to fresh criticism of the Inquisition whose notorious *autos de fe*, intended to put an end to such practices, were themselves an example of even more fanatical cruelty.

Pedro Romero   [671] c.1795-98. 84·1×65 cm. Kimbell Foundation, Forth Worth

most of the drawings in album B were executed in Madrid, after 1 April 1797 and before Goya started work on the *Caprichos* which in many cases developed from them, the change of 'accent' within the album seems almost certainly connected with the bitter deception of his passion. Already cut off from the outside world by his deafness, Goya withdrew into a private world of dreams and caricatures where fantasy and eroticism, which he had just experienced so painfully, were to combine in the creation of a new art.

Back in Madrid, he lost no time in following the path which had just opened up before him. He renewed contact with his friends, among them the Osunas who commissioned or bought from him six little scenes relating to witchcraft and sorcery for the decoration of the Alameda palace [659-664]. Four of the paintings are very closely connected with the

witchcraft prints in the second half of the *Caprichos* [659-662] and the remaining two Witchcraft scenes for the Osunas
illustrate scenes from two plays by Zamora: the bewitched priest in *El Hechizado por Fuerza*
and Don Juan with the stone guest in *El Burlador de Sevilla*. They were paid for by the Duke
of Osuna in 1798, and were probably the *seis caprichos raros* (six strange caprices) exhibited *See Appendix V*
at the Academy of San Fernando in the following year. Part comedy, part tragedy, they
reveal the artist in the process of transformation. It is significant that one of the pictures
even looks back to the composition of a tapestry cartoon [I.259, II.659]; Goya still had
many of the sketches for the cartoons in his collection and sold a group of them to the
Duke of Osuna in May of the same year [I.256-261, 272-275]. At the same time the literary
themes and the fashionable topic of witchcraft itself show that he is fully at home in the
cultured milieu of the Osunas and their friends. One can also point to the fact that while
he paints the portraits of toreadors such as the great Pedro Romero, creator of the modern
form of bullfighting [671], he is also the portraitist of his 'enlightened' friends who dream *Ill. p. 123   See p. 132*
of making Spain something more than a country of *corridas* and *seguidillas*.

1797-1799. Goya is 51 to 52 years old. Draws and engraves the first of his great series of prints (80 etchings), published in 1799 as 'Caprichos de Goya'. Liberal interlude: Jovellanos and the 'ilustrados' in power. Reign of Charles IV.

Los Caprichos are a series of eighty satirical prints in etching and aquatint which Goya published in book form in 1799. Original in conception, masterly in execution, they place Goya in the tradition of the greatest painter-engravers such as Dürer and Rembrandt. It was as the creator of the *Caprichos* that he was first known and appreciated in France and England, and their unique blend of dream and fantasy with social criticism, of evasion and flight from reality with commitment and harsh realism, continues to fascinate all students of Goya and of the troubled times when these prints first appeared.

El sueño de la razon produce monstruos.
(The dream of reason brings forth monsters)
Caprichos 43   [536] 1797-98.
Etching and aquatint 21·6 × 15·2 cm.

The print shows Goya himself at his work table, with the creatures of darkness swarming from the shadows behind him. An owl has grasped his pencil and seems to be urging him to set to work to portray the 'monsters' of his dreams.

    Goya designed this composition as the original title page to a series of *Sueños* (dreams). The preparatory drawing [537] shows the projected title page which has an explanation of the composition: 'The Author dreaming. His only intention is to banish harmful common beliefs and to perpetuate with this work of *caprichos* the sound testimony of truth'.

    Goya's ideas developed and changed as he worked on the prints and in the end he prefaced the series with the famous self-portrait (see p. 103). 'The Author dreaming' became plate *43* and acts as an introduction to the prints mainly concerned with witch-craft and sorcery. The evocative title was 'written' by Goya himself in the aquatint.

El sueño de la razon produce monstruos.   *Caprichos 43*   [536]

When Goya returned to Madrid after his long absence in Andalusia and his stay with the Duchess of Alba, some time during the spring of 1797, he found an atmosphere of political excitement and change in the capital. Godoy, who had always been his supporter, was momentarily forced to withdraw behind the scenes and the *ilustrados*, the group of 'enlightened' men led by Jovellanos, saw their dreams of reform and good government become reality. In November Jovellanos took office as Minister of Grace and Justice. Although the liberal interlude was very brief and Jovellanos lost his position within a year, it produced an upsurge of optimism and activity among the *ilustrados*, and their criticism and discussion of social and political questions must have taken on a quite new sense of purpose and practicability.

In 1795, after the death of Francisco Bayeu, Goya seems to have solicited through Iriarte, but without success, the post of First Court Painter. Since 1792 he had executed no commissions for the royal family, because of his ill-health, and his links with the court had become much less strong. It was therefore natural that he should be drawn into the active circle of the *ilustrados* among whom he had so many friends. He no doubt showed them the drawings of the so-called Madrid album [377-450] and discussed with them his project to engrave and offer to the public a collection of satirical prints, in which he could express his views and criticism of contemporary society. *Bibl. 144, pp. 335-337*

See pp. 117-121

In April 1797 Goya wrote to the Royal Academy to resign his directorship of the painting classes. This meant that he was relieved of most of his official duties, and before the end of the year he had completed the Madrid album of some one hundred drawings and had so far progressed with the project for the album of prints that he had designed and dated the title page; not the plate which finally served as frontispiece to the series – the sardonic, top-hatted self-portrait [451] – but the design [537] which records his original idea to produce a series of prints entitled *Sueños* (Dreams) and which in the final arrangement of the prints became plate 43, with the title *El sueño de la razon* (The dream of reason) [536]. *Bibl. 72, p. 59*

Ill. p. 103

Ill. p. 125

In the later drawings of the Madrid album, Goya played with different titles such as *Caricatures*, *Masquerades*, but to many of the preparatory drawings which he made for the prints he gave the general title *Sueño*, as well as an individual caption. Most of these drawings are numbered above the composition, and to some extent the original 'dream' sequence can be reconstructed. The *1st Dream* [537] was the drawing already referred to, in which we see Goya himself asleep at his work table, almost overwhelmed by the night creatures which crowd in upon him from the darkness. The second dream is the amusing drawing [572] for the plate which became *Capricho 60*, showing two novice witches making their first flight. The third [592] shows another apprentice witch making her oath of allegiance, and this composition was taken directly from page 56 of the Madrid album [416]. The first ten dream drawings are all illustrations of witchcraft and sorcery – the 'harmful common beliefs' which Goya wished to chase away, according to the inscription on the *1st Dream*. By the fifteenth dream [480], Goya has turned his satire and ridicule to the direct criticism of social evils, in this case the sacrifice of a young and beautiful girl to a marriage with one of a choice of rich but repellent old suitors. This subject introduces a group of mild satires on current conventions of marriage and courtship, and it is not until dream 25 [477], which became *Capricho 13*, that the Church comes under attack, followed by the medical profession [531] (*Capricho 40*), and the law which leaves time-honoured ills untended – in this case the abuse of the so-called 'tobacco guards' turned bandits [473] (*Capricho 11*). The *Sueños* or Dreams

Ill. p. 128

Ill. p. 120

José López-Rey and other writers have shown that this first idea of presenting his criticism and satire as a series of dreams belongs in the tradition of Spanish writers such as Quevedo, whose *Sueños* were republished in 1726 with a frontispiece very similar to the design chosen by Goya. The fact that Goya's 'dreams' began with a group of light-hearted scenes of witches busy with their duties and diversions (see plates 60, 62, 63, 65, *Bibl. 93, p. 49; 108, p. 114, pl. 16; 115, pp. 99-101*

Gallant quizzing a maja. Album B.*19* [389] 1796-97. Indian ink wash 21·9×13·5 cm. Prado Museum, Madrid

Por aberle yo dicho, q.ᵉ tenia buen mobimiento no puede ablar sin colear (Just because I told her she moved nicely she can't talk without wiggling). *Sueño 21* [464] Preparatory drawing for *Caprichos 7*. Pen and sepia ink with Indian ink wash. Title written below in pencil.
Prado Museum, Madrid

Ni asi la distingue (Even so he cannot make her out) *Caprichos 7* [463] 1797-98. Etching and aquatint 20×15 cm.

In this sequence from Madrid album to *Caprichos* print, we can follow the working out not only of the design but also of Goya's satirical intention. After the conversational title on the preparatory drawing, he tried out a much more cryptic phrase on one of the working proofs: *Ya la percivo* (Now he can see what she is). He finally settled for the cynical comment engraved on the plate, which is amplified in his commentary (from the manuscript in the Prado): 'How could he make her out? In order to know what she is a monocle is not enough; judgment and experience of the world are necessary and these are precisely what this poor gentleman is lacking'.

Gallant quizzing a maja. Album B.*19*   [389]

These three illustrations show a typical sequence in the elaboration of one of the early *Caprichos* prints, starting with a drawing in the Madrid album whose composition was elaborated in a drawing prepared for the *Sueños* series and etched as plate 7 of the *Caprichos*.

A sketch in the Madrid album (left) showing a couple on the *paseo* – seen perhaps in Cadiz or on Goya's return to Madrid in the spring of 1797 – served as the basis for a detailed pen and ink drawing (lower left), in which he added many more figures, including a man reclining against a seated girl, and the suggestion of a building. The drawing was made as number *21* in the *Sueño* (Dream) series which Goya initially planned to publish, and it was given a long and amusing title.

This pen drawing was then damped and transferred to the copperplate (the pen lines are blurred and the imprint of the copperplate is visible on the drawing). The etched design (lower right) is therefore identical with the outlines and proportions of the preparatory drawing, but Goya reduced the height of the composition and left out the background, retaining only the seated girl and the face which peeps between the two main figures. He then added an Indian ink wash to the drawing and freely interpreted the wash effect in aquatint on the plate. In the early plates of this series, Goya had not yet fully mastered the aquatint technique, and the tonal effect in the print is much less bold than that of the wash on the drawing.

Finally, having decided on the title of the composition, this was engraved on the copperplate, with the number, and the plate was then ready for publication.

Por aberle yo dicho ... Preparatory drawing   [464]

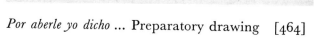
Ni asi la distingue.   Caprichos 7   [463]

127

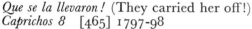

Que se la llevaron! (They carried her off!)
Caprichos 8 [465] 1797-98

Ensayos. (Trials) *Caprichos 60*
[571] 1797-98

Que se la llevaron!
Etching and aquatint 21·7×15·2 cm.
Although the composition is derived from one of the caricatures in the Madrid album [421], the treatment of the print suggests that it was one of the latest which Goya engraved for the *Caprichos*. The subject is without humour, a harsh comment on 'the woman who cannot take care of herself' and exposes herself to the hazards of kidnap and rape, expressed by the contrast of the dark aquatint and the violent, dramatic highlights.

Ensayos
Etching and aquatint 21×16·6 cm.
This print was designed as the second in the series of *Sueños* (Dreams) with which Goya intended to 'banish harmful common beliefs', namely superstition and witchcraft. The composition recalls one of the witchcraft scenes painted by Goya for the Duchess of Osuna (see p. 122), and the light-hearted treatment of the print suggests the amused and sceptical interest taken by the aristocracy and intelligentsia in the widespread popular belief in witchcraft in eighteenth-century Spain.

66, 68-70) suggests that he was deliberately sugaring the pill and obscuring his more serious aim of social satire and criticism. In the final arrangement of the *Caprichos* plates, the sequence is more or less illogical. Scenes of witchcraft and sorcery are intermingled with social satire, and if coherent groups emerge – the education of children (plates *3* and *4*), prostitution (plates *15-17*), secular and religious 'justice' (plates *21-24*), they continue for no more than three or four compositions and are then broken off, to reappear later in another guise. The longest series within the *Caprichos* is that of the asses: plates *37* to *42* [522-535]. In these, Goya attacks the so-called leaders of society: the aristocrats (plate *39*), the teachers (plate *37*), the doctors (plate *40*), the self-important people who have their portraits painted by servile artists (plate *41*), the cultural snobs who applaud what they do not understand (plate *38*) and, finally, all the rulers and exploiters of the long-suffering people (plate *42*).

Goya did not etch all the subjects for which he made preliminary drawings, nor did he publish all the plates which he in fact engraved. Among the unpublished plates [614-621] is the *Sueño. De la mentira y la ynconstancia* (Dream. Of lying and inconstancy) [619] where Goya recalled the agony of his passion for the Duchess of Alba in such unequivocal terms that he decided not to include it in the published series, although another reference to her, where she appears wearing the same symbolic butterfly wings and flying away with an expression of cold disdain, was included as plate *61* [573]. Another plate which Goya excluded from the series appears to be a savage caricature of the dissolute Queen María Luisa [618]. Furthermore, two drawings for a design which satirized en bloc all the Royal Academies and would have been included among the 'asinine' prints, were apparently never engraved [630, 631].

On 6 February 1799, the *Diario de Madrid* carried on its front page a long announcement of the publication of the *Caprichos* prints. The original text was written after the decision to call the series *Los Caprichos* and is, in effect, an expanded version of the long

Ill. p. 130

Ill. p. 131

Publication of the *Caprichos* prints
Ill. p. 129
Bibl.: 88, I, p. 95; 115, p. 185

inscription at the foot of the *1st Dream* drawing [537]: *The Author dreaming. His only intention is to banish harmful common beliefs and to perpetuate with this work of* caprichos *the sound testimony of truth*. The announcement was no doubt written with the help of his friends who played so large a part in the conception of the whole work. Goya specifically paid tribute to Jovellanos by making the first of the *caprichos* subjects the illustration to one of his satirical poems and using a fragment of his verse as the title [454], and the very close connection which exists between Goya and his friend, the dramatist Moratín, has been pointed out by Edith Helman. The announcement stated that painting as well as eloquence and poetry should concern itself with the censure of the vices and errors of society, and was careful to say that the satire in the prints was general and all-embracing, and was not aimed at the particular defects of individual persons. This would have been a natural disclaimer on the part of anyone publishing a contemporary satire, but Goya emphasized not only the general aims of his satire – the title on the original frontispiece was *Ydioma universal* (Universal language) [537] – but also the creative rôle of his own genius in expressing 'forms and attitudes that have so far existed only in the human mind' and in combining 'in a single fantastic personage, circumstances and characteristics which nature has divided among many'. Nevertheless, as we have already suggested, there are clear individual references in some of the prints and drawings.

Bibl. 92

The very fact that Goya drew equally from the dark recesses of his mind and from the variety of life which he observed around him, gives to the prints both their timeless quality of irrationality and obsession and their immediacy and extraordinary sense of reality. This dual quality is interdependent and in a sense interchangeable; the early scenes of witchcraft, made from the *Sueño* drawings, look as if they have been observed from life, whereas some of the later scenes of social satire have a dream-like, nightmare quality – for example plates *3, 8* and *22*. It is typical of Goya's way of plunging into his subject and developing it as he went along that as his satire became profounder so his images became more dramatic and more abstract. At the same time, his technical progress within the

Ill. p. 128

Núm. 37   149

DIARIO DE MADRID

DEL MIERCOLES 6 DE FEBRERO DE 1799.

Santa Dorotea Virgen. = Q. H. en la Iglesia de San Felipe Neri.

Observacio. meteorolog. de ayer.				Afecciones astronomicas de hoy.
Epocas.	Termom.	Barometro.	Atmosfera.	El 30 de la Luna. Sale el sol á las 7 y 59 m. de la m. y se pone á las 5 y un m. de la tarde.
7 de la m.	3 s. o.	25 p. 4⅛ L	O. y Nub.	
12 del d.	3½ s. o.	25 p. 8¼ L	O. y Nub.	
5 de la t.	3 s. o.	25 p. 8¼ L	O. y Nub.	

Coleccion de estampas de asuntos caprichosos, inventadas y grabadas al agua fuerte, por Don Francisco Goya. Persuadido el autor de que la censura de los errores y vicios humanos (aunque parece peculiar de la eloqüencia y la poesia), puede tambien ser objeto de la pintura: ha escogido como asuntos proporcionados para su obra, entre la multitud de extravagancias y desaciertos que son comunes en toda sociedad civil, y entre las preocupaciones y embustes vulgares, autorizados por la costumbre, la ignorancia ó el interes, aquellos que ha creido mas aptos á subministrar materia para el ridiculo, y exercitar al mismo tiempo la fantasia del artifice.

Como la mayor parte de los objetos que en esta obra se representan son ideales, no será temeridad creer que sus defectos hallarán, tal vez, mucha disculpa entre los inteligentes: considerando que el autor, ni ha seguido los exemplos de otro, ni ha podido copiar tampoco de la naturaleza. Y si el imitarla es tan dificil, como admirable quando se logra; no dexará de merecer alguna estimacion el que apartandose enteramente de ella, ha tenido que exponer á los ojos formas y actitudes que solo han existido hasta ahora en la mente humana, obscurecida y confusa por la falta de ilustracion ó acalorada con el desenfreno de las pasiones.

Seria suponer demasiada ignorancia en las bellas artes el advertir al público, que en ninguna de las composiciones que forman esta coleccion se ha propuesto el autor, para ridiculizar los defectos particulares á uno ú otro individuo: que seria en verdad, estrechar demasiado los limites al talento y equivocar los medios de que se valen las artes de imitacion para producir obras perfectas.

150

La pintura (como la poesia) escoge en lo universal lo que juzga mas á proposito para sus fines: reune en un solo personage fantastico, circunstancias y caracteres que la naturaleza presenta repartidos en muchos, y de esta convinacion, ingeniosamente dispuesta, resulta aquella feliz imitacion, por la qual adquiere un buen artifice el titulo de inventor y no de copiante servil.

Se vende en la calle del Desengaño nº 1, tienda de perfumes y licores, pagando por cada coleccion de á 80 estampas 320 rs. vn.

NOTICIAS PARTICULARES DE MADRID.

LITERATURA.

Conservaciones de Emilia, escritas en francés por Madama Live de Espinai, para instruccion de su familia, y proporcionar á los que tienen semejante cuidado, un medio facil y eficaz de cumplir tan importante obligacion, y procurar á sus hijos y domesticos una crianza christiana y politica: desempeña este importante objeto con cuentos ingeniosos, dichos oportunos, y sencillas reflexiones propias para entretener sin fastidio los niños, y fixar en su alma las sólidas maximas que contiene, é inspiran el conocimiento del corazon humano: cómo obra las mas á proposito y acomodadas para este fin, se imprimió repetidas veces en Francia, y se prefirió á otras por órden de Luis XVI, para las escuelas y colegios de ambos sexôs, y se traduxo en varias lenguas, y ahora en la nuestra sobre la quinta edicion para utilidad principalmente de las madres de familia: dos tomos en octavo con laminas alusivas á la materia. Se hallará en la Libreria de Alonso, frente á las gradas de S. Felipe el Real.

Suplemento á la Coleccion de Pragmáticas, Cédulas, Provisiones, Circulares, y otras providencias del presente Reynado; cuya observancia corresponde á los Tribunales y Justicias ordinarias del Reyno, y á todos los vecinos en general. Comprende las respectivas á los años de 1797, y 1798, con las quales se dá principio al tomo tercero de esta Coleccion, y quinto de toda la obra segun la segunda edicion. Se hallará en la Libreria de la Viuda de Fernandez, frente á las gradas de San Felipe: y se previene á los sugetos que han tomado el quaderno del año de 1794, y no los de 95, y 96 que forman el tomo segundo del actual Reynado, que acudan á recogerlos, en inteligencia de que pasados los primeros ó meses de este año, se completarán tomos y no se darán sueltos dichos suplementos.

Obra utilisima para Comerciantes en granos y semillas, Administradores de Rentas consistentes en ellos, Alondigas, Labradores, Panaderos, Renteros &c. del valor de celeminas y quartillos desde medio quartillo hasta tres, y desde un celemin ó almud hasta doce, á los precios desde un real, uno y quartillo, uno y medio y uno y tres quartillos, hasta ciento y tres quartillos, reales vellon la fnega. Por Don Clemente Rodriguez, Director en Zamora de la provision de vi-

The announcement of the *Caprichos* in the *Diario de Madrid* of 6 February 1799

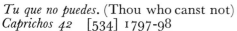

Tu que no puedes. (Thou who canst not)
Caprichos 42 [534] 1797-98

Que pico de Oro! (What a golden beak!)
Caprichos 53 [557] 1797-98

series enabled him in the later plates to express, by means of a perfectly bitten etched line and superbly controlled shades of rich, dark aquatint, the whole conflict between light and dark, between right and wrong, between 'enlightenment' and ignorance, which was the fundamental meaning of the rationalist cause.

These qualities in the finest *Caprichos* plates recall the emotional drama of some of Rembrandt's etchings, of Piranesi's *Carceri* (Prisons) – where an orchestration of light and shade and architectural forms creates a universe of cruelty and despair – and above all the world of the Tiepolos, the Venetian world of spectacle and masquerade conjured up in the great frescoes of Giambattista and in so many drawings by his son Domenico (of whose relationship with Goya we know nothing except that he possessed examples of most of Goya's prints made up to the time of his death in 1804, including a set of the *Caprichos*). It is also the strange, private world of Giambattista's etchings, the *Vari Capricci* and the *Scherzi di fantasia*, whose titles alone speak of the influence they must have had on Goya. In the *Scherzi*, the element of mystery and drama, the sorcerers, the snakes and night birds, and the stillness of the figures, is recalled in such *Caprichos* etchings as plates *22* and *43* and the unpublished *Dream. Of lying and inconstancy* [496, 536, 619]. Many of the technical devices in the *Caprichos* prints come straight from Giambattista's style, such as Goya's use of the dramatic foreground close-up, where the figures appear almost within the spectator's world, standing on the very edge of the picture space or leaning against the frame, the dividing line between the real and the imaginary world. The artistic and dramatic power of a drawing like number *80* from the Madrid album [438] and of plate *6* of the *Caprichos* [461] shows that Goya understood the example of Tiepolo as his study of Velázquez led him to understand the 'magic of the atmosphere'.

The eighty copperplates were expertly printed and the first edition was offered for sale privately at the beginning of 1799 (the Duchess of Osuna bought four copies in

The influence of the Tiepolo family

Bibl. 88, I, p. 13

Ill. pp. 125, 131

Ill. pp. 118, 131

See Appendix V

Bibl. 72, pp. 55-56

Bibl. 72, p. 55; 173, pp. 113-114

The commentaries

January) and was announced in two Madrid newspapers on February 6 and 19. Nothing more is known of Goya's venture until 1803 when he offered the copperplates and two hundred and forty unsold sets of the first edition to Charles IV. Although there are no records of any proceedings having been taken against him, there was no doubt an outcry from the Church which, coupled with the uncertain political situation and the defeat of his liberal friends, induced him to withdraw the prints from sale. A text by Goya, written perhaps in his own hand and now preserved in the Prado, provides a commentary for each plate. However, it is impossible to say whether these commentaries, which explained the satire of the *Caprichos* in very general terms, succeeded in convincing his enemies, when the scenes represented could so easily be interpreted as personal attacks and when other manuscript commentaries of unknown authorship appeared, to demonstrate such an intention.

The *Caprichos* offer something for everyone. For the Osunas and their friends they must have appeared as grotesque caricatures and provided an amusing game in trying to identify the victims, in spite of Goya's denials. For the romantic artists and writers of the nineteenth century they were a revelation of the wild forces of the unconscious mind. And for our own day they remain a masterpiece and a challenge: no one believes in witchcraft, but the forces of evil and oppression and the follies of mankind are apparently eternal, and in the *Caprichos* engravings one can ponder every aspect of deceit and self-deception.

Nadie se conoce (Nobody knows anybody)
Etching and aquatint 21 × 15 cm.
One of the many plates which exploit the Tiepolesque theme of masque and carnival. Here Goya summarizes and generalizes a theme which runs through all the prints concerning the relationship of men and women. His commentary on the print expresses his disillusion and pessimism: 'The world is a masquerade. Face, dress and voice, all are false. All wish to appear what they are not, all deceive and nobody knows anybody'.

Dream. Of lying and inconstancy
1797-98. Etching and aquatint 18 × 12 cm.
Biblioteca Nacional, Madrid
The title comes from Goya's inscription on the preparatory drawing [620] and the composition is generally interpreted as a direct allusion to the cruel deception of his relationship with the Duchess of Alba (see pp. 114, 115). The symbolism is complex but the action of the drama seems to concern the secret arrival of a new lover, towards whom the double heads of the duchess and her servant are turned, while Goya grasps his mistress's arm in anguish, as yet unaware of the full extent of her treachery.

Nadie se conoce. Caprichos P. 6 [461] 1797-98

Dream. Of lying and inconstancy [619] 1797-98

131

Everyone who has studied the Spain of the second half of the eighteenth century has emphasized the essential rôle played by a handful of men whose patriotic and reforming zeal was inspired by a single aim: to arouse their great country from the deep lethargy which, for the last hundred years, had paralysed its once vigorous body and brilliantly lively mind. These 'enlightened' men, the *ilustrados*, had turned their faces towards the great wind of cosmopolitanism and rationalism then sweeping Europe and they dreamed of recreating a great and prosperous Spain. This heroic task met with opposition on almost every side, from the ignorant and superstitious masses, from a clergy whose hostility was a matter of both principle and habit, and above all from the Inquisition, now considerably weakened but still fearful and much feared. In the eyes of these men, everything needed reform: education, religion, industry, agriculture, the whole economy. 'Imbued with culture like the men of the Renaissance, energetic and impartial, their knowledge and their good faith gave them an influence over the government and over public opinion.' They included statesmen like Campomanes, Cabarrús, Floridablanca and Aranda, and above all writers and scholars like Cadalso, Meléndez Valdés, Ceán Bermúdez, Moratín, Azara, Olávide, the two Iriarte brothers and the outstanding Don Gaspar Melchor de Jovellanos who embodied in himself all the virtues and talents of these 'crusaders' of enlightened Spain. Many of them (and by no means the least important, since they included Meléndez Valdés, Moratín, Bernardo de Iriarte) who had been *afrancesados* by inclination long before the War of Independence were later persuaded, in perfectly good faith, into collaborating with Joseph Bonaparte. One therefore feels all the more admiration for the integrity of Jovellanos who remained faithful to his ideas throughout his life and maintained to the end an unwavering patriotism, even in the face of threats. His reply to the proposals of General Sebastiani in 1809 is a model of dignity and courage.

And what of Goya? What part did he play in this Spain of light and darkness? Was he just 'Francisco de los toros', the charming or ironical painter of *manolas*, of weird witches' sabbaths, of girls who deck themselves out at nightfall – and nothing more? Without going to the opposite extreme and making him into a 'philosopher', we should not forget that he had met Jovellanos as soon as he became a member of the Academy, in 1780, and that the latter's constant help and support had made of the artist a faithful friend. In 1798 Goya painted a melancholy portrait of Jovellanos [675], as if he wished, during these crucial years in Spain's history, to affirm with his brush his sympathy with those who were fighting against the forces of darkness. Between 1797 and 1799 all his 'enlightened' friends sat for him and there are portraits of Bernardo de Iriarte [669], Meléndez Valdés [670], Moratín [685], Saavedra [676], most of them in the particular, intimate style sometimes referred to as 'portraits de bibliothèque'*.

Even more important is the fact that from a very early date – probably by 1781 when Jovellanos delivered his *Elogio de las Bellas Artes* and Meléndez Valdés read his poem 'In honour of the Arts' in the Academy – Goya became involved through his friends with the new ideas which were discussed at the *tertulias* (regular meetings of groups of friends) in the coffee-houses of Madrid. The talk was all of economics, agriculture, philosophy, the mechanical arts and, of course, poetry. At the same time, his entry around 1785 into the circle of the aristocracy, and in particular his contact with the Altamiras and the Osunas, widened still more the field of his experience. The Osunas were fully conversant with European cosmopolitan culture and ideas and the duchess was a member of the Royal

1780-1800. Goya is 34 to 54 years old. Influence of the French 'siècle des lumières'. Goya's 'enlightened' friends (ilustrados): Meléndez Valdés, Ceán Bermúdez, Moratín, Jovellanos, Iriarte. Reign of Charles IV.

Bibl. 170, quotation p. 113

Bibl. 142, p. 95

*Ill. p. 133   * Ill. p. 109, 135*

Arms of Jovellanos   [747] c.1798? Etching

Gaspar Melchor de Jovellanos (1744-1811)
He was the most upright and liberal of
men and the most eminent representative
of enlightened eighteenth-century Spain.
Born in Gijón in 1744, into a family of the
old Asturian nobility, his early career was
protected by his uncle, the Duke of
Losada, Charles III's Lord Chamberlain.
In 1778 he was appointed Alcalde de
Casa y Corte in Madrid. He already had
a high reputation and in 1780, on the
proposal of Campomanes, he was received
into the Academy of History, and became
an honorary member of the Academy of
San Fernando a month before the election
of Goya. He was elected director of the
Royal Economic Society of Madrid in
1784.

As faithful to his ideals as to his friends,
his defence of Cabarrús, who was persecuted in 1789, led to his exile from the
capital for several years. In 1797 Cabarrús
was back in favour with Godoy and
advised the all-powerful favourite to
choose ministers from among the most
eminent *ilustrados*. In November of that
year Jovellanos was made Minister of
Grace and Justice while Francisco Saavedra became Finance Minister. In March
1798 Godoy was momentarily ousted from
power, but both Jovellanos and Saavedra
fell seriously ill – poisoned, according to
some historians – and had to withdraw
altogether from public affairs in August.

Jovellanos was exiled until 1801 in
Gijón where seven years before he had
founded an Asturian Institute which was
later to bear his name. He was then sent
to Majorca as a prisoner of the State until
1808. He proudly rejected the terms offered
by General Sebastiani and in 1810 became
a member of the Regency Council appointed by the central junta in Cadiz. He
died the following year at the age of
sixty-seven.

Jovellanos probably met Goya for the
first time at the Academy in 1780 and for
twenty years he proved the best of friends
and, whenever possible, his patron and
protector. This portrait, painted in 1798
at the time of Jovellanos' ministry, is
movingly intimate in character and reveals
the melancholy and meditative nature of
the sitter who appears as a man of ideas
rather than a man of action.

Arms of Jovellanos
This little etching (4·7×6·1 cm.) was
probably intended to serve as an ex-libris.
Only two proofs are known including this
one, with a pen and ink inscription, in the
Biblioteca Nacional, Madrid.

Gaspar Melchor de Jovellanos   [675] 1798. 205×133 cm. Viscountess of Irueste, Madrid

Ferdinand Guillemardet (1765-1809)
It is significant that the first foreigner painted by Goya should
have been the French ambassador
in Madrid, an envoy from the
neighbouring republic, who was
known as a revolutionary and a
regicide. Guillemardet took back
to France a copy of the *Caprichos*
which has become famous as the
first copy seen and studied by a
great artist outside Spain, his
young godson, Eugène Delacroix,
about the years 1818-1820.

Ferdinand Guillemardet   [677] 1798. 185×125 cm. Musée du Louvre, Paris

Leandro Fernández de Moratín (1760-1828)
Juan Antonio Meléndez Valdés (1755-1817)
These two men were among Goya's most
faithful friends and were also two of the most
outstanding representatives of French classicism in Spain.

Moratín played a particularly important
rôle in Goya's life, especially at the time when
the artist was working on the *Caprichos* prints
which owe so much to his influence. On the
recommendation of Jovellanos he became
secretary to Cabarrús in Paris in 1787, and
he later enjoyed the patronage and protection
of Godoy which earned him many favours
and enabled him to stage his comedies in
Madrid, in particular *La comedia nueva o El
café* (1792) and *El sí de las niñas* (1806). Like
Meléndez Valdés, Moratín was a confirmed
afrancesado and was made director-general
of libraries by Joseph Bonaparte. He subsequently went into exile in France and
settled in Bordeaux where he founded a
college with Manuel Silvela [III.891]. Goya
painted a second portrait of Moratín (see
p. 334) after his return from Paris in 1824.

Meléndez Valdés, poet and lawyer, was
appointed attorney in Madrid in the year
this portrait was painted. He was particularly
concerned with the conditions in prisons and
lunatic asylums which form the subject of so
many of Goya's most personal works.

Leandro Fernández de Moratín [685] 1799.
73×56 cm. Academy of San Fernando, Madrid

Juan Antonio Meléndez Valdés [670] 1797.
73·3×57·1 cm. Bowes Museum, Barnard Castle

Economic Society of Madrid. Rousseau, Diderot, Condillac, Ward, the Abbé Raynal
and the English economists were on everyone's lips. Despite the frequent blacklists compiled by the Inquisition and the efforts of the police who, after 1789, attempted to set up
an effective 'iron curtain' along the Pyrenees, a flood of books entered Spain and the more
they were forbidden the more avidly they were read. Libraries were filled with all the
latest works published in London or Paris, among which Diderot's *Encyclopedia* was one
of the most popular. There was a passionate interest in everything which concerned man
and society. Physiognomy became fashionable and so did witchcraft which was denounced
for its diabolical hold over so many minds as yet unenlightened by Divine Reason. Goya
listened (at least until his illness), questioned and learned. The inscription on one of his
Ill. p. 354 last drawings [V.1758] applies to his whole life – *Aun aprendo* (I am still learning) – but
above all to this last decade of the eighteenth century. We have already referred to his
See p. 68 clumsy expression of this new awareness in a letter of 1790 addressed to Zapater. In it
he spoke of 'a certain dignity which a man ought to possess'. By 1797 Goya had realized
that this dignity implied certain obligations not only in his life but also in his art and with
Bibl. 92 the help of his friends, Moratín in particular, he began to spell out the famous 'universal
language' of the *Caprichos*. He was not good at expressing himself well or writing elegantly
– his letters are ample proof of this – but he found that with a brush or an etching needle
it was possible to say more and to say it much more forcefully.

Liberal interlude. Jovellanos becomes
Minister of Justice

At that same moment, the cause for which he was preparing to fight in his own way
seemed about to triumph. Spain was caught in a complicated game of political intrigue,
both internal and foreign, which brought to power the party of the *ilustrados* or liberals.
In November 1797, Jovellanos and Saavedra became ministers and then, when they withdrew, were replaced by Urquijo and Caballero. But this liberal interlude was short-lived.
At the end of the year 1800, Godoy resumed control of the state, more powerful and more
machiavellian than ever.

While he was working on the *Caprichos* prints and painting a series of witchcraft scenes
See pp. 122-124 for the Osunas [659-664], the splendid frescoes of the *Miracle of St Anthony* for the church

135

Time flying with Truth
The drawing (far left) is connected with the preparatory drawings made for the *Caprichos*. It may have been a project for an engraving or a first idea for the allegory in the Boston sketch (see p. 137) and the large painting in Stockholm (at left).

Truth, Time and History
The sketch on the opposite page is closely linked to the *Caprichos* prints. The owls and bats in the darkness behind the dazzling apparition of Truth are the same as the 'monsters' engendered by the *Dream of reason* in plate *43* of the *Caprichos* (see p. 125), and the graceful little nudes recall the figures in the Sanlúcar album [356-376].

The naked figure symbolizing Truth in the sketch is transformed, in the large painting, into a richly dressed woman who accords with the description of Philosophy in Ripa's *Iconologia*. This canvas, with its pendant, an allegory of *Poetry* [694], was probably made, like the four circular allegories (see p. 138), to decorate the palace of Godoy and his young wife, the Countess of Chinchón.

Time flying with Truth(?) [642] 1797-98. Red chalk, sanguine wash. Prado, Madrid

Truth, Time and History   [695] 1797-1800. 294×244 cm. Nationalmuseum, Stockholm

Drawings for the Dictionary of Ceán Bermúdez

Juan Agustín Ceán Bermúdez (1749-1829) [697] 1798-99. Red chalk 12·2×9·8 cm. Carderera collection, Madrid

Portrait of Zurbarán [707] 1798-99. Red chalk 15·2×11·8 cm. Musée du Louvre, Paris

Don Juan Agustín Ceán Bermúdez was a protégé of Jovellanos and one of the best art historians of his time. In 1785 he encountered Goya in connection with an important portrait commission for the Bank of San Carlos (see p. 61). Goya visited him in Seville in 1792 and 1796, admiring the finest works of art in the town in his company. Ceán returned to favour at the same time as Jovellanos and was elected to the Academy of San Fernando in 1798. He was then working on his famous *Historical dictionary of the most illustrious masters of the fine arts in Spain* which was to have been illustrated with engravings after portrait drawings by Goya. This project came to nothing but a number of preparatory drawings are known, executed in a rather conventional style, as well as the very lively portrait of Ceán himself.

Juan Agustín Ceán Bermúdez   [697] 1798-99

Portrait of Zurbarán   [707] 1798-99

Truth, Time and History – sketch   [696] 1797-1800. 42×32·5 cm. Museum of Fine Arts, Boston

Commerce
Four large circular allegories were painted by Goya to decorate the palace of Godoy in Madrid (now the War Ministry): *Agriculture, Industry, Commerce* and *Science* (the last picture now lost). Executed between the years 1797-1800, they symbolize the preoccupations of Goya's enlightened friends, especially Jovellanos, as well as the chief interests of the celebrated Economic Societies which were created throughout the length and breadth of Spain in the last third of the eighteenth century. Godoy, who protected the *ilustrados* for his own political ends, liked to pose as an enlightened statesman and connoisseur and he may also have commissioned the two large allegories now in the museum at Stockholm (see p.136).

The painting of *Commerce* is a good example of the way in which, after 1793, Goya was able to dominate his subject-matter – even in a difficult case like this – in order to achieve the most remarkable artistic effects, far removed from the traditional treatment of such themes. This allegory becomes essentially an interior scene where the strong light floods in through the wide open door to challenge the shadows in which the figures are working. The curious presence of the stork in the foreground again suggests Goya's use of Ripa's *Iconologia* in which this bird appears as one of the attributes of Mercury, the god of merchants.

Commerce   [692] 1797-1800. 227 cm. diameter. Prado Museum, Madrid

of San Antonio de la Florida [717-735] and a dashing portrait of Ferdinand Guillemardet, the French Directory ambassador, in his red, white and blue plumes [677], Goya also decorated the palace of the Prince of the Peace, Godoy, with allegorical paintings representing *Commerce, Agriculture, Industry* and *Science* (now lost) [690-692] and possibly also with the two large canvases now identified as an *Allegory of Poetry* and *Allegory of Philosophy* [694, 695]. The knowledge of iconography demonstrated in the careful working-out of these important pieces of 'intellectual' painting shows that Goya had learnt a great deal over the years. He had also seen and reflected a great deal, and it is this which gives his art its remarkable and sometimes disconcerting diversity. Portraits, drawings, etchings, imaginative scenes, allegories, religious canvases or frescoes, everything seemed to come easily to him, in spite of his physical handicaps. The reason must have been that after a long and hard journey along the road which leads through success to ultimate freedom, he was at last in a position to paint as he pleased, and the proof of his greatness lies in the fact that he was to apply this freedom not only to subjects of his imagination and *capricho* but also to commissions of the most official kind which were soon to come his way.

Ill. p. 134

Bibl. 136, pp. 95-115

1798. Goya is 52 years old. Jovellanos and
Saavedra at the head of a liberal government.
Frescoes for the hermitage of San Antonio de
la Florida in Madrid: 'The miracle of
St Anthony of Padua'. Reign of Charles IV.

Bibl. 154, doc. 184
Bibl. 154, doc. 158

See p. 108 and Appendix IV

On 28 March 1798, Jovellanos and Saavedra, who had been ministers since the previous November, replaced Godoy at the head of the government. Goya was to benefit at once from their support and patronage, at a time when his financial position seems to have been rather shaky. Although he continued to receive his regular income of fifteen thousand reales, his poor health since 1793 meant that he had been able to carry out no royal commissions and only a few private ones. In a memorandum presented to the king in March 1798 he declared that 'for six years I have been completely bereft of good health and in particular of my hearing, and I am so deaf that without using sign language I cannot understand anything, for which reason I have not been able to attend to the business of my profession . . .' He had even fallen into debt and in 1793 was forced to ask the Duke of Osuna for ten thousand reales. The little pictures which he sent to Bernardo de Iriarte in 1794 [317-330] were in fact painted, as he said, not only 'in order to occupy my imagination mortified by the contemplation of my sufferings', but also 'in order to compensate in part for the considerable expense which they have caused me . . .'

The church of San Antonio de la Florida
Two identical little churches in the neo-classical style stand today between the hill of Príncipe Pío and the river Manzanares, just below the Northern Station; the one nearest to Madrid is the church, or hermitage, of San Antonio de la Florida; the other is an exact replica of the first, built to take over as the shrine of St Anthony of Padua when the eighteenth-century church was transformed into a museum after Goya's remains had been reinterred there on 19 November 1919. Goya's pantheon now belongs to the Royal Academy of San Fernando and its original function is evoked only once a year, on 16 April, the anniversary of the artist's death, when a solemn mass is celebrated by the Academy in faithful remembrance of its most illustrious member.

The church was built by the Italian architect Felipe Fontana between 1792 and 1798, after Charles IV had added considerably to the royal estates which surrounded the previous church built by Sabatini. The present state of the area no longer gives any idea of the extent and delightful appearance of this huge domain of La Florida which was still intact in the nineteenth century.

The church of San Antonio de la Florida in Madrid

Sketch for the cupola of San Antonio de la Florida. A miracle of St Anthony of Padua
[718] 1798. 26×38 cm. Countess of Villagonzalo, Madrid

Sketch for San Antonio de la Florida
Only two sketches certainly attributable to Goya's brush are known for the San Antonio frescoes, both in the Villagonzalo collection in Madrid. The sketch showing the scene with the miracle of St Anthony of Padua affords clear evidence of the artist's search for a definitive solution, not only in the details of the attitudes but in the whole idea of the composition. Whereas in the fresco the background consists of a very freely painted landscape, the sketch shows a group of angels in the sky above the figure of the saint, in accordance with the classic formula of baroque religious art. In the end, Goya opted for a very personal solution which 'secularizes' the scene of the miracle and makes the whole composition into a sort of realistic and yet timeless tapestry cartoon stretched over the cupola of the church.

Jovellanos first commissioned a portrait of himself, which was painted at Aranjuez in the spring [675]; he then made sure that Goya received a favourable response to the application he had made in October 1797 for the reimbursement of the wages owing to his colour grinder over twenty-seven months and of his studio expenses. But a much more important consequence of the protection of his friend the minister was the commission to decorate the hermitage of San Antonio de la Florida, at the gates of Madrid [717-735]. The site, between the river Manzanares and the hill known as Príncipe Pío, a stone's throw from the present Northern Station, had for many years been consecrated to St Anthony of Padua and in the reign of Philip V there was already a church of brick built there by Churriguera. Charles III had ordered its demolition in order to widen the road and lay out the banks of the river, and the great architect Sabatini was commissioned to build a new church. However, under Charles IV, when all the surrounding land had become part of the royal estates, the whole site was replanned as a pleasant recreation area and Sabatini's church was demolished in its turn and replaced by the present chapel. The architect Felipe Fontana was in charge of the work which lasted until 1798, and the solemn inauguration took place on 11 July 1799. Meanwhile a brief from Pope Pius VI had attached the hermitage to the chapel of the royal palace which had been granted the status of an independent parish, under the sole authority of the First Chaplain of the Army, the Patriarch of the Indies and the priest of the royal palace.

This explains why the frescoes which Goya was commissioned to paint in the spring of 1798 were not subject to the approval of either chapter or academy. For the first time he was given a major official commission which left him free to paint as he pleased. This was an extraordinary opportunity, almost unique in the life of any painter, and he took advantage of it to the full extent of his brilliant gifts. We do not know whether the subject was imposed on him or whether he chose it himself but, as in the case of his altarpiece for San Francisco el Grande, he used the text of Father Croisset's *Christian Year* which had been translated into Spanish and was then in current use among artists as an iconographical

Ill. p. 133

Bibl. 154, docs 181-190

Construction of the hermitage

Ill. p. 139

The subject of the fresco

Ill. p. 55

A miracle of St Anthony of Padua (detail)   [717] 1798. Fresco. San Antonio de la Florida, Madrid

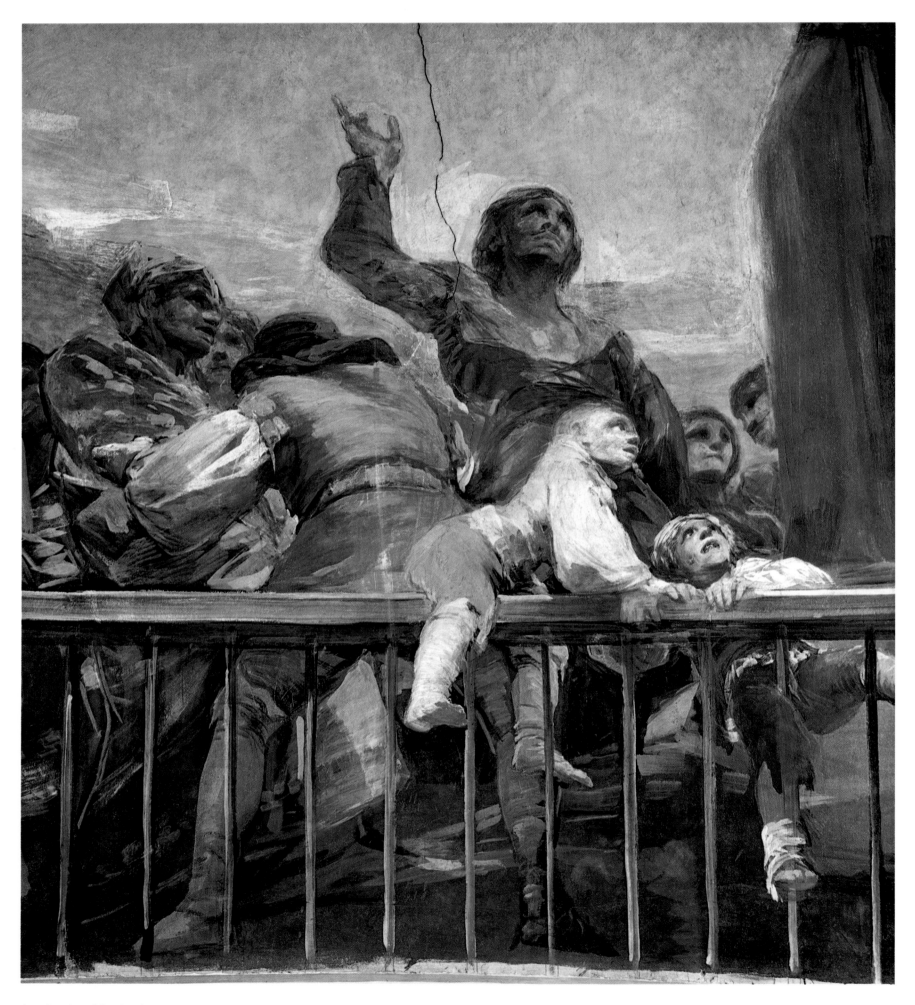

A miracle of St Anthony of Padua (detail)   [717] 1798. Fresco. San Antonio de la Florida, Madrid

A miracle of St Anthony of Padua   [717] 1798. Fresco, diameter about 5·5 m. View of the whole cupola. San Antonio de la Florida, Madrid

View of the interior of the church
The plan of San Antonio de la Florida is of classic simplicity. It takes the form of a Greek cross with very short arms, thus giving maximum importance to the central square above which the cupola, supported on pendentives, has a diameter of approximately 5.5 metres. Apart from the cupola where the scene of the miracle is depicted, Goya decorated the pendentives, arches and side walls with his celebrated female angels and flying cherubim, and painted an *Adoration of the Trinity* in the apse.

View of the interior of the church of San Antonio de la Florida, Madrid

source-book. It told the story of the miracle of St Anthony, which Goya was to represent on the walls and cupola of the church, in a few lines. But from the very start, Goya upset all the iconographic traditions and stylistic rules regarded as essential to this kind of religious painting. The miracle had taken place in Lisbon in the thirteenth century and, according to the *Christian Year*, had occurred in the court-room where the saint's father, wrongfully accused of murder, was about to be condemned to death. There is nothing in the fresco to suggest either the time or the place. Should we then accept the often repeated assertion that Goya transposed the scene into eighteenth-century Spain, making the miracle of St Anthony into a sort of huge tapestry cartoon hung round the dome of the church? Though some elements of the composition, such as the distant sierra, the tree standing out against the sky, the balustrade with children clinging to it and several *manolas*, might seem to confirm this theory, the other figures in the cupola and the strange garments worn by almost all of them make this very unlikely.

Bibl. 105, p. 23

The essential quality of this fresco is its *unreality*. Goya created through it a strange universe peopled by figures of his imagination, outside time and outside his own familiar world. The miracle was no more than a pretext which he interpreted as he pleased, without paying any attention to the rules normally observed in this type of painting. Instead of showing the miracle in the lower areas of the church (on the arches, pendentives and lateral walls) and filling the cupola with piles of clouds and bursts of celestial glory thronging with angels and cherubim, in keeping with the baroque technique still practised by Tiepolo, he reversed the whole scheme and placed round the cupola about fifty life-size figures set behind a balustrade with a wooden hand-rail. As for the angels, whose presence affords the only evidence of the sacred nature of the scene, they are placed on the less important, lower surfaces and appear as beautiful young women draped in long dresses splashed with many shades of colour.

Bibl. 112

144

Bibl. 154, doc. 191

The sketches
Ill. p. 140

Bibl. 105, p. 137

Cp. Bibl. 154, doc. 109

Ill. p. 146

Ill. p. 147

See pp. 313-320

Relatively little is known about the actual execution of the fresco. The long list of expenses presented by Goya on 20 December 1798 is undoubtedly very exaggerated, as Lafuente Ferrari has pointed out, and the hire of a coach every day for four months is surely no indication of the actual time taken by the artist over his work. There are two vivid little sketches, very rapidly brushed in, for the *Miracle of St Anthony* in the cupola [718] and the *Adoration of the Trinity* in the apse [723]. In addition, the thorough study of the fresco carried out from scaffolding by the late Ramón Stolz shows that Goya traced the main lines of his composition in the fresh plaster but in most cases painted over the top without keeping to these original indications. This means that he certainly could not have used, as has recently been maintained, a study on canvas, painted in four separate pieces, which reproduces the whole of the fresco almost down to the last detail [721]; the lines drawn in the plaster condemn both this hypothesis and, in consequence, the supposed study. Moreover, if Goya had executed such a large preparatory study in oils, he would certainly have included it, as he always did with the tapestry cartoons, in his list of expenses; and there is no mention of canvas or stretcher in the account.

However, the design sketched out in broad lines in the plaster but rarely followed in the fresco gives us an idea of the verve and brio with which Goya painted the cupola in San Antonio during that summer in Madrid, assisted by Asensio Juliá who no doubt prepared his colours and laid in the ground tone and of whom Goya has left a lively and affectionate portrait [682] which is at the same time one of his most sensitive and brilliant little pictures, full of the 'magic of the atmosphere'.

The feeling for atmosphere and the dramatic sweep of a picture, whether on a large or small scale, is also found in the *Prendimiento*, the 'Taking of Christ', which he painted for the cathedral at Toledo in the same year. The astonishing brio of the sketch [737] was considerably subdued in the final painting [736] which was no doubt subject to the approval of the cathedral chapter, whereas the frescoes in San Antonio remain, together with the 'black paintings' [iv.1615-1627a], the freest and fullest expression of the painter's genius, where

Two angels
Details of the frescoes on the walls and arches below the cupola. It has rightly been pointed out that these figures of angels, whose presence outside the cupola is an almost revolutionary innovation, are of great importance. The heavy draperies which they support or pull aside in order to reveal the scene of the miracle add to the disturbing nature of these frescoes where a rather theatrical solemnity is blended with mystical sweetness and with an element of sensuality in the clinging dresses which suggest rather than conceal the youthful forms of these 'angels'.

Angel [728] San Antonio de la Florida, Madrid   Angel [729] San Antonio de la Florida, Madrid

Asensio Juliá (1767-1830)
Asensio, or Asensi, Juliá was the son of a Valencian fisherman, hence his nickname of 'El pescadoret' (the little fisherman). He was Goya's only pupil or at least his only really close assistant, according to Carderera.

In this picture his 'friend Asensi' is usually said to be standing at the foot of the scaffolding in San Antonio de la Florida where he worked with Goya. This theory is supported by his dress – a sort of long painter's robe – and the brushes and mixing bowl on the ground beside him. Another portrait of Juliá, dated 1814, has unfortunately been affected by damage and restoration [III.902].

Asensio Juliá also copied portraits painted by Goya, decorated the façade of the house belonging to Tadeo Bravo de Rivero [854] according to a design by Goya in 1808, and made a number of paintings and engravings of the War of Independence. However, his own œuvre is little known and remains to be studied.

Asensio Juliá 'El pescadoret'   [682] 1798. 56×42 cm. Formerly Arthur Sachs, Paris

the subject of the work is of minor importance. The unusual colour harmonies, dominated by blue and yellow-ochre, and the rhythm of the figures crowding behind the balustrade create that 'magic of the atmosphere' which is the hallmark of Goya's greatest works. At once nostalgic and timeless, it pulsates, a century in advance, with the spirit of the painting of our time.

146

The taking of Christ

The large painting of the *Prendimiento de Cristo* [736] may have been commissioned by the cardinal-archbishop of Toledo as early as 1789, to decorate the cathedral sacristy. Many reasons including Goya's illness and long convalescence, his private work, his mistrust of church authorities after the experience with the Pilar building committee in Saragossa in 1781, may account for the fact that this painting was only completed at the end of 1798. It was shown to the San Fernando academicians on 6 January 1799 and received with high praise, and two days later it was installed in the cathedral at Toledo.

One could apply to this painting the lines in which Jovellanos praised the three altarpieces (now destroyed) in the church of Monte Torrero at Saragossa [738-740], which were painted at the same period: the 'force of the chiaroscuro' is indeed the dominant impression in this painting in which Sánchez Cantón points out the strong influence of Rembrandt.

The sketch, illustrated here, was recently acquired by the Prado. It is one of the finest examples of the Spanish *veta brava* (impetuous style), and in its vigour and creative power gives us the full measure of Goya's genius.

The taking of Christ – sketch [737] 1798. 40×23 cm. Prado Museum, Madrid

147

Goya's career at the court of Spain, which had begun when Mengs summoned him in 1774, reached its climax twenty-five years later. On 31 October 1799, Mariano Luis de Urquijo, prime minister since the departure of Jovellanos and Saavedra in August 1798, informed Goya of the royal decree which appointed him First Court Painter with an annual, tax-free salary of fifty thousand reales and five hundred ducats for the maintenance of a carriage.* After the difficult years which he had recently experienced, this coveted title brought him not only official recognition of his talents but above all an extremely comfortable financial position if one compares the new salary with the fifteen thousand reales he had been earning since 1786 as Painter to the King and which at the time had seemed to him a veritable gold mine.

Moreover, further royal commissions followed the completion of the San Antonio frescoes, suggesting that the artist's health was now fully restored. In September, when the court was as usual at La Granja, Goya painted *Charles IV in hunting dress* [774] and *María Luisa in a black mantilla* [775], of which we know that copies were made for Godoy. In October, at El Escorial, María Luisa posed for him again but this time on horseback [777], a revealing whim on the part of the queen who wished to have a reminder of her favourite horse, Marcial, who was a present from her 'dear Manuel' Godoy. Finally, in the spring of 1800, Goya tackled the most important but also the last of his royal commissions before the war, the *Family of Charles IV* [783]. One could also include among these official tasks the portrait of the Countess of Chinchón, the wife of Godoy, painted in April of the same year [793]. By this marriage, arranged by the diabolical María Luisa in 1797, the obscure hidalgo from Badajoz, nicknamed 'the sausage-maker' by the people of Madrid, had become a cousin of the king. He nevertheless remained the lover of Pepita Tudó – she too was granted titles and the privileges of a grandee – and continued to force his attentions shamelessly on all the female visitors who attended his 'audiences'.

In order to paint the large royal family portrait, Goya travelled to Aranjuez at considerable expense with his canvases, stretchers and painting materials, taking no less than four journeys to transport the whole lot. At the end of May and beginning of June he made ten studies from life, in oil on canvas, of the principal members of the royal family [784-788]; first the king and queen, then the Infanta Doña María Josefa and the Infante Don Antonio Pascual, the sister and brother of Charles IV, and finally the king's children, Don Carlos María Isidro, Don Fernando, prince of Asturias and future Ferdinand VII, Doña María Isabel, Don Francisco de Paula and Doña María Luisa beside her husband Don Luis de Borbón, prince of Parma and future king of Etruria. There were no individual studies for three of the figures who appear in the large painting: the mysterious princess who turns away her head, Doña Carlota Joaquina, the eldest daughter of Charles IV, whose profile is just visible, and the little Don Carlos Luis who lies in his mother's arms.

From the regular exchange of letters between the queen and Godoy, we know that all the sitters were delighted with these studies. The next step was to arrange them on the large canvas to produce a great showpiece. As for many of his royal portraits, Goya looked to the work of Velázquez. He was familiar with the *Meninas* which he had engraved in 1778 [I.107] and, like everyone who sees this picture, he remained fascinated by it. Like Velázquez he posed his figures in a room in the palace and showed himself in front of his easel, in the background to the left; but there the resemblance ends. Goya was after something different. Standing grouped around the queen, who occupies her appropriate

1799-1808. Goya is 53 to 62 years old. Appointed First Court Painter (1799). Paints 'The family of Charles IV' and the 'Majas'. Godoy triumphs over Portugal in the War of the Oranges (1801). Reign of Charles IV.

* *Bibl. 154, docs 193-195*

Bibl. 166, p. 69
Ill. p. 104

Ill. pp. 149, 150
Ill. p. 19

Ill. p. 104

Bibl. 49, 50
The royal family portrait

Bibl. 154, doc. 213

Bibl. 166, p. 71

The 'Family of Charles IV' and two studies

The large group portrait of the family of Charles IV marks the summit of Goya's official career after his appointment the previous year as First Court Painter.

From Goya's account we know that ten studies for the principal figures were painted at the palace of Aranjuez where the court always spent the period from Easter until the month of July. The studies, sketched in over a red ground which they do not completely cover, were made from life towards the end of May and beginning of June 1800.

From left to right in the large picture, the members of the royal family represented are: the Infante Don Carlos María Isidro (aged 12), died at Trieste in 1855; study [784]; the prince of Asturias, future Ferdinand VII (aged 16), died in Madrid in 1833; no study is known but see [791]; the Infanta Doña María Josefa, sister of Charles IV (aged 56), died in Madrid in 1801; study [785], illustrated above; an unknown princess, the bride-to-be of the prince of Asturias, who was not present and whose face could therefore not be shown; the young Infanta Doña María Isabel (aged 11) who was to marry Francis I of the Two Sicilies in 1802 and died in Portici in 1848; no study is known but see [792]; Queen María Luisa (aged 48), died in Naples in 1819; no study is known but see [790]; the little Infante Don Francisco de Paula Antonio (aged 6) who was to marry Luisa Carlota de Borbón in 1819 and died in Madrid in 1865; study [786], illustrated above; King Charles IV (aged 52), died in Naples in 1819; no study is known but see [789]; the Infante Don Antonio Pascual, the king's brother (aged 45), who had married his niece Doña María Amalia in 1795 and died in Madrid in 1817; study [787]; the Infanta Doña Carlota Joaquina, eldest daughter of Charles IV, Queen of Portugal (aged 25), died in Quelez in 1830; her head is glimpsed in profile and no study is known; Don Luis de Borbón, prince of Parma (aged 27), king of Etruria in 1802, died in Florence in 1803; study [788]; and finally his wife, the Infanta Doña María Luisa Josefina (aged 18), died in Rome in 1824; she holds in her arms the baby Don Carlos Luis, born in December 1799, king of Etruria from 1803 to 1807, died in 1883; only attributed studies of the mother and child are known.

The portrait of Goya himself, who appears at his easel in the background, is similar to two bust portraits [680, 681], and suggests a conscious imitation of Velázquez's *Meninas* – compare [1.107].

The Infanta María Josefa   [785]
1800. Study 74×60 cm. Prado Museum, Madrid

The Infante Francisco de Paula Antonio   [786]
1800. Study 74×60 cm. Prado Museum, Madrid

The family of Charles IV   [783] 1800-01. 280×336 cm. Prado Museum, Madrid

The family of Charles IV (detail) [783] 1800-01. Prado Museum, Madrid (See p. 149)

position in the centre of the canvas, the members of the royal family are spread out across a limited space in depth, their backs to the wall, pinned like great insects to the neutral ground which is dimly broken by two pictures. Velázquez's depth and above all the opening up of the background towards the light no longer exists here; this is a closed world, without escape, and with only just enough air to breathe. Apart from the youngest children, the faces are neither beautiful nor ugly, only 'real', which means terrifying in their intense reality. María Luisa herself, decked out in the richest silks and her most precious jewels, parades the forty-eight years of her insatiable and obdurate flesh in a flood of light. It seems in this picture as if the friend of Jovellanos is making his own pitiless appraisal and behind the puppets decked with gold has an intuition of the final catastrophe. One could apply to it the title of the first plate of the *Disasters of War* [III.993], 'Sad forebodings of what is going to happen'. However, the last act was to drag on for another eight years.

Between 1 July 1800 and June 1801, Goya painted an equestrian portrait of Charles IV [776], as a pendant to that of the queen, and two further, life-size portraits of Their Majesties executed as a gift to be sent to Paris but finally retained in Madrid [781, 782]. After this the First Court Painter never painted anything more for Charles IV. There has been much speculation about this sudden end to Goya's official activities, but no one has produced a satisfactory explanation. One cannot really speak of his 'disgrace'; it was more a question of his 'withdrawal' from the court. Did Godoy intervene against Goya? It is most unlikely, since he had commissioned several works from the artist: the *Allegories* of 1797-1800 [690-696], the portrait of his wife, the Countess of Chinchón, in 1800 [793] and his own portrait as hero of the War of the Oranges in 1801 [796]. Moreover, there is a superb copy of the *Caprichos*, with the ex-libris of the Prince of the Peace, in a library in Paris. Besides all this, it seems very probable that the celebrated *Majas* [743, 744] were painted for Godoy between 1800 and 1805. There is nothing to prove that they belonged to the Duchess of Alba – and still less that they represented her. On the other hand, they appear in the 1808 inventory of Godoy's possessions, just before these were sequestrated. Only Godoy was powerful enough to keep in his own home or in that of his mistress, 'la Tudo', such scandalous paintings which were so perfectly in accordance with his tastes. The provocative and delicately erotic nude was to enchant Baudelaire who kept a small version of it beside him until his death, believing, as so many others have done, that it represented the Duchess of Alba: 'The banality of the pose increases the charm of the pictures . . . I would describe the duchess as a very strange creature, with a wicked expression . . . and a 'squinting' bosom which rises and at the same time diverges until it hides the armpits . . . Think of a Bonington or a ferociously passionate Devéria'. The two pictures, described as 'obscene paintings', led the Inquisition in 1815 to 'summon the said Goya to appear before this Tribunal to identify them and declare whether they are by his hand, for what reason they were painted, at whose order and to what end'. Unfortunately, the sequel to this affair remains unknown.

In conclusion, it is impossible to find any evidence of hostility towards Goya on the part of Godoy; rather the contrary. It is therefore more plausible to imagine that Goya, who always moved with caution over the shifting sands of politics, decided to refrain from showing himself at court after his friends Jovellanos and Urquijo had been imprisoned in 1801 and above all after the death in very unnatural circumstances of the Duchess of Alba in 1802. However, he still had in his possession a weapon which might well prove explosive: the *Caprichos*, of which two hundred and forty copies remained unsold after their publication in 1799. The Inquisition was undoubtedly interested in them, since Goya referred to the fact years later, in Bordeaux. By presenting the eighty copperplates and the remaining first edition copies to the king, in exchange for an annual pension of twelve thousand reales for his son, Goya did a good piece of business and so did the king; but this 'settling of the accounts' marked the end of relations between the artist and the court.

Detail ill. p. 104
Bibl. 154, doc. 218

Ill. pp. 136-138

Ill. pp. 19, 104
Bibl. 88, I, p. 10
The Majas

See note to [744]

Bibl. 166, pp. 75-76; 88, I, p. 106

The naked maja   The clothed maja
Very little is known about these celebrated pictures. They were included in the inventory of Manuel Godoy's collection, dated 1 January 1808, and in 1814 were handed over to the Grand Inquisitor together with three other 'obscene' paintings, two of which also belonged to Godoy. In the 1808 inventory the figures are referred to as *Gitanas* (gypsies). Louis Viardot was the first, in 1845, to suggest that they represented the Duchess of Alba, but there is nothing to support this theory. The most likely hypothesis is that they were painted for Godoy who acquired Velázquez's *Toilet of Venus* from the estate of the Duchess of Alba at her death in 1802.

The naked maja   [743] c.1798-1805. 97×190 cm. Prado Museum, Madrid

The clothed maja   [744] c. 1798-1805. 95×190 cm. Prado Museum, Madrid

The years leading up to the War of Independence were quiet ones for Goya. He seems to have decided not to become involved, whether directly or indirectly, in the intrigues at court, whose outcome he already suspected. In his view there was no longer any hope of reforming Spain and it would be mad to attempt to play a game that was already lost. Since his salary as First Court Painter freed him from all material worries, he was content to paint portraits or private works which he kept for himself and his family. The bourgeois tranquillity into which he settled as he approached his sixties contrasts with the dark years of passion and bitterness which he had experienced between 1792 and 1799. The storms in his heart and senses had momentarily subsided and the powerful head, which no sound could reach, seemed filled with a deep serenity. One thinks inevitably of his musical brother, Beethoven.

The experience of the *Caprichos* was far from forgotten and Goya now began to turn his gaze, so penetrating under the heavy eyelids of the self-portrait in the frontispiece [451] (ill. p. 103), to the people around him. Painting and engraving were cumbersome and sometimes dangerous, so he would devote himself to drawing, for his own pleasure, with no particular aim, just recording whatever struck him and made him think. These were

1800-1808. Goya is 54 to 62 years old. Marriage of his son Javier with Gumersinda Goicoechea (1805). Birth of their son Mariano (1806). Family portraits, drawings and miniatures. 'The capture of the bandit El Maragato' (1806). Various portraits. Reign of Charles IV.

Gumersinda Goicoechea   [842] 1805. Black chalk 11×8·2 cm. Formerly Carderera, Madrid

Javier Goya   [844] 1805-06. Copper 8·1 cm. diam. Private collection, Paris

Juana Galarza   [841] 1805. Black chalk, pen and ink 11·4×8·2 cm. Casa Torres, Madrid

not the sketches and studies from life that every painter makes; they formed a kind of private journal which he kept up with his brush. The tentative development from the Sanlúcar to the Madrid album [356-450] had opened up a new path which he now determined to follow. These albums of drawings were an underground work, almost unknown to his contemporaries and still very little reproduced today. Although it is

In 1805 Javier, only son of Goya and his wife Josefa (see p. 246), was married to Gumersinda Goicoechea and a year later their son Mariano was born. Goya made many portraits of the two families in 1805-1806, and also painted his beloved grandson three times between the ages of three and twenty-one.

Francisca Sabasa y García   [816] c.1804-08. 71×58 cm. National Gallery of Art, Washington

difficult, if not impossible, to date them with any precision, they seem to have been begun in the early years of the century. However, since the different series form together an inseparable whole, the discussion of all these private albums has been postponed until the third part of this book. *See pp. 230-239*

In 1803 Goya acquired a fine house in the centre of Madrid, at number 7 Calle de los Reyes. His son Javier was then nineteen years old and was probably already engaged to a certain Gumersinda Goicoechea, the daughter of a prosperous merchant family which had settled in the capital. The marriage took place on 8 July 1805. The young couple were to live with the Goya parents for as long as they pleased, otherwise the house in the Calle de los Reyes was to be made over to them. The separation came hardly six months after the wedding and on 11 July 1806 a son, Mariano, was born in the home of Javier.

At the time of these important family events, Goya made a whole series of drawings [840-843], miniatures on copper [844-850] and portraits on canvas [851, 852], representing the young couple, the Goicoechea parents-in-law, his wife Josefa and Gumersinda's sisters. Of the two large portraits, that of Javier Goya is outstanding, its polished elegance recalling a number of male portraits of English inspiration. As for the miniatures, all of the same circular format, they have nothing in common with traditional miniature technique; they are small pictures, handled with the same freedom as the large canvases. *Ill. pp. 154, 246*

Before concluding this family episode, a few words should be said about Javier, the artist's only son, who was already living apart from him. Everything that is known about him shows how little he took after his father; there was not a spark of temperament in this methodical, selfish, cautious man. Throughout his life (he died in 1854) his only interest was in selling off his father's works on the best possible terms and in quietly increasing his capital, by usury if necessary. *Bibl. 102, p. 294*

Finally, it should be noted that it was at Javier's wedding that Goya met for the first time, among the innumerable relations of the Goicoechea and Galarza clans, an extremely pretty and perhaps rather provocative young girl of seventeen, called Leocadia Zorrilla y Galarza. Two years later it was her turn to get married, to a German merchant in Madrid, Isidoro Weiss. At this new family celebration, Goya scrutinized the lovely girl who was about to fall into the arms of a dull shopkeeper – undoubtedly an arranged marriage – and told himself that nothing had changed: *El si pronuncian y la mano alargan al primero que llega* Leocadia Zorrilla

El Maragato points a gun at Friar Pedro   [864]   Friar Pedro averts El Maragato's gun   [865]

Friar Pedro wrests the gun from El Maragato   [866]

Friar Pedro clubs El Maragato   [867]

Friar Pedro shoots El Maragato   [868]

Friar Pedro binds El Maragato   [869]

The capture of the bandit called El Maragato by Friar Pedro de Zaldivia. 1806-07. Six panels 29·2×28·5 cm. Chicago Art Institute

The capture of El Maragato
Bibl. 62

(They say yes and give their hand to the first comer). A pity! But suppose she had accepted her Weiss like the 'many women [who] consent to marry, hoping thereby to live in greater freedom'? What might follow then?

Before discussing the long and important series of portraits painted between 1802 and 1808, we should consider a series of little pictures devoted to a piece of topical news which created a great stir at the time and was illustrated in a number of widely circulated prints. These are the six panels representing the various stages in the *Capture of the bandit El Maragato by Friar Pedro de Zaldivia* [864-869], an event which had taken place on 10 June 1806 near Oropesa in the province of Estremadura. Goya found in these scenes of violence a new material for his art: popular realism. One has only to compare these sturdy little figures with the refined 'populace', the majos and majas, of earlier years; elegance has given way to brutality, rustic amusements to harsh, everyday reality. Goya was already painting another world, and yet the war had still not begun. Hence the importance of this little 'news report', painted about 1806 or 1807, which proves that realism had already appeared in Goya's work before the start of the napoleonic invasion.

For their part, Goya's portraits become penetrating character studies in which the essential qualities are dashed onto canvas with an impetuous verve and no concessions are any longer made to attractiveness or rank. Some of the men are among the best posed of Goya's portraits: *Fernán Núñez* [808], *San Adrián* [818], *Bartolomé Sureda* [813], while the bust portraits, set against a neutral background, have an intensity of expression which is life itself: *Juan de Villanueva* [803], the *Conde de Teba* [812], *Pérez de Castro* [815], *Mocarte* [834], *Máiquez* [858].

Portraits 1803-1807

Although some of the women are less successful than their male counterparts, notably the *Condesa de Fernán Núñez* [807], *Teresa de Sureda* [814] and *Josefa de Garcini* [821], this period of calm creativity produced some unforgettable faces. Everyone knows the sensuous *Isabel de Porcel* [817], regarded as the embodiment of Spanish womanhood in the full bloom of her beauty. But at the same time one should not overlook the proud and sensitive reserve of the women of Madrid, immortalized by Goya in the *Bookseller's wife* [835] and above all *Doña Francisca Sabasa y García* [816]. These, it should be noted, are all young women of the middle classes and not great ladies, like the *Marquesa de Villafranca* [810] or the *Marquesa de Santa Cruz* [828], whom Goya surrounds with the attributes of their talent or their rank. More and more he tended to take as his models people from the middle and lower classes, whose blood flowed generously in their veins and was soon to be spilt fearlessly in the cause of liberty.

Ill. p. 155

Bartolomé Sureda   [813] c. 1804-06

Isabel de Porcel   [817] 1804-05

Bartolomé Sureda
[813] c.1804-06. 119·7×79·4 cm.
National Gallery of Art, Washington

Isabel de Porcel
[817] 1804-05. 82×54 cm.
National Gallery, London

Don Antonio Porcel and his wife Doña Isabel both had their portraits painted by Goya. The husband's, which shows him in hunting dress [855], is a mark of the friendship between the two men. That of his wife, shown here, was exhibited at the Academy of San Fernando in 1805 and is a splendid example of the *majismo* which was so fashionable with the Spanish aristocracy in the second half of the eighteenth century and still persisted in the early years of the nineteenth. The elegance of the costume and the ripe beauty of the sitter create an image of the ideal Spanish woman whose lively intensity is far removed from the frail figures of the tapestry cartoons.

The same natural quality appears in most of the portraits of this period, including that of Don Bartolomé Sureda y Miserol. After a stay at Sèvres, he was appointed director of the Buen Retiro porcelain factory by Charles IV in 1804. According to his son, he learnt the process of mezzotint engraving in London and taught it to Goya who painted his portrait and that of his wife Teresa [814] in gratitude.

CATALOGUE II 1792-1808

INTRODUCTION

PAINTINGS The second part of this catalogue opens with one of the most difficult problems which has faced all students of Goya's work and which is now almost entirely resolved. This is the identification of the famous 'cabinet pictures' which Goya sent to Bernardo de Iriarte on 4 January 1794 and which were shown in the Academy of San Fernando on the following day and described in the minutes as 'eleven pictures . . . of various scenes of national diversions'.

It has often been thought that the five panels bequeathed to the Academy by Manuel García de la Prada in 1839 [III.966-970] were part of this group. However, Beruete and Sánchez Cantón as well as other critics suggested a much later date, around 1808-1812, for these five genre scenes. The 1793 pictures still remained to be identified. Then in 1967 Xavière Desparmet Fitz-Gerald rediscovered the *Yard with lunatics* [330] whose subject exactly corresponds with the description given by Goya in his second letter to Iriarte, of 7 January 1794, and this led to the identification of other paintings of almost identical dimensions, all executed in a very similar style on sheets of tinplate. A recent study by Xavier de Salas established a connection between this group of paintings and the description given in a list of pictures drawn up for Godoy about 1805. The list included 'fourteen little pictures' by Goya among which the 'various scenes of *fiestas de toros*' could well correspond with the 'various scenes of national diversions' shown in the Academy in 1794. According to Salas, these would be the eight bullfighting scenes formerly in the Torrecilla collection in Madrid [317-324]. Five of these scenes take place in a bullring whose architecture recalls the famous Maestranza in Seville, built in 1760, and one of the others [318] is set in an urban landscape where we feel confident in identifying the Torre del Oro which rises on the banks of the river Guadalquivir in Seville, very close to the Maestranza. These episodes of the 'national sport' of Spain would therefore be direct souvenirs of the beginning of Goya's stay in Seville, towards the end of 1792.

Three other titles in the list correspond with known paintings in this series on tinplate [327-329]; we believe the remaining three in the list of fourteen, whose subjects were not specified, to be the *Strolling players*, the *Marionette seller* and the *Yard with lunatics* [325, 326, 330]. In this way, the problem of the identification of the 'cabinet pictures' sent to Iriarte in 1794 would now seem settled.

From 1793 until his illness in 1819, portraiture was to occupy the major place in Goya's paintings. Apart from the series of royal portraits in the years 1799-1801, they were mostly commissions from the great families of Spain or the ever more numerous portraits of his 'enlightened' friends. The remarkable development of his art in the years 1794-95, when his health was still very precarious, can be appreciated in the *Marquesa de la Solana* [341] and the half-length *Tirana* in the March collection [340].

As far as the Duchess of Alba is concerned, there is a romantic tradition which insists on discovering her features in earlier scenes (see note to [I.248-255]) and in works which are not here accepted as by Goya, but she can only be identified with certainty in the two famous portraits in the Alba collection [351] and the Hispanic Society of America [355] and in one of two little intimate scenes painted in 1795 [352]; she may also appear in the *Coloquio galante* [354] which recalls several of the tapestry cartoons. There is no solid basis for any of the other identifications proposed.

On his return from Andalusia in 1797, Goya launched into a brief period of 'militant liberalism' and painted a whole series of portraits of his friends, the *ilustrados*: Iriarte, Meléndez Valdés, Jovellanos, Saavedra, Moratín, Urquijo and the French ambassador and regicide Guillemardet – see [669-689].

At the same time Goya painted some of his most important religious works. The three paintings in the Santa Cueva at Cadiz [708, 709, 711], for many years almost unknown, pose some problems which have not yet been resolved. They may have been conceived in 1792-93, at the time of his first visit to Andalusia, but were probably not painted until the second journey in 1796-97, although the oratory was consecrated on 31 March 1796. It is not known whether the subjects, two of which are rare in christian iconography, were imposed on him or whether he chose them himself and if so for what reasons.

The frescoes of San Antonio de la Florida [717-735] are the outstanding work of this period and are presented in the catalogue in relation to the plan of the church which is oriented with the apse to the north-east. Lafuente Ferrari has made an authoritative and magnificently presented study of this great work. One point remains to be settled, the question of the so-called sketch in Pittsburgh [721]. We are certainly not confronted here with 'the sketch which Goya used for San Antonio de la Florida', as has been maintained. Such a view ignores the earlier design of the composition, traced by Goya in the fresh plaster and photographed in a raking light by the late Ramón Stolz in 1956. This first design, which the painter did not always follow, is incompatible with the Pittsburgh 'sketch' which is identical in all respects with the final fresco. It must therefore be a later reduction and does not appear to be by Goya's hand.

There is no longer any doubt concerning the seven paintings acquired for the Duchess of Osuna's study and for which the duke paid ten thousand reales in 1799 (see Appendix V). The documents published by Sambricio prove that they were all sketches for tapestry cartoons, painted in 1786 and 1788 – see [I.256-261, 272-275] – and not later reductions after the cartoons, made in 1799 for the duchess, as has often been maintained on apparently reasonable grounds. This is a further instance of the sure taste of the Osunas who recognized the exceptional qualities in Goya's sketches at the very time when he was beginning to apply them to major compositions, where they become the hallmark of his personal style.

The third group of portraits (1799-1808) begins with Goya's nomination as First Court Painter; it includes a series of official portraits of the king and queen, of which several copies were made by Agustín Esteve, and above all the *Family of Charles IV*

[783], together with the preparatory studies of which only the five in the Prado are of indisputable authenticity [784-788].

Also in this section is a group of portraits made by Goya on the occasion of the marriage of his son Javier in 1805 [840-852] and which consists of portrait drawings in black chalk and pen and ink, miniatures on copper and two large canvases. Besides Javier and his young wife Gumersinda, there is the only known representation of Goya's wife, Josefa [840].

DRAWINGS   More than half of this part of the catalogue is taken up by the extensive group of drawings in the so-called Sanlúcar and Madrid albums, followed by the etchings of the *Caprichos* and their preparatory drawings, as well as many additional drawings connected with this series [356-656]. These graphic works were produced in a very short space of time, beginning with Goya's stay at Sanlúcar with the Duchess of Alba, no earlier than the summer of 1796, and ending with the final *Caprichos* plates in 1798.

Goya's first two albums of drawings were described in 1860 by Carderera who may have seen them intact. The sheets (with drawings on both sides) were dispersed, and in 1928 Sánchez Cantón reconstructed the two series from the pages preserved in the Prado and the Biblioteca Nacional in Madrid. In 1953 López-Rey reproduced the sheets known at that time (six in album A, twenty-four in album B). In 1958 Eleanor Sayre defined the technical characteristics of these two albums (as well as those of all Goya's other albums – see Part III, p. 252), and in 1964 she published a detailed study with a catalogue (eight sheets in album A, thirty-five in album B). Our catalogue corresponds with hers but includes three more drawings (known from copies) for album A [374-376] and two previously unpublished sheets for album B [425/426, 441/442].

The Sanlúcar album (or album A) was a small album of sketches; eight sheets with drawings recto and verso are generally recognized as authentic [356-371]; another sheet [372/373], published by Pierre Gassier in 1953, is on different paper but of similar dimensions and may be a copy, perhaps made by Goya himself. Several copies on larger sheets (drawn on one side only) were possibly made by Carderera; we have illustrated only those which record lost drawings [374-376]. It is probable that this sketchbook contained more than a dozen pages and that Goya drew other scenes which were not referred to by Carderera, either because he had never seen them or because they were of too intimate a nature to be described. These are the very first drawings which Goya executed with a brush and Indian ink wash. The technique, which he rapidly learnt to exploit for a wide range of effects, is handled with some hesitation and even clumsiness in these early drawings and was clearly more appropriate to drawings made from memory than to sketches from life.

The Madrid album (or album B) was Goya's first major album, with page numbers inscribed in the upper corner of the sheets, right on the recto pages, left on the verso, and from number 55 [415] onwards there are autograph titles and inscriptions. On some drawings the number has disappeared, either because it has faded with time [377-380] or because the sheet was later cut down [419/420]. The inscriptions are sometimes written with the brush and Indian ink, sometimes with a pen and sepia ink; in the latter case the title was probably added after the completion of the drawing. Sometimes the two techniques are used on the same sheet: the pen and ink inscription then completes the word or words written with the brush [415/416, 417/418, 419, 429, etc.],

substitutes a more exact word for another [428] and even, in a curious instance, corrects a spelling mistake [434]. At the same time, the pen was often used to retouch or alter the drawing itself.

Among the drawings known and catalogued at the present time, a total of ten sheets are missing in the album: 1/2, 9/10, 11/12, 29/30, 41/42, 47/48, 51/52, 53/54, 73/74 and 91/92, always accepting that the drawings [419/420], which lack page numbers, do in fact fill the empty space 59/60.

For reasons of convenience and unity of presentation, the drawings from four other albums (C, D, E and F) are catalogued in Part III. However, in spite of the very great difficulty in establishing any precise chronology for these large series of drawings, it is quite possible that a number of them were executed before 1808, in particular perhaps the whole of album D [III.1368-1384] which takes up the themes of the *Caprichos* and uses the same paper as the Madrid album, but seems to have been abandoned in favour of album E. This problem will be discussed again in the introduction to Part III of the catalogue (see pp. 251-252).

ENGRAVINGS   The chapter on the *Caprichos* (pp. 125-131) described the development of this series from the drawings in the Sanlúcar and Madrid albums through the *Sueño* (Dream) drawings to the final arrangement of the published prints. The preparatory drawings in the Prado have not yet been studied in detail, but it appears that the twenty-six drawings in pen and sepia ink used for the *Caprichos* prints were probably all made for the original *Sueño* series: nineteen of them have the *Sueño* numbering (up to 28) and of the seven without visible numbers, two have the *Sueño* title. Fourteen out of the twenty-six are wholly or partly based on drawings from the Madrid album and there is clearly a very close relationship between the two series. The other preparatory drawings are in brush and sanguine wash or – by far the largest group – in red chalk. Many additional drawings were apparently prepared for the series but not engraved [629-656].

Technically, the *Caprichos* engravings carry on from the point which Goya had reached in the *Copies after Velázquez* [I.88-112] some twenty years before. In the first plates, made from the *Sueño* drawings, the etched line is light and sketchy and the aquatint, with which he had so much trouble in the Velázquez plates, is handled with caution, usually being limited to producing a single, pale tone. However, Goya soon acquired confidence and mastery, handling the etching needle with great decision and biting and burnishing the aquatint to produce a rich variety of tones.

The series was complete and at least partially printed by January 1799 when the Duchess of Osuna bought four copies from Goya (see Appendix V). On 6 February 1799, the series was announced in the *Diario de Madrid* and was again advertised, on the back page of the *Gaceta de Madrid*, on 19 February. The sale of the prints seems to have been stopped almost immediately. In 1803 Goya wrote to offer the copperplates, together with two hundred and forty copies already printed, to Charles IV. Yriarte maintained that he had written evidence from Javier Goya to show that the king in fact ordered Goya to hand over the plates and prints, as a means of saving him from trouble with the Inquisition (Bibl. 193, p. 105). This would confirm Goya's own statement in a letter to Ferrer, written in 1825 (see p. 346).

Of the total of 290 known prints by Goya – engravings and lithographs – 85 for the *Caprichos* and 4 others [747, 748, 750, 772] are catalogued within this second period of his career.

NOTES TO CATALOGUE II   [317-873a]

317-330 For the identification of the group of pictures sent by Goya to Iriarte, see Salas (Bibl. 149; also 151, p. 30, for the complete text of the inventory entry). His views and interpretation of the documents cited have in the main been accepted by the authors. He did not, however, identify [326] as part of this series; and the *Prison scene* in the Bowes Museum is here excluded from it and placed much later [III.929] (but see note to [330]). Eleven paintings were shown to the Academicians on 5 January 1794: *El S.or D.n Fran.co Goya remitió para que se viesen en la Academia once quadros pintados por él mismo de varios asuntos de diversiones nacionales, y la Junta se agradó mucho de verlos, celebrando su merito y el del S.or Goya* (Real Academia de San Fernando, *Juntas Ordinarias*, Libro IV, 5 January 1794; see Bibl. 149, p. 8). A twelfth painting, the *Yard with lunatics* [330], was sent to Iriarte two days later. Fourteen pictures, listed together, were in the Chopinot collection in 1805 (Bibl. 151); eleven of them are identified with pictures catalogued here, but they are not necessarily the eleven which were sent to the Academy. If the fourteen pictures were painted as a group, and if the twelfth was described by Goya as the last, it seems likely that he would have added [328] and [329] as afterthoughts, since they are the most advanced in style and subject matter. For Goya's letters to Iriarte concerning this group of paintings, see Appendix IV.

317-324 According to Salas, these would be the *varios pasajes de fiestas de toros* mentioned in the Chopinot inventory (Bibl. 151, p. 30) and it would have been to this group of eight pictures that the Academy referred in describing the eleven paintings presented for its approval as *varios asuntos de diversiones nacionales* (Bibl. 149, p. 8). The series of bullfights apparently belonged at one time to Ceán Bermúdez.

317 Exhibited in 1961-62 (Bibl. 24, no. 12), but no photograph was available. Reproduced from the catalogue of the *Vente Candamo*, Galerie Charpentier, Paris, 14-15 Dec. 1933, lot 35 (acquired Thierry-Delanoue).

318 The building on the right has been identified by Pierre Gassier as the Torre del Oro at Seville.

322 *Vente Candamo*, lot 34 (see note to [317]). Exhibited 1951 (Bibl. 17, no. 2). The painting was in the collection of Paul Lefort, together with [317], and Yriarte had no hesitation in identifying 'le cirque de Séville, dont on reconnaît l'architecture' (Bibl. 193, p. 149).

325 Inscription identified as an abbreviation of *Alegoria menandrea* – used by the Commedia dell'Arte in homage to the Greek actor Menander. For the official Prado catalogue description, see Bibl. 2, p. 27. Viñaza gave this picture the title *Los volatineros*, describing it as 'una compañia de cómicos de la legua, entre cuyos sujetos adivínase una punzante alusión a María Luisa y Godoy' (Bibl. 190, p. 295, no. CXVII). Lafond believed that this was a reference to another picture; he listed [325] as *La baraque de foire* (Bibl. 97, p. 113, no. 98) and translated Viñaza's title as *Les danseurs de corde* to make his no. 99. Mayer echoed Lafond (M.652).

326 Exhibited and reproduced in 1970 (Bibl. 30, no. 13 [15]) for the first time since the *Vente Lefèvre-Bougon*, Hôtel Drouot, Paris, 2 April 1895, lot 19, ill.

327 Presumably represents the *asaltos de ladrones* listed in the Chopinot inventory (Bibl. 151, p. 30). Compare with the painting for the Alameda de Osuna [I.251].

328 Presumably represents the *naufragios* listed in the Chopinot inventory (Bibl. 151, p. 30). Possible sources were discussed by Salas (Bibl. 149, p. 5, n. 9, giving previous references). Given the reminiscences of Saragossa – certain in [330] and possible in [329] – it seems not unlikely that this picture may represent the great flood in Aragon in 1787.

329 Presumably the *yncendios, un fuego de noche* listed in the Chopinot inventory (Bibl. 151, p. 30). Also possibly identifiable with the 'canvas' described by Father López, representing 'el incendio del teatro de [Zaragoza], ocurrido á fines del siglo pasado [in fact, November 1778]. Es de unos cinco palmos y sobre siete de alto y tiene muchísimas figuras' – with bibliographical references for contemporary accounts of the disaster (Bibl. 190, p. 464). Exhibited 1970 (Bibl. 30, no. 14).
Gudiol publishes a small panel representing the burning of the theatre (Appendix, no. 770) but it does not in any case correspond with the format of the picture described by Father López.

330 (Yard with lunatics). Described in detail by Goya in his letter to Iriarte of 7 January 1794: *un corral de locos, y dos q.e estan luchando desnudos con el q.e los cuida cascandoles, y otros con los sacos; (es asunto q.e he presenciado en Zaragoza)*. See Appendix IV and ill. p. 110. Unseen since it was sold at the Hôtel Drouot on 30 December 1922, the painting was published as a rediscovery by Xavière Desparmet Fitz-Gerald, 'Una obra maestra desconocida', *Goya*, 76, 1967, pp. 252-255.
It was no doubt the *Casa de locos* exhibited with [III.929] in 1846 from the Quinto collection in Madrid (Bibl. 102, p. 342, no. 51). It had already left the Quinto collection by 1862 when the Goya pictures were sold in Paris (Bibl. 57, II, p. 260) and appeared in a Paris sale in 1876 (Bibl. 57, II, p. 264). Exhibited in 1970 (Bibl. 30, no. 15 [13]).

331 One of the most difficult works to date. Gudiol places it as early as 1775-80; Sánchez Cantón (Bibl. 166, p. 45) suggested 1790; Held (Bibl. 89, no. 59) dated it c.1795. Last exhibited in 1928 (Bibl. 10, no. 25) and very little studied since then, the subtle handling and atmospheric quality suggest a relationship with the cabinet pictures of 1793-94 [317-330] and two small pictures of 1795 [352, 353]. For the explanation of the metal clips on the hat, see Bibl. 34, p. 100: 'los ultimos toques para el mejor efecto de un cuadro los daba de noche, con luz artificial'. Detail reproduced in colour, Bibl. 64, p. 38.

332 Drawing used by Loizelet for the portrait of Goya on the frontispiece to the third edition of *La Tauromaquia* (1876). Exhibited 1941 (Bibl. 16, no. 18, ill.).

333 Inscribed on paper: *Dn Sebastian/Martinez/Por su Amigo/Goya/1792*.
Replica or copy cited by Lafuente (Bibl. 102, p. 175).

334 Listed by Carderera (Bibl. 148, nos 24 and 61). Compare Goya's portrait drawing of Ceán [697].

335 Listed by Carderera together with [334] (Bibl. 148, nos 24 and 62). Both identification and attribution have been questioned and Lafuente (Bibl. 102, p. 162) discussed Mayer's statement (Bibl. 128, p. 46) that the portrait was originally larger and was signed by Joaquín Inza. Mayer, however, maintained the attribution to Goya (and Carderera's list at least proves that a portrait of Ceán's wife existed). If it is by Goya, this portrait can be seen as a continuation of Goya's 'rococo' manner – cp. [I.220, 221, 278] and [336].

336 Date given by Viñaza (Bibl. 190, p. 261, no. CXII).

337 Dated between 7 November 1793 – when the general was still at the front (having been awarded a decoration, which he is wearing in the portrait, after the battle of Truilles on 22 September) – and his death on 13 March 1794. See Bibl. 166, p. 51. Boadilla no. 83 (Bibl. 37). Listed by Carderera (Bibl. 148, no. 31).
Replica: Cudillero (Asturias), heirs of D.F. de Selgas M.397a, DF.305n.
Copy: 95·9×75 cm. Baltimore, Walters Art Gall. (37.283) Gaya Nuño 927 (Bibl. 65).

338 First catalogued in 1961 (Bibl. 23, no. VI).

339 Inscribed on title page of open book: *JUZGADOS/ MILITARES / DE ESPAÑA / POR D. FELIX COLON DE/ LARRIATEGUI / TOMO V.* and on paper behind *Año 1794*. See Trapier (Bibl. 188, p. 10). Described by Father Tomás López as a full-length portrait (Bibl. 190, p. 464). The dimensions were given as 120×85 cm. by Viñaza who praised the drawing of the legs but specified that it was not a full-length portrait (Bibl. 190, p. 241, no. LXXIII).

340 Inscribed on paper: *María / del rosario / La Tirana / Por Goya/1794*. For a previous alteration to the inscription see Bibl. 10, no. 28. Probably the portrait listed by Carderera (Bibl. 148, no. 26). Painted in the year of the actress's retirement; see [684] for a later portrait. Her nickname 'la Tirana' came from the fact that her actor husband usually played the rôle of tyrant.

341 Also known as the Condesa del Carpio, she married in 1775 and died in November 1795. For dating of the portrait, cp. Sánchez Cantón (Bibl. 166, p. 46) and Held (Bibl. 89, no. 54). Exhibited 1970 in Paris (Bibl. 30, Appendice, 16 bis).

342 For the identification of the sitter as a Mexican who came to Spain and visited Goya in 1794, see Diego Angulo Iñiguez, 'Un testimonio mejicano de la sordera de Goya', *Archivo Español de Arte*, XVII, 1944, p. 391. For the previous identification see Bibl. 8, no. 35.

343 Elected Director of the Royal Academy of History in 1795; died in 1801. See Trapier (Bibl. 188, pp. 11-12). Exhibited 1970 (Bibl. 30, no. 16).

344 Possibly the sketch referred to in Goya's letter to Zapater, written before the death of Francisco Bayeu in August 1795 but dated in jest 2 August 1800. See Bibl. 72, p. 43, and Sánchez Cantón (Bibl. 161, p. 88). Cantón has tentatively suggested that this sketch may be identifiable with the *boceto de un ginete* – no. 26 in the 1812 inventory of Goya's effects (*op. cit.* p. 106; Bibl. 166, p. 55), but this description could equally well apply to [I.255] or [III.876]. See Appendix I, no. 26.

345 Bayeu died on 4 August 1795 and the portrait was exhibited 'sin concluir' at the Royal Academy later the same month – see Sentenach (Bibl. 177) and Sánchez Cantón (Bibl. 166, p. 59 and figs 24, 25 for the Bayeu self-portrait which Goya used as a model, also Bibl. 159, pp. 40/41, figs 11, 12). See note to [640]. The Prado catalogue says the posthumous portrait was commissioned by Bayeu's sister Feliciana and her husband Pedro Ibáñez. Lafuente mentioned a copy by Fortuny (Bibl. 102, p. 257).

346 Exhibited 1961 (Bibl. 23, no. LXXXII).

347 Exhibited 1961 (Bibl. 23, no. XXXVIII). Held dated it c.1795 (Bibl. 89, no. 95).

348 Mother of the XIth Marqués, husband of the Duchess of Alba. Probably painted as a companion to [349]. She was sixty in 1795 and died in 1801.
Replica: 85×70 cm. Madrid, Duque de Sueca.

349 XIth Marqués de Villafranca, he married the Duchess of Alba in 1775 and died on 9 June 1796, at the age of forty. Ezquerra del Bayo dated this portrait c.1790-92 and reproduced the engraving by Carmona which the duchess had made as a memorial gift for their friends (Bibl. 58, p. 201, pl. XXXVIII).
Replica: 89×75 cm. Madrid, Duque de Sueca G.336.

350 Inscribed on cover of book: *Cuatro canc.s / con Acomp.to de Fórzp.o / del S.r Haydn*. Companion portrait to [351].
Replica or copy: Madrid, Marquesa de Caltabuturu Cited by Beruete (Bibl. 36, I, p. 61, no. 156); M.191n.

351 Inscribed in the sand at left: *A la Duquesa/de Alba Fr.co de/Goya 1795*. Born in 1762, she was thirty-three years old. Portrait listed by Carderera (Bibl. 148, nos 7 and 40).
Replicas or copies:
As [350] M.193a.
86·3×68·5 cm. (half-length, as companion to [349]) Chicago, Chauncey McCormick M.193b, DF.363, Soria 75 (Bibl. 180).
Copy by Esteve: 193×123 cm. Luton Hoo, Sir Harold Wernher M.193n., DF.362, Soria 74 (Bibl. 180). See Bibl. 27, no. 41.

352 Inscribed in lower right corner, according to Bibl. 8, no. 102. Ezquerra del Bayo identified the duenna as D.ª Rafaela Luisa Velázquez, known as 'La Beata' (Bibl. 58, pp. 190-191).
This and the following picture, together with [665], remained in the family of the duchess's majordomo and his son Luis. See Ezquerra (*op. cit.* pp. 190 and 281) and Wehle (Bibl. 192, p. 7).

353 Inscribed *Luis Berganza año 1795 Goya*, according to Bibl. 8, no. 103. The two children are the little negro girl María de la Luz (cp. [360]) and Luis Berganza, both named in the duchess's will of 1797. See note to [352].

354 The woman has often been identified with the Duchess of Alba, and the figures recall many of the drawings in the Sanlúcar and Madrid albums [356-450].
Copy: 52×38 cm. Agen, Mus. G.325, Tormo 145 (Bibl. 184).
Mayer published a drawing (by Lucas?) after the painting (Bibl. 129, pl. 133.2).

355 Inscribed in the sand — facing the Duchess *Solo Goya*, facing the spectator *1797*, on the two rings on her finger *Alba* and *Goya*. Listed in the 1812 inventory as *Un retrato de la de Alva con el numero catorce* (Bibl. 161, pp. 84 and 106; see Appendix I, no. 14). Listed by Carderera (Bibl. 148, nos 1 and 41), both before and after it passed to the Louis-Philippe collection in Paris (Bibl. 6, no. 103; 31, no. 444). Painted at the country palace of Rocío, near Sanlúcar, between January and April, and/or on Goya's return to Madrid. See Ezquerra del Bayo (Bibl. 58, p. 211) and Trapier (Bibl. 188, pp. 13-14).

356-376 The album, probably still in its original form, was described by Carderera (Bibl. 45, [II], pp. 223-224). The sheets are now dispersed and the album reconstructed and catalogued by Sayre (Bibl. 171 and 172, giving previous references) and partially reproduced by López-Rey (Bibl. 115, II).

356 The sheet is shown without the additional 17 mm. added at the bottom after 1867.

358 Drawing described by Carderera (Bibl. 45, [II], p. 223).

360 . . .holding María de la Luz. Drawing described by Carderera (Bibl. 45, [II], p. 223). Cp. the painting of 1795 where María de la Luz appears [353].

365 Cp. *Caprichos* plate 17 [485].

369 Cp. *Caprichos* plate 20 [491].
Copy: 16·7×10 cm. Inscribed below in pencil, by Carderera: *del 1er libro de Goya cuando fue a la de Alba*, and on the backing sheet *[Copia] de Goya* (the first word has been erased) Madrid, Prado (486) First published by Salas (Bibl. 152, p. 33, C).

371 Cp. *Caprichos* plate 15 [481].

372 The sheet, which differs from the others in the type of paper, was published by Gassier (Bibl. 62a). It is not accepted by Sayre (Bibl. 172, p. 20, n. 3). Drawing described by Carderera (Bibl. 45, [II], p. 223).
Copy: 21·2×14·3 cm. Inscribed *Duquesa de Alba* Madrid, Fund. Lázaro (M.I-10,618) Reproduced in Bibl. 107, II, p. 420, no. 940, and discussed by Mayer (Bibl. 129, pl. 130.2).

374 Inscribed below *Goya San Lucar*. Drawing described by Carderera (Bibl. 45, [II], p. 223). See Sayre (Bibl. 172, p. 20, n. 3). Reproduced in Bibl. 107, II, p. 420, no. 938, and discussed by Mayer (Bibl. 129, pl. 130.1).

375 Inscribed below in pencil by Carderera: *Copia de*

[partly erased] *Goya del 1er Libro cuando fue a S. Lucar con la Duquesa de Alba*. First published by Salas (Bibl. 152, p. 33, B). See note to [743 and 744].

376 Original described by Carderera (Bibl. 45, [II], p. 223). Inscribed below in pencil by Carderera: *del 1er libro de Goya con la de Alba*. First published by Salas (Bibl. 152, p. 33, A). Cp. *Caprichos* plate 9 [467].

377-450 The sheets are now widely dispersed and the album has been reconstructed and catalogued by Sayre (Bibl. 171 and 172, giving previous references) and largely reproduced by López-Rey (Bibl. 115, II).

377/378 Identified by Sayre as pages *5* and *6* (Bibl. 172, p. 24). Juliet Wilson reads the partially effaced numbers as *3* and *4*.
378 Copy (by Carderera?): Madrid, Fund. Lázaro (M. I-10, 617) Reproduced in Bibl. 107, II, p. 421, no. 939, and discussed by Mayer (Bibl. 129, pl. 128.2).

379/380 Unnumbered, but with the triangular tear which affects the first four sheets. Identified by Sayre (Bibl. 172) with the letters *a* and *b* and suggested as pages *3* and *4*, but see note to [377/378].
379 Cp. *Caprichos* plate 5 [459].
380 Cp. *Caprichos* plate 16 [483].

382 Inscribed in pencil, apparently by Goya: *Ay muñecos* (There are puppets).

387 Dimensions given by museum.

389 Cp. *Caprichos* plate 7 [463].

390 Cp. *Caprichos* plate 27 [504].

391 Cp. the painting of 1786-87 for the Alameda de Osuna [I.249].

395 Cp. *Caprichos* plate 31 [513].

396 Cp. the etching by Rembrandt, *Woman with an arrow* (Hind 303). Reproduced together by Salas (Bibl. 152, p. 40).

401/402 Exhibited 1970 (Bibl. 30b, no. 1, ill.).

403 Reproduced in Bibl. 78. Cp. *Caprichos* plate 10 [469].

408 Cp. *Caprichos* plate 27 [504] and additional plate [618].

409 . . .with a man across her lap.

415/416 Reproduced here for the first time

417 (Old auntie Bellows lights the fire. Witches about to gather again).

418 (. . .The woman is asking her husband for an explanation).

419 (Masquerades. He notes her down as an hermaphrodite). Sheet cut; catalogued by Sayre (Bibl. 172) with the letters *c* and *d*. From the subject and title it would fit in here or as pages *73/74*. See Gassier (Bibl. 63, pp. 32-34). Cp. *Caprichos* plate 57 [565] and additional drawing [624].

420 For an interpretation of the subject, see José López-Rey, 'Goya's vision of mid-Lent merriment', *Art Quarterly*, IX, 1946, pp. 141-143, and Gassier (Bibl. 63, pp. 34-36). Cp. the late drawing [V.1722].

421 (Caricatures. It's her saint's day). See Gassier (Bibl. 63, pp. 36-37).

422 *Carracas* means rattles and, figuratively, old crocks. According to Pierre Gassier it was used as a slightly contemptuous name for the inhabitants of Carraca, near Cadiz. See also Gassier (Bibl. 63, p. 37).

423 Cp. *Caprichos* plate 13 [476].

425/426 Published here for the first time. Exhibited 1970 (Bibl. 30b, no. 2).
425 (. . .for the one who made it up).

428 (Every word is a lie. The charlatan who pulls out a jaw and they believe it). Cp. *Caprichos* plate 33 [517].

429/430 Exhibited 1970 (Bibl. 30b, no. 3).
429 . . ./*se pone como un tigre* (Just because she is asked if her mother is well, she acts like a tiger).

431/432 Exhibited 1970 (Bibl. 30b, no. 4).
432 (. . .There are also Asses masquerading as men of letters). Cp. *Caprichos* plate 39 [526].

433 (Humility versus Pride).

434 (Generosity versus Greed).

435 . . .*matan a su amante/y ella/se mata despues* (Her brothers kill her lover, and afterwards she kills herself).

436 (They got the confessor to climb in by the window).

437 . . .*bayá estese V. quieto* (She is bashful about taking her clothes off, 'Go along, keep still will you').

438 (. . .in the year 94). This is the only date given in relation to the series, and it is the only drawing known to record an actual event, with the possible exception of [450].

439/440 Exhibited 1970 (Bibl. 30b, no. 5, ill).
439 Cp. *Caprichos* plate 36 [521] and additional drawing [622].
440 . . ./*que á de ser, q.e las lleban a S.n Fernando*. (Poor things, how many would deserve it more? but what is this? What else but that they are being taken off to San Fernando). The old Hospicio de San Fernando in Madrid (now the Museo Municipal) must have contained a penitentiary for prostitutes. Cp. *Caprichos* plate 22 [496].

441/442 This sheet has recently reappeared in a private collection and is reproduced here for the first time. It was in the collection of E. Calando (Lugt 837). Exhibited 1970 (Bibl. 30b, no. 16 bis).
441 (Apprehensive girls with a very black tom). Inscribed below with the pen: *Las miedosas* in Indian ink, the remainder in sepia. Thieves and also natives of Madrid are called 'cats'. Catalogued by Lafond (Bibl. 97, p. 156, no. 65).
442 Inscribed below: *S.n Fernando* in brush and Indian ink, the rest in pen and sepia ink. This drawing follows on from [440] and shows the girls in the penitentiary workroom, their heads now shaved. Cp. the three spinning Fates in *Caprichos* plate 44 [539].

443 . . .*y se espulgan/al tiento* (It is summer and in the moonlight they take the air and get rid of their fleas by feel).

444 (. . .where was it celebrated?) Cp. *Caprichos* plate 18 [487].

446 Cp. *Caprichos* plate 11 [472]. Closely connected with the tapestry cartoon of 1779, the *Tobacco guard* [I.136] — see note.

447 . . .*tan dañino como/como* [sic] *un Medico malo* (This one never spares anybody, but he's not as harmful as a bad doctor).

448 (A wise and repentant fiancée shows herself to her parents in this manner). Cp. *Caprichos* plate 14 [479].

449 . . .*y dice ola? y empieza/a palos con las mascaras/ellos huyendo, claman la injusticia del poco respeto/a su representacion* (The oil vendor recognizes them and cries Hey! and begins to cudgel the masqueraders; they, fleeing, protest the injustice of such lack of respect for their performance).

450 . . .*y / arranca el pelo y patéa / Porq.e el abate Pichurris, le á dicho en sus ocicos, q.e/estaba descolorida* (She orders them to send away the carriage, spoils her coiffure and tears her hair and stamps. Because Abbé Pichurris told her to her face that she was pale). Probably a record of one of the Duchess of Alba's tantrums. Cp. *Caprichos* additional plate [621].

451-613 The prints and their preparatory drawings have been published by Sánchez Cantón (Bibl. 165) and López-Rey (Bibl. 115, II). The series of prints is reproduced, with Goya's commentaries, in Bibl. 78. For Goya's and other contemporary commentaries on the plates, see Bibl. 93, pp. 219-241; 115, I, pp. 187-212; 88, II, nos 36-115.

451 (Francisco Goya y Lucientes, Painter). The first six prints have the letter *P*. engraved before the plate number in the top right corner.

452 Exhibited 1963-64 (Bibl. 27, no. 144) and reproduced in Bibl. 78, frontispiece.

453 It has been suggested that these two self-portrait sketches are connected with plate 43 [536], but they were probably made at the same time as the drawing on the other side of the sheet [452] and reflect a first intention to engrave a frontal self-portrait.

454 (They say yes and give their hand to the first comer) Two lines from the poem *A Arnesto* by Jovellanos. See Helman (Bibl. 93, p. 126).

460 *...p.r q.e/saben q.e el no lleba un cuarto* (The old women laugh themselves sick because they know he hasn't a bean). Title in pencil below the design. Cp. the old women in Madrid album, B.5 [379].

464 *...buen mobimiento / no puede ablar sin colear* (Just because I told her she moved nicely, she can't talk without wiggling). Title in pencil below design.

472 See notes to [446] and [I.136].

473 Title in pencil below design.

477 (Dream. Of some men who were eating us up). Title in pencil below design.

480 Title in pen and ink and beneath it a pencil inscription (the second line repeated below the platemark): *...son Senoritos a cual mas rico; y la pobre / no sabe a qual escoger* (...they are young gentlemen each richer than the other, and the poor girl doesn't know which to choose).

482 Drawing first published by Salas (Bibl. 152, p. 34, D).

483 (...And it was her mother). Probably a play on the phrase *Dios la perdone* which could mean 'God forgive her' or 'Excuse me'. The latter reading is borne out by the inscription on the drawing [484].

484 *.../en publico, y le dice, perdone Vm p.r Dios.* (She is ashamed that her mother should speak to her in public, and says, Please excuse me). Title in pencil below design. Although no number is visible at the top of the drawing, this is almost certainly one of the *Sueños*.

488 *...y/dando buenos consejos a un candil yncendia/la casa.* (Drunken mat maker who can't manage to undress himself, and sets fire to his house while giving good advice to the oil lamp). Title in pencil below the design. Trace of a number at top of drawing.
Another drawing in pen and sepia ink with wash is listed by Harris (Bibl. 88, II, p. 88) who also mentions the attributed drawing in sanguine wash, with title and as engraved, reproduced by Sánchez Cantón (Bibl. 165).

489 For a discussion of the iconography, see Levitine (Bibl. 108, p.109).

491 The foreground girl with a broom is based on the Sanlúcar album A[n] – see [369].

498 The title comes from the Spanish proverb *Aquellos polvos traen estos lodos* (From that dust this dirt must come). For the first etching and preparatory drawing of this subject, see [614, 615].
A drawing in red chalk is recorded in the collection of Herbert L. Matthews (photograph in N.Y., Metropolitan Museum files).

502 The title is a complicated play on the word *asiento*: seat, bottom, chair, judgment; *tener asiento* to be established, settled. Cp. additional *Caprichos* drawing [629].

505 (Past and present, the origin of pride). Title written in ink over a partly illegible pencil inscription: *Pintor de [?] miniatura. 7 [?] minutos le costa de / cruzar la Plaza de*

San Antonio de Cadiz (Miniature painter. It takes him 7 minutes to cross the Plaza de San Antonio at Cadiz). Edith Helman has queried the reading of this inscription, but it is transcribed as faithfully as possible. Cp. Madrid album, B. 20 [390].

515 Cp. the painting in the series belonging to the Marqueses de la Romana [III.915].

517 The title is a play on the word *palatino*, meaning palatine or palatal. The nobleman is portrayed as a quack dentist at work on his unfortunate patients.

518 The reproduction of the print has been cut, by mistake, to correspond with the format of the drawing [519].

519 On the verso are several brush and Indian ink strokes representing a head(?) Prado (447) SC.460.

520 Cp. the similar subject in additional *Caprichos* drawing [639].

521 For the drawing for an unknown first etching of this subject, based on Madrid album, B.81 [439], see [622].

528 Title in pencil below design. Although there is no sign of a number, this is probably one of the *Sueños* drawings. It may in fact be the drawing for an unknown first etching of this subject – bleaching and pressing may have removed traces of the platemark, and the proportions of the design differ from those of the published etching [526].

531 (Witches disguised as ordinary doctors). Title in pencil below design. This may be a drawing for an unknown first etching, although no trace of a platemark is visible.

533 Title written on the block on which the monkey is sitting. Araujo Sánchez (Bibl. 33, p. 135) mentions a preparatory drawing with the inscription *Hará carrera* (He will make a career), but as he misquotes many titles, this may be an error.

534 The title comes from the Spanish proverb *Tu que no puedes, llévame a cuestas* (Thou who canst not, carry me on thy shoulders). Cp. the later drawing [III.1355].

536 (The dream of reason brings forth monsters). Title made by stopping-out the aquatint on the front of the the artist's work bench. For an iconographical study of this composition, see Levitine (Bibl. 108, pp. 114-131) and Nordström (Bibl. 136, pp. 116-132, giving previous references), also the views of Eleanor Sayre (Bibl. 78, p. 2).

537 Inscribed in pencil *Sueño 1o* (1st Dream) at top centre; *Ydioma univer/sal. Dibujado/y Grabado p.r/F.co de Goya / año 1797* (Universal language. Drawn and Engraved by Francisco de Goya in the year 1797) on the front of the work table; *El Autor soñando./Su yntento solo es desterrar bulgaridades / perjudiciales, y perpetuar con esta obra de / caprichos, el testimonio solido de la verdad.* (The Author dreaming. His only intention is to banish harmful common beliefs and to perpetuate with this work of *caprichos* the sound testimony of truth) below the drawing.
Araujo Sánchez (Bibl. 33, p. 135) described a drawing in pen and ink, with Goya's self-portrait as a great head appearing through mists in the background, and inscribed below: *Sueño del autor que quiere con estos Caprichos censurar y corregir ridículas preocupaciones y contribuir al triunfo de la verdad.* But see note to [533].

547 *Soplones* means 'blowers' and also 'talebearers', 'informers'.

551 For the drawing for an unknown first etching of this subject, and a discussion of the subject, see [623] and the note.

560 *...q.e tenia la/cara yndecente se puso los calzones en la/cabeza y solo p.a comer se descubre, y/con razon, qe ay caras qe debian yr en calzones* (This is a man who, because he was told he had an indecent face, put his breeches on his head and only uncovers it to eat, and rightly so for there are faces which ought to go in breeches). Title written in pencil below the design; the last *e* of *descubre* written over *ia*. The *Sueño* number at the top is illegible.

565 For the drawing for an unknown first etching of this subject, based on Madrid album B.59 [419], see [624].

567 For the title of this plate, see Nigel Glendinning, 'The Monk and the Soldier in Plate 58 of Goya's *Caprichos*', *Journal of the Warburg and Courtauld Institutes*, XXIV, 1961, pp. 115-120.

572 *...de primer / buelo, y con temor se prueban p.a trabajar.* (Trial of novice witches on their first flight, and they set to work with fear). Title written in pencil below the design. The word *Sueño* may have been erased in front of the *2o* at top centre.

573 This was a contemporary Spanish meaning of the latin word.

576 *...son arrojadas las / soberbias Brujas* (From the highest point of their flight the arrogant Witches are hurled down). Title written in pencil below the design.

578 (Dream. The Witches' Drones). Title written in pencil below the design.

582 *...sacan a paseo las mejores boladoras* (Dream. Mighty witch who because of her dropsy is taken for an outing by the best flyers). Title written in pen and sepia ink below the design.

584 *...a su discipula del primer buelo.* (Dream. A witch teacher giving instruction to a pupil on her first flight), written below in pen and sepia ink, and below this in pencil *Brujas en ensayo* (Witches practising).

585 Cp. one of the six witchcraft paintings [662].

588 (Dream. Of Witches... running an errand... [?]). The title is written below in pencil and the second line seems to be repeated. It is almost illegible.
A very doubtful drawing is known from a photograph: red chalk 20×17 cm. Mexico City, Museo de San Carlos.

590 (Dream of Witches consumed...). The title, written below in pencil, is partly illegible.

592 (Dream of a novice Witch). Title written below in pencil – the last word barely legible. The drawing was traced through from the earlier one on the other side of the sheet, omitting the flying demons.

593 Title written in pencil below the design.

595 Inscription written below in chalk – as final engraved title.

597 Traced through from the first drawing on the other side of the sheet.

605 (Are you with me, Sir? ...well then, as I say...eh! Look out! if not...).

614 Unique proof found in a set of mixed proofs, probably made up by Goya as a presentation volume (and now dispersed). First published by Jean Adhémar, 'Une épreuve unique d'un "Caprice" de Goya...', *Gazette des Beaux-Arts*, LV, 1960, pp. 185-187.

616 Cp. *Caprichos* plate 32 [515].

618 Bound at the end of a trial proof set with letters (A.10467). First published by Jean Adhémar, *Les Caprices de Goya*, Paris, 1948, and reproduced by Sánchez Cantón (Bibl. 165). Cp. the bowing man in Madrid album, B.40 [408].

619 *...and inconstancy.* For an iconographical study of this composition, see Nordström (Bibl. 136, pp. 142-152).

620 (Dream. Of lying and inconstancy). The title of the Madrid album drawing, B.71 [431], is *Lo mismo* (The same) and follows on from the preceding one, *Confianza* (Trust) [430]; there seems to be a clear relationship of form and content with the *Sueño* composition.

621 This etching, recalling the tantrums of the Duchess of Alba recorded in the Sanlúcar and Madrid albums [358, 450], was a technical failure.

622 (Wind. If there is anything to blame in the scene it is the dress). Title written below in pencil. The composition was repeated in plate 36 [521].

623 The title is written in pen and ink over a pencil inscription: *Pesadilla soñando qe. no me podia despertar* *ni desen-/redar de la nobleza en donde...* [illegible] (Nightmare dreaming that I could not wake up nor free myself from the nobility in which...). For an identification of the subject, see Edith Helman, 'Los "Chinchillas" de Goya', *Goya*, 9, 1955, pp. 162-167. The composition, with considerable variants, was repeated in plate 50 [551].

624 ...*p.ʳ su significado*[?] (Masquerades of caricatures which they note down according to their significance). Title written below in pencil. The composition, with considerable variants, was repeated in plate 57 [565]. See Gassier (Bibl. 63, pp. 32-34).

625 ...*proibiendo a las / q.ᵉ no pasan de treinta años p.ʳ mas merito q.ᵉ tengan* (Dream. Proclamation of Witches banning those under thirty however great their merit). Title written below in pencil. No number is visible at the top.

626 This was no doubt the second drawing for the unknown plate, made as a guide for the aquatint.

627 (Dream. Growing after death). Title written in pencil below the design.

629 Cp. *Caprichos* plate 26 [502].

630 The inscription appears below and to the left, in red chalk, and is presumably a parody on the customary titles of academic discourses. The composition is a simplified version of [631].

631 The signature *Goya* is probably false.

635 and 636 Cp. the paintings of twenty years later in the Quinta del Sordo [IV.1624, 1625].

638 Cp. *Caprichos* plates 3 and 52 [455, 555] and *Proverbios* plate 2 [IV.1572].

639 Compare *Caprichos* plate 35 [520].

640 On the verso are some verses referring to the 1795 portrait of Francisco Bayeu [345], cited by Sánchez Cantón (Bibl. 168).

641 Cp. *Caprichos* plates 64-66 [579, 581, 583].

642 Probably made for the *Caprichos* series, but used for the allegorical painting of 1797-1800 [695, 696].

648-653 See López-Rey (Bibl. 115, I, pp. 66-72) and Nordström (Bibl. 136, pp. 76-94).

654 The drawing was traced through from the other side of the sheet in pen and sanguine ink; the padlocked 'belt' in sepia; various sanguine brush strokes; and a slight pencil sketch of a head with its tongue out.

656 Title written in red chalk in the lower right corner.

657 With contemporary(?) inscription *por Goya 1798*. Traditionally said to have been drawn by Goya at the *tertulia* of the IXth Marqués de Santa Cruz. Last seen and catalogued by Boix in 1922 (Bibl. 9, no. 179).

658 Exhibited 1963-64 (Bibl. 27, no. 153). The attribution to Goya was rejected by López-Rey (Bibl. 118, p. 365).

659-664 Goya's account, dated 27 June 1798, for 6,000 reales for *seis quadros de conposición de asuntos de Brujas*, and a note concerning its payment were published by Miguel Herrero, 'Un autógrafo de Goya', *Archivo Español de Arte*, XLIII, 1941, p. 176. The Duke of Osuna's order for payment, dated 29 June 1798, was published by Loga (Bibl. 109, p. 166, n. 183). See Appendix V.
These pictures were probably the *seis caprichos raros* exhibited at the Academy of San Fernando in 1799 (Bibl. 177). They were all included in the Osuna sale in 1896 (Bibl. 32, nos 83-88). For a discussion of the series, see Nordström (Bibl. 136, pp. 153-171, giving previous references).

659 Cp. the walking figure with his head covered and the mule behind him with the *Winter* tapestry cartoon of 1786-87 and its sketch which Goya sold to the Duke of Osuna the following year, 1799 [I.259, 265]. Osuna no. 83.

660 Cp. *Caprichos* plates 47 and 60 [545, 571]. Osuna no. 84. Exhibited 1970 (Bibl. 30, no. 27).

661 Osuna no. 86.

662 Cp. *Caprichos* plate 67 [585]. Osuna no. 85.

663 The inscription on the paper represents lines from the comedy *El Hechizado por Fuerza* by Zamora: *Lámpara descomunal...* (Monstrous lamp...).

664 A scene from another of Zamora's plays *El Burlador de Sevilla*, showing Don Juan and the arrival of the 'stone guest'. Osuna no. 87. Reproduced in Bibl. 72, pl. 318.

665-689 For a special study of the portraits of this period, see Trapier (Bibl. 187).

665 Ezquerra del Bayo (Bibl. 58, p. 281) said that this small picture (or a replica?) remained in the family of the Duchess of Alba's majordomo, Tomás de Berganza. It is almost identical with the portrait drawing [666].

666 See Wehle (Bibl. 192, p. 7, ill. frontispiece).

667 Inscribed *Goya a su Amigo Altamirano Oidor/de Sevilla*. Probably painted during Goya's stay in Andalusia between the summer 1796 and spring 1797.

668 Inscribed *Goya. A su Amigo Marñ Zapater. 1797.* The painting was with Durand-Ruel, and has not been seen for many years. According to Desparmet, it was cut down to its present oval shape. Cp. the earlier portrait [I.290].

669 Inscribed *D.ⁿ Bernardo Yriarte Vice prot.ʳ de la R.ᶦ Academia de las tres nobles / Artes, retratado por Goya en testimonio de mutua estimac.ⁿ y afecto. año de / 1797.* Shown to the Academicians on 1 November 1797 and praised for its resemblance (Bibl. 157, p. 17). Exhibited 1970 (Bibl. 30, no. 18).
Replica or copy: 108×85·1 cm. Inscr. (same text, differently spaced) New York, M.M.A. (59.145.19) M.451 See Trapier (Bibl. 187, pp. 9-10).
The two versions were exhibited together in 1953 (Bibl. 18, nos 11, 12) and are discussed in Bibl. 25, no. 115.

670 Inscribed *A Melendez Valdes su amigo Goya./1797.* Exhibited 1970 (Bibl. 30, no. 17).
Replica: 72×58 cm. Inscribed with the same text Madrid, Banco Español de Crédito M.347, G.372.

671 Replicas and copies of this portrait have led to some confusion in the literature. The original portrait was listed in the 1812 inventory of Goya's effects as *El retrato de Perico Romero con el no. diez y nueve* and Sánchez Cantón suggested that this was the painting acquired by Don Sebastián de Borbón, which passed to the Sachs collection and is now at Fort Worth (Bibl. 161, pp. 85, 106; see Appendix I, no. 19). An old Otero photograph, made when the picture was in the Lafitte collection in Madrid (not mentioned by Salas, Bibl. 147, p. 109), shows no sign of the inventory mark; the dimensions are given as 84×65 cm. See the note on the picture when it was acquired from the Kann collection (*Burlington Magazine*, XII, 1907-08, p. 232, ill. p. 233). Exhibited 1970 (Bibl. 30, no. 19).
In 1795 Pedro Romero was forty-one. This portrait or a replica was probably a pendant to that of his brother [672].
Replica(?): 85×64 cm. Geneva, priv. coll. (ex-Eissler, Vienna) M.405, DF.427, G.404 Reproduced in the *Burlington Magazine*, XIII, 1908, p. 99, pl. III, with a review of the Galerie Miethke exhibition.
Copy(?): 80×60 cm. Formerly New York, Charles Deering M.407.

672 In 1795 José Romero was forty-four. An inscription on the back of the painting says that he is shown wearing the *traje de luces* given to him by the Duchess of Alba. See Ezquerra del Bayo (Bibl. 58, p. 171) and the 1928 exhibition catalogue (Bibl. 10, no. 23).

673 Exhibited at the Academy of San Fernando in August 1798 and noticed in the *Diario de Madrid* on August 17 – see Sentenach (Bibl. 177) and Helman (Bibl. 93, p. 19; 94, pp. 30, 33). The sitter's identity has been established by Nigel Glendinning, 'Goya's portrait of Andrés del Peral', *Apollo*, LXXXIX, 1969, pp. 200-202. Peral was a collector of Goya's paintings and according to Carderera he commissioned many small genre scenes from the artist (Bibl. 102, pp. 303, 306).

674 Inscribed on paper *El Duque de/Osuna/Por Goya*. Osuna no. 63? (Bibl. 32). See Trapier (Bibl. 188, p. 17). Cp. the earlier portraits [I.219, 278].

675 Inscribed on paper *Jovellanos/por/Goya*. Documented by Goya's letter to Zapater (Bibl. 72, p. 44 – wrongly identified as a reference to Godoy), by Jovellanos' note of payment on 19 July 1798, and the text of his will in which he left to his 'protector', Arias de Saavedra, *el retrato original de cuerpo entero, que hizó de mí D. Francisco Goya en 1798* (Bibl. 36, II, pp. 151-152). See Trapier (Bibl. 187, p. 17) and Nordström (Bibl. 136, pp. 133-141). For a note of a copy, see Bibl. 27, no. 81. Cp. the earlier portrait [I.217] and the note.

676 Inscribed on side of table *Savedra/por/Goya*. Painted after [675] – see Bibl. 72, p. 44 – and before his illness and enforced retirement in August. Portrait discussed by Trapier (Bibl. 187, pp. 15-16).

677 Guillemardet was Ambassador of the French Directory to the Court of Madrid in 1798. The portrait was shown at the Academy of San Fernando in 1799 (Bibl. 177). Cleaned and exhibited 1970 (Bibl. 30, no. 21).

678 The portrait has been described as signed and dated 1799, but this inscription appears on the reduction (see below). The sitter's identity is uncertain, but the death of the Marquesa de la Mercedes in 1797-98 is documented by the publication of an elegy (see Bibl. 10, no. 44, and Trapier, Bibl. 187, p. 8). The fact that Guillemardet owned a reduction of this portrait and must therefore have known the sitter, as well as the advanced style of the original, suggest that it can hardly have been painted before 1798. Exhibited 1970 (Bibl. 30, no. 22).
Reduction: inscr. on verso *Goya 1799*. 52×34 cm. Paris, Louvre (M.I.698) M.351, DF.385, Held (Bibl. 89, p. 189). This picture was bequeathed to the Louvre by Guillemardet's son, together with [677].

679 Inscribed on ground at lower right *Goya al General/Urrutia*. Commissioned by the Osunas. Goya's account is dated 27 June 1798 (Bibl. 36, I, pp. 72-73) and the order for payment is dated 29 June (Bibl. 109, p. 166, n. 182), together with a document suggesting that a copy was made by Esteve in 1803; also 176, p. 215, n. 1). See also an apparently contradictory, probably misprinted, document cited in Bibl. 174, p. 199. (All documents given in Appendix V.) Listed by Carderera (Bibl. 148, no. 21). Osuna no. 77 (Bibl. 32). See Trapier (Bibl. 187, pp. 13-14). Replica or copy mentioned by Lafuente (Bibl. 102, p. 175).

680 Signed half-way up left side. See Salas for a suggestion that the portrait was painted while the artist was at work on the *Caprichos* prints (Bibl. 146, pp. 318-319). It has also been thought to be a study for the self-portrait in the *Family of Charles IV* [783]. Exhibited 1970 (Bibl. 30, no. 31).

681 Sometimes considered a replica or copy of [680], it is much less finished and of different colouring (the jacket is blue). Discussed in Bibl. 25, no. 114. See also Held (Bibl. 89, p. 189).

682 Inscribed on ground at lower left *Goya a su/Amigo Asensi*. The picture is now generally identified as a portrait of Asensio Juliá, nicknamed 'El pescadoret' – the little fisherman – because he was the son of a Valencian fisherman. He is standing, wearing a painter's(?) robe, among scaffolding, presumably in San Antonio de la Florida. See Lafuente (Bibl. 102, p. 152 ff; 105, p. 108), Trapier (Bibl. 187, pp. 18-19) and Boix (Bibl. 39) who did not believe this portrait represented Asensio Juliá. Cp. the portrait of 1814 [III.902]. Exhibited 1970 (Bibl. 30, no. 20). Sold at Sotheby's, London, 24 March 1971, lot 17; acquired by Baron Thyssen, Lugano.

683 Inscribed on ground *D. Manuel Lapeña / P. Goya 1799*. The portrait was probably commissioned by the Duchess of Osuna. See Trapier (Bibl. 187, pp. 20-21; 188, p. 18).

684 The signature and date, first noted by Mayer (Bibl. 128, p. 55) but dismissed as unauthentic and later pointed out by Sambricio (Bibl. 156, p. 97), appear in the lower left corner in large letters, lightly pencilled as if they were to serve as a guide for a painted inscription: *La TIRANA / Por Goya â 1799*. Listed by Carderera (Bibl. 148, no. 44). María del Rosario Fernández died in 1803. Cp. the 1794 portrait and note [340]. Exhibited 1970 (Bibl. 30, no. 26).

685 Documented by the entry in Moratín's diary for 16 July 1799: *A casa de Goya: retrato*. See Sánchez Cantón

(Bibl. 166, p. 68), Helman (Bibl. 92, p. 103) and Viñaza (Bibl. 190, p. 250, no. LXL). Cp. the 1824 portrait [V.1661].

686 The traditional identification of the sitter as Goya's wife seems unlikely. She was born in 1747, and would therefore have been fifty at this date, or over forty if one accepts Gudiol's date of c.1790. The only certain likeness of her is the drawing of 1805 [840], where she looks her age of nearly sixty. A half-length portrait of *D.ª Josefa* was listed in the Brugada inventory of 1828 (Bibl. 57, I, p. 53; see Appendix II, no. 14).
Copy: Madrid, Sra Viuda de Lorenzo Pardo – exhibited Madrid 1961 (Bibl. 23, hors catalogue).

687 The attribution of this portrait is uncertain.
A three-quarter length standing portrait of the same sitter is reproduced by Calleja (Bibl. 72, pl. 98) and Calvert (Bibl. 41, pl. 150).

688 The sitter is now identified as Antonio Gasparini, the son of Matias, the Neapolitan (Bibl. 23, no. XL). Gudiol dates the portrait c.1786-88. Exhibited and published by Tomás Harris, *From Greco to Goya*, London 1938, no. 23.
Replica: Madrid, Aldama   G.267.

689 The attribution of this portrait is in doubt. It is known that Goya painted two portraits of Urquijo, who replaced Saavedra in August 1798 and was awarded the Order of Charles III. In 1800 the Junta of the Royal Academy of History decided to have a copy made of the most faithful existing portrait of Urquijo which was 'el segundo que ha executado don Francisco Goya'. Sánchez Cantón published all the documents, which would seem to show that this is the copy referred to, but he maintained the attribution to Goya (Bibl. 162, pp. 12-16).

690-696 The significance and iconography of the allegories were discussed by Martín S. Soria, 'Goya's allegories of fact and fiction', *Burlington Magazine*, XC, 1948, pp. 196-200, and by Nordström (Bibl. 136, pp. 95-115). See also F. J. Sánchez Cantón, 'La Elaboración de un cuadro de Goya', *Archivo Español de Arte*, XVIII, 1945, pp. 301-307.

693 The early provenance of this attributed sketch is not known. The composition differs considerably from that of the final painting [692]. Sánchez Cantón suggested that item 27 in the inventory of 1812 referred to four sketches (Bibl. 161, p. 86), and they could have been for these allegories. Cp. Appendix I, no. 27.

695 Nordström suggested that the picture was an allegory representing Philosophy, citing Ripa's *Iconologia* and discussing the differences between the sketch [696] and the final painting. Cp. Goya's drawing of *Philosophy* in album E [III.1399].
López-Rey compared this painting with the *Allegory of the Town of Madrid* of 1810 [III.874], and dated it c.1810-12 (see note to [III.875-902], *op. cit.* p. 59). However, the style of the painting does not bear out this late dating.

696 Exhibited in 1963-64 (Bibl. 27, no. 83). The exhibition catalogue refers to another sketch for [695] in a private collection in Paris.

697-707 The drawings were discussed by Xavier de Salas, 'Portraits of Spanish artists by Goya', *Burlington Magazine*, CVI, 1964, pp. 14-19, and by Jutta Held, 'Two portrait drawings by Goya', *Master Drawings*, IV, 1966, pp. 294-298, giving previous references.

697 Inscribed below *Don Juan Agustín Cean Bermúdez, dibujado del natural por Don Francisco Goya*. The inscription, not now visible beneath the mount, is transcribed from the 1922 catalogue (Bibl. 9, no. 184). Cp. the earlier portrait of Ceán [334].

699 The artist's name rewritten in red ink over Goya's red chalk inscription.

700 The artist's name is rewritten in red ink over Goya's red chalk inscription. Based on a drawing in black chalk 19·8×14·5 cm., Madrid, B.N. (2098) – v. Held, *op. cit.* n. 8.

704 The artist's name rewritten in red ink over Goya's red chalk inscription.

705 Same remark as [704].

707 Catalogued in the Cabinet des Dessins as a self-portrait by Zurbarán. Based on a drawing in black chalk in Madrid, coll. Amunátegui.

708-712 See Ezquerra del Bayo (Bibl. 59) for a full account, and Sánchez Cantón (Bibl. 166, pp. 60-61); also René Taylor, 'Goya's Paintings in the Santa Cueva at Cadiz', *Apollo*, LXXIX, 1964, pp. 62-66, and Held (Bibl. 89, nos 16-18). For Goya's presence in Seville and Cadiz in 1796-97, see text pp. 114-116.

710 Published by A. L. Mayer, 'Goyas Gemälde für die Santa Cueva in Cadiz', *Cicerone*, XX, 1928, p. 501. Sold at auction by Lempertz, Cologne, 27-28 November 1935 (lot 146). Since all the pre-war auction records have been destroyed, the firm was unable to identify the buyer, and the sketch has not been seen since the date of the sale. Photograph kindly made available by Enriqueta Frankfort-Harris.

712 Published by Mayer, *op. cit.* p. 500 (see note to [710]). The sketch was with Kleinberger in Paris in 1932, according to the photograph made available by Enriqueta Frankfort-Harris.

713-716 See Sánchez Cantón, Bibl. 163, pp. 295-296; 166, p. 61. Gudiol dates this series c.1781-85.

713 Acquired from the Contini-Bonacossi collection (Bibl. 110, no. 28) in 1969 and to be published by Ann T. Lurie, *Cleveland Museum of Art Bulletin*, LVII, 1970.

716 Torrigiano's terracotta *Saint Jerome* (now in the museum at Seville) was described by Ceán Bermúdez who commented on Goya's lengthy study of it (Bibl. 47, V, pp. 65-66).

717-735 See López-Rey (Bibl. 112), Lafuente (Bibl. 105) and Christian Baur, *Die Fresken Francisco de Goyas in San Antonio de la Florida* (doctoral thesis for the Ludwig-Maximilian University, Munich), 1968.

719 Entirely different in style from the Villagonzalo sketch [718], the attribution of this and the following picture to Goya seems very questionable but they may possibly record a further stage in the working out of the design. Mentioned by Glendinning (Bibl. 67, p. 12).

720 See note to [719].
Replica: 27×40 cm.   Madrid, Fund. Lázaro (M.2521).

721 First published as a sketch for the whole cupola by E. Lafuente Ferrari, 'El boceto para la cúpula de San Antonio de la Florida', *Arte Español*, XXIII, 1961, pp. 133-138, and included in Bibl. 105, 1964 and later editions. See also Xavière Desparmet Fitz-Gerald, 'L'esquisse qui servit à Goya pour San Antonio de la Florida', *Connaissance des Arts*, 132, 1963, pp. 32-33. Reproduced in colour in Bibl. 169, pp. 40-41. Considered by Gudiol, Baur (*op. cit.*) and the authors to be a copy from the fresco.

726 A possible sketch (more probably a reduction from the fresco) of the section shown on the left was exhibited in 1953 (Bibl. 18, no. 14): 38×13·6 cm.   Paris, David-Weill   G.386.

736 For the 1788 commission, see Goya's letter (Bibl. 72, p. 39) and Beruete (Bibl. 36, II, p. 35). Sánchez Cantón gives the documented dates (Bibl. 157, p. 17; 166, pp. 66, 169).

737 First officially catalogued by the Prado in Bibl. 2, p. 29. Exhibited 1970 (Bibl. 30, no. 25).

738-740 See Sánchez Cantón (Bibl. 163, pp. 300-301), Paulina Junquera, 'Un lienzo inédito de Goya en el Palacio de Oriente', *Archivo Español de Arte*, XXXIII, 1959, p. 186, n. 2), quoting Jovellanos' description, and Enrique Pardo Canalis, 'La iglesia zaragozana de San Fernando y las pinturas de Goya', *Goya*, 84, 1968, pp. 358-365, for a fully documented account.

738 . . . a sick woman. Sketch for the painting which hung on the Gospel side of the choir, i.e. to the left of the altar.
A wash drawing, attributed to Goya, was reproduced by Pardo Canalis (*op. cit.* p. 364, ill. p. 362).

739 . . . to Saint Ferdinand. Sketch for the largest painting which hung over the altar. The church was dedicated to Saint Ferdinand.

740 Sketch for the painting which Jovellanos described hanging on the Epistle side of the choir, i.e. to the right of the altar.

742 The traditional attribution to Goya is not accepted by Held (Bibl. 89, p. 191). The butterfly wings and masks suggest a relationship with the *Caprichos* prints and with the cherubs in the allegory of *Poetry* [694] and the frescoes of San Antonio de la Florida [726-735].

743 and 744 Beruete specifically denied that the *Majas* were painted for Godoy and said (without giving details) that they were acquired by him and first appeared in an inventory of his paintings in 1803 as 'Número 122: Dos cuadros . . . representa uno una Venus sobre el lecho, otro una maja vestida, autor Francisco Goya' (Bibl. 36, I, p. 65). They could, therefore, have been acquired by him from the Duchess of Alba's collection after her death in 1802, together with pictures which included the *Venus* of Velázquez (London, N.G.).
Although there are no documents to prove that the paintings belonged to the duchess, Ezquerra del Bayo believed that they represented her and were done from life in 1797 during Goya's stay at her country palace near Sanlúcar (Bibl. 58, pp. 216, 247). The recent publication of a copy after a lost drawing from Goya's Sanlúcar album, showing a standing nude [375] (Bibl. 152, p. 33, B), perhaps lends some support to the theory that they may have been painted for the duchess at that time, although she was certainly not the model.
It is sometimes suggested that the *Maja vestida*, which was no doubt intended as a cover for the *desnuda* (cp. Bibl. 193, p. 88), was painted some years later but if both were in Godoy's collection in 1803 and if the provenance from the Alba collection is ever proved, they would have been painted together, before Goya's rupture with the duchess. Goya's son referred to the pictures as 'las Venus que tenía el Principe de la Paz' (Bibl. 34, p. 100), and his grandson Mariano gave a fanciful account of their origin (Bibl. 36, I, p. 67).
On 1 January 1808, Frédéric Quilliet dated his inventory of Godoy's collection, three months before the latter's downfall. They appear in the third category, relating to 'second rate' pictures, as 'Gitana vestida' and 'Gitana desnuda' (i.e. gypsies) (Bibl. 138, p. 114). Between 1803 and 1808 they were no doubt seen by many people, since the author of a review of the *Caprichos*, published in 1811, referred to Goya's much admired Venuses (Bibl. 86, p. 42). They were next mentioned in 1814 in a document relating to Goya's denunciation to the Inquisition on account of two obscene paintings representing 'una mujer desnuda sobre una cama' and 'una mujer vestida de maja, sobre una cama' (Bibl. 166, pp. 75-76). Carderera listed the two paintings as 'una manola, o maja, echada; otra, desnuda' (Bibl. 148, no. 47) when they were in the Academy of San Fernando where the *desnuda* was kept hidden away for many years (Bibl. 193, p. 89). They were exhibited in 1900 (Bibl. 8, nos 8, 9) and were transferred to the Prado in 1901.

744 Reduction: 57×86 cm.   Rotterdam, Mus. Boymans (2578)   M.634?, DF.388n.
Yriarte mentioned a reduced copy of the *Maja desnuda* often seen in the sale-rooms (Bibl. 193, p. 89). Possibly these were the two pictures known to Baudelaire (Œuvres complètes, Club Français du Livre, Paris, 1966, pp. 810, 811, 814). Yriarte (*op. cit.* p. 136) also listed a *Maja*, 'esquisse très lumineuse achetée au fils de Goya', in the collection of Valentín Carderera, which may be identifiable with the *maja vestida echada (mas de una vara)* in the Brugada inventory of 1828 (Bibl. 57, I, p. 53, n. 1). See note to [III.1563] and cp. Appendix II, no. 7.

745 See F. J. Sánchez Cantón, *La Colección Cambó*, Barcelona, 1955, pp. 87-88.

746 Almost unknown until its acquisition by Dublin in 1970, this picture has been assigned widely differing dates. Gudiol suggests that it was the third over-door painted for Sebastián Martínez – cp. [I.307 308] – and dates it c.1790; Mayer suggested c.1800-10, and it may have been painted as late as the portraits of *Mariano Goya* and the *Duchess of Abrantes* in 1815-16 [III.1553, 1560]. Exhibited in 1970 (Bibl. 30, no. 32).

747 The dimensions given are those of the etched design. Probably designed as a book-plate for Jovellanos whom Goya first met in 1780. Velasco y Aguirre (Bibl. 189, pp. 7-8) dates it to the period of the *Copies after Velázquez* [I.88-188] – i.e. around 1778. It could in fact have been made at any time between 1780 and 1798 when Goya painted a portrait of Jovellanos [675] and when his friend and patron withdrew from public life. This proof is inscribed in ink – not by Goya – del S.or Jovellanos (above) and Goya (below).
Preparatory drawing in pencil (Velasco *op. cit.*) or

pen and ink (Mayer) Formerly Madrid, Julio Somoza M.739.

748 The copperplate was cut in half about 1810 when two war scenes were engraved on the verso: plates 13 and 15 of the *Desastres* (III.1011, 1015]. A third proof, not recorded by Harris, is in a private collection in Germany (first catalogued in 1966, Bibl. 28, no. 32).

750 The copperplate was cut in half about 1810 when two war scenes were engraved on the verso: plates 14 and 30 of the *Desastres* (III.1013, 1044]. A second proof, not recorded by Harris, is in a private collection in Germany (first catalogued in 1966, Bibl. 28, no. 34).

755 Signed *Goya* by another hand. Cp. this and [756] with the painting at Agen [III.955].

756 Doubted by Mayer and tentatively attributed to Carnicero.

758 It is not known when or for what purpose this monument or mausoleum was projected. Inscribed lower right in chalk by Goya *Baras castella.s* (Castilian varas) below a scale measure (1 *vara* = 83·5 cm.), and lower left in pen and ink, not by Goya, *Goya invento y dibujo*. Discussed by Fernando Chueca Goitia, 'Goya y la Arquitectura', *Revista de Ideas Estéticas*, IV, 1946, pp. 431-448, see p. 437.

759 Project for the tomb of the Duchess of Alba in the church of the Noviciado in Madrid, described by Ezquerra del Bayo (Bibl. 58, pp. 249, 300). The existence of the projected grisaille painting would seem proved by an architectural drawing of the whole monument incorporating Goya's painted design and with the words 'Aprobado por la Junta' and the signature of one of the duchess's heirs. But see Tormo's comments on Ezquerra's text (Bibl. 185, pp. 234-241). Goya's drawing and the architectural elevation were reproduced by Ezquerra (*op. cit.* plates LV, LVI) and Tormo (*op. cit.* pp. 234/235). See also Bibl. 166, p. 58.

760-765 Drawings made up of figures copied singly or in groups from the engravings published from Flaxman's classical outline drawings to the three parts of Dante's *Divine Comedy*. The extremely rare first edition was published in Rome in 1793, the second edition in Rome in 1802, and the first English edition in 1807 (see G. E. Bently, *The Early Engravings of Flaxman's Classical Design. A Bibliographical Study*, New York, 1964).
Salas implies that Goya's drawings were made as early as 1795 (Bibl. 152, p. 34), but in view of the very restricted publication of the Flaxman designs before 1802, this seems unlikely. On the other hand, the later plates of the *Caprichos* have a strength and clarity of line which may prove to have been due in part to the influence of Flaxman (see note to [763]).

760 Based on three designs for the *Inferno*: left figure from plate 2, centre pair from plate 1, right-hand pair from plate 16.

761 The only drawing clearly based on a single Flaxman design: *Inferno* plate 25.

762 Probably based on the figures in *Inferno* plate 34.

763 Apparently adapted from figures in *Inferno* plates 22 and 26, with a possible reminiscence of the prostrate figure in plate 6. This design inevitably recalls *Caprichos* plate 8 [465] but is also very close to some of the *Desastres* plates and particularly to the background group in one of the 'X. 9' paintings [III.931].

764 Based on two figures from designs for *Purgatory*: left figure from the Dante in plate 6 and the kneeling figure from plate 14. Catalogued by Lafond (Bibl. 97, p. 155, no. 56). Sold at Galerie Charpentier, Paris, 24 March 1955, lot 5, ill.

765 Drawing first published by Salas (Bibl. 152, p. 34, E.) and based on six of Flaxman's designs for *Paradise*: the extreme left figure not identifiable (plate 5?), the next two from plates 1 and 3, the centre pair from plate 7, the left figure in the right-hand group from plate 17 and the other two from plate 26; the mother and child in bed from plate 15.

766 Described by Barcia as belonging with the Flaxman group of drawings, its attribution requires further study.

767 Although the paper has not been checked, the size, technique and style of this drawing suggest that it may be closely connected with the Flaxman group. The design recalls some of the famine scenes from the *Desastres* plates, e.g. [III.1078, 1080].

768 Inscribed below in pencil. This drawing has something in common with the 'black border' series, album E [III.1385-1430], but is so much weaker that its attribution to Goya has been doubted.

769 Head and shoulders in grey ink, silhouetted, and additions over the backing sheet in sepia ink. Signature in red chalk. Wrongly identified in the Boix catalogue as Juan Martín de Goicoechea (see [I.277]), it is no doubt a portrait of the father-in-law of Goya's son. Cp. the miniature on copper [850].

770 Inscribed below in ink *J. B. CASTI / cui miro carmine dicere verum / nihil vetuit / muerto en Paris en 1802 de edad de 83 años.* (J. B. Casti, whom nothing hindered from speaking the truth in marvellous verse, died in Paris in 1802 at the age of 83). Inscription *por D.n Fran.co Goya Pintor* at lower right is not by Goya. See Boix (Bibl. 9, no. 182) and the 1963-64 exhibition catalogue (Bibl. 27, no. 154). Probably based on a print and designed to be engraved. Various dates have been suggested.
This drawing and another version, probably a copy, were reproduced and discussed by F. J. Sánchez Cantón, 'Una docena de dibujos goyescos', *Archivo Español de Arte*, XXVII, 1954, pp. 288-289, pl. VIII. (The other drawings published in the article are not included here as part of Goya's œuvre.)

771 Inscribed below in ink *Erasmus Rotterdamus*. The pencil inscription *Goya dibujó* at lower left is by another hand. The drawing was copied from the etching in van Dyck's *Iconography* and the inscription is copied from that engraved on the print (M. Mauquoy-Hendrickx, *L'Iconographie d'Antoine van Dyck – Catalogue raisonné*, Brussels, 1956, no. 5. III).
Another version: pen and sepia ink 23×17·5 cm. Inscribed below in pencil *Goya copió* Formerly Madrid, Lázaro Bx.177 Reproduced in the unpublished facsimile catalogue of the Lázaro collection (no. 44).

772 A contemporary proof has a MS title *Barbara dibersion* (Barbarous entertainment), possibly written by Ceán Bermúdez (the proof is bound with the *Tauromaquia* proof set given to him by Goya). The print was published in the *Gazette des Beaux-Arts*, XXII, 1867, facing p. 388, entitled *AVEUGLE ENLEVÉ SUR LES CORNES D'UN TAUREAU* (Blind man caught up on the horns of a bull) and has not been republished since that date. The copperplate is in the collection of Dr Zdenko Bruck in Buenos Aires.
The terminus ante quem is suggested by the fact that Domenico Tiepolo, who owned a proof of this etching, died in 1804. If it were not for this, one would be inclined to place the print close to the *Tauromaquia* of 1815, given the similarity of style and its inclusion in Ceán's copy.

774-782 See Sambricio (Bibl. 156). Six copies of (unspecified) full-length portraits by Goya were made by Esteve and included in his account dated 20 July 1800 (Bibl. 154, doc. 209). Four of them were painted for Godoy and were included in the 1808 inventory of his collection as originals by Goya (Bibl. 138, p. 144). They are discussed by Sambricio (*op. cit.* pp. 95, 105-107).

774 Copies by Agustín Esteve:
209×126 cm. Naples, Musei Nazionali de Capodimonte (121) M.129, DF.420 See Held (Bibl. 89, p. 188). Painted for Godoy. The Madrid and Capodimonte versions are reproduced together in *Museum*, III, 1913, pp. 168-169.
Parma, Palazzo del Governo See note to [774-796].
Reduction by Esteve(?): 46×30 cm. Washington, N.G. (Mellon 86) G.416.

775 This picture or Goya's lost sketch for it is referred to in María Luisa's letter to Godoy of 24 September 1799 (Bibl. 156, p. 91).
Copies by Agustín Esteve:
209×125 cm. Madrid, Prado (728) M.152, DF.415, G.420 Painted for Godoy and mentioned in María Luisa's letter of 15 October 1799 (Bibl. 156, pp. 94-95).
Parma, Palazzo del Governo See note to [774-796].
Reduction by Esteve(?): 46×30 cm. Washington, N.G. (Mellon 87) G.417.
A full-size copy and a reduction, painted by Francisco Lameyer, were exhibited in 1932; mentioned by Lafuente (Bibl. 102, pp. 217, 364, nos 66, 67).

776 Included with [781-783] in Goya's account for painting materials supplied between 1 July 1800 and 1 June 1801 (see Sambricio, Bibl. 154, doc. 218). Listed by Carderera (Bibl. 148, no. 55).
Reduction: 34×26 cm. Collection unknown M.133a, DF.393, G.421.

777 Painted at San Lorenzo del Escorial. The horse, Marcial, was a present to the queen from Godoy. María Luisa's letters to Godoy of October 5, 8 and 9 describe her sittings for the sketches by Goya who was to begin the final version on the 10th. Her letter of October 15 refers to a copy to be made for Godoy by Esteve. It is not known. (See Bibl. 156 for letters.) The portrait was listed by Carderera (Bibl. 148, no. 56).

778 This sketch, mentioned but not studied by recent writers, would be one of the studies made between October 5 and 9 (see note to [777]), and is so referred to by Sambricio (Bibl. 156, p. 94). Mayer considered it a false copy.

779 Possibly a study for a projected double portrait of Charles IV and María Luisa. Mayer no. 680.

781 Sambricio identified this and the companion portrait [782] as the two referred to in María Luisa's letter to Godoy of 9 June 1800: 'Goya ha hecho mi Retrato q.e dicen es el mejor de todos; está haciendo el del Rey en la Casa del Labrador' (Bibl. 156, p. 100). According to him, they were intended as gifts for Napoleon (in return for the portrait of *Napoleon crossing the Alps*, sent to Spain in July 1802, and now at Malmaison). The portraits were included in Goya's account dated 10 January 1802: *Dos Retratos de SS.MM. de Cuerpo entero de tamaño natural para emviar â Paris* (Bibl. 154, doc. 218) but were never despatched to France (see documents quoted by Sambricio, Bibl. 156, pp. 100-102).
Engraved busts after these portraits were used as the frontispiece to the *Kalendario Manual, y Guía de Forasteros en Madrid para el año 1802* (Bibl. 4, no. 1712-51). Cp. [I.289].
Copy by Agustín Esteve: 204×125 cm. Naples, Musei Nazionali de Capodimonte Painted for Godoy. See Held (Bibl. 89, p. 188) and note to]774-796].
Copies (three-quarter length):
114×81 cm. Madrid, Prado (740e) M.143, DF.408 Pendant to Prado 740d now at La Coruña (M.120) See Held (Bibl. 89, p. 188);
110×83 cm. New York, M.M.A. (29.100.11) M.149, DF.407;
153×110 cm. Madrid, Marqués de Casa Torres M.146, DF.548s Pendant to a modified copy of [I.283].
Reduction·47×30 cm. Madrid, MacCrohon Exhibited 1928 (Bibl. 10, no. 30).

782 See note to [781].
Copy by Agustín Esteve: 202×126 cm. Madrid, Prado (727) M.132, DF.412, G.415 Painted for Godoy. See note to [744-796].
Desparmet mentioned two more replicas or copies: University of Salamanca and Madrid, Duque de Tamames. Attributed by Sambricio to Esteve or other assistants (Bibl. 156, p. 112).

783 See Salas (Bibl. 143) and Sambricio (Bibl. 154, doc. 218). For an identification of the picture in the background, see Priscilla E. Muller, 'Goya's *The Family of Charles IV*: An Interpretation', *Apollo*, XVI, 96, 1970, pp. 132-137, and the note to [I.168].

784-788 Goya's account for the ten sketch portraits of the royal family, painted at Aranjuez, includes the cost of canvases, cases for their transportation, his journeys to Aranjuez and living expenses, and also the cost of the canvas for the large painting (Bibl. 154, doc. 213). The original sketches of the king and queen and the heir to the throne and his sister María Isabel are not known (see note to [789-792]).
For the portrait studies outside Spain, see Salas (Bibl. 143, p. [31]); Gaya Nuño (Bibl. 65, nos 983, 985-987); Bibl. 110, no. 29; 14, no. 19; 21, no. 118, together with Sambricio's review in *Goya*, 13, 1956, p. 37.

787 A so-called sketch, which comes into the same category as those discussed in relation to [784-788], is catalogued in Bibl. 110, no. 30.

789-792 Sambricio suggested that these four portraits, which were in the collection of the daughter of Ferdinand VII, were based on Goya's lost sketches for the royal family portrait (Bibl. 156, p. 98). They are tentatively attributed to Esteve by Gudiol. The portraits were later over-painted with an oval 'frame' which has been removed in the case of [790].

791 Mayer pointed out that the identical portrait reproduced by Richard Oertel (*Goya*, Bielefeld and Leipzig, 1929, p. 95) is erroneously described as being in the collection of the Vizconde de Val de Erro.

792 Castañeda (Bibl. 46, no. XXIV) listed an engraving after a lost portrait of the Infanta María Isabel by Goya, but one of the known prints (Bibl. 4, no. 1243-2) is lettered *Antonio Carnicero lo dib.º*, thus disproving Goya's authorship.

793 Painted in Madrid and referred to in María Luisa's letters to Godoy of 22 and 24 April 1800 (Bibl. 166, p. 71. 156, pp. 96-97). Listed by Carderera (Bibl. 148, no. 38). Boadilla no. 231 (Bibl. 37). Exhibited 1970 (Bibl. 30, no. 29); Measurements checked at the time of the exhibition.
Half-length copy by Agustín Esteve: 101·5×78·7 cm. Shelburne (Vermont), Mus. Soria 62 (Bibl. 180).
A full-length standing portrait of the Condesa, with a half-length copy, was described in detail and catalogued by Viñaza (Bibl. 190, p. 229). They were also seen by Tormo at Boadilla del Monte (Bibl. 182, p. 206, n. 1) – see note to [I.206-212] – but are otherwise unknown. The date of this portrait is uncertain but it was probably painted between the marriage of the Condesa with Godoy in 1797 and the fall of the latter in 1808, and more probably before 1802 when Goya virtually ceased to work for the Royal family: 195×130 cm. Formerly Boadilla del Monte (139) Viñaza XL, M.185.
Half-length copy: 74×56 cm. Formerly Boadilla del Monte (230) Viñaza XLI, M.186 Described by Tormo as a poor copy.

794 Dimensions given by museum; catalogued in Bibl. 10, no. 46 (195×130 cm.) and in 1954, *Masterpieces from the São Paulo Museum of Art*, Tate Gallery, London, no. 27 (200×114 cm.). Listed by Carderera (Bibl. 148, no. 37). Boadilla no. 135 (Bibl. 37).
Copy by Esteve(?): 200×214 cm. Madrid, Marqués de Casa Torres M.177, DF.312, Soria 99 (Bibl. 180).
A so-called study for the head (which in any case more closely resembles Archbishop Company [798-800]) comes into the same category as those discussed in relation to [784-788].

796 With Portuguese banners alluding to the 'War of the Oranges' which began on 27 February 1801. Painted after 7 July 1801 when Godoy was awarded the banners and before 4 October when he was made Generalissimo, with a blue sash. See Sánchez Cantón (Bibl. 166, p. 74).
Copy of the head: 67×50 cm. Chicago, Chauncey McCormick M.280, DF.422, G.435bis Exhibited 1953 (Bibl. 18, no. 6, although the catalogue states it is not recorded by Mayer or Desparmet).

798 Inscribed at lower right: *El Exmo S.ʳ D.ⁿ Fray/Joaquin Company, Na-/tural de Penaguila Reyno/de Valencia. Ministro/Gral. del Orden de S.ⁿ/Fran.ᶜᵒ efecto Arzobispo/de Zaragoza en 30/de Junio de 1797./y trasladado al Arzo-/bispado de Valencia/en 11 de Agosto de 1800*. The original was no doubt painted when the Archbishop was 'translated' to Valencia in 1800, and not in Saragossa in 1790 as suggested by Sánchez Cantón (Bibl. 166, p. 45). It is mentioned and very poorly reproduced by González Martí (Bibl. 69, pp. 436, 445).
Replica or copy: 212×130 cm. Saragossa, Palacio Arzobispal Described by Tormo as much less fine than the Valencia version (Bibl. 183, p. 284). Exhibited 1961 (Bibl. 23, hors catalogue, no. 120).
Soria (Bibl. 180, no. 164) attributed the Saragossa version to Goya and the Valencia picture to Esteve. M. Gómez-Moreno ('Más obras inéditas de Goya', *Archivo Español de Arte*, XXVII, 1954, p. 63) agreed with Sánchez Cantón that the Saragossa portrait was earlier than the Valencia version, pointing out that in the latter the archbishop is wearing the Order of Charles III. However, the style of the portrait suggests that it was not painted before 1799-1800 and the Order could have been added later to the Valencia picture.

800 Original, or replica, or copy of a lost original by Goya, which was drawn by J. Piquer and engraved by V. Capilla. The print was published in Valencia in 1818 as an illustration to the funeral oration for Company, spoken on 11 March 1815, and is catalogued by Castañeda

(Bibl. 46, no. XXIII). The painting is mentioned in the Prado catalogue as a later study than [799], but also made for the Valencia portrait. It could equally well have been made posthumously.

801 Inscribed on letter *el S.ᵒʳ D.ⁿ / Antonio / Noriega / Tesorero / General / F. Goya / 1801.* and on side of table with a long and virtually illegible list of his official positions. See Trapier (Bibl. 188, p. 23).

802 Inscribed on letter. Sánchez Cantón (Bibl. 166, p. 171), followed Mayer's original misreading of the date as 1809 (corrected in the 1930 catalogue of the Alte Pinakothek). Queralto, a military doctor, died in 1805.

803 Inscribed on paper by dividers *Villanueva/por Goya*. Architect of the Prado Museum, he wears the uniform of the Royal Academy of San Fernando of which he was Director General.

804 Inscribed on paper *D.ⁿ / Thomas Perez / Estala. / P. Goya.* See Beruete (Bibl. 36, I, p. 43) who related it to the 1792 portrait of Sebastián Martínez [333], and Held (Bibl. 89, no. 52) who dated it c.1794. Mayer, who identified the sitter as a cloth-maker from Segovia, suggested the late nineties, rejecting Logas's date of 1805 (Bibl. 128, p. 53). A date within this period seems appropriate to the vigorous, open style of this portrait where the famous yellow sofa makes perhaps its first appearance – cp. [853 and III.892].
Mayer refers to a sketch or copy in Madrid M.383.

805 The little countess was born in 1787, married in 1802 at the age of fifteen, and died in January 1805. See Bibl. 10, no. 49; 20a, no. 105 (catalogued but not exhibited).

806 Inscribed in pencil *El Ministro D.* [blank] *Soler*. The signature *Goya* at lower left is by another hand. Preparatory drawing for the engraving (reproduced) by Rafael Esteve (Bibl. 4, 8981.1).
A letter from Goya to the minister on 9 October 1803 (Bibl. 72, p. 56) apparently refers to a lost portrait of him and to a copy made by Esteve: M.424, DF.428.

807 and 808 Listed by Carderera (Bibl. 148, no. 52). See Bibl. 23, nos XII, XIII; 27, nos 89, 90, for inscriptions on verso of portraits.

809 Listed by Carderera (Bibl. 148, no. 49). The portrait belongs to the Real Academia de Bellas Artes de San Carlos. See Bibl. 23, no. XXXV; 27, no. 91 for discussion of the sitter's identity.
Reduction: 102×74·5 cm. Paris, Stavros S. Niarchos M.225, DF.433, G.520n. Exhibited *The Niarchos Collection*, Arts Council, London, 1958, no. 30.
Copy of the head: 40×30 cm. Paris, G. Neumans M.226, Gaya Nuño 1008 (Bibl. 65).

810-812 Three brothers and sisters, children of the VIth Countess of Montijo.

810 Signed and dated on arm of chair; inscribed *Maria Teresa / Palafox* on palette (error in Prado catalogue). Exhibited at the Academy of San Fernando in 1805 (Bibl. 177).

811 Listed by Carderera (Bibl. 148, no. 58). See Trapier (Bibl. 188, p. 26). At one time attributed by Soria to Esteve (Bibl. 178, no. 62), but not in Bibl. 180. Sambricio considered it certainly by Goya (Bibl. 23, no. IX).

812 See Trapier (Bibl. 188, p. 26).

813 See Cook (Bibl. 51, pp. 156-160) and Trapier (Bibl. 188, pp. 31-32) who dated the portrait c.1807-08. See also Boix (Bibl. 38, pp. 280-281).

815 See the 1970 exhibition catalogue (Bibl. 30, no. 38) for a discussion of the sitter's identity. See also Bibl. 25, no. 117 for the original identification in 1900. According to Cook, the portrait was painted in 1808 (Bibl. 51, p. 161). See note to [III.983a].

816 A niece of Pérez de Castro [815?], she was said by Cook to have been eighteen years old when this portrait was painted in 1808, and to have married Manuel García de la Prada [819] in 1811 (Bibl. 51, p. 161). Trapier recorded that she married a Toledan (Bibl. 188, p. 33).

817 Exhibited at the Academy of San Fernando in 1805 (Bibl. 177). For the discovery of the sitter's real name,

Isabel Lobo de Porcel, see Nigel Glendinning, 'Goya's portrait of Andrés del Peral', *Apollo*, LXXXIX, 1969, p. 202 and n. 36. The portrait of her husband was signed and dated in 1806 [855].

818 Inscribed on block *El Marques de / S.ⁿ Adrian / por Goya 1804*. Listed by Carderera (Bibl. 148, no. 42).

819 He bequeathed to the Academy the five genre panels [III.966-971]. See note to [816].

820 Inscribed at lower left *D.ⁿ Ignacio Garcini por Goya 1804*. See Trapier (Bibl. 188, p. 25).

821 Inscribed at lower right *D.ª Josefa Castilla de/Garcini. p.ʳ Goya. 1804*.

822 The curiously modern appearance of this pendant to [823] is possibly due to heavy restoration. Both portraits were reproduced in *Museum*, III, 1913, pp. 190, 440, as from the collection of D.J.M[ontespines], Valencia.

824 Inscribed at lower right *Alberto Foraster Por Goya 1804*. The portrait was painted over a portrait of Godoy by another hand. See Trapier (Bibl. 188, p. 24).

825 Known until very recently only from an old Moreno photograph, this painting would have been listed as a copy. The original has not been seen by the authors.

826 Inscribed on paper *D.ⁿ Felix de/Azara/P.ʳ Goya./1805*.

827 Inscribed at lower left *D.ⁿ Josef de Vargas. / Por Fran.ᶜᵒ de Goya/año de 1805*. See Sánchez Cantón (Bibl. 162, pp. 23-26) and Trapier (Bibl. 188, p. 30).

828 Inscribed at lower left *D.ª Joaquina Giron, Marquesa de Santa Cruz / Por Goya 1805* (according to the 1928 catalogue, Bibl. 10, no. 54). Listed by Carderera (Bibl. 148, no. 32). She is the little girl at her mother's side in the Osuna family portrait [I.278]. See note to [829].

829 This portrait differs considerably from [828] and its authenticity has been contested by Desparmet and by López-Rey (Bibl. 117, p. 283). See the extensive analysis in *Bulletin of the Art Division - Los Angeles County Museum*, vol. 10, no. 1, 1958, with an answer to López-Rey on p. 26, n. 44, and the latter's 'Letter to the Editor', *Gazette des Beaux-Arts*, LIV, 1959, pp. 287-288.

830 Inscribed at lower left *D.ª Maria Vizenta / Baruso Valdes./P.ʳ Goya año 1805*.

831 Inscribed at lower right *D.ª Leonor Valdes / de Barruso/Por Fr.ᶜᵒ Goya año/1805*.

833 Inscribed on the ground *Clara de Soria de 6 años*. Published, together with [831], by Lafuente (Bibl. 102, pp. 36-37, ill. facing p. 32) giving useful references. See Held (Bibl. 89, no. 104) who dates them c.1805-06.

834 Inscribed on verso *P.D. Pedro Mocarte cantante en la catedral de Toledo. Pinto por Goya su intimo amigo* by another hand. See E. du Gué Trapier, 'Goya's Portrait of Pedro Mocarte, Choir Singer in Toledo Cathedral', *Studies in the History of Art*, 1959, p. 368, and Bibl. 188, pp. 28-29.
Lafuente mentioned a copy by Fortuny (Bibl. 102, pp. 257 and 364, nos 66, 67).

835 The sitter was traditionally identified as the wife of a bookseller in the Calle de las Carretas, and Sánchez Cantón, citing Sambricio (*Arriba*, 31 March 1936), suggested that he might have been Antonio Bailó, who had a shop at no. 4, and who testified on Goya's behalf at his 'purification' in 1814 (see Bibl. 166, pp. 79-80 and Sambricio, Bibl. 154, doc. 234).

836 and 837 Lorenza Correa and Manuel García were two of the most famous singers of their day. The two portraits were sold together in the Vente Salamanca in 1867 (Bibl. 57, II, p. 261), where [837] was described as having come from 'la Galerie de Goya' (i.e. from Javier or Mariano's collection). They have the same dimensions and in style and pose appear to form a pair. They may therefore have been painted by Goya for his own collection, and it is possible the the un-named *Retrato de señora con abanico, medio cuerpo* listed in the Brugada inventory of 1828 (Bibl. 57, II,

Notes continued on page 374

TABLE OF WORKS IN CATALOGUE II   1792-1808

ABBREVIATIONS AND SIGNS

[   ]   Numbers within square brackets refer to the works listed in the catalogue. The number is preceded by a roman numeral (I-V) referring to the section of the book in which the work appears. (This is omitted if the reference is to a work within the same section.)

TITLE

Goya's autograph titles are given in *italics*. Where there is no room for the whole title or its translation in the catalogue legend, it is continued in the note.

DATE

Examples: *1797*   dated by Goya
1797   certain date
1797?   probable date
c.1797   about 1797
1797-99   executed during the period indicated

d.   Dated
Doc.   Date indicated by a document

SIGNATURE

s.   Signed

INSCRIPTION

italics   Title or inscription by Goya
Inscr.   Inscription
/   Change of line in an inscription
MS.   Manuscript

TECHNIQUE

All works are in oil on canvas unless otherwise specified

Aq.   Aquatint
L.   Lithograph

DIMENSIONS

cm.   Centimetres
approx.   Approximately
vis.   Visible dimensions (e.g. where work is partly covered by a mount or frame)
diam.   Diameter

Dimensions of the drawings are those of the sheet of paper.
Dimensions of the engravings are those of the copperplate.

COLLECTION

A.I.   Art Institute
B.M.   British Museum, London
B.N.   Biblioteca Nacional / Bibliothèque Nationale
C.   Calcografía Nacional, Madrid (see Bibl. 5)
Fund. Lázaro   Fundación Lázaro Galdiano, Madrid (the indication M = Museum, B = Biblioteca)
Gal.   Galerie / Gallery
Inst.   Institut / Institute / Instituto
Hispanic Soc.   Hispanic Society of America, New York
K.K.   Kupferstichkabinett (Print room)
Min.   Ministère / Ministerio / Ministry
Mus.   Musée / Museo / Museum (of Fine Arts, unless otherwise indicated)
M.F.A.   Museum of Fine Arts, Boston
M.M.A.   Metropolitan Museum of Art, New York
N.G.   National Gallery
Patr. Nac.   Patrimonio Nacional, Madrid
R.A.   Real Academia / Royal Academy
P. Palais   Petit Palais (Musée des Beaux-Arts de la Ville de Paris)
Rhode Is. S. D. Mus.   Museum of the School of Design, Providence (Rhode Island)

V. and A.   Victoria and Albert Museum, London
coll.   Collection (a capital C indicates a public collection, e.g. Frick Coll., New York)
priv.   Private
destr.   Destroyed

Acquisition or inventory numbers are given in brackets after the name of the collection. See Index of Collections, page 394.

BIBLIOGRAPHICAL REFERENCES

Bibl.   See the numbered Bibliography, page 386. The most frequently used abbreviations are:
B.   Barcia, *Catálogo de la Colección de Dibujos Originales de la Biblioteca Nacional* (Bibl. 3)
D.   Delteil, 'Francisco Goya', *Le Peintre graveur illustré* (Bibl. 55)
DF.   Desparmet Fitz-Gerald, *L'Œuvre peint de Goya* (Bibl. 57)
G.   Gudiol, *Goya* (catalogue raisonné) (Bibl. 85)
H.   Harris, *Goya. Engravings and lithographs* (Bibl. 88)
M.   Mayer, *Francisco de Goya* (Bibl. 128)
S.   Sambricio, *Tapices de Goya* (Bibl. 154)
SC.   Sánchez Cantón, *Museo del Prado: Los dibujos de Goya* (Bibl. 168)

ILLUSTRATION

Ill. p. (or p.)   See the reproduction in the text at the page indicated.

NOTE

*   Reference to a note on the pages preceding the illustrated catalogue.

CATALOGUE II
1792-1808

[317-873a]

CABINET PICTURES
1793-1794

Series of little paintings made during convalescence and sent to Iriarte to be shown to the Academicians.
4 January 1794: Goya's letter to Iriarte referring to his 'set of cabinet pictures'.
5 January: minutes of the Royal Academy recording the presentation of 'eleven paintings . . . of various scenes of national diversions'.
7 January: Goya's letter describing the 'yard with lunatics' [330] which he was still painting and would send 'in order to complete the work'.
In these small pictures Goya said that he had 'managed to make observations for which there is normally no opportunity in commissioned works which give no scope for fantasy and invention'. From the bullfights to the scene which Goya had witnessed in the madhouse at Saragossa [330], they represent the decisive move towards a private art where violence and tragedy were to find such powerful expression.

[317-330] *

317

Bulls rounded up 1793.
Tinplate 42·5×31·5 cm.
Paris, priv. coll.
M.654a, DF.137 *

318

Capture of a bull 1793.
Tinplate 43×31 cm.
Madrid, Marqués de la Torrecilla
M.667a, DF.130, G.273 *

319

Placing the banderillas 1793.
Tinplate 43×31 cm.
Madrid, priv. coll.
M.667d, DF.132, G.274 p.110

320

Clearing the bullring 1793.
Tinplate 43×31 cm.
Madrid, priv. coll.
M.667b, DF.131, G.275

321

A pass with the cape 1793.
Tinplate 43×31 cm.
Madrid, priv. coll.
M.667c, DF.133, G.276

322

Picador caught by the bull 1793.
Tinplate 40×30 cm.
New York, Cotnareanu
M.660, DF.136, G.277 p. 110 *

323

Matador killing the bull 1793.
Tinplate 43×32 cm.
Madrid, Duquesa de Cardona
M.667e, DF.134, G.278

324

Mules dragging off the bull
1793. Tinplate 43×32 cm.
Seville, Duquesa de Medinaceli
M.667f, DF.135, G.279

325

Strolling players 1793. Inscr.
ALEG. MEN Tinplate 43×32 cm.
Madrid, Prado (3045)
M.621, DF.128, G.344 p. 110 *

326

Marionette seller 1793.
Tinplate 42×32 cm.
Switzerland, priv. coll.
M.646, DF.189 Ill. p. 110 *

327

Brigands attacking a coach
1793-94. Tinplate 50×32 cm.
Madrid, Marqués de Castro Serna
M.601, DF.127, G.347 *

328

The shipwreck or The flood
1793-94. Tinplate 50×32 cm.
Madrid, Marqués de Oquendo
M.688, DF.126, G.346 *

329

The fire at night 1793-94.
Tinplate 50×32 cm.
San Sebastian, José Várez
M.689, DF.129, G.345 *

330

Corral de locos Doc. Jan. 1794.
Tinplate 43·8×32·7 cm.
Dallas, Meadows Mus.
M.695, G.343 Ill. p. 111 *

PORTRAITS 1792-1797

The series includes some of Goya's finest portraits of women: 'La Tirana' [340], the Marquesa de la Solana [341] and the Duchess of Alba [351, 355]. Physical and spiritual presence of the model, the 'magical effect of atmosphere', and a virtuosity of touch which makes light of difficulties. Contrast between the inspired portraits and the ordinary official commissions.

[331-355]

331

Self-portrait in the studio
c.1790-95. 42×28 cm.
Madrid, Condesa de Villagonzalo
M.293, DF.352, G.96 p. 63 *

332

Self-portrait in a cocked hat
c.1785-95.
Pen and sepia ink 10×8·7 cm.
New York, Coll. Lehman *

333

Sebastián Martínez   s.d. *1792*
with inscr.   92·9×67·6 cm.
New York, M.M.A. (06.289)
M.339, DF.350, G.310   p.107   *

334

Juan Agustín Ceán Bermúdez
c.1792-93.   122×88 cm.
Madrid, Marqués de Perinat
M.235, DF.391, G.318   *

335

The wife of Ceán Bermúdez(?)
c.1792-93.   121×84·5 cm.
Budapest, Museum (3792)
M.236, DF.329, G.319   *

336

Tadea Arias de Enríquez
c.1793-94.   190×106 cm.
Madrid, Prado (740)
M.251, DF.355, G.339   *

337

General Antonio Ricardos
1793-94.   112×84 cm.
Madrid, Prado (2784)
[M.398], DF.305, G.328   *

338

General Antonio Ricardos
c.1794.   225×150 cm.
Seville, Marqués de Valencia del
Alcor   G.329   *

339

Felix Colón de Larriategui
d.*1794*, inscr.   110·7×84·1 cm.
Indianapolis, estate of J. K. Lilley
M.239, DF.356, G.331   *

340

María del Rosario Fernández
'La Tirana'   s.d. *1794* with inscr.
112×79 cm.   Madrid, Juan March
M.433, DF.358, G.330   *

341

Marquesa de la Solana
c.1794-95.   183×124 cm.
Paris, Louvre (Beistegui)
M.423, DF.414, G.341   *

342

Ramón Posada y Soto   s.   179·
113×87·5 cm.   San Francisco,
De Young Memorial Mus. (K.197:
M.392, DF.426, G.342

343

Marqués de Sofraga   c.1795.
108·3×82·6 cm.
San Diego, Fine Arts Gall. (38.244)
G.337   *

344

Equestrian sketch of Manuel
Godoy(?)   c.1794-95.
55·2×44·5 cm.
Dallas, Meadows Mus.   G.332   *

345

Francisco Bayeu   Aug.1795.
112×84 cm.
Madrid, Prado (721)
M.211, DF.357, G.335   *

346

Gil de Tejada   c.1794-95(?)
112×84 cm.
Madrid, Duque del Infantado
M.431, G.453   *

347

Juan José Arias de Saavedra
c.1794-95(?)   82×55 cm.
Madrid, Conde de Cienfuegos
G.409   *

348

Marquesa viuda de Villafranca
c.1795.   87×72 cm.
Madrid, Prado (2447)
M.445, DF.309/313, G.444   *

349

Duque de Alba   c.1795.
86·3×68·5 cm.
Chicago, Chauncey McCormick
M.192, DF.345, G.[336]   *

350

Duque de Alba   1795.   Inscr.
195×126 cm.
Madrid, Prado (2449)
M.191, DF.346, G.333   *

351

Duquesa de Alba   s.d. *1795*
with inscr.   194×130 cm.
Madrid, Alba Coll.
M.193, DF.361, G.334   *

Two little pictures of 1795 suggest the charm and liveliness of the duchess's ways. The traditional identification of the figures in a third painting as Goya and the duchess is unconvincing. After the light-hearted mood of the 1795 pictures and the Sanlúcar sketches of the following year [356-376], the magnificent and enigmatic 'Solo Goya' portrait of 1797 [355].

352

Duchess of Alba and her duenna
s.d. *Goya año 1795.* 31×25 cm.
Madrid, Berganza de Martín
M.699, DF.180, G.368 *

353

The duenna with two children
s.d. *1795* with inscr. 31×25 cm.
Madrid, Berganza de Martín
M.700, DF.181, G.367 *

354

Coloquio galante (The flirtation)
c.1793-97. 41×31 cm.
Madrid, Marqués de la Romana
M.306a, DF.182, G.324 *

355

Duquesa de Alba s.d. *1797*
with inscr. 210·2×149·3 cm.
New York, Hispanic Soc.(A.102)
M.194, DF.374, G.371 p. 115 *

SANLÚCAR ALBUM - A
1796-1797

Goya's first series of private drawings, made during his stay with the Duchess of Alba at her Sanlúcar estate, probably during the summer of 1796. The duchess appears in several of these intimate little scenes, as do various members of her entourage. The figures are sometimes awkwardly drawn, but are full of life and movement.
Eight sheets from the sketchbook are known, with drawings on both sides [356-371]. Another possible sheet is listed [372/373]. In addition, a number of copies are known, probably made by Carderera and including three drawings of which Goya's

originals are unknown [374-376]. The eighteen drawings are in brush and Indian ink wash; size of the uncut sheets 17·2×10·1 cm. Drawings related to the *Caprichos* etchings are indicated in the notes.

Abbreviations and signs, see p. 168.
LR = López-Rey, Bibl. 115, II, fig.
SC = Sánchez Cantón, Bibl. 168
ES = Eleanor Sayre, Bibl. 172, fig.

[356-376] *

356 A[a] recto of 357

The Duchess of Alba 1796-97.
Indian ink wash 17×9·7 cm.
Madrid, B.N. (B.1270)
LR.1 Ill. p. 117 *

357 A[b] verso of 356

Young woman lifting up her skirts Indian ink wash
See [356] LR.2, ES.12

358 A[c] recto of 359

The Duchess of Alba tearing her hair 1796-97.
Indian ink wash 17·1×10·1 cm.
Madrid, B.N. (B.1271) LR.7 *

359 A[d] verso of 358

Young woman bathing at a fountain Indian ink wash
See [358] LR.8

360 A[e] recto of 361

The Duchess of Alba... 1796-97.
Indian ink wash 10·6×9·2 cm.
(vis.) Madrid, Prado (426)
SC.221, LR.5 Ill. p. 117 *

361 A[f] verso of 360

Girl dancing to a guitar
Indian ink wash See [360]
Prado (468) SC.220, LR.6

362 A[g] recto of 363

Maja on the paseo 1796-97.
Indian ink wash 10·6×8·9 cm.
(vis.) Madrid, Prado (466)
SC.216, LR.3

363 A[h] verso of 362

The siesta Indian ink wash
See [362] Prado (428)
SC.217, LR.4

364 A[i] recto of 365

Young woman with arms uplifted 1796-97. Indian ink wash
10·6×9·2 cm. (vis.)
Madrid, Prado (427) SC.219, LR.9

365 A[j] verso of 364

Young woman pulling up her stocking Indian ink wash
See [364] Prado (467)
SC.218, LR.10 *

366 A[k] recto of 367

Two young women naked on a bed 1796-97. Indian ink wash 17·2×10·1 cm. Formerly Rome, Clementi LR.11, ES.10

367 A[l] verso of 366

Old woman tending a girl on a bed Indian ink wash
See [366] LR.12

368 A[m] recto of 369

Young woman arranging her hair beside another woman on a bed 1796-97. Indian ink wash 17·2×10·1 cm. Paris, priv. coll.

369   A[n]   verso of 368

Young woman sweeping
Indian ink wash   See [368]   *

370   A[o]   recto of 371

Woman weeping behind a
carriage   1796-97.
Indian ink wash 17·2×10·1 cm.
Paris, priv. coll.

371   A[p]   verso of 370

Majas sitting on the paseo
Indian ink wash   See [370]   *

372   A[q]   recto of 373

The Duchess of Alba with hand
raised   1796-97.
Indian ink wash 17·1×8·8 cm.
Rotterdam, Boymans Mus. (S.2)   *

373   A[r]   verso of 372

Group of shepherds(?)
Indian ink wash
See [372]

374   A [copy a]

The Duchess of Alba writing
Inscr.   Indian ink wash
19·4×12·7 cm.   Madrid,
Fund. Lázaro (M.I-10, 619)   *

375   A [copy b]

Standing nude woman
Indian ink wash 20·1×11·5 cm.
Madrid, Prado (485)   *

376   A [copy c]

Woman fainting in an officer's
arms   s. Goya.
Indian ink wash 20×10·7 cm.
Madrid, Prado (487)   *

MADRID ALBUM - B
1796-1797

Larger and much more ambitious
album. The drawings, again
recto and verso on the sheets
and this time numbered, show the
rapid evolution of Goya's ideas
and technique leading up to the
Caprichos etchings, many of
which were based on drawings in
the album.   Titles appear on the
drawings from number 55 [415]
onwards: Goya adds his ironic
commentary to the caricature.
Thirty-seven sheets with seventy-
four drawings are known, the
highest page number being 94.
Drawn with the brush and Indian
ink, the designs are sometimes
retouched with the pen and sepia
ink, especially when the pen was

used to add or alter a manuscript
title. These retouches are not
indicated in the catalogue, but the
use of the pen for the titles is
indicated in the notes. Size of
the uncut sheets 23·7×14·8 cm.
Drawings related to the Caprichos
etchings are indicated in the
notes.

Abbreviations and signs, see p. 16
LR = López-Rey, Bibl. 115, II, fig
SC = Sánchez Cantón, Bibl. 168
ES = Eleanor Sayre, Bibl. 172, fig
W = Wehle, Bibl. 192, fig.

[377-450]

377   B.3   recto of 378

Couple making love in the dark
1796-97.   Indian ink wash
23·6×14·7 cm.   Hamburg,
Kunsthalle (38544)   ES.14   *

378   B.4   verso of 377

Maja and celestina waiting under
an arch   Indian ink wash
See [377]   LR.33   *

379   B.5?   recto of 380

Majas on the paseo   1796-97.
Indian ink wash 23·4×14·5 cm.
Madrid, B.N. (B.1262)   LR.30   *

380   B.6?   verso of 379

Old woman begging from a maja
Indian ink wash   See [379]
LR.29   *

381   B.7   recto of 382

Picnic in the country   1796-97.
Indian ink wash 21·9×13·3 cm.
(vis.)   Madrid, Prado (464)
SC.223, LR.13

382   B.8   verso of 381

Maja and man with tricorn
Inscr.   Indian ink wash
See [381]   Prado (422)
SC.222, LR.14   *

383   B.13   recto of 384

Two women embracing
1796-97.   Indian ink wash
22·2×14·6 cm.   Princeton,
University Art Mus.   LR.15

384   B.14   verso of 383

Maja parading in front of three
others   Indian ink wash
See [383]   LR.16

385   B.15   recto of 386

Majo laughing as two girls fight
1796-97.   Indian ink wash
22·8×14 cm.   New York,
Hispanic Soc. (A.3309)   ES.15

386   B.16   verso of 385

Majas and majos conversing
Indian ink wash   See [385]
Hispanic Soc. (A.3310)

87 B.*17* recto of 388	388 B.*18* verso of 387	389 B.*19* recto of 390	390 B.*20* verso of 389	391 B.*21* recto of 392

Weeping woman and three men 1796-97. Indian ink wash 3·5×14·6 cm. New York, M.M.A. (35.103.4) LR.17, W.I *	A maja and two companions Indian ink wash See [387] M.M.A. (35.103.5) LR.18, W.II	Gallant quizzing a maja 1796-97. Indian ink wash 21·9×13·5 cm. (vis.) Madrid, Prado (424) SC.5, LR.19 Ill. p. 127 *	Maja standing before three companions Indian ink wash See [389] Prado (462) SC.D, LR.20 *	The swing 1796-97. Indian ink wash 23·7×14·6 cm. New York, M.M.A. (35.103.2) LR.21, ES.16, W.III *

92 B.*22* verso of 391	393 B.*23* recto of 394	394 B.*24* verso of 393	395 B.*25* recto of 396	396 B.*26* verso of 395

Maja and an officer Indian ink wash See [391] M.M.A. (35.103.3) LR.22, W.IV	Girl and bull 1796-97. Indian ink wash 23·5×14·6 cm. New York, M.M.A. (35.103.7) LR.23, W.V	Lovers sitting on a rock 1796-97. Indian ink wash See [393] M.M.A. (35.103.6) LR.24, W.VI	Maid combing a young woman's hair 1796-97. Indian ink wash 23·4×14·5 cm. Madrid, B.N. (B.1263) LR.25 *	Naked woman holding a mirror or After the bath Indian ink wash See [395] LR.26 *

97 B.*27* recto of 398	398 B.*28* verso of 397	399 B.*31* recto of 400	400 B.*32* verso of 399	401 B.*33* recto of 402

Concert at the clavichord 1796-97. Indian ink wash Madrid, Prado (425) SC.224, LR.27	Group of majas on the paseo Indian ink wash See [397] Prado (469) SC.225, LR.28	Corner of a tertulia 1796-97. Indian ink wash Madrid, Prado (429) SC.226, LR.31	Encounter on the paseo Indian ink wash See [399] Prado (465) SC.227, LR.32	Young woman running up steps to see soldiers 1796-97. Indian ink wash 23·7×14·7 cm. Zurich, Anton Schrafl p. 121 *

02 B.*34* verso of 401	403 B.*35* recto of 404	404 B.*36* verso of 403	405 B.*37* recto of 406	406 B.*38* verso of 405

Young man beating a girl Indian ink wash See [401]	Woman holding up her dying lover 1796-97. Indian ink wash 23·6×14·6 cm. Cambridge (Mass.), Philip Hofer ES.17 *	Couple conversing on the paseo Indian ink wash See [403] ES.18	Couple with a parasol on the paseo 1796-97. Indian ink wash 22×13·4 cm. Hamburg, Kunsthalle (38545)	Two majas parading on the paseo Indian ink wash See [405] LR.34

407 B.*39* recto of 408

Gallant with two majas in a park
1796-97. Indian ink wash
21·6×13 cm. (vis.) New York,
Benjamin Sonnenberg ES.19

408 B.*40* verso of 407

Majo watching a petimetre bowing
Indian ink wash
See [407] ES.20 *

409 B.*43* recto of 410

Seated maja . . . 1796-97.
Indian ink wash 23·3×14·5 cm.
Cambridge (Mass.), Fogg
Mus. (1943.551.a) LR.35 *

410 B.*44* verso of 409

Young woman taking an infant
from a nurse Indian ink wash
See [409] Fogg (1943.551.b)
LR.36

411 B.*45* recto of 412

Three washerwomen 1796-97.
Indian ink wash 23·5×14·6 cm.
New York, M.M.A. (35.103.8)
LR.37, W.VII

412 B.*46* verso of 411

Girl at a well Indian ink wash
See [411] M.M.A. (35.103.9)
LR.38, W.VIII,

413 B.*49* recto of 414

Young woman with a potbellied
man 1796-97.
Indian ink wash 23·6×14·6 cm.
Formerly Rome, Clementi LR.39

414 B.*50* verso of 413

Young woman wringing her hands
over a man's body Indian ink
wash See [413] LR.40

415 B.*55* recto of 416

Mascaras /crueles (Masks, cruel
ones) 1796-97.
Indian ink wash 23·7×15 cm.
Paris, priv. coll. Ill. p. 119 *

416 B.*56* verso of 415

Brujas á bolar (Witches, about
to fly) Indian ink wash
See [415] Ill. p. 120

417 B.*57* recto of 418

*La tia chorriones enciende la
Óguera / Brujas á recoger*
1796-97. Indian ink wash
Coll. unknown *

418 B.*58* verso of 417

*Caricat.ˢ / Le pide cuentas la
muger al marido* (Caricatures. . . .)
Indian ink wash See [417] *

419 B.*59?* recto of 420

Masc.ˢ / La apunta p.ʳ ermafrodita
1796-97. Indian ink wash
20·9×12·5 cm. Paris,
Louvre (1870.6914) LR.45 *

420 B.*60?* verso of 419

Parten la Vieja (They are cutting
the old woman in two)
Indian ink wash See [419]
LR.46 Ill. p. 121 *

421 B.*61* recto of 422

Caricat.ˢ / Es dia de su Santo
1796-97. Indian ink wash
23·5×14·6 cm. Paris,
Louvre (1870.6912) LR.41 *

422 B.*62* verso of 421

Caricatura /d[e] las carracas
(Caricature of the old crocks or
carracans) Indian ink wash
See [421] LR.42, ES.21 *

423 B.*63* recto of 424

Caricatura alegre (Merry
caricature) 1796-97. Indian
ink wash 19×13 cm. (vis.) Madrid,
Prado (443) SC.20, LR.43 *

424 B.*64* verso of 423

Aguarda q.ᵉ benga (She is
waiting for him to come)
Indian ink wash See [423]
Prado (452) SC.212, LR.44

425 B.*65* recto of 426

Cantan para el q.ᵉ lo hizo
(They are singing . . .) 1796-97.
Indian ink wash 23·3×14·6 cm.
Lille, priv. coll. Ill. p. 118 *

426 B.*66* verso of 425

Sueña de un tesoro
(She is dreaming of a treasure)
Indian ink wash See [425]

427 B.*67* recto of 428

Se emborrachan (They are getting drunk) 1796-97. Indian ink wash 23·5×14·6 cm. New York, M.M.A. (35.103.11) LR.47, W.IX

428 B.*68* verso of 427

Tuto parola e busia / El Charlatan q.ᵉ arranca una quijada y lo / creen Indian ink wash See [427] M.M.A. (35.103.10) LR.48, W.X *

429 B.*69* recto of 430

Solo p.ʳ q.ᵉ le pregunta, si esta buena su Madre . . . 1796-97. Indian ink wash 23·4×14·6 cm. Switzerland, priv. coll.   *

430 B.*70* verso of 429

Confianza (Trust) Indian ink wash   See [429]

431 B.*71* recto of 432

lo mismo (the same) 1796-97. Indian ink wash 23·7×14·4 cm. Switzerland, priv. coll.   *

432 B.*72* verso of 431

Mascaras de B. / Tambien ay mascaras de Borricos / Literatos (Masquerades of A[sses] . . .) Indian ink wash   See [431] *

433 B.*75* recto of 434

Humildad contra soberbia 1796-97. Indian ink wash 23·5×14·6 cm. New York, M.M.A. (35.103.13) LR.49, W.XI *

434 B.*76* verso of 433

Largueza contra Abaricia Indian ink wash   See [433] M.M.A. (35.103.12) LR.50, W.XII   *

435 B.*77* recto of 436

Los hermanos de ella . . . 1796-97. Indian ink wash 23·6×14·7 cm. New York, M.M.A. (35.103.14) LR.51, W.XIII   *

436 B.*78* verso of 435

An echo subir al confesor por la bentana Indian ink wash See [435] M.M.A. (35.103.15) LR.52, W.XIV   *

437 B.*79* recto of 438

Tiene cortedad de desnudarse, . . . 1796-97. Indian ink wash 23·2×14·1 cm. San Francisco, William M. Roth ES.22   *

438 B.*80* verso of 437

Mascaras de semana santa del año de 94 (Masquerades of Holy Week . . .) Indian ink wash See [437] ES.23 Ill. p. 118 *

439 B.*81* recto of 440

Jesus q.ᵉ Aire (Lord what a wind) 1796-97. Indian ink wash 23·6×14·7 cm. Paris, priv. coll. LR.53   *

440 B.*82* verso of 439

Pobres, ¡quantas lo mereceran mejor? ¡pues q.ᵉ es esto? . . . Indian ink wash   See [439] LR.54   *

441 B.*83* recto of 442

Las miedosas á un Gato muy negro 1796-97. Indian ink wash 23·6×14·7 cm. Belgium, priv. coll. ·   *

442 B.*84* verso of 441

.n Fernando ¡como hilan! (San Fernando - how they spin!) Indian ink wash   See [441] *

443 B.*85* recto of 444

Es berano y a la luna, toman el fresco, . . . 1796-97. Indian ink wash 23·6×14·5 cm. Formerly Rome, Clementi LR.55   *

444 B.*86* verso of 443

Buen sacerdote ¿donde se ha celebrado? (Good priest, . . .) Indian ink wash   See [443] LR.56, ES.11   *

445 B.*87* recto of 446

¿Ay Pulgas? (Are there fleas?) 1796-97. Indian ink wash 23·7×14·7 cm. New York, Hispanic Soc. (A.3316)

446 B.*88* verso of 445

Buena Jente, somos los / Moralistas (What good people we moralists are) Indian ink wash   See [445] Hispanic Soc. (A.3317)   *

447   B.*89* recto of 448

El Abogado. / Este a nadie perdona,
pero no es ...   1796-97.
Indian ink wash 21·6×12·7 cm.
London, priv. coll.   LR.57   *

448   B.*90* verso of 447

Nobia Discreta y arrepentida a
sus Padres / se presenta en esta
forma   Indian ink wash
See [447]   LR.58   *

449   B.*93* recto of 450

Conocélos el aceitero ...   1796-97.
Indian ink wash 23·5×14·6 cm.
New York, M.M.A. (35.103.17)
LR.59, W.XV   *

450   B.*94* verso of 449

Manda q.ᵉ quiten el coche, se
despeina, ...   Indian ink wash
See [459]   M.M.A. (35.103.16)
LR.60, W.XVI   *

**LOS CAPRICHOS
(The Caprices) Drawn and
engraved 1797-1798**

Eighty plates first published by
Goya in 1799 and combining
scenes of witchcraft with social
satire. The series grew out of the
caricatures in the Madrid Album
[377-450] and many of the
designs are directly based on
these drawings. In the prints
the dream-like and dramatic
quality of the etchings of Tiepolo
and Piranesi are combined with
the gross humour of contemporary satirical prints.

Seventy-nine preparatory drawings
are known for the eighty
published plates. They are in
three techniques: pen and sepia

ink, red chalk and sanguine
wash. The pen and ink drawings
were made as a series to be
entitled *Sueños* (Dreams) and
were numbered accordingly.
Sueño 1 became plate 43 [536].
The engraved titles are reproduced
textually in the catalogue legends.
Preparatory drawings are
reproduced after the engravings,
and the manuscript numbers on
the *Sueño* drawings are indicated
in the same way as the engraved
numbers on the prints. Drawings
from the Sanlúcar and Madrid
albums which were used for the
Caprichos designs are also shown.
Unique proofs and additional
drawings are reproduced after
the eighty published plates - see
[614-628]

Twelve editions were printed
from the original copperplates
between 1799 and 1937.
The copperplates are in the
Calcografía Nacional, Madrid,
and their dimensions are given in
the catalogue legends (Bibl. 5,
Goya, 1-80).

All the plates are in etching
and/or aquatint; drypoint and
burin retouches are not mentioned.

Abbreviations and signs, see p. 168
Aq. = aquatint
D = Delteil, Bibl. 55
H = Harris, Bibl. 88
SC = Sánchez Cantón, Bibl. 168

[451-613]   *

451   Cap. *P.1.*

Fran.ᶜᵒ Goya y Lucientes, / Pintor.
1797-98.   Etching and
aquatint 21·9×15·2 cm.
D.38, H.36   Ill. p. 103   *

452   recto of 453

Drawing for [451].
Red chalk 17·8×12·7 cm.
New York, Walter C. Baker   *

453   verso of 452

Studies for [451]?
See [452]   *

454   Cap. *P.2.*

El si pronuncian y la mano
alargan / Al primero que llega.
1797-98.   Etching and aq.
21·8×15·4 cm.   D.39, H.37   *

455   Cap. *P.3.*

Que viene el Coco. (Here comes
the bogey-man)   1797-98.
Etching and aquatint
21·7×15·3 cm.   D.40, H.38

456

Drawing for [455].
Red chalk
Madrid, Prado (48)   SC.1

457   Cap. *P.4.*

El de la rollona. (Nanny's boy)
1797-98.   Etching and
aquatint 20·7×15·1 cm.
D.41, H.39

458

Drawing for [457].
Red chalk
Madrid, Prado (49)   SC.4

459   Cap. *P.5.*

Tal para qual. (Two of a kind)
1797-98.   Etching and
aquatint 20×15·1 cm.
D.42, H.40

460   Sueño *19*

Las viejas se salen de risa ...
Drawing for [459].   Pen and
sepia ink, Indian ink wash
Madrid, Prado (27)   SC.3   *

461   Cap. *P.6.*

Nadie se conoce. (Nobody
knows anybody)   1797-98.
Etching and aq. 12·8×15·3 cm.
D.43, H.41   Ill. p. 131

462   recto of 538

Drawing for [461].   Red chalk
Madrid, Prado (471)   SC.4

463 Cap.7.

Ni asi la distingue. (Even so he
cannot make her out) 1797-98.
. Goya Etching and aquatint
20×15 cm.   D.44, H.42   p. 127

464 Sueño *21*

Por aberle yo dicho, q.ᵉ tenia . . .
Drawing for [463].   Pen and
sepia ink, Indian ink wash
Madrid, Prado (29) SC.6 p.127 *

Madrid Album B.19 - see [389]

465 Cap.*8.*

Que se la llevaron! (They
carried her off!) 1797-98.
Etching and aq. 21·7×15·2 cm.
D.45, H.43   Ill. p. 128

466

Drawing for [465].
Sanguine wash
Madrid, Prado (93)   SC.17

Madrid Album B.61 - see [421]

467 Cap.*9.*

Tantalo. (Tantalus) 1797-98.
Etching and aquatint
20·8×15·1 cm.   D.46, H.44

468

Drawing for [467].   Red chalk
Madrid, Prado (51)   SC.8

469 Cap.*10*

El amor y la muerte. (Love and
death) 1797-98.   Etching and
aquatint 21·8×15·3 cm.
D.47, H.45

470

Drawing for [469].   Red chalk
Madrid, Prado (50)   SC.18

471

Drawing for [469].
Sanguine wash
Madrid, Prado (92)   SC.7

Madrid Album B.35 - see [403]

472 Cap.*11.*

Muchachos al avío. (Lads
getting on with the job)
1797-98.   Etching and aquatint
21·5×15 cm.   D.48, H.46   *

473 Sueño *28.*

Los Mercaderes silbestres.
(Rustic traders)   Drawing for
[472].   Pen and sepia ink
Madrid, Prado (19)   SC.23   *

474 Cap.*12.*

A caza de dientes. (Out hunting
for teeth) 1797-98.
Etching and aquatint
21·8×15·1 cm.   D.49, H.47

475 recto of 604

Drawing for [474].   Red chalk
Madrid, Prado (438)   SC.19

476 Cap.*13.*

Estan calientes. (They are
hot-headed) 1797-98.
Etching and aquatint
21·8×15·4 cm.   D.50, H.48

477 Sueño *25.*

*Sueño / De unos hombres q.ᵉ se
nos comian.*   Drawing for [476].
Pen and sepia ink
Madrid, Prado (20)   SC.21   *

478

Drawing for [476].
Sanguine wash
Madrid, Prado (94)   SC.174

Madrid Album B.63 - see [423]

479   Cap.14.

Que sacrificio! (What a sacrifice!)   1797-98.
s. *Goya.*   Etching and aquatint
20·1×15·1 cm.   D.51, H.49

480   Sueño 15.

Sacrificio del Ynteres (Sacrifice of interest)   Drawing for [479].
Pen and sepia ink
Madrid, Prado (22)   SC.24   *

481   Cap.15.

Bellos consejos. (Fine advice)
1797-98.   Etching and aquatint
21·8×15·3 cm.   D.52, H.50
Ill. p. 17

482

Drawing for [481].
Red chalk 19·5×12·9 cm.
Madrid, Prado (484)   *

Sanlúcar Album A [p] - see [371]

483   Cap.16.

Dios la perdone: Y era su madre.
('So sorry'...)   1797-98.
Etching and aquatint 20×15 cm.
D.53, H.51   *

484   Sueño ?

Se aberguenza de q.ᵉ su Madre le able ...   Drawing for [483].
Pen and sepia ink, Indian wash
Madrid, Prado (28)   SC.9   *

Madrid Album B.6 - see [380]

485   Cap.17.

Bien tirada está. (It is well pulled up)   1797-98.   Etching and aquatint 21·8×15·3 cm.
D.54, H.52

486

Drawing for [485].   Red chalk
Madrid, Prado (52)   SC.10

Sanlúcar Album A [j] - see [365]

487   Cap.18.

Ysele quema la Casa. (And his house is on fire)   1797-98.
Etching and aquatint
21·8×15·4 cm.   D.55, H.53

488   Sueño ?

Espartero Borracho q.ᵉ no acierta a desnudarse ...   Drawing for
[487].   Pen and sepia ink
Madrid, Prado (21)   SC.12   *

Madrid Album B.86 - see [444]

489   Cap.19.

Todos Caerán. (All will fall)
1797-98.   Etching and aquatint
21·9×14·5 cm.   D.56, H.54   *

490

Drawing for [489].   Red chalk
Madrid, Prado (53)   SC.13

491   Cap.20.

Ya van desplumados. (There they go plucked)   1797-98
Etching and aquatint
21·7×15·2 cm.   D.57, H.55   *

492   recto of 633

Drawing for [491].   Red chalk
Madrid, Prado (434)   SC.14

493

Drawing for [491].
Sanguine wash
Madrid, Prado (95)   SC.15

494 Cap.*21.*

¡Qual la descañonan! (How they pluck her!) 1797-98. Etching and aquatint 21·7×14·8 cm. D.58, H.56.

495

Drawing for [494]. Sanguine wash Madrid, Prado (104) SC.11

496 Cap.*22.*

Pobrecitas! (Poor little things!) 1797-98. Etching and aquatint 21·8×15·2 cm. D.59, H.57

497

Drawing for [496]. Red chalk Madrid, Prado (54) SC.16

Madrid Album B.82 - see [440]

498 Cap.*23.*

Aquellos polbos. (That dust) 1797-98. Etching and aquatint 21·7×14·8 cm. D.60, H.58 *

Drawing for additional plate - see [615]

499 Cap.*24.*

Nohubo remedio. (There was no remedy) 1797-98. Etching and aquatint 21·7×15·2 cm. D.61, H.59

500 Cap.*25.*

Si quebró el Cantaro. (But he broke the pitcher) 1797-98. Etching and aquatint 20·7×15·2 cm. D.62, H.60

501

Drawing for [500]. Red chalk Madrid, Prado (55) SC.25

502 Cap.*26.*

Ya tienen asiento. (Now they are sitting pretty) 1797-98. Etching and aquatint 21·7×15·2 cm. D.63, H.61 *

503

Drawing for [502]. Red chalk Madrid, Prado (56) SC.27

504 Cap.*27.*

Quien mas rendido? (Which is the more overcome?) 1797-98. s. *Goya* Etching and aquatint 19·5×15 cm. D.64, H.62

505 Sueño *18.*

Antiguo y moderno, Origen del orgullo Drawing for [504]. Pen and sepia ink Madrid, Prado (23) SC.26 *

Madrid Album B.40 - see [408]

506 Cap.*28.*

Chiton. (Hush) 1797-98. Etching and aquatint 21·8×15·2 cm. D.65, H.63

507

Drawing for [506]. Red chalk Madrid, Prado (57) SC.28

508 Cap.*29.*

Esto si que es leer. (This certainly is reading) 1797-98. Etching and aquatint 21·5×15 cm. D.66, H.64

509

Drawing for [508]. Red chalk Madrid, Prado (58) SC.29

510 Cap.*30.*

Porque esconderlos? (Why hide them?) 1797-98. Etching and aquatint 21·8×15·2 cm. D.67, H.65

511   recto of 512

Drawing for [510].   Red chalk
Madrid, Prado (445)   SC.30

512   verso of 511

Sketches for [510].   Red chalk
See [511].
Prado (450)   SC.458

513   Cap.*31.*

Ruega por ella. (She prays for her)
1797-98.
Etching and aquatint
20·8×15·2 cm.   D.68, H.66

514

Drawing for [513].   Red chalk
Madrid, Prado (59)   SC.32

Madrid Album B.25 - see [395]

515   Cap.*32.*

Por que fue sensible. (Because
she was susceptible)   1797-98.
Aquatint 21·8×15·2 cm.
D.69, H.67   *

516

Drawing for [515].
Red chalk and sanguine wash
Madrid, Prado (106)   SC.16B

517   Cap.*33.*

Al Conde Palatino. (To the Count
Palatine)   1797-98.
Etching and aquatint
21·8×15·2 cm.   D.70, H.68   *

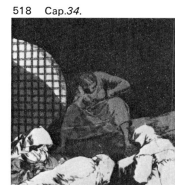

Madrid Album B.68 - see [428]

518   Cap.*34.*

Las rinde el Sueño. (Sleep over-
comes them)   1797-98.
Etching and aquatint
21·8×15·3 cm.   D.71, H.69   *

519

Drawing for [518].
Red chalk with Indian ink and
sepia wash
Madrid, Prado (440)   SC.31   *

520   Cap.*35.*

Le descañona. (She fleeces him)
1797-98.
Etching and aquatint
21·7×15·3 cm.   D.72, H.70   *

521   Cap.*36.*

Mala noche. (A bad night)
1797-98.
Etching and aquatint
21·8×15·2 cm.   D.73, H.71   *

Series of six satirical plates
representing asses. The theme first
appeared in the drawings of the
Madrid album.

[522-535]

522   Cap.*37.*

Si sabrá mas el discipulo?
(What if the pupil knows more?)
1797-98.   Etching and aquatint
21·6×15·4 cm.   D.74, H.72

523

Drawing for [522].   Red chalk
Madrid, Prado (107)   SC.16A

524   Cap.*38.*

Brabisimo! (Bravissimo!)
1797-98.
Etching and aquatint
21·8×15·2 cm.   D.75, H.73

525

Drawing for [524].   Red chalk
Madrid, Prado (60)   SC.34

526   Cap.*39.*

Asta su Abuelo. (As far back
as his grandfather)   1797-98.
Aquatint 21·5×15 cm.
D.76, H.74

527

Drawing for [526].
Red chalk and sanguine wash
Madrid, Prado (96)   SC.35

528 Sueño ?

El Asno Literato (The Literate Ass) Drawing for [526].
Pen and sepia ink
Madrid, Prado (25)   SC.36   *

Madrid Album B.72 - see [432]

529 Cap.40.

De que mal morira? (Of what ill will he die?) 1797-98.
Etching and aquatint
21·7×15·1 cm.   D.77, H.75

530

Drawing for [529].
Red chalk and sanguine wash
Madrid, Prado (97)   SC.38

531 Sueño 27.

Brujas disfrazadas en fisicos comunes. Drawing for [529].
Pen and sepia ink
Madrid, Prado (26)   SC.37   *

---

532 Cap.41.

Ni mas ni menos. (Neither more nor less) 1797-98.
Etching and aquatint 20×15 cm.
D.78, H.76

533

No moriras /de ambre (You will not die of hunger)
Drawing for [532].   Red chalk
Madrid, Prado (61)   SC.39   *

534 Cap.42.

Tu que no puedes. (Thou who canst not) 1797-98.
Etching and aq. 21·7×15·1 cm.
D.79, H.77   Ill. p. 130   *

535

Drawing for [534].
Red chalk and sanguine wash
Madrid, Prado (98)   SC.40

The *Dream of reason* [536] is the design which Goya originally drew as a frontispiece [537] to his projected series of *Dreams*, to be entitled *Universal language*. The etched plate, placed near the middle of the *Caprichos* series, introduces the scenes of witches and demons which predominate in the second half.
It is the only plate where the title is 'written' by Goya himself, within the design.

---

536 Cap.43.

El sueño/de la razon/produce/monstruos. 1797-98.
Etching and aq. 21·6×15·2 cm.
D.80, H.78   Ill. p. 125   *

537 Sueño 1.º

Ydioma univer/sal. ... /año 1797 // El Autor soñando ... Drawing for [536].   Pen and sepia ink
Madrid, Prado (34)   SC.41   *

538 verso of 462

Drawing for [536].
Pen and sepia ink
Madrid, Prado (470)   SC.42

539 Cap.44.

Hilan delgado. (They spin finely)
1797-98.   Etching and aquatint
21·8×15·4 cm.   D.81, H.79

540

Drawing for [539].   Red chalk
Madrid, Prado (62)   SC.43

Madrid Album B.84 - see [442]

541 Cap.45.

Mucho hay que chupar. (There is a lot to suck) 1797-98.
Etching and aquatint
20·8×15·1 cm.   D.82, H.80

542

Drawing for [541].   Red chalk
Madrid, Prado (63)   SC.44

543 Cap.46.

Correccion. (Correction)
1797-98.
Etching and aquatint
21·7×14·9 cm.   D.83, H.81

544

Drawing for [543].   Red chalk
Madrid, Prado (66)   SC.45

545 Cap.*47.*

Obsequio á el maestro.
(Hommage to the master)
1797-98. Etching and aquatint
21·7×15 cm. D.84, H.82

546

Drawing for [545]. Red chalk
Madrid, Prado (67) SC.46

547 Cap.*48.*

Soplones. (Squealers) 1797-98.
Etching and aquatint
20·7×15·1 cm. D.85, H.83 *

548

Drawing for [547]. Red chalk
Madrid, Prado (68) SC.47

549 Cap.*49.*

Duendecitos. (Little goblins)
1797-98.
Etching and aquatint
21·8×15·2 cm. D.86, H.84

550

Drawing for [549]. Red chalk
Madrid, Prado (69) SC.48

551 Cap.*50.*

Los Chinchillas. (The Chinchillas)
1797-98.
Etching and aquatint
20·8×15·1 cm. D.87, H.85 *

552

Drawing for [551].
Sanguine wash
Madrid, Prado (99) SC.50

553 Cap.*51.*

Se repulen. (They spruce themselves up) 1797-98.
Etching and aquatint
21·4×15·1 cm. D.88, H.86

554

Drawing for [553]. Red chalk
Madrid, Prado (70) SC.51

555 Cap.*52.*

Lo que puede un Sastre! (What
a tailor can do!) 1797-98.
Etching and aquatint
21·7×15·2 cm. D.89, H.87

556

Drawing for [555].
Sanguine wash
Madrid, Prado (101) SC.40B

557 Cap.*53.*

Que pico de Oro! (What a golden
beak!) 1797-98.
Etching and aq. 21·7×15·1 cm.
D.90, H.88 Ill. p. 130

558

Drawing for [557]. Red chalk
Madrid, Prado (71) SC.52

559 Cap.*54.*

El Vergonzoso. (The shame-faced
man) 1797-98.
Etching and aquatint
21·8×15·2 cm. D.91, H.89

560 Sueño *?*

*Este es un hombre q.e p.r q.e le
digeron . . .* Drawing for [559].
Pen and sepia ink, sanguine wash
Madrid, Prado (108) SC.53 *

561 Cap.*55.*

Hasta la muerte. (Till death)
1797-98.
Etching and aquatint
21·8×15·2 cm. D.92, H.90

562

Drawing for [561]. Red chalk
Madrid, Prado (72) SC.54

563 Cap.*56.*

Subir y bajar. (Ups and downs)
1797-98.
Etching and aquatint
21·7×15·1 cm. D.93, H.91

564

Drawing for [563]. Red chalk
Madrid, Prado (73) SC.55

565 Cap.57.

La filiacion. (The lineage)
1797-98.
Etching and aquatint
21·7×15·2 cm.   D.94, H.92   *

566

Drawing for [565].
Sanguine wash
Madrid, Prado (102)   SC.56A

567 Cap.58.

Tragala perro. (Swallow that, dog)
1797-98.
Etching and aquatint
21·7×15·1 cm.   D.95, H.93   *

568

Drawing for [567].
Red chalk and sanguine wash
Madrid, Prado (103)   SC.53B

569 Cap.59.

Y aun no se van! (And still they
don't go!) 1797-98.
Etching and aquatint
21·7×15·2 cm.   D.96, H.94

570

Drawing for [569].   Red chalk
Madrid, Prado (74)   SC.57

571 Cap.60.

Ensayos. (Trials) 1797-98.
s. *Goya*
Etching and aquatint 21×16·6 cm.
D.97, H.95 Ill. p. 128

572 Sueño 2.º

Ensayo de Brujas primerizas . . .
Drawing for [571].
Pen and sepia ink
Madrid, Prado (36)   SC.58   *

573 Cap.61.

Volaverunt. (Gone for good)
1797-98.
Etching and aquatint
21·7×15·2 cm.   D.98, H.96   *

574

Drawing for [573].   Red chalk
Madrid, Prado (75)   SC.59

575 Cap.62.

Quien lo creyera! (Who would
believe it!) 1797-98.
Etching and aquatint
20·7×15·2 cm.   D.99, H.97

576 Sueño 10?

De lo mas alto de su buelo . . .
Drawing for [575].
Pen and sepia ink
Madrid, Prado (37)   SC.60   *

577 Cap.63.

Miren que grabes! (Look how
serious they are!) 1797-98.
s. *Goya*   Etching and aquatint
21·5×16·3 cm.   D.100, H.98

578 Sueño 8.

*Sueño / Los Zanganos de las
Brujas*   Drawing for [577].
Pen and sepia ink
Madrid, Prado (38)   SC.61   *

579 Cap.64.

Buen Viage. (Bon voyage)
1797-98.
Etching and aquatint
21·8×15·2 cm.   D.101, H.99

580 recto of 644

Drawing for [579].   Red chalk
Madrid, Prado (441)   SC.62

581 Cap.65.

Donde vá mamá? (Where is
mother going?) 1797-98.
s. *Goya*   Etching and aquatint
20·9×16·7 cm.   D.102, H.100

582 Sueño 9.

*Sueño. / Bruja poderosa que por
ydropica . . .*   Drawing for [581].
Pen and sepia ink
Madrid, Prado (39)   SC.64   *

583 Cap.66.

Allá vá eso. (There it goes)
1797-98.
Etching and aquatint
20·9×16·6 cm.   D.103, H.101

584 Sueño 5.

*Sueño. / Bruja maestra dando
lecciones . . .*   Drawing for [583].
Pen and sepia ink
Madrid, Prado (40)   SC.65   *

585 Cap.*67*.

Aguarda que te unten. (Wait till you've been anointed) 1797-98. Etching and aquatint 21·7×15·1 cm   D.104, H.102   *

586

Drawing for [585].   Red chalk Madrid, Prado (76)   SC.66

587 Cap.*68*.

Linda maestra! (Pretty teacher!) 1797-98.   s. *Goya* Etching and aquatint 21·3×15cm.   D.105, H.103

588 Sueño ?4

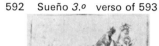

Sueño / De Brujas . . . Agente en diligencia . . .   Drawing for [587].   Pen and sepia ink Madrid, Prado (41)   SC.67   *

589 Cap.*69*.

Sopla. (Blow)   1797-98. s. *Goya* Etching and aquatint 21·3×14·8 cm.   D.106, H.104

590 Sueño *7*

Sueño de Brujas/consu[madas] ? Drawing for [589]. Pen and sepia ink Madrid, Prado (16)   SC.68   *

Madrid Album B.57 - see [417]

591 Cap.*70*.

Devota profesion. (Devout profession)   1797-98.   s. *Goya* Etching and aquatint 21×16·6 cm.   D.107, H.105

592 Sueño *3.º*   verso of 593

Sueño/de Bruja principianta Drawing for [591]. Pen and sepia ink Madrid, Prado (451)   SC.69   *

593 recto of 592

Sueño / De Brujas (Dream. Of witches)   First drawing for [59· Pen and sepia ink Madrid, Prado (444)   SC.73

Madrid Album B.56 - see [416]

594 Cap.*71*.

Si amanece; nos Vamos. (If day breaks, we go)   1797-98. Etching and aquatint 20×15 cm.   D.108, H.106

595

Drawing for [594].   Inscr. Red chalk Madrid, Prado (82)   SC.70   *

596 Cap.*72*.

No te escaparás. (You won't escape)   1797-98. Etching and aquatint 21·6×15·1 cm.   D.109, H.107

597 verso of 598

Drawing for [596].   Red chalk Madrid, Prado (458)   SC.71

598 recto of 597

First drawing for [596]. Red chalk Madrid, Prado (432)   SC.74

599 Cap.*73*.

Mejor es holgar. (It's better to be idle)   1797-98. Etching and aquatint 21·7×15·2 cm.   D.110, H.108

600 Cap.*74*.

No grites, tonta. (Don't scream, stupid)   1797-98. Etching and aquatint 21·6×15 cm.   D.111, H.109

601

Drawing for [600].   Red chalk Madrid, Prado (78)   SC.75

602 Cap.*75*.

¿No hay quien nos desate? (Is there no one to untie us?) 1797-98.   Etching and aquatint 21·7×15·2 cm.   D.112, H.110

603

604   verso of 475

605   Cap.*76.*

606

607   Cap.*77.*

Drawing for [602].   Red chalk
Madrid, Prado (79)   SC.76

Sketch for [602].   Red chalk
Madrid, Prado (449)   SC.72

*¿Está Vm̃d . . . pues, Como
digo . . eh! Cuidado! si nó . . .*
1797-98.   Etching and aquatint
21·6×15·1 cm.   D.113, H.111   ✱

Drawing for [605].   Red chalk
Madrid, Prado (80)   SC.78

Unos á otros. (One to another)
1797-98.
Etching and aquatint
21·7×15·2 cm.   D.114, H.112

608

609   Cap.*78.*

610   recto of 645

611   Cap.*79.*

612

Drawing for [607].   Red chalk
Madrid, Prado (81)   SC.79

Despacha, que dispiertan.
(Be quick, they're waking up)
1797-98.   Etching and aquatint
21·7×15·1 cm.   D.115, H.113

Drawing for [609].   Red chalk
Madrid, Prado (442)   SC.80

Nadie nos ha visto. (No one
has seen us)   1797-98.
Etching and aquatint
21·6×15·1 cm.   D.116, H.114

Drawing for [611].   Red chalk
Madrid, Prado (77)   SC.81

613   Cap.*80.*

ADDITIONAL PLATES

Five plates made for the
Caprichos series but rejected by
Goya or accidentally destroyed.
Only one proof is known from
each plate.

[614-621]

614

615

616

Ya es hora. (Time is up)
1797-98.
Etching and aquatint
21·7×15·2 cm.   D.117, H.115

[*Aquellos polbos.*]   First version
of plate 23 [498]   1797-98.
Aquatint 21·5×15 cm.
Paris, B.N. (A.11036)   H.116   ✱

Drawing for [614].
Red chalk and sanguine wash
Madrid, Prado (105)   SC.40A

Woman in prison   1797-98.
Aquatint 18·5×12·5 cm. (cut)
Madrid, B.N. (45621)
D.34, H.117   ✱

617

618

619   recto of 621

620   *Sueño ?*

Drawing for [616].
Red chalk and sanguine wash
Madrid, Prado (100)   SC.203

Old woman and a gallant
1797-98.   Etching and aquatint
21·5×15 cm.
Paris, B.N.   H.118   ✱

Dream. Of lying . . .   1797-98.
Etching and aq. 18×12 cm. (cut)
Madrid, B.N. (45673)
D.118, H.119   Ill. p. 131   ✱

*Sueño / De la mentira y la
ynconstancia*   Drawing for [619].
Pen and sepia ink with wash
Madrid, Prado (17)   SC.82   ✱

Madrid Album B.71 - see [431]

621   verso of 619

Women weeping over an injured
dog   1797-98.
Etching and aquatint
See [619].   D.119, H.120   *

Madrid Album B.94 - see [450]

ADDITIONAL DRAWINGS

Five *Sueño* drawings which show
the mark of the copperplate and
must have been etched, although
no proofs are known. The first
three designs, perhaps accidentally destroyed, were repeated
in new drawings and plates.

[622-628]

622   Sueño *22.*

*Viento. | Si ay culpa en la escena
la tiene/el trage.*   1797-98.
Pen and sepia ink   Madrid,
Prado (24)   SC.33, H.120a   *

Madrid Album B.81 - see [439]

623   Sueño *?*

La enfermedad de la razon
(Sickness of reason)   1797-98.
Pen and sepia ink   Madrid,
Prado (35)   SC.49, H.120b   *

624   Sueño *11.*

*Mascaras de caricaturas | q.ᵉ
apuntaron*[?] . . .   1797-98.
Pen and sepia ink   Madrid,
Prado (30)   SC.56, H.120c   *

625   Sueño *?*

Madrid Album B.59 - see [419]

Sueño. | Pregon de Brujas . . .
1797-98.   Pen and sepia ink
Madrid, Prado (477)
SC.211, H.120d   *

626

Proclamation of witches.
1797-98.   Red chalk and
sanguine wash
Madrid, Prado (476)   SC.207   *

627   Sueño *16.*

Sueño | Crecer despues de morir.
1797-98.   Pen and sepia ink
Madrid, Prado (18)
SC.B, H.120e   *

628   verso of 638

Sketch for [627]?
Red chalk and sanguine wash
Madrid, Prado (479)   SC.273

Drawings in red chalk or red chalk
and sanguine wash which were
undoubtedly prepared for the
Caprichos series. Further
examination of these drawings
may show that some of them
were transferred to copperplates
for etching.

[629-647]

629

Dressing upside-down   1797-98
Red chalk
Madrid, Prado (84)   SC.195   *

630

De todo (Concerning everything)
1797-98.   Red chalk
Madrid, Prado (480)   SC.197   *

631

Academic session   1797-98.
Red chalk
Madrid, Prado (481)   SC.199   *

632

Girl and flying guitarist   1797-98.
Red chalk
Madrid, Prado (64)   SC.200

633   verso of 492

Giant figure on a balcony
1797-98.   Red chalk
Madrid, Prado (456)   SC.198

634

Domestic work   1797-98.
Red chalk
Madrid, Prado (83)   SC.196

635

Saturn devouring his sons
1797-98.   Red chalk
Madrid, Prado (85)   SC.202   *

36	637	638 recto of 628	639	640

modern Judith(?) 1797-98. ed chalk ladrid, Prado (65) SC.201 *	Orator haranguing a crowd 1797-98. Sanguine wash Madrid, Prado (115) SC.206	Crowd spying at a phantom 1797-98. Red chalk and sanguine wash Madrid, Prado (478) SC.204 *	The barber 1797-98. Red chalk and sanguine wash Madrid, Prado (111) SC.56C *	Witches' swing 1797-98. Red chalk and sanguine wash Madrid, Prado (114) SC.215 *

41	642 recto of 643	643 verso of 642	644 verso of 580	645 verso of 610

 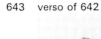

ight flight of witches 1797-98. ed chalk and sanguine wash ladrid, Prado (116) SC.208 *	Time flying with Truth(?) 1797-98. Red chalk and sanguine wash Madrid, Prado (423) SC.451 *	Sketch for [642]? Sanguine wash Madrid, Prado (463) SC.452	Sketch of old man 1797-98. Red chalk Madrid, Prado (446) SC.63	Sketch of hooded woman 1797-98. Red chalk Madrid, Prado (453) SC.77

46		647		648

Series of drawings possibly prepared for the *Caprichos,* and certainly made at the same time.

MIRROR IMAGES
Six drawings showing four human types looking at their symbolical counterpart in a mirror or on a canvas before them.
[648-653]   *

LOCKS
Linked to the 'mirror' drawings are three drawings on the symbolic sexual theme of locks. These found no echo in the etchings.
[654-656]

PHYSIOGNOMIC STUDIES
Two drawings attributed to Goya.
[657, 658]

allant watching a girl undress 797-98. ed chalk and sanguine wash ladrid, Prado (4) SC.210	Madrid Album B.79 - see [437]	Girl with gesticulating gallant 1797-98. Sanguine wash Madrid, Prado (3) SC.205	Serpent / Woman - Melancholy temperament 1797-98. Pen and brush with sepia ink Madrid, Prado (32) SC.268, LR.70

49	650	651	652	653 recto of 654

erpent / Woman 1797-98. ed chalk ladrid, Prado (482) C.E, LR.69	Ape / Gallant - Sanguine temperament 1797-98. Pen and brush with sepia ink Madrid, Prado (31) SC.270, LR.68	Tortured fop 1797-98. Brush and sepia wash Madrid, Prado (112) SC.56D, LR.67	Cat / Constable - Choleric temperament 1797-98. Pen and sepia ink Madrid, Prado (33) SC.269, LR.75	Frog / Student - Phlegmatic temperament 1797-98. Brush and sepia ink Madrid, Prado (439) SC.271, LR.72

654 verso of 653

Padlocked man and frog
Pen and brush, sanguine and
sepia
Prado (448)   SC. 272   *

655

Frog / Humans embracing
1797-98.   Sanguine wash
Madrid, Prado (110)   SC.209

656

La confianza (Trust)   1797-98.
Red chalk and sanguine wash
Madrid, Prado (109)   SC.213   *

657

Sixteen caricature heads   1798?
Pen and sepia ink 29·8×40·4 cm.
Coll. unknown (formerly Madrid,
Scláfani)   LR.61   *

658

Group of caricature heads
1797-98.   Pen and sepia ink
21×15 cm.
Paris, priv. coll.   *

WITCHCRAFT PAINTINGS FOR THE OSUNAS 1797-1798

Six paintings made for the
Duchess of Osuna's study in the
country palace of La Alameda,
and probably executed at the same
time as the *Caprichos* prints.
Witchcraft was a fashionable
topic and Goya's friends, especially
Moratín, were fascinated by it.
Two of the subjects are from
comedies by Antonio de Zamora,
and the other paintings may
also be scenes from plays.
27 June 1798: Goya dated his
account for the six pictures.

[659-664]   *

659

Flying witches   1797-98.
43·5×30·5 cm.
Madrid, Min. de la Gobernación
M.550, DF.169, G.360   *

660

'El aquelarre' (The witches'
sabbath)   1797-98.   44×31 cm.
Madrid, Fund. Lázaro (M.2004)
M.548, DF.170, G.356   p. 122   *

661

The spell   1797-98.
45×32 cm.
Madrid, Fund. Lázaro (M.2016)
M.552, DF.172, G.358   *

662

The witches' kitchen   1797-98.
45×32 cm.
Mexico City, priv. coll.
M. 549, DF.171, G.361   *

663

The bewitched   1797-98.
Inscr. *LAM DESCO*   42×30 cm.
London, N.G. (1472)
M.557, DF.174, G.359   *

664

Don Juan and the Comendador
1797-98.   45×32 cm.
Coll. unknown
M.558, DF.173, G.357   *

PORTRAITS   1797-1799

Series dominated by portraits of
men and in particular of Goya's
liberal friends: Iriarte, Meléndez
Valdés, Jovellanos, Saavedra
and Moratín. Intimate portraits,
whose style recalls the French
type of 'portrait de bibliothèque'
and also the informal manner of
Gainsborough and the English
school.

[665-689]   *

665

Self-portrait   c.1795-97.
s. *Goya*   20×14 cm.
Formerly Madrid, Alejandro Pidal
M.299, G.338   *

666

Self-portrait   c.1795-97.
s. *Goya*   Brush and Indian ink
23·3×14·4 cm.   New York,
M.M.A.(35.103.1.)   Ill. p. 114

667

Judge Altamirano   c.1796-97.
Inscr.   82·8×61·9 cm.
Montreal, Mus. (61)
M.202, DF.353, G.403   *

668

Martín Zapater   s.d. *1797* with
inscr.   83×64 cm. (oval)
Bilbao, Sota
M.455, DF.376, G.370   *

669

Bernardo de Iriarte   s.d. *1797*,
with inscr.   108×84 cm.
Strasburg, Mus. (308)   M.[451],
DF.375, G.373   Ill. p. 109   *

670

J. A. Meléndez Valdés   s.d. *1797*,
inscr.   73·3×57·1 cm.   Barnard
Castle, Bowes Mus. (26)   M.345,
DF.378, G.[372]   Ill. p. 135   *

671

Pedro Romero   c.1795-98.
84·1×65 cm.   Fort Worth,
Kimbell Foundation   M.404,
DF.427n., G.405   Ill. p. 123   *

672
José Romero   c.1795-98.
63×76 cm.
Philadelphia, Mus. (63.116.8)
M.402, DF.470, G.406   *

673
Andrés del Peral   c.1797-98.
Panel 95×65 cm.
London, N.G. (1951)
M.377, DF.366, G.377   *

674
IX Duque de Osuna   c. 1797-99.
Inscr.   113×83·2 cm.
New York, Frick Coll. (A.523)
M.368, DF.327, G.399   *

675
Gaspar Melchor de Jovellanos
1798.   Inscr.   205×133 cm.
Madrid, Vizcondesa de Irueste
M.323, DF.372, G.376   p. 133 *

676
Francisco de Saavedra   1798.
Inscr.   196×118 cm.
London, Courtauld Inst. Galleries
M.409, DF.371, G.400   *

677
Ferdinand Guillemardet   1798.
185×125 cm.   Paris,
Louvre (M.I.697)   M.317,
DF.380, G.375   Ill. p. 134   *

678
Marquesa de las Mercedes?
c.1797-98.   142×97 cm.
Paris, David-Weill
M.350, DF.385, G.340   *

679
General José de Urrutia   c.1798.
Inscr.   200×132 cm.
Madrid, Prado (736)
M.440, DF.383, G.374   *

680
Self-portrait   c.1797-1800.
s. Goya   63×49 cm.
Castres, Mus. Goya
M.297, DF.331, G.426   *

681
Self-portrait   c.1797-1800.
54×39·5 cm.
Bayonne, Mus. Bonnat (9)
M.298, DF.379, G.427   *

682
Asensio Juliá 'El Pescadoret'
1798.   Inscr.   56×42 cm.
Paris, Arthur Sachs   M.325,
DF.382, G.378   Ill. p. 146   *

683
Marqués de Bondad Real
s.d. 1799, inscr.   225×140 cm.
New York, Hispanic Soc. (A.99)
M.215, DF.386, G.412   *

684
La Tirana   s.d. 1799 with inscr.
206×130 cm.
Madrid, R.A. San Fernando (677)
M.434, DF.384, G.315   *

685
Leandro Fernández de Moratín
1799.   73×56 cm.   Madrid,
R.A. San Fernando (671)   M.358,
DF.390, G.411   Ill. p. 135   *

686
Unknown woman (Josefa Bayeu?)
c.1798.   81×56 cm.
Madrid, Prado (722)
M.307, DF.425, G.320   *

687
Man in a brown coat
c.1797-1800.   105×84 cm.
Boston, M.F.A. (10.33)
G.525   *

688
Antonio Gasparini   c.1790-1800.
107×81·5 cm.
Madrid, Marquesa de Zurgena
M.274, DF.324, G.268   *

689
Mariano Luis de Urquijo
c.1798-99?   128×97 cm.
Madrid, R.A. de la Historia
M.439, DF. 347, G.401   *

ALLEGORICAL PAINTINGS 1797-1800

Four circular allegories painted
for the palace of Godoy in Madrid.
One of the four - Science - was
badly damaged and completely
overpainted, and there is no
record of its original form.
The two large paintings now in
Stockholm were probably painted
for the same palace, and the
second of them is closely related
in theme and composition to some
of the prints and drawings in the
Caprichos series.

[690-696]   *

690
Agriculture   1797-1800.
227 cm. diam.
Madrid, Prado (2547)
M.89a, DF.92, G.480

691

Industry   1797-1800.
227 cm. diam.
Madrid, Prado (2548)
M.89b, DF.93, G.479

692

Commerce   1797-1800.
227 cm. diam.
Madrid, Prado (2546)
M.89c, DF.94, G.478   Ill. p. 138

693

Sketch for [692].
31·8 cm. diam.
New York, priv. coll.
DF.94n, G.477   *

694

Poetry   1797-1800.
300×326 cm.
Stockholm, Nationalmus. (5592)
M.91, DF.85, G.484

695

Truth, Time and History?
1797-1800.   294×244 cm.
Stockholm, Nationalmus. (5593)
M.86, DF.87, G.483   p. 136   *

696

Sketch for [695].   42×32·5 cm.
Boston, M.F.A. (27.1330)
M.87, DF.86, G.482   Ill. p. 137 *

Drawing for [696]? - see [642]

Drawing for the figure of Truth -
see [643]

**DRAWINGS FOR THE
DICTIONARY OF CEÁN
BERMÚDEZ   1798-1799**

Series of drawings made for
engravings to illustrate the
*Diccionario de los más ilustres
profesores de las Bellas Artes* by
Juan Agustín Ceán Bermúdez.
The Dictionary was finally
published in 1800, without
illustrations. The portrait of Goya's
friend, Ceán, would have formed
the frontispiece to the work.
Ten portraits of artists have so
far been identified, copied by
Goya from prints or drawings.
The articles in the Dictionary are
indicated by the volume and page
number after the artists' names.

[697-707]   *

697

Juan Agustín Ceán Bermúdez
1798-99.   Inscr.
Red chalk 12·2×9·8 cm.   Madrid,
Carderera   M.682   Ill. p. 136   *

698

Cesar Arbasia. / Pint.   (I,42)
1798-99.   Red chalk 17×12·5 cm.
Formerly London, H.M. Calmann

699

*Alónso Cáno. Pint. Escul. / y
Arqui.º*   (I,208)   1798-99.
Red chalk 22×15·7 cm.
Madrid, Amunátegui   *

700

Pablo de Céspedes. Pint.   (I,316)
1798-99.
Red chalk 21·9×15·6 cm.
Madrid, Amunátegui   *

701

Luis Fernandez Pint.   (II,88)
1798-99.
Red chalk 16×11·6 cm.
Madrid, B.N. (2101)

702

*Juan Fernandez Navarrete / el
Mudo Pint.*   (II,93)   1798-99.
Red chalk 17·1×12·3 cm.
London, C.R. Rudolf

703

Felipe Liaño Pint.   (III,36)
1798-99.
Red chalk 17·1×12·3 cm.
London, C.R. Rudolf

704

Pedro Roldán. Escult.   (IV,240)
1798-99.
Red chalk 17·4×12·6 cm.
London, Enriqueta Frankfort   *

705

Cornelio Schut. Pint.   (IV,359)
1798-99.
Red chalk 17·5×12·7 cm.
Madrid, Amunátegui   *

706

Luis de Vargas Pint.   (V,135)
1798-99.
Red chalk 15·6×11·7 cm.
Madrid, B.N. (2102)

707

Retrato de Zurbaran   (VI,44)
1798-99.
Red chalk 15·2×11·8 cm.
Paris, Louvre (18.482)   p. 136

RELIGIOUS PAINTINGS 1792-1801

Second great period of religious paintings, culminating in the frescoes of San Antonio de la Florida.

[708-740]

CADIZ   SANTA CUEVA
c.1796-1797

Goya may have gone to Cadiz in 1792 in connection with this commission for three large scenes from the New Testament for an oratorio then under construction. If so, his long illness delayed the execution of the paintings.

31 March 1796: consecration of the oratorio.
May 1796: Goya probably left Madrid for Andalusia.
Said to have been absent in Seville 'the whole of the year '96', his presence in Cadiz is documented in January 1797.
The paintings were executed either in Madrid before March 1796 or in Andalusia between

May 1796 and April 1797. The two known sketches are as freely handled as those for San Antonio de la Florida [718, 723].

[708-712]   *

708

Parable of the guest without a wedding garment c.1796-97. 146×340 cm.   Cadiz, Santa Cueva   G.362   Ill. p. 113

709

Miracle of the loaves and fishes c.1796-97.   146×340 cm. Cadiz, Santa Cueva DF.534s, G.364   Ill. p. 112

710

Sketch for [709]. 22·4×38·7 cm. Collection unknown DF.534s(n), G.363   *

711

The Last Supper   c.1796-97. 146×340 cm. Cadiz, Santa Cueva DF.535s, G.366

712

Sketch for [711].   25×42 cm. Formerly Paris, Kleinberger D.535s(n), G.365   *

DOCTORS OF THE CHURCH
c.1796-1799

Probably painted during or after the second visit to Andalusia in 1796-97. Clear influence of Murillo's *Saint Isidore* and *Saint Leander* in the Cathedral at Seville and of Torrigiano's terracotta *Saint Jerome*.

[713-716]   *

713

Saint Ambrose   c.1796-99. 190×113 cm. Cleveland, Mus. (69.23) G.179   *

714

Saint Augustine   c.1796-99 190×115 cm. Madrid, Manuel Monjardín M.31, DF.72, G.178

715

Saint Gregory the Great c.1796-99.   190×115 cm. Madrid, Museo Romántico (21) M.47, DF.71, G.180

716

Saint Jerome   c.1796-99. 93×114·3 cm. Fullerton (Calif.), Norton Simon Found.   M.48, G.181   *

MADRID   SAN ANTONIO DE LA FLORIDA   1798

Goya's third and last great fresco painting. The commission for the newly rebuilt hermitage on the outskirts of Madrid came through Jovellanos.
1 August 1798: Goya began work, and is said to have completed it in one hundred and twenty days. The *Miracle of Saint Anthony of Padua* is represented in the cupola, and the *Adoration of the Trinity* in the apse.
The rest of the upper areas - pendentives, vaults, lateral walls - are painted with angels and cherubim.

[717-735]   *

717

Miracle of Saint Anthony of Padua 1798.   Fresco 5·5 m. diam. Madrid, San Antonio de la Florida M.8, DF.89, G.381   pp. 141-143

Half of cupola with miracle

Sections of the fresco

Half of cupola with tree

Sections of the fresco

718

719

721

Sketch for half of cupola [717]
with the miracle   26×38 cm.
Madrid, Condesa de Villagonzalo
M.10, DF.88, G.380   Ill. p. 140

Sketch for [717]? - the miracle
26×36·8 cm.
Johannesburg, H.Oppenheimer
M.12   *

Reduction of [717].
55·3×26·6 cm.   Pittsburgh,
Carnegie Inst. (65.15)   *

720

722

723

724

Sketch for [717]? - the tree
26×36·8 cm.
Johannesburg, H. Oppenheimer
M.11   *

Adoration of the Trinity   1798.
Fresco 5·5 m. diam. (approx.)
Madrid, San Antonio de la Florida
M.2, DF.89, G.396

Sketch for [722].   26×38 cm.
Madrid, Condesa de Villagonzalo
M.13, DF.90, G.395

Angels on north-east vault
1798.   Fresco 900×160 cm.
(approx.)   Madrid, San Antonio
de la Florida   G.390

etail of [724] - centre section

Detail of [724] - lower left
section (seen from south-west)

Detail of [724] - lower right
section (seen from south-west)

725

Angels on south-west vault
1798.   Fresco 900×160 cm.
(approx.)   Madrid, San Antonio
de la Florida   G.387

etail of [725] - centre section

Detail of [725] - lower left
section (seen from south-west)

Detail of [725] - lower right
section (seen from south-west)

726-728

Angels on north-west vault and
lateral walls   1798.   Fresco -
vault 900×140 cm. (approx.)
Madrid, San Antonio de la Florida

726

Angels and cherubs on north-west
vault - lower sections   G.388   *

ngel on left half of north-west
nette
50×200 cm. (approx.)
.391

728

Angel on right half of north-west
lunette
250×200 cm. (approx.)
G.392   Ill. p. 145

729-731

Angels on south-east vault and
lateral walls   1798.   Fresco -
vault 900×140 cm. (approx.)
Madrid, San Antonio de la Florida

729

Angels on south-east vault -
lower sections   G.389   Ill. p. 145

730

Angel on left half of south-east
lunette
250×200 cm. (approx.)
G.393

31

ngel on right half of south-east
nette
50×200 cm. (approx.)
.394

732

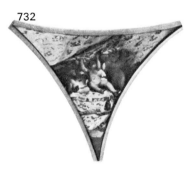

Cherubim 1798.   Fresco - west
pendentive 300 cm. wide (approx.)
Madrid, San Antonio de la Florida
G.382

733

Cherubim 1798.   Fresco -
north pendentive 300 cm. wide
(approx.)   Madrid, San Antonio
de la Florida   G.384

734

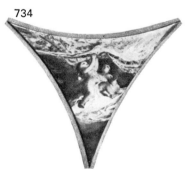

Cherubim 1798.   Fresco - east
pendentive 300 cm. wide
(approx.)   Madrid, San Antonio
de la Florida   G.383

735

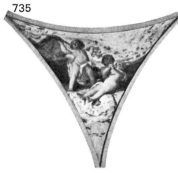

Cherubim 1798.   Fresco -
south pendentive 300 cm. wide
(approx.)   Madrid, San Antonio
de la Florida   G.385

'EL PRENDIMIENTO' 1798

Painted for the Archbishop of Toledo, this representation of the betrayal of Christ may have been commissioned ten years previously.
6 January 1799: painting shown to the Academicians of San Fernando and duly praised.
8 January 1799: delivered to the Cathedral sacristy at Toledo.

The painting is full of the expressive deformations which first appear in the Madrid album and *Caprichos* prints. The sketch, which is very different from the final version, is remarkable for its extraordinary vigour.

736

'El prendimiento de Cristo' (The taking of Christ) 1798.
300×200 cm. Toledo, Cathedral sacristy M.21, DF.80, G.398 *

737

Sketch for [736]. 40×23 cm.
Madrid, Prado (3113)
M.22, DF.80n, G.397 p. 147 *

MONTE TORRERO (Saragossa) CHURCH OF SAN FERNANDO c.1798-1800

The three altarpieces were destroyed in 1808, and are known from the sketches and from the description in Jovellanos' diary in 1801. His note might be applied to many works of this period and the succeeding years: 'force of the *claro-oscuro*, inimitable beauty of the colouring and a certain magic of lights and tones, which no other brush seems able to attain'.

[738-740]   *

738

Saint Elizabeth tending . . .
c.1798-1800 33×23 cm.
Madrid, Fund. Lázaro (M.2021)
M.41, DF.100, G.460 *

739

Apparition of Saint Isidore . . .
c.1798-1800. 44·2×23·5 cm.
Buenos Aires, Mus. (2563)
M.56, DF.104, G.459 *

740

Saint Hermengild in the prison
c.1798-1800. 33×23 cm.
Madrid, Fund. Lázaro (M.2017)
M.49, DF.101, G.461 *

CLASSICAL AND GENRE SUBJECTS c.1797-1808

The two celebrated *Majas* [743, 744] are certainly not portraits of the Duchess of Alba. They may have been commissioned by Godoy, and were seized among his effects in 1808.
In 1814 Goya was summoned to appear before the Holy Inquisition on account of these two 'obscene paintings'.

The *Cupid and Psyche* [745] is Goya's only known mythological painting after the *Hercules and Omphale* of 1784 [I.198].

The *Sleeping woman* [746] recalls a painting of c.1792 [I.308] but the dark ground and broad

technique suggest that it may even have been painted after 1810.

[742-746]

742

Children's masquerade
c.1798-1800. 31×95 cm.
Florence, Contini-Bonacossi
M.723, DF.96, G.466 *

743

La maja desnuda (Naked maja)
c.1798-1805. 97×190 cm.
Madrid, Prado (742)
M.625, DF.389, G.539 p. 153 *

744

La maja vestida (Clothed maja)
c.1798-1805. 95×190 cm.
Madrid, Prado (741)
M.624, DF.388, G.540 p. 153 *

745

Cupid and Psyche c.1800-05.
221×156 cm.
Barcelona, Mus. (Cambó 33)
M.69, DF.67, G.541 *

746

El sueño (Sleeping woman)
c.1798-1808. 44·5×76·5 cm.
Dublin, N.G. (1928)
M.637, DF.183, G.323 *

PRINTS AND DRAWINGS c.1798-1808

This group of works includes a magnificent series of landscapes [748-754], two attributed drawings showing the ascent of a balloon [755, 756], a project for the tomb of the Duchess of Alba who died in 1802 [759] and a group of drawings after Flaxman's illustrations to Dante's *Divine Comedy* [760-765]. The dating of many of these drawings is uncertain.
Two more landscapes are known only from the descriptions in the Boix catalogue (Bibl. 9, nos 206A, 209).

Abbreviations and signs: see p.168
Aq. = aquatint
Bx = Boix, Bibl. 9
D = Delteil, Bibl. 55
H = Harris, Bibl. 88
M = Mayer, Bibl. 128
SC = Sánchez Cantón, Bibl. 168
If not a print from an edition:
1/1 = unique proof; 1/3 =one of three proofs known.

[747-773]

747

Coat of arms of Jovellanos
c.1798? Etching 4·7×6·1 cm.
(design) 1/2 Madrid, B.N.
(45608) D.36, H.22 p. 132 *

748

Landscape with buildings and trees c.1800-08. Etching and aq.
16·5×28·5 cm. 1/3 Chicago,
A.I. D.22, H.23 p. 216 *

749

Drawing for [748].
Red chalk 15·1×25·7 cm.
Madrid, Prado (190) SC.457

750

751

752

753

754

Landscape with waterfall
c.1800-08. Etching and aq.
15·6×28·5 cm. 1/2 Madrid,
B.N. (45610) D.23, H.24 *

Drawing for [750].
Red chalk 15·2×25·8 cm.
Madrid, Prado (191) SC.456

Landscape c.1800-08.
Red chalk 18·3×12·9 cm.
Madrid, Carderera Bx.210

The bridge c.1800-08.
Black chalk 29·7×41·2 cm.
Madrid, Marqués de Casa Torres
Bx.205B, M.738

The pyramid c.1800-08.
Black chalk 29·1×41·4 cm.
Madrid, Marqués de Casa Torres
Bx.205A, M.737

755

756

757

758

759

The balloon c.1800-08.
Black chalk 38·3×27·3 cm.
Hamburg, Kunsthalle (38546)
M.722a *

The balloon c.1800-08.
Pen and sepia ink 30×22·7 cm.
Madrid, Marqués de Casa Torres
Bx.208, M.722b *

A street c.1800-08.
Red chalk, pen and Indian ink,
grey paper 11·5×19·5 cm.
Madrid, Prado (411) SC.465

Commemorative monument(?)
c.1800-08. Inscr. Pen and
Indian ink, grey paper
Madrid, Prado (407) SC.449 *

Design for the Duchess of Alba's
tomb c.1802-03. Brush and
Indian ink 12×16·5 cm.
Madrid, Berganza de Martín *

760

761

762

763

764

DRAWINGS AFTER FLAXMAN
[760-765] *

Five men with cloaks and hats
c.1800-08. Brush and Indian
ink 15·6×25·9 cm.
Madrid, B.N. (B.1276) *

Three pairs of hooded figures
c.1800-08. Brush and Indian
ink 17·5×26·9 cm.
Madrid, B.N. (B.1275) *

Two men conversing
c.1800-08. Brush and Indian
ink 14·5×23·6 cm.
Madrid, B.N. (B.1277) *

Two men carrying off a woman
c.1800-08. Brush and Indian
ink 18·4×26 cm.
Madrid, B.N. (B.1279) *

Religious submission c.1800-08.
Brush and Indian ink 17×22·5 cm.
Paris, priv. coll. M.673 *

765

766

767

768

769

Eight figures and a mother and
child c.1800-08. Brush and
Indian ink 19·5×26·6 cm.
Madrid, Prado (488) *

The Mass c.1800-08. Brush
and Indian ink 19·3×25(?) cm.
Madrid, B.N. (B. 1278) *

Four figures round a dying man
c.1800-08. Brush and
Indian ink 18×24·5 cm.
Paris, priv. coll. *

Se hizo á obscuras (It happened
in the dark) c.1800-08.
Brush and Indian ink 22×17·1 cm.
Madrid, B.N. (B.1261) *

Martín Miguel de Goicoechea(?)
c.1805-08. s. Goya f.t Pen
12·4×9 cm. Madrid, Fund Lázaro
(M.I-4018) Bx.188, M.685a *

770

J.B. Casti c.1803-08? Inscr.
Pen and sepia ink 19·2×12 cm.
Madrid, Fund. Lázaro (M.I-4058) *

771

Erasmus of Rotterdam
c.1800-08? Inscr.
Pen and sepia ink 19·8×14·5 cm.
Madrid, Carderera Bx.178 *

772

May God reward you c.1800-04.
Etching and aq. 17·5×21·5 cm.
D.24, H.25 *

773

Dios se lo pague a uste (May God reward you) Drawing for [772].
Red chalk 17×19 cm.
Madrid, Prado (133) SC.455

PORTRAITS 1799-1808

[774-863]

I. ROYAL FAMILY 1799-1801

The letters of María Luisa to Godoy refer to the progress of the different portraits: that of the Queen wearing a mantilla [775] in September 1799; the equestrian portraits [776, 777] in October; the Condesa de Chinchón, Godoy's wife [793], in April 1800; and in May and June the sketches for the great family portrait [783] and the portraits in court dress [781, 782] which were destined for Napoleon. The group is completed by the portraits of the brother and husband of the Condesa de Chinchón [794-796].

[774-796]

PORTRAITS OF CHARLES IV AND MARÍA LUISA

Second series of official portraits of Charles IV and María Luisa, begun in the autumn of 1799 when Goya became Primer Pintor de Cámara. Treating the same subjects at ten years' interval, cp. [I.279-288], the ceremonial character of the royal effigies is now dominated by the freedom and strength of Goya's style and execution.

[774-782] *

774

Charles IV in hunting dress
1799. 210×130 cm.
Madrid, Palacio Real
M.130, DF.419, G.418 *

775

María Luisa in a mantilla 1799.
210×130 cm.
Madrid, Palacio Real
M.151, DF.416, G.419 *

776

Charles IV on horseback 1800-0
305×279 cm.
Madrid, Prado (719)
M.133, DF.394, G.422 p. 104

777

María Luisa on horseback
1799. 335×279 cm.
Madrid, Prado (720)
M.153, DF.392, G.424 p. 104 *

778

Study for [777]? 63×52 cm.
England, priv. coll.
M.154, DF.530s/549, G.423 *

779

Study for a double equestrian portrait 1799-1801. Pencil, brush and sepia wash 24×20·6 cm.
London, B.M. (1895.9.15.892) *

780

Sketch for [779]. Brush and sepia wash 13·5×13·8 cm.
Madrid, Prado (7) SC.459

781

María Luisa in court dress
June 1800. 210×130 cm.
Madrid, Palacio Real
M.148, DF.409, G.414 *

782

Charles IV as Colonel of the Life Guards 1799. 202×126 cm.
Madrid, Palacio Real
M.131, DF.412n, G.413 *

THE FAMILY OF CHARLES IV
1800-1801

The culmination of Goya's career as official court painter.
May-June 1800: to Aranjuez to make sketches for the portraits.
23 July: dated his account for the ten sketches.
December 1801: presented his account for the large painting which was executed in Madrid between July 1800 and June 1801. Inspired by Velázquez's *Meninas*, it is painted with exceptional virtuosity.

783

The family of Charles IV
1800-01. 280×336 cm.
Madrid, Prado (726) M.103,
DF.406, G.434 pp. 149, 150 *

SKETCHES FOR THE ROYAL FAMILY PORTRAIT

Five of the ten sketches are in the Prado. Vividly brushed in on a red-brown ground, they are the fruit of pitiless realism.
A number of portrait studies in collections outside Spain have been described as sketches for the family portrait, but they are of doubtful authenticity when compared with those in the Prado.

[784-788] *

784

Infante Carlos María Isidro - sketch for [783]. 74×60 cm.
Madrid, Prado (731)
M.109, DF.396, G.428

785
Infanta María Josefa -
sketch for [783]. 74×60 cm.
Madrid, Prado (729)
M.115, DF.404, G.429   Ill. p. 149

786
Infante Francisco de Paula
Antonio - sketch for [783].
74×60 cm.   Madrid, Prado (730)
M.110, DF.397, G.430   p. 149

787
Infante Antonio Pascual -
sketch for [783].   74×60 cm.
Madrid, Prado (733)
M.111, DF.395, G.431   *

788
Luis de Borbón, Prince of Parma -
sketch for [783].   74×60 cm.
Madrid, Prado (732)
M.112, DF.405, G.432

Four portraits possibly painted
by Agustín Esteve from Goya's
lost original sketches for the
royal family portrait [783].

[789-792]   *

789
Charles IV   1800.   84×67 cm.
Collection unknown
M.105, DF.399, G.439   *

790
María Luisa   1800.
81·5×66·9 cm.
Cincinnati, Taft Mus. (1931.446)
M.106, DF.400, G.440   *

791
Ferdinand, Prince of Asturias
1800.   83·2×66·7 cm.
New York, M.M.A. (51.70)
M.108, DF.401, G.441   *

792
Infanta María Isabel   1800.
84×67 cm.
Collection unknown
M.113, DF. 402, G.442   *

THE ROYAL FAMILY CIRCLE

The Condesa de Chinchón, wife
of the favourite Godoy, and her
brother the Cardinal Luis María
de Borbón, the children of the
Infante Don Luis, Goya's
first royal patron. Goya had
painted them seventeen years
before at Arenas de San Pedro
[I.209, 210]. The portrait of the
expectant Chinchón is full of
tenderness and the contrast with
the bombastic portrait of her
husband, Godoy, is telling.

[793-796]

793
Condesa de Chinchón
April 1800.   174·2×144 cm.
Madrid, Duque de Sueca
M.187, DF.308, G.425   p. 19   *

794
Cardinal Luis María de Borbón
c.1800.   200×106 cm.
São Paulo, Mus.
M.175, DF.297, G.447   *

795
Cardinal Luis María de Borbón
c.1800.   214×136 cm.
Madrid, Prado (738)
M.176, DF.318, G.448

796
Manuel Godoy   July-Sept. 1801.
180×267 cm.
Madrid, R.A. San Fernando (670)
M.278, DF.423, G.435   p. 104 *

VARIOUS PORTRAITS
1800-1805

group which includes some of
Goya's most accomplished
portraits. The men (Fernán-
úñez [808], San Andrián [818],
or example) have a very English
avour. Among the women, the
omantic 'maja' type of portrait
807, 809] gives way to a cooler,
eo-classical style [814, 828].
s he concentrates more and
ore on the world of everyday
eality, Goya finds a superbly
orceful and direct but unpreten-
ous style with portraits such as
ose of Francisca Sabasa García
16], Pedro Mocarte [834] and
he bookseller's wife [835].

98-839]

798
Archbishop Joaquín Company
c.1800.   Inscr. 212×130 cm.(?)
Valencia, Church of San Martín -
destr.   M.240, G.[450]   *

799
Study for [798].
44×31 cm.
Madrid, Prado (2995)
G.449

800
Joaquín Company   c.1800?
72×55 cm.
Louisville, J.B. Speed Mus.
(58.16)   *

801
Antonio Noriega   s.d. 1801 with
inscr.   102·6×80·9 cm.
Washington, N.G. (Kress 1626)
DF.547s, G.436   *

802

José Queralto   s.d. *D.ⁿ Josef Queralto/Por/Goya./1802.*
101·5×76·1 cm.   Munich, Alte Pinakothek (9334) G.550 *

803

Juan de Villanueva   c.1800-05.
Inscr.   90×67 cm.
Madrid, R.A. San Fernando (678)
M.446, DF.448, G.529   *

804

Tomás Pérez de Estala   c.1800-05.
Inscr.   102×79 cm.
Hamburg, Kunsthalle (239)
M.382, DF.364, G.531   *

805

Condesa de Haro   c.1802-03.
59×36 cm.
Switzerland, priv. coll.
M.320, DF.431, G.517   *

806

Miguel Cayetano Soler   1803?
Inscr.   Pencil 11·7×8·1 cm. (vis.
Madrid, Carderera

Engraving by Rafael Esteve
after [806]

807

Condesa de Fernán Núñez   s.d.
Goya f. a 1803.   211×137 cm.
Madrid, Duques de Fernán Núñez
M.257/357, DF.430, G.487   *

808

Conde de Fernán Núñez   s.d.
Goya f. 1803.   211×137 cm.
Madrid, Duques de Fernán Núñez
M.256, DF.429, G.486   *

809

Joaquina Candado   c.1802-04.
169×113·5 cm.
Valencia, Mus. (583 - R.A.)
M.224, DF.434, G.520   *

810

Marquesa de Villafranca   s.d.
Goya 1804, inscr.   195×126 cm
Madrid, Prado (2448)
M.444, DF.435, G.490

811

Marquesa de Lazán   c.1804.
193×115 cm.
Madrid, Alba Coll.
M.330, DF.447, G.445   *

812

Conde de Teba(?)   c.1804.
63·2×48·9 cm.
New York, Frick Coll. (A.301)
M.432, DF.424, G.535   *

813

Bartolomé Sureda   c.1804-06.
119·7×79·4 cm.
Washington, N.G. (548)
M.427, DF.509, G.533   p. 158 *

814

Teresa Sureda   c.1804-06.
119·7×79·4 cm.
Washington, N.G. (549)
M.428, DF.510, G.534

815

Evaristo Pérez de Castro(?)
c.1804-08.   99×69 cm.
Paris, Louvre (RF 1476)
M.381, DF.445, G.530   *

816

Francisca Sabasa y García
c.1804-08.   71×58 cm.
Washington, N.G. (Mellon 88)
M.499, G.527   Ill. p. 155   *

817

Isabel de Porcel   1804-05.
82×54 cm.
London, N.G. (1473)
M.391, DF.453, G.509   p. 158 *

818

Marqués de San Adrián   s.d.
1804 with inscr.   209×127 cm.
Pamplona, Diputación Foral
M.410, DF.437, G.493   *

819

Manuel García de la Prada
c.1804-08.   212×128 cm.
Des Moines, Art Center (53.15)
M.271, DF.475, G.572   *

820

Ignacio Garcini   s.d. *1804* with
inscr.   104·1×83·2 cm.
New York, M.M.A. (55.145.1)
M.272, DF.438, G.491   *

821

822

823

824

825

…sefa Castilla Portugal de Garcini
d. *1804*, inscr.   104·1×82·2 cm.
ew York, M.M.A. (55.145.2)
.273, DF.439, G.492   *

Marquesa de Castrofuerte
c.1804-08.   91×71 cm.
Montreal, Mus. (45.955)
M.502a, DF.463, G.563   *

Marqués de Castrofuerte
c.1804-08.   91·5×71·1 cm.
Montreal, Mus. (45.954)
M.476a, G.564

Alberto Foraster   s.d. *1804* with
inscr.   138·5×109·5 cm.
New York, Hispanic Soc. (A.103)
M.267, DF.436, G.489   *

Study for [824]?
46×37·4 cm.
New York, priv. coll.
M.268, DF.436n, G.488   *

26

827

828

829

830

…lix de Azara   s.d. *1805* with
scr.   212×124 cm.
aragossa, Mus. (165)
.205a, G.494   *

José de Vargas Ponce   s.d. *1805*
with inscr.   104×82 cm.
Madrid, R.A. de la Historia
M.441, DF.440, G.495   *

Marquesa de Santa Cruz   s.d.
1805 with inscr.   130×210 cm.
Bilbao, Valdés
M.416, DF.441, G.496   *

Marquesa de Santa Cruz   1805?
s. *Goya*   126·5×207·6 cm.
Los Angeles, County Mus.
(M.58.8)   G.497   *

María Vicenta Baruso Valdés   s.d.
1805 with inscr.   104·7×83·7 cm.
Johannesburg, H. Oppenheimer
M.210, DF.443, G.498   *

1

832

833

834

835

…eonora Valdés de Baruso   s.d.
805 with inscr.   104·7×83·7 cm.
ohannesburg, H. Oppenheimer
.209, DF.442, G.499   *

Boy of the Soria family
c.1804-08.   112×80 cm.
Paris, priv. coll.
M.426a, DF.348, G.519

Clara de Soria   c.1804-08
Inscr.   112×80 cm.
Paris, priv. coll.
M.426, DF.349, G.518   *

Pedro Mocarte   c.1805-06.
78×57 cm.   New York,
Hispanic Soc. (A.1890)
M.354, DF.381, G.532   *

The bookseller's wife   c.1805-08.
109·9×78·2 cm.
Washington, N.G. (1903)
M.502, DF.455, G.522   *

36

837

838

839

…orenza Correa   c.1802-03?
J×58 cm.   Paris,
eirs of Comtesse de Noailles
.242, DF.444, G.446   *

Manuel García   c.1802-08.
81·5×58 cm.
Boston, M.F.A. (48.558)
M.270, G.647   *

Condesa de Frutos
c.1804-08.
New York, priv. coll.
M.492   *

Leona de Valencia(?)
c.1804-08.   75·2×52·7 cm.
Dallas, Meadows Mus.
M.503/513, DF.457, G.443

III. GOYA AND THE GOICOECHEA FAMILY 1805-1806

Drawings, miniatures and portraits executed for the marriage of his only son Javier with Gumersinda Goicoechea in 1805. The miniatures in oil on copper show a superb freedom of touch and he captures the Goicoechea family with great sympathy. The drawing of his wife [840] is her only certainly authentic portrait.

Abbreviations and signs: see p. 168
Bx = Boix, Bibl. 9

[840-852]   *

840

Josefa Bayeu d. *AÑO 1805*.
Black chalk 11·1×8·1 cm.
Madrid, Marqués de Casa Torres
Bx.186D, M.688   Ill. p. 246 *

841

Juana Galarza d. *AÑO 1805*
Black chalk and pen 11·4×8·2 cm.
Madrid, Marqués de Casa Torres
Bx.186C, M.685   Ill. p. 154 *

842

Gumersinda Goicoechea d. *AÑO 1805*, inscr. Black chalk 11×8·2 cm.
Formerly Madrid, Carderera
Bx.186A, M.689   Ill. p. 154 *

843

Javier Goya 1805. Inscr.
Black chalk 11·7×8 cm.
Madrid, Marqués de Casa Torres
Bx.186B, M.690   *

844

Javier Goya 1805-06.
Copper 8·1 cm. diam.
Paris, priv. coll.   Ill. p. 154 *

845

Gumersinda Goicoechea
1805-06.   Copper 8 cm. diam.
Paris, priv. coll.   *

846

Manuela Goicoechea
1805-06.   Copper 7·6 cm. diam.
Madrid, X. de Salas G.506 *

847

Gerónima Goicoechea s.d. *1805*, inscr.   Copper 8 cm. diam.
Providence, Rhode Is. S.D.
Mus. (34.1366) G.504   *

848

Cesárea Goicoechea s.d. *1806*, inscr.   Copper 8 cm. diam.
Providence, Rhode Is. S.D.
Mus. (34.1365) G.505   *

849

Juana Galarza 1805-06.
Copper 8 cm. diam.
Formerly Madrid, Alejandro Pidal
M.286, G.502   *

850

Martín Miguel de Goicoechea
1805-06.   Copper 8 cm. diam.
Formerly Madrid, Alejandro Pidal
M 284, G.503   *

851

Gumersinda Goicoechea
1805-06.   192×115 cm.   Paris, heirs of Comtesse de Noailles
M.311, DF. 454, G.500   *

852

Javier Goya 'L'homme en gris'
1805-06.   192×115 cm.   Paris, heirs of Comtesse de Noailles
M.309, DF.367, G.501   *

IV. VARIOUS PORTRAITS 1806-1808

[853-863]

853

Francisca Vicenta Chollet y Caballero s.d. *1806*   103×81 cm.
Paris, Comtesse de Bismarck
M.216, DF.449, G.524   *

854

Tadeo Bravo de Rivero s.d. *1806* with inscr.   208×125 cm.
Brooklyn, Mus. (34.490)
M.400, DF.451, G.508   *

855

Antonio Porcel s.d.*1806* with inscr.   113×82 cm.
Buenos Aires, Jockey Club - destr.
M.390, DF.452, G.510   *

856

Manuel Godoy as Patron of Education 1806.   242×170 cm.
New York, priv. coll.
M.281, G. 538n.   *

857

Students from the Pestalozzi Institute - fragment 1806.
55×96·8 cm.
Dallas, Meadows Mus.   G.538

858

Isidro Máiquez s.d. *Mayquez / Por Goya / 1807*. 77×58 cm. Madrid, Prado (734) M.335, DF.473, G.542 *

859

Isidro González Velázquez s.d. *1807*? with inscr. 93·3×67·2 cm. U.S.A., priv. coll. (loan to Boston, M.F.A.) M.287, DF.417, G.437 *

860

Marquesa de Caballero s.d. *1807* with inscr. 105·3×84·4 cm. Bavaria, priv. coll. M.219, DF.456, G.543n. *

861

Marqués de Caballero s.d. *1807* with inscr. 105·5×84 cm. Budapest, Mus. (3274) M.217, DF.458, G.544 *

862

Antonio Raimundo Ibáñez c.1805-08. 96·5×72·4 cm. Baltimore, Mus. (51.222) M.321 *

863

Portrait of a woman c.1808-12. s. *P.r Goya* 95×69 cm. Collection unknown M.322a, DF.496, G.560 *

GENRE SUBJECTS 1806-1812

The works which Goya painted for his own pleasure remained in his house or studio and were inventoried in 1812. Among them were the six scenes describing the capture of the bandit known as El Maragato in 1806 [864-869], a kind of strip-cartoon, based on contemporary prints. As in many of the drawings from his various albums [Ill.1244-1516], Goya was concerned to express the realism of an actual incident, and after the events of 1808 would turn his reportage to the description of the horrors of the war.

[864-871] *

864

El Maragato points a gun . . . [X.8] 1806-07. Panel 29·2×38·5 cm. Chicago, A.I. (1933.1071) M.597a, DF.215, G.511 p. 156 *

865

Friar Pedro averts . . . [X.8] 1806-07. Panel 29·2×38·5 cm. Chicago, A.I. (1933.1072) M.597b, DF.216, G.512 p. 156 *

866

Friar Pedro wrests the gun . . . [X.8] 1806-07. Panel 29·2×38·5 cm. Chicago, A.I. (1933.1073) M.597c, DF.217, G.513 p. 157 *

867

Friar Pedro clubs El Maragato 1806-07. Panel 29·2×38·5 cm. Chicago, A.I. (1933.1074) M.597d, DF.218, G.514 p. 157

868

Friar Pedro shoots El Maragato 1806-07. Panel 29·2× 38·5 cm. Chicago, A.I. (1933.1075) M.597e, DF.219, G.515 p. 157 *

869

Friar Pedro binds El Maragato 1806-07. Panel 29·2×38·5 cm. Chicago, A.I. (1933.1076) M.597f, DF.220, G.516 Ill. p. 157

870

Women spinning c.1806-10. 95×107 cm. Formerly, Trieste, Francesco Basilio M.653, G.584 *

871

The topers c.1806-12. Inscr. 101·5×80 cm. Raleigh, North Carolina Mus. (G.56.13.1) M.673, G.581 *

LOST WORKS
known from prints

872

Condesa-Duquesa de Benavente d. 1794. Engraving by Fernando Selma from a drawing by Goya *

873

Ramón Cabrera c.1797-99. Lithograph by J. Oton from a painting by Goya *

873a

Device for the Real Instituto Militar Pestalozziano, Madrid 1806. Engraved by Albuerne from a painting by Goya M.90 *

Part three

1808-1819

CHRONOLOGICAL TABLE 1808-1819

Dates	Life of Goya	Spanish History	History outside Spain	The Arts	Literature and Science
1808	The *Majas* inventoried in Godoy's collection (1 Janv.) The Academy commissions Goya to paint the portrait of Ferdinand VII (28 March) At General Palafox's request Goya leaves for Saragossa (2 October) Jovellanos and Ceán Bermúdez return to Madrid	Aranjuez riots (17 March) Charles IV abdicates and Godoy arrested (19 March) Murat enters Madrid (22 March) Ferdinand VII leaves for Bayonne (10 April) Uprising in Madrid (2 May) Joseph made king (6 June) First Siege of Saragossa (June-August) Bailén surrenders (22 July) Napoleon in Spain (5 Nov.) Second Siege of Saragossa (December-February 1809)		Girodet: *The burial of Atala* Beethoven: *Pastoral Symphony* Daumier († 1879) Death of Hubert Robert (aged 75)	Gérard de Nerval († 1855) Barbey d'Aurevilly († 1889)
1810	*Allegory of the Town of Madrid* General Guye, Victor Guye First *Disasters of War* etchings	Spanish colonies in revolt	Marriage of Napoleon and Marie-Louise Napoleon publishes the Penal Code	Chopin († 1849) Schumann († 1856)	Musset († 1857)
1811	Goya awarded the Royal Order of Spain Marriage of Isidoro Weiss and Leocadia breaks down	Death of Jovellanos (aged 67) Moratín made Director-General of Libraries	Birth of the king of Rome	Liszt († 1886)	Théophile Gautier († 1872) Le Verrier († 1877) Ambroise Thomas († 1896)
1812	Death of Josefa Bayeu Inventory and division of the parents' property between Goya and his son Javier *Portraits of Wellington*	Constitution of Cadiz (18 March) Battle of Arapiles (22 July) Wellington in Madrid (Aug.) The French return (3 Nov.)	Russian campaign Moscow taken and burned (September) Retreat from Russia (October-December)	Turner: *Hannibal crossing the Alps* Théodore Rousseau († 1867)	Byron: *Childe Harold* Dickens († 1870) R. Browning († 1889)
1813		Joseph Bonaparte leaves Madrid (17 March) Battle of Vitoria (21 June) Treaty of Valençay (11 Dec.) Ferdinand VII to Spain	Declaration of war by Russia (16 March) and Austria (12 Aug.) against Napoleon Battle of Leipzig (16-19 Oct.)	Wagner († 1883) Verdi († 1901)	Kierkegaard († 1855) Claude Bernard († 1878)
1814	Goya paints the scenes of the 2 and 3 May 1808 *Portraits of Ferdinand VII General Palafox* Birth of María del Rosario Weiss (2 Oct. † 1843) The two *Majas* denounced to the Inquisition as obscene	Decree against the Liberals The Constitution is abolished (4 May) Ferdinand enters Madrid (7 May) Inquisition re-established (21 July)	Paris surrenders (30 March) Napoleon abdicates and Louis XVIII returns (6 Apr.) Pius VII re-establishes the Jesuits Napoleon on Elba (3 May) Peace of Paris (30 May) Treaty of Ghent (24 Dec.)	Ingres: *The Grande Odalisque; Portrait of Mme de Sénones*	Stephenson invents the steam locomotive Byron: *The Corsair* W. Scott: *Waverley* Lermontov († 1841)
1815	Goya summoned to appear before the Inquisition *Self-portraits Duke of San Carlos Miguel de Lardizábal Ignacio Omulryan José Luis Munárriz Rafael Esteve* First *Tauromaquia* prints (published 1816)	Jesuits return (May)	The Hundred Days (1 March-22 June) Waterloo (18 June) Return of Louis XVIII The Holy Alliance		Schlegel: *History of Literature*
1817	Stay in Seville *Saints Justa and Rufina*	Death of Meléndez Valdés in Montpellier (aged 63) Death of Urquijo in Paris	Monroe, President of the United States of America	Daubigny († 1878)	
1818		Dismissal of Finance Minister Garay; Spain falls into anarchy	Congress of Aix-la-Chapelle	Constable: *A cottage in a cornfield*	Keats: *Endymion* Shelley: *The Revolt of Islam* K. Marx († 1883) Turgenev († 1883) Gounod († 1893) Leconte de Lisle († 1894)
1819	Goya buys the 'Quinta del Sordo' (27 February) Goya's first lithographs *The last Communion of St Joseph of Calasanz Juan Antonio Cuervo* Goya seriously ill	Death of Charles IV and María Luisa in Rome The United States buys Florida from Spain Opening of the Prado Museum		Géricault: *Raft of the Medusa* Gérard: *Corinna at Cape Misena* Chassériau († 1856) Offenbach († 1880)	First Atlantic crossing by steamship Laënnec: *De l'auscultation médicale* W. Scott: *Ivanhoe* G. Eliot († 1880) Ruskin († 1900)

NAPOLEON AND SPAIN. JOSEPH BONAPARTE
THE SECOND AND THIRD OF MAY 1808

1808. Goya is 62 years old. The Treaties of Basle (1795) and San Ildefonso bound Spain to the French Republic. The War of the Oranges against Portugal (1801). Trafalgar and Austerlitz (1805). Entry of the French troops into Spain (1807). The Aranjuez plot: Charles IV abdicates in favour of his son Ferdinand VII. Godoy is dismissed. The revolt of the second of May (1808). Meeting at Bayonne: Joseph Bonaparte is made king of Spain.

Self-portrait (detail) [1551] 1815
Academy of San Fernando, Madrid

The events which overwhelmed Spain in 1808 signalled the beginning of one of the most terrible slaughters which Europe had ever known; like the Spaniards we shall call it the War of Independence. For five years Napoleon and Spain opposed each other in a pitiless struggle which saw the birth of a type of combat well known to us today: guerilla warfare. During this War of Independence things were made even more complicated by the countless intrigues which, long before 1808, had been slowly corrupting the politics of the Spanish court and which became more and more complex during the course of the war. For it was not just a question of a face to face confrontation between Napoleon and Spain; England was also involved. During this round in the gigantic contest between the two most powerful nations in Europe, neither the French nor the English, with very few exceptions, were at all concerned with the well-being of Spain for which most of them felt no more than a condescending contempt – a sad privilege of great powers!

On the Spanish side, it is fair to say that the shameful 'Trinity', with Godoy at its head, did everything to hasten the downfall of the kingdom. By the Treaty of Basle (22 July 1795), which had earned the favourite the pompous title of Prince of the Peace, and by the first Treaty of San Ildefonso (19 August 1796), Spain had bound herself to the fortunes of the French Republic and Godoy, fired by ambition and self-interest, did not hesitate to launch the country into ventures which were well beyond its capacities and of which the end result was the Napoleonic invasion.

In reality, Napoleon's main objective in the Iberian peninsula was Portugal, the traditional ally of England, which he wanted to neutralize with a view to negotiating with Pitt. Hence the comic opera of the so-called War of the Oranges in 1801, with the Prince of the Peace blustering and swaggering as never before. Entirely convinced, as was the doting Queen María Luisa, that he was the greatest strategist in Europe, he had himself appointed Generalissimo of the Armies on Land and Sea, which led Talleyrand to say of Charles IV and the queen, 'Before they had a favourite, now they take him for a warrior'. Bonaparte, who was not taken in by this ridiculous comedy and who held Godoy in profound contempt, tried to open the eyes of the king. But the confidential message in which he described Manuel as an 'intruding king' fell into the hands of María Luisa and her lover who managed to persuade the poor Charles to return it to the sender *without reading it.* One cannot help recalling the phrase attributed to the old king, Charles III: 'Que tonto eres, Carlos!' (What an idiot you are, Charles).

All the while, in the shadows of the royal palace, an implacable enemy of Godoy was silently biding his time. At the age of twenty, the prince of Asturias, future King Ferdinand VII, was well aware of his mother's shameful behaviour. How can he be accused of being a bad son when he had such parents? Under the weight of continual reproach and reprimand, which became more and more vexatious for a prince who was no longer a child, he sought support within the court and outside Spain. He was convinced, and not without good reason, that in the event of a vacancy of the throne María Luisa and Godoy would do everything in their power to prevent his accession. Seeing that the favourite was hand-in-glove with Napoleon, he at first turned towards London for help.

Trafalgar, Austerlitz (1805)

Meanwhile, however, the war declared against England had come to a disastrous end for the Franco-Spanish fleet at the battle of Trafalgar (21 October 1805). On the continent, a victory was won at Austerlitz (2 December), followed immediately by the invasion of the kingdom of Naples where Joseph Bonaparte became king (27 December). Charles IV,

The second of May 1808 [982] 1814. 266×345 cm. Prado Museum, Madrid

The second of May and *The third of May 1808*
Painted six years after the tragic events which they represent, these two pictures were executed by Goya, at his own request, 'to perpetuate by means of the brush the most notable and heroic actions and scenes of our glorious insurrection against the tyrant of Europe'. The Regency, 'in consideration of the great importance of so praiseworthy an enterprise and of the artist's well-known talents which will enable him to bring it to a successful conclusion', accorded him, in addition to the expenses of his canvases, stretchers and paints, an allowance of fifteen hundred reales per month while he was working on the pictures.

The first scene is generally said to represent a furious struggle between the people of Madrid and a detachment of Mamelukes of the Imperial Guard in the Puerta del Sol. The second, showing the pitiless repression which followed the uprising, is set beside the hill of Príncipe Pío, in the area known today as the Moncloa. However, topographical accuracy was not Goya's aim; in these two paintings the dramatic action takes place on a level far beyond this kind of photographic realism.

deeply grieved to see his brother dethroned without so much as an excuse from his ally Napoleon, was so hopelessly naïve that he never suspected that it was his 'dear Manuel' who had informed the emperor of a dark plot hatched by the queen of Naples, the mother of the first wife of the prince of Asturias.

It was at this stage that Godoy, by way of a precaution against Ferdinand's possible accession to the throne, dreamed of seizing Portugal with the help of Napoleon and becoming regent there or even king. Then, annoyed because nothing seemed to happen, thinking that he had been made a fool of and seeing the emperor engaged against both Prussians and Russians, he made a spectacular volte-face and attempted to avenge himself by launching a back-handed attack on France. Jena and Auerstedt put an end to the generalissimo's *élan* and he submitted to Napoleon's policies with greater docility than ever.

On his side, Ferdinand, with the support of the Dukes of Infantado and San Carlos, was seeking to avoid a second marriage (his first wife had died in January 1805) with Godoy's sister-in-law, María Josefa de Borbón y Vallabriga, the youngest daughter of Goya's beloved Infante Don Luis. He turned for help to Napoleon and in a secret letter, signed with his own hand on 11 October 1807 at El Escorial, asked to be allowed to marry a Bonaparte.

At the end of 1807 events took a sudden turn. The emperor made up his mind to bring the Portuguese question to an end by conquest and partition, as Godoy himself had suggested, and he marched his troops into Spain even before the Treaty of Fontainebleau had been signed. The French troops were greeted everywhere with enthusiasm by the Spanish for whom the enemy to be struck down was the universally detested Prince of the Peace. The general belief at that time was that Napoleon was coming to support the prince of Asturias, the idol of a nation now thoroughly sick of the corruption which had prevailed in Spain for nearly twenty years. Meanwhile, however, the 'Trinity' – that is Godoy –

Entry of the French into Spain

The third of May 1808 (detail) [984] 1814. Prado Museum, Madrid. See ill. p. 20

attempted to forestall events and had Ferdinand arrested in the palace at El Escorial under the pretence of a plot to usurp the throne. Charles IV informed Napoleon of 'this crime so heinous that it must be punished with the full rigour of the law' and declared that the law of succession should be revoked. In the end the guilty prince 'acknowledged' his crimes and was pardoned, whereupon the court moved to Aranjuez in accordance with its immutable custom.

The masquerade at the Escorial only succeeded in heightening the sympathy of the whole nation for 'poor little Ferdinand' and more especially in irritating Napoleon to such a degree that he became absolutely determined to eliminate the reigning clique in Spain and replace it by a member of his own family.

On the night of 17 to 18 March 1808, at Aranjuez, the prince of Asturias had his revenge: the carefully conditioned mob rose against Godoy and threatened to put everything to the fire and the sword. The king took fright, remembering the fate of his cousin Louis XVI, and after prudently dismissing Godoy – who was only just saved from a lynching – decided, on 19 March, to abdicate in favour of the prince. The Spanish people, freed at last from the infamous 'Trinity', acclaimed their new king, Ferdinand VII.

Aranjuez plot. Godoy dismissed. Ferdinand VII succeeds Charles IV (1808)

Their joy was to be short-lived. Napoleon summoned everyone to Bayonne for a final settlement. Meanwhile Murat, contrary to the Emperor's orders, had entered Madrid. The departure of Ferdinand had already led the inhabitants of the capital to believe that the emperor was taking their young sovereign away from them. On an order from Charles IV, the queen of Etruria and the little Infante Don Francisco de Paula made ready in their turn to leave the royal palace for Bayonne on 2 May. Riots at once broke out; Murat lost his head and ordered the grenadiers and the Polish light infantry to clear the approaches to the royal palace. A little later a squadron of Mamelukes, coming from the Retiro, entered the Puerta del Sol where there were a large number of demonstrators. There followed a short but violent engagement, a furious orgy of slashing, disembowelling and butchering which Goya was to immortalize in the first of his two pictures painted in 1814, the *Second of May in the Puerta del Sol* [982].

The revolt of the second of May in Madrid

Ill. p. 206

The news immediately spread throughout the kingdom and was brought by special messenger to Bayonne. After a degrading family scene in the presence of the emperor,

Victor Guye   [884] N.G., Washington

Pepito Costa   [895] Metropolitan, New York

Victor Guye
[884] 1810. 106·7×85·1 cm.
National Gallery of Art, Washington

Pepito Costa y Bonells
[895] 1813? 105·1×84·5 cm.
Metropolitan Museum of Art, New York

General Nicolas Guye

Children occupy an important place in Goya's work and the earliest commissioned portraits are already filled with the tenderness he felt for his young sitters [I. 209, 210, 231, 233] (see p. 59). The portrait of Pepito Costa y Bonells is one of Goya's most moving canvases; painted at the same time as that of his mother [894], it evokes memories of the Duchess of Alba since the boy's grandfather, Jaime Bonells, was her family doctor. The charming, serious little Pepito's sister, Rafaela Costa, later married the painter Antonio Brugada who was Goya's companion during his last years in Bordeaux.

General Guye and his nephew Victor were among the French whom Goya seems to have had no reluctance in painting under the Napoleonic occupation. The young Victor is wearing the uniform of a page to Joseph I.

General Nicolas Guye   [883] 1810. 106×84·7 cm. Mrs Marshall Field, New York

Ferdinand abdicated in favour of his father; the latter at once handed the crown to Napoleon who ordered his brother Joseph to be proclaimed king of Spain and the Indies on 6 June 1808. Ferdinand, the king of a moment, began a life of golden exile at Valençay. For the Spanish people he became the *Deseado*, the 'desired one'. A government was hastily formed with Mariano Luis de Urquijo as Secretary of State, assisted by such experienced men as Pedro de Ceballos, Cabarrús, Admiral Mazarredo and Azanza. They had all been *afrancesados* from the beginning – long before there was a single French soldier in Spain – and were now 'collaborators' in good faith, convinced that there was no other way of saving the kingdom from the ruin into which twenty years of intrigue and ignominy had plunged it.

Joseph Bonaparte king of Spain

But in Madrid the second of May was only a beginning, the fatal spark which was to set everything ablaze, with the inevitable succession of chain reactions always kindled by the infernal cycle of provocation and repression. After the Puerta del Sol came the Moncloa episode where the rioters who had been caught with weapons in their hands were shot during the night, beside the hill of Príncipe Pío. The scene formed the second part of the bloody diptych painted by Goya, the *Executions of the third of May* [984]. Did he witness these actual scenes? It seems unlikely. However, it may not be out of place to try to dispose once and for all of the tenacious legend, so often repeated by fanciful biographers, which describes Goya in the Quinta del Sordo (House of the deaf man), watching the executions through a telescope, then going off with his gardener, armed with a lantern, to sketch the blood-spattered bodies of the victims on the spot. It makes a very colourful tale but unfortunately Goya did not buy the Quinta until eleven years later. However, like everyone else in Madrid, he must certainly have had the opportunity during those days of rioting to see scattered instances of stabbing or shooting. It was not difficult to do so, and when one remembers Goya's liking for street scenes it is easy to imagine him prowling around the Madrid in which he had lived for more than thirty years, which he loved so well and which had become unrecognizable.

The executions of the third of May

Ill. pp. 20, 207

Bibl. 100, pp. 15-17
See p. 313

Nevertheless, there is a lesson to be drawn from these legends which still cling round the artist's life. In almost every case they are concerned to make him a kind of 'naturalist' before his time, taking the subjects of almost everything he painted or drew directly from life. It is certainly true that Goya was a realist artist and that he was the first to succeed in transcribing reality with a ruthlessness which at first shocks and then convinces us. But it should not be forgotten that his eye was capable of recording what he saw in the most extraordinary way and that his memory enabled him to recreate years later, as if he were still there, many of the scenes which he had witnessed. The famous canvases of the *Second of May* and the *Third of May* are proof of this, since they were painted in 1814, six years after the events which they record.

During the two weeks which Ferdinand spent in Madrid before leaving for Bayonne, he had time to pose for Goya for three-quarters of an hour at two separate sittings. This was the first and last time he sat for him. An equestrian portrait had been commissioned by the Academy of San Fernando [875] and in spite of the troubled times in the capital the artist continued to work on it until October. When informing the Academy that the picture was ready, he apologized for not personally supervising its hanging, 'having been called by his Excellency Señor Don José Palafox to go this week to Saragossa to see and study the ruins of that town for the purpose of painting the glorious exploits of its inhabitants, which I cannot refuse, given the great interest I take in my country's glory'. On 23 December, after his return to Madrid, he swore 'love and lealty' to King Joseph, together with thirty thousand heads of families.

Bibl. 166, p. 86
Bibl. 167, p. 87

1808-1814. Goya is 62 to 68 years old. Death of his wife Josefa (1812). Paintings of the war. Portraits of Spanish, French and English generals: Palafox, Guye, Wellington. 'The Colossus'. Joseph Bonaparte is king of Spain.

Napoleon had written to Murat on 29 March 1808: 'If war breaks out, all will be lost . . .' Through the accumulated mistakes of the man whom the Spanish people – never at a loss for witticisms against their oppressors – had already baptized the 'great cabbage head', the war began on 2 May in front of the royal palace and in the Puerta del Sol. From that moment on, through five years of battles, sieges and guerilla warfare, of heroism matched by equal brutality, everything was indeed lost, in the first place for Napoleon whose abdication was to coincide with the return of Ferdinand VII and in the second place for Spain which suffered the long after-effects of such a devastating blood bath.

The guerilla war

The new phenomenon which, as already mentioned, gave this War of Independence a unique quality was guerilla warfare. In a very short time the whole country was swept into the struggle by the ever-increasing number of provincial juntas. False rumours spread with incredible speed and, passed on by word of mouth, succeeded in creating a permanent state of terror in which the people, normally peaceful but murderous when angered, cried out for revenge. The Spaniard loves blood and death; if he believes his cause to be just, he can be remorselessly cruel. Besides, in a country of almost universal poverty, it was the all-powerful Church and not 'Divine Reason' which ruled. In the eyes of some of the clergy, and especially the regular clergy – it should not be forgotten that there were then more than one hundred thousand monks and nuns in the convents of Spain – the French were abominable atheists, the spiritual sons of Voltaire and Rousseau, and Napoleon himself was Antichrist. Often it was the monks who led the juntas or incited true patriots to murder

Bibl. 142, p. 239

in the name of Christ. And they were not afraid to set the example.

The fury of the Spanish was in reality due to the over-simple belief that the French had stolen their king from them. Having had to endure that the Spain of Charles the Fifth should be governed by a Godoy for twenty years, they had made an absolute idol of Ferdinand. And now Napoleon held him captive at Valençay and had put a usurper on the throne. In these conditions, Joseph could be the most gracious of kings, the most ardent admirer of Spain and the author of the most liberal reforms which the country

Shooting in a military camp
This scene must have been inspired by the War of Independence and was no doubt painted after the year 1808. The picture probably belongs to the series of 'Twelve horrors of the war' listed in the inventory of 1812 under the number 12 (see Appendix I).

Shooting in a military camp　[921] c.1808-12. 32×58 cm. Romana coll., Madrid

had yet known, it was all to no avail. For the Spanish, 'their' king was Ferdinand VII and anyone who supported the usurper became an enemy of the motherland.

Yet how astonished these patriots would have been if they could have seen how shamefully the *Deseado* behaved in exile. Comfortably installed in Talleyrand's superb château at Valençay, Ferdinand was not content to amuse himself as best he could in the company of his brother the Infante Don Carlos, his old uncle the Infante Don Antonio and his retinue but stooped to demonstrations of the most abject servility. Having in his turn sworn loyalty to King Joseph, he then asked to be accorded the honour of wearing the Royal Order of Spain (the notorious 'Aubergine' whose bearers were persecuted by him on his return in 1814). He missed no opportunity of acclaiming Napoleon and when offered a means of escape by the English he promptly betrayed the scheme to his warders; finally he expressed the desire to become 'the adoptive son of H.M. the Emperor, our August sovereign'. Unhappy Spain who shed her blood for such a figure of straw! As long as the fiction of the wretched king, a victim of 'infamous treatment', 'surrounded by jailors and spies' and 'ignobly kept in irons' by the tyrant, continued to be piously maintained by the juntas, the whole of Spain prayed for its beloved monarch and his return to the throne became the very symbol of liberty, dearly paid but finally recovered. The moment of truth came in 1814 and we shall see how cruel it was to be for those who had suffered so much and hoped so fervently.

As far as Goya is concerned, we know that he spent the whole of the war in Madrid, with the exception of his hasty journey to Saragossa in the autumn of 1808, at the invitation of Palafox [901], after the first siege of the town. In Madrid he lived not in the Puerta del Sol and still less at the Quinta del Sordo (which he did not acquire until February 1819) but in a house at number 15 Calle del Valverde, which he had bought in 1800. His wife Josefa was the only one who shared his home, since Javier and Gumersinda had left them in 1806. What kind of life did he lead in this semi-solitude aggravated by his deafness? Only the inventory of their joint possessions, drawn up six years later, after the death of his wife, gives us a glimpse into his home life. It reveals the interior of a well-to-do bourgeois of the period, though some details are rather striking: first, the considerable amount of jewelry and silver which, in a total estate – including the house and ready cash – worth 357,700 reales, were valued at 52,060 reales while all the paintings and prints together were estimated at only 11,939 reales. Then, there was the curiously large number of seats: no less than fifty-six chairs, armchairs and stools, to which must be added the famous 'yellow damask sofa' on which he posed his sitters on several occasions. It has been concluded that the *tertulias* in Goya's home were frequent and well-attended. These meetings of friends or neighbours must have played an important rôle during the war years when there was a greater need than ever to exchange news and views concerning the events of the day. In spite of his deafness, the master of the house could understand most of what was said by lip-reading, and for anyone who has ever frequented *tertulias* in Madrid it is easy to imagine what kind of subjects were discussed at these gatherings, in the midst of the chaotic political situation and the war. Goya undoubtedly saw many scenes of violence himself but since he remained in Madrid he absorbed far more from this exchange of news which day by day wove a kind of fabulous, epic chronicle of Spain at war.

Apart from the etchings of the *Disasters of War* [993-1148], which are the subject of the following chapter, Goya made many small pictures which he kept for himself or those closest to him and which represent scenes of murder, shooting, prisoners, rape and fire, besides those almost indecipherable scenes, certainly among the finest, where figures moulded from light and shadow seem to writhe or fly from the threat of some unknown, monstrous horror [914-921]. In these, Goya goes beyond the conventional limits of a painting or a print to cry aloud rather than portray his pity and his indignation. But it should be noted that he never painted a single scene to glorify the regular Spanish army, still less the forces of Wellington; the only heroes in his eyes were the common people, the brave

Ferdinand at the Château de Valençay

Bibl. 142, p. 242

Goya in Madrid during the war

Bibl. 153, p. 13. Appendix VIII

Death of Josefa Bayeu de Goya (1812)
Bibl. 161, pp. 79-91 and Appendix III

Bibl. 161, p. 82

Making shot in the Sierra de Tardienta
The two little panels showing the manufacture of gunpowder and of shot in the Sierra de Tardienta are records of the guerilla war. In 1810 Don José Mallén, a shoemaker from the Aragonese village of Almudevar, near the Sierra de Tardienta, set up a clandestine munitions factory. Goya's memories of his journey to Saragossa in 1808 probably inspired these two landscapes – a theme rarely found in his œuvre – which are handled in the sketch-like style characteristic of his most personal works.

women and the men without uniforms, almost without arms, who fought in the shadow of the crushing boot of the conqueror.

From this passionate protest against the French invasion and above all against its 'fatal consequences' for Spain, we might conclude that Goya belonged to those good patriots who saw in Napoleon a henchman of the French Revolution and thus of the devil, who ridiculed 'Pepe Botella' – Jo Bottles – and prayed daily for the return of the *Deseado*. Surely the author of the *Disasters of War*, the painter of the *Second of May* and the *Third of May*, the portraitist of Palafox and Wellington [896-901] must have taken sides? The answer is that Goya did not take sides in the sense in which this is understood today. Although the mutilated, dismembered, quartered bodies of so many anonymous martyrs aroused his rightful anger against the cruel foreigners, he was nevertheless caught, like so many of his friends and compatriots, in such a web of contradiction and internal conflict that he could not be resolutely for or resolutely against anyone or anything. For more than twenty years he and his dearest friends had dreamed of a better Spain, released at last from its medieval straight-jacket; he had, so to speak, 'militated' with them in his own way by publishing the *Caprichos*; and he had just seen Napoleon issue in a few days a series of decrees which could only give the *ilustrados* overwhelming satisfaction: the suppression of the tribunal of the Inquisition, the abolition of feudal rights and privileges, the closing of two-thirds of the convents. Later on, in spite of the instability of his storm-tossed passage, Joseph attempted to continue the policy of liberal reform so much desired by the Spanish intel-

Ill. p. 214

Making shot in the Sierra de Tardienta [981] c.1810-14. Panel 33×52 cm. Royal Palace, Madrid

213

Don José Rebolledo de Palafox y Melci (1775-1847) was Aragonese, like Goya, and distinguished himself by his heroic defence of Saragossa during the two sieges of 1808 and 1809, which later earned him the title of Duke of Saragossa with the status of a grandee of the first rank. It is known that the young general summoned Goya, after the lifting of the first siege, to 'see and study the ruins of that town for the purpose of painting .the glorious exploits of its inhabitants'. However, no works are known which would correspond with this intention.

The group of portraits and drawings of the Duke of Wellington was executed by Goya after the battle of Arapiles on 10 August 1812 and probably in Madrid following the victorious general's triumphal entry into the city on 12 August.

Equestrian portrait of General Palafox (detail) [901] 1814. Prado Museum, Madrid

The Duke of Wellington   [897] 1812-14. Panel 60×51 cm. National Gallery, London

ligentsia, and some of the men Goya had known best or admired most now 'collaborated' with this policy: Meléndez Valdés, Manuel Silvela, Urquijo, Moratín, Melón, Arnao, García de la Prada, Bernardo de Iriarte and many more. In 1810, at the very time when he was dating the first plates of the *Disasters of War*, he was commissioned to execute a large *Allegory of the Town of Madrid* [874], with a portrait of Joseph I in a medallion; he painted one of his most vigorous portraits, of General Guye [883], the companion in arms of General Hugo, and at the same time the portrait of his nephew, Victor Guye [884], in the dress of a page to King Joseph, which is so close in its melancholy charm to the little Pepito Costa y Bonells [895]; he also painted the portraits of two notorious *afrancesados*, General José Manuel Romero, Minister of Justice and of the Interior [882] and Canon Juan Antonio Llorente [881] who was commissioned to write an official history of the Inquisition when the dreaded tribunal was abolished, and whose portrait is one of the most intensely 'alive' which Goya ever painted. Finally, although he was no longer referred to as Court Painter, Goya was awarded the Royal Order of Spain in 1811.

Portraits of Frenchmen and 'afrancesados'
Ill. p. 209

Ill. p. 208

A fresh contradiction seems to lie in his depiction, about the same period, of two celebrated scenes of the guerilla war, the *Making of gunpowder* and *Making of shot* [980, 981] in the Sierra de Tardienta. These afford unusual examples of landscape painting in his work and probably derive from memories of his journey to Saragossa in 1808. Finally, when Wellington arrived to liberate Madrid in August 1812, it is hard to tell whether he was anxious or merely willing to paint the victor of Ciudad Rodrigo. He made several portraits, based on a red chalk drawing [898]; the bust study in the National Gallery, London, is greatly superior to the large equestrian portrait which was painted in haste and exhibited at the Academy of San Fernando September [896-900].

Scenes of the guerilla war
Ill. p. 213

This disconcerting swing of the pendulum characterizes the whole of Goya's life but is hardest to understand at a period when people generally took sides with violent conviction. Some biographers give up the attempt and, unable to demonstrate his allegiance to one side or the other, draw a discreet veil over all the apparent contradictions. But the very greatness of Goya, the mark of his most personal and most powerful works – the *Caprichos*, the frescoes of San Antonio, the *Disparates*, the 'black paintings' and the enigmatic *Colossus* – may indeed reside in just this quality of ambiguity.

The colossus
This painting appears in the inventory of 1812 under the number 18, with the title *A giant*, and was therefore one of the many important works which Goya painted for himself and kept in his house. It has often been suggested that this enigmatic figure may symbolize war, from which men and beasts are flying in wild disorder. Whatever its true significance, it remains one of Goya's most impressive and most tragic works.

The colossus   [946] c.1808-12. 116×105 cm. Prado Museum, Madrid

Landscape with buildings and trees   [II.748] c.1800-08. Etching and aquatint 16·5×28·5 cm. Art Institute, Chicago

Duro es el paso! (Hard is the way!) *Desastres 14*   [1013]

Estragos de la guerra (Ravages of war) *Desastres 30*   [1044]

1810-1823. Goya is 64 to 77 years old. The 82 engravings of the 'Disasters of War' (published 25 years after his death, in 1863). Scenes of the war and the famine of 1811-12; satirical 'caprichos'. Reign of Joseph Bonaparte; return of Ferdinand VII (1814); the Constitution (1820-23).

* Ill. p. 218

Ill. p. 211

Bibl. 154, doc. 225

Bibl. 88, I, p. 139

*Ill. p. 219

Landscape with buildings and trees
This print and its companion, *Landscape with waterfall* [750], show two motifs which recur throughout Goya's work: a great rock, and a building or town set high up on a hill. These motifs appear in many of his paintings and prints and find their grandest form in the 'black paintings' of the Quinta del Sordo (see p. 23). The landscape etchings are known only from a few impressions. In 1810 Goya cut the copperplates in half and used the backs for four war scenes.

Duro es el paso!   Estragos de la guerra
c. 1810-11. Etching and aquatint
These two prints were etched on the back of the *Landscape with waterfall*, after Goya had cut the copperplate in two, and they are certainly among the earliest plates which he engraved for the war series. The four compositions engraved on the backs of the landscape plates show the atrocities suffered by the Spanish people at the hands of the French soldiers – the women raped, the men hanged or shot, and whole families killed by the bombardment of the heavy artillery (see also plates *13* and *15* [1011, 1015]).

The War of Independence against the French gave rise to a spate of patriotic publications, both literary and artistic. In 1808 Goya was called by General Palafox to Saragossa in order to record the 'glorious exploits' of the inhabitants during the first siege of the town by the French. The results of this project are unknown but one of the eighty-two prints of the *Disasters of War* recalls perhaps the most celebrated act of heroism during the siege, the manning of a cannon by the young Agustina of Aragon, illustrated by Goya in plate *7* [1000].*

Goya apparently began work on his series of prints in 1810, the date which is engraved on three of the copperplates. The small paintings of violence and atrocities mentioned in the previous chapter [914-935] may represent his private conflict and distress during the early stages of the French occupation. By 1810 there could no longer be any illusions about the real intentions of the 'tyrant of Europe'. There was a general uprising early in that year, and a wave of savagery and brutality engulfed the whole country as the Spanish people turned like wild beasts against their oppressors. On either side atrocities were met with the most horrifying reprisals. The people armed themselves with pitchforks and knives to resist the guns and sabres of the French troops whose brutal raping of their wives and daughters – the subject of so many scenes at the beginning of the *Disasters* series – was symbolic of the rape of their motherland. Goya could not remain quiet. He took up his engraver's tools which had lain virtually abandoned since his work on the *Caprichos* twelve years before and began the series which was to show the 'fatal consequences of the bloody war in Spain with Bonaparte'. He set about his project with the same haste and enthusiasm with which he had worked on the earlier set of prints. Harris has shown how he started by using any copperplates which came to hand: since materials were scarce he made do with odd sizes and with imperfect plates and even went so far as to cut up and re-use two of the most beautiful plates which he ever engraved, the landscapes of which only a very few proofs are known [II.748, 750], and on the backs of which he engraved four of the *Disasters*, plates *13* to *15* and *30* [1011-1015, 1044].

The plates dated 1810, which were probably among the very earliest to be engraved, show scenes such as Goya might have observed in and around Saragossa when he went there in 1808, the wounded being roughly patched up in the open, in plate *20* [1024], piles of dead lying in the desolate countryside, in plate *22* [1029]*, and then stripped of their clothes and thrown into an open pit: *Charity* is the terse caption on plate *27* [1038], and it has been suggested that the figure standing with his arms folded, an impassive expression on his face, may be Goya himself. He certainly lent support to the belief that he actually witnessed the scenes, by his captions on two plates showing civilians fleeing from the invaders with their children and their belongings: *I saw this*, *And this too* on plates *44* and *45* [1064, 1066]. Yet however immediate and real the source of Goya's inspiration, he managed to combine the impact of what often appears to be direct reportage with a deep concern for the artistic force and validity of the image he was creating.

As in all the other series of engravings, his mastery of the technical problems paralleled the development of his style which gradually became more powerful and more abstract. The early plates with their numerous small figures and lack of structure in the design give way to the most moving and horrifying of the war scenes, in plates *31* to *39* [1046-1055], where the strength and sureness of the etched line and the dramatic handling of the aquatint recall the later plates of the *Caprichos*, although the freedom with which they are now

Que valor ! (What courage !) *Desastres 7*　[1000]　c.1810-15. Etching and aquatint

Que valor !
This print recalls the heroic action of the girl known as Agustina of Aragon, during the first siege of Saragossa in 1808. She fired a cannon against the French when all who manned it had fallen or fled, and the incident was celebrated in many contemporary accounts and popular prints. Goya eliminates all but the essential elements: the pile of bodies, the iron strength of the cannon, the delicate, graceful figure of the girl, and thus creates an image of deep pathos and timeless validity.

Con razon ó sin ella (Rightly or wrongly) *Desastres 2*　[995]　c.1812-15. Etching and lavis

Con razon ó sin ella
Probably one of the latest war scenes engraved by Goya, it is almost a synthesis of the left and right halves of the two great paintings of 1814 which commemorate the events of the second and third of May 1808 (see pp. 20, 206). On the left are the Spanish people fighting savagely against the foreign intruders and on the right the line of soldiers, their muskets with fixed bayonets at the ready. The setting in the print is highly abstract and Goya achieves a close-knit design of great drama and power.

used shows the length of Goya's stride into the nineteenth century. This group of plates was probably etched around the years 1812 to 1814, at the time when he was working on the prints recording the famine which killed thousands and reduced the people of Madrid to living skeletons, begging and dying in the streets – see plates *48* to *64* [1070-1103].

Goya must have intended to publish the prints as soon as circumstances were favourable. While the albums of drawings discussed in chapter six constituted his private journal, the

See pp. 230-239

Tanto y mas

One of the three plates which Goya signed and dated in 1810. This pathetic 'still-life' of human bodies may have been inspired by scenes which Goya himself saw on his journey to Saragossa in 1808. The figure lying prostrate in the centre of the group, his arms outstretched in front of him, recurs in many of the war scenes and in both the large paintings of the second and third of May 1808 (as a French soldier in one, a civilian in the other). This pathetic figure is a counterpart to another which recurs throughout Goya's work: the dramatic, gesticulating figure of which the most celebrated example is the man in *The third of May* (see p. 207).

Tanto y mas (All this and more) *Desastres 22* [1029] 1810. Etching and lavis 16·1×25·4 cm.

Barbaros!

Again, in this late war scene, Goya underlines the helplessness of the civilian population and the cruelty of the well-armed French. This scene, too, recalls the great painting of *The third of May 1808* but there is no heroism, no dignity here. The wretched victim is bound with cords to a tree while two soldiers fire at point blank range into his back. The broad handling of the aquatint suggests a lowering sky; the officer in the middle distance watches and records; the atmosphere is doom-laden and Goya's brief cry – *Barbarians!* – sets off the nightmare quality of the scene.

Barbaros! (Barbarians!) *Desastres 38* [1053] c.1812-15. Etching and aquatint

See pp. 227-229 etchings were made as a public protest. However, the return of Ferdinand two years after Wellington's decisive victory in 1812 only succeeded in bringing about the most 'fatal consequence' of all, the triumph of the forces of reaction and the re-subjection of Spain to a régime of cruelty and terror. Goya was probably still working on the war and famine scenes when Ferdinand began his purges and organized persecution of the liberals. Instead of publishing these prints, he started work in 1815 on the series of etchings illustrating

Lo peor es pedir   Lo mismo
Two details from the later war and famine scenes, made between 1812 and 1815. One of the simplest and most conclusive demonstrations of Goya's graphic genius is that the whole or an isolated detail of such works can be enlarged without any loss of intensity. The tiny compositions of the *Disasters of War* are as monumental in conception and as firm in execution as the large paintings of the second and third of May.

Lo peor es pedir (The worst is to beg)
Desastres 55 (detail)   [1084]   c.1812-15.

Lo mismo (The same) *Desastres 3* (detail)
[996] c.1810-15. Etching and lavis

the art of bullfighting, which he issued the following year (see chapter five). At the same time, however, he bought a new supply of copperplates and began to add a group of savagely satirical prints to the war and famine scenes. Largely anti-clerical in theme, they castigate the antics and machinations of the Church which deceived and betrayed the people and actively encouraged every kind of repression [1104-1138].

Ill. p. 221

The final form which Goya intended the whole work to take is known from a complete set of numbered proofs which he gave to his friend Ceán Bermúdez. The title page has the inscription already mentioned: 'Fatal consequences of the bloody war in Spain with Bonaparte and other striking *caprichos*' (the 'striking caprichos' being the satirical plates just referred to). In Ceán's copy, the titles are written in pencil below the etchings, most probably by Goya himself. They are an integral part of the compositions and help to establish their relationship with the spectator who is listening to the artist's exclamations and comments on the scenes before them: What courage! – They don't want to – That's tough! – Barbarians! – It's no use crying out – What madness! Most effective are the sequences where the titles follow on from one plate to the next: They don't want to – Nor do these – Nor these – of women being attacked and raped by French soldiers (plates *9* to *11*); For having a knife – No one can tell why – Not in this case either – of men being garrotted or hanged on suspicion of guerilla activity (plates *34* to *36*).

Bibl. 103, pp. 95-103

In the end the plates were never published in Goya's lifetime and the first edition was issued by the Royal Academy of San Fernando in 1863, with the title *Los Desastres de la Guerra*. For this edition, Goya's manuscript titles were faithfully engraved on the copperplates. But one inscription proved too much for the susceptibilities of the academicians. On the famous etching – plate *69* [1112] – where the skeleton rises from his grave to inscribe the single word *Nada* (Nothing) on a sheet of paper, Goya's original title read *Nada. Ello lo dice* (Nothing. That's what it says). The Academy decided to soften the extreme and possibly atheistic pessimism of this title by altering it to *Ello dirá* (The event will tell).

Publication of the *Disasters of War* in 1863

The series as published ended with plates *79* and *80* which show the death of Truth and imply that if she tries to rise she will again be struck down by the forces of evil and reaction, among which the Church figures so prominently [1132, 1134]. But the final print which Goya designed for the series, plate *82* [1138], is a vision of peace and plenty which can be interpreted as a reaffirmation of his hope for mankind. This optimistic ending, after the dark pessimism of the preceding plates, parallels the moving sequence of drawings [1350-1353] which are linked to the last, brief liberal triumph from 1820 to 1823, before the iron hand of repression forced the remaining liberals into hiding and exile and Goya decided to go to France, leaving behind the unpublished plates of the *Disasters*.

See pp. 238-239

Gracias á la almorta
Where the war scenes are stark and brutal, Goya creates in many of the famine scenes an atmosphere of gentle pathos and resignation which expresses the weakness and suffering of the starving people. This print, with its dreamlike quality and masterly handling of the aquatint, is one of the most moving and beautiful in the series.

Gracias á la almorta (Thanks to the millet) *Desastres 51* [1076] Etching and aquatint

El buitre carnívoro
This is one of the satirical *caprichos enfáticos* which Goya added to the series of war and famine scenes. The plates immediately preceding and following this one suggest that the 'vulture' in question is the Church herself, and a visual trick shows the pope (who also appears in the following plate) as her 'golden egg', or perhaps something worse. The hideous bird is staggering away, its wings clipped and ragged, prodded by the pitch-fork of a Spaniard who had earlier fought against the French (see p. 218) and was now combating a worse evil which threatened to enslave the people.

El buitre carnívoro (The carnivorous vulture) *Desastres 76* [1126] c.1815-20. Etching 17·5×22 cm.

221

Ferdinand VII

In 1796 there had been secret negotiations between Jovellanos and the Marquis of Santa Cruz with a view to Goya's painting the portrait of the young prince of Asturias, the future Ferdinand VII. Nothing came of this project and before 1808 Goya seems only to have represented the young prince in the large group picture of the *Family of Charles IV* (see pp. 149, 150).

In 1808, during the tragic and eventful days which shaped the fate of the nation, Ferdinand became king for a brief period, after the abdication of his father on 19 March. He accorded Goya two brief sittings for an equestrian portrait which had been commissioned by the Academy of San Fernando and was completed on 2 October of the same year, when Ferdinand had already abdicated in his turn at Bayonne [875].

When the *Deseado* mounted the throne again in 1814, Goya executed several portraits of him, using the studies made in 1808 [1536-1541]. The portrait reproduced here was painted for one of the ministries and shows the king wearing his regal robes with the great collar of the Golden Fleece and the sash of the Order of Charles III. It is significant that Ferdinand VII himself never commissioned his portrait from Goya, an indication of the antipathy which the two men certainly felt for each other.

Ferdinand VII with royal mantle   [1540] 1814. 212 × 146 cm. Prado Museum, Madrid

Chapter 4

THE RETURN OF FERDINAND VII. THE REACTION
LAST OFFICIAL COMMISSIONS

1814-1819. Goya is 68 to 73 years old. Departure of King Joseph (1813). Regency council and return of Ferdinand VII to Madrid. Purge of the liberals. Self-portraits, the 'Session of the Royal Company of the Philippines' (1815).

King Joseph finally left Madrid at the head of an exhausted and demoralized army on 17 March 1813. He was given the *coup de grâce* at Vitoria on 21 June by Wellington who carried off a fabulously rich booty, including more than two hundred pictures seized from the palaces, convents and churches of Spain: paintings by Velázquez, Titian, Giulio Romano, Correggio, Murillo and many other sixteenth – and seventeenth – century artists. The then president of the Royal Academy in London was amazed at the sight of these treasures and observed that the Correggios and the Giulio Romanos deserved to be framed in diamonds and that it was worth having fought a battle for them. The taste of the time accounts for the lack of interest accorded to a group of fifty to sixty canvases which included 'several fine paintings by modern masters, which are worth preserving'. Among them may have lurked a rare pearl: one of the two known versions of Goya's *Marquesa de Santa Cruz* [II.829]. Wellington must have had some qualms about carrying off such plunder which, though seized from the enemy according to the rules of war, nevertheless formed part of the artistic heritage of his ally Spain. He insisted that the pictures should be handed back to the government in Madrid, but to no avail; Ferdinand VII refused the offer and made him a present of what amounted to a veritable museum.

While awaiting the return of the *Deseado*, a regency council was set up in Madrid on 6 January 1814, headed by a man whom Goya had known for many years, Cardinal Don Luis María de Borbón, the son of the Infante Don Luis and brother of the Countess of Chinchón. Goya must have recalled how more than thirty years ago he set out as a hopeful and enthusiastic young man for Arenas de San Pedro. No one could then have imagined, in the clear autumn atmosphere, at the foot of the misty blue sierra, that the two enchanting children whom he had just painted were destined to lead such fateful lives. The little María Teresa became the wife of Godoy, the most detested man in all the kingdom, and was now in exile [I.210, II.793]; her elder brother, his long locks then tied with a velvet ribbon, now dressed in the cardinal's red robes in which Goya had also painted him as a younger man [I.209, II.794], was preparing to hand the throne of Spain back to the man whom his brother-in-law Godoy hated so much. Ferdinand made his solemn entry into Madrid on 7 May 1814, in final triumph over Godoy, and the popular rejoicings knew no bounds. Triumphal arches were set up everywhere and one of them may have been decorated with the two canvases which Goya had just painted, representing the *Second of May in the Puerta del Sol* and the *Executions of the third of May* [982, 984]. As early as 24 February, Goya had informed the Regency of 'his burning desire to perpetuate by means of the brush the most notable and heroic actions and scenes of our glorious insurrection against the tyrant of Europe'. But the chief aim of his petition seems to have been financial: he said that he was in 'a state of absolute penury' and requested some help from public funds in order to be able to carry out this noble project. Deprived of his salary as Court Painter under Joseph I, he hoped by this means to attract the attention of the palace and to be reinstated with all his former rights and prerogatives as soon as possible. In fact, the wily old *baturro* was no doubt hoping to elicit both sympathy and a pardon. It is difficult to believe that he was really impoverished when only a little more than a year before he had received, as his share of the property which was divided after his wife's death, more than a hundred and forty thousand reales in cash, without counting the furniture, silver and jewels.

But this patriotic fervour was not enough to wipe out the past. Even before he entered Madrid, Ferdinand VII had signed the first decrees against the liberals. He abolished the

Prisoner   [986] c.1810-20. Etching

Bibl. 154, doc. 225

See p. 212

The reaction

Session of the Royal Company of the Philippines
It is now generally agreed that this painting, of impressive dimensions, represents a meeting of the Royal Company of the Philippines which had been founded by Charles III in 1785. The session is presided over by the king, Ferdinand VII, who is surrounded by the directors of the company among whom one can make out the figure of Don José Luis Munárriz. Munárriz, a friend of Goya, had given up his post as secretary of the Academy of San Fernando in May 1815 in order to take on his directorship of the Royal Company of the Philippines, and it is possible that the portrait of him which Goya signed and dated in 1815 (see p. 226) is closely connected with the execution of this huge canvas.

However, historical and documentary data are of secondary importance. What counts above all in this painting is the impression of boredom, of torpor, which fills the cavernous, bare room where the harsh light from the tall bay window invades the shadows, and accentuates figures and setting with vigorously applied touches of paint.

Session of the Royal Company of the Philippines   [1534] c.1815. 327×417 cm. Musée Goya, Castres

Constitution which the junta of Cadiz, the most obdurately anti-Napoleonic of them all, had drawn up and voted for in 1812; and the cheers and demonstrations of joy had hardly died down before a period of merciless repression began. Not only the *afrancesados* but also the liberals who upheld the Constitution of Cadiz were hunted like wild beasts. Men were imprisoned, tortured and killed with revolting sadism. The more fortunate went into exile in France where they joined the partisans of Joseph who had preceded them there. In this way Goya lost some of his best friends: Moratín and Meléndez Valdés became exiles, the actor Máiquez was imprisoned and went mad.

On 21 May 1814 the Duke of San Carlos [1542] was made responsible for a 'purge' of the employees of the royal palace, who included Goya. The affair dragged on for several months and it was not until April 1815 that the artist and his son were officially listed in the first category of 'purified' persons who were thereby reinstated in all their rights, including their salary and pension. The documents in Goya's dossier provide a good deal of information concerning his life under the occupation: not only had he not received any money from the 'intruding government' but, as he declared, he had preferred to sell his jewels cheaply in order to live; according to the evidence of Antonio Bailó, a bookseller at number 4 Calle de las Carretas – whose young wife may have been painted by Goya [II.835] – he avoided all contact with those connected with the 'intruding government'; finally, a very little known detail, he had left Madrid for Piedrahita (mid-way between the capital and the Portuguese border) 'with the intention of making his way from there to a free country'. This plan was not pursued as a result of a plea from his children and a warning from the Minister of Police that the property of the whole family would be seized if he did not return to Madrid within a given period. It nevertheless affords a dramatic proof of the courage of this sixty-five year old man, stone-deaf, who set out in the midst of the war to cross the sierras which surrounded Madrid, in search of a free country. So much of his life was inspired by the *Divina Libertad* whom one of his figures kneels to adore [1350].

The purges

Bibl. 154, docs 226-248

See p. 249

Ill. p. 301

Session of the Royal Company of the Philippines (detail) [1534]   c.1815. Musée Goya, Castres (see p. 224)

Ill. p. 153

See p. 152

Ill. p. 222

Ill. p. 205

Goya and the Inquisition

For Goya the return of the *Deseado* was in no sense synonymous with liberty and joy. His purge which had already been dragging on for a whole year was already causing him grave concern when a completely unexpected threat materialized in November 1814. Since 1808 the collection of paintings which had belonged to the Prince of the Peace had lain, together with other works, in the General Repository of sequestrated property. In 1814 five 'obscene paintings', including four from Godoy's collection, were brought out and handed over to the Grand Inquisitor. Godoy had acquired some superb 'erotic' paintings, including Velázquez's *Toilet of Venus*, Correggio's *Mercury instructing Cupid*, *The rape of Lucretia* after Tintoretto and above all Goya's two celebrated *Majas* [II.743, 744]. All nude paintings came under the jurisdiction of the Holy Office and in 1815 Goya was summoned to appear before its fearful tribunal, which had been reinstated by Ferdinand, to account for the *Majas*. The sequel to the affair is unknown and the case was probably suppressed. Nevertheless, one can imagine Goya's feelings towards the new régime. Though he laboured to produce a whole series of portraits of Ferdinand VII for various official bodies [1536-1541], he was not looked upon with any favour by the king. He was nearing the age of seventy; most of those who had appreciated his painting and contributed to his fame and fortune over more than twenty years, from 1785 to 1808, had died or been scattered by the war. He was the grand old man of a previous age and was no longer in fashion with the court which preferred Vicente López. This in itself was proof that Goya had had no influence either on his period or on his immediate successors; on the contrary, the heights to which he had attained were only equalled by the depths to which taste and art descended after him.

And yet this old 'has-been' was younger than ever and the works which he produced in 1815 alone are evidence of his unshakeable vitality. He marked each major stage in his life with a self-portrait, and the two painted at this time, in the Academy of San Fernando and the Prado Museum [1551, 1552], are the most powerful of them all. The expression

Miguel de Lardizábal   [1546] 1815. 86×65 cm.
National Gallery, Prague

José Luis Munárriz   [1545] 1815. 85×64 cm.
Royal Academy of San Fernando, Madrid

Miguel de Lardizábal
For a long time it was thought that this portrait of Miguel de Lardizábal in fact represented the famous guerilla leader Espoz y Mina, on account of the uniform and the inscription on the paper: *Fluctibus Reipublicae expulsus* (Expelled through the vicissitudes of the State). The real sitter was identified through an engraving and he wears the uniform of a minister of the Indies, a post which he occupied in 1814 and 1815 when he was dismissed and banished.

José Luis Munárriz
Goya has left us an image of Munárriz which exactly reflects the studious life of this refined and cultured man. A lawyer in the Council of State, a member of the Spanish Academy and secretary of the Academy of San Fernando, he became a director of the Royal Company of the Philippines in May 1815 and this portrait was probably painted to mark the occasion. The book, on the cover of which appears Goya's signature and dedication, is a volume of the works of Hugh Blair whose lectures on aesthetics he had translated in 1798. In 1804 he published a translation of Addison's essay *On the Pleasures of Imagination* and the books behind him include *The Spectator* as well as works by Horace, Petrarch, Boileau and Cervantes' *Don Quixote*.

is one of mingled bitterness and calm, with the eyes as deep-set as ever beneath the strong brow, but his face now has the quiet assurance of a man who has run the full cycle of passion and illusion.

At about this same period he undertook a monumental work which has not always been accorded the importance it deserves because it does not occupy a star position in one of the major European museums: the *Session of the Royal Company of the Philippines* in the Musée Goya at Castres [1534]. There are few paintings in which the subject-matter counts for less. In this picture the 'subject' to which everything else is sacrificed is the vast emptiness which fills the canvas and the play of light and shade in the great council chamber. The powerful portraits of *Ignacio Omulryan y Rourera* and *Miguel de Lardizábal* [1546, 1547], ministers of Ferdinand VII, and the hardly less austere image of *José Luis Munárriz* [1545], have the expressive strength which is characteristic of most of Goya's post-war works.

But whatever the expressive possibilities of a painting, its language remains limited and Goya now needed to state, to cry aloud what he felt and thought when confronted with the new wave of cruelty which was engulfing Spain, even if he had to keep his dangerous message hidden for posterity to read. From 1815 onwards he was almost entirely absorbed by his 'underground' production of drawings and prints which included the final plates of the *Disasters of War* and the *Disparates*.

The Royal Company of the Philippines
Ill. pp. 224, 225

1815-1816. Goya is 69 to 70 years old. Series of 33 etchings illustrating 'La Tauromaquia', the art of bullfighting, from its origins to the most celebrated events of Goya's own day. Published in 1816. Reign of Ferdinand VII.

* *Bibl. 72, p. 42; 102, p. 36; 134, p. 73*

Ill. pp. 43, 110, 123

Bibl. 101, p. 180

Bibl. 66

Ill. p. 228

Ill. p. 228

Bibl. 101, pp. 207-208

Bibl. 101; 80, pp. 2-3

History of bullfighting

Goya was an ardent *aficionado* of the bullfight, the national sport of Spain. He wrote about it in his letters to Zapater; Carderera recorded his dressing up on bullfight days with Francisco Bayeu and another friend, and keeping company with the most celebrated toreros; and Moratín recorded Goya's statement at the end of his life that he had fought bulls himself, sword in hand.* Testimony is not lacking in his own works: in the *Novillada* [I.133], the tapestry cartoon painted in 1779, he showed himself as a toreador, a gay and burly young man of thirty-three; in 1793 he executed a whole series of little bullfight scenes [II.317-324]; and he painted the portraits of famous bullfighters like the brothers Pedro and José Romero [II.671, 672].

In 1815, at the age of sixty-nine, he decided to publish a series of prints showing aspects of the sport of which he was so fond. Various motives have been suggested for this decision. Was it to forget his post-war depression when the restoration of Ferdinand ushered in a period of violent anti-liberal reaction? Could there have been, as with the *Caprichos*, a moral and satirical intention behind the publication of these prints illustrating the sport which so many of his friends, Jovellanos among them, had rejected as barbarous and degrading? Or was the publication of these thirty-three prints of 'popular' subjects part of his attempt to reinstate himself as the leading artist at court and to gain a new following when the situation in Spain made it impossible to publish the *Disasters of War*?

Whatever the reason, Goya once again invested in a large number of best quality copperplates, set to work, and published a series of thirty-three prints in 1816. Seven of the copperplates have engravings rejected by Goya on the other side [1219-1232] and these suggest that the artist started with the contemporary scenes showing various passes and dramatic moments in the ring. The style of these rejected scenes is similar to that of the three engravings dated 1815, plates *19, 29* and *31* [1188, 1208, 1212], and all are characterized by the small scale of the figures and the fierce, dramatic quality of the action. This is particularly true of one of the rejected plates – later published with the letter *E* [1227] – which shows the death of the great matador Pepe Illo in the ring at Madrid. Goya engraved two other versions of this tragic event, one which was also rejected and later published as plate *F* [1229] and the one finally chosen as the last plate in the series of thirty-three [1217]. The incident had occurred on 11 May 1801; it caused a great impression at the time and Queen María Luisa, who was among those present, gave a blood-curdling description of the tossing and goring of the unfortunate matador in a letter to 'friend Manuel' Godoy. Goya's final composition in plate *33* is of moving simplicity compared with the hectic activity of the first two versions, and the sparse, abstract quality of the design is typical of the later plates which he engraved for the series.

Lafuente Ferrari has shown the extent to which Goya's *Tauromaquia* is based on the famous *Carta histórica* – the 'Historical letter on the origins and progress of bullfighting in Spain' – written by Nicolás Fernández de Moratín, the father of Goya's friend Leandro [II.685], and on the *Tauromaquia* of José Delgado, known as Pepe Illo, which first appeared in Cadiz in 1796 and was republished with illustrations in 1804, after the author's tragic death. It seems that Goya at first intended to describe the different stages and passes of the art of bullfighting and some of the feats of the great toreros of his own time but that he eventually decided to illustrate the elder Moratín's account of the origins of bullfighting as well. In a magnificent series of plates, remarkable for the assurance and economy of their handling, Goya shows how the primitive hunting of bulls in the open country was

El Cid Campeador lanceando otro toro (The Cid Campeador spearing another bull) *Tauromaquia 11* [1171] 1815-16

Otra locura suya en la misma plaza (Another madness [of Martincho] in the same ring) *Tauromaquia 19* [1188] 1815. Etching and aquatint

The death of Pepe Illo (2nd composition) *Tauromaquia E* [1227] 1815. Etching and aquatint 25×35 cm.

Pedro Romero matando a toro parado (Pedro Romero killing the halted bull) *Tauromaquia 30* [1210] 1815-16. Etching and aquatint

elaborated and refined by the Moors and became the sport of kings and princes under Charles V, after El Cid, in the eleventh century, had introduced the fighting of bulls on horseback – plates *1* to *11* [1149-1177]. More spectacular, however, are the prints which represent thrilling moments of the bullfights of Goya's own day: Juanito Apiñani leaping over the bull's back in plate *20* [1190], the picador Fernando del Toro defying the bull in plate *27* [1204], Martincho the Basque and Mariano Ceballos, the South American Indian, holding the crows spell-bound with their mad, exuberant feats – among plates *15* to *24* [1180-1198].

As in the *Caprichos* prints, the combination of Goya's masterly technique and the beautiful quality of the printing of the first edition emphasizes the purely artistic qualities of the prints and enables them to be appreciated as great works of art even by those who have a natural aversion to the subject-matter. Goya's love of bullfighting remained with him to the end and provided the inspiration for his last masterpieces in the field of print-making, the lithographs known as the *Bulls of Bordeaux* [v.1707-1710], which are in large part based on the *Tauromaquia* prints.

Contemporary episodes

Rafael Esteve
This portrait of the engraver and printer Esteve is signed and dated on the copperplate which he is holding. He was a friend of Goya and may have printed the *Caprichos* in 1798 as well as the first edition of the *Tauromaquia* in 1816; both are remarkable for their expert and beautiful printing technique.

228

El Cid Campeador lanceando otro toro
One of the last, historical prints made for the series, it illustrates the text of Nicolás Fernández de Moratín who described El Cid as the first to spear bulls on horseback. It was engraved on the back of a copperplate which Goya had already used for the rejected composition illustrated below.

The death of Pepe Illo (2nd composition)
Probably one of the earliest plates in the series, it was no doubt rejected by Goya on account of the defective aquatint. It is one of three versions of the tragic death of José Delagado, known as Pepe Illo, in 1801. The bull was finally killed by José Romero, brother of Pedro, who was a matador in Pepe Illo's *cuadrilla*.

Otra locura suya en la misma plaza
Signed and dated 1815, this is an early plate in the series, showing one of the fantastic feats of Martincho the Basque in the ring at Saragossa, where Goya no doubt saw him as a young man. Martincho stands on a table, facing the charging bull with his feet in irons. A number of chulos are watching, ready to run to his aid.

El esforzado Rendon picando un toro de cuya suerte murió en la plaza de Madrid (The forceful Rendon stabbing the bull with his pique from which pass he died in the ring at Madrid) *Tauromaquia 28* [1206]

Pedro Romero matando a toro parado
The classical restraint and dignity of Pedro Romero contrasts with the exuberance and spectacular style of toreros like Martincho and Pepe Illo. Here he performs his most famous feat, the *suerte de matar*, standing alone with the animal in the ring. (See p. 123.)

El esforzando Rendon picando un toro...
An example of the bullfights which Goya had seen in Saragossa and Madrid (the only rings referred to in the *Tauromaquia*). The composition shows a large number of figures in the ring, silhouetted against the barrier which separates them from the densely packed rows of spectators, and is characteristic of the early plates in the series.

Desgracias acaecidas en el tendido...
(Dreadful incidents which occurred in the front rows of the ring at Madrid, and death of the mayor of Torrejon) *Tauromaquia 21*. The print illustrates another drama which occurred only a month after the terrible death of Pepe Illo, in 1801 (see opposite page), and recalls many of the scenes from the *Disasters of War*.

Rafael Esteve [1550] 1815. Valencia Museum

Desgracias acaecidas en el tendido de la plaza de Madrid, y muerte del alcalde de Torrejon Plate 21 [1192]

Drawings occupy a place of special importance in Goya's work. Until 1796, that is until his second stay in Andalusia and more particularly at Sanlúcar de Barrameda where he made, with no particular aim in view, his first little album of sketches known as the Sanlúcar album or album A [II.356-376], he seems only to have made a very few drawings. Although some have probably been lost or are unidentified, this is in keeping with the tradition of Spanish art which is renowned for its poverty in this field.

For thirty years Goya treated drawing as a poor relation and used it only to make studies before beginning a painting or an engraving. In the latter case he usually applied the moistened drawing to the copperplate and transferred the main lines of the composition, in reverse, on to the surface to be engraved. He used the classic techniques of black, red or white chalk, separately or together, and of pen and ink. These early drawings included a number of preparatory studies for the tapestry cartoons [I.71-73, etc.] and the important group of drawings made in 1778, after paintings by Velázquez, in preparation for the series of etchings [I.88-117]. All these drawings show considerable mastery and those after Velázquez are characterized by a sensitivity to the originals which is far superior to that of the etchings, where he was still unfamiliar with the technique. Even so, there is nothing to give any indication of the masterpieces to come and no comparison with the three colour crayon or red chalk drawings of Watteau and Boucher.

It was not until he was fifty years old that Goya first used the brush and wash technique which appears in the Sanlúcar album. This major discovery was accompanied by a quite new tendency in his drawing, at first timidly explored in the first little album of sketches from life and soon developed in the so-called larger Madrid album or album B [II.377-450]. From then on a drawing for Goya was no longer an isolated study, such as all artists make when preparing to paint a picture, or a sheet of more or less detailed sketches intended to serve as a reference library of forms; on the contrary the drawing became a work of art in its own right, what might be called a 'pure drawing', with its own formal balance and its own meaning. Goya's most important innovation was the addition of titles to his drawings and their arrangement within 'albums', each with its own distinctive characteristics and with the pages numbered by the artist himself. The term 'album' is somewhat misleading since only the drawings from the Sanlúcar and Madrid albums show traces of having been bound and they are the only ones in which the sheets were drawn on both sides. In the case of the other six 'albums', it is probable that the drawings were kept loose in portfolios, and it would be more correct to describe them as 'series' or 'cycles', as has already been done. The widespread use of the term 'album' is relatively recent and is a convenient but not altogether exact description.

Of the eight albums which have been identified, the first two, discussed in Part two, are easy to date; on the one hand, documents recently discovered have established the dates of Goya's visit to Sanlúcar with greater precision, and on the other hand the period at which he was working on the *Caprichos* is well known. We shall see that the last two, albums G and H [v.1711-1822], are also easy to assign to the period of Goya's stay in Paris and Bordeaux from 1824 to 1828. The remaining four albums, identified with the letters C, D, E and F, which are the subject of this chapter, are much more difficult to date. Like the Sanlúcar and Madrid albums, they are drawn with the brush, sometimes with Indian ink and sometimes with sepia, or a mixture of the two. They must originally have formed a group of at least three hundred and thirteen drawings, of which two hundred and

1801-1823. Goya is 55 to 77 years old. The Sanlúcar and Madrid albums (1796-97), precursors of the series of drawings known as albums C, D, E and F. Current events, satires, victims of the repression, hymn to Liberty. Reign of Ferdinand VII. The revolt of Riego (1820). The Constitution (1820-23).

Ill. p. 46
Ill. p. 50

Sanlúcar and Madrid albums (1796-97)
See pp. 117-121

Bibl. 116, 126 and 192
Bibl. 171

See pp. 117-124

Albums G and H (1824-28)   *See pp. 337-348*

Albums C to F

seventy-one are known today. The numerical size of the albums varied considerably, the largest being album C in which the highest known page number is *133*.

Album D (c.1801-1803)

Bibl. 171, pp. 130-131

The smallest album is identified with the letter D [1368-1384]. Its highest known page number is only *22* and it may well have been abandoned in favour of album E which is of better proportions. It is significant that album D is drawn on the same paper as the Madrid album and this coincidence, which is only repeated in the case of albums G and H, executed together in France, leads us to date this album to the first years of the nineteenth century, about 1801 to 1803. After completing the Madrid album, probably in 1797, Goya was kept very busy with a large number of important commissions which left him no time to draw for his own pleasure. The years 1801 and 1802, however, were a period of respite and even of semi-retirement for reasons which are not entirely clear but were probably connected with the political reaction against Jovellanos and Urquijo who were imprisoned in 1801, the death of the Duchess of Alba in 1802 and above all with the probable denunciation of the *Caprichos* to the Inquisition which led Goya, in 1803, to dispose of the copperplates and the remaining unsold copies to the king, in order to avoid serious trouble. It was therefore during the years 1801 to 1803 that Goya's more or less enforced seclusion gave him the opportunity to start drawing again. He took up the paper which had served for the Madrid album and set to work, using the same upright format and the same technique of Indian ink wash, but drawing on one side of the paper only. The subjects have much in common with those of the *Caprichos*: witches floating up into the air [1368-1370, 1378] or gloating over the tender young flesh of babies [1374, 1379], figures piled one on another [1376, 1384], allusions to marriage [1375], and so on.

Album E: 'black border' series (c.1806-1812)

Bibl. 171 and 192

Album E, known as the 'black border series' [1385-1430], has a unique characteristic in that all the drawings are surrounded by a 'frame' consisting of a single or double ruled ink line. Goya had already used this kind of border, though in a much less geometric form,

Drawings from album D. 15 and 4

D.*15* *Sueño de buena echizera* (Dream of a good witch) [1374] c.1801-03. Indian ink wash 23·4×14·4 cm. Kupferstichkabinett, Berlin-Dahlem

D.*4* *regozijo* (mirth) [1370] c.1801-03. Indian ink wash 23·7×14·7 cm. Hispanic Society of America, New York

The drawings in this album are very close to those of the so-called Madrid album, both in their dimensions and technique and in their subject-matter. The hideous old witch who carries a bunch of new-born babies on her back would be at home in several of the *Caprichos* plates [II.539, 541, 545] as well as in the *Witches' sabbath* from the Alameda de Osuna [II.660], which dates from the same period. They are examples of the witchcraft practices which were denounced by Moratín in his commentaries on the *auto de fe* at Logroño (see pp. 120, 122, 128).

The two witches frolicking in the air likewise recall the flying figures and animals drawn or etched by Goya at the period of the *Caprichos* and later on. Three other drawings in this album show similar subjects [1368, 1369, 1378], and the group of three at the beginning of the album show pairs of merry witches playing tambourines, a guitar and, here, the castanets.

Album D.*15*   *Sueño de buena echizera*   [1374]   Album D.*4*   *regozijo* (mirth)   [1370]

Album E.*16*   *Despreciar los ynsultos*   [1391]

E.*16* *Despreciar   los   ynsultos* (Contemptuous   of   the insults)   [1391]   c.1806-12.   Indian   ink   wash 26·5×18·5 cm. Private collection, France

E.*32* *Son colericos* (They are angry)   [1401] c.1806-12. Indian ink wash 27×19 cm. Private collection, Basle

E.[d]   *Trabajos   de   la   guerra* (Hardships   of   the war) [1420] c.1806-12. Indian ink wash 24×17 cm. Baronne de Gunzburg, Paris

The dark borders which Goya carefully traced round the drawings in this series show that he considered them in effect as little pictures, and it is significant that the autograph numbers and titles show none of the crossing out and alteration which affect those in the other albums. The finest and most 'finished' of Goya's drawings, they were assiduously sought after by collectors from the middle of the nineteenth century, and are now widely dispersed throughout the world.

Each drawing expresses a particular idea which is illustrated by one or two figures and emphasized by the manuscript legend. The angry men fly at each other with such comic fury that any moral comment becomes superfluous; the Spanish bourgeois snaps his fingers contemptuously at two dwarfs dressed in the Napoleonic army uniform; but the invasion and war give rise to tragedy and suffering symbolized by the poor crippled man forced to become a beggar.

Album E.*32*   *Son colericos*   [1401]

Album E.[d]   *Trabajos de la guerra*   [1420]

Album E.19 No sabe lo q.ᵉ hace
c.1806-12. Indian ink wash 26·9×17·9 cm.
This man of the people, peasant or worker, is
poised on a ladder, pointing, though his
eyes are closed, towards the remains of a
statue which he has just sent crashing to the
ground with a swing of his pick. The legend
comments 'He doesn't know what he's doing',
and although the exact significance of the
female bust which he has destroyed is not
clear, the drawing probably alludes to the
unconscious destruction by the people of their
own liberty and happiness. This drawing
belongs in the same popular vein as the
realist paintings of the period 1808-1819
[962-970] and is one of the finest in the
'black border' series.

E.*19*   *No sabe lo q.ᵉ hace* (He doesn't know what he's doing) [1392] Kupferstichkabinett, Berlin-Dahlem

Ill. p. 127

for the pen and ink drawings used for the *Caprichos* prints, for example [II.464, 480, 505, 578, 620, 622-624]. The page numbers and titles are usually written outside the border which serves to make the figure or scene into a picture complete in itself. In the 'black border' album these qualities are transformed and heightened by its format, the largest of all the albums, by the brush and wash technique which is handled with complete mastery and

Drawing from album F.13
The first part of this album, which is executed entirely in sepia wash, includes a group of six drawings devoted to duelling [1438-1443]. They represent Goya's protest against an archaic custom – emphasized by the old-fashioned dress worn by some of the figures – which was particularly deadly among Spaniards whose highly touchy notions of honour were very easily offended.

In this drawing the standing gentleman and his victim both wear the ruff and plumed hat which were the fashion in El Greco's time. The duel has taken place in the open country and the winner is savouring his triumph, hand on hip, his rapier pointing towards the still warm corpse of his adversary. As with the rest of the series, there is no title but the meaning of the drawing is sufficiently clear and it expresses Goya's opinion of these ridiculous *desafíos* (duels).

Victory without witnesses. Album F.*13*   [1441] c.1812-23. Sepia. Prado, Madrid

above all by the robust realism of the figures whose shapes are thrown into relief against the whiteness of the paper. Although no precise date can be advanced for this album, the style of the figures suggests a connection with paintings such as the *Maragato* series of 1806-1807 [II.864-869], the *Water-carrier* and *Knife-grinder* [963, 964] and the *Young women with a letter* [962], painted between 1808 and 1814. Moreover, the allusions to war and banditry in several drawings [1391, 1410, 1420] as well as to the problems of child education [1389] add weight to the hypothesis that the album was executed between 1806, the year in which Godoy founded a Pestalozzi Institute in Madrid, and the end of the war in 1812. Finally, it is worth noting the exceptional trouble which Goya took over this series, for which he chose a very fine quality Dutch paper, undoubtedly a luxury in Madrid at that time.

The cycle of drawings known as album C [1244-1367] is the largest of all. There is a sheet numbered *133* [1367] and of the one hundred and twenty-four drawings now known, all but four are in the Prado Museum, the most complete existing collection from a single

Ill. pp. 156, 157
Ill. pp. 243, 245

Cp. notes to [856, 857]

Album C (c.1814-1823)
Bibl. 171, p. 131

Drawing from album F.61

This scene, which appears to have no specific meaning, shows the perfection and economy of handling which Goya achieved with the brush and wash technique. The easy, natural movement of the two figures, on what could well be a stage set, is admirably conveyed and everything concentrates on the essential theme of this drawing, which is the perfect balance of the bodies caught at the most transitory moment of their movement from one position to another.

Cavalier helping a woman to climb steps. Album F.*61* [1482] c.1812-23. Sepia wash 20·8×14·2 cm. Private collection, Paris

Bibl. 190, p. 463

Bibl. 116; 122, pl. 17-133 and Appendix II

series. These drawings entered the Prado collection in the nineteenth century without passing through the trade, which means that they are still in virtually the same condition as when Javier Goya classified them in his own way and pasted them on to the pages of three large volumes. Goya's autograph numbers have made it possible to reconstruct the series in the actual order intended by the artist, though not without hesitation over the sequence of some drawings. In fact, whole sections were shifted by one or more numbers within the series, which proves how much importance Goya attached to the relationship between the drawings. A careful study of the additional numbers even suggests that in some cases, if not in all, the numbers were written at the top of the sheets before the titles

Drawing from album F.72
This drawing belongs to a group which came, as did those in the Metropolitan Museum, from the collection of Federico de Madrazo, and it was published with the other ten by Elizabeth du Gué Trapier in 1963.

Like many of the drawings in this album, it is in the popular, realist vein of many of the paintings and prints of this same period. The powerful stance of the peasant who lifts a frightened woman in his arms to carry her across a waterfall, recalls the figures in the *Forge* and the *Knife-grinder* (see pp. 244, 245). The landscape, a rare element in Goya's art, is conceived in the simplest terms and its stark horizontality serves to emphasize the lifting movement of the main figure.

Peasant carrying a woman. Album F.72 [1491] c.1812-23. Sepia wash 20·5 × 14·3 cm.
Hispanic Society of America, New York

were added, and that new drawings were inserted to complete a particular group, for example C.42 [1280].

In establishing the sequence of the drawings, we also referred to the numbers written with a fine pen in the lower right corner of many of the sheets and which may correspond to Javier Goya's classification. The sequence of these numbers is exactly the reverse of the artist's numbering and, in spite of a few inexplicable cases where the sequence breaks down, it helps to establish the position of this or that drawing where the original number is illegible, and also suggests that a number of sheets were lost or deliberately destroyed before Javier's classification.

Ill. p. 239

Drawings from album C. 85, 88 and 94

Por descubrir el mobimiento de la tierra (For discovering the motion of the earth) Album C.*94* [1330] c.1814-23. Sepia wash 20·6×14·2 cm. Prado Museum, Madrid (right)

P.ʳ haber nacido en otra parte (For being born somewhere else) Album C.*85* [1321] c.1814-23. Sepia wash 20·3×14·1 cm. Prado Museum, Madrid (below left)

P.ʳ linage de Ebreos (For being of Jewish ancestry) Album C.*88* [1324] c.1814-23. Sepia wash 20·5×14·2 cm. British Museum, London (below right)

It is in the long series of drawings known as album C that Goya expressed his political ideas most openly, taking the side of the victims of the Inquisition and of the repression instigated by Ferdinand VII. In some thirty drawings, from number *85* onwards, the true liberal which he had always been cries out his pity and his indignation in the face of the atrocities committed in the name of morality and religion, after the return of Ferdinand in 1814. It is the *J'accuse!* of an old artist of nearly seventy who had the courage to throw his brush into the scales on the side of Justice and Liberty.

The first drawings show those condemned by the Inquisition, wearing the *sanbenito* and with the *coroza* on their heads. Goya cites the grounds of their indictment, each more absurd than the next: 'For being born somewhere else' is a typical example; in another he stigmatizes the persecution of the Jews: 'For being of jewish ancestry'.

Besides the anonymous contemporary victims, Goya also evokes three historical cases in this series: the Italian sculptor Torrigiano and Diego Martín Zapata, both designated by name in the titles [1336, 1345], and the great Galileo (above right) who is clearly alluded to in the title: 'For discovering the motion of the earth'.

Finally, although the series does not at first sight seem to have much unity or plan, we can nevertheless distinguish three major groups. Up to and including number *84* the scenes, or rather the figures – since all the albums without exception represent only human figures – illustrate a wide variety of themes: physical deformity or infirmity [1248, 1260, 1273, 1274, 1302, 1318], satire against the religious orders [1249, 1250, 1257, 1268], women, marriage and love [1246, 1251, 1255, 1259, 1265], prisoners and victims of violence [1270, 1289, 1291, 1292]. One homogeneous group emerges from this variety, the nine drawings numbered *39* to *47* [1277-1285], representing a series of visions seen in the course of a single night, which are a perfect example of the 'monstrueux vraisemblable' engendered by dreams.

See p. 121

Number *85* [1321] marks the beginning of an important and very clearly defined series: C.*85* to *92* [1321-1328] show victims of the Inquisition with the *coroza* on their heads and the sinister *sanbenito* inscribed with the reasons for their condemnation, which Goya's titles take up like a monotonous refrain, all starting with the word *Por . . .* (For . . .); then, from C.*93* to *114* [1329-1349], comes a long and fearful procession of prisoners and tortured men, victims of the repression which clamped down on Spain when Ferdinand returned in 1814; the mood changes with the optimistic titles of C.*111* to *114* [1346-1349], culminating in an outburst of joy for liberty regained in C.*115*, the libations of C.*116* and the allegorical figures, of which Goya was so fond, in C.*117* and *118* [1346-1353], all undoubtedly alluding to the revolt of Riego in January 1820.

Ill. p. 237

Ill. pp. 301, 302

The third group, which follows on the act of indictment and the hymn to liberty, from C.*119* to *131* [1354-1366], includes a lively satire on the 'defrocking' of monks and nuns, presumably a reference to the secularization laws of the years 1820-1823 (always assuming that the cycle of drawings does in fact follow the chronological order of these historical events).

Ill. p. 302

The last two parts of the album thus appear to be closely related to the contemporary events which had such a profound effect on the lives of Goya and his fellow countrymen. Nevertheless, the difficulty of dating the whole series remains just as great for there is nothing to prove that the drawings were executed at the time of the events to which they refer. Indeed, it is very likely, as was so often the case with Goya, that the majority of these fragile works were made from memory. We are therefore inclined to assign to album C a fairly broad period extending from about 1814 to 1823, which would make it contemporary with the final plates of the *Disasters of War* [1104-1139] where we also find the radiant figure of a young woman in white, symbolizing Reason and Truth as opposed to the dark forces of stupidity and oppression [1132, 1134, 1138].

The final album from this period, known as album F [1431-1518], differs markedly from the others in its almost total lack of titles. The technique is still brush and wash, but this time exclusively in sepia ink. The highest page number known today is *106* [1518] and we have been able to catalogue eighty-eight drawings in all, of which the first twenty-four, with the numbers *1* to *28* [1431-1454], are preserved in the Prado Museum and the Biblioteca Nacional in Madrid. An important group of twenty-nine, acquired by the Metropolitan Museum in New York in 1935, come from one of the albums made up by Javier Goya and which later passed to Mariano Fortuny. Three drawings help to suggest an approximate date for the whole album: F.*12* [1440] is the first idea for a lithograph made in 1819 [IV.1644]; F.*45* [1470] shows the same allegorical figure of Truth which appears in the last *Disasters* prints, engraved about 1820; and F.*51* [1472] is very close to the painting of *The forge* [965], generally dated between 1812 and 1816. Besides the scenes of violence and of monks, which occur frequently in this period, album F includes two homogeneous sequences, the first devoted to different types of duel, on sheets *10* to *15* [1438-1443], the second to Goya's favourite sport, hunting, on the final sheets *97* to *106* [1510-1518]. But perhaps the most impressive feature of this album is those drawings where the *chiaroscuro* effects are on a level with those of Goya's acknowledged master,

Album F (c.1812-1823)
Bibl. 171, p. 133

Bibl. 122, pl: 134-155 and Appendix III

Bibl. 192, pl. XXI-XLVIII

Ill. p. 244

Ill. p. 234
Ill. p. 231

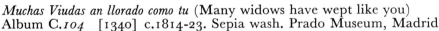

Muchas Viudas an llorado como tu (Many widows have wept like you)
Album C.*104* [1340] c.1814-23. Sepia wash. Prado Museum, Madrid

Quien lo puede pensar (Who can think of it!) Album C.*105* [1341]
c.1814-23. Sepia and Indian ink wash. Prado Museum, Madrid

Drawings from album C. 104 and 105
The first drawing is an open indictment of the Holy Office whose arms appear in the background over the door which no doubt leads to the prison. The moving title expresses Goya's pity not only for the victims themselves but also for those who wait and weep. The following drawing sums up with an extraordinary economy of means the whole weight of human cruelty, in the woman's figure which appears crushed beneath the heavy chain fixed to a great iron ring.

* Ill. p. 303

Rembrandt, [1434, 1448, 1459, 1466, 1476, 1480] or a drawing like F.*56* [1477] which goes far beyond the horrors evoked by Callot and Magnasco.*

In conclusion, we should emphasize one of the most original aspects of Goya's albums: their titles. Inscribed by the artist on a majority of the sheets, they are not just an explanation or a witty comment like those of Hogarth or Daumier, but a barbed shaft which pins the drawing to the pity or the shame in our hearts. In the privacy of his studio, far from prying and inquisitive eyes, Goya seems to be conversing sometimes with his future admirers and sometimes with his own figures whom he addresses with affectionate familiarity: You'll see later [1397] – You won't get anywhere by shouting [1408] – Think it over well [1263, 1412] – God deliver us from such a bitter fate [1410] – If I am not mistaken he is going to throw off his habit [1257] – Just look at her expression, but the husband doesn't believe it [1258] – Are you going very far? [1275] – Don't eat, great Torrigiano [1336] – You will soon be free [1349]. Like a man with a magic lantern show, Goya projects for us in these albums the images culled from his wide experience of life and adds his commentary. By turns amazed, ironic, indignant, vengeful, consoling, his voice runs through the whole range of emotions to assert, over and above everything else, his boundless confidence in Man, the sole theme of these drawings which reach the highest levels of expression as works of art.

Genre paintings occupy a particularly important place in Goya's work, not only because of their numbers but also because it was these paintings, many of them small in size, which like the engravings found their way most readily outside Spain in the nineteenth century and largely contributed to the incomplete but still deeply compelling image evoked by the artist's name throughout the world. The majority of these paintings were not commissioned works, and they therefore count among the artist's most personal creations, made for his own pleasure, without any external restrictions or requirements. In 1793-1794, as we have already seen in Part two, he worked on a series of such paintings during his convalescence and submitted them to the Academy of San Fernando [II.317-330]. This marked the beginning of his taste for compositions on a wide variety of themes but whose common source he defined by describing them as his *caprichos*. In fact it was the tapestry cartoons which lay behind the appearance of the first genre paintings in his work. These scenes of Spanish popular life, destined to decorate the walls of the royal residences, inspired him to paint a number of small pictures of which the most remarkable

1810-1817. Goya is 64 to 71 years old. Death of his wife Josefa (1812). Panels in the Academy of San Fernando: 'The burial of the sardine', 'The procession of flagellants', etc. 'Les jeunes' (Lille), 'The water-carrier' (Budapest), 'The forge' (Frick, N.Y.). The War of Independence. Reigns of Joseph Bonaparte and Ferdinand VII.

Bullfight in a village   [969] c.1812-19. Panel 45×72 cm. Royal Academy of San Fernando, Madrid

F.*99* Hunter loading his gun [1512]
c.1812-23. Sepia wash 20·5 × 14·2 cm.

F.*100* Hunter and his dog on the alert
[1513] c.1812-23. Sepia wash 20·5 × 14·5 cm.

F.*102*? Hunter with his dog running [1514]
c.1812-23. Sepia wash 20·5 × 14·2 cm.

F.*103* Rabbit hunter with retriever [1515]
c.1812-23. Sepia wash 20·6 × 14·6 cm.

Goya naturally reserved a special place for
his favourite sport, shooting. His first tapestry
cartoons were already devoted to this theme,
but that was only a coincidence with the
tastes and decorative traditions of the time
(see p. 44). The nine known drawings which
form a coherent group at the end of album F
were executed by an expert shot who produced a connoisseur's guide to the various
stages of the shoot: the loading of the gun
(F.*99*), the dog on the alert (F.*100*), the dog
dashing off in search of the game (F.*102*)
and finally bringing the rabbit back to his
master (F.*103*).

Bullfight in a village
The five superb paintings on panel, bequeathed in 1839 to the Academy of San Fernando by Don Manuel García de la Prada
[II.819], constituted for many years one of the
major problems in the dating of Goya's
works. It is now clear that these paintings
were not among the 'various scenes of
national diversions' which the convalescent
artist sent to Don Bernardo de Iriarte in
January 1794 and which were shown to his
colleagues in the Academy (see pp. 110, 111).
However, the date of their execution is still
uncertain, and although their style corresponds to the period 1812-1820, they could
equally well have been painted during the
early years of the war, around 1808-1810.
According to Xavier de Salas, the *Bullfight
in a village* was probably the last to be executed, after the *Burial of the sardine* (see frontispiece) which Goya modified to achieve a
circular composition characteristic of many
of his later works. Here, the circular movement is perfectly suited to the subject where
the crowd marks out the traditional *plaza*
in a Spanish village. Goya has come a long
way since the little bullfight scenes painted in
1793 (see p. 110); where 'fantasy and invention' were latent in the early works, they
find their full expression in the freedom and
originality of this masterly painting.

F.*99* Hunter loading his gun
[1512] Private collection, Paris

F.*100* Hunter and his dog on the alert
[1513] Private collection, Milan

F.*102*? Hunter with his dog running
[1514] Private collection, Paris

F.*103* Rabbit hunter with retriever
[1515] Metropolitan Museum, New York

form a series of *Children's games* [I.154-159], painted about 1776-1786. Later on, his technique evolved to achieve a sometimes astonishing freedom, with the use of knives, spatulas,
his fingers and so on, and the subjects became more varied and more dramatic, especially
during the period of the War of Independence. But the basic idea always remained the
same: to recreate from memory on a small canvas, panel or sheet of metal scenes from
popular life which he actually witnessed or imagined from accounts which he had heard
or read. These works find their ultimate expression in a series of monumental compositions
which are among his greatest masterpieces [957-965].

These groups of paintings are the most difficult of Goya's works to date. For many of them there are no points of reference and what documentation exists is often vague. This means that most art historians have had to resort to a study of their style and technique in order to establish a chronology, and this difficult method has very often proved misleading in Goya's case. A typical example is that of the five panels in the Academy of San Fernando, *The burial of the sardine*, *The bullfight in a village*, *The Inquisition scene*, *The procession of flagellants* and *The madhouse* [966-970]. It was long believed that these were the paintings sent by Goya to his friend Don Bernardo de Iriarte to be shown to the academicians in 1794. The validity of this hypothesis was first called in question by very convincing stylistic arguments and by the differences between the Academy *Madhouse* [968] and the description given by Goya in his letter to Iriarte; the recent reappearance of the original *Yard with lunatics* [II.330], described in his letter, furnished the final proof.

The panels in the Academy of San Fernando
Ill. frontispiece and p. 240

Bibl. 166, p. 52
Ill. pp. 110, 111

The five panels in the Academy cannot be dated with any certainty but their lively and vibrant handling suggests a comparison with the two small pictures of the *Making of gunpowder* and the *Making of shot* [980, 981] and with the *Colossus* [946]. At the same time, we could also apply Salas' observations concerning the circular composition of the *Burial of the sardine* and the *Bullfight in a village* [969, 970] to a drawing from album F in the Metropolitan Museum, showing a *Crowd in a circle* [1467], in which the arrangement is very similar. The group of paintings would thus be contemporary with drawings in album F, and the *Bullfight in a village* would therefore be close to the *Tauromaquia* etchings which were made in 1815, about the same period as the latest of the war and famine scenes from the series of prints which Goya had begun in 1810.

Ill. pp. 213, 215
Bibl. 149, pp. 4-5

Ill. pp. 228, 229, 240

So we see that although realism appears early on in Goya's work, it was not until after 1808, under the impact of the war and the misery which it caused, that it came to occupy an increasingly important place in his creative activity. It was the source not only of a large number of paintings, including the still-lifes [903-912], but also of the engravings and the impressive mass of drawings which compose the albums executed during this period. Central to the realism which predominates in Goya's work during the war years is Man, the pawn and the victim in a pitiless struggle; he is the major theme, ever-present, even when it is stated in very different keys. Goya's Man is universal and as anonymous as the masses whom he represents; in his vigour and muscular solidity he foreshadows the work of Daumier, Millet and the Van Gogh of the Brabant period.

Ill. p. 248

This popular realism finds its full expression in three paintings, the large canvas of the *Young women with a letter* [962], in which both strength and grace are united, and the smaller *Water-carrier* and *Knife-grinder* [963, 964] where the first real 'proletarians' in the history of art make their appearance. These last two pictures were painted before 1812 since they were listed together as a pair, with the same number, in the inventory made in that year after the death of Goya's wife Josefa. The painting of *Time and the old women* [961], which was also listed in the 1812 inventory, is no doubt a pendant to the *Young women with a letter*, and the fact that this latter picture was not included in the inventory suggests that it was painted shortly after 1812 or had already been removed from Goya's studio. From the same period, and also included in the inventory, come two more large-scale paintings, the *Maja and celestina on a balcony* [958] and the *Majas on a balcony* [959], where Goya recreates in an entirely new technique the forms of the graceful young women who had filled his work since his earliest days with the tapestry factory of Santa Bárbara. The *Young women*, which has an almost magical charm, is composed entirely of figures of women including, in the background, a number of washerwomen who recall the tapestry cartoon of 1779-80 [I.132] and more particularly a drawing of robust sensuality from album E entitled *Useful work* [1406]. We are inclined to see in this group of pictures of seductive young women a discreet allusion to Leocadia Weiss who was twenty-four years old in 1812, the year in which her liaison with the old artist may have brought a fresh taste of youth into his life.

Ill. pp. 243, 245

See p. 246

Ill. p. 250

Ill. p. 21

See pp. 246-249

'Les jeunes'

This picture was acquired by Baron Taylor in Madrid between 1835 and 1837, together with a number of other large subject pictures, several of which were inventoried in Goya's house in 1812 [III.957, 959, 961, 965]. All these pictures were exhibited in Louis-Philippe's celebrated *Galerie espagnole* in Paris (with the exception of *'Les vieilles'* [961]) and were then sold in London in 1853. *'Les jeunes'* and *'Les vieilles'* were bought by subscription in 1874 and offered to the museum at Lille.

We believe that the charming young woman reading a letter may well be Leocadia Weiss who was twenty-four years old in 1812. The picture does not appear in the 1812 inventory and may therefore have been painted after the death of Goya's wife and the drawing up of the inventory.

'Les jeunes' – Young women with a letter   [962] c.1812-14. 181×122 cm. Musée des Beaux-Arts, Lille

243

The forge   [965] c.1812-16. 181·6×125 cm. Frick Collection, New York

Three men digging. Album F.*51*
[1472] c.1812-23. Sepia wash
20·6×14·3 cm.   Metropolitan
Museum, New York
One of the very few drawings
from the albums which are
directly related to Goya's paintings, it is an independent composition on a similar theme.

The water-carrier　[963] c.1808-12. 68×52 cm. Budapest Museum

The knife-grinder　[964] c.1808-12. 68×50·5 cm. Budapest Museum

The forge　The water-carrier　The knife-grinder
The inventory of 1812 lists 'A water-carrier and her companion' under the number 13, valued at three hundred reales. Like the figures in *The forge*, the water-carrier is also the subject of a drawing, this time from album C [1314]. The sympathetic knife-grinder is shown in action, his shirt-sleeves rolled up to reveal muscular forearms. In *The forge*, painted a few years later, the physical effort of the workers is emphasized more violently and the use of black anticipates Goya's palette in the years 1819-1824.

Already by 1812 Goya had painted the two striking figures of the *Water-carrier* and the *Knife-grinder* [963, 964], which were listed in the inventory of his property. These two little pictures, which were therefore painted during the War of Independence, mark a turning point in nineteenth-century art. With them the figure of the worker takes his place, as an individual person, alongside the bourgeois, the ministers, the generals. They lead on to one of the great masterpieces in Goya's 'black' manner, *The forge* [965] which has its counterpart in an equally vigorous sepia wash drawing in album F, the *Three men digging* [1472]. A naturalist before his time, Goya heralds with this canvas both the *Stone-breakers* of Courbet and the workers of Zola, with the same rejection of good-breeding and bourgeois conventions. It is of particular significance that this great painting, together with the two pendant canvases of the young and the old women (now known as *Les jeunes* and *Les vieilles*), the *Majas on a balcony* and other important works listed in the inventory of Goya's possessions, were acquired for Louis-Philippe and sent to Paris where they were exhibited in the famous 'Galerie espagnole' in the Louvre in 1838. More than any other works, they look forward to the great achievements of French art and literature during the nineteenth century.

We must now return to an earlier period in Goya's private life in order to understand the chain of events which led to the Quinta del Sordo (House of the deaf man) and the last years in Bordeaux.

It is now known that the unassuming Josefa Bayeu left Goya's home for ever on 20 June 1812, as discreetly as she had entered it in 1773 and as she had lived there for nearly forty years. Hardly anything is known about her, not even exactly how many children she had, and there is no certainty that the somewhat melancholy portrait in the Prado represents her [II.686]. Her features are known only from one small drawing in black chalk, made at the time of Javier's marriage in 1805 when she was fifty-eight [II.840]. On 3 June 1811, Goya and his wife signed their will, making Javier residuary legatee. Whether this was due to a premonition or because Josefa was in ill-health, she died a year later. In October, after the inheritance had been inventoried and valued, it was divided between father and son, according to the terms of the will. The documents, published by Sánchez Cantón, provide invaluable information concerning Goya's possessions in 1812 and in particular concerning all the pictures which he kept in his home and whose subsequent identification has often upset the previous dating based on stylistic considerations.

The most striking thing about this amicable division is the way in which the property was apportioned. The artist kept virtually all the furniture, most of the linen and silver, and 142,627 reales in cash. Javier received a little linen, almost no furniture, some jewelry and a few silver dishes but, very surprisingly, all the paintings and prints as well as the library of several hundred volumes and finally the house itself in the Calle de Valverde, valued at 126,000 reales, as well as 13,838 reales in cash to make up his equal share of the property. The valuation figures are also surprising and suggest that the assessment was merely nominal. The entire collection of seventy-eight paintings and prints was valued at 11,939 reales as against 13,332 reales for a single medallion set with diamonds.

A number of Goya's paintings are easily identifiable in the inventory: the portraits of the Duchess of Alba [II.355] and Pedro Romero [II.671], the *Maragato* series [II.864-869], the *Water-carrier* and *Knife-grinder* [963, 964], the *Colossus* [946], two paintings of *Young women on a balcony* [958, 959], the *Lazarillo de Tormes* [957], *Time and the old women* [961] and perhaps four sketches for the allegories painted for Godoy [II.690-696]. For the rest, one can only make guesses, except for the 'series' of pictures identified with the same inventory number (which again points to Goya's fondness for making 'series', whether of paintings, drawings or prints). A very interesting study by Salas has thrown fresh light on the inventory.* He noticed that a number of Goya's paintings were marked with an X followed by a number, painted in white in one of the lower corners, and he concluded that this was the initial of Javier (who also spelt his name Xavier) with the inventory number. Salas then put forward this very persuasive theory: that all the pictures were marked by Javier because, although they were allotted to him in the division of the property, he left them in his father's studio. The reason for the son's lack of trust, in marking them in this way, would, Salas suggested, be due to the fact that his father was already involved with Leocadia Weiss and that Javier was afraid that part of his inheritance might be made over to her. These same fears continued to be expressed up to and after the time of Goya's death in Bordeaux.

Although this takes us into the rather hazardous realms of conjecture, a great many things are thereby clarified. Between 1807, the year of Leocadia's marriage with Isidoro

1812. Goya is 66 years old. Death of his wife Josefa. Division of their property: furniture, linen, silver and cash to Goya; pictures, prints, library and the house to his son Javier. The inventory; the pictures marked with an X. Leocadia Weiss. Birth of Rosario (1814). Wellington enters Madrid and is expelled by the French. Reign of Joseph Bonaparte.

The will of Goya and his wife

The inventory of 1812
Bibl. 161. Appendix I
The pictures in Goya's own collection

* Pictures marked with an X   *Bibl. 147*

Josefa Bayeu   [II.840] 1805. Black chalk

Mariano Goya   [1553] c.1815. Panel 59×47 cm. Duke of Alburquerque, Madrid

Weiss, and 1812, Goya had many opportunities of meeting this young woman who was related to the Goicoechea family and belonged, like them, to the business world of Madrid. After the birth of two sons, the Weiss ménage began to break up and in 1811 the husband lodged a complaint against his twenty-three year old wife, which was renewed in 1812, on the grounds of 'infidelity, illicit relations and misconduct . . . coupled with a high-handed and threatening disposition'. He could hardly have made his meaning clearer and one can only assume that before taking such a serious step, Isidoro Weiss had reached the end of his patience and decided that he could no longer tolerate the 'relations' which had become public knowledge. Then, in October 1814, Leocadia gave birth to a daughter, María del Rosario, for whom Goya showed the most remarkable affection right up to his death. According to a posthumous biography of Rosario, she was even entrusted to his care as a young child for some time in 1821. But it is difficult to imagine an old man of seventy-five living alone with a child of seven, without a woman's presence in the background. The most that some writers have admitted is that Leocadia was an *ama de llaves*, or housekeeper, to the artist, as if this impetuous young woman was a mature and respectable matron, and there have even been attempts, in the interests of propriety, to show that Isidoro Weiss died before 1824, which would have lessened the embarrassment of this illicit relationship. Unfortunately, it is known that Leocadia's legal husband died long after Goya. Final proof seems to be provided by the letter which Goya wrote from Bordeaux on 28 October 1824 to his friend Joaquín Ferrer in Paris; there is the typically paternal blindness of the old artist's faith in Rosario's talent and above all the phrase, which is tantamount to a confession, 'I want to send her to Paris for some time but I want you to treat her as if she were my own daughter . . .'

If we admit Goya's paternity we also have to admit that there must have been 'illicit relations' between Goya and Leocadia at least as early as 1813 and that it was probably these relations which led Isidoro Weiss to lodge his complaint against his wife. It is easy

Leocadia Weiss

Bibl. 164, p. 60; 166, pp. 123-124

Birth of Rosario Weiss

Bibl. 102, pp. 337-338

Bibl. 72, p. 54

Sheep's head and joints   [903] c.1808-12. 45×62 cm. Musée du Louvre, Paris

Sheep's head and joints
Matheron, in his biography, recorded that Goya 'executed a very large number of little still-life pictures' in Bordeaux, and the known still-life paintings were generally attributed to this late period.

However, the 1812 inventory included a group of twelve still-lifes, under the number 11; they were valued at a total of twelve hundred reales, suggesting that they were all the same size and worth a hundred reales each. Of the ten pictures of identical dimensions catalogued together here, the one in the Louvre furnished the proof that they were the inventory pictures since it was recently found to show a trace of the X (for Xavier) with which it was marked at the time the inventory was made.

Six of the paintings are signed, sometimes with a flourish as part of the design, and this would lend support to the anecdote according to which Goya painted them to give to his guests instead of offering them the food itself.

Procession in Valencia

The 1812 inventory includes 'Four similar paintings with the number one', valued at eighteen hundred reales. The X I mark, in white paint, is still visible on two pictures [951, 952], including this one whose pendant appears to be the *Bullfight in a divided ring* now in the Metropolitan Museum [953].

Processions were a theme often treated by Goya, particularly in his drawings, but the most striking element is the artist's taste, more pronounced here than in similar paintings, for the massive architectural forms which he often placed in the background of his compositions. They seem to overwhelm the tiny figures and introduce an element of disproportion into the picture which dramatizes the otherwise unremarkable scene, evoking the blind forces which threaten mankind.

Procession in Valencia   [952] c.1810-12. 105×126 cm. Bührle Foundation, Zurich

to imagine the scandal in the two families who were certainly aware of this relationship and the anxiety of Javier and his wife, after Josefa's death, at the thought that Leocadia might drive the artist to extravagant expenses just at the time when he was no longer receiving his salary as Court Painter. Hence the division of the property which gave to Javier the most substantial items, the house and all the paintings – carefully marked in order that there should be no possibility of confusion.

See Appendix VIII

The fact that Goya was content to remain without a house of his own (while Javier already had one), without a library and without his paintings and prints, and took as his share a large sum of money and 162,127 reales worth of jewelry (out of a total collection valued at 178,864 reales) suggests that it may have been at this time that he left Madrid 'to make his way to a free country' as the Postmaster General declared in his evidence given in 1814. The division of the property took place on 28 October 1812 and on 3 November the French reoccupied Madrid. Goya had just painted the large equestrian portrait of Wellington [896] which was placed on public exhibition in the galleries of the Academy between 2 and 11 September, and he therefore had reason to fear the French. It is quite possible that he thought of escaping with Leocadia, taking his money and jewels, to some country where they could live without fear of scandal, prison, starvation or death each time the political situation changed. Moreover, the same witness specified that if he did not continue with his plan but stopped at Piedrahita, it was 'at his children's request' and on receipt of a warning from the Minister of Police that the property of the whole family would be seized and sequestrated if he did not return to Madrid. This episode in Goya's life may seem fantastic but it is not so surprising when we recall his lone departure into the unknown ten years later and his final settling in Bordeaux with Leocadia.

Bibl. 154, doc. 238

See p. 224

249

Maja and celestina on a balcony
The two paintings of 'young women on a balcony' listed under the number 24 in the 1812 inventory have both now been identified by the X 24 marks on the canvases.

This picture is a direct descendant of the *Caprichos* and of some of the young women who lean on the balcony painted round the cupola of San Antonio de la Florida (see pp. 17, 141, 143). The return of these sensual majas in Goya's work around 1808-1812 was probably connected with his relationship with the young Leocadia Weiss (see p. 243).

Maja and celestina on a balcony [958] c.1808-12. 166 × 108 cm. Bartolomé March Servera, Madrid

CATALOGUE III 1808-1819

INTRODUCTION

PAINTINGS This period of Goya's artistic activity covers only eleven years of his life but it is by far the richest since the catalogue includes nearly seven hundred works. However, we should point at once to the phenomenon already mentioned in the general introduction in relation to Goya's work as a whole (see p. 72) and which is particularly striking in the period 1808 to 1819; the overwhelming numerical superiority of the graphic work which here accounts for four-fifths of the whole. As far as the paintings are concerned, although there are almost no religious works, portraits continue to occupy an important place alongside the series of genre paintings, most of them of small dimensions and almost all inspired by the War of Independence and its accompanying horrors. It is this part of Goya's œuvre which poses the most difficult problems of chronology and classification. Like the drawings and most of the engravings, all these pictures are the fruit of the artist's 'fantasy and invention' and were intended to remain in his studio; there are therefore none of the useful documents which normally accompany the commissioned works.

Thanks to the publication of Sánchez Cantón, we do, however, have the inventory of Goya's property which was drawn up on his wife's death so that it could be divided between him and his son Javier. This document is one of the most informative and revealing which has ever been published in relation to Goya and it led to the demonstration by Xavier de Salas that all the paintings in the artist's studio in 1812, which were allotted to Javier, were marked with a white-painted X followed by the inventory number. On the basis of these facts and discoveries, we have systematically grouped together a large number of paintings which are now widely dispersed throughout the world, many of which had already been pointed out by Sánchez Cantón and Salas. Among those which they had already identified with the inventory paintings, we can confirm the group of still-lifes [903-912], of which twelve were inventoried in 1812 with the number 11. The discovery by Juliet Wilson of traces of the inventory mark XII on the still-life in the Louvre [903] and on that in the David-Weill collection [907] proves that these were two of the inventory pictures, together, in all probability, with eight others of the same format and technical characteristics. There is therefore no question of dividing the group and assigning some of the pictures to the artist's last years in Bordeaux, as has often been done.

Among the scenes of war, violence and famine, Sánchez Cantón proposed the identification of the eight pictures from the Romana collection [914-921] with the group of twelve 'Horrors of the War' with the number 12 in the 1812 inventory, and Salas identified the group of 'six of various subjects' marked X.9, of which we have been able to localize three of the original panels [930-935]. José Gudiol identified the X.28 group [947-950], and information communicated or published by him and by Salas has enabled us to identify the group of four paintings which head the inventory list [951-954].

To the large figure paintings identified by Sánchez Cantón and Salas with the inventory pictures, we have added the version of the *Majas on a balcony* [959] which is the pair, with the same inventory number, to the *Maja and celestina* in the March collection [958]. This version of the *Majas on a balcony* was studied for the first time on the occasion of the Goya exhibition at The Hague in 1970.

All these discoveries and identifications are summed up in Appendix I at the end of the volume, where we have reprinted the 1812 inventory and listed all the paintings which have so far been identified with it.

Other pictures have been connected, though with a much lesser degree of certainty, with the works mentioned in the inventory of the Quinta del Sordo, drawn up by Antonio Brugada after Goya's death in 1828. This inventory and the pictures identified with it are published in Appendix II. Among these pictures, Sánchez Cantón suggested the identification of four of the five panels in the Academy of San Fernando [966-969], which were bequeathed to the Academy in 1839 by Manuel García de la Prada whose portrait Goya had painted around 1804-1808 [II.819]. Unfortunately it is impossible to assign a precise date to these important works. The violent anticlericalism of two of them suggests that they may be connected with the secularization laws decreed by Napoleon when he arrived in Madrid in 1808 and which must have delighted Goya and his 'enlightened' friends at a time when the 'horrors of the war' had not yet tainted their hopes with bitterness and anger. On the other hand, the fact that they do not appear in the inventory of 1812 and the very close resemblance between the bullfight scene [969] and the prints of the *Tauromaquia* executed by Goya in 1815 [1149-1243] may indicate a date between 1812 and 1815.

The first group of portraits, executed between 1808 and 1814, includes a number of Frenchmen and *afrancesados* who sat for Goya around 1810. The lost *Joseph Bonaparte* which originally appeared in the medallion in the *Allegory of the Town of Madrid* [874], then *Juan Antonio Llorente* [881], the celebrated canon, author of a history of the Inquisition, who was decorated by Joseph, *General Manuel Romero* [882] who held several ministries under the intruder king, the Frenchman *General Nicolas Guye* [883] and his nephew *Victor Guye* [884], *Juan Bautista de Goicoechea* [888], a relative of Javier Goya's wife, who wears Joseph's Royal Order of Spain, and finally *Manuel Silvela* [891], the intimate friend of Moratín, who became mayor of Madrid in 1808.

DRAWINGS During the period 1808 to 1819, Goya executed a very large number of drawings, of which 275 come from the four albums which are now generally designated by the letters C, D, E and F. It should, however, be noted that the term 'album' does not strictly apply to these series of drawings of which we have no proof that they were in fact originally grouped together in the form of albums; in addition, the order of the letters given to these four 'albums' does not indicate their chronological order.

We have suggested overall dates for the different series in the text (pp. 230-239).

The albums in question owe the definition of their basic characteristics to two fundamental studies. In 1938, H. B. Wehle published an article accompanying the superb reproductions of the fifty drawings acquired in 1935 by the Metropolitan Museum of New York, and he identified for the first time the series of 'black border' drawings (album E) and another series apparently abandoned by Goya (album D). He also connected the Metropolitan Museum's drawings from album F with those in the Prado and the Biblioteca Nacional in Madrid.

In 1947, Pierre Gassier added an 'essai de catalogue' to the book by André Malraux devoted to a selection of drawings from the Prado. Of the 195 drawings reproduced, 116 sheets from album C were shown for the first time according to the order of the artist's manuscript numbers. The drawings from the other albums were also grouped together, and the two late albums made in Bordeaux were defined and classified (see Part V, p. 355), although the scope of the study was limited to the drawings in the Prado collection.

In 1958, Eleanor Sayre studied the problem of the 'journal-albums', suggesting that the artist kept them as loose sheets so that he could change their order and renumber them at will, and making a special study of album E for which she catalogued 17 drawings. Her most important contribution was the rigorous definition, in an 'essai de catalogue' appended to the same article, of the technical characteristics of the eight 'albums' (which she designated by the letters A to H): the type and format of the paper, watermarks (given in tracing), techniques used, and so on.

Today, thanks to all these studies, Goya's albums of drawings are clearly defined and research must now be directed to the identification of further drawings which may still exist to fill the vacant spaces within each series.

A drawing in its original state can be classified according to the following criteria: its relationship to the given characteristics (paper, technique, etc.); the existence or lack of a manuscript title and, if there is one, its position in relation to the drawing and its technique; the position and technique of the manuscript number; the existence of a single or double dark border round the design. A summary of these characteristics is given in the Analytical Index at the end of the book.

Unfortunately, some drawings have been cut down or over-cleaned or are time-stained or faded so that numbers, titles, even the black borders may have disappeared. These alterations tend to make their identification and classification a very difficult matter. All the drawings which lack a manuscript number have been grouped at the end of each series and classified with the letters a, b, c, etc., unless other factors made it possible to assign them a place within the album, with a minimum risk of error.

ENGRAVINGS   A further large group of drawings (nearly 130) was made in preparation for two series of engravings. The prints known as the *Disasters of War* [993-1148] were created over a period of perhaps more than ten years (1810-1820/23). They include scenes of the war (plates *2-47*) – three of them dated 1810 (plates *20, 22* and *27*) – scenes of the famine of 1811-12 (plates *48-64*), and the group of mainly satirical *caprichos* which Goya later added to conclude the series (plates *65-82*). Almost all the preparatory drawings are in a rather hard, unsympathetic red chalk technique, like the majority of those made for the *Caprichos*. (Goya presumably found it particularly well-suited to the transfer process.)

The *Disasters* plates show an even greater variation in style and technique than do those of the *Caprichos*: the early engravings were improvised on damaged or previously used plates and Goya, perhaps lacking the materials necessary for a conventional aquatint, applied an acid 'lavis' directly to the plate, with a brush or feather, to achieve a light tone. The later scenes of the war (e.g. plates *31-39*) as well as those recording the famine achieve both monumentality and an extraordinary freedom and command of technique. The *caprichos enfáticos* (plates *65-82*) which develop this freedom and assurance are similar to and probably contemporary with the *Disparates* prints [IV.1571-1613].

The plates were numbered by Goya himself; two series of numbers are engraved on the war and famine scenes – the earlier in the lower left, the final in the upper left corners. The copperplates were stored away in the Quinta del Sordo when Goya left for France in 1824. Eighty plates were first published in 1863; the final two were mislaid for many years and only a few impressions have been printed.

During an interlude in the long preparation of the *Disasters of War*, Goya drew, engraved and published the series of prints illustrating *La Tauromaquia* [1149-1243] in the space of less than two years. The earliest plates are dated 1815 and the edition of 33 prints was advertised for sale on 28 October 1816. Goya prepared at least 45 plates for this series: rejected engravings on the other side of 7 of the 33 copperplates were first published in 1876 [1219-1232]; four additional compositions are known from rare or unique proofs, and a unique proof of a fifth composition known from a preparatory drawing was identified in 1966 [1241]. As already indicated, the drawings for this series are in red crayon, four of them (sometimes considered of doubtful authenticity and yet to be studied in detail) with the addition of sanguine wash [1205, 1215, 1228, 1240].

Of the total of 290 known prints by Goya – engravings and lithographs – 131 (83 for the *Disasters*, 45 for the *Tauromaquia*, the *Colossus* and the three small etchings of *Prisoners* [985-991]) are catalogued within this third period of his career.

NOTES TO CATALOGUE III   [874-1570]

874 See Beruete for a concise account (Bibl. 36, I, pp. 114-117) and Bibl. 23, no. I, for full bibliographical references. Listed by Carderera (Bibl. 148, no. 51) when the portrait of Ferdinand by Vicente López was painted in the medallion.

875-902 For a study of some of the portraits, see José López-Rey, 'Goya's cast of characters from the Peninsular War', *Apollo*, LXXIX, 1964, pp. 54-61.

875 Commissioned by the Academia de San Fernando on 28 March 1808; Ferdinand sat twice to Goya in April; on October 2 Goya wrote to the Academia to say that the portrait was finished, and would be hung as soon as it was dry. See Sánchez Cantón (Bibl. 157, p. 18; 166, pp. 85-86), and all the documents published by Narciso Sentenach, 'Fondos selectos del archivo de la Real Academia de Bellas Artes de San Fernando', *Boletín de la R.A. de B.A. de San Fernando*, 1923, pp. 205-211.

876 Tormo suggested that the model was Javier Goya (Bibl. 183, no. 144), whom Goya certainly used for [1558, 1559]. Federico de Madrazo apparently acquired this sketch from Goya's son (Bibl. 193, p. 137), and it may be identical with the *boceto de un ginete* listed in the 1812 inventory (Bibl. 161, p. 106; see Appendix I, no. 26). See note to [II.344].

877 Probably a study made during the two sittings in April 1808. It may have been used for all the later portraits [1536-1541].

878 Inscribed on scabbard *Don Pantaleon Perez de Nenin / Por Goya 1808*. For the identity of the sitter and references, see Bibl. 23, no. III; last exhibited 1963-64, Bibl. 27, no. 95.

879 Inscribed on ground at right *La Marquesa de / Sn Tiago Goya 1809*. This very little known portrait has never been exhibited, and Mayer does not give the inscription which is invisible in some photographs.

880 Although the style of dress suggests a relationship with the portraits of 1805 [II.828-831], the robust plasticity and solid stance of the figure relate it to the portrait of Llorente [881] and the large figure compositions of 1808-14 [958-963]. Dated c.1812-13 in the Ganay sale catalogue, 1922 (Bibl. 57, II, p. 275). Exhibited 1961-62 (Bibl. 24, no. 26).

881 Wearing the Royal Order of Spain which he was awarded by Joseph Bonaparte on 20 September 1809, the year in which he was appointed archivist and historian of the suppressed Inquisition. He left Madrid when Joseph fled in August 1812. See Sánchez Cantón (Bibl. 166, pp. 99-100).

882 See Trapier (Bibl. 188, p. 36). The general was made Minister of Justice in 1809, and the appointment was announced in the *Diario de Madrid* on December 24.

883 Inscribed on verso (before relining) *Sor Dn Nicolas Guye, Marquis de Rio-Milanos, Général Aide de Camp de S.M. Catholique. Membre de la Légion d'Honneur de l'Empire Français, Commandeur de l'Ordre des Deux-Siciles et Commandeur de l'Ordre Royal d'Espagne, etc. Né à Lons-le-Saunier (Jura) le 1er mai 1773. Donné à Vincent Guye, son frère. A Madrid le 1er Octobre 1810 et Pintado por Goya* (Bibl. 36, I, p. 119). See Trapier (Bibl. 188, pp. 36-37).

884 Inscribed on verso (before relining) *Ce portrait de mon Fils a été peint par Goya pour faire le pendant de celui de mon Frère le Général. / Vt Guye* (Bibl. 36, I, p. 120).

885 The son of Javier and Gumersinda, he was born on 11 July 1806, and appears to be between two and four years old in this portrait. Apparently listed by Carderera, although he identified it as Javier (Bibl. 148, no. 25). Cp. the later portraits [1553] and [V.1664].

886 Inscribed at lower right *D.ª Juana Galarza por Goya 1810*. Cp. the drawing and miniature of 1805-06 [II.841, 849]. See note to [II.840-852.]

887 Inscribed at lower right *D. Martin de Goicoechea Pr Goya 1810*. Cp. the miniature of 1805-06 [II.850] and the drawing which may also represent him [II.769].
See note to [840-852]. Born in 1755, he was 55 years old when this portrait was painted. He later emigrated to France (Bibl. 137, pp. 241-242) and died in Bordeaux in 1825. He has frequently been confused with Juan Martín de Goicoechea, Goya's friend and protector in Saragossa. See the 1928 exhibition catalogue (Bibl. 10, no. 74). Desparmet referred to a replica at Saragossa, but this is the portrait of Juan Martín [I.277 replica].

888 Lafuente suggested a date around 1810, since the sitter is wearing Joseph Bonaparte's Royal Order of Spain, and he discussed the possible identity of this member of the Goicoechea family (Bibl. 102, p. 291). Exhibited together with [889] in 1900 (nos 170, 171, hors catalogue — see Bibl. 57, I, p. 53, n. 3; 182, p. 200, n. 1).

889 Signed on the ring. The authenticity of this portrait has been questioned and Trapier did not include it among her *Sitters* (Bibl. 188). See note to [888].

890 The sitter has been identified as Gumersinda Goicoechea by Salas, but he did not then know of the miniature [845], here identified as Gumersinda. The miniature [846], previously identified as Gumersinda, is here identified as her elder sister Manuela.
The picture was probably one of the two half-length portraits of a lady with a fan (one identified as Catalina Viola) listed in the Brugada inventory of 1828 (Bibl. 57, I, p. 53, n. 1; see Appendix II, no. 10). It appeared in the first Salamanca sale in 1867 with the indication 'provient de la Galerie de Goya' (Bibl. 57, II, p. 261). Cp. note to [II.836, 837]. See Bibl. 25, no. 118; 30, no. 37.

891 Born 1781. See Núñez de Arenas (Bibl. 137, p. 233) and Sánchez Cantón (Bibl. 166, p. 100).

892 and 893 There has been considerable confusion over the dates of the two portraits, although Carderera listed them together in the collection of the sitter's son, Antonio Gil y Zárate, and said that one was painted in 1810 and the other in 1811 (Bibl. 148, no. 22). Unfortunately he did not specify the earlier and the later portrait. Sánchez Cantón dated [893] c.1808 and [892] c.1810-11 (Bibl. 166, p. 104); the 1963-64 catalogue reversed the order, dating [892] c.1805 and [893] c.1810-11 (Bibl. 27, no. 94). The famous actress died on 4 March 1811.
The vigorous portrait with the yellow sofa (cp. [II.804]) is possibly the earlier [892]. The bust portrait [893] belongs to the daughter of Marshall Field and was exhibited in New York in 1955 (Bibl. 20, no. 176); it is reproduced in Bibl. 159, pl. 45.

894 The recent identification of the sitter (formerly known as the Condesa de Gondomar) shows her to have been the mother of [895] (both portraits came from the Gondomar collection). She was the daughter of the Alba family doctor who died in 1813, and it is possible that her sombre black clothing may connect the date of the portrait with his death. She is referred to by Ezquerra del Bayo (Bibl. 58, p. 279), Núñez de Arenas (Bibl. 137, p. 252) and Trapier (Bibl. 188, pp. 27-28). See also Xavier de Salas, 'Los retratos de la familia Costa', *Archivo Español de Arte*, XXXVIII, 1965, pp. 64-65.

895 Inscribed *Pepito Costa y Bonells / Por Goya. 18[?]*. The date, partially obliterated, has been variously read as 1804, 1808 or 1813. Beruete read it as 1813 or 1818, and opted for the former (Bibl. 36, I, p. 127) which would link up with the date suggested for [894].
A Moreno photograph (no. 290) shows what appears to be a miniature of the same boy, holding a sword over his right shoulder and the reins of a hobby horse(?) in his left hand. Cp. the miniatures of 1805-06 [II.844-850].

896-900 Following the victory of Salamanca on 22 July 1812, the Duke entered Madrid on August 12 and left again on September 1. He returned in May 1814, as ambassador to Ferdinand VII. It is generally agreed that the red chalk drawing [898] was Goya's original study, made from life. The equestrian portrait [896] was exhibited at the beginning of September, and the bust portrait [897], which shows extensive alterations, was probably reworked in 1814. For references to Goya's relationship with the duke, see Glendinning (Bibl. 67, pp. 5-6).

896 Using the red chalk drawing [898] as the model for the head, the painting was executed over a previously painted canvas with an equestrian portrait of Godoy. See Allan Braham, 'Goya's Equestrian Portrait of the Duke of Wellington', *Burlington Magazine*, CVIII, 1966, pp. 618-621.
On 27 August Goya wrote that Wellington had visited him the previous day to discuss the exhibition of the portrait in the Real Academia de San Fernando, and on 1 September a notice appeared in the *Diario de Madrid*, announcing the public exhibition of the portrait between September 2 and 11 in the galleries of the Academia. The letter, in the Lázaro Galdiano Foundation, Madrid (Biblioteca 15648.3), is reproduced in Bibl. 107, I, p. 219, and translated into English by Trapier (Bibl. 188, p. 38); the text of the *Diario* announcement appears in Bibl. 36, I, p. 122. See also Bibl. 177.

897 For the complicated history of the alterations to this portrait, which in its original state was very close to the red chalk drawing [898], see Allan Braham, 'Goya's Portrait of the Duke of Wellington in the National Gallery', *Burlington Magazine*, CVIII, 1966, pp. 78-83. He suggested that the many alterations which Goya had to make may lend some support to the often-repeated tale of Goya's violent behaviour during one of the sittings, which Matheron said occurred during the reign of Ferdinand VII (on Wellington's return to Madrid in 1814?).

898 Inscribed by Carderera *Lord Welingn estudio p.a el retrato / equestre q.e pinto Goya*. A note by Mariano Goya, acquired with the drawing, describes it as *Un dibujo hecho en Alba de Tormes despues de la batalla de Arapales* [sic] *del Duque de Weelingthon por el q.e se hizo el retrato* (see Appendix VI).
It has generally been denied that Goya would have gone to Alba de Tormes (where the Duke is known to have been on the day following the battle of Arapiles, or Salamanca), but Braham suggested that he may have been summoned to make the drawing before Wellington's entry into Madrid on August 12 (*op. cit.* in note to [897]).
Besides being used as a model for [896] and [897], this drawing was undoubtedly designed to be engraved. The blank space below must have been intended for an engraved inscription, and the double platemark all round the design shows that the drawing was transferred to a copperplate measuring 19×14 cm. (see Bibl. 88, p. 39). No proof is known, and if an etching by Goya or engraving by another artist was made from the drawing, it may have been disapproved by the Duke since the dress and decorations were 'incorrect' (see Braham, *op. cit.*). The two drawings of Wellington [898, 899] were described in Carderera's collection by Gustave Brunet, *Etude sur Francisco Goya. Sa vie et ses travaux*, Paris, 1865, p. 15.

899 Inscribed by Carderera *Lord Wellington p.r Goya*. The relationship of this drawing to the painted portraits is not entirely clear, and even its authenticity has been questioned. However, Braham has shown that it corresponds to the second stage in the development of [897] (*op. cit.*

in note), and since, like [898], it has a blank margin below, it is possible that it may represent another attempt to produce an engraving of the Duke, correctly attired and decorated. It must be dated after Wellington had received permission to accept the Order of the Golden Fleece, at the end of August or beginning of September, and before its addition, in a different form, to [897]. See note to [898]. Catalogued in Bibl. 28, no. 135. The provenance from an Englishman in Spain is referred to by Glendinning (Bibl. 67, p. 10).

900 Inscribed at lower left (not by Goya) *A.W. Terror Gallorum* (A[rthur] W[ellesley] Terror of the French). This portrait, which belonged to the Spanish general Alava who fought beside Wellington, does not appear to have been made from the life. See the 'Appendix' to Braham's article cited in the note to [896].

901 Inscribed at lower left *El Exmo. S.or D.n Josef Palafox y Melci, / por Goya, año de 1814.* Listed by Carderera (Bibl. 148, no. 60).

Another portrait of Palafox, generally attributed to Goya, is not included in this catalogue. See references in Bibl. 23, no. XLI, and Gudiol no. 568.

902 Inscribed in lower left corner. The portrait, which has been almost entirely repainted, can be considered only as a record of Goya's original painting. Yriarte described the portrait when it was in the collection of Federico de Madrazo: 'coiffé d'un chapeau semblable [*Caprichos* pl. 1], une cocarde tricolore fixée au chapeau et un accent presque cruel donnent à cette toile un caractère particulier' (Bibl. 193, p. 137).

A copy by Fortuny, described as 'Portrait de Julia de Valence *(d'après Goya)*' in the 1875 sale catalogue, was identified by Lafuente as a reference to a copy of [II.863] (Bibl. 102, p. 257).

903-912 The 1812 inventory lists *Doce bodegones con el n.o once en . . . 1.200* (i.e. each still-life valued at 100 reales), and last but one in the list of paintings was *Unos pájaros con el n.o veinte y nueve en . . . 25*, which may also refer to a still-life (Bibl. 161, p. 106; see Appendix I, nos 11 and 29). Juliet Wilson recently identified traces of the inventory mark on [903] and [907], and since communicating this information to Jeannine Baticle of the Musée du Louvre, the latter has discovered that several of the still-lifes listed here have wooden battens nailed to the stretcher to make an identical, simple frame.

Saltillo published a list of paintings by Goya in the collection of the Conde de Yumuri in Carabanchel (Bibl. 153, p. 48). The group of still-lifes which decorated the Conde's dining-room was acquired from Mariano Goya as security against a loan which he did not repay. Saltillo's transcript of the original document suggests that there was some inaccuracy in the descriptions, but six of the nine still-lifes listed can definitely be identified with those catalogued here. The description included: *un bodegón de caza muerta, dos representando un pollo muerto y un pato, uno con frutas y pescado, un pavo sin pelar y otro pelado, y una naturaleza muerta con trozos de costilla, lomo y cabeza de carnero . . . tres ruedas de salmón y tres chochas muertas.* Interestingly, the list concluded with *dos bodegones apaisados, de tres cuartos, originales de Eugenio Lucas, con caza muerta.*

Sánchez Cantón had already proposed the identification of these still-lifes with those of the 1812 inventory (Bibl. 161, p. 106) and all the evidence now makes it clear that this group of still-lifes (all of the same size) was executed before 1812, probably as a series to decorate the artist's dining room, and that none of the pictures can be attributed to the Bordeaux period (as has been done by many writers, citing the evidence of Matheron in Bibl. 124, ch. XI, [pp. 91-92]).

The paintings have been discussed by José López-Rey 'Goya's Still-Lifes', *Art Quarterly*, XI, 1948, pp. 250-261, pointing out the relationship of the Prado pictures [904, 905] with the 'still-lifes' of dead bodies in the earliest designs for the *Desastres* prints, dated 1810, such as plate 22 [1029] (*op. cit.* figs 1-3), and publishing [909] and [910] for the first time. See the latest study by Jeannine Baticle in Bibl. 30, nos 35, 36.

903 Signature very small, in red, in the shadow below the sheep's head. Damaged along the lower edge, but with a clear trace (confirmed by laboratory examination) of the white inventory X at lower right. The *trozos de costilla, lomo y cabeza de carnero* in the Yumuri collection (see note to [903-912]). The authenticity of this picture has been doubted by several scholars, including López-Rey. Mayer described it as from the O'Rossen collection (*op. cit.* in note to [911]). Exhibited 1970 (Bibl. 30, no. 35).

904 Signed on the ground in the centre, almost vertically. The *pavo sin pelar* in the Yumuri collection (see note to [903-912]).

905 Possibly identifiable with the *pollo muerto* in the Yumuri collection (see note to [903-912]).

906 The large signature *Goya* appears in the background at upper left. This is the *otro* [pavo] *pelado* in the Yumuri collection (see note to [903-912]).

907 Signed diagonally at lower right. Saltillo cited a still-life of *frutas y pescado* in the Yumuri collection (see note to [903-912]). It is possible that the reference should indicate two pictures. Cp. note to [912]. At the exhibition in The Hague in 1970 (Bibl. 30, no. 36), Juliet Wilson found a trace of the inventory X in the lower right corner of the picture.

908 Signed in the background, diagonally along the line of the duck's wing. The *pato* in the Yumuri collection (see note to [903-912]).

909 Possibly the *caza muerta* in the Yumuri collection (see note to [903-912]). First published by López-Rey in 1948 (see the note already cited), together with [910]. Compare the two paintings with the hares and woodcocks in Goya's first known still-life, in a tapestry cartoon of 1775 [I.69]. Exhibited with [910] in 1963-64 (Bibl. 27, nos 125, 126).

910 Presumably the *tres chochas muertas* in the Yumuri collection. See note to [909].

911 The *tres ruedas de salmón* in the Yumuri collection (see note to [903-912]). First published, together with [912], by August L. Mayer, 'Three pictures by Goya', *Burlington Magazine*, LXXV, 1939, p. 240. He said that the pictures had been 'entrusted to a French officer in Paris'.

(The portrait published in the same article is not included in this catalogue of Goya's œuvre.)

912 Signed vertically on the label of the central bottle. Possibly the *frutas y pescado* in the Yumuri collection. See notes to [903-912] and [907] and [911]. This picture is quite different from the others in its conventional type of still-life composition.

913 This painting seems to bear no relationship, either in size or technique, to those listed above. Its attribution, in the absence of any documents or established provenance, remains tentative. Exhibited in 1959-60 (Bibl. 22, no. 156).

914-984 For the publication of the 1812 inventory by Sánchez Cantón and the subsequent identification by Salas of further paintings listed in the inventory, see Bibl. 161 and 147. Cp. Appendix I.

914-921 If Sánchez Cantón's identification is correct, these are some of the *Otros doce de los Horrores de la Guerra con el número doce en . . . 2.000* (i.e. valued at about 167 reales each) listed in the 1812 inventory (Bibl. 161, pp. 86, 106; Appendix I, no. 12). Alternatively, they may be identified with the *Diez cuadritos, horrores de la guerra* listed in the Brugada inventory of 1828 (Bibl. 57, I, p. 53, n. 1; Appendix II, no. 3). See note to [936-944]. Their date has been the subject of much discussion. Gudiol now places them in the same period as the cabinet pictures of 1793-94 [II.317-330], and they may have been painted before 1808. Held dated them c.1810 on stylistic grounds (Bibl. 89, nos 209-216). The series was last exhibited in 1928 (Bibl. 10, nos 62-69).

914 Cp. album F.55 and 59 [1476, 1480].

915 Very close in composition to *Caprichos* plate 32 [II.515].

918 Replica: 39×30 cm. Formerly Vienna, Eissler M.604/608, DF.195, Gaya Nuño 971 (Bibl. 65). Exhibited Galerie Miethke, Vienna, March-April 1908, no. 10 (as from the Romana collection).

919 Recalls one of the famine scenes in the *Desastres*, plate 57 [1088], and also plates 49, 58, 59.

921 Replica: 33·5×57·5 cm. Seville, Gonzalo Bilbao DF.(ill.173) Exhibited 1928 (Bibl. 10, no. 72).

922-925 Four paintings on panels of nearly the same size, they may have formed a series. There is no real proof that the first two represent the martyrdom of Jesuit missionaries by the Iroquois in Canada; Yriarte first identified one of the scenes as 'l'Archevêque de Québec' (Bibl. 139, p. 151), which Sánchez Cantón showed was impossible (Bibl. 166, p. 155). Following Cantón's identification, the 1963 exhibition catalogue discussed the relationship of the compositions to contemporary accounts of the Jesuit missionaries' fate (Bibl. 25, nos 120, 121). Cp. the discussion in the 1970 exhibition catalogue (Bibl. 30, nos 23, 24). The authors of the present work are inclined to see all four pictures as variations on the theme of 'savages', similar to the outrages performed by bandits in the Romana series [914-921] and Pierre Gassier points out the similarity with the 'savages' in the drawing F.57 [1478]. See note to [926, 927].

926 and 927 These are almost exact replicas of [924, 925] and the repetition could be explained by Goya's intention to create series of pictures, some for his own collection and some for sale. Cp. Carderera's references to the many small subject pictures in the collection of Andrés del Peral (Bibl. 102, pp. 303, 306). Also on sheets of tinplate of the same dimensions are [928, 929, 976 and 978].

927 is incorrectly listed in the 1963 Prado catalogue as no. 740º.

928 Formerly in the Marqués de la Torrecilla collection (together with [976], also on tin). Exhibited in 1961-62 (Bibl. 24, no. 86). Cp. the large painting [965].

Replica: 31·5×40·5 cm. Bilbao, Elosua Miquelena.

929 First recorded in the Quinto collection in Madrid when it was exhibited in 1846 together with *Una casa de locos* (Bibl. 102, p. 342, nos 50, 51). It is possible that the latter may have been the 1793-94 picture, which is on a sheet of tinplate of almost the same size [II.330] (see note), and the prison scene has sometimes been included with the series of 1793-94. However, its style and its close relationship with the three etchings of prisoners [986, 988, 990] and with drawings from the albums (cp. [1428]) and prints from the *Desastres* (cp. [1011]) suggest a considerably later date.

930-935 The *otros seis de varios asuntos con el n.o nueve en . . . 800* – i.e. valued at 133 reales each (Bibl. 161, p. 106; see Appendix I, no. 9). This group of paintings was identified by Salas (Bibl. 147). Father Tomás López referred to *una colección de* tablas*, como de un palmo de altas y palmo y medio de anchas, que representan los* horrores de la guerra*, los cuales tenía el mismo Goya en mucho aprecio* (Bibl. 190, p. 463). The paintings are probably contemporary with the earliest of the *Desastres* etchings – i.e. 1810.

930 and 931 These two panels were described in detail by Araujo (Bibl. 33, nos 97, 98). They passed from the Lafitte collection (where they were photographed by Otero – prints in the Prado library) to J. Böhler of Munich and were catalogued by Mayer. (He erroneously described them as on canvas, but the inventory marks are visible in the reproductions.) The compositions recall some of the *Desastres* plates, e.g. [997, 1006, 1007].

930 Replica(?): panel 31·3×40 cm. Paris, Nat Leeb G.608.

Poor copy: 30·5×41 cm. Sold at Christie's, London, 5 December 1961, lot 45.

931 The woman being carried off by soldiers is very close to the 'Flaxman' drawing [II.763], and also recalls *Desastres* plate 50 [1074].

Replicas(?):

Panel 47·7×31·7 cm. Madrid, X. de Salas G.609 Reproduced by Lafuente (Bibl. 102, p. 33). Exhibited 1963-64 (Bibl. 27, no. 101, with dimensions 30·5×39·5 cm.).

30·5×40·5 cm. France, priv. coll. From the Stchoukine and Zuloaga collections (see note to [936-944]). The existence of this painting was kindly communicated by Xavière Desparmet Fitz-Gerald. It was at one time in the collections of Santamarina and Acevedo in Buenos Aires.

932 Cp. *Desastres* plate 14 [1013].

Replicas or copies:

Panel 29×38 cm. Formerly Paris, Barroilhet DF. 231 (known only from the sale catalogue reference, see Bibl. 57, II, p. 263)

19×29 cm. Zumaya, Zuloaga Coll. DF.232 See note to [936-944].

933 With the X.9 repeated on the verso. First published by Salas (Bibl. 147, p. 108, figs 6, 6a).

934 Published by Salas from a photograph made by Otero (print in the Prado library) when the painting was in the Lafitte collection (Bibl. 147, fig. 7). The picture was in the collection of the Marqueses de Villatoya and passed to J. Böhler of Munich (cp. note to [930 and 931]) and in 1912 to the Langaard collection.

935 This picture was mentioned by Araujo as a pendant to [930, 931] which had belonged to Constantino Ardanaz, and described as *unos frailes echando libros y papeles en una hoguera* (Bibl. 33, no. 98). Reference quoted by Salas (Bibl. 147, p. 109), giving the dealer's name as Ardamar.

936-944 These paintings are known to the authors only from photographs. The greater number appear to be the canvases (in poor condition) which were acquired by Zuloaga at the Stchoukine sale in 1908 (lot 41) *'La Débâcle* – Dix petits tableaux... 19×29' (Bibl. 57, II, p. 271) and which included replicas or copies of two of the X.9 pictures [931, 932]. Doubts concerning the attribution of this group have been suggested by the quality of the paintings and their very close similarity with compositions from the *Desastres* etchings. If it were not for these doubts, it would be tempting to identify them with the *diez cuadritos, horrores de la guerra* listed in the Brugada inventory of 1828 (Bibl. 57, I, p. 53, n. 1; see Appendix II, no. 3). They certainly seem too slight to be identified with the 'twelve Horrors of War' listed in the 1812 inventory (see note to [914-921]).
The other paintings in this group look more like original works, but until they can be studied at first hand their attribution remains tentative. The paintings are listed in the order of the *Desastres* etchings to which they are related.
A further canvas is known only from a poor photograph. It shows women being attacked by soldiers in an interior and has some similarities with [930, 931 and 942] 40×48·2 cm. Montreal, van Horne Cp. [936 replica].

936 Similar to *Desastres* pl. 5 [998]. Authenticity doubted by Soria who noted that it was said to have been stolen and burnt (photographic collection, Instituto Diego Velázquez, Madrid). Cp. [939] and note.
Replica (with variants): panel 37×50 cm. Montreal, van Horne M.76.

937 Figures identical with *Desastres* pl. 16 [1017]. Exhibited 1961-62 (Bibl. 24, no. 66; not DF.238, as stated in the catalogue).

938 Identical with *Desastres* pl. 18 [1020]. Published by Juan Lafora, 'Goya: Estudio biográfico crítico', *Arte Español*, IX, 1928, p. 12, fig. 31.

939 The corpses are similar to those in *Desastres* pl. 18 [1020]. Authenticity doubted by Soria who noted that it was said to have been stolen and burnt (photographic collection, Instituto Diego Velázquez, Madrid). It was in the Traumann collection, with [936]; both are characterised by a vigorous, impasted technique.

940 Identical with *Desastres* pl. 25 [1035].

941 Identical with *Desastres* pl. 41 [1058]. Probably one of the Stchoukine-Zuloaga pictures, it has recently reappeared and a photograph was kindly made available by Xavière Desparmet Fitz-Gerald, enabling it to be reproduced for the first time.

942 Apparently painted from the drawing reproduced, which was not used for the *Desastres* series. It was shown in the *Exposición Histórica del Centenario 1808* in Madrid, but the authors were unable to consult this catalogue.

943 Apparently painted from the drawing reproduced, which was not used for the *Desastres* series.

944 Compare the drawing which was not used for the *Desastres* series [1148].
Replica: panel 98×125 cm. Paris, priv. coll.
Painting discovered and a photograph kindly made available by Xavière Desparmet Fitz-Gerald. The technique is very free and sketchy.

945 Known only from a Moreno photograph (no. 82a).

946 *Un gigante con el n.o diez y ocho en... 90* (Bibl. 161, p. 106; see Appendix I, no. 18). The different interpretations of this picture were summarized and a new theory proposed by Nigel Glendinning, 'Goya and Arriaza's *Profecia del Pirineo*', *Journal of the Warburg and Courtauld Institutes*, XXVI, 1963, pp. 363-366. Exhibited 1970 (Bibl. 30, no. 40).

947-950 The inventory lists *Quatro de otros asuntos con el n.o veinte y ocho en... 60* (Bibl. 161, p. 106; see Appendix I, no. 28). These are therefore, at 15 reales each, the least valuable pictures in the inventory (apart from number 5 *Una cabeza*). They come at the end of the list, following numbers 26 *Un boceto... en 30* and 27 *Otros quatro de las Artes... en 80* (i.e. at 20 reales each), and one would assume that the description *boceto* would also apply to these very modestly valued pictures. The pictures catalogued here were identified as the X.28 group by Gudiol (Bibl. 84), who described the inventory number on [947] as a large, half-erased *28*.
They first appeared in 1866 in the Eustaquio López sale, with a provenance from Mariano Goya (Bibl. 57, II, pp. 260-261), and Viñaza recorded that they were acquired by Sr. Ferrándiz (Bibl. 190, pp. 292-293, nos CIV-CVII). Viñaza did not refer to their sale in 1868 by Luis de Madrazo. Both Araujo (Bibl. 33, pp. 136-137) and Beruete (Bibl. 36, II, p. 97) referred to the legal dispute concerning their authenticity which arose on this occasion and for which Mariano Goya was called to Madrid to give his opinion. They were duly authenticated by Mariano who recalled seeing Goya paint one of them, [949] (although he would have been only six years old at the time the inventory was made). The paintings later passed to Argentina.
These paintings are almost the same size as the X.1 pictures [951-954], valued at 450 reales each. It seems more likely that they correspond with pictures listed in the Brugada inventory of 1828 (see Bibl. 57, I, p. 53, n. 1 and Appendix II, as well as the notes below). These, together with the X.1 and similar pictures, could be the group mentioned by Father Tomás López (see note to [951-956]). If they were painted after 1812, Mariano Goya's statement appears plausible. The number 28 on [947] nevertheless remains to be explained.
Gudiol was the first to take seriously the often repeated testimonies that Goya painted with the palette knife and in particular with the split canes described by Mariano Goya and Tomás López, and the identification of the 1812 inventory mark on paintings previously considered of doubtful authenticity (cp. [951-956]) bears out his analysis of this technique in the article cited above.

947 Possibly the painting listed in the 1828 Brugada inventory as *Incendio de un pueblo (una vara)* – i.e. 83·5 cm. See Appendix II, no. 22. The inventory mark is in the lower left corner. (The much smaller painting catalogued by Desparmet in the Miethke collection, Vienna, cannot be the one which came from the Eustaquio López collection and passed to Buenos Aires.) Cp. the earlier *Incendio* of 1793-94 [II.329].

948 The 1828 Brugada inventory lists *Dos Escenas de bandoleros, bocetos*, but the qualification 'sketch' seems to rule out an identification with this composition. See Appendix II, no. 28. Both this picture and the identical replica in Budapest have been attributed to Lucas (cp. Trapier, Bibl. 186, p. 40, pl. XXVIII), and the replica is now described in the Budapest catalogue as a copy by Lucas of the Goya original in Buenos Aires.
Gudiol discussed the problem of Lucas copies and variants, illustrating a painting which is a mixture of elements from [948] and [949] (Bibl. 84, p. 16, fig. 25); this composite painting was also mentioned by Trapier (*op. cit.* p. 62, pl. XLVI, erroneously identifying it as one of this group; also confusing [947] with [II.329]), and by Lafuente (Bibl. 102, p. 229). Mayer 650 gave the dimensions as about 98×126 cm.
Replica or copy: 69×107·5 cm. Budapest, Mus. (4121) See Held (Bibl. 89, p. 193).

949 The Brugada inventory lists *Un baile, cuadro* which may be this picture. See Appendix II, no. 29. Mayer gave the dimensions as 98×126 cm.
A copy by Lucas in the Carles collection, Barcelona, was discussed by Gudiol (Bibl. 84, p. 16, fig. 17). For a variant by Lucas, see note to [948].

950 Published in colour by the Jockey Club in 1928, *Tres cuadros de Goya*, with the dimensions. Dimensions given by Mayer 538: 98×126 cm.; Mayer 687: 80×180 cm; Desparmet: 80×110 cm.; Gudiol echoes Mayer 538.
This was the painting which Mariano Goya, in 1868, recalled seeing his grandfather paint with 'cañas finas, abiertas en su extremo' (thin canes, open at the end) (Bibl. 36, II, p. 97).
This type of scene with torrential rain was frequently imitated by Lucas – cp. the signed and dated painting of 1856 in the Musée Goya, Castres.

951-956 The 1812 inventory lists *Quatro quadros iguales con el numero primero, en 1800* – i.e. valued at 450 reales each (Bibl. 161, p. 106; see Appendix I, no. 1). Three of them are possibly identifiable in the Brugada inventory of 1828 (see Bibl. 57, I, p. 53, n. 1, Appendix II, and the individual notes). Together with similar paintings [954-956] and possibly the preceding group of pictures [947-950], they may constitute the group described by Father Tomás López who saw among other pictures in Javier Goya's house *ocho ó diez en lienzo (como de una vara)* [83·5 cm.], *pintados* sin pinceles, *puesto el color con unos cuchillitos de caña, que él mismo se hacía, y de cuyo método se preciaba él de ser el inventor. Representan corridas de toros y asuntos de costumbres* (Bibl. 190, p. 463). Two of the paintings appeared together in the Salamanca sales [952, 953], as noted by Salas in Bibl. 149, pp. 9-11 (cp. Bibl. 57, II, pp. 261-262, 263-264). The full history of the other two is not known. The additional paintings [955, 956], which are of the same size but do not appear to be recorded in the 1812 inventory, were probably painted after that date. One of them seems to be listed in the 1828 inventory and certainly came from the Goya collection [956]; the early provenance of the other is not known, and its attribution to Goya has often been disputed [955]. See remarks at end of note to [947-950].
A landscape painting was certified by Mayer who related it to [946] and [950] and described it as a pendant to [956]. It seems in our opinion to have no connection with Goya's work, either in composition, handling or colour; it is mentioned here because it has so frequently been reproduced and exhibited: 106×86 cm. Sold at Sotheby's, London, 3 December 1969 Mentioned in Bibl. 15, no. 22; reproduced in Bibl. 166, fig. 47; exhibited in 1955 (Bibl. 20, no. 189).
Another work attributed to Goya, although the violence of its technique suggests (in a photograph) the hand of an imitator, is the *Fight with bars*: panel 62·5 ×69·7 cm.(?) Indianapolis, Clowes Fund Inc. DF.263, G.673 (described as a small canvas).

951 This painting was virtually unknown until its recent identification by José Gudiol who kindly provided the information concerning its existence and the inventory mark which is still visible. The painting was reproduced by Manuel Gómez-Moreno, 'Los fondos de Goya', *Boletín de la Real Academia de la Historia*, 1946, following pp. 30-41, and a Moreno photograph (no. 6983) shows the X.1 very clearly.
Replica or copy: 81·7×103·5 cm. Berlin, N.G. (A I 785) M.579, DF.269, G.672 Discussed by Held (Bibl. 89, p. 192).
The Berlin version (from the Casa Torres collection) has frequently been attributed to Lucas, but a comparative study of the two paintings is now required. A version of this painting, from the collection of Luis Quer, Barcelona, was reproduced in *Hispania*, 31, 1900, p. 171.

952 Possibly the painting listed in the Brugada inventory of 1828 as *Una procesion (de una vara y media)* – i.e. 126 cm. See Appendix II, no. 19. The 1812 inventory mark, which is clearly visible, was first described by Salas who also discussed the description of the painting in the two Salamanca sales, first as 'Procession de Valence' and secondly as 'Procession à Lambas' (Bibl. 149, pp. 9-11; 57, II, pp. 261-262, 263-264). Until the identification of the inventory number, this painting was often considered of doubtful authenticity – cp. Held (Bibl. 89, p. 191).

953 Possibly the painting listed in the Brugada inventory of 1828 as *Dos corridas de toros, cuadro* – i.e. a picture showing two simultaneous bullfights. See Appendix II, no. 30. This is the painting which appeared as the pendant to [952] in the Salamanca sales (Bibl. 57, II, pp. 261-262, 263-264). Cp. the bullfight on panel [969].

954 Possibly the painting listed in the 1828 Brugada inventory as *Baile de mascaras (de una vara)* – i.e. 83·5 cm. It could also be the fourth of the X.1 group, although its provenance requires some clarification (there seems to be a possible confusion with [949]). See Appendix I, no. 1 and II, no. 18. It has not been seen since it was exhibited on loan at the National Gallery, London, in 1938-39, together with [I.254] and [II.871].

955 The authenticity of this picture has been very much discussed, but with the documentation of the preceding paintings [951-954] it should now be possible to make a conclusive comparative study, and Gudiol accepted it unhesitatingly in the context of this group (Bibl. 84, p. 15). The connection with the *Disparate* print of the 'Flying men' [IV.1591] is obvious, and the print and its preparatory drawing may have been designed as early as 1815. Cp. the rock with [951] and [IV.1620].

A reduction is known from a photograph: 56×68 cm. Barcelona, Luis Rei (1935) Photo Mas 80891.

956 Possibly the painting listed in the 1828 Brugada inventory as *Un globo*. See Appendix II, no. 20. Cp. the drawings of balloons [II.755, 756], and see Bibl. 25, no. 122, for a discussion of the subject. This painting was acquired by Federico de Madrazo from Javier Goya, together with [975] (also apparently listed in the 1828 inventory) and another painting which is not included in this catalogue, in spite of its provenance:

Capricho 37×49 cm. Agen, Mus. (272 Ch.) DF.175, G.616. This work has often been considered a pastiche (cp. Held, Bibl. 89, p. 194), particularly since it includes motifs such as a flying bull and an elephant which occur in two *Disparate* prints [IV.1603, 1604] and a drawing [1533], and animals which are very close to the Goya-Weiss drawings of a dog and a fox [V.1867, 1869]. It is also curious that the Agen painting does not correspond with the painting belonging to Madrazo as described by Viñaza: 'Tres aerostáticos ascienden por la atmósfera, suspendiendo un asno, un toro y un elefante, cada uno de aquellos respectivamente' (Bibl. 190, p. 297, no. CXXVI) – there are no balloons in the Agen picture. Cp. Tormo (Bibl. 184, nos 141, 143).

957-965 For the identification of these paintings with those of the 1812 inventory, see Sánchez Cantón (Bibl. 161) and Salas (Bibl. 147) as well as Appendix I and the individual notes. The most important were acquired by Louis-Philippe, together with the portrait of the Duchess of Alba [II.355], and shown in the Galerie Espagnole in the Louvre in 1838 (Bibl. 6). All the figure paintings sold at Christie's in 1853 were described in the catalogue as having been obtained from the son of the artist (Bibl. 31). See the discussion of some of these pictures in Bibl. 30, nos 41-43.

957 Listed in the 1812 inventory as *El lazarillo de Tormes con el n.o veinte y dos en . . . 100* (see Appendix I, no. 22) and identified by Salas (Bibl. 147, pp. 105-106, fig. 2). Catalogued in the Galerie Espagnole in 1838 as 'Lazarille de Tormes', but apparently with wrong dimensions (Bibl. 6, no. 102). Sold at Christie's for £11.10 in 1853 (Bibl. 31, lot 171). Catalogued by Yriarte in 1867 in the collection of M. Comartin (for Caumartin), from the Galerie Espagnole. The 1963-64 exhibition catalogue (Bibl. 27, no. 80) suggested that the Galerie Espagnole picture was another, larger version, but it seems more likely that the dimensions in the 1838 catalogue were erroneous (they were given as 161×105 cm., the same as for the full-length figure paintings).

958 The X.24 is no longer visible on the picture, but it is visible in the lower left corner in a Moreno photograph. The 1812 inventory lists *Dos quadros de unas jovenes al balcon con el n.o veinte y quatro en . . . 400* (see Appendix I, no. 24). There has been considerable confusion over the different versions of the *Majas on a balcony*, but the identification of the two inventory paintings – [958] by Salas (Bibl. 147, p. 108, fig. 5) and [959] by Juliet Wilson – has clarified the position. This picture was acquired by Francisco Acebal y Arratia and first exhibited in 1846 (Bibl. 7, and 102, p. 341, no. 9). It was fully catalogued in 1928 (Bibl. 10, no. 84).

959 An old Durand-Ruel photograph, kindly made available by Enriqueta Frankfort Harris, shows the picture with the X.24 clearly visible in the lower left corner and gives the dimensions as 162×108 cm. (as in Desparmet), i.e. the same size as its companion [958] and considerably smaller than [961, 962, 965].
Mayer confused the provenance of this picture with that of [960]. This one [959] was the picture acquired by Louis-Philippe and shown in the Galerie Espagnole as '*Manolas* au balcon (Femmes de Madrid)' (Bibl. 6, no. 99). It was bought in for £70 at Christie's in 1853 (Bibl. 31, lot 352) and passed to the Duc de Montpensier in Seville. Reproduced by Sánchez Cantón (Bibl. 161, fig. 14, described as the New York picture [960]; 159, pl. 63, described as the Groult picture [960 copy]). The different versions were clarified in a later article: F. J. Sánchez Cantón, 'Las versiones de "Las majas al balcón"', *Archivo Español de Arte*, XXV, 1952, pp. 336-338 (but incorrectly identifying the two versions of the picture as the two paintings listed in the 1812 inventory under no. 24). See note to [958].
The painting remained virtually unknown, and incomplete photographs and erroneous dimensions led to the assumption that it had been reduced in size. However, its exhibition in 1970 (Bibl. 30, no. 42/41) showed that this was not the case and that it still has the inventory mark. The dimensions given in this catalogue were taken at the time of the exhibition.

960 Larger than [959] and in a smoother, sweeter style and technique, this version may have been painted as a pair to the replica of [961] – see note. Exhibited 1963-64 (Bibl. 27, no. 84). It was in the collection of the Infante Don Sebastián by 1867 (cp. Bibl. 193, p. 90) and may have been acquired at the first Salamanca sale that year; the sale catalogue gave as its provenance 'la vente Goya'. Another version, the copy listed below, was included in the second sale (Bibl. 57, II, pp. 261, 264).

Copy by Alenza(?): 192×130 cm. Sold Galerie Charpentier, Paris, 24 May 1955 (formerly Groult, Salamanca) M.148 Described in the catalogue of the second Salamanca sale as from the collection of Séraphin de la Huerta (Bibl. 57, II, p. 264).

Copy by Lameyer(?): see Lafuente (Bibl. 102, p. 218, fig. 40).

961 Inscribed *Que tal?* (How goes it?) on back of mirror. Listed in the 1812 inventory as *El tiempo con el n.o veinte y tres en . . . 150* (see Appendix I, no. 23) and identified by Salas (Bibl. 147, pp. 107-108, fig. 3). It passed to the collection of Louis-Philippe, but was not exhibited in the Galerie Espagnole. It was included in the Christie sale in 1853 and sold for £4.15 (Bibl. 31, lot 169). It has often been described as a pair to [962], but this whole group of paintings was probably conceived as a series. Exhibited 1970 (Bibl. 30, no. 41/43).

Replica(?): 192×125 cm. Formerly Madrid, Marqués de la Torrecilla M.691, DF.190 Yriarte dismissed it as apocryphal (Bibl. 193, p. 135), but this painting, which has never been exhibited or studied, has similar dimensions to [960] and (from a photograph) something of the same softer quality. The 1963 exhibition catalogue suggested that it might have been painted as a pendant to the larger version of the *Majas on a balcony* [960] (Bibl. 25, no. 123).

962 Not included in the 1812 inventory, but certainly part of this series, and often considered to be a pendant to [961]. Malraux considered it a portrait rather than a genre painting (Bibl. 25, no. 126), and Pierre Gassier suggests that it represents Leocadia Weiss (see text, and cp. [IV. 1622]). It was acquired by Louis-Philippe and exhibited in the Galerie Espagnole as 'Femmes de Madrid en costume de *Majas*' (Bibl. 6, no. 100), before being sold at Christie's for £21 in 1853 (Bibl. 31, lot 353), as from the collection of Goya's son. Exhibited 1970 (Bibl. 30, no. 43/42).

963 and 964 The 1812 inventory lists *Una aguadora y su compañero con el número trece en . . . 300* (see Appendix I, no. 13). It has always been assumed that these two paintings are those referred to in the inventory, but if so it is curious that each of these fairly small pictures was given the same valuation as the Lille painting [961]. (The inventory valuations appear to some extent to reflect the size of the pictures and the complexity of their compositions.) It is therefore just possible that an original pair of paintings, of the same size as the others in this group, has been lost and that the Budapest pictures are reductions. (They were already in the Prince Kaunitz collection, Vienna, by 1820.)
Several replicas or copies of the *Water-carrier* are known, and it must have been greatly in demand. A further curious fact is that the sketch for a tapestry cartoon on the same theme [I.295] was found, when examined by Juliet Wilson, to have a large X.13 painted on the back of the canvas, suggesting that it was added in with the inventory pair (its value would have been very slight).
963 Replicas or copies:

56×42 cm. Fullerton (Calif.), Norton Simon Found. M.678?, DF.240?, G.578 Described as from the Castelar and Rodríguez collections.

Mexico City, Museo de San Carlos Gaya Nuño 1064 (Bibl. 65), with the same provenance as the Norton Simon picture. Described by the museum as a copy.

Madrid, Marqués de la Montesa G.577.

The provenance and characteristics of these replicas require further study.
There is a clear relationship between the *Water-carrier* and the drawing from album C, reproduced after it.

965 Probably the last of the series, this picture was acquired by Louis-Philippe and exhibited in the Galerie Espagnole in 1838 (Bibl. 6, no. 101), before being sold at Christie's in 1853 for £10. Like the other paintings, it came from the collection of the artist's son (Bibl. 31, lot 354).

966-971 It is now certain that these paintings were not the 'cabinet pictures' sent to Iriarte in 1794 (cp. [II.317-330]). They do not appear in the 1812 inventory and were probably executed after that date. Sánchez Cantón suggested that the four first pictures might be the *Quatro cuadritos fiestas y costumbres* listed in the Brugada inventory of 1828 (Bibl. 166, pp. 100-101). If this is likely, one might also identify [970] with the *Baile de mascaras* listed in the same inventory. See Appendix II, nos 5 and 18. All five paintings were acquired by Manuel García de la Prada, who was painted by Goya as a young man [II.819]; he left them to the Academy in his will.

Tormo mentioned copies of all five paintings, exhibited as originals in Saragossa, from the collection of the Baronesa de Areyzaga (Bibl. 183, p. 285).

Lafuente mentioned copies of the first four paintings by Francisco Lameyer (Bibl. 102, p. 217).

Other replicas and copies are mentioned in the individual notes.

967 Cp. the early Madrid album drawing [II.438] and the two versions of [974].

A poor copy in the Spanish Embassy in Paris is known from a photograph.

968 Cp. the 1793-94 painting [II.330].

Replica or copy: panel 44×69 cm. Vienna, Kunsthistorisches Museum, Neue Galerie (109) M.694 From the collection of Beruete who discussed and reproduced it (Bibl. 36, II, p. 94, pl. 35).

969 Cp. the larger and presumably earlier painting [953].

970 Dimensions as given by Salas in a study analysing the changes in the composition of this painting which was originally very close to the preparatory drawing [971] (Bibl. 149, pp. 1-5). Possibly the *Baile de mascaras (de una vara)* – i.e. 83·5 cm. – in the 1828 inventory (see note to [966-971]).

Copy: 83×62 cm. Paris, private coll. DF.243n Exhibited 1961-62 (Bibl. 24, no. 70).

Free copy by Lucas, discussed by Lafuente (Bibl. 102, p. 234, fig. 60).

972-979 Paintings which were formerly considered of doubtful authenticity and which have now been connected with the inventories of 1812 and 1828 [947-956] may help to determine the attribution of those listed here.

972 Cp. the dancing figures in [970]. Held dated it c.1806, together with [966-971] (Bibl. 89, no. 206).

973 Known only from a photograph (Moreno 415).

974 The two versions of this composition have both been attributed to Lucas, but Gudiol definitely ascribed the Buenos Aires picture to Goya (Bibl. 84, p. 15, fig. 19), relating it to the technique of the X.28 and X.1 pictures [947-956]. The Lázaro picture was discussed by Vicente Marrero, 'Los "Disciplinantes" de Goya', *Goya*, no. 27, 1958, pp. 172-175, colour ill.

Replica: 46·5×54·5 cm. Madrid, Fund. Lázaro (M.2016) M.534a, DF.213, G.676 See Held (Bibl. 89, p. 193), giving the dimensions cited here.

975 The Brugada inventory of 1828 lists *La misa de parida* (see Appendix II, no. 31) which is probably this painting, acquired by Federico de Madrazo from Javier Goya (see note to [956]). The largest of the different versions known (see [976] and replicas), it was discussed by Tormo (Bibl. 184, no. 142), Gudiol (Bibl. 84, p. 15) and Held (Bibl. 89, p. 187).

A copy by Fortuny was mentioned by Beruete (Bibl. 36, II, p. 97).

976 Known only from a photograph (Moreno 52), this picture is the same format as [926-929] and may form part of a series on tin. Lafond catalogued a replica on tin(?) in the Esteban Collantes collection (now Lázaro), and described both as sketches for [975] (Bibl. 97, p. 104, nos 62, 63).

Replicas:

37×45·5 cm. Madrid, Fund. Lázaro (M.8093) Pair to [977 replica] M.531, DF.262 Described in the Lázaro

museum catalogue as from the Groult collection. See Held (Bibl. 89, p. 187), giving dimensions cited here.
49×61 cm. Formerly Cassel, Kleinschmidt M. 531a, DF.262n.
35×41 cm. Formerly Madrid, Castelar DF.266n.
A version in the Museo de San Carlos, Mexico City, was described in the Paní collection catalogue (1921, no. 6) as from the Groult collection (sold at Galerie Georges Petit, Paris, 21 March 1920). Cp. Lázaro replica above. Described by the museum as a copy by Lucas.
The provenance and characteristics of all these versions require further study.

977 Replica: 37×45 cm. Madrid, Fund. Lázaro (M. 2514) Pair to [976 replica]; see note for provenance DF.266 See Held (Bibl. 89, p. 186).
A version in the Museo de San Carlos, Mexico City, is a pair to the one described in the note to [976]. Paní catalogue no. 7.
The provenance and characteristics of all these versions require further study.

978 This picture has often been attributed to Lucas. Its format is the same as [976] and the group of pictures on tin [926-929]. See Held (Bibl. 89, p. 192), giving the dimensions as 32×39·5 cm.
The original version of this composition was first exhibited and published in 1970 (Bibl. 30, no. 28):
Tinplate 29×41 cm. Paris, Louvre (RF 1970.33) Repr. in colour in *Revue du Louvre*, 1970, nos 4-5, p. 261.
This picture appeared too late to be included in the illustrated catalogue. Its quality suggests a much earlier date than that indicated for the other paintings in this group.
Copy: 25×35 cm. Madrid, Museo Romántico Exhibited 1951 (Bibl. 17, no. 24) Reproduced in *Museum*, V, 1917, p. 83.

979 Copy by Lucas, together with a drawing, discussed and reproduced by Lafuente (Bibl. 102, p. 232, figs 54, (55.
Copy by Fortuny mentioned by Lafuente (*op. cit.* p. 257).

980 and 981 It has been suggested that these pictures were painted as a result of Goya's visit to Saragossa in 1808, but the inscriptions on the verso suggest a later date. Both the landscape and the scenes of guerilla activity may be recollections from the 1808 journey. Held (Bibl. 89, nos 221, 222) dated them c.1811 on stylistic grounds.
980 Inscribed on verso *N.º 1 / Fábrica de pólvora establecida / por don Josef Mallen en la / Sierra de Tardienta en Aragón / en los años de 1811, 12 y 13* (Bibl. 23, no. LV).
981 Inscribed on verso *Número 2 / Fábrica de balas de fusil / establecida por don Josef Mallen / en la Sierra de Tardienta / en Aragón / en los años de 1811, 12 y 13* (Bibl. 23, no. LIV).

982-984 For a full account see Lafuente (Bibl. 100). The origin of the pictures was discussed by Lafuente (*op. cit.* p. 22) and Sánchez Cantón (Bibl. 166, pp. 96-97). Sambricio published the document, dated 9 March 1814, in which the Regency acceded to Goya's request to be allowed to paint *las mas notables y heroicas acciones ó escenas de nuestra gloriosa insurreccion contra el tirano de Europa*, allowing him 1,500 reales per month in addition to his expenses (Bibl. 154, doc. 225).
Mayer recorded Cristobal Férriz's statement that Goya had painted not two but four scenes of the May uprising, the other two being the revolt before the Royal Palace and the defense of the Artillery Park (Bibl. 128, p. 66). Both Mayer and Lafuente (*op. cit.* p. 23) who recalled Mayer's note emphasized that no trace of these two additional compositions had been found.
Beroqui also pointed out that there was no evidence to support Ferriz's statement, echoed by Beruete, that the *Dos* and *Tres de Mayo* were displayed on a triumphal arch (Bibl. 35, p. 72, n. 2; cp. Lafuente, *op. cit.* p. 23).
Beroqui indicated that at the death of Ferdinand in 1834 the paintings were in the reserves of the Prado Museum, and Lafuente pointed out that they were not included in the museum catalogue until the edition of 1872 (*op. cit.* p. 23, n. 32). See also Beroqui (*op. cit.* p. 101) for a reference to the rapturous reception accorded to the two similarly heroic paintings by José Aparicio, which were installed among the modern pictures in the Prado in 1828 (Bibl. 1, nos 303, 310). See note to [1568].

982 Inscribed in the sky *MADRID / DOS DE MAYO*; see Lafuente (Bibl. 100, p. 32 and n. 40) for a detailed discussion. Prado title: 'El 2 de Mayo de 1808 en Madrid: la lucha con los Mamelucos'; the catalogue points out that

there is no proof of the traditional belief that the scene is the Puerta del Sol. See Demerson (Bibl. 56) for the evidence that Goya was not living in the Puerta del Sol in 1808, but could have witnessed the event from his son's house or the street which led from it.

983 It is possible that this sketch was painted in 1808, as a direct record of the event. Demerson analysed the differences between this and the final version, and concluded that it may represent the Puerta del Sol which was then much smaller (Bibl. 56, pp. 183-184). Its exact relationship to [982] requires further study (see note to [983a]). Exhibited 1970 (Bibl. 30, no. 44).

983a This attributed sketch, which has not been discussed in the Goya literature, is closer to the final picture but the background is closed off on the right with a wall which ends abruptly near the centre of the picture. This is also visible in [983] but appears to have been overpainted to open up the perspective view. A note (no source given) in the Witt Library, London, says that the sketch was given by Goya to Evaristo Pérez de Castro (cp. note to [II.815]).

984 Prado title: 'El 3 de Mayo de 1808 en Madrid: los fusilamientos en la montaña del Príncipe Pío'. The executions took place beside the hill in the area known as Moncloa.
A possible sketch, once attributed to Goya, is no longer considered authentic: New York, Hispanic Society (A.100) M.74a, DF.226n.

985 There is still some doubt over the exact technique of this print, unique in Goya's œuvre. The son of Bartolomé Sureda said that his father learnt the technique of mezzotint engraving in England and that he taught it to Goya who painted his portrait and that of his wife in gratitude [II.813, 814] – see Trapier (Bibl. 188, p. 32). If the print is a mezzotint, it can in any case hardly have been made before 1810, which does not accord with the probable date of the Sureda portraits. A note by Mariano Goya, preserved in the British Museum (see Appendix VII), listed a proof which he said had been stored away, with other works and papers, in 1818. In 1964 a sixth proof, in the first state, was found and is now in the Museum of Fine Arts, Boston.

986-992 Proof prints of these etchings, with manuscript titles in pencil, were included in the complete set of the *Desastres* proofs which Goya gave to Ceán Bermúdez (Bibl. 88, I, p. 140). Cp. the prisoners in the small painting on tin [929]. López-Rey has discussed the preparatory drawings (Bibl. 117, pp. 20-23).

986 (The custody is as barbarous as the crime). First published from the original copperplate in the *Gazette des Beaux-Arts*, XXII, 1867, p. 196. See note to [992]. The copperplate, now heavily reworked, is in a Paris collection.

987 Much cruder than the other drawings for these prints, it recalls the Goya-Weiss drawings [V.1842-1870] and is attributed to Rosario Weiss, as a copy after Goya's lost preparatory drawing, by López-Rey (Bibl. 117, pp. 21-22).

988 (The custody of a criminal does not call for torture). First published in a limited edition about 1859, together with [990]. It is not known whether the copperplate still exists.

989 Exhibited in 1937 (Bibl. 14, no. 40, ill.) and 1941 (Bibl. 16, no. 135, ill.).

990 (If he is guilty let him die quickly). Published together with [988]. It is not known whether the copperplate still exists.

992 Possibly made as a first study for [990], or may have been used for [986].

993-1148 The prints and their preparatory drawings have been published by Lafuente (Bibl. 104). The complete set of first edition prints is reproduced actual size, together with facsimile reproductions of the title page and introduction (and English translations), in Bibl. 79.

993 (Sad forebodings of what is to come). One of the *caprichos enfáticos*.

1000 This is the print which recalls the heroism of Agustina, the Maid of Saragossa, who manned the cannon during the first siege of the city. The aquatint was added in 1863, before the printing of the first edition, to conceal the very damaged and pitted background.

1003 One of the *caprichos enfáticos*.

1011 Etched on the back of a cut plate [II.748].

1013 Etched on the back of a cut plate [II.750].

1015 Etched on the back of a cut plate [II.748].

1026 Cp. [1142-1145] for two pairs of drawings of very similar compositions. In each case, one drawing has a platemark and of the other a painting is known. It may be that this drawing was also made for an unknown painting.

1028 Catalogued by Harris as a drawing for an unknown plate, but in spite of considerable variations it was probably used for this etching.

1040 One of the *caprichos enfáticos*.

1042 One of the *caprichos enfáticos*.

1044 Etched on the back of a cut plate [II.750].

1049 Cp. the group of drawings in album C [1321-1328], and the earlier etchings [I.122] and [II.498, 614].

1054 Not reproduced by Sánchez Cantón in Bibl. 168.

1055 (A great feat! With dead men!)

1056 One of the *caprichos enfáticos*.

1060 One of the *caprichos enfáticos*.

1098 The size of the plate corresponds with the *caprichos enfáticos*.

1105 Possibly a first drawing for [1104].

1106 and 1108 The subject was discussed by Nigel Glendinning, 'El asno cargado de reliquias en los *Desastres de la Guerra*, de Goya', *Archivo Español de Arte*, XXXV, 1962, p. 221-230.

1112 Inscribed *Nada*, as if by the corpse, on the sheet of paper. The original MS. title *Nada. Ello lo dice*. (Nothing. That's what it says) was altered to make it less emphatic. This plate may have been designed to end the series of war and famine scenes, before Goya thought of adding the *caprichos enfáticos*.

1113 Entirely different from the other drawings in the series, it may represent a first idea for the design.

1120 The title suggests a play on the word *gato* – cat, but also a sneak-thief (cat burglar) and a native of Madrid. Cp. [II.441].

1122 Inscription *Misera humanidad / la culpa es tuya / Casti* (Miserable humanity, the fault is thine. Casti), written by the wolf on the sheet of paper. The source of the quotation from the poet Casti has not been identified–see Sánchez Cantón, 'Una docena de dibujos goyescos', *Archivo Español de Arte*, XXVII, 1954, pp. 287-288, and the note to [II.770].

1134 The iconography of this composition was discussed by Levitine (Bibl. 108, p. 110). See note to [1352].

1141 The title is no longer visible on the drawing.

1142 Shows a platemark.

1143 Drawing used for [942].

1144 Shows a platemark.

1145 Drawing used for [943].

1146 Shows a platemark.

1147 Shows a platemark.

1148 Cp. the painting [944], with its larger replica.

1149-1243 The prints and their preparatory drawings were published by E. Lafuente Ferrari, *Francisco Goya y Lucientes. La Tauromaquia*, Paris (Le Club français du Livre), 1963. The complete set of 33 plates from the first edition (together with a facsimile, and translation, of the title page) and the 7 additional plates A-G are reproduced actual size in Bibl. 80. For a discussion of the sources and development of the series, see Lafuente (Bibl. 101). See also P. Beroqui, 'La fecha de la ''Tauromaquia'' de Goya', *Archivo Español de Arte*, V, 1929, p. 287.

1149 ...*cazaban los toros á caballo en el campo.* (The way in which the ancient Spaniards hunted bulls on horseback in the open country). Engraved on the verso of plate A [1219].

1151 Engraved on the verso of plate B [1221].

1152 Published and reproduced in *Hispania*, 1900, no. 31, pp. 178, 184 (from the Cabot collection). Exhibited 1963-64 (Bibl. 27, no. 146).

1153 ...*prescindiendo de las supersticiones de su Alcorán, adoptaron esta caza y arte, y lancean un toro en el campo.* (The moors settled in Spain, giving up the superstitions of the Koran, adopted this art of hunting and spear a bull in the open).

1155 (...in an enclosure).

1157 (The spirited moor Gazul was the first to spear bulls according to rules).

1158 Reproduced from the facsimile in *L'Art*, 1877, II, p. 79.

1159 (The moors make a different pass, playing [the bull] in the ring with their burnous). Engraved on the verso of plate C [1223].

1161 (...or banderillas). Engraved on the verso of plate D [1225].

1163 (...by the bull in the ring).

1165 ...*despues de haber perdido el caballo.* (A Spanish knight kills the bull after having lost his horse).

1167 (Charles V spearing a bull in the ring at Valladolid). This plate and [1171] are in the wrong historical order.

1171 (The Cid Campeador spearing another bull). Engraved on the verso of plate E [1227]. See note to [1167].

1174 ...*banderillas y otras armas.* (The rabble hamstring the bull with lances, sickles, banderillas and other weapons).

1176 ...*sin auxilio de los chulos.* (A Spanish mounted knight in the ring breaking short spears without the help of assistants).

1178 ...*burla al toro con sus quiebros.* (The highly skilful student of Falces, wrapped in his cape, tricks the bull with the play of his body).

1180 (The famous Martincho places the banderillas *al quiebro* [as he dodges the bull]).

1182 (The same [Martincho] throws a bull in the ring at Madrid).

1184 ...*para defenderse del toro embolado.* (The moors use donkeys as a barrier to defend themselves against the bull whose horns are tipped with balls). Engraved on the verso of plate F [1229].

1186 (Recklessness of Martincho in the ring at Saragossa). Cp. plate [H] [1233].

1188 (Another madness of his in the same ring).

1190 (Agility and audacity of Juanito Apiñani in the [ring] at Madrid).

1192 ...*de la plaza de Madrid, y muerte del alcalde de Torrejon.* (Dreadful incidents which occurred in the front rows of the ring at Madrid, and death of the mayor of Torrejon).

1194 ...*en la de Zaragoza.* (Manly courage of the celebrated Pajuelera in the [ring] at Saragossa). Engraved on the verso of plate G [1231].

1196 (Mariano Ceballos, alias the Indian, kills the bull from his horse). Ceballos was a South-American Indian,

most renowned for the feat illustrated in [1198] (see the note for other versions). Cp. Lafuente (Bibl. 101, p. 201) and Xavier de Salas, 'Sobre las laminas 29 y 43 J de la ''Tauromaquia'' ', *Archivo Español de Arte*, XXVIII, 1955, pp. 145-147.

1198 ...*en la plaza de Madrid* (The same Ceballos mounted on another bull breaks short spears in the ring at Madrid). Cp. the first version of this subject [1237] and the lithograph [V.1707]. See note to [1196].

1200 A second version of plate C [1223].

1202 (A picador is unhorsed and falls under the bull).

1204 ...*con su garrocha.* (The celebrated picador, Fernando del Toro, inciting the wild beast with his pique).

1206 ...*de cuya suerte murió en la plaza de Madrid.* (The forceful Rendón stabbing a bull with the pique from which pass he [or the bull?] died in the ring at Madrid).

1207 Exhibited 1963-64 (Bibl. 27, no. 147) and 1966 (Bibl. 29, no. 129).

1208 (Pepe Illo making the pass of the *recorte* with the bull).

1210 (Pedro Romero killing the halted bull).

1211 Exhibited 1963-64 (Bibl. 27, no. 148). Reproduced in Bibl. 80, frontispiece.

1214 (Two teams of picadors thrown one after the other by a single bull).

1215 Exhibited 1963-64 (Bibl. 27, no. 149) and 1966 (Bibl. 29, no. 130).

1217 (The unfortunate death of Pepe Illo in the ring at Madrid). Cp. the two earlier versions [1227, 1229].

1219 (A Spanish knight breaking short spears with the help of assistants). Engraved on the recto of plate 1 [1149].

1221 Engraved on the recto of plate 2 [1151].

1223 Engraved on the recto of plate 6 [1159]. Cp. the second version in plate 25 [1200].

1225 (A bullfighter mounted on the shoulders of an assistant, spearing a bull). Engraved on the recto of plate 7 [1161].

1227 (Death of Pepe Illo). Cp. plates F [1229] and 33 [1217]. Engraved on the recto of plate 11 [1171].

1228 Exhibited in 1963-64 (Bibl. 27, no. 150) and 1966 (Bibl. 28, no. 19; 29, no. 132).

1229 Cp. plates E [1227] and 33 [1217]. Engraved on the recto of plate 17 [1184].

1231 (Fight in a carriage harnessed to two mules). Engraved on the recto of plate 22 [1194].

1233 Cp. plate 18 [1186]. The proof catalogued was listed by Harris as 'I.2. Formerly Paris, Lefort'.

1235 ...using a hat instead of the cape. Cp. plate 30 [1210].

1237 ...on a bull breaking spears. Cp. plate 24 [1198]. Proof undescribed by Harris: state I.3.

1239 ...with his back turned.

1240 Exhibited 1966 (Bibl. 29, no. 133).

1241 ...while gripping the bull's horn. Additional plate unrecorded in previous catalogues and first published by François Lachenal in Bibl. 28 (before no. 107) and in a note 'Tauromaquia working proofs in the Musée du Petit Palais, Paris', *Burlington Magazine*, CVIII, 1966, pp. 390, 393.

1243 Drawing for an engraving of which no proof is known.

1244-1518 An attempt has been made to give previous references and provenance for drawings in private collections.

1244-1367 The technical characteristics of this album were defined by Sayre (Bibl. 171, Appendix I, p. 131, 'Journal-album C'). It has been catalogued by Gassier (Bibl. 122, pl. 17-133, catalogue II) and by López-Rey (Bibl. 116, pp. 149-156, pl. 1-113). See note to [1252].

1244-1262 The inscriptions are written with the pen and sepia ink.

1246 (...of the skirt and pantaloons?)

1248 (This one was a cripple who had a title).

1249 (Into the desert to be a saint, Amen). Pierre Gassier points out that this drawing, like several others in the first part of the album, e.g. [1250, 1257, 1268, 1286, 1289, 1295, 1296, 1300, 1305, 1311, 1317], contains a direct allusion to monastic life. Several of them are clearly anti-clerical in nature and may date from the period of Joseph Bonaparte's secularization measures. Compare also the group of drawings on a similar theme [1354-1367].

1250 (At least he's doing something). See note to [1249].

1251 (A good woman, apparently).

1252 (Paternal embrace).
The drawing which should follow this one, C.11, has mistakenly been placed in album E. See [1388].

1253 *la guebera* written to the left and partially effaced.

1254 (What stupidity! to settle their destinies from childhood).

1255 (This one claims her career is selling radishes). *Rabanera* also means a slut, a shameless woman.

1256 (This is how useful men often end).

1257 (If I am not mistaken, he is going to throw off his habit).

1258 (Just look at her expression, but the husband doesn't believe it).

1259 (Her lover is dead and she is going to a convent).

1262 The glass and bottle are added in sepia ink.

1263 A drawing by Rosario Weiss appears to be a reverse copy of this composition: New York, Hispanic Society (A.733) – see Bibl. 181, pl. XXXVIII. Also reproduced by López-Rey (Bibl. 117, p. 26).

1264-1311 The inscriptions are written in black chalk.

1266 (I won't interfere with these).

1267 Missing in López-Rey's sequence; he read the number as 23. The inscription is in black chalk; see notes to [1244-1262] and [1264-1311].

1268 (Let's leave this as it was).

1270 (What horror for the sake of revenge).

1271 (These believe in the flight of birds).

1273 (He carries his inheritance in his sack of flesh).

1276 López-Rey translated the title as 'That lesbian of an aunt Gila', but the meaning of *maricón* is unequivocal and can only indicate a man.

1286 See note to [1249].

1288 ...*hasta q.e le dan algo* (Poor man in Asia who sets his head aflame until they give him something).

1289 See note to [1249].

1290 (This one has lots of relatives and some of them rational).

1293-1295 Not included in López-Rey's sequence. The order suggested here by Gassier is supported by the title of the first which is related to C.53 and 54, and by the secondary number on [1295] which follows that on C.58 (see text p. 236).

1295 and 1296   See note to [1249].

1299   Not included in López-Rey's sequence. The position is suggested by the secondary number (see text p. 236). It might otherwise be placed as C.110.

1300   (It may be that he's a good man). See note to [1249].

1301   (. . . not a matter of pulling up turnips).

1303   Not included in López-Rey's sequence. The position is suggested by the secondary number (see text p. 236).

1304   (There is much of this but one doesn't see it).

1305   See note to [1249].

1306 and 1307   An example of drawings connected by their titles: the second is a negative reply to the affirmation in the first.

1308   First published in 1963 by Trapier (Bibl. 187a, p. 20, n. 9, pl. 12a). Cp. album G.2 [V.1712] drawn in Bordeaux; both drawings represent a peep-show, called *mundonuevo* in Spain, and are reproduced by Trapier (*op. cit.*).

1310   López-Rey suggested that the drawing has been partially reworked with the pen by María del Rosario Weiss (Bibl. 117, p. 102).

1311   (Away with that rubbish). See note to [1249].

1312-1361   The inscriptions are written in pen and ink or with the brush.

1312   Not included in López-Rey's sequence. The position is suggested by the secondary number (see text p. 236).

1313   (. . . and sleep, loaf and stroll about).

1314   (. . . have something else to do). Not included in López-Rey's sequence. Cp. the painting listed in the inventory of 1812 [963].

1315   (These outdo themselves at the tavern).

1316   (A great hand at stealing little bells (because [his hand] was shaky).) The intended sense of the word *sonajas* is not clear, but the composition and title imply a pun on the theme of the thieving barber who shaves too close and 'fleeces' his victim. Cp. the *Caprichos* print and drawing [II.520, 639].

1317   See note to [1249].

1319   (Shameless, with all [women], all).

1321   (For being born somewhere else).

1322   (For bringing diabolical tales from Bayonne). An allusion to the banned news and writings which were smuggled into Spain from Bayonne.

1323   . . . // Y le di / eron / palos / en la cara // Yo la bi / en Zaragoza á / Orosia Moreno / P.ʳ q.ᵉ sabia hacer / Ratones (They put a gag on her because she talked. And hit her about the head. I saw her in Saragossa, Orosia Moreno. Because she knew how to make mice). Evidently a record of the trial of a witch.

1324   (For being of Jewish ancestry).

1325   (For wagging his tongue in a different way).

1326   . . . q.ᵉ no tenia pies, / y dicen q.ᵉ le [. . .] cuando salia de[?] Zaragoza / y en la calle de / Alcala cuando entraba pidiendo[la?] (For having no legs. I knew this crippled man who had no feet and they say that . . . when he left Saragossa, and when one went into the calle de Alcalá one found him there begging). The final title *Por no tener piernas* is written over the long, original inscription in which the phrase *quando salia de Zaragoza* is inserted before *y en la calle* by means of a little double cross.

1327   (Many have ended like this).

1329   (For marrying whom she wanted).

1330   (For discovering the motion of the earth). A reference to Galileo's condemnation by the Inquisition.

1332   (Because he didn't write for fools) is probably the meaning of the title, rather than the translation given by López-Rey: 'You shouldn't have written for fools'.

1333   Not included in López-Rey's sequence. The position is suggested by the secondary number (see text p. 236).

1334   The word 'liberal' was first used in this sense in Spain after 1814.

1336   The Italian sculptor who died in prison in Spain for having broken a statue of the Virgin for which he was not paid the price he asked. See Ceán Bermúdez (Bibl. 47, V, p. 65) and José López-Rey, 'Goya's drawing of Pietro Torrigiano', *Gazette des Beaux-Arts*, XXVII, 1945, pp. 165-170, also Bibl. 116, pp. 119-122.

1340   (Many widows have wept like you). Above the door in the background is the emblem of the Holy Office or Inquisition.

1345   (Zapata. Thy glory will be eternal). Probably a double reference, to the doctor Diego Martín Zapata, imprisoned and condemned by the Inquisition in the mid-eighteenth century and to the hero of Voltaire's *Les Questions de Zapata* – see Bibl. 116, pp. 127-129.

1348   (You are going to escape from your sorrows).

1350   The inkwell and the sheet of paper on the ground show that the drawing is concerned with freedom of expression, symbolised by the rays of light which the figure receives on his knees, his arms outstretched, in a gesture which frequently recurs in Goya's work (cp. [II.328, III.984, IV.1640]).

1351   Not included in López-Rey's sequence. The position is suggested by the secondary number (see text p. 236).
    A drawing with the same title was reproduced by Mayer as a fake (Bibl. 129, pl. 133.1).

1352   (Light out of the darkness). Cp. this and the following drawing [1353] with the final plates of the *Desastres* [1132, 1134, 1138] where the same symbolism of the dazzling light of Truth and Justice fighting against the dark forces of ignorance and oppression is used and see the article cited in the note to [1134].

1354-1367   Group of drawings discussed by José López-Rey, 'The "Unfrocking" Drawings of Francisco de Goya', *Gazette des Beaux-Arts*, XXVII, 1945, pp. 287-296.

1354   (We've been known for a long time).

1355   (Will you never known what you're carrying on your back?). Inscription almost illegible in lower left corner. López-Rey read the number as 128 – see [1363]. Cp. *Caprichos* plate 42 [II.534].

1357   (Divine Reason – Don't spare one of them).

1358   (What does this great phantom want?).

1362-1366   Inscriptions written in black chalk.

1362   (He gets undressed for good).

1363   First published in 1964 by Trapier (Bibl. 187a, p. 20, n. 12, pl. 13a). See note to [1355].

1366   (This one takes it off pensively).

1367   Inscription written with the brush.

1368-1384   The technical characteristics of this album were defined by Sayre (Bibl. 171, Appendix I, p. 131, 'Journal-album D'). See also Gassier (Bibl. 63, pp. 39-41).

1368   Pierre Gassier was informed by the previous owner that the number on the drawing was removed in cleaning, before its acquisition by the Louvre in 1950. Cp. his article (Bibl. 63, p. 41).

1369   Catalogued by Count Antoine Seilern, *Paintings and Drawings. . . at 56 Princes Gate London*, London, 1961, III, p. 135, no. 256, pl. LXXXII.

1370   First published in 1963 by Trapier (Bibl. 187a, p. 20, n. 6, pl. 14).

1372   Reproduced here for the first time.

1375   (. . . to be still thinking of marriage).

1376   The word *Vision* was written to the left and then scored through. Cp. the drawing without a number [1384].

1382   Cp. album E.36 [1405].

1383   (She won't get up till she's finished her prayers).

1385-1430   The technical characteristics of this album were defined by Sayre (Bibl. 171, Appendix I, p. 131, 'Dark border' Journal-album E), cataloguing seventeen drawings (*op. cit.* Appendix II, p. 135). Wehle was the first to identify this series which he called 'black border' drawings (Bibl. 192). See note to [1388].

1385   Discussed by Gassier (Bibl. 62a, fig. 15).

1386   *Tiempo* could mean weather, time or age. Sold by Ader and Boisgrand, Paris, 14 May 1936, lot 38, ill.

1387   Sold by Ader and Boisgrand, Paris, 14 May 1936, lot 39, ill.

1388   (. . . makes the most of her time). Exhibited 1941 (Bibl. 16, no. 68, ill.). This drawing, known only from the description and reproduction in the exhibition catalogue, does not form part of album E and should probably have been catalogued in album C. See note to [1252].

1389   (Severity is not always good). Exhibited 1961-62 (Bibl. 24, no. 169) and 1966 (Bibl. 28, no. 11), incorrectly identified and dated. Catalogued by Sayre (Bibl. 171, p. 135).

1390   (You know a lot and you're still learning) written below the drawing; (Everything is a trade) inscribed by the old man on the slab. On the verso is a slight sketch of a mythological scene.

1391   An allusion to the presence of the Napoleonic troops in Spain.

1395   . . . ó el Españoleto, por los años de 1640 (This woman was painted in Naples by José Ribera called Lo Spagnoletto around the year 1640). Reproduced by Mayer (Bibl. 127, p. 379). Sold at Sotheby's, London, 29 June 1960, lot 19. The painting by Ribera is the full-length portrait of *Magdalena Ventura of the Abruzzi* (Duchess of Lerma collection, Toledo), discussed and illustrated by Elizabeth du Gué Trapier, *Ribera*, New York, 1952, pp. 71-72.

1398   (. . . Pet[rarch]). The last word is cut. The title, in faulty Italian, gives the line from Petrarch 'Povera e nuda vai filosofia' (*Rime*, sonnet VII, line 10), which appears in Ripa's *Iconologia* of 1630 in the description of 'Philosophy'. Nordström cited the text and reproduced Ripa's representation of Philosophy, in discussing the allegorical painting of 1797-1800 [II.695] (Bibl. 136, p. 112, fig. 57). The provenance of this hitherto unpublished drawing is unknown. Exhibited 1970 (Bibl. 30b, no. 6).

1400   Cp. the sketch drawing [1418].

1401   From the collection of Mariano Fortuny y Madrazo who owned, bound in an album, the fifty drawings now in the Metropolitan Museum (Bibl. 192). Published by Crispolti (Bibl. 52, fig. 8).

1402   Published in 'Centennial Acquisitions', *Boston MFA Bulletin*, LXVIII, 1970, no. 55, p. 87, ill. Reproduced here from a photograph without the black border.

1403   Exhibited 1941 (Bibl. 16, no. 67, ill.). Catalogued by Sayre (Bibl. 171, p. 135).

1404   Exhibited 1961-62 (Bibl. 24, no. 170) and 1966 (Bibl. 28, no. 12), incorrectly identified and dated. Catalogued by Sayre (Bibl. 171, p. 136). Recto and verso drawings reproduced here for the first time.

1406   Published by Xavière Desparmet Fitz-Gerald, 'Deux dessins inédits de Francisco Goya', *Pantheon*, XXIII, 1965, pp. 111-115. Exhibited 1970 (Bibl. 30b, no. 7, ill.). Cp. the washerwomen in the background of the painting *Les jeunes* [962].

Notes continued on page 375

TABLE OF WORKS IN CATALOGUE III   1808-1819

ABBREVIATIONS AND SIGNS

[ ]   Numbers within square brackets refer to the works listed in the catalogue. The number is preceded by a roman numeral (I-V) referring to the section of the book in which the work appears. (This is omitted if the reference is to a work within the same section.)

TITLE

Goya's autograph titles are given in *italics*. Where there is no room for the whole title or its translation in the catalogue legend, it is continued in the note.

DATE

Examples:	*1797*	dated by Goya
	1797	certain date
	1797?	probable date
	c.1797	about 1797
	1797-99	executed during the period indicated

d.   Dated
Doc.   Date indicated by a document

SIGNATURE

s.   Signed

INSCRIPTION

italics   Title or inscription by Goya
Inscr.   Inscription
/   Change of line in an inscription
MS.   Manuscript

TECHNIQUE

All works are in oil on canvas unless otherwise specified

Aq.   Aquatint
L.   Lithograph

DIMENSIONS

cm.   Centimetres
approx.   Approximately
vis.   Visible dimensions (e.g. where work is partly covered by a mount or frame)
diam.   Diameter

Dimensions of the drawings are those of the sheet of paper.
Dimensions of the engravings are those of the copperplate.

COLLECTION

A.I.   Art Institute
B.M.   British Museum, London
B.N.   Biblioteca Nacional / Bibliothèque Nationale
C.   Calcografía Nacional, Madrid (see Bibl. 5)
Fund. Lázaro   Fundación Lázaro Galdiano, Madrid (the indication M = Museum, B = Biblioteca)
Gal.   Galerie / Gallery
Inst.   Institut / Institute / Instituto
Hispanic Soc.   Hispanic Society of America, New York
K.K.   Kupferstichkabinett (Print room)
Min.   Ministère / Ministerio / Ministry
Mus.   Musée / Museo / Museum (of Fine Arts, unless otherwise indicated)
M.F.A.   Museum of Fine Arts, Boston
M.M.A.   Metropolitan Museum of Art, New York
N.G.   National Gallery
Patr. Nac.   Patrimonio Nacional, Madrid
R.A.   Real Academia / Royal Academy
P. Palais   Petit Palais (Musée des Beaux-Arts de la Ville de Paris)
Rhode Is. S. D. Mus.   Museum of the School of Design, Providence (Rhode Island)

V. and A.   Victoria and Albert Museum, London
coll.   Collection (a capital C indicates a public collection, e.g. Frick Coll., New York)
priv.   Private
destr.   Destroyed

Acquisition or inventory numbers are given in brackets after the name of the collection. See Index of Collections, page 394.

BIBLIOGRAPHICAL REFERENCES

Bibl.   See the numbered Bibliography, page 386. The most frequently used abbreviations are:
B.   Barcia, *Catálogo de la Colección de Dibujos Originales de la Biblioteca Nacional* (Bibl. 3)
D.   Delteil, 'Francisco Goya', *Le Peintre graveur illustré* (Bibl. 55)
DF.   Desparmet Fitz-Gerald, *L'Œuvre peint de Goya* (Bibl. 57)
G.   Gudiol, *Goya* (catalogue raisonné) (Bibl. 85)
H.   Harris, *Goya. Engravings and lithographs* (Bibl. 88)
M.   Mayer, *Francisco de Goya* (Bibl. 128)
S.   Sambricio, *Tapices de Goya* (Bibl. 154)
SC.   Sánchez Cantón, *Museo del Prado: Los dibujos de Goya* (Bibl. 168)

ILLUSTRATION

Ill. p. (or p.)   See the reproduction in the text at the page indicated.

NOTE

*   Reference to a note on the pages preceding the illustrated catalogue.

CATALOGUE III
1808-1819

[874-1570]

ALLEGORY OF THE TOWN
OF MADRID   1810

23 December 1809: the Town
Council of Madrid resolved to
have a portrait made of 'our
present sovereign' - Joseph
Bonaparte - and delegated the
commission to Tadeo Bravo de
Rivero [II.854].
27 February 1810: he reported
that the painting had been
completed by Goya, who used an
engraving for the head of the
absent king.
1812: when the French withdrew
from Madrid, the word
Constitución was painted over the
portrait, but a new one was made
when Joseph returned.
1813: the word Constitución was
again substituted for the portrait.

1814: a portrait of Ferdinand VII
was painted in the medallion.
1823: a better portrait was made
by Vicente López, in the year of the
final defeat of liberalism in Spain.
1843: the words El libro de la
Constitución were painted over
the portrait.
Finally, after an unsuccessful
attempt to recover Goya's original
portrait of Joseph Bonaparte, the
words DOS DE MAYO were
painted in the medallion.
The painting's history is a striking
reflection of the political situation
in Madrid between 1808 and 1824
when Goya finally left Spain to
end his life in France.

874

Allegory of the Town of Madrid
1810.   260×195 cm.
Madrid, Ayuntamiento (1048)
M.88, DF.97, G.555   *

PORTRAITS   1808-1814

Between the first official portrait
of Ferdinand VII in 1808 [875]
and the various portraits of
Wellington in 1812 [896-900]
is a notable group which
includes the bust of the Intruder
King, Joseph Bonaparte, now
over-painted, in the Allegory
[874] and portraits of the
afrancesados who supported his
rule [881-883], all executed
around 1810.
At the same time Goya painted
the parents of his son's wife
[886, 887] and the first of the
moving portraits of his grandson,
Mariano [885].

[875-902]   *

875

Ferdinand VII on horseback
1808.   285×205 cm.
Madrid, R.A. San Fernando (679)
M.157, DF.483, G.547   *

876

Sketch for [875].   40×28 cm.
Agen, Mus. (271 Ch.)
M.158, DF.482, G.546   *

877

Ferdinand VII   1808?
Black chalk, blue paper
26·9×20·1 cm.
Madrid, B.N. (B.1266)   *

878

Pantaleón Pérez de Nenín   s.d.
1808 with inscr.   206×125 cm.
Madrid, Banco Exterior de España
M.384, DF.464, G.548   *

879

Marquesa de Santiago   s.d. 1809
with inscr.   212×125 cm.
Madrid, Duque de Tamames
M.417, DF.467, G.549   *

880

Marquesa de Monte Hermoso
1808-10.   170×103 cm.
Paris, priv. coll.
M.356, DF.322   *

881

Juan Antonio Llorente
c.1810-12.   189·2×114·3 cm.
São Paulo, Mus.
M.332, DF.478, G.570   *

882

General Manuel Romero
c.1810.   105·3×87·6 cm.
Chicago, Chauncey McCormick
M.403, DF.468, G.569   *

883

General Nicolas Guye   1810.
106×84·7 cm.   New York,
Mrs. Marshall Field   M.318,
DF.550s, G.553   Ill. p. 209   *

884

Victor Guye   1810.
106·7×85·1 cm.
Washington, N.G. (1471)
M.319, DF.551s, G.554   p. 208 *

885

Mariano Goya   c.1809-10.
93×78 cm.
Malaga, Marqués de Larios
M.312, DF.552s, G.536   *

886

Juana Galarza de Goicoechea
s.d. 1810 with inscr.   82×59 cm.
Madrid, Marquesa de Casa Riera
M.286a, DF.471, G.552   *

887

Martín Miguel de Goicoechea
s.d. 1810 with inscr.   82×59 cm.
Madrid, Marquesa de Casa Riera
M.284a, DF.472, G.551   *

888

Juan Bautista de Goicoechea
c.1810.   112×80 cm.
Karlsruhe, Staatliche Kunsthalle
(2515)   M.282, DF.469, G.663 *

889

Narcisa Barañana de Goicoechea
c.1810.   s. Goya   112·3×78 cm.
New York, M.M.A. (29.100.180)
M.283, DF.368, G.528   *

890

Young woman with a fan
c.1805-10.   103×83 cm.
Paris, Louvre (RF 1132)
M.505, DF.466, G.659 *

891

Manuel Silvela   c.1809-12.
95×68 cm.
Madrid, Prado (2450)
M.421, DF.505, G.567   *

892

Antonia Zárate   1810?
103·5×81·9 cm.   Blessington
(Eire), Sir Alfred Beit
M.457, DF.446, G.562   *

893

Antonia Zárate   1811?
71×58 cm.
Paris, Comtesse de Flers
M.456, DF.365, G.561   *

894

Fernanda Bonells de Costa
c.1808-13.   87·3×65·4 cm.
Detroit, Inst. of Arts (41.80)
M.511/514, DF.499, G.523   *

895

THE DUKE OF WELLINGTON

12 August 1812: Wellington
entered Madrid in triumph after
the battle of Arapiles.
27 August: Goya's letter to Durán
about the exhibition of the
equestrian portrait [896].
1 September: announcement of
the exhibition in the *Diario de
Madrid*.
2 to 11 September: portrait on
show at the Real Academia de
San Fernando.

[896-900]   *

896

897

898   recto of 1562

Pepito Costa y Bonells   s.d.
1813?, inscr.   105·1×84·5 cm.
New York, M.M.A. (61.259)
M.243, DF.460, G.662   p. 208 *

Duke of Wellington on horseback
1812.   294×240 cm.   London,
Wellington Mus. (WM 1566.1948)
M.448, DF.476, G.557   *

Duke of Wellington   1812-14.
Panel 60×51 cm.
London, N.G. (6322)
M.449, G.556   Ill. p. 214   *

Duke of Wellington   1812.
Red chalk over pencil
23·2×17·5 cm.   London,
B.M. (1862.7.12.185)   *

899

900

901

902

STILL-LIFES   c.1808-1812

'Twelve still-lifes with the numbe
eleven at . . . 1200 reales'.
The following ten pictures are
probably those of the 1812
inventory. The Louvre painting
still shows a trace of the X mark,
and all are of the same size and
technique. Several have the
signature *Goya* curiously worke
into the design.
The last picture does not seem
to belong with the others.

[903-913]

Duke of Wellington   1812?
Pencil 22·7×15·8 cm.
Hamburg, Kunsthalle (38547)   *

Duke of Wellington   1812?
Inscr.   105·5×83·7 cm.
Washington, N.G. (1902)
M.450, DF.477, G.558   *

General Palafox on horseback
s.d. *1814*, inscr.   248×224 cm.
Madrid, Prado (725)
M.372, DF.487, G.620   p. 214 *

Asensio Juliá   s.d. *P.ʳ Fr. Goya
1814*.   73·4×57·3 cm.
Williamstown, Clark Art Inst. (83)
M.326, DF. 495, G.625   *

903

904

905

906

907

Sheep's head and joints   X.11
c.1808-12.   s. *Goya*   45×62 cm.
Paris, Louvre (RF 1937.120)
G.596   Ill. p. 248   *

Dead turkey   c.1808-12.
s. *Goya*   45×63 cm.
Madrid, Prado (751)
M.731, DF.177, G.589   *

Dead birds   c.1808-12.
46×64 cm.
Madrid, Prado (752)
M.730, DF.176, G.590   *

Plucked turkey and frying pan
c.1808-12.   s.   44·8×62·4 cm.
Munich, Alte Pinakothek (8575)
M.732, G.593   *

Golden bream   X[11]
c.1808-12.   s. *Goya*   45×63 cm
Paris, David-Weill
G.592

| 08 | 909 | 910 | 911 | 912 |

Duck c.1808-12.
. *Goya* 44·5×62 cm.
urich, Mme Anda-Bührle
DF.540s, G.586   *

Hares c.1808-12.
45·1×62·9 cm.
New York, priv. coll.
DF.541s, G.588 *

Woodcocks c.1808-12.
45·1×62·9 cm.
New York, priv. coll.
DF.542s, G.587   *

Salmon steaks c.1808-12.
44×62 cm.
Winterthur, Reinhart Coll. (79)
G.595   *

Still-life with bottles, fruit and
bread c.1808-12. s. *Goya*
45×62 cm. Winterthur,
Reinhart Coll. (78)   G.591   *

| 13 | | | 914 | 915 |

GENRE SUBJECTS
1808-1820

Most of the paintings in this
large section were made by Goya
for his own pleasure and remained in his house. Those painted
before 1812 were included in the
inventory made in that year and
were marked with an X and a
number (cp. [II.864-871] and
[III.903-913]). These inventory
numbers, still visible on some of
the paintings, are included in the
catalogue legends.
The paintings take up the realism
of the cabinet pictures of 1793-94
[II.317-330] and a large number
are devoted to themes of violence.

[914-984]   *

THE 'ROMANA' PAINTINGS
c.1808-1812

Eight small pictures, belonging to
the Marqueses de la Romana,
were identified by Sánchez
Cantón as some of the 'twelve
[paintings] of the Horrors of the
War' listed in the 1812 inventory.
If the first two scenes are
reminiscent of the *Caprichos*
prints, the remainder are closer
to the *Disasters of War*.

[914-921]   *

Calf's head c.1808-12?
7×70.5 cm.
Copenhagen, Nationalmus.
DF.543s., G.594   *

The monk's visit c. 1808-12.
40×32 cm.
Madrid, Marqueses de la Romana
M.539, DF.209, G.351

Interior of a prison(?)
c.1808-12. 42×32 cm.
Madrid, Marqueses de la Romana
M.545, DF.206, G.352   *

| 16 | 917 | 918 | 919 | 920 |

Brigand stripping a woman
.1808-12. 41×32 cm.
Madrid, Marqueses de la Romana
M.605, DF.197, G.348

Brigand murdering a woman
c.1808-12. 40×32 cm.
Madrid, Marqueses de la Romana
M.607, DF.196, G.350

Brigands shooting their prisoners
c.1808-12. 41×32 cm.
Madrid, Marqueses de la Romana
M.604, DF.194, G.349   *

Plague hospital(?)
c.1808-12. 32×56 cm.
Madrid, Marqueses de la Romana
M.692, DF.192, G.353   *

Vagabonds resting in a cave
c.1808-12. 32×56 cm.
Madrid, Marqueses de la Romana
M.603, DF.193, G.354

| 21 | | 922 | 923 | 924 |

A pair of paintings which have been
identified as the martyrdom of
two French missionaries by
Iroquois Indians, and a further
pair, with replicas, showing
similar scenes with 'savages'.
The replicas on tinplate are of the
same dimensions as the *Forge*
[928] and the *Prison* [929]. Cp.
[976, 978] and the cabinet
pictures of 1793-94 [II.317-330].

[922-929]

Shooting in a military camp
.1808-12. 32×58 cm.
Madrid, Marqueses de la Romana
M.606, DF.222, G.355 p. 211 *

Martyrdom(?)-I c.1808-14.
Panel 31×45 cm.
Besançon, Mus. (896.1.176)
M.706, DF.249, G.475   *

Martyrdom(?)-II c.1808-14.
Panel 31×50 cm.
Besançon, Mus. (896.1.177)
M.707, DF.250, G.476   *

Savages murdering a woman
c.1808-14. Panel 33×47 cm.
Madrid, Condesa de Villagonzalo
M.555, DF.198, G.474   *

925

Savages by a fire   c.1808-14.
Panel 33×47 cm.
Madrid, Condesa de Villagonzalo
M.553, DF.200, G.472   *

926

Savages murdering a woman
c.1808-14.   Tinplate 29×41 cm.
Madrid, Prado (740i)
M.556, DF.199, G.473   *

927

Savages by a fire   c.1808-14.
Tinplate 32×43 cm.
Madrid, Prado (740j)
M.554, DF.201, G.471   *

928

The forge   c.1808-14.
Tinplate 31·5×40·5 cm.
Madrid, priv. coll.
DF.264, G.681   *

929

Interior of a prison   c.1808-14.
Tinplate 42·9×31·7 cm.
Barnard Castle, Bowes Mus. (29
M.544, DF.207, G.470

SIX PAINTINGS X.9
c.1808-1812

These are the 'six [paintings] of
various subjects with the
number nine' listed in the 1812
inventory, and may perhaps also
be identified with the 'collection
of panels . . . representing the
horrors of the war' which Father
Tomás López saw in the house of
Goya's son. The five known
paintings from this series all show
the inventory number. The
sixth is listed from a description.

[930-935]   *

930

Scene of rape and murder   X.9.
c.1808-12.   Panel 30·5×39·8 cm.
Frankfort, Kunstinstitut (1980)
M.79, DF.210/233, G.[608]   *

931

Women attacked by soldiers   X.9.
c.1808-12.   Panel 30·5×39·8 cm.
Frankfort, Kunstinstitut (1981)
M.78, DF.211/234, G.[609]   *

932

The hanged monk   X.9.
c.1808-12.   Panel 31×39·2 cm.
Chicago, A.I. (1936.225)
DF.230, G.607   *

933

Prison scene   X.9.   c.1808-12.
Panel 31·5×40 cm.
Guadalupe (Extremadura),
Monastery   G.606   *

934

Procession   X.9.   c.1808-12.
Panel 30·5×39·5 cm.
Oslo, N.G. (1347)
M.82b, DF.221, G.605   *

935

No reproduction is known

Monks throwing books and
papers on the fire   Panel
Coll. unknown (formerly Madrid,
Constantino Ardamar)   *

DISASTERS OF WAR
c.1808-1814

A group of paintings whose
subjects are very similar to those
of the etchings [993-1148].
Known mainly from inadequate
photographs, they could be
considered to be copies based
on the prints. However, the facts
that at least three paintings of
larger dimensions on panel are
known and that several of the
scenes are based on drawings
which Goya prepared for the
Disasters series but did not
engrave, suggests that the whole
group calls for further examination.

[936-944]   *

936

Women attacking soldiers
c.1808-14.   20×28 cm.
Formerly Madrid, Traumann
M.75, DF.235, G.600   *

937

Stripping the dead
c.1808-14.   21×35 cm.
France, priv. coll.
M.77a, G.604   *

938

Searching among the corpses
c.1808-14.   19×29 cm.
Formerly Madrid, Juan Lafora
DF.237, G.603   *

939

Heap of corpses   c.1808-14.
20×28 cm.
Formerly Madrid, Lázaro
M.77, DF.236, G.601   *

940

The wounded in a hospital
c.1808-14.   31×41 cm.
Zumaya, Zuloaga
DF.238.3   *

941

Escape through the flames
c.1808-14.   20·5×31 cm.
Madrid, priv. coll.
DF.238.4?   *

942

Women surprised by soldiers
c.1808-14. Panel Formerly
Madrid, Duque de Tamames
M.77c, G.599

943

944

945

[D]rawing for *Disasters of War*
[se]ries - see [1143]

Carrying the wounded
c.1808-14.   19×29 cm.
Buenos Aires, priv. coll.
M.77b, DF.238.1, G.602   *

Drawing for *Disasters of War*
series - see [1145]

The shooting   c.1808-14.
31×41 cm.
Zumaya, Zuloaga
DF.238.2   *

Officer with his horse
c.1808-14.   Panel
Coll. unknown
M.82a, G.598   *

[T]HE COLOSSUS

[T]his painting was listed in the
[18]12 inventory as 'A giant with
[th]e number eighteen'.
[It] is closely connected with the
[en]graving of a similar colossus
[9]85].
[O]ne of Goya's most dramatic
[w]orks, its symbolism has been
[th]e subject of much discussion.

946

FOUR PAINTINGS   X.28?
c.1808-1812?

The inventory of 1812 lists
'four of other subjects with the
number twenty-eight'.   One
painting which appears to show
the inventory number and three
others of the same size have
been identified as the inventory
pictures, but the inventory description suggests some doubts
(see notes).   The style and technique are violent and the paint
impasted in a manner often
adopted by Goya's imitators.

[947-950]   *

947

948

The colossus   c.1808-12.
116×105 cm.
Madrid, Prado (2785)
DF.539s, G.610   Ill. p. 215   *

Village on fire   X.28?
c.1808-12.   72×100 cm.
Buenos Aires, Mus. (6986)
DF.278, G.614   *

Scene of bandits   c.1808-12.
72×100 cm.
Buenos Aires, Mus. (6985)
M.611/650, DF.164, G.611   *

[9]49

950

FOUR PAINTINGS   X.1
AND SIMILAR PAINTINGS
c.1810-1816

'Four similar paintings with the
number one' heads the list of
pictures in the 1812 inventory.
Two paintings with the inventory
mark are known, and a third has
recently been identified.

Further paintings of similar
dimensions and technique may
have been added to the series
after 1812.   A number of them
are apparently described in the
Brugada inventory of 1828.

[951-956]   *

951

952

[Fi]esta   c.1808-12.
[7]2·5×100 cm.
[B]uenos Aires, Mus. (2561)
[G].589, G.612   *

The hurricane   c.1808-12.
73×100 cm.
Buenos Aires, Jockey Club - destr.
M.538/687?, DF.256, G.613   *

The maypole   X.1.
c.1810-12.   80×103 cm.
Madrid, Duque de Tamames
G.671   *

Procession in Valencia   X.1.
c.1810-12.   105×126 cm.
Zurich, Stiftung Bührle
M.536, DF.267, G.668   p. 249   *

[9]53

954

955

956

[B]ullfight in a divided ring   [X.1]
[c.]1810-12.   98·4×126·3 cm.
[N]ew York, M.M.A. (22.181)
[G].659, DF.244, G.615   *

Carnival scene
c.1812-16.   84×104 cm.
Formerly Budapest, Baron Herzog
M.591, DF.259, G.669   *

City on a rock   c.1812-16.
83·8×104·2 cm.
New York, M.M.A. (29.100.12)
M.551, DF.251, G.674   *

The balloon   c.1812-16.
105·5×84·5 cm.
Agen, Mus. (335 Ch.)
M.710, DF.268, G.667   *

FIGURE PAINTINGS
c.1808-1816

A group of figure paintings, most of which were included in the 1812 inventory. The inventory numbers are included in the catalogue legends. See also [II. 864-871]. The paintings take up the themes of the *Caprichos*, giving them a new breadth and vigour. These subjects, together with the monumental figures of working-people [963-965], may have been conceived as a unified series (see notes).

[957-965]   *

957

El Lazarillo de Tormes   X.25.
c.1808-12.   80×65 cm.
Madrid, Marañon   G.585   *

958

Maja and celestina on a balcony
[X.24]   c.1808-12.   166×108 cm.
Madrid, Bartolomé March
DF.536s, G.574   Ill. p. 250   *

959

Majas on a balcony   X.24.
c.1808-12.   162×107 cm.
Private collection
M.626/627, DF.186, G.575   *

960

Majas on a balcony   c.1800-1
194·8×125·7 cm.
New York, M.M.A. (29.100.10)
M.626/627, DF.187 ,G.576

961

'Les Vieilles' - Time and the old women   X.23.   Inscr. c.1810-12.
181×125 cm.   Lille, Mus. (350)
M.690, DF.191, G.582   *

962

'Les Jeunes' - Young women with a letter   c.1812-14.
181×125 cm.   Lille, Mus. (349)
M.630, DF.242, G.583   p. 243 *

963

La aguadora (The water-carrier)
[X.13]   c.1808-12.   68×52 cm.
Budapest, Mus. (760)   M.677,
DF.240n, G.579   Ill. p. 245   *

964

Album C.78 - see [1314]

El afilador (The knife-grinder)
[X.13]   c.1808-12.   68×50·5 c
Budapest, Mus. (763)
M.648, DF.248, G.580   p. 245

965

The forge   c.1812-16.
181·6×125 cm.
New York, Frick Coll. (A.1009)
M.649, DF.264n, G.682   p. 244 *

Album F.51 - see [1472]

FIVE PAINTINGS ON PANEL
c.1812-1819

These paintings, not apparently included in the 1812 inventory, were probably executed between 1812 and 1819. The scenes of the inquisition and of flagellants, and the drawing and first version of the *Burial of the Sardine* with their strong anti-clerical flavour are close to the etchings at the end of the *Disasters of War* [1104-1139], and the themes of the paintings recur again and again in the different albums of drawings [1244-1518].

[966-971]   *

966

Inquisition scene   c.1812-19.
Panel 46×73 cm.
Madrid, R.A. San Fernando (673)
M.543, DF.212, G.462

967

Procession of flagellants
c.1812-19.   Panel 46×73 cm.
Madrid, R.A. San Fernando (674
M.534, DF.214, G.463

968

The madhouse   c.1812-19.
Panel 45×72 cm.
Madrid, R.A. San Fernando (672)
M.693, DF.202, G.464   *

969

Bullfight in a village   c.1812-19.
Panel 45×72 cm.
Madrid, R.A. San Fernando (675)
M.658, DF.247, G.465   p. 240 *

970

The burial of the sardine
c.1812-19.   Panel 82·5×62 cm.
Madrid, R.A. San Fernando (676)
M.590, DF.243, G.467   p.2   *

971

Drawing for [970].   Inscr.
MORTVS on banner.
Pen and sepia ink 22×18 cm.
Madrid, Prado (272)   SC.461

VARIOUS SCENES
c.1808-1820

A number of pictures, mainly religious subjects, are here grouped together for reference and further study.   Several are known in two or three versions; some have been attributed to Lucas. The authenticity of the group as a whole has yet to be established with certainty.

[972-979]

972   973   974   975   976

...sked dancers beneath an arch
...808-20. 30×38 cm.
...drid, Duquesa de Villahermosa
...592, DF.239, G.468   *

Figures beneath an arch
c.1808-20. Coll. unknown
(formerly Madrid, Lafora)   *

Flagellants near an arch
c.1812-20. 51·5×57·5 cm.
Buenos Aires, Mus. (6987)
G.677   *

La misa de parida (The churching)
c.1812-20. 53×77 cm.
Agen, Mus. (276 Ch.)
M.529, DF.261, G.679   *

La misa de parida (The churching)
c.1812-20. Tinplate 32×42 cm.
Formerly Madrid, Torrecilla
M.530, DF.260, G.689   *

...7   978   979   THE WAR AGAINST BONAPARTE c.1810-1814   980

...ly Communion c.1812-20.
·3×43·3 cm.
...illiamstown, Clark Art Inst. (750)
...257?, G.688   *

Wedding of the ill-assorted couple
c.1812-20. Tinplate 32·5×41 cm.
Madrid, Fund. Lázaro (M.2022)
M.595, DF.265, G.690   *

The exorcism c.1812-20.
48×60 cm.
Madrid, Prado (747)
M.533, DF.272, G.678   *

Two small pictures showing the
clandestine making of powder
and shot in Aragon during the
war years, and Goya's two great
paintings of 1814, recalling the
events of May 1808 which symbolized the rising of the Spanish
people against the French.
24 February 1814: Goya
presented a petition to the
Regency Council.
9 March 1814: a Royal Order
granted him an allowance while
he was engaged in painting
these records of 'our glorious
insurrection against the tyrant of
Europe'

[980-984]

Making gunpowder in the sierra
c.1810-14. Panel 33×52 cm.
Madrid, Palacio Real
M.81, DF.227, G.618   *

...1   982   983   983a   984

...aking shot in the sierra
...810-14. Panel 33×52 cm.
...adrid, Palacio Real
...80, DF.228, G.619   p. 213   *

The 2nd of May 1808 1814.
Inscr. 266×345 cm.
Madrid, Prado (748)
M.72, DF.225, G.623   p. 206   *

Sketch for [982].
Oil on paper 24×32 cm.
Madrid, Duquesa de Villahermosa
M.73, DF.224, G.621   *

Sketch for [982]?
Panel 26·5×34 cm.
Formerly Madrid, Lázaro
DF.223   *

The 3rd of May 1808 1814.
266×345 cm.
Madrid, Prado (749) M.74,
DF.226, G.624   pp. 20, 207   *

RINTS AND DRAWINGS
1810-1820

...very large body of etchings
...th their preparatory drawings,
...cluding the *Disasters of War*
...d the *Tauromaquia* (Bullfighting)
...nts.
...e *Colossus* - Goya's only
...ezzotint engraving - is a
...m counterpart to the Prado
...inting [946], and the three
...le etched *Prisoners* are very
...milar to those in the Bowes
...useum painting [929] and
...call the series of drawings in
...um C. 93-114 [1329-1349].

...85-992]

Abbreviations and signs, see p. 260
D = Delteil, Bibl. 55
H = Harris, Bibl. 88
SC = Sánchez Cantón, Bibl. 168
If not a print from an edition:
1/1 = unique proof; 1/3 = one of
three proofs known

985   986   987

The colossus c.1810-18.
Mezzotint 28·5×21 cm.
1/6 Paris, B.N. (A.3122)
D.35, H.29   *

*Tan barbara la seguridad como el
delito* c.1810-20.
Etching and burin 11×8·5 cm.
D.31, H.26 Ill. p. 223   *

Drawing for [986]?
Pen and brush, sepia ink 11×8 cm.
Madrid, Prado (387)
SC.335   *

988

La seguridad de un reo no exige tormento c.1810-15. Etching and burin 11·5×8·5 cm. D.32, H.27 *

989

Drawing for [988]. Red chalk and sepia wash 10·2×6·7 cm. Boston, Russell Allen *

990

Si es delinquente q.ᵉ muera presto c.1810-20. Etching 11·5×8·5 cm. D.33, H.28 *

991

Drawing for [990]. Brush and sepia wash 10·3×6·5 cm. Madrid, Prado (389) SC.337

992

Prisoner - drawing for an etching c.1810-20. Brush and sepia wash 10·3×6·5 cm. Madrid, Prado (388) SC.336

LOS DESASTRES DE LA GUERRA (The Disasters of War)

Drawn and engraved 1810-1820, and entitled by Goya 'Fatal consequences of Spain's bloody war with Bonaparte and other striking *caprichos*'.
The first plates are dated 1810 [1024, 1029, 1038] and the series was executed over a number of years. It includes three main groups - the war scenes: plates 2-47 [995-1069], the scenes of the famine in Madrid in 1811-12: plates 48-64 [1070-1103], and the symbolic, essentially anticlerical *caprichos*: plates 65-82 [1104-1139].
Goya put together a complete set of proofs with manuscript titles,

but the plates were stored away when he left Spain in 1824 and were not published in his lifetime. The first edition was made in Madrid in 1863.
73 preparatory drawings are listed: 65 for the known plates, and 8 additional drawings. Almost all are in red chalk.
The two sets of numbers engraved by Goya on the plates are indicated (the earlier number in brackets).
The unique proof and seven additional drawings are reproduced after the published plates [1140-1148].
Seven editions of plates 1-80 were printed from the original copperplates between 1863 and 1937. Plates 81 and 82 became

separated from the others and a few proofs were printed about 1870 and again in 1957-58.
The dimensions given are those of the copperplates which are in the Calcografía Nacional, Madrid (Bibl. 5, *Goya*, 81-162).

Abbreviations and signs, see p. 260
Aq. = aquatint
D = Delteil, Bibl. 55
H = Harris, Bibl. 88
SC = Sánchez Cantón, Bibl. 168

[993-1148] *

993 Des.*1*

Tristes presentimientos de lo que ha de acontecer c.1814-20. Etching 17·5×22 cm. D.120, H.121 *

994

Drawing for [993]. Red chalk Madrid, Prado (117) SC.83

995 Des.*2 (36)*

Con razon ó sin ella. (Rightly or wrongly) c.1812-15. Etching and lavis 15·5×20·5 cm. D.121, H.122 Ill. p. 218

996 Des.*3 (48)*

Lo mismo. (The same) c.1810-15. Etching and lavis 16×22·1 cm. D.122, H.123 Ill. p. 220

997 Des.*4 (34)*

Las mugeres dan valor. (The women give courage) c.1810-15. Etching and aq. 15·5×20·6 cm. D.123, H.124

998 Des.*5 (28)*

Y son fieras. (And they are like wild beasts) c.1812-15. Etching and aquatint 15·6×20·8 cm. D.124, H.125

999 Des.*6 (26)*

Bien te se está. (It serves you right) c.1810-15. s. *Goya* Etching and lavis 14·4×20·9 cm. D.125, H.126

1000 Des.*7 (41)*

Que valor! (What courage!) c.1810-15. Etching and aquatint 15·5×20·8 cm. D.126, H.127 Ill. p. 218 *

1001 recto of 1002

Drawing for [1000]. Red chalk Madrid, Prado (430) SC.84

1002 verso of 1001

Sketch for [1000]. Red chalk Prado (455) SC.85

1003 Des.*8*

Siempre sucede. (It always happens) c.1814-20. Etching 17·7×21·9 cm. D.127, H.128 *

1004

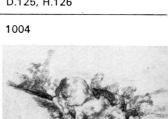

Drawing for [1003]. Red chalk Madrid, Prado (118) SC.86

05 Des.9 (29)

quieren. (They don't want to)
810-15. Etching and
uatint 15·5×20·9 cm.
28, H.129

1006 Des.10 (19)

Tampoco. (Nor do these)
c.1810-15. s. _Goya_
Etching 15×21·6 cm.
D.129, H.130

1007 - Des.11 (18)

Ni por esas. (Nor these)
c.1810-15. s. _Goya_
Etching and lavis 16·2×21·3 cm.
D.130, H.131

1008

Drawing for [1007]. Pen and
sepia ink with wash, red chalk
Madrid, Prado (167) SC.87

1009 Des.12 (24)

Para eso habeis nacido. (This is
what you were born for)
c.1810-12. s. Etching and lavis
16×23·5 cm. D.131, H.132

0

awing for [1009]. Red chalk
drid, Prado (119) SC.88.

1011 Des.13 (20)

Amarga presencia. (Bitter
presence) c.1810-11. s._Goya_
Etching and lavis 14·2×17 cm.
D.132, H.133 *

1012

Drawing for [1011]. Red chalk
Madrid, Prado (120) SC.89

1013 Des.14 (23)

Duro es el paso! (Hard is the
way!) c.1810-11.
Etching and lavis 14·3×16.8 cm.
D.133, H.134 III. p. 216 *

1014

Drawing for [1013]. Red chalk
Madrid, Prado (121) SC.90

15 Des.15 (22)

no hai remedio. (And it can't
helped) c.1810-11.
ching 14·1×16·8 cm.
134, H.135 *

1016 recto of 1045

Drawing for [1015].
Brush and sepia wash
Madrid, Prado (460) SC.333

1017 Des.16 (4)

Se aprovechan. (They take
advantage) c.1810-12.
s. _Goya_ Etching and lavis
16·2×23·2 cm. D.135, H.136

1018

Drawing for [1017]. Red chalk
Madrid, Prado (122) SC.91

1019 Des.17 (17)

No se convienen. (They do not
agree) c.1810-12. s. _Goya_
Etching 14·6×21·8 cm.
D.136, H.137

20 Des.18 (16)

terrar y callar. (Bury them and
ep quiet) c.1810-12.
Goya Etching and lavis
·3×23·8 cm. D.137, H.138

1021

Drawing for [1020]. Red chalk
Madrid, Prado (123) SC.92

1022 Des.19 (19)

Ya no hay tiempo. (There is no
longer time) c.1810-12.
s. _Goya_ Etching and lavis
16·6×23·9 cm. D.138, H.139

1023

Drawing for [1022]. Red chalk
Madrid, Prado (124) SC.93

1024 Des.20 (8)

Curarlos, y á otra. (Treat them,
and then on again) s.d. _Goya_
1810 Etching and lavis
16·1×23·8 cm. D.139, H.140

1025

Drawing for [1024]. Red chalk
Madrid, Prado (126) SC.95

1026

First drawing for [1024]?
Red chalk
Madrid, Prado (125) SC.94 *

1027 Des.21 (25)

Será lo mismo (It will be the
same) c.1810-12. s. Goya
Etching and lavis 14·7×21·8 cm.
D.140, H.141

1028

Drawing for [1027].
Brush and sepia wash
Madrid, Prado (168)
SC.151A; H.203e *

1029 Des.22 (7)

Tanto y mas (All this and more)
s.d. Goya 1810.
Etching and lavis 16·1×25·4 cm.
D.141, H.142 Ill. p. 219

1030

Drawing for [1029]. Red chalk
Madrid, Prado (127) SC.96

1031 Des.23 (14)

Lo mismo en otras partes (The
same elsewhere) c.1810-12.
s. Goya Etching and lavis
16·2×24 cm. D.142, H.143

1032

Drawing for [1031]. Red chalk
Madrid, Prado (128) SC.97

1033 Des.24 (12)

Aun podrán servir (They'll still be
useful) c.1810-12. s. Goya
Etching 16·8×26 cm.
D.143, H.144

1034

Drawing for [1033]. Red chalk
Madrid, Prado (129) SC.98

1035 Des.25 (13)

Tambien estos. (These too)
c.1810-12. s. Goya
Etching 16·5×23·6 cm.
D.144, H.145

1036

Drawing for [1035]. Red chalk
Madrid, Prado (130) SC.99

1037 Des.26 (27)

No se puede mirar. (One can't
look) c.1810-12. s.Goya
Etching and lavis 14·4×21 cm.
D.145, H.146

1038 Des.27 (11)

Caridad. (Charity)
s.d. Goya 1810
Etching and lavis 16·1×23·6 cm.
D.146, H.147

1039

Drawing for [1038]. Red chalk
Madrid, Prado (132) SC.100

1040 Des.28

Populacho. (Rabble) c.1814-20.
Etching and lavis 17·7×21·9 cm.
D.147, H.148 *

1041

Drawing for [1040]. Red chalk
Madrid, Prado (131) SC.101

1042 Des.29

Lo merecia. (He deserved it)
c.1814-20.
Etching 18×22 cm.
D.148, H.149 *

1043

1043
Drawing for [1042]. Red chalk
Madrid, Prado (134) SC.102

1044 Des.30 (21)

Estragos de la guerra. (Ravages
of war) c.1810-11. s. Goya
Etching and lavis(?) 14·1×17 cm
D.149, H.150 Ill. p. 216

1045 verso of 1016	1046 Des.*31 (32)*	1047 Des.*32 (49)*	1048 Des.*33 (42)*	1049 Des.*34 (1)*

…rawing for [1044].
…en and sepia ink with wash
…adrid, Prado (436) SC.103

Fuerte cosa es! (That's tough!)
c.1812-15.
Etching and aquatint
15·5×20·7 cm. D.150, H.151

Por qué? (Why?) c.1812-15.
Etching and lavis 15·6×21 cm.
D.151, H.152

Qué hai que hacer mas? (What more can one do?) c.1812-15.
Etching and lavis 15·8×20·8 cm.
D.152, H.153

Por una navaja. (For having a knife) c.1812-15.
Etching 15·6×20·8 cm.
D.153, H.154 *

…050 Des.*35 (2)*	1051 Des.*36 (39)*	1052 Des.*37 (32)*	1053 Des.*38 (57)*	1054

…o se puede saber por qué.
…ne can't tell why) c.1812-15.
…ching and lavis 15·5×20·8 cm.
…154, H.155

Tampoco. (Not [in this case] either) c.1812-15.
Etching and aquatint
15·8×20·8 cm. D.155, H.156

Esto es peor. (This is worse)
c.1812-15.
Etching and lavis 15·7×20·7 cm.
D.156, H.157

Bárbaros! (Barbarians)
c.1812-15. Etching and aquatint
15·8×20·8 cm.
D.157, H.158 Ill. p. 219

Sketch for [1053]. Red chalk
Madrid, Prado (454) *

…055 Des.*39 (51)*	1056 Des.*40*	1057	1058 Des.*41 (10)*	1059

…rande hazaña! Con muertos!
…1812-15. s. *Goya*
…ching and lavis 15·7×20·8 cm.
…158, H.159 *

Algun partido saca. (He makes some use of it) c.1814-20.
Etching 17·1×22 cm.
D.159, H.160 *

Drawing for [1056]. Red chalk
Madrid, Prado (135) SC.104

Escapan entre las llamas.
(They escape through the flames)
c.1810-12. s. *Goya* Etching
16×23·5 cm. D.160, H.161

Drawing for [1058]. Red chalk
Madrid, Prado (136) SC.105

…060 Des.*42*	1061	1062 Des.*43 (40)*	1063	1064 Des.*44 (15)*

…odo va revuelto. (Everything is
…psy-turvy) c.1815-20.
…ching 17·5×22 cm.
…161, H.162 *

Drawing for [1060]. Red chalk
Madrid, Prado (137) SC.106

Tambien esto. (So is this)
c.1815-20.
Etching and aquatint
15·5×20·5 cm D.162. H.163

Drawing for [1062]. Red chalk
Madrid, Prado (431) SC.C

Yo lo vi. (I saw this)
c.1810-12. s. *Goya*
Etching 16×23·5 cm.
D.163, H.164

1065

Drawing for [1064].   Red chalk
Madrid, Prado (138)   SC.107

Seventeen plates recording the
terrible *año del hambre* - the year
of the famine which lasted from
1811 to 1812 and in the course
of which thousands of people
died of hunger in the streets.

[1070-1103]

1066   Des.*45*

Y esto tambien. (And this too)
c.1812-15.   s. *Goya*
Etching and aquatint
16·5×22 cm.   D.164, H.165

1067

Drawing for [1066].   Red chalk
Madrid, Prado (139)   SC.108

1068   Des.*46 (53)*

Esto es malo. (This is bad)
c.1812-15.
Etching and aquatint
15.5×20.5 cm.   D.165, H.166

1069   Des.*47 (33)*

Así sucedió. (This is how it
happened)   c.1812-15.
Etching and lavis 15·5×20·5 cm
D.166, H.167

1070   Des.*48 (47)*

Cruel lástima! (A cruel shame!)
c.1812-15.
Etching and lavis
15·5×20·5 cm.   D.167, H.168

1071

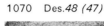

Drawing for [1070].   Red chalk
Madrid, Prado (140)   SC.109

1072   Des.*49 (36)*

Caridad de una muger.
(A woman's charity)   c.1812-15.
Etching and lavis 15·5×20·5 cm.
D.168, H.169

1073

Drawing for [1072].   Red chal
Madrid, Prado (141)   SC.110

1074   Des.*50 (55)*

Madre infeliz! (Unhappy mother!)
c.1812-15.
Etching and aquatint
15·5×20·5 cm.   D.169, H.170

1075

Drawing for [1074].   Red chalk
Madrid, Prado (142)   SC.111

1076   Des.*51 (46)*

Gracias á la almorta. (Thanks to
the millet)   c.1812-15.
Etching and aq. 15·5×20·5 cm.
D.170, H.171   Ill. p. 221

1077

Drawing for [1076].   Red chalk
Madrid, Prado (143)   SC.112

1078   Des.*52 (50)*

No llegan á tiempo. (They do n
arrive in time)   c.1812-15.
Etching and lavis 15·5×20·5 cm
D.171, H.172

1079

Drawing for [1078].   Red chalk
Madrid, Prado (144)   SC.113

1080   Des.*53 (43)*

Espiró sin remedio. (There was
nothing to be done and he died)
c.1812-15.   Etching and aquatint
15·5×20·5 cm.   D.172, H.173

1081

Drawing for [1080].   Red chalk
Madrid, Prado (145)   SC.114

1082   Des.*54 (45)*

Clamores en vano. (Vain laments)
c.1812-15.
Etching and lavis 15·5×20·5 cm.
D.173, H.174

1083

Drawing for [1082].   Red chalk
Madrid, Prado (146)   SC.115

1084   Des.*55 (37)*

1085

1086   Des.*56 (30)*

1087

1088   Des.*57 (5)*

Lo peor es pedir. (The worst is to beg) c.1812-15. s. *Goya* Etching and lavis 15·5×20·5 cm. D.174, H.175   Ill. p. 220

Drawing for [1084].   Red chalk Madrid, Prado (147)   SC.116

Al cementerio. (To the cemetery) c.1812-15. Etching and lavis 15·5×20·5 cm. D.175, H.176

Drawing for [1086].   Red chalk Madrid, Prado (148)   SC.117

Sanos y enfermos. (The sound and the sick) c.1812-15. Etching and aquatint 15.5×20.5 cm.   D.176, H.177

1089

1090   Des.*58 (34)*

1091

1092   Des.*59 (3)*

1093

Drawing for [1088].   Red chalk Madrid, Prado (149)   SC.118

No hay que dar voces. (It's no use crying out) c.1812-15. Etching and aquatint 15·5×20·5 cm.   D.177, H.178

Drawing for [1090].   Red chalk Madrid, Prado (150)   SC.119

De qué sirve una taza? (Of what use is one cup?)   c.1812-15. Etching and aquatint 15·5×20·5 cm.   D.178, H.179

Drawing for [1092]. Red and black chalk, sanguine wash Madrid, Prado (151)   SC.120

1094   Des.*60 (31)*

1095

1096   Des.*61 (35)*

1097

1098   Des.*62*

No hay quien los socorra. (There is no one to help them) c.1812-15.   Etching and aquatint 15·5×20·5 cm.   D.179, H.180

Drawing for [1094].   Red chalk Madrid, Prado (152)   SC.121

Si son de otro linage. (But they are of another breed)   c.1812-15. Etching and lavis 15·5×20·5 cm. D.180, H.181

Drawing for [1096].   Red chalk Madrid, Prado (153)   SC.122

Las camas de la muerte. (The beds of death)   c.1812-15. Etching and lavis 17·5×22 cm. D.181, H.182   *

1099

1100   Des.*63 (44)*

1101

1102   Des.*64 (38)*

1103

Drawing for [1098].   Red chalk Madrid, Prado (154)   SC.123

Muertos recogidos. (Dead bodies heaped together) c.1812-15. Etching and aquatint 15.5×20.5 cm.   D.182, H.183

Drawing for [1100].   Red chalk Madrid, Prado (155)   SC.124

Carretadas al cementerio. (Cartloads to the cemetery) c.1812-15.   Etching and aquatint 15·5×20·5 cm.   D.183, H.184

Drawing for [1102].   Red chalk Madrid, Prado (156)   SC.125

Plates 65-82 are the *caprichos enfáticos* — the striking caprices which Goya added to the war and famine scenes between 1815 and 1820. They are above all a savage and barely veiled attack on the clergy, the most powerful and dangerous of the forces of reaction which triumphed with the return of Ferdinand VII.

[1104-1139]

1104 Des.*65*

Qué alboroto es este? (What is this hubbub?) c.1815-20.
Etching and aquatint 17·5×22 cm.
D.184, H.185

1105

Drawing for [1104]? Red chalk
Madrid, Prado (180) SC.147 *

1106 Des.*66*

Extraña devocion! (Strange devotion!) c.1815-20.
Etching and aquatint 17·5×22 cm.
D.185, H.186   *

1107

Drawing for [1106]. Red chalk
Madrid, Prado (157) SC.126

1108 - Des.*67*

Esta no lo es menos. (This is no less so) c.1815-20.
Etching and aquatint 17·5×22 cm.
D.186, H.187   *

1109

Drawing for [1108]. Red chalk
Madrid, Prado (158) SC.127

1110 Des.*68*

Que locura! (What madness!)
c.1815-20.
Etching and lavis 16×22 cm.
D.187, H.188

1111

Drawing for [1110]. Red chalk
Madrid, Prado (159) SC.128

1112 Des.*69 (69)*

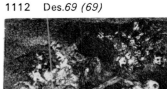

Nada. Ello dirá. (Nothing. The event will tell) c.1812-20.
Inscr. Etching and aquatint
15·5×20 cm. D.188, H.189   *

1113

Drawing for [1112]? Brush and sepia, heightened white, blue paper 20×25·6 cm.
Madrid, Prado (169) SC.129 *

1114 Des.*70*

No saben el camino. (They don't know the way) c.1815-20.
Etching 17·5×22 cm.
D.189, H.190

1115

Drawing for [1114]. Red chalk
Madrid, Prado (161) SC.130

1116 Des.*71*

Contra el bien general. (Against the common good) c.1815-20.
Etching 17·5×22 cm.
D.190, H.191

1117

Drawing for [1116]. Red chalk
Madrid, Prado (160) SC.131

1118 Des.*72*

Las resultas. (The consequences)
c.1815-20.
Etching 17·5×22 cm.
D.191, H.192

1119

Drawing for [1118]. Red chalk
Madrid, Prado (162) SC.132

1120 Des.*73*

Gatesca pantomima. (Feline pantomime) c.1815-20.
Etching 17·5×22 cm.
D.192, H.193   *

1121

Drawing for [1120]. Red chalk
Madrid, Prado (163) SC.133

1122 Des.*74*

Esto es lo peor! (This is the worst of all!) c.1815-20. Inscr.
Etching 18×22 cm.
D.193, H.194
    *

1157 Taur.*5*	1158	1159 Taur.*6*	1160	1161 Taur.*7*

   —

El animoso moro Gazul es el primero que lanceó toros en regla. 1815-16. Etching and aquatint 25×35 cm. D.228, H.208 *

Drawing for [1157]. Red chalk Coll. unknown (formerly Paris, Charles Yriarte) *

Los moros hacen otro capeo en plaza con su albornoz. 1815-16. Etching and aquatint 24·5×35 cm. D.229, H.209 *

Drawing for [1159]. Red chalk Madrid, Prado (212) SC.155

Origen de los arpones ó banderillas. (Origin of the harpoons...) 1815-16. Etching and aquatint 24·5×35 cm. D.230, H.210 *

1162	1163 Taur. *8*	1164	1165 Taur.*9*	1166

Drawing for [1161]. Red chalk Madrid, Prado (213) SC.156

Cogida de un moro estando en la plaza. (A moor caught...) 1815-16. Etching and aquatint 24·5×35 cm. D.231, H.211 *

Drawing for [1163]. Red chalk Madrid, Prado (214) SC.157

Un caballero español mata un toro... 1815-16. s. Goya Etching and aquatint 24·5×35 cm. D.232, H.212 *

Drawing for [1165]. Red chalk Madrid, Prado (215) SC.158

1167 Taur.*10*	1168	1169	1170 verso of 1172	1171 Taur.*11*

Carlos V. lanceando un toro en la plaza de Valladolid. 1815-16. s. Goya Etching and aquatint 25×35 cm. D.233, H.213 *

Drawing for [1167]. Red chalk Madrid, Prado (219) SC.160

First drawing for [1167]. Red chalk Madrid, Prado (216) SC.159

Sketch for [1167]? Red chalk Madrid, Prado (461) SC.161

El Cid Campeador lanceando otro toro. 1815-16. s. Goya Etching and aquatint 25×35 cm. D.234, H.214 Ill. p. 228 *

1172 recto of 1170	1173	1174 Taur.*12*	1175	1176 Taur.*13*

Drawing for [1171]. Red chalk Madrid, Prado (435) SC.162

Study for [1167] or [1171]. Red chalk Madrid, Prado (218) SC.163

Desjarrete de la canalla con lanzas, medias-lunas,... 1815-16. Etching and aquatint 25×35 cm. D.235, H.215 *

Drawing for [1174]. Red chalk Madrid, Prado (217) SC.164

Un caballero español en plaza quebrando rejoncillos... 1815-16. Etching and aquatint 25×35 cm. D.236, H.216 *

1177

The remainder of the series is concerned with the exploits of famous bullfighters and the illustration of the different stages and passes of the corrida, some of which Goya had portrayed years before in the little paintings of 1793 [II.317-324].

1178 Taur.*14*

1179

1180 Taur.*15*

Drawing for [1176]. Red chalk
Madrid, Prado (220) SC.165

El diestrísimo estudiante de Falces, embozado . . . 1815-16.
s. *Goya* Etching and aquatint
25 × 35·5 cm. D.237, H.217 ✳

Drawing for [1178]. Red chalk
Madrid, Prado (221) SC.166

El famoso Martincho poniendo banderillas al quiebro. 1815-1
Etching and aquatint 25 × 35 cn
D.238, H.218

1181

1182 Taur.*16*

1183

1184 Taur.*17*

1185

Drawing for [1180]. Red chalk
Madrid, Prado (222) SC.167

E mismo vuelca un toro en la plaza de Madrid. 1815-16.
Etching and aquatint 24·5 × 35 cm.
D.239, H.219 ✳

Drawing for [1182]. Red chalk
Madrid, Prado (223) SC.168

Palenque de los moros hecho con burros . . . 1815-16.
Etching and aquatint 24·5 × 35 cm.
D.240, H.220 ✳

Drawing for [1184]. Red cha
Madrid, Prado (224) SC.169

1186 Taur.*18*

1187

1188 Taur.*19*

1189

1190 Taur.*20*

Temeridad de Martincho en la plaza de Zaragoza.
1815-16. Etching and aquatint
24·5 × 35·5 cm. D.241, H.221 ✳

Drawing for [1186]. Red chalk
Madrid, Prado (226) SC.171

Otra locura suya en la misma plaza. s.d. *Goya 1815.*
Etching and aquatint 24·5 × 35 cm.
D.242, H.222 Ill. p. 228 ✳

Drawing for [1188]. Red chalk
Madrid, Prado (227) SC.172

Ligereza y atrevimiento de Juanito Apiñani en la de Madr
1815-16. Etching and aquatin
24·5 × 35·5 cm. D.243, H.223

1191

1192 Taur.*21*

1193

1194 Taur.*22*

1195

Drawing for [1190]. Red chalk
Madrid, Prado (229) SC.173

Desgracias acaecidas en el tendido . . . 1815-16. Etching
and aquatint 24·5 × 35·5 cm.
D.244, H.224 Ill. p. 229 ✳

Drawing for [1192]. Red chalk
Madrid, Prado (230) SC.174

Valor varonil de la célebre Pajuelera . . . 1815-16.
s. *Goya* Etching and aquatint
25 × 35 cm. D.245, H.225 ✳

Drawing for [1194]. Red cha
Madrid, Prado (231) SC.175

96 Taur.*23*   1197   1198 Taur.*24*   1199   1200 Taur.*25*

...ariano Ceballos, alias el Indio, ...ta el toro desde su caballo. ...15-16. Etching and aquatint ...×35 cm. D.246, H.226 ✳

Drawing for [1196]. Red chalk Madrid, Prado (232) SC.176

El mismo Ceballos montado sobre otro toro quiebra rejones . . . 1815-16. Etching and aquatint 24·5×35·5 cm. D.247, H.227 ✳

Drawing for [1198]. Red chalk Madrid, Prado (233) SC.177

Echan perros al toro. (They loose dogs on the bull) 1815-16. Etching and aquatint 24·5×35·5 cm. D.248, H.228 ✳

...01   1202 Taur.*26*   1203   1204 Taur.*27*   1205

...awing for [1200]. Red chalk ...adrid, Prado (234) SC.178

Caida de un picador de su caballo debajo del toro. 1815-16. Etching and aquatint 24·5×35·5 cm. D.249, H.229 ✳

Drawing for [1202]. Red chalk Madrid, Prado (235) SC.179

El célebre Fernando del Toro, barilarguero, obligando á la fiera... 1815-16. Etching and aquatint 24·5×35 cm. D.250, H.230 ✳

Drawing for [1204]. Red chalk and sanguine wash Madrid, Prado (236) SC.180

...06 Taur.*28*   1207   1208 Taur. *29*   1209   1210 Taur.*30*

...esforzado Rendon picando un ...ro . . . 1815-16. s. *Goya* ...ching and aquatint 25×35 cm. ...251, H.231 Ill. p. 229 ✳

Drawing for [1206]. Red chalk 18·7×31·3 cm. Hamburg, Kunsthalle (38534) ✳

Pepe Illo haciendo el recorte al toro. s.d. *Goya 1815.* Etching and aquatint 24·5×35 cm. D.252, H.232 ✳

Drawing for [1208]. Red chalk Madrid, Prado (237) SC.181

Pedro Romero matando á toro parado. 1815-16. Etching and aquatint 24·5×35·5 cm. D.253, H.233 Ill. pp. 123, 228 ✳

...11   1212 Taur.*31*   1213   1214 Taur.*32*   1215

...awing for [1210]. ...ed chalk 20×28·9 cm. ...ambridge (Mass.), Philip Hofer ✳

Banderillas de fuego. (Banderillas with firecrackers) s.d. *1815 Goya.* Etching and aquatint 24·5×35 cm. D.254, H.234

Drawing for [1212]. Red chalk Madrid, Prado (238) SC.182

Dos grupos de picadores arollados de seguida por un solo toro. 1815-16. Etching and aquatint 24·5×35 cm. D.255, H.235 ✳

Drawing for [1214]. Red chalk and sanguine wash 18·2×31·3 cm. Hamburg, Kunsthalle (38541) ✳

1216

Study for main group in [1214].
Red chalk
Madrid, Prado (239)   SC.183

1217   Taur.*33*

La desgraciada muerte de Pepe Illo en la plaza de Madrid.
1815-16.   Etching and aquatint
24·5×35 cm.   D.256, H. 236   *

1218

Drawing for [1217].   Red chalk
Madrid, Prado (240)   SC.184

PLATES A-G

Additional compositions engraved on seven of the plates and rejected by Goya who used the backs of the plates for designs included in the first edition.
In 1876 these rejected engravings were printed for the first time together with the third edition of the other thirty-three, and published in Paris.
They were engraved with the letters A to G, and French titles were invented for them.
They represent Goya's early attempts in this series, and are generally technically inferior to the thirty-three others.

[1219-1232]

1219   Taur.*A*

Un cavalier espagnol brisant des 'rejoncillos' avec l'aide des chulo
1815.   Etching and aquatint
25×35 cm.   D.257, H.237

1220

Drawing for [1219].   Red chalk
Madrid, Prado (241)   SC.185

1221   Taur.*B*

Cheval renversé par un taureau.
(Horse thrown by a bull)   1815.
s. *Goya*   Etching and aquatint
24·5×35 cm.   D.258, H.238   *

1222

Drawing for [1221].   Red chalk
Madrid, Prado (243)   SC.186

1223   Taur.*C*

Les chiens lâchés sur le taureau.
(Dogs let loose on the bull)
1815.   Etching and aquatint
24·5×35 cm.   D.259, H.239   *

1224

Drawing for [1223].   Red chalk
Madrid, Prado (244)   SC.187

1225   Taur.*D*

Un torero monté sur les épaules d'un chulo 'lancea[n]do' un taureau
1815.   Etching and aquatint
24·5×35 cm.   D.260, H.240   *

1226

Drawing for [1225].   Red chalk
Madrid, Prado (245)   SC.188

1227   Taur.*E*

Mort de Pepe Illo. (2e composition)
1815.   s. *Goya*
Etching and aquatint 25×35 cm.
D.261, H.241   Ill. p. 228   *

1228

Drawing for [1227].   Red chalk
and sanguine wash 19×31·3 cm.
Hamburg, Kunsthalle (38533)   *

1229   Taur. *F*

Mort de Pepe Illo. (3e composition)
(Death of Pepe Illo)   1815-16.
s. *Goya*   Etching and aquatint
24·5×35 cm.   D.262, H.242

1230

Drawing for [1229].   Red chalk
Madrid, Prado (246)   SC.190

1231   Taur. *G*

Combat dans une voiture attelée de deux mulets.   1815-16.
Etching and aquatint 25×35 cm.
D.263, H.243   *

1232

Drawing for [1231].   Red chalk
Madrid, Prado (247)   SC.191

ADDITIONAL PLATES
AND DRAWINGS

Five plates known only from rare or unique proofs.
(1/1 = unique proof; 1/3 = one of three proofs known.)
One additional drawing for which no proof is known.

[1233-1243]

1233   Taur.[*H*]

Recklessness of Martincho
1815-16.   Etching and aquatint
24·5×34·5 cm.   1/3   Paris,
P. Palais (5423b)   D.264, H.244

234

rawing for [1233]. Red chalk
adrid, Prado (225) SC.170

1235 Taur.[I]

Torero going in to kill . . . 1815-16.
Etching and aquatint 25×35 cm.
1/2 Madrid, Fund. Lázaro
(B.14866-6) D.265, H.245 *

1236

Drawing for [1235]. Red chalk
Madrid, Prado (248) SC.189

1237 Taur.[J]

Mariano Ceballos mounted . . .
1815-16. Etching and aquatint
24×36 cm. 1/2 Paris,
P. Palais (5431) D.266, H.246 *

1238

Drawing for [1237]. Red chalk
Madrid, Prado (242) SC.193

---

239 Taur.[K]

skillful fighter calling the bull . . .
315-16. Etching and aquatint
5×35 cm. 1/1 Madrid,
N. (45683) D.267, H.247 *

1240

Drawing for [1239]. Red chalk
and sanguine wash 19·2×29 cm.
Hamburg, Kunsthalle (38542) *

1241 Taur.[L]

A matador thrusts the sword
home . . . 1815-16. s. *Goya*
Etching and aq. 24·8×34·6 cm.
1/1 Paris, P. Palais (5439) *

1242

Drawing for [1241]. Red chalk
Madrid, Prado (228)
SC.192; H.247a

1243 verso of 1154

The bull charges a torero who
protects himself with a basket
1815-16. Red chalk Madrid,
Prado (437) SC.194; H.247b *

LBUMS OF DRAWINGS
, D, E, F c.1804-1823

our albums which originally
ontained at least 313 drawings.
71 are now known — more than
alf of them in the Prado Museum.
ome of the scenes suggest a few
pproximate dates, but a
ronology is difficult to establish.
ne whole group probably spans
period of some twenty years
efore Goya's departure for France.
ne technique is limited to use
the brush and wash, sometimes
dian ink, sometimes sepia.

244-1518] *

bbreviations and signs, see p. 260
R = López-Rey, Bibl. 116
C = Sánchez Cantón, Bibl. 168
/ = Wehle, Bibl. 192, fig.

ALBUM C c.1814-1823

The longest of all the albums.
The highest page number is 133.
Of the 124 known drawings,
120 are in the Prado.
Maximum known sheet size:
20·8×14·4 cm. Indian or sepia
ink wash, occasionally retouched
with pen and ink or crayon.
All the drawings have titles and
numbers written by Goya (some
of the numbers illegible or
effaced). Where the numbers
were altered by Goya, the first is
given in brackets after the final
number.

[1244-1367] *

1244 C.*1*

P.r no trabajar (Because he has no
work) Indian ink wash
20×14 cm. Madrid, Prado (86)
SC.228, LR.1 *

1245 C.*2*

Salvage menos q.e otros (Less
savage than some) Indian ink
wash Madrid, Prado (87)
SC.229, LR.2

1246 C.*3*

Á q.e bendra el faldellin y los
calzones? (What's the use . . .)
Indian ink wash Madrid,
Prado (88) SC.230, LR.3 *

---

247 C.*4*

las probecho saco de estar solo.
'm better off alone) Indian
k wash 20·5×13 cm. Madrid.
rado (89) SC.231, LR.4

1248 C.*5*

Este fue un cojo q.e tenia señoria
Indian ink wash 20·6×14·3 cm.
Madrid, Prado (90)
SC.232, LR.5 *

1249 C.*7*

Al desierto p.a ser santo, Amen
Indian ink wash 20·5×14·3 cm.
Madrid, Prado (207)
SC.233, LR.6 *

1250 C.*8*

A lo menos hace algo
Indian ink wash 20×14·3 cm.
Madrid, Prado (279)
SC.329, LR.7 *

1251 C.*9*

Buena muger. parece
Indian ink wash 20·5×14 cm.
Madrid, Prado (13)
SC.234, LR.8 *

1252   C.*10*

Habrazo Paternal.
Sepia wash 20·2×13·9 cm.
Madrid, Prado (410)
SC.323, LR.9   *

1253   C.*12* (*11*)

La huebera and *la guebera*
(The egg vendor)   Indian ink
wash 20·5×13·8 cm.   Madrid,
Prado (10)   SC.235, LR.10   *

1254   C.*13* (*12*)

¡Q.e Necedad! dar los destinos en
la niñez   Indian ink wash
20·5×14·3 cm.   Madrid,
Prado (15)   SC.236, LR.11   *

1255   C.*16*

*Esta pretende el destino de
rabanera*   Indian ink wash
20·5×14 cm.   Madrid,
Prado (11)   SC.237, LR.12   *

1256   C.*17* (*16*)

*Asi suelen acabar los hombres
utiles*   Indian ink wash
20·6×14·3 cm.   Madrid,
Prado (46)   SC.238, LR.13   *

1257   C.*18* (*17*)

*Si no me engano, ba á dejar el
avito*   Indian ink wash
20·5×14·3 cm.   Madrid,
Prado (278)   SC.325, LR.14   *

1258   C.*19* (*18*)

*Be V.d q.e expr.n, pues no lo cree
el marido*   Indian ink wash
20·5×14 cm.   Madrid,
Prado (14)   SC.239, LR.15   *

1259   C.*20* (*19*)

*Se le murio su amante y se ba al
comb.to*   Indian ink wash
20·5×14·1 cm.   Madrid,
Prado (209)   SC.244, LR.16   *

1260   C.*21* (*20*)

¡Que desgracia!
(What a misfortune!)   Indian
ink wash 20·6×14·3 cm.   Madrid,
Prado (91)   SC.245, LR.17

1261   C.*22* (*21*)

Culpable miseria
(Reprehensible poverty)   Indian
ink wash 20·5×14·3 cm.   Madri
Prado (43)   SC.246, LR.18

1262   C.*23* (*22*)

Muecas de Baco
(Bacchus's grimaces)   Indian
ink wash 20·6×14·3 cm.   Madrid,
Prado (42)   SC.247, LR.19   *

1263   C.*25* (*24*)

Piensalo bien (Think it over well)
Indian ink wash 20·5×14 cm.
Madrid, Prado (12)
SC.240, LR.20   *

1264   C.*26*

Malos Poetas (Bad poets)
Indian ink wash 20·5×14 cm.
Madrid, Prado (274)
SC.241, LR.21   *

1265   C.*27* (*26*)

Lo q.e puede el Amor!
(What Love can do!)   Indian
ink wash 20·5×14·3 cm.   Madrid,
Prado (206)   SC.242, LR.22

1266   C.*28* (*27*)

Con estos no me meto
Indian ink wash 20·5×14·1 cm.
Madrid, Prado (208)
SC.243, LR.23   *

1267   C.*29*

Mejor fuera vino (Wine would be
better)   Indian ink wash
20·5×14·3 cm.   Madrid,
Prado (47)   SC.248, LR.112   *

1268   C.*30* (*29*)

Esto degemoslo como estaba.
Indian ink wash 20·5×14·2 cm.
Madrid, Prado (277)
SC.330, LR.24   *

1269   C.*31* (*30*)

No lo encontraras. (You won't
find it)   Indian ink wash
20·5×14 cm.   Madrid,
Prado (419)   SC.315, LR.25

1270   C.*32*

Q.e orror p.r benganza
Indian and sepia ink wash
Madrid, Prado (329)
SC.324, LR.26   *

1271   C.*33* (*32*)

*Estos/creen/en los bu-/elos de
las/abes*   Indian ink wash
20·5×14·1 cm.   Madrid,
Prado (204)   SC.249, LR.27

72   C.34 (33)

ra penitencia (An odd sort of
nance)   Indian ink wash
drid, Prado (280)
.250, LR.28

1273   C.35 (34)

En el talego de carne lleba su
patrimonio
Indian ink wash   Madrid,
Prado (281)   SC.251, LR.29   *

1274   C.36 (35)

Misto de Mona (Part monkey)
Indian ink wash
Madrid, Prado (282)
SC.252, LR.30

1275   C.37 (36)

Bas mui lejos? (Are you going
very far?)   Indian ink wash
20·5×14·1 cm.   Madrid,
Prado (205)   SC.253, LR.31

1276   C.38 (37)

El Maricon de la tia Gila (Auntie
Gila's pansy)   Indian ink wash
Madrid, Prado (283)
SC.254, LR.32   *

roup of nine drawings of *comic*
sions, all apparently seen in the
urse of a single night.

277-1285]

1277   C.39 (38)

Vision burlesca (Comic vision)
Indian ink wash   Madrid,
Prado (264)   SC.255, LR.33

1278   C.40 (39)

Otra en la misma noche (Another
in the same night)   Indian
ink wash 20·5×14 cm.   Madrid,
Prado (265)   SC.256, LR.34

1279   C.41 (40)

3.ª en la/misma (3rd in the same)
Indian ink wash   Madrid,
Prado (266)   SC.257, LR.35

1280   C.42

4.ª/en la misma (4th in the same)
Indian ink wash 20·5×14 cm.
Madrid, Prado (267)
SC.258, LR.36

281   C.43 (41)

a (5th)   Indian ink wash
·4×14 cm.   Madrid,
ado (268)   SC.259, LR.37

1282   C.44 (42)

6.ª/con pesadi/lla (6th with
nightmare)   Indian ink wash
20·5×14 cm.   Madrid,
Prado (269)   SC.260, LR.38

1283   C.45 (43)

7.ª (7th)   Indian ink wash
20·5×14·1 cm.   Madrid,
Prado (270)   SC.261, LR.39

1284   C.46 (44)

8.ª (8th)   Indian ink wash
20·4×14·1 cm.   Madrid,
Prado (271)   SC.262, LR.40

1285   C.47 (45)

9.ª (9th)   Indian ink wash
20·5×14 cm.   Madrid,
Prado (276)   SC.264, LR.41

286   C.48

eligion en la Asia (Religion in
sia)   Indian ink wash
·5×14 cm.   Madrid,
ado (275)   SC.263, LR.42   *

1287   C.49 (46)

La misma (The same)   Indian
ink wash   Madrid, Prado (45)
SC.265, LR.43

1288   C.50

Pobre en Asia q.ᵉ se enciende/la
cabeza...   Indian ink wash
20·5×14 cm.   Madrid,
Prado (273)   SC.266, LR.44   *

1289   C.51

Esto/ya se be (This is now clear)
Indian ink wash   Madrid,
Prado (300)   SC.375, LR.45   *

1290   C.52

Este tiene/muchos pa-/rientes y/
algunos/racionales
Indian ink wash   Madrid,
Prado (44)   SC.267, LR.46   *

1291   C.53

No se sabe (One doesn't know)
Indian ink wash   Madrid,
Prado (298)   SC.321, LR.47

1292   C.54

Tan poco (Nor in this case)
Indian ink wash   Madrid,
Prado (299)   SC.360, LR.48

1293   C.55?

Menos (Still less)   Indian ink
and sepia wash   Madrid,
Prado (330)   SC.357   *

1294   C.56?

No ha muerto toda via (He's not
dead yet)   Indian ink and sepia
wash   Madrid, Prado (328)
SC.332   *

1295   C.57?

Bayan en ora buena (Good luck
go with them)   Sepia wash
Madrid, Prado (262)   SC.308

1296   C.58

Ya dispertará (He's going to
wake up)   Indian ink and sepia
wash 20·6×14 cm.   Madrid,
Prado (305)   SC.301, LR.49   *

1297   C.59

Sueño raro (Bizarre dream)
Sepia wash 20·5×14 cm.
Madrid, Prado (306)
SC.310, LR.50

1298   C.60

P.ª los q.ᵉ/estan en/P.ᵈᵒ Mortal
(For those in a state of deadly
sin)   Sepia wash   Madrid,
Prado (290)   SC.287, LR.51

1299   C.61?

Calla/El tiempo mu-/da las oras
(Be quiet. Time changes the
hours)   Sepia wash   Madrid,
Prado (261)   SC.358   *

1300   C.62

Puede ser q.ᵉ sea bueno
Indian ink and sepia wash
18·9×13·3 cm.   Madrid,
Prado (307)   SC.302, LR.52

1301   C.63

*Esto ya se/be qᵉ no es/arrancar
Nabos* (One can see that this
is...)   Sepia wash   Madrid,
Prado (289)   SC.286, LR.53   *

1302   C.64

Ciego ena/morado de/su potra
(Blind man in love with his
hernia)   Sepia wash   Madrid,
Prado (302)   SC.298, LR.54

1303   C.65?

Mal señal (A bad sign)
Sepia wash
Madrid, Prado (263)   SC.355   *

1304   C.67

de esto hay mucho, y no se be
Sepia wash 20·6×14·3 cm.
Madrid, Prado (260)
SC.284, LR.55   *

1305   C.68

Esto huele a/cosa de Magia
(This smacks of magic)   Sepia
wash 20·6×14·3 cm.   Madrid,
Prado (367)   SC.338, LR.56

1306   C.69

Estas Brujas lo diran (These
witches will tell)   Sepia wash
20·5×14·2 cm.   Madrid,
Prado (368)   SC.339, LR.57   *

1307   C.70

Nada dicen (They say nothing)
Sepia wash 20·5×14·2 cm.
Madrid, Prado (369)
SC.340, LR.58   *

1308   C.71

Tuti li mundi (All the world)
Indian ink and sepia wash
20·7×14·4 cm.   New York,
Hispanic Soc. (A.3314)   *

1309   C.73

No la engañas (You don't fool
her)   Sepia wash 20·5×14·3 cm.
Madrid, Prado (250)
SC.293, LR.59

1310   C.74

Tan vien aqui/hay amores
(There are amours here too)
Sepia wash   Madrid, Prado (30...
SC.303, LR.60

1311 C.75

Con la musica á otra parte
Indian ink and sepia wash
20·5×14 cm.   Madrid,
Prado (370)   SC.341, LR.61 *

1312 C.76?

Que sacrificio (What a sacrifice)
Sepia wash
Madrid, Prado (325)   SC.356 *

1313 C.77

Comer vien veber mejor y / dormir
olgar y pasear (To eat well, drink
better . . .)   Sepia wash   Madrid,
Prado (301)   SC.299, LR.62 *

1314 C.78

Lastima es qe no te ocupes en
otra/cosa (It's a pity you don't . . .)
Sepia wash 20 · 3×14 cm.
New York, Knoedler *

1315 C.79

Estos hacen raya/en la taberna
Sepia wash 20·6×14 cm.
Madrid, Prado (252)
SC.296, LR.63 *

1316 C.80

Gran mano para / hurtar sonajas
por qe era tremulo)   Sepia
wash 20·8×14·1 cm.   Madrid,
Prado (253)   SC.294, LR.64 *

1317 C.81

Ó Ste Brague (O Holy Breeches)
Sepia wash 20·6×14 cm.
Madrid, Prado (308)
SC.326, LR.65 *

1318 C.82

Edad con desgracias (The mishaps
of old age)   Sepia wash
Madrid, Prado (292)
SC.288, LR.66

1319 C.83

Desbergonzado, con todas, todas
Sepia wash 20·5×14·3 cm.
Madrid, Prado (251)
SC.292, LR.67 *

1320 C.84

Nada nos ynporta (Nothing
matters to us)   Sepia wash
20·5×14 cm.   Madrid,
Prado (249)   SC.295, LR.68

Group of eight drawings showing
victims of the Inquisition wearing
the san benito (tall hat) and the
coroza on which the inscriptions
give the reason for their
condemnation.

[1321-1328]

1321 C.85

P.r haber nacido en/otra parte
Sepia wash 20·3×14·1 cm.
Madrid, Prado (309)
SC.342, LR.69   Ill. p. 237 *

1322 C.86

Por traer cañutos/de diablos de
Bayona   Sepia wash
20·5×14 cm.   Madrid,
Prado (311)   SC.343, LR.70 *

1323 C.87

Le pusie/ron mor/daza p.r/q.e
habla/ba . . .   Sepia wash
20·5×14·1 cm.   Madrid,
Prado (312)   SC.344, LR.71 *

1324 C.88 (78)

P.r linage de Ebreos
Sepia wash 20·5×14·2 cm.
London, B.M. (1862.7.12.187)
LR.72   Ill. p. 237 *

1325 C.89 (79)

P.r mober la lengua de otro modo
Sepia wash 20·2×14 cm.
Madrid, Prado (313)
SC.345, LR.73 *

1326 C.90

Por no tener piernas // Yo lo
conoci á este baldado . . .
Sepia wash 20×14 cm.   Madrid,
Prado (314)   SC.346, LR.74 *

1327 C.91 (81)

Muchos an acabado asi
Indian ink and sepia wash
20·5×14·3 cm.   Madrid,
Prado (348)   SC.376, LR.75 *

1328 C.92 (82)

P.r querer á una burra (For loving
a she-ass)   Sepia wash
20·3×13·8 cm.   Madrid,
Prado (310)   SC.347, LR.76

Group of drawings representing
prisoners and tortured men,
victims of the cruel repression
ordered by Ferdinand VII against
the liberals between 1814
and 1820.   [1329-1345]

Group of drawings of prisoners
for whom the hour of liberation
is approaching.   [1346-1349]

Then a burst of joy as liberty is
regained. Probable allusion to the
revolt of Riego, 1 January 1820.
[1350-1353]

285

1329   C.93?

Por casarse con quien quiso
Indian ink and sepia wash
20·5×14 cm.   Madrid,
Prado (342)   SC.361, LR.113   *

1330   C.*94* (*85*)

*Por descubrir el mobimiento / de
la tierra*   Sepia wash
20·6×14·2 cm.   Madrid, Prado
(333)   SC.327, LR.77   p.237 *

1331   C.*95* (*86*)

No lo saben todos (Not everyone
knows it)   Indian ink and sepia
wash   Madrid, Prado (338)
SC.348, LR.78

1332   C.*96* (*87*)

No haber escrito para tontos
Indian ink and sepia wash
20·6×14 cm.   Madrid, Prado
(343)   SC.374, LR.79   *

1333   C.97?

Te comforma?
(Are you persuaded?)
Indian ink and sepia wash
Madrid, Prado (344)   SC.328

1334   C.*98*

P.r Liberal? (For being a liberal?)
Sepia wash 20·6×14·2 cm.
Madrid, Prado (335)
SC.349, LR.80   *

1335   C.*99*

Cayó en la trampa (He fell into
the trap)   Sepia wash
20·6×14.2 cm.   Madrid,
Prado (332)   SC.362, LR.81

1336   C.*100*

No comas celebre Torregiano
(Don't eat, great Torrigiano)
Indian and sepia wash   Madrid,
Prado (339)   SC.363, LR.82   *

1337   C.*101*

No se puede mirar (One can't
look)   Indian ink and sepia wash
20·5×14.2 cm.   Madrid,
Prado (336)   SC.331, LR.83

1338   C.*102*

Pocas óras te faltan (You've
only a few hours left)   Sepia
wash with Indian ink   Madrid,
Prado (352)   SC.364, LR.84

1339   C.*103*

Mejor es morir (It's better to die)
Indian ink and sepia wash
Madrid, Prado (341)
SC.365, LR.85

1340   C.*104*

*Muchas Viudas an llorado como
tu.*   Sepia wash and Indian ink
Madrid, Prado (254)
SC.359, LR.86   Ill. p. 239   *

1341   C.*105*

Quien lo puede pensar (Who
can think of it!)   Sepia wash and
Indian ink   Madrid, Prado (353)
SC.366, LR.87   Ill. p. 239

1342   C.*106*

No habras los ójos (Don't open
your eyes)   Indian ink and sepia
wash 20·5×14·2 cm.   Madrid,
Prado (337)   SC.367, LR.88

1343   C.*107*

El tiempo hablará (Time will tell)
Indian ink and sepia wash
Madrid, Prado (340)
SC.368, LR.89

1344   C.*108*

Que crueldad (What cruelty)
Sepia wash 20·5×14·2 cm.
Madrid, Prado (334)
SC.369, LR.90

1345   C.*109*

Zapata / Tu gloria será eterna
Indian ink and sepia wash
20·4×14·1 cm.   Madrid,
Prado (351)   SC.370, LR.91   *

1346   C.*111*

No te aflijas (Don't grieve)
Indian ink and sepia wash
20·6×14·5 cm.   Madrid,
Prado (349)   SC.371, LR.92

1347   C.*112*

Dispierta ynocente (Wake up,
innocent)   Indian ink and sepia
wash 20·5×14·5 cm.   Madrid,
Prado (350)   SC.378, LR.93

1348   C.*113*

Ya vas á salir de penas
Sepia wash with Indian ink
Madrid, Prado (354)
SC.373, LR.94   *

49 C.*114*

onto seras libre (You will soon free)   Sepia wash with Indian .372, LR.95   Madrid, Prado (355)

1350   C.*115*

Divina Libertad (Divine Liberty) Indian ink and sepia wash 20·6×14·4 cm.   Madrid, Prado (346)   SC.377, LR.96   p. 301   *

1351   C.116?

Dure la alegria   (May their joy last)   Indian ink and sepia wash Madrid, Prado (356)   SC.322   *

1352   C.*117*

LUX EX TENEBRIS Indian ink and sepia wash 20×13·8 cm.   Madrid, Prado (347)   SC.379, LR.97   *

1353   C.*118*

The light of Justice Indian ink wash 20·5×14·2 cm. Madrid, Prado (345) SC.381, LR.98   Ill. p. 302

---

ti-clerical drawings showing onks and nuns taking off their bits. Allusion to the seculari-ion laws of the liberal period 20-1823

354-1367]   *

1354   C.*119*

Ya hace mucho tiempo q.ᵉ som.ˢ conoci-ᵈᵒˢ   Indian ink and sepia wash   Madrid, Prado (358)   SC.306, LR.99   *

1355   C.*120*(?)

No sabras / lo q.ᵉ llebas a / quest / as?   Indian ink and sepia wash Madrid, Prado (361) SC.311, LR.107   *

1356   C.*121*

Busca un medico (She's looking for a doctor)   Indian ink and sepia wash   Madrid, Prado (363) SC.312, LR.100

1357   C.*122*

Divina Razon / No deges ninguno Indian ink and sepia wash 20·5×14·3 cm.   Madrid, Prado (409)   SC.380, LR.101   *

58   C.*123*

ue quiere este fantasmon? pia wash 21·6×16 cm. adrid, Prado (357) .320, LR.102   Ill. p. 302   *

1359   C.*124*

¿Qᵉ trabajo es ese? (What sort of work is that?)   Indian ink and sepia wash   Madrid, Prado (359)   SC.307, LR.103

1360   C.*125*

¿Cuantas baras? (How many yards?)   Indian ink and sepia wash   Madrid, Prado (362) SC.305, LR.104

1361   C.*126*

Sin camisa, son felices (Shirtless and happy)   Indian ink and sepia wash   Madrid, Prado (360) SC.304, LR.105

1362   C.*127*

Se desnuda p.ᵃ siempre Indian ink and sepia wash 20·6×14·2 cm.   Madrid, Prado (371)   SC.317, LR.106   *

63   C.*128*

ene prisa de ecapar [sic] (She's a hurry to escape)   Indian wash 20·2×14·2 cm.   New rk, Hispanic Soc. (A.3318)   *

1364   C.*129*

Tambien lo dejan estas (These also take it off)   Indian and sepia wash 20·5×14·4 cm.   Madrid, Prado (374)   SC.316, LR.108

1365   C.*130*

Lo cuelga ravioso (He hangs it up in a rage)   Indian ink and sepia wash 20·5×14·4 cm.   Madrid, Prado (372)   SC.318, LR.109

1366   C.*131*

Esta lo deja pensativa Indian ink and sepia wash 20·6×14·2 cm.   Madrid, Prado (373)   SC.319, LR.110

1367   C.*133*

Todo lo desprecia (She despises everything)   Indian ink and sepia wash 20·4×14 cm.   Madrid, Prado (418)   SC.309, LR.111   *

ALBUM D   c.1801-1803

The smallest of all the albums, it was perhaps abandoned by Goya in favour of album E which has better proportions and is also drawn with the brush and Indian ink. Highest page number: 22. Seventeen drawings are known. Maximum known sheet size: 23·5×14·5 cm.
Indian ink wash. Inscriptions in black chalk beneath the drawings; autograph numbers at the top of the sheets in the centre.

Abbreviations and signs, see p. 281

[1368-1384]   *

1368   D.2

Suben alegres (They rise up joyfully)   Indian ink wash 23·5×14·2 cm.
Paris, Louvre (29772)   *

1369   D.3

Cantar y bailar (Song and dance) Indian ink wash 23·5×14·5 cm. London, Count Seilern   *

1370   D.4

regozijo (mirth)   Indian ink wash 23·7×14·7 cm.
New York, Hispanic Soc. (A.3308) Ill. p. 231   *

1371   D.7

De esto nada se sabe (Nothing is known of this)   Indian ink wash 23·7×14·6 cm.   New Yo M.M.A. (35.103.24)   W.XIX

1372   D.11

Locura (Madness)   Indian ink wash 22·5×14 cm.   New York, Mr and Mrs E. V. Thaw   *

1373   D.13

Dispierta dando patadas (He wakes up kicking)   Indian ink wash 23·6×14·6 cm.   New York, M.M.A. (35.103.26)   W.XX

1374   D.15

Sueño de buena echizera (Dream of a good witch)   Indian ink wash 23·4×14·4 cm.   Berlin-Dahlem, K.K. (4396)   Ill. p. 231

1375   D.18

Que disparate, pensar/aun en matrimonio (What folly, . . .) Indian ink wash 23·4×14·4 cm. Paris, Louvre (6913)   *

1376   D.20

Pesadilla (Nightmare)
Indian ink wash 23·3×14·4 cm. New York, M.M.A. (19.27)   *

1377   D.22

La madre Celestina (Old mother Celestina)
Indian ink wash 23·3×14·5 cm. Boston, M.F.A. (59.200)

Drawings without numbers

Seven drawings which may fill some of the twelve gaps among the numbered pages.

[1378-1384]

1378   D.[a]

Sueño de azotes (Dream of a spanking)
Indian ink wash 23·3×14·2 cm. Chicago, A.I. (1961.785)

1379   D.[b]

Mala muger (Wicked woman) Indian ink wash 21·5×14·3 cm. Paris, Louvre (6910)

1380   D.[c]

Yo oygo los ronquidos (I can hear the snores) Indian ink wash 23·3×14·5 cm. Berlin-Dahlem, K.K. (4394)

1381   D.[d]

Estropeada codiciosa (Worn out with greed) Indian ink wash 21×14·5 cm. Madrid B.N. (B.1255)

1382   D.[e]

Tan bien riñen las viejas (The old women also fight) Indian ink wash 15·3×12·4 cm. Madrid B.N. (B.1256)   *

1383   D.[f]

No se lebantara, q.ᵉ no aca[be]/ sus debociones Indian ink wash 15·1×11·9 cm. Madrid B.N. (B.1257)   *

1384   D.[g]

Unholy union
Indian ink wash 17·6×12·7 cm. New York, Lehman Coll.

ALBUM E c.1806-1812

Album originally containing over
fifty drawings, which includes
some of Goya's finest and
most 'classic' designs.
Highest page number: 52. Forty
drawings and five sketches are
known. Maximum size of the
sheets: 27×19 cm. Drawn
with the brush and Indian ink,
with extensive use of scraping, to
alter the composition or to
produce a distinctive, rough-
textured effect.
The drawings have a ruled border
(single or double lines) drawn
round them in Indian ink, whence
the appellation 'black border
series', first coined by Wehle.
Titles are in pencil, usually below
the border; Goya's autograph

numbers, in sepia pen and ink,
are at the top of the sheet in the
centre. The series is now
widely dispersed throughout
the world.

Abbreviations and signs, see p. 281

[1385-1430]   *

1385   E.2

. . .con su . . .
(Title cut and illegible)
Indian ink wash 24×17·7 cm.
Rotterdam, Boymans Mus. (S.3) *

1386   E.6

Quejate del tiempo
(Complain about the weather)
Indian ink wash 21×15 cm.
Paris, priv. coll.   *

1387   E.8

No llenas tanto la cesta
(Don't fill the basket so full)
Indian ink wash 20×13·5 cm.
Paris, priv. coll.   *

1388   E?11

Esta pobre aprobecha el tiempo
(This poor woman . . .)
Indian ink wash 25·4×17·7 cm.
New York, priv. coll.   *

1389   E.13

No es siempre bueno el rigor
Indian ink wash 26·4×17·8 cm.
Madrid, heirs of Marqués de
Valdeterrazo   *

1390   E.15?

*Mucho sabes, y aun aprendes //
Tuto he/mestier*
Indian ink wash 26·4×18 cm.
Boston M.F.A. (58.359)   *

1391   E.16

Despreciar los ynsultos
(Contemptuous of the insults)
Indian ink wash 26·5×18·5 cm.
France, priv. coll.   III. p. 232 *

1392   E.19

No sabe lo q.e hace (He doesn't
know what he's doing)   Indian
ink wash 26·9×17·9 cm.   Berlin-
Dahlem K.K. (4391)   p. 233

1393   E.20

Pesadilla, (Nightmare)
Indian ink wash 26·4×17·1 cm.
New York, Pierpont Morgan
Library (1959.13)

1394   E.21

No se descuida el Borrico
(The donkey looks out for himself)
Indian ink wash 25·7×18·2 cm.
Madrid, B.N. (B.1254)

1395   E.22

*Esta Muger fue retratada en
Napoles por/Jose Ribera . . .*
Indian ink wash 26×17·8 cm.
U.S.A., priv. coll.   *

1396   E.23

Mother showing her deformed
child to two women
Indian ink wash 26·6×18·5 cm.
Paris, Louvre (6911)

1397   E.24

Despues lo beras (You'll see later)
Indian ink wash 26·7×18·7 cm.
New York M.M.A. (35.103.18)
W.XVII

1398   E.28

Pobre e gnuda bai filosofia / Pet
(poverty and bare-foot goes
philosophy . . .)   Indian ink wash
25×18·4 cm. Paris, priv. coll.   *

1399   E.30

Cuydado con ese paso
(Be careful with that step)
Indian ink wash 26·3×18·2 cm.
Chicago, A.I. (1958.42)

1400   verso of 1399

Sketch of girl dancing
Indian ink wash
See [1399]   *

1401   E.32

Son colericos (They are angry)
Indian ink wash 27×19 cm.
Basle, priv. coll.   III. p. 232 *

1402   E.33

La resignacion (Resignation)
Indian ink wash 25·5×18 cm.
Boston, M.F.A. (69.68)   *

1403   E.*35*

He doesn't wake up
Indian ink wash 25·4×17·7 cm.
New York, priv. coll.   *

1404   E.*36*

¿Quien bencera? no visible
Indian ink wash 25·8×18·4 cm.
Madrid, heirs of Marqués de
Valdeterrazo   *

1405   verso of 1404

Sketch for E.36
Indian ink wash
See [1404]

1406   E.*37*

Hutiles trabajos (Useful work)
Indian ink wash 26·3×18·6 cm.
Paris, priv. coll.   Ill. p. 21   *

1407   E.*38?*

¿Valentias? Quenta con los años
(Showing off?. . .)
Indian ink wash 26·1×18·5 cm.
Berlin-Dahlem, K.K. (4395)   *

1408   E.*39*

No haras nada con clamar (You
won't get anywhere by shouting)
Indian ink wash 26·5×18·1 cm.
Cambridge (Mass.), Philip Hofer *

1409   E.*40*

Dejalo todo a la probidencia
(Leave it all to providence)
Indian ink wash 26×18 cm.
U.S.A., priv. coll.   *

1410   E.*41*

*Dios nos libre de tan amargo
lance*   Indian ink wash
26·7×18·7 cm.   New York,
M.M.A. (35.103.50)   W.XVIII   *

1411   E.*43*

Penitencia (Penitence)
Indian ink wash 26×18·5 cm.
Paris, priv. coll.   *

1412   E.*48*

Piensalo bien (Think it over well)
Indian ink wash 26·5×18·6 cm.
Paris, priv. coll.

1413   verso of 1412

Sketch of a young nun
Indian ink wash
See [1412]

1414   E.*49*

Lo yerras, si te bue[l]bes á casar
Indian ink wash 26·7×18·1 cm.
Cambridge (Mass.), Fogg Art
Mus. (1949.7)   *

1415   E.*50*

Muy acordes (Perfect harmony)
Indian ink wash 26·2×18·5 cm.
New York, Mr and Mrs E. V.
Thaw   *

Eight black border drawings
(with two verso sketches) have
cut or illegible numbers.
Two further drawings do not
have a border, and three more
are tentatively included in this
album.

[1416-1430]

1416   E.[a]

Aprende á ver (He is learning
to see)   Indian ink wash
26·5×18·1 cm.
Berlin-Dahlem, K.K. (4393)

1417   E.[b]

El trabajo siempre premia.
Indian ink wash 24·2×17 cm.
Cambridge (Mass.), Fogg
Mus. (1943.550)   *

1418   verso of 1417

Sketch of girl dancing
Indian ink wash   See [1417]   *

1419   E.[c]

Cuidado con los consejos
(Beware of the advice)
Indian ink wash 25·4×17·1 cm.
Washington, Phillips Coll.

1420   E.[d]

Trabajos de la guerra (Hardships
of the war)   Indian ink wash
24×17 cm.   Paris, Baronne
de Gunzburg   Ill. p. 232   *

1421   E.[e]

El ciego trabajador
(The industrious blind man)|
Indian ink wash 23·8×17·1 cm.
Vienna, Albertina (45410)

1422   E.[f]

culpa es tuya
(...'s all your fault)
...dian ink wash 24·7×17·6 cm.
...ris, priv. coll.   *

1423   E.[g]

Artemisia (Artemis)
Indian ink wash
Collection unknown   *

1424   E.[h]

La novicia (The novice)
Indian ink wash 26·4×17·9 cm.
Fondation Custodia - Paris,
Inst. Néerlandais   *

1425   verso of 1424

Sketch of a nun
Indian ink wash
See [1424]   *

1426   E.[i]

Two women embracing
Indian ink wash 21·8×15·2 cm.
Bayonne, Mus. Bonnat (1415)   *

1427   E.[j]

...ained prisoner
...dian ink wash 21·8×15·1 cm.
...yonne, Mus. Bonnat (1416)   *

1428   E.[k]

Those who avoid work end up
like this
Indian ink wash 26·5×17 cm.
Collection unknown   *

1429   E.[l]

No reproduction is known

Lo mismo (The same)
Indian ink wash 26×18 cm.
Formerly Paris, A. Beurdeley   *

1430   E.?

La pescadera (The fish-wife)
Indian ink wash 23×15·5 cm.
Biarritz, J. Ballestero   *

ALBUM F   c.1812-1823

...umerically the most important
...er album C. The highest page
...mber: 106. Eighty-eight
...awings are known. Maximum
...own sheet size: 21×15 cm.
...pia wash. No titles (except in
...ree isolated and doubtful
...ses). Numbers are written with
...e brush in the top right corner.
...ey are frequently cut and where
...fficult to read are followed by a
...estion mark.
...ose connection between some
... the drawings in this album and
...e *Disasters of War*.

...breviations and signs, see p. 281

...431-1518]   *

1431   F.*1*

Dead from hunger
Sepia wash
Madrid, Prado (303)   SC.350   *

1432   F.*2*

In Turkey(?)
Sepia wash 18·7×13·3 cm.
Madrid, Prado (293)   SC.289

1433   F.5?

Death of a saint(?)
Sepia wash
Madrid, Prado (324)   SC.353

1434   F.6?

Women in church
Sepia wash 17·8×14·6 cm.
Madrid, B.N. (B.1259)   *

1435   F.7

...eet performers
...pia wash 18·7×13·3 cm.
...drid, Prado (294)   SC.290

1436   F.8?

People sheltering in a cave
Sepia wash
Madrid, Prado (326)   SC.354

1437   F.*9*

Two figures beside a rock
Sepia wash
Madrid, Prado (327)   SC.351

Group of six drawings showing
different duelling scenes. One of
the drawings was used for a
lithograph made in 1819 [IV.1644].

[1438-1443]

1438   F.*10*

Duel with shields
Sepia wash 19·2×13·5 cm.
Madrid, Prado (284)   SC.277

1439   F.11

'En garde'
Sepia wash 19×13·5 cm.
Madrid, Prado (285)   SC.278

1440   F.12

Sword-thrust
Sepia wash 19·2×13·5 cm.
Madrid, Prado (286)   SC.274   ∗

1441   F.13

Victory without witnesses
Sepia wash 19×13·3 cm.
Madrid, Prado (295)   SC.291
Ill. p. 234

1442   F.14

Gentlemen duelling in hats
Sepia wash 19·2×13·5 cm.
Madrid, Prado (287)   SC.275

1443   F.15

Duelling with knives
Sepia wash 19·2×13·5 cm.
Madrid, Prado (288)   SC.276

1444   F.16

El pelado/de Ybides
(The native of Ybides stripped)
Sepia wash 19×13·5 cm.
Madrid, Prado (296)   SC.279   ∗

1445   F.17

To market(?)
Sepia wash
Madrid, Prado (291)   SC.280   ∗

1446   F.18

Conjugal row
Sepia wash 20·8×14·6 cm.
Madrid, Prado (255)   SC.297

1447   F.19

A fine pair
Sepia wash 20·5×14·4 cm.
Madrid, Prado (256)   SC.352

1448   F.20 (?)

In the choir
Sepia wash 18·5×14·4 cm.
Madrid, Prado (317)   SC.314

1449   F.21

Protection
Sepia wash
Madrid, Prado (257)   SC.281   ∗

1450   F.22

Poverty
Sepia wash 20·5×14·6 cm.
Madrid, Prado (258)   SC.282   ∗

1451   F.23

Help
Sepia wash 20·9×14·6 cm.
Madrid, Prado (259)   SC.283   ∗

1452   F.25?

Group of women
Sepia wash 18·5×14·7 cm.
Madrid, B.N. (B.1258)

1453   F.27

Scene of exorcism
Sepia wash 20·2×14·4 cm.
Madrid, Prado (316)   SC.313

1454   F.28?

The visit to the hermit
Sepia wash 18·3×13·5 cm.
Madrid, Prado (315)   SC.285

1455   F.29?

Anglers   Inscr.
Sepia wash 19·7×13·7 cm.
New York, Frick Coll. (A.412)   ∗

1456   F.30

The skaters
Sepia wash 20·5×14·3 cm.
Boston, M.F.A. (61.166)

1457   F.31

Crowd in a park
Sepia wash 20·6×14·3 cm.
New York, M.M.A. (35.103.19)
W.XXI

1458   F.32(?)

Nude woman beside a brook
Sepia wash 20·6×14·3 cm.
New York, M.M.A. (35.103.25)
W.XXIV

1459   F.33

Monks in an interior
Sepia wash 20·5×14·3 cm.
New York, M.M.A. (35.103.20)
W.XXII

1460   F.34?

Monks reading
Sepia wash 20·2×14·1 cm.
Dresden, K.K. (C.1910.56)

1461   F.36

Man and woman on a mule
Sepia wash 20·5×14·3 cm.
New York, M.M.A. (35.103.21)
W.XXIII

1462   F.37

Monk on a mule beaten by a man
Sepia wash   Madrid, heirs of
Marqués de Valdeterrazo   *

1463   F.38

*Este caso sucedió en Aragon
sien/do yo muchacho,...*
Sepia wash 21·5×14 cm.
New York, priv. coll.   *

1464   F.39

Dogs chasing a cat on a man
on a donkey
Sepia wash 20×14 cm.
Merion (Pa.), Barnes Foundation

1465   F.40(?)

Hunting lice
Sepia wash 20·5×14·6 cm.
New York, M.M.A. (35.103.27)
W.XXV

1466   F.41

Interior of a church
Sepia wash 20·5×14·3 cm.
New York, M.M.A. (35.103.28)
W.XXVI

1467   F.42

A crowd in a circle
Sepia wash 20·6×14·3 cm.
New York, M.M.A. (35.103.29)
W.XXVII

1468   F.43(?)

Three people round a dying man
Sepia wash 20·5×14·5 cm.
Paris, priv. coll.   *

1469   F.44

Procession of monks
Sepia wash 20·4×13·8 cm.
Berlin-Dahlem, K.K. (4292)

1470   F.45

Truth beset by dark spirits
Sepia wash 20·5×14·3 cm.
New York, M.M.A. (35.103.30)
W.XXVIII   *

1471   F.46

Construction in progress
Sepia wash 20·5×14·3 cm.
New York, M.M.A. (35.103.31)
W.XXIX

1472   F.51

Three men digging
Sepia wash 20·6×14·3 cm.
New York, M.M.A. (35.103.32)
W.XXX   III. p. 244   *

1473   F.52?

Three men carrying a wounded
man
Sepia wash 20·5×14·5 cm.
Chicago, A.I. (1960.313)

1474   F.53

The stabbing
Sepia wash 20·5×14·3 cm.
New York, M.M.A. (35.103.33)
W.XXXI

1475   F.54

Don Quixote
Sepia wash 20·7×14·4 cm.
London, B.M. (1862.7.12.188)   *

1476   F.55

Woman kneeling before an old man
Sepia wash 20·5×14·3 cm.
New York, M.M.A. (35.103.34)
W.XXXII

1477   F.56

Torture of a man
Sepia wash 20·5×14·3 cm.
New York, Hispanic Soc. (A.3312)
III. p. 303   *

1478   F.57(?)

Naked savage about to cudgel
another
Sepia wash 20·7×14·1 cm.
Oxford, Ashmolean Mus.   *

293

1479   F.58

Man holding back a horse
Sepia wash 19·7×13·3 cm.
New York, John D. Herring   ∗

1480   F.59

Woman whispering to a priest
Sepia wash 20·5×14·3 cm.
New York, M.M.A. (35.103.35)
W.XXXIII

1481   F.60

Two men with bundles
Sepia wash 21×15 cm.
Paris, priv. coll.   ∗

1482   F.61

Cavalier helping a woman to
climb steps
Sepia wash 20·8×14·2 cm.
Paris, priv. coll.   III. p 235   ∗

1483   F.62?

Jacob and his sons with the
bloody tunic(?)   Inscr.
Sepia(?) wash   Formerly
Berlin, Gerstenberg - destr.   ∗

1484   F.63

Man drinking from a wine skin
Sepia wash 20·5×14·3 cm.
New York, M.M.A. (35.103.36)
W.XXXIV

1485   F.64

Glutton eating by himself
Sepia wash 20·3×14·9 cm.
Williamstown, Clark Art
Inst. (64.01)   ∗

1486   F.65

Nun frightened by a ghost
Sepia wash 20·5×14·5 cm.
New York, M.M.A. (35.103.37)
W.XXXV

1487   F.67

Acrobats
Sepia wash 20·5×14·6 cm.
New York, M.M.A. (35.103.38)
W.XXXVI

1488   F.69

Beggar holding a stick in his
right hand   Sepia wash
20·5×14·3 cm.   New York,
M.M.A. (35.103.39)   W.XXXV

1489   F.70

Beggar holding a stick in his
left hand   Sepia wash
20·5×14·3 cm.   New York,
M.M.A. (35.103.40)   W.XXXVIII

1490   F.71

Waking from sleep in the open
Sepia wash 20·5×14·6 cm.
New York, M.M.A. (35.103.41)
W.XXXIX

1491   F.72

Peasant carrying a woman
Sepia wash 20·5×14·3 cm.
New York, Hispanic Soc. (A.3315)
III. p. 236   ∗

1492   F.73

Two men fighting
Sepia wash
Formerly Rome, Clementi   ∗

1493   F.74

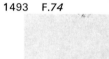

Woman spanking another with
shoe   Sepia wash 20·5×14·1
Rotterdam, Mus. Boymans (S.1

1494   F.75

Old people singing and dancing
Sepia wash 20×14 cm.
Merion (Pa.), Barnes Foundation

1495   F.76

Group with dishevelled woman
Sepia wash 20·6×14·5 cm.
New York, M.M.A. (35.103.42)
W.XL

1496   F.78

Women with children by a
wayside Cross   Sepia wash
20·5×14·3 cm   New York,
M.M.A. (35.103.43)   W.XLI

1497   F.79

Beggars in front of a door
Sepia wash 20·4×14·1 cm.
Berlin-Dahlem, K.K. (4397)   ∗

1498   F.80

Two prisoners in irons
Sepia wash 20·6×14·3 cm.
New York, M.M.A. (35.103.44)
W.XLII

99 F.81

nstable dragging a person
the arm
pia wash 20·5×14 cm.
ris, priv. coll.   *

1500 F.82

Man interfering in a street fight
Sepia wash 20·5×14·3 cm.
New York, M.M.A. (35.103.45)
W.XLIII   *

1501 F.83

Savages in a cave
Sepia wash 20·5×14 cm.
Paris, priv. coll.   *

1502 F.86(?)

Muerte del Alguacil Lampiños,...
Revenge upon a constable   Sepia
wash 20·5×14·5 cm.   New York,
M.M.A. (35.103.49)   W.XLIX *

1503 F.87

Woman murdering a sleeping man
Sepia wash 20·5×14·3 cm.
New York, M.M.A. (35.103.46)
W.XLIV

·04 F.88

e tambourine player
epia wash 20·5×14 cm.
ris, priv. coll.   *

1505 F.89

Provincial danse
Sepia wash 20·6×14·3 cm.
New York, M.M.A. (35.103.47)
W.XLV

1506 F.91

Woman and two men with a cart
Sepia wash 20·4×14·2 cm.
Berlin-Dahlem, K.K. (4398)

1507 F.92

Man with an enormous bundle
Sepia wash 20·5×14 cm.
Paris, priv. coll.   *

1508 F.93

Woman handing a mug to an old
man   Sepia wash 20·6×14·3 cm.
New York, M.M.A. (35.103.48)
W.XLVI

·09 F.94

e widow
epia wash 20·5×14·5 cm.
ris, priv. coll.   *

The last nine known drawings in
this album are devoted to the
hunt, Goya's favourite sport,
which had been the subject of his
first tapestry cartoons [I.57-69].

[1510-1518]

1510 F.97

Hunter shooting birds
Sepia wash 20·4×14 cm.
Rotterdam, Mus. Boymans (S.16)
                           *

1511 F.98

Hunter raising his gun
Sepia wash 20·6×14·6 cm.
Cambridge (Mass.), Fogg Art
Mus. (1954.30)

1512 F.99

Hunter loading his gun
Sepia wash 20·5×14·2 cm.
Paris, priv. coll.   III. p. 241 *

·13 F.100

unter and his dog on the alert
epia wash 20·5×14·5 cm.
ilan, priv. coll.   III. p. 241 *

1514 F.102?

Hunter with his dog running
Sepia wash 20·5×14·2 cm.
Paris, priv. coll.   III. p. 241

1515 F.103

Rabbit hunter with retriever
Sepia wash 20·6×14·6 cm.
New York, M.M.A. (35.103.22)
W.XLVII   III. p. 241

1516 F.104

Hunter loading his gun
Sepia wash 20·6×14·5 cm.
Formerly Rome, Clementi *

1517 F.105

Bird hunters with decoy
Sepia wash 20·5×14·3 cm.
New York, M.M.A. (35.103.23)
W.XLVIII

1518   F.*106*

Hunter in ambush
Sepia wash 20×14·3 cm.
New York, Paul Rosenberg and Co.
*

VARIOUS DRAWINGS
c.1810-1820

A group of drawings, most of
which show some relationship in
style or subject-matter with the
drawings in the albums or with
engravings and their preparatory
drawings in this section.
Many of the drawings, and others
of which no reproduction is
known, were included in the
Madrid exhibition of 1922. They
are indicated with the abbreviation
Bx (= Boix, Bibl. 9) and the
titles and dimensions given in the
exhibition catalogue are used.

[1519-1532]

1519

Three moors carrying off a woman
c.1810-20.   s. *Goya*
Indian ink wash 24×19 cm.
Paris, priv. coll.
*

1520

Before the Sultan   c.1810-15.
Black chalk
Madrid, Prado (413)   SC.421   *

1521a

Cronies reading   c.1810-20.
Sepia wash 15×9·2 cm.
Formerly Madrid, Marqués de
Casa Torres   Bx.192B   *

1521b

Pasiega (Pás valley dweller?)
c.1810-20.   Sepia wash
14·7×9·2 cm.   Formerly Madrid,
Marqués Casa Torres   Bx.192E   *

1521c

Shepherd   c.1810-20.
Sepia wash 14·7×9·3 cm.
Formerly Madrid, Marqués de Casa
Torres   Bx.192F   *

1521d

Dancing couple   c.1810-20.
Sepia wash 14·8×9·2 cm.
Formerly Madrid, Marqués de Casa
Torres   Bx.192G

1521e

The sawyers   c.1810-20.
Sepia wash 15×9·2 cm.
Formerly Madrid, Marqués de
Casa Torres   Bx.192C   *

1522

Witches' coven   c.1810-20.
Sepia wash
Madrid, Prado (113)   SC.214

1523

Nun at prayer   c.1810-20.
Indian ink wash 15·3×9·1 cm.
Madrid, Fund. Lázaro (M.I-4048)
Bx.201   *

1524

Old woman at prayer   c.1810-20.
Indian ink wash 15·3×9·8 cm.
Madrid, Fund. Lázaro (M.I-4049)
Bx.200   *

1525

Vinculos indisolubles   c.1810-20.
Black chalk and Indian ink wash
18·8×15·8 cm.
Madrid, B.N. (B.1253)   *

1526   recto of 1527

Woman weeping over a dying man
c.1810-20.
Indian ink wash 16×23 cm.
Madrid, B.N. (B.1260 r.)   *

1527   verso of 1526

Group of figures
Indian ink wash   See [1526]
B.N. (B.1260 v.)

1528

Ragged figures by a barred arch
c.1810-20.   Indian ink wash
Formerly Berlin, Gerstenberg -
destr.   *

1529

Celestina and maja   c.1810-20.
Indian ink wash, heightened
white 22·4×15 cm.   Madrid,
Marqués de la Scala   Bx.196   *

1530

Interior of a prison
s.d. *Por Goya. 1819.*   Black and
white chalk, black card 16×20 cm.
Madrid, Prado (408)   SC.448   *

1531

Monk   c.1810-20.
Brush and wash   Formerly
Berlin, Gerstenberg - destr.   *

1532

Two elephants   c.1815-19.
Pen and sepia ink 20·5×30 cm.
Madrid, Prado (420)   SC.453

HE ROYAL COMPANY
F THE PHILIPPINES c.1815

his enormous painting shows a
eeting of the Company presided
y Ferdinand VII, but its subject
now of little significance. It
above all remarkable for Goya's
nagic of the atmosphere'
vhich here attains an intensity
omparable with the greatest
vorks of Rembrandt.
t the high table the king is
urrounded by the directors of
f the Company, and the
hareholders, in an astonishing
ariety of pose, are ranged on
ther side of the room. The scene
the gloomy chamber recalls the
nquisition Scene [966] of
erhaps almost the same date.

1534

1535

Session of the Company of the
Philippines c.1815. 327×417 cm.
Castres, Mus. Goya (49)
M.84, DF.246, G.666 p. 224 *

Sketch for [1534].
54×70 cm. Berlin-Dahlem,
Staatliche Mus. (1619)
M.85, DF.245, G.665

PORTRAITS 1814-1819

With the restoration of Ferdinand,
Goya turned again to portraiture
and the year 1815 is remarkable
for a series of masterpieces
including the great self-portrait in
the Royal Academy of San
Fernando [1551]. The use of a
black ground gives many of them
a new depth and intensity.
None of the portraits of Ferdinand
was commissioned by the king
who had only posed for Goya
very briefly in 1808.
The studies made at that time
had to serve for all the other
portraits commissioned by loyal
town councils and corporations.

[1536-1566] *

1536

Ferdinand VII June-July 1814.
Inscr. 103×82 cm.
Pamplona, Diputación Foral
M.164, DF.479, G.629 *

537

erdinand VII 1814?
ormerly Madrid, Duque de
amames *

1538

Ferdinand VII Oct.-Dec. 1814.
225·5×124·5 cm.
Santander, Mus. G.630 *

1539

Ferdinand VII in an encampment
1814. s. *Goya* 207×140 cm.
Madrid, Prado (724)
M.159, DF.502, G.631 *

1540

Ferdinand VII with royal mantle
1814. 212×146 cm.
Madrid, Prado (735)
M.161, DF.480, G.632 p. 222 *

1541

Ferdinand VII with royal mantle
Sept. 1814-July 1815. s. *Goya*
280×125 cm. Saragossa, Mus.
(172) M.162, DF.481, G.633 *

542

uque de San Carlos s.d. *1815*
vith inscr. 280×125 cm.
aragossa, Mus. (168)
1.413, DF.490, G.635 *

1543

Study for [1542].
Panel 59×43 cm.
Madrid, Condesa de Villagonzalo
M.415, DF.488, G.634

1544

Reduction of [1542].
77×60 cm.
Madrid, Marquesa de Santa Cruz
M.414, DF.489, G.636

1545

José Luis Munárriz s.d. *1815*
with inscr. 85×64 cm.
Madrid, R.A. San Fernando (680)
M.362, DF.507, G.644 p.226 *

1546

Miguel de Lardizábal s.d. *1815*
with inscr. 86×65 cm.
Prague, N.G. (01577)
M.471, DF.494, G.643 p. 226 *

547

nacio Omulryan s.d. *1815*
vith inscr. 83·8×64·8 cm.
ansas City, Nelson Gall.-Atkins
lus. (30.22) M.364, G.641 *

1548

Miguel Fernández Flores s.d.
1815 with inscr. 100·3×84·1 cm.
Worcester (Mass.), Mus.(1911.25)
M.258, DF.450, G.642 *

1549

Manuel Quijano s.d. *1815*
with inscr. 85×58·5 cm.
Barcelona, Mus. (Cambó 34)
G.646 *

1550

Rafael Esteve s.d. *1815* with
inscr. 99·5×74·5 cm.
Valencia, Mus. (584)
M.254, DF.493, G.645 p. 229 *

1551

Self-portrait (age 69) s.d. *Goya*
1815 Panel 51×46 cm.
Madrid, R.A. San Fernando (669)
M.302, DF.492, G.637 p. 205 *

1552

Self-portrait 1815? Inscr.
Fr. Goya / Aragones / Por el mismo
46×35 cm. Madrid, Prado (723)
M.303, DF.500, G.638   *

1553

Mariano Goya c.1815. Inscr.
Panel 59×47 cm.
Madrid, Duque de Alburquerque
M.313, DF.503, G.617   p. 247   *

1554

Francisco del Mazo c.1815.
Inscr. 90×71 cm.
Castres, Mus. Goya (50)
M.344, G.573   *

1555

Friar Juan Fernández de Rojas
c.1815. 75×54 cm.
Madrid, R.A. de la Historia
M.408, DF.465, G.640   *

1556

Franciscan monk c.1810-15.
82×68 cm. Formerly Berlin,
Kaiser Friedrich Mus. (16.19.B) -
destr. 1945 M.470, G.537   *

1557

Xth Duque de Osuna [s.d.] 1816.
202×140 cm.
Bayonne, Mus. Bonnat (10)
M.370, DF.497, G.649   *

1558

Sketch for [1557].
Panel 32·5×24·5 cm.
Formerly Bremen, Kunsthalle -
destr. M.371, DF.497n., G.648   *

1559

Drawing for [1557]. Inscr.
Pen and sepia ink
Madrid, Prado (297)   SC.464   *

1560

Duquesa de Abrantes s.d. *1816*
with inscr. 92×70 cm. Madrid,
Conde del Valle de Orizaba
M.189, DF.498, G.650   *

1561

Juan Antonio Cuervo s.d. *1819*
with inscr. 120·2×87 cm.
Cleveland, Mus. (43.90)
M.248, DF.508, G.691   *

1562   verso of 898

Friar Juan Fernández de Rojas
1817-20. Inscr. Black chalk
23·4×17·7 cm. London, B.M.
(1862.7.12.185 v.)   M.693n.   *

1563

Condesa de Baena(?)
s.d. *Goya 1819.*   92×160 cm.
Zumaya, Zuloaga
M.206, DF.531s, G.692   *

1564

Lady in a black mantilla
c.1815-24. 54×43 cm.
Dublin, N.G. (572)
M.520, DF.524, G.722   *

1565

Rita Luna c.1814-18.
43×35·5 cm.
Fort Worth, Kimbell Foundation
M.331, DF.461, G.656   *

1566

Portrait of a woman
c.1815-24. 61×51 cm.
U.S.A., priv. coll.
M.516, DF.521, G.721   *

RELIGIOUS PAINTINGS 1812-1817

The moving grisaille, discovered
some ten years ago in the Royal
Palace, was Goya's last royal
commission. Not strictly religious,
it was part of a series of semi-
allegorical paintings ordered to
decorate the apartments of the
second wife of Ferdinand VII.
The painting of *Saints Justa and
Rufina* for Seville Cathedral was
commissioned through Goya's
friend Ceán Bermúdez. It caused
a sensation in the town; sonnets
were written in praise of the
painting, and Ceán published
a glowing critique of it.

[1567-1570]

1567

The Assumption of the Virgin
1812? 311×240 cm.
Chinchón, parish church
M.28, DF.74 cit., G. 559   *

1568

Saint Elizabeth tending a sick
woman 1816-17.
Tempera grisaille 169×129 cm.
Madrid, Palacio Real   G.652   *

1569

Saints Justa and Rufina s.d. *1817*
with inscr. 309×177 cm.
Seville, Cathedral sacristy
M.58, DF.99, G.654   *

1570

Sketch for [1569].
Panel 47×29 cm.
Madrid, Prado (2650)
M.59, DF.98, G.653   *

Part four

1819-1824

Dates	Life of Goya	Spanish History	History outside Spain	The Arts	Literature and Science
1820	*Goya and his doctor Arrieta* Goya's last attendance at the session of the Academy to swear allegiance to the Constitution (4 April) *Tiburcio Pérez* Goya begins work on the 'black paintings' (1820-23)	The revolt of Riego (1 January) Ferdinand VII forced to accept the Constitution (9 March)	Assassination of the Duc de Berry Death of George III Accession of George IV	Constable: *Stratford Mill*	Lamartine: *Méditations* Keats: *Tales and Poems* Shelley: *Prometheus Unbound* Engels († 1895)
1821	Goya works on the 'black paintings' and on the *Disparates* prints		Napoleon dies on Saint Helena (aged 52)	Constable: *The Haywain* Weber: *Der Freischütz*	Death of Keats (aged 26) Mariette-Pacha († 1881) W. Scott: *Kenilworth* Flaubert († 1880) Dostoievsky († 1881)
1822		Ferdinand VII prisoner of Spanish liberals (30 June)	Greece declares her independence (13 January) Massacre at Chios (April) Congress of Verona	Delacroix: *The Barque of Dante* Schubert: *Unfinished Symphony* César Franck († 1890)	Champollion deciphers hieroglyphics Stendhal: *On Love* Pushkin: *The Prisoner of the Caucasus* Schliemann († 1890) Pasteur († 1895) E. de Goncourt († 1896)
1823	Goya gives the 'Quinta del Sordo' to his grandson Mariano (17 September) *Ramón Satué*	France sends the 'Cent Mille Fils de Saint Louis' into Spain (7 April) Taking of Trocadero (31 August) Surrender of Cadiz (30 Sept.)	Death of Pius VII Monroe doctrine enunciated	Death of Prud'hon (aged 65) Beethoven: *Ninth Symphony* Schubert: *Rosamunde*	Lamartine: *Nouvelles Méditations* W. Scott: *Quentin Durward* Th. de Banville († 1891) Niepce discovers the principle of photography E. Renan († 1892)
1824	Goya in hiding in the house of José Duaso y Latre (January-April) *José Duaso y Latre* *María Martínez de Puga* Goya asks for six months leave of absence to go to Plombières (2 May) Leaves for France in June			Death of Géricault (aged 33) Puvis de Chavannes († 1898) Smetana († 1884) Delacroix mentions Goya in his *Journal* (19 March)	Vigny: *Eloa* Death of Byron at Missolonghi (19 April)

Chapter I

THE REVOLT OF RIEGO. THE CONSTITUTION
1823: RENEWED REPRESSION AND REIGN OF TERROR

1819-1823. Goya is 73 to 77 years old. Revolt of Riego (January 1820). Ferdinand VII swears allegiance to the Constitution proclaimed by the liberals in Cadiz in 1812. Military action of the Holy Alliance. Abolition of the Constitution and new White Terror. Reign of Ferdinand VII.

On 1 January 1820 the revolt led by Rafael Riego put a temporary stop to the narrow-minded absolutism of Ferdinand VII. The men who had risked their lives to prepare for his return during the Napoleonic occupation, who had proclaimed the Constitution of Cadiz in 1812, who, for the first time in History, had borne the noble name of 'liberals', and whom the *Deseado* had pursued with his hatred for six years, these men were now triumphant and they promised the Spanish people that the shadows of oppression would be chased away and the dazzling light of liberty and justice would radiate at last.

Self-portrait (detail) 1820. See ill. p. 307

Self-portrait Divina Libertad
At the end of the year 1819 Goya fell very seriously ill; he was then seventy-three years old and for some time he seems to have hovered between life and death. Saved by his friend, Doctor Arrieta, he was so grateful for his miraculous return to health that he dedicated to him a picture in which he shows himself lying in his doctor's arms (see p. 307). It is the most moving image he has left of himself; the robust figure of the self-portrait of 1815 (see p. 205) appears here stricken by his sufferings, the penetrating gaze now veiled by the approach of death.

As he regained his health he no doubt learnt with profound joy of the revolt of Riego on 1 January 1820, which forced Ferdinand VII to abide by the Constitution of Cadiz and to relax the tyrannical grip which had been strangling Spain since 1814. He expressed his delight in one of the drawings in album C, where a kneeling figure, poet or writer, salutes 'Divine Liberty'.

Divina Libertad Album C.115 [III.1350] Brush and wash. Prado, Madrid

The light of Justice. Album C.*118* [III.1353] c.1820-23. Indian ink wash 20·5×14·2 cm. Prado Museum, Madrid

Que quiere este fantasmon? (What does this great phantom want?) C.*123* [III.1358] c.1820-23. Sepia wash 21·6×16 cm. Prado, Madrid

In the face of this sudden political reversal, Ferdinand VII took fright and accepted all Riego's demands. On 9 March he finally swore allegiance to the loathed Constitution and made a series of decrees which went even farther than those of Joseph. The Jesuits were again driven out, most of the convents were closed, the property of the Church was secularized and the Inquisition abolished. On 4 April, although he was seventy-four years old and had virtually retired from public life, Goya could not resist the pleasure of making a last attendance at the solemn session of the Academy where he too swore allegiance to the Constitution.

Unhappily for Spain, what could have been the birth of a real constitutional monarchy rapidly foundered in the chaos of civil strife and personal vendettas. Faced with the development of another civil war in the kingdom, Ferdinand VII appealed to the powers of the Holy Alliance who took the advice of Chateaubriand and decided at the Congress of Verona in 1822 to organize a military action in Spain in order to restore absolute monarchy there. This became known as the expedition of the 'Cent Mille Fils de Saint Louis', the political stroke of genius from the author of *Les Martyrs*.

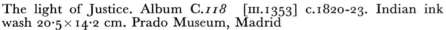

Expedition of the 'Cent Mille Fils de Saint Louis'

The French troops, composed partly of veterans from Napoleon's Grande Armée and commanded by the Duke of Angoulême, marched across Spain in three months, virtually without striking a single blow, from the Pyrenees to Cadiz. Ferdinand was held prisoner

In the drawings of this period, Goya savagely satirized the dark forces which oppressed the people and above all the clergy which lent its support to the worst period of repression which Spain had ever experienced. Justice, Truth and Liberty, which for Goya remained inseparable, appear in his graphic work in symbolic form, as rays of light or as a beautiful young woman whose dazzling purity puts to flight the sinister shapes among which the cassocks and birettas are clearly distinguishable.

In the drawing C.*118* (far left), the only one in the album without a title, the scales of Justice are suspended at the centre of a blaze of light; among the dense crowd over which it sheds its rays some figures are dancing for joy while others, in particular a priest in the foreground, run away in terror.

With an even more violent contrast of light and shade, the drawing C.*123* (left) silhouettes against a dark wash background the ghostly apparition of a monk with arms outstretched and a macabre expression on his face, of whom Goya ironically asks: 'What does this great phantom want?' It is the first image in a group of drawings showing monks and nuns 'defrocking' themselves, which Goya treats with a certain vengeful pleasure [III.1359-1366].

The great hopes born in 1820 were to be short-lived but they led the Spanish liberals to believe that they would never again see re-established in their country the reign of terror and torture which Goya had so often denounced. This drawing (right) shows a wretched victim being subjected to the torture of the strappado which had been illustrated by Callot and Magnasco and was still in current practice in the dungeons of the Inquisition. As in the drawings from album C (see pp. 237, 239) Goya expresses his sense of outrage at these barbarous practices.

Torture of a man. Album F.*56* [III.1477] c.1815-20. Sepia wash 20·5 × 14·3 cm. Hispanic Society of America, New York

there by the liberals in the island of León where eleven years before the Cortes had voted for the Constitution. On 30 August 1823 the capture of the fort at Trocadero marked the end of this route march and the king was restored to his throne. Despite the Duke of Angoulême's urgent appeals for moderation, he again gave way to the pathological hatred which had filled his heart when he was prince of Asturias. Another White Terror spread across Spain and the liberals were hunted down, deported or executed. Thousands of Spaniards, realizing that no help could be expected either from within or outside the country, again took the road to exile.

Goya too must have felt himself seriously compromised and threatened, to judge from the fact that he made over his house, the Quinta del Sordo, as a gift to his grandson Mariano

New White Terror

Ill. p. 313

Tiburcio Pérez y Cuervo
Goya seems to have felt a special sympathy for architects. Having painted the portraits of Ventura Rodríguez and perhaps Sabatini [I.205, 214], of Villanueva and of Isidro González Velázquez [II.803, 859], he executed those of Juan Antonio Cuervo, director of the Academy of San Fernando, in 1819 [III.1561] and of his nephew, Tiburcio Pérez, in 1820.

The portrait of Tiburcio Pérez, like that of Ramón Satué [1632], is one of the finest examples of his informal style; it was painted after Goya's grave illness, but his brush is as vigorous as ever. Four years later, when he left to go to France, he entrusted the little Rosario Weiss to his friend's care.

Tiburcio Pérez y Cuervo   [1630] 1820. 102·1×81·3 cm. Metropolitan Museum of Art, New York

only a few days after the capture of Trocadero, and went into hiding in the house of a trustworthy friend, Don José Duaso y Latre, whose portrait he painted in gratitude [1633]. It is not known what happened to Leocadia Weiss at that time, though it seems likely that she was imprisoned or had to go into hiding herself, since her little daughter Rosario was placed in the care of an architect friend of the artist, Don Tiburcio Pérez [1630], in that same year. Realizing that it was no longer possible to live and work in Spain, Goya decided to leave his native land, as so many of his friends had already done, in order to end his days in peace with the two creatures who still remained attached to him, Leocadia and her daughter.

Bibl. 167.   Cp. pp. 336-338

See pp. 248, 335

1817-1819. Goya is 71 to 73 years old. Altarpiece for the cathedral at Seville (1817). 'The last Communion of St Joseph of Calasanz' and the 'Christ on the Mount of Olives' for the Escuelas Pías in Madrid (1819). Reign of Ferdinand VII.

See p. 51
See pp. 139-146

Christ on the Mount of Olives [1640] 1819

This little painting was a gift from Goya to the fathers of the Escuelas Pías de San Antón who in May 1819 had commissioned from him the *Last Communion of St Joseph of Calasanz* for the chapel attached to their community (see p. 306). These two works are the most profoundly religious which Goya ever painted. The great altarpiece showing the dying saint suggests an intuition of the artist's own agony (see p. 307) and the *Christ* is overwhelming in its spontaneity and impassioned execution. It expresses all the emotion with which the old artist thanked the *escolapios* from whom he had received his basic education as a child in Saragossa.

Contrary to what many people have long believed, or wished to believe, religious painting forms an important part of Goya's œuvre, and this is confirmed even today by the reappearance of many youthful works painted before or during the period of the first tapestry cartoons and which played a major rôle in his artistic formation. It is noticeable, however, that some periods of his life are richer in religious works than others, though it is difficult to say whether this was due to the random receipt of commissions, to financial need or to spontaneous surges of religious fervour. Whatever the answer, Goya does not seem to have felt any particular attraction for religious subjects and whenever he tackled them, as an immature young artist or in the full possession of his powers, he inevitably went beyond the traditions and conventions appropriate to this kind of painting. This led to the violent quarrels with his brother-in-law at Saragossa in 1781, but also, when he was given a free rein, to the magnificent freedom of the frescoes in the hermitage of San Antonio de la Florida [II.717-735].

After the years 1797-1799, in which he created this masterpiece and other remarkable paintings such as those for the Santa Cueva in Cadiz, the four *Doctors of the Church*, the *Taking of Christ* in Toledo and the paintings for Monte Torrero in Saragossa [II.708-740], there are no further religious works until the rather mediocre *Assumption* in the church at Chinchón [III.1567], which was painted in or before 1812, and the group of works painted about 1817-1819: *St Elizabeth of Hungary* [III.1568], *Saints Justa and Rufina* [III.1569], the *Last Communion of St Joseph of Calasanz* and the *Christ on the Mount of Olives* [1638-1640].

This scarcity of religious subjects over a long period of time may be due to a number of causes: lack of commissions (perhaps on account of the *Caprichos*), a slowing down in the construction of churches, but above all the war and the simultaneous hardening of Goya's anti-clerical feelings which he expressed in his drawings and prints. Nevertheless, the large altarpiece representing *Saints Justa and Rufina* [III.1569], commissioned for the cathedral at Seville, enabled him to make a last journey to Andalusia, as Ceán Bermúdez recorded, in order to study the setting and make detailed preparations for the work which was executed in Madrid in 1817 (Bibl.48).

In May 1819, when he was working on the final plates of the *Disasters of War* [III.1104-1139] and on the *Disparates* [1571-1613], the fathers of the Escuelas Pías de San Antón in Madrid commissioned from him a great altarpiece in honour of the patron saint of the community, St Joseph of Calasanz [1638]. Goya wrote a moving letter when the painting was half-finished, sending back almost all the money from the first instalment which he had received and saying, 'I am returning this to the person ordererd to make the payment, or to the rector, and tell him that D. Francisco Goya must do something in homage to his countryman the Saintly Joseph of Calasanz.' This work is probably unequalled in its spiritual and pictorial intensity and is suffused with all the magical qualities of his art. In the play of light and shade, in the ecstatic congregation, in the figures of the priest and the saint caught at the most fleeting and solemn moment of the sacrament, in the richness of the blacks which set off the singing reds and golds, Goya expresses the ultimate peace which fills the soul before death.

A few months later, he himself fell seriously ill and only recovered through the devoted care of his doctor Arrieta [1629]. We feel a strange presentiment of his own agony in that of the *Christ on the Mount of Olives* [1640] which he had just given to the fathers of the Escuelas Pías. Like the unknown man waiting to be shot on the third of May, the Son of man appears with arms outstretched, a frail, white figure in the darkness, questioning the will of Heaven.

The last Communion of St Joseph of Calasanz   [1638] 1819. 250 × 180 cm. San Antón Abad, Madrid (See p. 305)

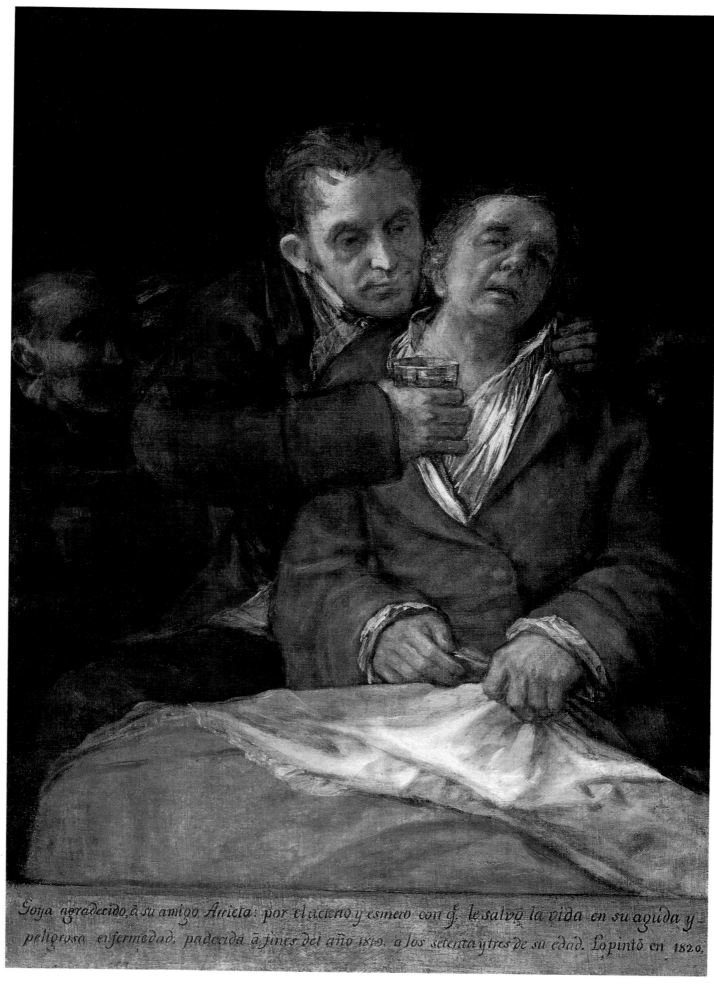

Goya agradecido, á su amigo Arrieta: por el acierto y esmero con q. le salvó la vida en su aguda y peligrosa enfermedad, padecida á fines del año 1819, a los setenta y tres de su edad. Lo pintó en 1820.

Goya and his doctor Arrieta [1629] 1820. 117×79 cm. Institute of Arts, Minneapolis (See p. 305)

The year 1819 was one of considerable activity for Goya and he opened it by learning a completely new technique to add to his already extensive repertoire. Lithography had been discovered at the turn of the century by Aloys Senefelder in Germany and lithographic presses were soon set up in most of the major cities of Europe. In 1811 Bartolomé Sureda [II.813] was in Paris where he made four little pen lithographs, but it was not until 1816, when Charles de Lasteyrie and Godefroi Engelmann opened their lithographic printing works there, that the new process really began to flourish as an art form. Three years later the first lithographic establishment was opened in Madrid by José María Cardano and Goya at once tried his hand at the new technique.

In February 1819 he signed and dated what was probably his first attempt in this medium and the first artistic lithograph printed in Spain: an *Old woman spinning* [1643], crudely drawn with the pen and printed by Cardano. He soon narrowed the gap between this primitive essay and the masterly style in which he was working at the time, for example in the albums of drawings [III.1244-1518]. The composition which he entitled *Expression of double force* [1648] shows a considerable stride forward, although the lithograph, made by the transfer process, loses much of the sensitivity and detail of the preparatory drawing [1649]. Cardano himself was an unadventurous lithographer and it was not until Goya went to France that he found the guidance and help which enabled him to exploit to the full all the potentialities of this new black and white technique.

1819-1824. Goya is 73 to 78 years old. First experiments with the technique of lithography, introduced into Spain in 1819. Series of 22 etchings entitled by Goya 'Disparates' (18 are published in 1864 as 'Los Proverbios'). Reign of Ferdinand VII.

Bibl. 38 and 132

See pp. 345-349

Espresivo doble fuerza (Expression of double force)   [1648] 1819? Lithograph 8 × 11·5 cm.

Espresivo doble fuerza
Proof in the Biblioteca Nacional, Madrid. The two known proofs of this early lithograph were printed by José Cardano, founder of the Establecimiento Litográfico in Madrid, on the back of proof prints of his own lithographs. Goya made a brush drawing with lithographic ink [1649] and this was transferred to the stone. The transfer was not entirely successful and both proofs were retouched by the artist. The ambiguous title is written on the proof in the New York Public Library. Another lithograph, known only from a unique proof [1650], appears to show the same girl — a symbolic figure? — struggling even more violently with a rough-looking man who is trying to overpower her.

Disparate Femenino
The composition of this plate is almost a synthesis of two of Goya's last tapestry cartoons, the *Blind man's buff* of 1788-89 [I.276] and the *Pelele* of 1791-92 [I.301] (see pp. 69 and 70).

Goya still had a collection of sixteen of his tapestry cartoon sketches among his possessions in the Quinta del Sordo and he probably used them as a starting point for a number of the *Disparate* designs. In the preparatory drawing, which is much less close to the cartoons, a man is lying spread-eagled in the sheet. In the print he is replaced by a donkey over whom the straw manikins are tossed. The charm and treachery of women who 'play' with men is a theme which constantly recurs in Goya's work.

Disparate Femenino (Feminine Folly) *Proverbios 1* [1571] c.1815-24. Artist's proof with manuscript title. Etching and aquatint 24×35 cm. Lázaro Galdiano Museum, Madrid

The 'Disparates' or 'Proverbios'

Bibl. 36, III, p. 106

Bibl. 88, II, nos 248-269

See pp. 313-320

During the years between 1815 and his departure for France in 1824, Goya engraved the most enigmatic of all his series of prints, whose very title has been the subject of much confusion and doubt [1571-1613]. The plates were not published during his lifetime, but on many of the proofs which he took in the course of work he wrote a title in pen and ink. These titles always include the word *Disparate*, which means 'folly', 'absurdity', and they are as brief as they are unenlightening: *Feminine Folly*, *Ridiculous Folly*, *Flying Folly*, *Carnival Folly*, *Well-known Folly*. However, the most cursory study of the prints themselves shows that something is going on in them, and this is confirmed by the preparatory drawings which often differ considerably from the prints, suggesting that Goya altered and clarified – or deliberately obscured – the significance of the designs as he worked on them. The Royal Academy of San Fernando, which acquired eighteen of the copperplates together with those of the *Disasters of War*, and which was probably unaware of the existence of the proofs with Goya's titles, published them in 1864 with the title *Los Proverbios* [1571-1600]. Presumably the academicians were able to identify at least a number of proverbs – Harris has suggested a complete list – but they gave no titles to the prints whose full significance will always remain obscure.

The series was probably begun about 1815 and was engraved on the same batch of copperplates as the *Tauromaquia* etchings [III.1149-1243]. At this period, between 1815 and 1824, Goya was very much occupied with his own private work. He continued his 'private journal' in the albums of drawings, completed the prints of the war with Bonaparte by the addition of the *caprichos enfáticos* [III.1104-1139], and decorated the walls of his house on the outskirts of Madrid, the celebrated Quinta acquired in 1819, with powerful and fantastic scenes [1615-1627a]. The execution of the *Disparates* prints probably covered most of this period. Twenty-two plates are known and fourteen of the contemporary proofs so far recorded have *Disparate* titles. The earliest plates to be engraved were probably those whose style is closest to the war scenes and the *Tauromaquia* and whose subject-matter seems the least complex: for example, the design with the flying men [1591], which was included in the set of *Tauromaquia* proofs given by Goya to Ceán Bermúdez; the *Fools' Folly* [1604] where all the bulls of the *Tauromaquia* go flying through the air; the scene where soldiers are terrified by a phantom [1573], which recalls many of the *Disasters of War* and also plates *3* and *52* of the *Caprichos* [II.455, 555]. As Goya worked on the series, the images became stranger and more distorted, while his use of very dark aquatint backgrounds intensifies their atmosphere of terror or black comedy.

Ill. p. 311

The large size of the copperplates which Goya had chosen for the *Tauromaquia* etchings, in order to show scenes in the crowded bullring, enabled him to achieve a style of impressive monumentality when he reduced the number of figures, and he exploited this to the full in the *Disparates* plates. The *Disparates* have much in common with the *Caprichos* in terms of mood and theme, but there is a very striking difference in scale. In the earlier series, in spite of the bold handling of the later plates (*Caprichos 8, 42, 53* for example), the designs are controlled and contained within the small format of the copperplates and are characterized by an almost classical balance in the setting of the figures within a defined space. The *Disparates* designs, on the other hand, offer a sense of limitless space, with the figures appearing in the foreground as if caught in the wide lens of a roving camera. The designs are composed entirely in terms of the figures which either achieve a precarious off-centre balance or are whirled into the circular movement which is such a characteristic feature of Goya's later work and is found, for example, in the *Feminine Folly* [1571] and even more markedly in the dancing figures of *Merry Folly* [1589]. The most 'monumental' figure in the series is another dancer, the grinning giant clicking his castanets and filling two-thirds of the design as he towers over two cowering figures in plate *4* [1576].

See pp. 227-229

Ill. pp. 128, 130

Ill. p. 309

One of the prints which most strongly evokes the paintings in the Quinta del Sordo, on which Goya was probably working at the same time, is the *Disorderly Folly* [1581] where a monstrous 'couple' of siamese twins confronts a crowd of figures whose mis-shapen forms and distorted features are extraordinarily close to those in the witches' sabbath, one of the largest and most terrifying of the 'black paintings' [1623]. The symbolism here recalls the theme of the ill-assorted couple which Goya had treated in one of the *Caprichos* plates [II.602] and which appears again in a late drawing made in Bordeaux [v.1723].

Ill. p. 312

Goya seems to have crowded into the *Disparates* prints, memories and allusions and ideas drawn from the whole of his life and work – from the tapestry cartoons of his youth, from the *Caprichos*, from the war and its 'fatal consequences' and from many other sources which he had always used: proverbs and sayings, literary texts, traditional allegory and symbolism. The *Disparates* are also so close to the *caprichos enfáticos* at the end of the *Disasters of War* and to the themes and imagery of the *Caprichos* that it seems inevitable that they must contain something of the same blend of ideas and satire, and one is tempted to conclude that the *Disparate* titles were a deliberate screen to cover Goya's real meaning. Some of the plates seem to be harmless satires: on the nature of women, for example, in the *Feminine Folly* [1571] where women are tossing straw manikins into the air, as they did in the tapestry cartoon of 1792 [I.301], and in the strange plate where an ecstatically smiling girl is carried off by a horse and which has been shown to be closely based on traditional emblematic representations of unbridled sexual passion. On the other hand, compositions like those of the *General Folly*, the *Clear Folly* and the impressive *Animal Folly* [1583, 1594, 1603] seem to carry elements of social or political satire within their complex imagery. Plate *4*, with the dancing giant [1576], was clearly designed as an anti-clerical satire, since in the preparatory drawing the man on the far left is wearing a cassock and is half-embracing, half-hiding behind a woman who may be a nun. The etching was altered, in the course of work, to remove the priest's skirts and make him into an old man with breeches. In the end, however, rather than through recognizable meanings and allusions, it is through their purely artistic qualities and their powerful suggestion of mood that these prints make their impression, evoking deep, intuitive responses and leaving unforgettable images in the mind.

Ill. p. 309
Ill. p. 70

Ill. p. 312
Bibl. 108, pp. 111-114

Preparatory drawing for Proverbios 13
This drawing was only recently discovered and is published here for the first time. The red wash technique is characteristic of all the drawings in this series, and the dirty black marks at the edge of the sheet show that the drawing was transferred to the surface of the copperplate as a guide for etching. Two artist's proofs are known, made before the dark aquatint was added to the background. One of them has the manuscript title *Modo de volar*. The realism and objectivity of the scene suggest that it may have been inspired by some contemporary account or actual event, and it was probably one of the early plates engraved for this series.

Preparatory drawing for *Proverbios 13* [1591] entitled *Modo de volar* (A way of flying)   [1592] c.1815-24.
Red chalk and sanguine wash 24·5×35 cm. Lázaro Galdiano Library, Madrid

Disparate de Tontos
Artist's proof with manuscript title
Lázaro Galdiano Museum, Madrid
One of the four plates which became separated from the remainder of the series and were never included in the *Proverbios* editions. They were published in 1877, in the French periodical *L'Art*. Like the flying men shown above, this other 'flying folly' was probably one of the earlier compositions which Goya etched, and is no doubt closely connected with the *Tauromaquia* prints, engraved and published in 1815-16. It has been suggested that the print may illustrate the popular saying 'Make way for bulls and wind', and there does not seem to be a deeper meaning to this absurd but magnificent composition.

Disparate de Tontos (Fools' Folly)   [1604] c.1815-24. Etching and aquatint 24·5×35 cm.

Unbridled Folly
Three artist's proofs before aquatint are known, but none with a *Disparate* title. This is one of the plates where the striking differences between the preparatory drawing and the final engraving suggest that Goya was deeply concerned with expressing a particular meaning. In the drawing [1586], a man lies dead or dying in the wake of the horse, and this seems to reinforce the interpretation referred to in the text, which identifies the woman and the horse with traditional representations of sexual passion.

Unbridled Folly. *Proverbios 10* [1585] c.1815-24. Etching and aquatint 24·5 × 35 cm.

Disparate Desordenado (Disorderly Folly) *Proverbios 7* [1581] c.1815-24. Etching and aquatint

Disparate Desordenado
Artist's proof with manuscript title
24·5 × 35 cm. Art Institute, Chicago
One of the strangest in the series, this composition recalls some of the *Caprichos* prints – the grotesque audience in plate *53* (see p. 130), the unhappy couple bound together for life in plate *75* [II.611]. The powerful handling and the overwhelming sense of drama (which we experience but cannot understand), suggest that the print was made while Goya was actually painting the ground-floor room in the Quinta, which he decorated with the 'blackest' and most macabre of his visions (see p. 316). One of them shows a crowd of witches [1623] and is very similar to the print reproduced here.

1819-1823. Goya is 73 to 77 years old. Acquires a country house near Madrid, known as the Quinta del Sordo (House of the deaf man), and decorates the two main rooms with fourteen mural paintings: his 'Descent into Hell'. Reign of Ferdinand VII.

* Bibl. 161, pp. 93, 108
** Ill. p. 66

Ill. p. 46
See pp. 51-52   Ill. p. 56

See pp. 48-50

On 27 February 1819 Goya acquired for sixty thousand reales a country property of about twenty-five acres of gently sloping land on the right bank of the river Manzanares, just outside Madrid, on which a single-storey house had been built in 1795.* From the Quinta there was one of the best views of Madrid, especially on a fine, spring day when it was almost the same as that in the *Meadow of San Isidro* [1.272]**: on the far left the gardens of La Florida and the foliage of the Casa de Campo, then the luminous mass of the royal palace where the setting sun kindles a thousand fires in the tall windows, and just opposite the imposing cupola of San Francisco el Grande. Finally, on the same side of the river, to the right, the meadow itself with the hermitage of San Isidro where every year, on 15 May, all the people of Madrid came in pilgrimage to honour their patron saint. Down below, the banks of the Manzanares re-echoed with the laughter and songs of the washerwomen, their sturdy figures silhouetted against the shimmering mosaic of coloured linen drying in the sun.

At a single glance the new proprietor could evoke the principal stages in his long career: the *Dance on the banks of the river Manzanares* [1.74], one of his first tapestry cartoons painted more than forty years before; San Francisco el Grande, the scene of his first official triumph [1.184]; the royal palace where he had received so many marks of favour from kings and princes, where he had studied the paintings by Velázquez and in which some of his finest portraits now hung; the *Hermitage of San Isidro* [1.273], a glowing memory of the time when

'La Quinta de Goya'
This illustration, a facsimile after a pen drawing by Saint-Elme Gautier, appeared with an article by Charles Yriarte in *L'Art*, 1877, vol. II, p. 9. Yriarte gave a detailed description of the position of the mural paintings in the two principal rooms on the first floor and ground floor in the Quinta. Unfortunately, all the known illustrations of the exterior of the Quinta show the larger wing added after Goya's death, rather than the original building. The house which he renovated and decorated with the 'black paintings' appears on the left.

'La Quinta de Goya' – Goya's country house on the banks of the Manzanares

La Leocadia   [1622] 1820-23. 147×132 cm. Prado Museum, Madrid

life was sweet and when the Duchess of Osuna, who acquired so many of his works, brought together the best 'enlightened' minds of the time at her country house at La Alameda; the cupola of San Antonio de la Florida on which he had left, for all time, the imprint of his genius in its freest and most original form [II.717-735]; and, in the distance, the tower of the church of San Bernardino which stood close to the spot where everything had been shattered by the invaders' bullets in the early hours of the third of May [III.984]; finally, among the washerwomen by the river, the graceful forms of a seductive young woman reading a letter and of her companion with a parasol, the *Young women with a letter* [III.962], representing perhaps the promise of a new life.

See pp. 139-145

Ill. p. 20

Ill. p. 243

Goya had chosen this retreat, which he at once began to extend and renovate, to escape the oppression, hypocrisy and denunciations which for the last five years had been the order of the day in the capital. The atmosphere there had become unbearable. The Inquisition had reopened their file on him and at any moment might interfere in his private life. Nothing definite is known about his relationship with Leocadia Weiss but it seems likely that she was living with him under the convenient title of *ama de llaves*, or housekeeper. The situation was scandalous and fraught with danger, and was further complicated by the constant vigilance of his family who were afraid that the inheritance might one day slip through their hands. Amidst the political and economic chaos into which Spain was sinking, the isolated Quinta, in its country setting, represented a haven of peace which would perhaps be his last home. There he could live and work, far from prying eyes, with the youthful companion whose elegant and melancholy figure was to decorate one of the walls in the main room, nearest the entrance to the house [1622]. The young painter Antonio Brugada, who was a friend and companion of Goya in Bordeaux, made an inventory of the contents of the Quinta, which was drawn up in the presence of Javier and Mariano shortly after Goya's death and in which this painting is identified as *La Leocadia*. Such direct evidence cannot be questioned, and the graceful *manola* could easily be thirty-two years old, as Leocadia was in 1820.

The Quinta del Sordo

Ill. p. 314
See plan p. 320 and Appendix VI

Appendices II and VI

The 'black paintings'

It was about that date, when the work on the house had been finished, that Goya began to decorate the walls of the two main rooms, on the ground floor and first floor, with paintings whose subjects were as strange as the technique he used [1615-1627a]. They were painted in oils directly on the plaster, filling the spaces between the windows and the doors. Intended as the decoration of his principal living rooms, they are the crowning achievement after fifty years of battle against the constraints and servitude imposed by his career and, fifty years before Impressionism, the most splendid example of artistic freedom.

After the serious illness which almost caused his death at the end of 1819, it is quite natural that he should have decided to 'paint' his will, to leave to posterity a final work which would sum up everything which he had so far expressed only incompletely through his paintings, drawings and prints. As soon as he had regained his health, shortly after painting the self-portrait with his doctor Arrieta [1629] in 1820, he devoted all his energies to this prodigious undertaking. There are fourteen paintings, some of them measuring more than six square metres, and all probably dashed onto the walls of his house in a single burst of inspiration. But the unity of inspiration and the violence of the technique should not be misunderstood. Like all great artists, Goya thought out the whole scheme of the 'black paintings' and apparently made sketches of the main designs. Those which are attributed to him at the present time are not altogether convincing, but Brugada's inventory listed seven which would correspond to the seven largest paintings.*

Ill. p. 307

* *Appendix II*
** *Bibl. 136, pp. 185-221*
*** *Bibl. 166, pp. 120-121*

There have been attempts to explain these 'black paintings', to give them a philosophical, even esoteric, interpretation and to identify their symbolism in order to prove that they constitute a coherent scheme.** But as Sánchez Cantón so rightly pointed out,*** this attributes to Goya an intellectual approach which he did not possess and which is certainly not found in any of his previous works. Nevertheless, we feel convinced that there is a single thread, however tenuous, linking these fourteen carefully worked out paintings,

La Leocadia
Of all the 'black paintings', this one alone, which was the first on the left as one entered the ground-floor room, remains apart from the nightmare world created by Goya. The young and beautiful *manola*, veiled in black, is Leocadia Weiss who came to live with the aging artist in the isolated Quinta, beyond the gates of Madrid. Leocadia is leaning beside a tomb, and this solemn image of life associated with the idea of his own death is the key to the 'black paintings'.

La Romería de San Isidro (The pilgrimage of San Isidro)   [1626] 1820-23. 140×438 cm. Prado Museum, Madrid

just as *The dream of reason*, in spite of its final position as plate *43*, in the middle of the *Caprichos* [II.536], nevertheless provides the key to the whole work.

Although such an undertaking may seem over bold, we shall attempt to identify this linking thread or theme in the 'black paintings', and we must first take into account the circumstances surrounding the creation of these extraordinary scenes, since even the most fantastic of Goya's works always have their source in reality, whether directly or indirectly experienced. At this particular time his life was dominated by two diametrically opposed images: that of youth and hope as personified by Leocadia and that of death as represented by his own figure in the arms of Arrieta. This was the dual inspiration behind the 'black paintings' which he undertook in the knowledge that they might be his last great work and that he must say in them everything which still remained to be said.

Everyone who looks at these fourteen paintings from the Quinta del Sordo is struck by the horror which pervades the scenes and by the nightmare atmosphere in which the figures move. The very title, 'black paintings', applies more to their mood than to their actual colouring. There is one painting, however, which remains untouched by the horror and nightmare: *La Leocadia* [1622], painted on the first wall to the left on entering the main room downstairs. She thus appears as a kind of 'frontispiece' to the whole work, and it is from her that we must follow the thread towards an understanding of the other paintings.

Leocadia: the key to the whole scheme
Ill. p. 314   See p. 320

Ill. p. 318

La Romería de San Isidro
Together with *The great he-goat* [1623] which faced it in the ground-floor room, this is the largest of all the 'black paintings'. Goya had long ago represented the feast of San Isidro in one of his gayest and most enchanting pictures (see p. 66), but here the scene is transformed into a nightmare procession which winds its way through a nocturnal landscape until it reaches the group of hideously bestial faces in the foreground. Only the agony of Goya's illness in 1819 and the nearness of his escape from death can account for this fantastic vision from another world.

Leocadia is shown as a beautiful but very solemn young woman; dressed entirely in black, her face completely covered by a veil, she is leaning against a mound on which appear the iron railings of a tomb. It seems to us that Goya has represented her in full mourning, standing by his own tomb, an image which must have haunted him during his recent fight with death and remained with him afterwards since he was to give it such powerful expression. By placing this *real* scene at the entrance to his house, Goya intended us to understand that the other thirteen paintings are in a sense scenes from beyond the grave, visions of the afterworld such as he may himself have glimpsed when he lay on the brink of death.

We believe, therefore, that the 'black paintings' are a *Descent into Hell*, such as another great visionary creator, Gérard de Nerval, was to experience. Moreover, if we move on to the painting next to this one, we find a crowd of monstrous beings huddled together in terror and dread of the devil – a huge, black he-goat – and also, outside this group and looking at the scene as a spectator, the silhouette of an elegant young woman, dressed in black, sitting on a chair to the right. It is quite possible that this again is Leocadia, placed there by Goya as an impassive witness to his own nightmare. On the wall opposite the *Leocadia* was the terrifying, bloodstained *Saturn* [1624], symbol both of time and death which devour us all. Its pendant represents *Judith and Holofernes* [1625], and the two subjects recall drawings on the same themes, executed in red chalk, at the time when Goya was

Saturn   Judith and Holophernes
The mythical figure of *Saturn* and the biblical theme of *Judith and Holophernes* were painted on the wall facing the entrance to the ground-floor room in the Quinta. The subjects were identified in the inventory of the house made after Goya's death by the young artist Antonio Brugada.

The theme of Saturn undoubtedly plays an essential rôle in the conception of the 'black paintings', as a symbol of melancholy and destruction. The pendant image of Judith combines death and blood with the sombre violence of unappeased desire.

Goya seems to have responded to the significance of these saturnine themes as early as the period of the *Caprichos* since he made two drawings of the same subjects in the years 1797-98 [II.635, 636]. A comparison with the paintings from the Quinta shows the extent to which these later, visionary works must have been the outcome of his close encounter with death.

Saturn   [1624] 1820-23. 146×83 cm.
Prado Museum, Madrid

Judith and Holophernes   [1625] 1820-23.
146×84 cm. Prado Museum, Madrid

working on the *Caprichos* prints [II.635, 636]; the pile of heads attacked by the Judith in the earlier drawing reappears again in one of Goya's last drawings made in Bordeaux, page *51* from album G, entitled *Comico descubrimiento* (Comic discovery) [v.1756].

The other paintings are all fantastic visions – painted *Disparates* – and often take up themes which Goya had already treated but which are here transposed into an infernal world to which death alone affords access. The *Pilgrimage of San Isidro* [1626], in the downstairs room, is a distant souvenir of the tapestry cartoons, but their absolute antithesis in its dark and terrifying intensity. In the upper room, where the paintings are rather brighter in colour and seem more closely related to the real world, the *Two young people laughing at a man* [1618] recalls, in its eroticism, a drawing from album E [III.1419]; the landscape and the firing soldiers of the *Asmodea* [1620] evoke earlier scenes of the War of Independence, but here the soldiers are aiming at a pair of flying demons; the *Duel* [1616] would be a barbarous but straightforward fight with cudgels between two peasants if it were not for the nightmare suggestion that the combattants are sinking into quicksand as they bludgeon each other to death; and the *Dog* [1621], perhaps the strangest of all the scenes, produces its powerfully disturbing effect by leaving everything to the spectator's imagination, with no possible answer to the question of the artist's own intention.

Ill. p. 316

Ill. pp. 20, 23
Ill. p. 320

We can sum up, therefore, by saying that it is the first image of Leocadia which gives the 'black paintings' their true meaning and coherence. Once we have crossed the threshold of the grave, under the gaze of the young 'widow', the other scenes unfold before our eyes like a series of visions of an afterworld forbidden to the living and glimpsed only by a few exceptional beings 'marked by the finger of God'.

The dog
This is one of the paintings from the first-floor room which also included the *Duel* (see below). It is the most extraordinary and certainly the most audacious of all the paintings in the Quinta: a dog is sinking into quicksand, only his head still visible, alive – for how much longer? – in a totally bare and abstract setting. Such a subject defies analysis and belongs to the irrational world of dream and hallucination.

Duel with cudgels (see p. 320)
This is one of the four large paintings, including the *Asmodea* (see p. 23), which were painted in the first-floor room in the Quinta. In the inventory drawn up by Brugada in 1828, this painting is entitled *Dos forasteros* (Two provincials), and Charles Yriarte, in 1867, identified them as cattle herdsmen from Galicia. The two peasants are engaged in a battle to the death as they sink up to their knees into the ground.

The dog   [1621] 1820-23. 134×80 cm. Prado Museum, Madrid

Duel with cudgels   [1616] 1820-23. 123×266 cm. Prado Museum, Madrid (See text p. 319)

THE QUINTA DEL SORDO   PLAN OF THE TWO ROOMS WITH THE 'BLACK PAINTINGS'   (See Appendix VI)

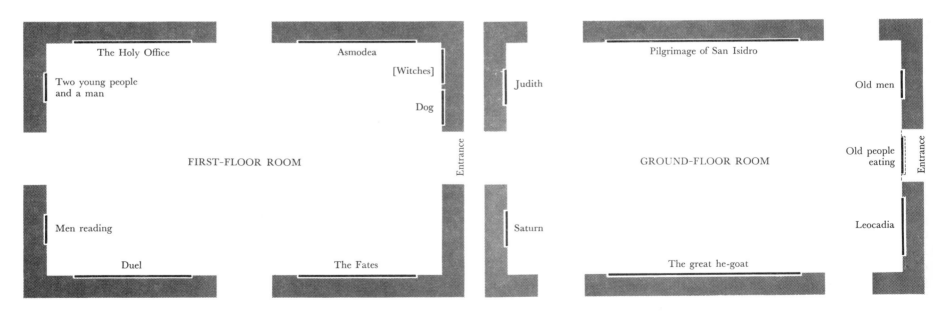

FIRST FLOOR
Atropos or The Fates   [1615]
Duel with cudgels   [1616] Ill. p. 320
Men reading   [1617]
Two young people laughing at a man   [1618]
Promenade of the Holy Office   [1619]
Asmodea   [1620] Ill. p. 23
[Painting by Javier Goya, lost]
The dog   [1621] Ill. p. 319

GROUND FLOOR
La Leocadia   [1622] Ill. p. 314
The great he-goat   [1623]
Saturn   [1624] Ill. p. 318
Judith and Holophernes   [1625] Ill. p. 318
The pilgrimage of San Isidro   [1626] Ill. p. 318
Two old men   [1627]
Two old people eating   [1627a]

CATALOGUE IV 1819-1824

INTRODUCTION

PAINTINGS   The five years which began with the acquisition of the Quinta del Sordo in February 1819 and ended with the departure for France in June 1824 were years of retirement, of withdrawal, in Goya's life and in his art. He produced far fewer works, partly because of his age but also on account of his preoccupation in 1819 with his new country property. He tended the estate of some twenty-five acres and enlarged and renovated the house, making it into a large, solid home on two floors. It is very unlikely that he intended at that time to decorate the walls of the two main rooms himself, and it was probably only after the almost fatal illness which he suffered at the end of the year that he felt the urgent need to recreate on the walls of his house the visions which had assailed him during his agony. It is generally agreed that the execution of the 'black paintings' [1615-1627a] was not begun before 1820 and was completed by 1823 when Goya gave the Quinta to his grandson Mariano as a result of the political situation and the return of Ferdinand VII.

On the basis of the inventory drawn up by Brugada in 1828 and of the description published by Charles Yriarte in 1867, we have indicated, in the notes to the catalogue and in Appendix VI, the distribution of the fourteen paintings in the two main rooms in the house, one on the ground floor, which may have been used as a dining-room, and the other on the first floor.

Any interpretation of the 'black paintings' must take into account two important facts: the visitor who entered the ground-floor room was confronted by two symbolic subjects on the wall opposite the door, *Saturn* and *Judith and Holophernes* [1624, 1625], which set the tone for the whole scheme; but if he looked at the paintings in the usual order, going clockwise round the room, he found the *Leocadia* [1622] on the first wall, to the left of the entrance, and she thus becomes the frontispiece and the key to the 'black paintings' (see the text, p. 315).

After Goya's death, the Quinta remained in Mariano's possession until he sold it, in 1859, to Rodolphe Coumont from whom it was acquired, in 1873, by the German banker from Ingelheim, Baron Emile Erlanger, who had all Goya's paintings transferred to canvas. In 1878 the paintings were exhibited in Paris, at the Palais du Trocadéro, during the Exposition Universelle; no one paid any attention to them and the only critical notice which has come to light is a violent attack by the English critic, P. G. Hamerton, in *The Portfolio* in 1879, where he accused Goya of corruption and immorality in his art. The 'black paintings' were finally given to the Prado Museum by Baron Erlanger in 1881. The history of the Quinta and its paintings is summed up in the fully documented study by F. J. Sánchez Cantón and Xavier de Salas, published in 1963.

There are only five religious paintings in this period, including a preparatory sketch, but they are Goya's most intensely mystical works [1638-1642]. The *Last Communion of St Joseph of Calasanz* and the *Christ on the Mount of Olives* which accompanied it, were executed only a few months before his illness, since the large altarpiece was unveiled on 27 August, the saint's feast day, and Goya wrote of the small picture '. . . it is the last which I shall paint in Madrid'. The *Repentant Peter* and the pendant *St Paul* were probably painted during these years before the departure for France.

The portraits include one, possibly two, which evoke the three months which Goya spent in hiding in a friend's home: *Don José Duaso y Latre* [1633] has an inscription which gives the artist's age, seventy-eight years, and proves that the portrait was completed after 30 March 1824, the date of his birthday, as a token of his gratitude. The pencil drawing of Duaso's nephew, *Don Francisco Otín* [1634], was made at the same time, and both works have remained in the collection of their descendants.

We have placed at the end of this fourth part of the catalogue two series of small pictures whose authenticity is unproven and which have sometimes been attributed to other hands. Nevertheless, the example of the series of pictures in the preceding period, which have been authenticated by the X mark of the 1812 inventory, suggests that one should be extremely careful in examining such works. We know that Goya was particularly fond of making series of pictures and these two groups appear to offer a typical example in that each is identical in its size and technical characteristics. The first is a series of *caprichos* painted on panel [1651-1656] and the second is on sheets of tinplate [1657a-d], like the 'cabinet pictures' of 1793-94. Both groups are related on the one hand to the 'black paintings', on the other hand to lithographs dating from 1819 or 1824-25 (compare the *Duel* [1653] with the two lithographs [1644] and [v.1702] and the *Woman reading* [1657a] with the lithograph [v.1699] where the almost identical composition appears in the reverse). The four scenes in the second group belonged to the painter-lithographer Gigoux who bequeathed them to the Museum at Besançon, together with the two celebrated scenes of savages [III.922, 923].

DRAWINGS AND ENGRAVINGS   During this period, Goya was still very much occupied with the large body of graphic work discussed in Part III. Some of the prints and drawings – the later plates of the *Disasters of War*, a sequence of drawings in album C – seem almost certainly connected with the political events of 1820-1823 (see p. 238), and the series of drawings and etchings on which Goya began to work around 1808-1810 were probably only interrupted by the restoration of the absolutist régime in 1823.

The series of prints which opens this part of the catalogue was possibly begun as early as 1815 but is also contemporaneous with the late *caprichos enfáticos* of the *Disasters* engravings [III.1104-1139] and with the paintings in the Quinta del Sordo [1615-1627a]. It was almost certainly incomplete when Goya stored away all his copperplates in chests in the Quinta (see Appendix II) before leaving for France in 1824. The existence of eight preparatory drawings for the *Disparates* of which no prints are known [1605-1612] suggests that the series was interrupted, and this would perhaps account for the lack of any explanation of the meaning of the prints which, if Goya had been ready to publish them, would surely have been accompanied by some kind of explanatory title or statement of the artist's intention. Eighteen of the twenty-two copperplates were acquired by the Academy of San Fernando and first published in 1864, the year after the issue of the *Disasters of War*. The four other plates were acquired by the painter Eugenio Lucas and published for the first and only time in the French periodical *L'Art* in 1877.

All the drawings for this series are executed with the brush and sanguine wash over a very sketchy red chalk base. Two hitherto unknown drawings provide an example of the range of Goya's drawing style in this series: the first is the bold and firmly detailed drawing for the early print of the flying men [1592] (reproduced on p. 311); the second is a drawing which was never engraved and which is so freely handled that it is difficult to make out the subject [1612]. The later drawings for the series are extraordinarily free and serve only as a starting point for Goya's work on the copperplate, but the etchings made from them acquire an impressive strength of line and tone and an intensity of expression which underline their enigmatic and surrealist qualities (see plates *3, 7, 16* and *17*). The *Disparate* titles were added on the working proofs with a pen and sepia ink, and are curiously reminiscent of the neat inscriptions which Goya added to the drawings and proofs of his first series of prints, the *Copies after Velázquez* [I.88-117].

LITHOGRAPHS   The lithographs which Goya made during this period [1643-1650] were probably all executed within a very short space of time, from the moment when José Cardano opened his atelier in Madrid in 1819 and Goya dated his first known lithograph in February that same year. Only five lithographs are here attributed to this period. They were all made by the transfer process: Goya's original drawings were transferred to the lithographic stone and printed by Cardano, with varying degrees of success. The retouching of most of the known proofs with the pen or crayon is proof of Goya's dissatisfaction with the limitations of the medium as practised by Cardano. Even so, he evidently grasped the possibilities inherent in this new technique and the two groups of lithographs and preparatory drawings [1645-1647, 1648-1650] suggest that he at once began to think in terms of series of prints with titles to be added for publication.

Of the total of 290 known prints by Goya – engravings and lithographs – 27 (22 for the *Disparates* and 5 lithographs) are catalogued within this fourth period of his career.

NOTES TO CATALOGUE IV   [1571-1657d]

1571-1613 The prints and their preparatory drawings have been published by Camón Aznar (Bibl. 42). The complete set of first edition prints is reproduced actual size, with the title page dated 1864, together with the four additional plates [1601-1604], in Bibl. 81. Where no *Disparate* title by Goya is known, titles invented by Camón or the authors, or traditional titles, are used. For an attempt at identifying proverbs to fit the plates, see Harris.

1571   Title on the proof in Madrid, Fund. Lázaro (M.I-11.588).

1573   Title invented by Beruete (Bibl. 36, III).

1575   Title on the proof in Madrid, Fund. Lázaro (M.I-11.592). No drawing is known unless, in spite of its considerable differences, the additional drawing [1605] was used for this plate.
Pierre Gassier has suggested that the girl with her hands in a muff may be connected with the figure tentatively identified as Leocadia Weiss in one of the 'black paintings' of the same period (see notes to [1622, 1623]).

1576   Title invented by Camón Aznar. Generally known as *Bobalicón* (Silly idiot).

1578   Title on the proof in Madrid, Fund. Lázaro (M.I-11.589).

1579   Title on an unpublished proof (U.S.A., priv. coll.), unknown to Harris.

1581   Title on the proof in Chicago, Art Institute. It is possible that the additional drawing [1606] was used for this plate, although it shows very considerable variations.

1582   Title invented by Camón Aznar. Cp. the similar subject in the additional drawing [1607].

1583   Title on the Beurdeley proof (present collection unknown) illustrated by Delteil.

1585   Title invented by the authors. Generally known by Beruete's title *El caballo raptor*. The emblematic significance of this composition was discussed by Levitine (Bibl. 108, pp. 111-114).

1587   Title on the proof in a German private collection (listed by Harris as 'formerly Madrid, Gerona').

1589   Title on the proof in Cambridge (Mass.), Philip Hofer. Reproduced in Bibl. 81, pl. 12a.

1591   Title on the proof included in the complete set of *Tauromaquia* proofs which Goya gave to Ceán Bermúdez (see Harris, Bibl. 88, I, pp. 173-174).

1592   A hitherto unrecorded drawing which came to light when Juliet Wilson was examining Goya's working proofs in the library of the Fundación Lázaro Galdiano, thanks to the kindness and co-operation of Sr. Felipe C. R. Maldonado. The signature in pencil in the lower right corner is probably apocryphal.

1593   Title on the proof in Madrid, B.N. (45692).

1594   Title on the proof in Cambridge (Mass.), Philip Hofer. Reproduced in Bibl. 81, pl. 15a. The falling soldier, added on the left in the course of work, recalls the demon in the additional drawing [1608].

1596   Title invented by Camón Aznar (perhaps with reference to the three-faced head on the figure to the left).

1598   Title invented by Camón Aznar.

1600   Title invented by Camón Aznar. It is conceivable that the additional drawing [1608] was used for this plate which appears to have been considerably altered in the course of work. See note to [1608].

1601-1604   The proofs with Goya's titles are in the Lázaro Foundation (museum) in Madrid, and the inventory numbers are given in the individual legends. The copperplates were exhibited in 1966 (Bibl. 28, nos 165-168) and 1970 (Bibl. 30b, nos 70-73).

1601   Lázaro proof (M.I-11.591). Engraved on plate *QUE GUERRERO! / (Quel guerrier)* (What a warrior!).

1602   Lázaro proof (M.I-11.587). Engraved on plate *UNA REINA DEL CIRCO / (Une reine du Cirque)* (A circus queen).

1603   Lázaro proof (M.I-11.590). Engraved on plate *OTRAS LEYES POR EL PUEBLO / (Autres lois pour le peuple)* (Different laws for the people).
The elephant was copied from the pen and ink study [III.1532], possibly made from life. The second elephant in the drawing was partially etched and then abandoned; traces of the outline can be seen in the shaded rocks to the left.

1604   Lázaro proof (M.I-11.586). Engraved on plate *LLUVIA DE TOROS / (Pluie de Taureaux)* (Raining bulls). There has been disagreement over the second word in the MS. title which has often been read as *Toritos* (little bulls). Careful examination of all the proofs with Goya's inscriptions has convinced Juliet Wilson that the only possible reading is *Tontos*.

1605   It is possible that this drawing was used for plate 3 [1575].

1606   It is possible that this drawing was used for plate 7 [1581].

1607   This drawing is very close to the design of plate 8 [1582].

1608   Camón Aznar has interpreted the demon as a falling figure and suggested the title 'La desesperación de Satán' (Satan's despair), whereas the drawing is usually reproduced the other way up. Camón's view, which enables the lightly sketched, flying figures to the right to be distinguished more easily, suggests a very strong connection with the falling figure which Goya added to plate 15 [1594] in the course of work. It is also possible that the design of this drawing, if viewed the other way up, may be connected with plate 18 [1600].

1612   This drawing, unrecorded in the Goya literature, was reproduced by the owner in Bibl. 81, frontispiece.

1613   This drawing has been interpreted as a caricature of Wellington (cp. [III.896-900]), and if the interpretation is correct it is probably connected with his second, ambassadorial visit to Madrid in 1814 and the alterations which Goya made to one of his portraits at that time – see note to [III.897].

1615-1627a The paintings in the Quinta have been studied, in the context of Goya's life and work and in the light of all the available documentation, by Sánchez Cantón and Salas (Bibl. 169). The first record of the paintings is the inventory of the Quinta, made by Antonio Brugada in 1828 after Goya's death, which listed all the wall paintings as well as the other works of art in the house. It was first published in Bibl. 57, I, p. 53, n. 1 and has been reprinted in Bibl. 169, pp. 71-72. See also Appendices II and VI. The paintings were also described *in situ* by Yriarte in 1867 and in several cases he gave the pictures the same titles as the 1828 inventory, which suggests that his description was based on information handed down by Javier and Mariano Goya (Bibl. 193, pp. 91-96). Both Brugada's list and Yriarte's much more detailed description make clear the disposition of the paintings in the two rooms. The analysis of these indications, published in Appendix VI, should be compared with the plans in Bibl. 169, p. 81, and 136, p. 191. The paintings in both rooms are listed here in order, starting from the left on entering the room.

1615-1621 Yriarte described two paintings to the right of the central door on entering (see Appendix VI), and there was apparently no painting to the left of the door.

1615 Brugada title *Atropos* – the name of one of the three Fates. Prado title 'El Destino' (Fate); also known as 'Las Parcas' (The Fates) – the title in Yriarte's catalogue.

1616 Brugada title *Dos forasteros* (Two foreigners). Yriarte catalogued them as 'Cowherds', adding that they were traditionally said to be *gallegos* – Galicians. In this context the Brugada title means 'provincials', men from one of the remotest and most primitive corners of Spain. Prado title (used here) 'Duelo a garrotazos'.

1617 Brugada title *Dos hombres* (Two men), a quite inaccurate description probably due to the darkness of the painting on an ill-lit wall. Yriarte, who identified the group of men reading a paper, called it 'Political gossip'. Prado title 'La lectura' (Reading).

1618 Brugada title *Dos mujeres* (Two women). Prado title 'Two women and a man'. Gudiol's title 'Two men and a woman' – he sees the figures on the left as a young couple (rather than two women) mocking the masturbating man. Cp. Sánchez Cantón (Bibl. 169, p. 44).

1619 Brugada title *El san[to] officio* (The Holy Office, i.e. Inquisition). Yriarte echoed this title, calling it 'Promenade du saint-office'. Prado title 'Peregrinación a la fuente de San Isidro' (Pilgrimage to the Fountain of San Isidro). For a possible sketch see [1628a].

1620 Brugada title *Asmodea* (a feminine version of the oriental demon of sensual desire). Yriarte wrote 'On peut intituler cette composition *Asmodée*' – perhaps the clearest proof of his access to information which can only have come from Javier or Mariano Goya. Prado title 'Al aquelarre' (To the witches' sabbath). Cp. the large landscape paintings [III.955, 956]. For a possible sketch see [1628b].

1621 Brugada title *Un perro*. Yriarte considered the painting unfinished and described the head of the swimming dog visible on the grey surface (Bibl. 193, p. 94). Prado title 'Perro semihundido' (Half-submerged dog). The dog has been thought to be swimming in water or half-buried in sand, and forms including a huge demon-like head have been tentatively identified in the damaged area above the dog's head.
Yriarte stated that there were originally two paintings on the wall to the right of the door on entering. On the right, the *Dog*; on the left, i.e. in the corner, there had been a painting by Javier which had been detached from the wall and taken by the banker M. de Salamanca. (He acquired important pictures from the collection in the Quinta, including [II.836, 837, 851, 852, III.890, 952, 953].) Yriarte added that this was not the best wall painting, but was the best preserved (Bibl. 193, pp. 92, 94, 140). See Appendix VI. Concerning Javier Goya's artistic activity, see Sánchez Cantón (Bibl. 161, pp. 78-79).

1622-1627a The paintings in this room were studied by Diego Angulo Iñíguez, 'El "Saturno" y las pinturas negras de Goya', *Archivo Español de Arte*, XXXV, 1962, pp. 173-177, and Nordström (Bibl. 136, pp. 185-221). Cp. Nordström's plan of the room (*op. cit.* p. 191) with that in Bibl. 196, p. 81, where the two paintings opposite the door have been transposed (against the evidence of Yriarte's description). See Appendix VI.

1622 Brugada title *La Leocadia*; also so identified by Yriarte who added that it was said to be the portrait of a mistress of Goya (Bibl. 193, p. 140). See the note to the portrait [III.1566]. (Saltillo illustrated a portrait of Leocadia by Rosario Weiss in Bibl. 153, facing p. 62.) Nordström pointed out the remarkable similarity between this composition and Ribera's etching of the Poet as a melancholy genius (Bibl. 136, pp. 208-209, figs 102, 103). For Gassier's interpretation of the representation of Leocadia as Goya's 'widow', and the other scenes in the room as visions from beyond the tomb, see text pp. 315-318.

1623 Title from the Brugada inventory, repeated (in Spanish) by Yriarte in his catalogue (Bibl. 193, p. 140). Prado title 'Aquelarre' (Witches' sabbath). Sánchez Cantón and Gassier agree in suggesting that the girl sitting on a chair to the right is also Leocadia. See note to [1575]. Cp. the painting of nearly a quarter-century earlier, painted for the Alameda de Osuna [II.660].

1624 Brugada title *Saturno*. Prado title 'Saturno devorando a un hijo' (Saturn devouring one of his sons). Cp. the drawing made at the time of the *Caprichos*, in 1797-99 [II.635]. It is reproduced by Nordström (who dated it to the period under discussion) together with the painting of Saturn by Rubens which may have provided a source for Goya's composition (Bibl. 136, pp. 193, 195).

1625 Brugada title *Judith y Oloferno*. Only part of Holofernes' head is visible, at the right edge. Yriarte wrote that according to tradition the model was one whom Goya often used and whose name was Ramera Moreno. As Salas has pointed out, 'ramera' is not a proper name but a reference to her class and profession, indicating that she was a prostitute (Bibl. 169, p. 74). Cp. the drawing of c.1797-99 [II.636] and the miniature of 1824-25 [V.1681]. Nordström suggested that the source for this composition was a painting by an unknown seventeenth-century artist in the cupola of San Andrés Apóstol, Madrid (Bibl. 136, p. 205, reproducing a wash design for the cupola).

1626 (The pilgrimage of San Isidro) – Brugada title, repeated in Spanish by Yriarte.

1627 Brugada title *Dos viejos*. Prado title 'Dos frailes' (Two monks). For a possible sketch see [1628c].

1627a Having worked round the lower room (in the opposite order to this catalogue), Yriarte completed his list of paintings with the *Leocadia*, followed by 'Deux vieilles femmes mangeant à la gamelle' (Two old women eating from a bowl) (Bibl. 193, p. 140). He had not described this painting in the text (p. 93), but the catalogue reference seems to correspond with the *Dos mujeres* (Two women) also listed in the Brugada inventory following the *Leocadia* painting. The two lists suggest that this painting (quite small and therefore not meriting a description in Yriarte's text) was next to or near the *Leocadia*, and its size and shape make it very likely that it was painted as an overdoor. Nordström suggested that it was an overdoor painted outside the room, as an introduction to the scenes within (Bibl. 136, pp. 190-191), and this view is supported by Yriarte's text which specified that there were six compositions within the room (*op. cit.* p. 92). However, its position in the Brugada inventory, between the *Leocadia* and the *Saturn*, seems to weight the balance in favour of its inclusion within the room. See Appendix VII.

1628a-d Three of the sketches listed here are almost identical with the Quinta compositions (whereas it has been seen that all Goya's known sketches tend to differ markedly from his final pictures), and a fourth [1628b]– the only one which the authors have had an opportunity of studying – is in a style quite unlike that of the Quinta or other paintings of the period. It came from the collection of Alphonse Kann and was exhibited in 1935 (Bibl. 18, no. 355) together with two sketches of witchcraft scenes, described as studies for the Quinta (no. 352). The latter are unknown to the authors even from photographs.

A painting sometimes connected with the Quinta is not included here as part of Goya's œuvre. It was in the collection of the Duc de Montpensier at San Telmo and later passed to the Contini-Bonacossi collection in Florence. Published by August L. Mayer, 'Dos bocetos de Juan Bautista Tiepolo y una obra perdida de Goya que aparece', *Revista Española de Arte*, IV, 1935, pp. 300-301. M.560, DF.273, G.717. Not accepted by Held (Bibl. 89, p. 192).

1628a Exhibited 1961-62 (Bibl. 24, no. 88).

1628b Not accepted by Held (Bibl. 89, p. 194). Reproduced in colour in Bibl. 169, p. 78, fig. 118.

1629 Inscribed *Goya agradecido, á su amigo Arrieta: por el acierto y esmero con q.e le salvó la vida en su aguda y- / peligrosa enfermedad, padecida á fines del año 1819. a los setenta y tres de su edad. Lo pintó en 1820.* (Goya in gratitude to his friend Arrieta, for the care and attention with which he saved his life in his acute and dangerous illness suffered at the end of the year 1819 at the age of 73. He painted it in 1820.) The portrait appears to have been exhibited at the Real Academia de San Fernando, although it is not clear in which year (cp. Bibl. 190, p. 253, no. LXLIII and 36, I, p. 141). See Trapier (Bibl. 188, pp. 42-43). First catalogued in 1928, from the collection of Lucas-Moreno (Bibl. 10, Appendix I).

Copies by Asensio Juliá: two were recorded in the 1928 exhibition catalogue (*op. cit.*) and by Desparmet, in collections in Madrid and Irun. See also Bibl. 39, p. 140.

1630 Inscribed at lower left *A Tiburcio Perez*. An architect like his uncle [III.1561], he looked after Rosario Weiss when Goya went to France in 1824 (1823, according to her biography in Bibl. 102, p. 337). See Trapier (Bibl. 188, p. 42). Exhibited 1970 (Bibl. 30, no. 51).

1631 Inscribed on verso before relining *El célebre ciego fijo* (The celebrated, totally blind man) – see Viñaza (Bibl. 190, p. 260, no. CIX) who described the picture as a portrait of the well-known old fellow Paquete, the blind beggar who usually sat on the steps of the church of San Felipe el Real, and was famous for his guitar-playing and singing. Goya's friend, the Augustinian friar Fernández de Rojas, died in the monastery at San Felipe el Real in 1817 or 1819 (see notes to [III.1555, 1562]). Held has dated this picture c.1815 (Bibl. 89, no. 123), but there seems to be a close connection with the 'black paintings' of c.1820-23 and also with the late *Monk* and *Nun* of 1827 [V.1668, 1669]. Exhibited in 1963-64 (Bibl. 27, no. 116) and 1970 (Bibl. 30, no. 53).

1632 Inscribed at lower left *D. Ramon Satue / Alcalde d[e] corte / P.r Goya 1823.* A nephew of Duaso y Latre [1633], his portrait was painted, according to Viñaza (Bibl. 190, p. 265, no. CXXVII), when Goya took refuge in Duaso's home in 1823. The date on the portrait has been questioned but there seems to be no doubt that the *3* is original, and the reference to Satué's office as city councillor, which ended in 1820, would be a record of his past position. See the discussion in Bibl. 27, no. 115. Viñaza's reference to the circumstances in which the portrait was painted appears to conflict with documents published by Sánchez Cantón which show that Goya went into hiding with Duaso y Latre at the beginning of 1824 (Bibl. 167). Cp. notes to [1633, 1634]. Exhibited 1970 (Bibl. 30, no. 52).

1633 Inscribed at lower right *D. José Duaso / Por Goya de 78 años*. This portrait was known only from a reference in a biography of the sitter (published 1849), until it was identified and published by Sánchez Cantón (Bibl. 167). The story of Goya's repeated attempts to get a good likeness and his rage when he could not succeed (cp. Viñaza, Bibl. 190, p. 65), supports his son's statement that his best portraits were those which he finished in one sitting (Bibl. 34, p. 100). Goya's relationship with Duaso, who saved him from the anti-liberal persecution as Arrieta [1629] had saved him from his physical illness, was fully discussed by Cantón (*op. cit.*). First exhibited in 1961 (Bibl. 23, no. XLII).

1634 Inscribed at left *Dn Fr.co Otin / De 25 / años* and at right *P.r Goya / 1824*. Otín was another nephew (cp. [1632]) of Duaso y Latre, and this portrait drawing belongs, together with the oil painting of his uncle [1633], to the family of the sitter. First published by Sánchez Cantón (see note to [1633]).

1635 Beruete identified the sitter who belonged to a middle class family with whom Goya was friendly (Bibl. 36, I, p. 142). Pierre Gassier has suggested that she was perhaps related to the D. Dionisio Antonio de Puga who witnessed the power of attorney which Goya signed on 19 February 1824 (document published by Sambricio, Bibl. 154, doc. 250).

Beruete also referred to the portrait drawing, signed and dated 1824, which Goya made of her son and which was then in the collection of Félix Boix. Mayer included it in his catalogue of drawings (691b) but without giving

Notes continued on page 378

ABBREVIATIONS AND SIGNS

[ ]   Numbers within square brackets refer to the works listed in the catalogue. The number is preceded by a roman numeral (I-V) referring to the section of the book in which the work appears. (This is omitted if the reference is to a work within the same section.)

TITLE
Goya's autograph titles are given in *italics*. Where there is no room for the whole title or its translation in the catalogue legend, it is continued in the note.

DATE
Examples: *1797*   dated by Goya
1797   certain date
1797?   probable date
c.1797   about 1797
1797-99   executed during the period indicated

d.   Dated
Doc.   Date indicated by a document

SIGNATURE
s.   Signed

INSCRIPTION
italics   Title or inscription by Goya
Inscr.   Inscription
/   Change of line in an inscription
MS.   Manuscript

TECHNIQUE
All works are in oil on canvas unless otherwise specified
Aq.   Aquatint
L.   Lithograph

DIMENSIONS
cm.   Centimetres
approx.   Approximately
vis.   Visible dimensions (e.g. where work is partly covered by a mount or frame)
diam.   Diameter

Dimensions of the drawings are those of the sheet of paper.
Dimensions of the engravings are those of the copperplate.

COLLECTION
A.I.   Art Institute
B.M.   British Museum, London
B.N.   Biblioteca Nacional / Bibliothèque Nationale
C.   Calcografía Nacional, Madrid (see Bibl. 5)
Fund. Lázaro   Fundación Lázaro Galdiano, Madrid (the indication M = Museum, B = Biblioteca)
Gal.   Galerie / Gallery
Inst.   Institut / Institute / Instituto
Hispanic Soc.   Hispanic Society of America, New York
K.K.   Kupferstichkabinett (Print room)
Min.   Ministère / Ministerio / Ministry
Mus.   Musée / Museo / Museum (of Fine Arts, unless otherwise indicated)
M.F.A.   Museum of Fine Arts, Boston
M.M.A.   Metropolitan Museum of Art, New York
N.G.   National Gallery
Patr. Nac.   Patrimonio Nacional, Madrid
R.A.   Real Academia / Royal Academy
P. Palais   Petit Palais (Musée des Beaux-Arts de la Ville de Paris)
Rhode Is. S. D. Mus.   Museum of the School of Design, Providence (Rhode Island)

V. and A.   Victoria and Albert Museum, London
coll.   Collection (a capital C indicates a public collection, e.g. Frick Coll., New York)
priv.   Private
destr.   Destroyed

Acquisition or inventory numbers are given in brackets after the name of the collection. See Index of Collections, page 394.

BIBLIOGRAPHICAL REFERENCES
Bibl.   See the numbered Bibliography, page 386. The most frequently used abbreviations are:
B.   Barcia, *Catálogo de la Colección de Dibujos Originales de la Biblioteca Nacional* (Bibl. 3)
D.   Delteil, 'Francisco Goya', *Le Peintre graveur illustré* (Bibl. 55)
DF.   Desparmet Fitz-Gerald, *L'Œuvre peint de Goya* (Bibl. 57)
G.   Gudiol, *Goya* (catalogue raisonné) (Bibl. 85)
H.   Harris, *Goya. Engravings and lithographs* (Bibl. 88)
M.   Mayer, *Francisco de Goya* (Bibl. 128)
S.   Sambricio, *Tapices de Goya* (Bibl. 154)
SC.   Sánchez Cantón, *Museo del Prado: Los dibujos de Goya* (Bibl. 168)

ILLUSTRATION
Ill. p. (or p.)   See the reproduction in the text at the page indicated.

NOTE
*   Reference to a note on the pages preceding the illustrated catalogue.

CATALOGUE IV
c.1815-1824

[1571-1657d]

**LOS DISPARATES or
LOS PROVERBIOS
(Follies or Proverbs)**

Drawn and engraved between 1815 and 1824.

In style and technique this series spans the period between the completion of the *Tauromaquia* engravings in 1816 [III. 1149-1243] and the decoration of the *Quinta del Sordo* [1615-1627a] after 1819 and before Goya's departure for Bordeaux in 1824. The copperplates were stored away with those of the *Disasters of War* when Goya left Spain, and the first edition was not published until 1864.
20 preparatory drawings are listed: 12 for the 22 published plates and

8 additional drawings of which no engravings are known. All are in red chalk and brush and sanguine wash.
14 of the artist's proofs have *Disparate* titles and a number in pen and ink in Goya's hand, but these titles and sequence were not followed by the Academicians when the plates were published under the title *Los Proverbios*. The numbers were engraved on the plates for the second edition. (Invented *Disparate* titles are given in square brackets.)
Nine editions were printed from 18 of the original copperplates between 1864 and 1937. These plates are in the Calcografía Nacional, Madrid (Bibl. 5, *Goya*, 163-180).
The remaining four plates became

separated from the others and were first published in the French periodical *L'Art* in 1877. See [1601-1604].
The plates are in etching and aquatint; drypoint and burin retouches are not recorded. The dimensions given are those of the copperplates.

Abbreviations and signs, see p. 324
Aq. = aquatint
D = Delteil, Bibl. 55
H = Harris, Bibl. 88
SC = Sánchez Cantón, Bibl. 168

[1571-1613]   *

1571   Prov.1

Disparate Femenino (Feminine Folly)   c.1815-24.   s. *Goya*
Etching and aquatint 24×35 cm.
D.202, H.248   Ill. p. 309   *

1572

Drawing for [1571].
Red chalk and sanguine wash
Madrid, Prado (185)   SC.382

1573   Prov.2

[Disparate de miedo] (Fearful Folly)   c.1815-24.
Etching and aquatint 24·5×35 cm.
D.203, H.249   *

1574

Drawing for [1573].
Red chalk and sanguine wash
Madrid, Prado (186)   SC.383

1575   Prov.3

Disparate Ridiculo (Ridiculous Folly)   c.1815-24.
Etching and aquatint 24·5×35 cm.
D.204, H.250   *

1576   Prov.4

[Disparate de bobo] (Simpleton's Folly)   c.1815-24.   s. *Goya*
Etching and aquatint 24·5×35 cm.
D.205, H.251   *

1577

Drawing for [1576].
Red chalk and sanguine wash
Madrid, Prado (188)   SC.384

1578   Prov.5

Disparate Volante (Flying Folly)
c.1815-24.
Etching and aquatint 24·5×35 cm.
D.206, H.252   *

1579   Prov.6

Disparate Cruel (Cruel Folly)
c.1815-24.   s. *Goya*
Etching and aquatint 24·5×35 cm.
D.207, H.253   *

1580

Drawing for [1579].
Red chalk and sanguine wash
Madrid, Prado (192)   SC.385

1581   Prov.7

Disparate Desordenado (Disorderly Folly)   c.1815-24.   s. *Goya*
Etching and aquatint 24·5×35 cm.
D.208, H.254   Ill. p. 312   *

1582   Prov.8

[Disparate de entalegados] (Folly in sacks)   c.1815-24.
Etching and aquatint 24·5×35 cm.
D.209, H.255   *

1583   Prov.9

Disparate General (General Folly)
c.1815-24.
Etching and aquatint 24·5×35 cm.
D.210, H.256   *

1584   recto of 1613

Drawing for [1583].
Red chalk and sanguine wash
Madrid, Prado (433)   SC.399

1585   Prov.10

[Disparate desenfrenado] (Unbridled Folly)   c.1815-24.   s.
Etching and aquatint 24·5×35 cm.
D.211, H.257   Ill. p. 312   *

1586

Drawing for [1585].
Red chalk and sanguine wash
Madrid, Prado (189)   SC.386

1587 Prov.11

Disparate Pobre (Poor Folly)
c.1815-24.
Etching and aquatint 24·5×35 cm.
D.212, H.258 *

1588

Drawing for [1587].
Red chalk and sanguine wash
Madrid, Prado (187) SC.390

1589 Prov.12

Disparate Alegre (Merry Folly)
c.1815-24.
Etching and aquatint 24·5×35 cm.
D.213, H.259 *

1590

Drawing for [1589].
Red chalk and sanguine wash
Madrid, Prado (193) SC.388

1591 Prov.13

Modo de volar (A way of flying)
c.1815-20.
Etching and aquatint 24·5×35 c
D.214, H.260

1592

Drawing for [1591]. Red chalk
and sanguine wash 24·5×35 cm.
Madrid, Fund. Lázaro (B.14866-22)
Ill. p. 311 *

1593 Prov.14

Disparate de Carnabal (Carnival
Folly) c.1815-24.
Etching and aquatint 24·5×35 cm.
D.215, H.261 *

1594 Prov.15

Disparate Claro (Clear Folly)
c.1815-24.
Etching and aquatint 24·5×35 cm.
D.216, H.262 *

1595

Drawing for [1594].
Red chalk and sanguine wash
Madrid, Prado (201) SC.397

1596 Prov.16

[Disparate triple] (Triple
Folly) c.1815-24.
Etching and aquatint 24·5×35 cr
D.217, H.263

1597

Drawing for [1596].
Red chalk and sanguine wash
Madrid, Prado (194) SC.389

1598 Prov.17

[Disparate quieto] (Still Folly)
c.1815-24
Etching and aquatint 24·5×35 cm.
D.218, H.264 *

1599

Drawing for [1598].
Red chalk and sanguine wash
Madrid, Prado (199) SC.395

1600 Prov.18

[Disparate fúnebre] (Funereal
Folly) c.1815-24.
Etching and aquatint 24·5×35 cm.
D.219, H.265 *

ADDITIONAL PLATES

Four of the twenty-two known copperplates were acquired by Eugenio Lucas and were published in the periodical *L'Art* in 1877 (Tome II, facing pp. 6, 40, 56 and 82). French titles were engraved on the plate as well as the letters *Goya inv. et sc.* and *F.çois Liénard. Imp. Paris.* The plates have apparently not been printed since 1877 and now belong to the heirs of Madame Le Garrec, Paris. All four unique contemporary proofs have *Disparate* titles.

[1601-1604]

1601

Disparate Conocido (Well-known
Folly) c.1815-24. Inscr.
Etching and aquatint 24·5×35 cm.
D.220, H.266 *

1602

Disparate Puntual (Precise Folly)
c.1815-24. Inscr.
Etching and aquatint 24·5×35 cm.
D.221, H.267 *

1603

Disparate de Bestia (Animal Folly)
c.1815-24. Inscr.
Etching and aquatint 24·5×35 cm.
D.222, H.268 *

Drawing used for [1603].
See [Ill.1532]

1604

Disparate de Tontos (Fools' Folly)
c.1815-24. Inscr.
Etching and aquatint 24·5×35 cm
D.223, H.269 Ill. p. 311 *

ADDITIONAL DRAWINGS

Eight drawings are listed. The first three show the mark of the copperplate on the sheet, which proves that they were used for engravings. The remainder are identical in style and technical characteristics. A ninth drawing shows an idea which does not recur in the prints.
The drawings for the *Disparate* series are so broadly and freely handled, and Goya apparently made such extensive alterations to the plates in the course of work, that it is not impossible that some of these additional drawings may have been used for the known plates.

[1605-1613]

1605

Crowd of figures in a tree(?) c.1815-24.   Red chalk and sanguine wash   Madrid, Prado (202)   SC.387; H.269a   *

1606

Giant pointing towards a crowd c.1815-24.   Red chalk and sanguine wash   Madrid, Prado (195)   SC.391; H.269b   *

1607

Figures enveloped in sacks c.1815-24.   Red chalk and sanguine wash   Madrid, Prado (198)   SC.394; H.269c   *

1608

Falling demon   c.1815-24. Red chalk and sanguine wash Madrid, Prado (200)   SC.396; H.269d   *

1609

The fire-eater   c.1815-24. Red chalk and sanguine wash Madrid, Prado (196) SC.392; H.269e

1610

Two figures pointing to a bright opening   c.1815-24.   Red chalk and sanguine wash   Madrid, Prado (197)   SC.393; H.269f

1611

Figures climbing over a reclining giant   c.1815-24.   Red chalk and sanguine wash   Madrid, Prado (203)   SC.398; H.269g

1612

Procession(?)   c.1815-24. Red chalk and sanguine wash 22·8×32·9 cm. Cambridge (Mass.), Philip Hofer *

1613   verso of 1584

The vain peacock   c.1815-24. Sanguine wash Madrid, Prado (457)   SC.454   *

THE BLACK PAINTINGS in the Quinta del Sordo 1820-1823

27 February 1819: Goya acquired the country-house on the outskirts of Madrid, and extensive repairs and alterations were made to the property.
Winter 1819: his serious illness is documented by the portrait of his doctor [1629].
17 September 1823: he made the Quinta over to his grandson Mariano.
The decoration of the Quinta was probably carried out between Goya's recovery from his illness in 1820, and his gift of the Quinta to Mariano. It consisted of fourteen oil paintings on plaster, seven in an upper room and six or

seven in the ground-floor room immediately below. Sánchez Cantón has suggested that the upper room was the first to be decorated since there is a considerable variety in style and subject between one painting and another, whereas the lower room presents a unified scheme.
The paintings were listed by Brugada in the inventory of 1828 (see Appendix VI). The 1963 edition of the Prado catalogue gives some of the Brugada titles beside the traditional Prado titles. All the alternative titles are indicated in the notes.

[1615-1627a]   *

FIRST-FLOOR ROOM

Seven paintings ranging from the colour and movement of the *Duel* [1616] and the *Asmodea* [1620] to the cold greys and yellows of the *Fates* [1615]. The paintings are listed in order, starting from the left as the room was originally entered.

[1615-1621]   *

1615

Atropos or The Fates   1820-23. 123×266 cm. Madrid, Prado (757) M.559d, DF.111, G.708   *

1616

Duel with cudgels   1820-23. 123×266 cm. Madrid, Prado (758)   M.559e, DF.112, G.709   Ill. p. 320 *

1617

Men reading   1820-23. 126×66 cm. Madrid, Prado (766) M.559n, DF.120, G.710   *

1618

Two young people laughing at a man   1820-23.   125×66 cm. Madrid, Prado (765) M.559m, DF.119, G.711   *

1619

Promenade of the Holy Office
1820-23.   123×266 cm.
Madrid, Prado (755)
M.559b, DF.109, G.713   *

1620

Asmodea   1820-23.
123×265 cm.
Madrid, Prado (756)   M.559c,
DF.110, G.715   Ill. p. 23   *

1621

The dog   1820-23.
134×80 cm.
Madrid, Prado (767)   M.559o,
DF.121, G.716   Ill. p. 319   *

GROUND FLOOR ROOM

Seven paintings which are now
generally thought to have a
common thematic unity: the
concept of Saturn as the symbol
of old age and melancholy, of
witchcraft and saturnalian revelry,
of darkness and destruction.
Since Beruete, the room has
usually been described as a
dining-room, but there is no
proof that it was.
The paintings are listed in the
same order as those of the upper
room.

[1622-1627a]   *

1622

La Leocadia   1820-23.
147×132 cm.
Madrid, Prado (754)   M.559a,
DF.108, G.699   Ill. p. 314   *

1623

El gran cabrón (The great
he-goat)   1820-23.
140×438 cm. Madrid, Prado (761)
M.559h. DF.115, G.700   *

1624

Saturn   1820-23.
146×83 cm.   Madrid, Prado (763)
M.68/559k, DF.117, G.702
Ill. p. 318   *

1625

Judith and Holofernes   1820-23.
146×84 cm. Madrid, Prado (764)
M.17/5591, DF.118, G.701
Ill. p 318.   *

1626

La Romería de San Isidro
1820-23.   140×438 cm.
Madrid, Prado (760)   M.559g,
DF.114, G.703   Ill. p. 316   *

1627

Two old men   1820-2
144×66 cm.
Madrid, Prado (759)
M.559f, DF.113, G.705

1627a

Two old people eating   1820-23.
53×85 cm.
Madrid, Prado (762)
M.559i. DF.116, G.707   *

SKETCHES FOR THE QUINTA DEL SORDO

In the inventory of the Quinta
made by Brugada in 1828 is an
item *Siete caprichos (bocetos de
la casa de campo)* - that is,
seven sketches for the paintings
in the Quinta. In recent years a
number of paintings have
appeared which may represent
this group of hitherto unknown
sketches. They have not been
studied together and their
authenticity has yet to be
established. They are listed here
pending further investigation.

[1628a-d]   *

1628a

Pilgrimage to the Fountain of San
Isidro - sketch for [1619]?
33×57·5 cm.   Paris, priv. coll.
DF.109n, G.712   *

1628b

Vision - sketch for [1620]?
20×48·5 cm.
Basle, Kunstmuseum (G. 1958.75)
G.714   *

1628c

Two old men - sketch for [1627
65×15 cm.
Salamanca, priv. coll.   G.704

28d

o old people eating - sketch
[1627a].   15×65 cm.
lamanca, priv. coll.
706

PORTRAITS   1820-1824

The last portraits before Goya's
departure for France. Portraits of
friends and above all of the two
men who saved him: Dr Arrieta
who in 1819 kept him alive during
his grave illness, and Don José
Duaso y Latre who in 1824 took
him into his house to escape
from Ferdinand's savage
repression.
Soon afterwards he left for France,
no doubt taking with him the
little drawing of his son Javier.

[1629-1637]

1629

Goya and his doctor Arrieta   s.d.
1820 with inscr.   117×79 cm.
Minneapolis, Inst. of Arts (52.14)
M.305, DF.270, G.697   p. 307 *

1630

Tiburcio Pérez y Cuervo   s.d. *Goya
1820* with inscr.   102·1×81·3 cm.
New York, M.M.A. (30.95.242)
M.380, DF.511, G.698   p. 304 *

1631

Tío Paquete   c.1820-23.   Inscr.
on verso 39×31 cm.   Lugano,
Baron Thyssen-Bornemisza
M.375, DF.512, G.723   *

32

món Satué   s.d. *1823*, inscr.
7×83·5 cm.   Amsterdam,
ksmuseum (988.BI)
418, DF.514, G.718   *

1633

José Duaso y Latre   s.[d.] 1824
with inscr.   74×59 cm.
Madrid, J. Rodríguez Babé
G.719   *

1634

Francisco Otín   s.d. *1824* with
inscr.   Pencil 14×9·5 cm. (vis.)
Madrid, J. Rodríguez Babé   *

1635

María Martínez de Puga
s.d. *Goya 1824*.   80×58·4 cm.
New York, Frick Coll. (A.302)
M.393, DF.517, G.720   p. 337 *

1636

Javier Goya   s.d. *P.r Goya año
1824*.   Black chalk 9×8 cm.
New York, Lehman Coll.   *

37

an Antonio Melón   c.1820-24.
hograph by Gillivray from a
awing by Goya   *

RELIGIOUS PAINTINGS
1819-1824

The greatest of all Goya's religious
paintings is undoubtedly the *Last
Communion of Saint Joseph of
Calasanz,* painted for the chapel
of the Escuelas Pías de San
Antón in Madrid, the religious
teaching order which had been
responsible for his education as a
child in Saragossa.
The small painting of *Christ on
the Mount of Olives,* was given by
Goya to the fathers as a gesture
of gratitude.
Two more works of strong
emotional intensity are the
pendant pictures of *Saint Peter*
and *Saint Paul.*

[1638-1642]

1638

The last Communion...   s.d.
1819.   250×180 cm.
Madrid, San Antón Abad
M.53, DF.103, G.694   p. 306 *

1639

Sketch for [1638].
Panel 45·5×33·5 cm.
Bayonne, Mus. Bonnat (11)
M.54, DF.102, G.693   *

1640

Christ on the Mount of Olives
s.d.*1819*   Panel 47×35 cm.
Madrid, Escuelas Pías
M.20, DF.105, G.696   p. 305 *

41

e repentant Peter   c.1820-24.
Goya   72·4×64·2 cm.
ashington, Phillips Coll.
66, DF.107, G.725   *

1642

Saint Paul   c.1820-24.
s. *Goya*   74×64·5 cm.
U.S.A., priv. coll.
M.65, DF.106, G.726   *

LITHOGRAPHS   1819

In 1819 José María Cardano
opened the first 'lithographic
establishment' in Madrid, and
Goya's earliest known lithograph
was dated in February of that
same year. All his early lithographs
were made by the transfer
process. The results were far
from satisfactory and very few
proofs are known, most of them
being retouched with pen and
ink or black chalk to make good
the defective printing. It was
not until he went to Bordeaux
that Goya learnt to master this
new medium - see [V.1698-1710].

Abbreviations and signs, see p. 324
D = Delteil, Bibl. 55
H = Harris, Bibl. 88
L = lithograph
If not a proof from an edition:
1/1 = unique proof; 1/3 = one
of three proofs known.
Dimensions of lithographs without
a border are approximately those
of the worked area

[1643-1650]   *

1643

Old woman spinning   d. *Madrid
Febrero 1819*.   L. pen and ink
20·5×25·5 cm.   1/4   Madrid,
X. de Salas   D.268, H.270

1644

1645

1646

1647

1648

Old style duel   1819.
L. pen and ink transfer 13×23 cm.
1/5   Madrid, B.N. (45626)
D.269, H.271   *

Inferno   1819?
L. ink wash transfer 12×24 cm.
1/1   Madrid, B.N. (45629)
D.271, H.272   *

Drawing for [1645].   Lithographic
ink wash 15·5×23·3 cm. (vis.)
London, B.M. (1876.5.10.374)

The road to hell - drawing
for a lithograph?   Lithographic
ink wash 18·8×26·7 cm.
Madrid, B.N. (B.1252)   *

Espresivo doble fuerza 1819?
L. ink. wash transfer 8×11·5 cm
1/2   Madrid, B.N. (45627)
D.272, H.274   Ill. p. 308   *

1649

1650

PAINTINGS ON PANEL
c.1820-1824?

A group of small paintings whose
authenticity has been questioned.
Recently, some more paintings
in the same series have come to
light, and the group now calls
for further study. If the
attribution is upheld, it is not easy
to say whether they should be
dated to Goya's last years
in Madrid, or to the Bordeaux
period. They recall many of the
drawings from albums C and F,
and are also close to the spirit and
technique of the Bordeaux
miniatures of 1824-25 - see
[V.1676-1697].

[1651-1656]   *

1651

Drawing for [1648].
Lithographic ink wash
8·6×17·5 cm.
London, priv. coll.   *

The outrage   1819?   L. ink
wash transfer 11×13·5 cm.   1/1
Berlin-Dahlem, K.K. (200.1905)

Monk preaching   c.1820-24.
Panel 31·1×21 cm.
Munich, Alte Pinakothek (8615)
M.526, DF.205, G.732

1652

1653

1654

1655

1656

Execution of a witch   c.1820-24.
Panel 31×21 cm.
Munich, Alte Pinakothek (8616)
M.546, DF.p.305, G.733

The duel   c.1820-24.
Panel 31·3×21 cm.
Munich, Alte Pinakothek (8617)
M.616, DF.208, G.731   *

The wounded man   c.1820-24.
Panel 31·1×20·8 cm.
Munich, Alte Pinakothek (8618)
M.615, DF.p.305, G.730

Brigands killing men and women
c.1820-24.   Panel 31×20 cm.
Rosario (Arg.), Mus. Castagnino
M.610, G.729

Carnival   c.1820-24.
Panel 31×20·5 cm.
Madrid, Rafael Lafora García
G.728   *

PAINTINGS ON TINPLATE
c.1820-1824

Four small paintings re-attributed
to Goya by Gudiol who points
out their similarity with the
technique of the 'black paintings'
[1615-1627a] and the evident
relationship of the *Woman
reading* with the lithograph of
1819 or 1825 [V.1699].
The paintings entered the Museum
at Besançon as part of the Gigoux
bequest, and were listed together
with [III. 922, 923] in the
inventory of his effects. They
were later attributed to Lucas.

[1657a-d]

1657a

1657b

1657c

1657d

Woman reading   c.1820-24.
Tinplate 22×32·5 cm.
Besançon, Mus. (896.1.342)
DF.[250n.], G.684   *

Joseph's tunic   c.1820-24.
Tinplate 22×32·5 cm.
Besançon, Mus. (896.1.330)
M.14, DF.[250n.], G.685 *

The fight   c.1820-24.
Tinplate 22×32·5 cm.
Besançon, Mus. (896.1.331)
M.609, DF.[250n.], G.686   *

The victim   c.1820-24.
Tinplate 22×32·5 cm.
Besançon, Mus. (896.1.343)
M.609, DF.[250n.], G.687   *

Part five   1824-1828

Dates	Life of Goya	History of Spain	History outside Spain	The Arts	Literature and Science
1824	Goya arrives in Bordeaux Stays with Moratín Leaves three days later for Paris (30 June) Stay in Paris (30 June-1 Sept.) *Joaquín Ferrer, Manuela Alvárez Coiñas de Ferrer* Paints a *Corrida* for Ferrer Settles in Bordeaux with Leocadia Weiss and her children (September) *Leandro Fernández de Moratín* Winter 1824-25: forty miniatures on ivory Drawings: *Albums G and H* (1824-28)	Period of absolutist repression under Ferdinand VII († 1833)	Frontier treaty between Russia and the U.S.A. Death of Louis XVIII, succeeded by Charles X (16 September) Bolivar frees Peru from Spanish domination	25 August: opening of the Paris Salon (Delacroix: *The massacre of Chios*; Ingres: *The Vow of Louis XIII*; Lawrence: *The Duke of Richelieu*; landscapes by Constable and Bonington) Beethoven: *Late quartets* (1824-26)	W. Scott: *Redgauntlet* Heine: *Harzreise*
1825	First renewal of Goya's leave of absence (13 January) Spring: Goya seriously ill Second renewal of Goya's leave of absence (4 July) Death of Martín Miguel de Goicoechea, father-in-law of Javier Lithographs known as the *Bulls of Bordeaux*		Death of Alexander I Nicholas I Bolivar frees Bolivia End of Spanish colonial rule in South America	Publication of copies after the *Caprichos* in Paris (Motte, éditeur) Death of David in Brussels Boïeldieu: *La Dame Blanche* C. F. Meyer († 1898) Constable: *The leaping horse* Hokusai: *The wave*	Thierry: *History of the Conquest of England* Pushkin: *Boris Godunov* Laplace: *Mécanique céleste*
1826	*Jacques Galos* Visit to Madrid: Goya is granted his retirement on full pay as Court Painter Portrait of Goya by Vicente López			Mendelssohn: *A Midsummer Night's Dream*	Vigny: *Poèmes antiques et modernes*; *Cinq-Mars* Fenimore Cooper: *The Last of the Mohicans* Leopardi: *Versi* Heine: *Reisebilder* (1826-31)
1827	Summer: second visit to Madrid *Mariano Goya* *Juan Bautista Muguiro* Moratín and Silvela move to Paris		Battle of Navarino; destruction of Turkish fleet by combined forces of England, France and Russia	Delacroix: *Sardanapalus* Corot: *Le Pont de Narni* Ingres: *Apotheosis of Homer* Schubert: *Trout Quintet* Death of Beethoven (aged 57) Death of William Blake	Hugo: Preface to *Cromwell* F. Cooper: *The Prairie* Manzoni: *I Promessi Sposi* Ohm's law on electric currents
1828	*José Pio de Molina* (unfinished) Gumersinda and Mariano in Bordeaux (28 March) Goya's last letter to Javier (1 April) Paralysis sets in (2 April) Death of Goya (16 April) Arrival of Javier (20 April) Death of Moratín in Paris (21 June) Inventory of the 'Quinta del Sordo' by Antonio Brugada		Wellington and Peel in office	François Rude: *Mercury putting on his heel wings* Schubert: *Symphony in C-Major* Berlioz: *Symphonie fantastique* Death of Bonington Catalogue of the Prado Museum: autobiographical note by Goya and exhibition of three of his paintings among works of the modern Spanish school	W. Scott: *The Fair Maid of Perth* D. G. Rossetti († 1882) Taine († 1898) Ibsen († 1906) Meredith († 1909) Tolstoy († 1910) Jules Verne († 1905)

Chapter 1

THE POLITICAL SCENE. GOYA LEAVES SPAIN. VISIT TO PARIS
LIFE IN BORDEAUX. ROSARIO WEISS. DRAWINGS AND MINIATURES

1823-1828. Goya is 77 to 82 years old. Reaction of Ferdinand VII after three years of constitutional monarchy. Goya gives the Quinta to his grandson Mariano, hides for three months in a friend's house, decides to emigrate. Obtains official leave of absence. Journey to France. Stay in Paris (July-August 1824). Settles in Bordeaux with Leocadia Weiss. Two last 'albums' of drawings. Reign of Ferdinand VII in Spain. The Restoration (Charles X) in France.

Self-portrait   [1658] 1824. Drawing
Prado Museum, Madrid

Gift of the Quinta to Mariano

Bibl. 161, pp. 93, 108-109

The expedition of the 'Cent Mille Fils de Saint Louis' culminated in the capture of Trocadero at the end of August 1823 and marked, as we have already seen, a return to despotism and oppression in Spain, as a new wave of brutality and terror swept across the kingdom. On 7 November 1823 Riego was executed and on 13 November Ferdinand VII made a triumphal entry into Madrid in a chariot drawn by twenty-four young men. The crowds welcomed him with cries of 'Death to the Constitution', 'Long live the Inquisition', 'Down with the Nation'. There followed another period of arbitrary arrests, personal vendettas, summary executions, torture and hanging, carried out with even greater savagery and more refined sadism. Then, after this initial outburst of blind hatred, a system of organized repression was set up in January 1824. In every province, permanent military commissions with executive powers were established to judge the enemies of absolute power. Strict censorship was imposed and all writings, lampoons, pamphlets and caricatures printed between 1820 and 1823 had to be handed over to the parish priests. Political 'purification' committees were established to inquire into the behaviour of officers and civil servants and then of the whole army, the teaching body, students and even school children. In short, not a single Spaniard was safe from the suspicions of the secret police or from an anonymous informer. The reign of fear had begun and was to last for ten years, until the death of Ferdinand VII.

It is easy to understand Goya's agitated feelings when the Duke of Angoulême's success was announced and particularly when the 'absolutists', whom he believed to have been driven away for good in 1820, returned in force. He had accumulated a large number of unpublished etchings in his home, including the final plates of the *Disasters of War* and the *Disparates* series, as well as dozens of drawings which amounted to enough pieces of evidence to send him to the galleys and justify the confiscation of all his property. Since 1808 he had harboured no illusions concerning the *Deseado*. During the two short sittings which the king had granted him he had gauged the depths of his royal model's soul. Brought up amid intrigue and enmity in the royal palace, the king was dominated by fear and could himself rule only by intrigue and enmity. As long as he remained on the throne there was no hope for Spain, and in 1823 he was only thirty-nine years old.

Faced with such bleak prospects for the future and aware of the serious threats which hung over him, Goya decided to emigrate, as so many of his friends had done since 1814. In 1823 he was seventy-seven, but in spite of his infirmities his will to live remained indomitable, his curiosity insatiable, and he was ready to go anywhere provided that he might end his life in a free country. But for the time being it was a question of saving the essentials, his life and his property.

Scarcely three weeks after the capture of Trocadero, he made over the Quinta del Sordo to his grandson Mariano who was then seventeen. The deed of gift specifies that he had taken this decision because he wished 'to give a proof of the affection which he felt for his grandson' and also that 'he does not need the donated property because he still owns enough to be able to live decently'. This operation was clearly intended to exempt the Quinta from any eventual confiscation of his property and to put his affairs in order before his final departure, and it had the advantage of leaving him the use of his home for as long as he wished.

By far the most difficult question which Goya had to settle during the winter of 1823-1824 was that of his official position as Court Painter and in particular the continued payment of his salary. He was still in the service of the king and any prolonged absence from court without official leave would deprive him of the fifty thousand reales which he received each year. He was now an old man and there was no question – it was also a matter of pride – of leaving secretly, like any poor *émigré*. His attempted escape to Piedrahita around 1812 had been an act of 'youthful' impulse when he thought he had nothing to lose, given that he did not draw his salary between 1808 and 1814. But the experience had shown that the police had formidable means of retaliation at their disposal when dealing with men in his position. So the only course open to him was to achieve the difficult feat of emigrating legally, retaining all the preferments and advantages of his office.

See pp. 224, 249

The circumstances surrounding Ferdinand VII's return to Madrid were far from favourable to such a plan. The repression grew fiercer every day and the decrees of

Leandro Fernández de Moratín   [1661] 1824. 54×47 cm. Museum of Fine Arts, Bilbao

Leandro Fernández de Moratín
This portrait was painted twenty-five years after the one in the Academy of San Fernando (see p. 135) and shows Moratín as Goya found him in Bordeaux, an old man with puffy, thickened features, almost unrecognizable in spite of the same gentle equanimity in his expression. Writing to his friend Juan Antonio Melón in Madrid, on 20 September 1824, Moratín made fun of his appearance, saying that Goya 'wants to paint my portrait so you can imagine how handsome I must be when such expert brushes wish to multiply my image'. Moratín's letters to Melón are one of the richest sources of information concerning Goya's years in Bordeaux. In 1827 he left Bordeaux, with Manuel Silvela, to settle in Paris where he died the following year, two months after Goya.

Yo lo he visto en Paris
Black chalk 19·4 × 14·8 cm.
Private collection, Paris
This album executed in Bordeaux includes a curious group of drawings showing various picturesque methods of transport which must have struck Goya. This one is a direct record of his stay in Paris, from 30 June to 1 September 1824, and it proves that he was interested above all in what went on in the streets rather than in the *salons*.

Yo lo he visto en Paris (I saw it in Paris) Album G.*31*   [1736] 1824-28

January 1824 concerning the activities of the police and the military commissions seem to have led Goya to fear for his own safety. One may indeed be justified in thinking that it was not so much Goya himself who was directly threatened as Leocadia Weiss, who was known for her violently anti-absolutist political opinions. Her eldest son Guillermo was in fact a member of the voluntary militia in Madrid and as a result he also had to seek refuge in France. Although little is known about the Weiss family before 1824, the documents found in the Bordeaux archives specify 'that in 1823 [Leocadia Weiss] was forced to seek asylum in France to escape the persecution to which she was subjected on account of her political opinions'. This apparently contradicts the only official report of her entry into France via Bayonne on 14 September 1824, accompanied by two children, but it seems quite logical that Leocadia should have tried to escape from the absolutist reaction in 1823 and while she may have gone into hiding in Spain she could equally

Bibl. 137, p. 263
Bibl. 137, pp. 256-257

well have crossed the frontier secretly into France. Although her own movements are not known, it is nevertheless recorded in a biography of her daughter Rosario that the little girl, then nine years old, was entrusted to the care of the architect Don Tiburcio Pérez (whose portrait Goya had painted in 1820 [IV.1630]), 'when Goya went to Bordeaux in 1823'. The date may be a mistake, but it does coincide with that mentioned in the document quoted above, concerning Leocadia's flight to France. It is also curious that the child should have been entrusted to someone who did not belong to the family, while her legal, if not her actual, father was living in Madrid at the time. It seems in any event that Leocadia, whose impetuous temperament is well known, was the first to suffer persecution and that Goya, with whom she was living, was so seriously worried about the possible repercussions that he went into hiding for three months in the home of an Aragonese friend, Don José Duaso y Latre. He left as a souvenir of his enforced stay a portrait of his

Ill. p. 304
Bibl. 102, p. 337

Goya hides with Duaso y Latre

Mendigos q.ᵉ se lleban solos en Bordeaux Album G.*29*   [1734] 1824-28

Mendigos q.ᵉ se lleban solos en Bordeaux
(Beggars who get about on their own in Bordeaux). Black chalk 18·4 × 14·2 cm.
Private collection, Paris
In Bordeaux as in Paris, Goya strolled about the streets and found much to interest his insatiable curiosity. The beggars and the legless cripples whom he had seen in Madrid dragged themselves miserably around on crutches [III.1256] or at best on a board with little wheels [III.1273]. In France there are beggars who can 'get about on their own. . .' on an ingenious little three-wheeled cart.

María Martínez de Puga
The portrait of María Martínez de Puga is signed and dated 1824. The sitter may be a relation, or possibly the wife, of the Dionisio Antonio de Puga whose signature appears as witness to the power of attorney drawn up in Madrid at Goya's request on 19 February 1824 and intended to insure the continued payment of his salary as Court Painter during his absence. It was in this year that Goya went into hiding in the house of his friend Don José Duaso y Latre, whose portrait he painted in gratitude [IV.1633]. That of María de Puga was probably painted in the same way, before he left for France. It is one of the most strikingly modern of all Goya's portraits and would have enchanted Manet with its harmonies of black and grey.

María Martínez de Puga [IV.1635] 1824. 80×58·4 cm. Frick Collection, New York

host [IV.1633] and a drawing of Duaso's nephew [IV.1634], both made after his seventy-eighth birthday on 31 March 1824 since in signing the works he mentioned his age, as he so often did in his later years. This means that he remained in hiding from about the third week in January until mid-April 1824. On 1 May an amnesty was proclaimed and the very next day, without losing a moment, Goya presented a request for six months' leave so that he might 'take the mineral waters at Plombières to alleviate the sufferings and infirmities which are such a burden to his old age'. Duaso and other friends had probably prepared the ground and the Duke of Hijar, the Lord Chamberlain, seems to have advised that the royal assent be given to the request, without consulting the Secretary of State. Ferdinand VII indicated his surprise but nevertheless gave his authorization on 30 May, and on 24 June the Sub-prefect of Bayonne informed the French Minister of the Interior that Goya had passed through on his way to Paris.

Probably before leaving Madrid, in the early months of 1824, Goya executed one of his most remarkable portraits, that of *Doña María Martínez de Puga* [IV.1635], which anticipates Manet in its use of black. Only the sitter's name is known, but there may be a connection between this young woman and the Don Dionisio Antonio de Puga whose name appears among the witnesses who countersigned the power of attorney drawn up for Goya on 19 February 1824 in anticipation of his imminent departure.

He stopped for three days in Bordeaux to see his friends Leandro Fernández de Moratín and Manuel Silvela who had already settled there in exile. In spite of his seventy-eight years and his many infirmities, the 'young traveller', as they called him, set out again at once for Paris. The fact that he went off so hastily, forgetting all about Plombières, is not really surprising when one realizes that the waters of Plombières, like those of Bagnères whose benefits he later extolled when asking for an extension of leave, were no more than medical pretexts which fooled no one. On the other hand one can well understand his desire to get as soon as possible to Paris, the artistic and literary capital where a new kind of painting was making its appearance and giving rise to much discussion. He was welcomed there by a cousin of his daughter-in-law, Jerónimo Goicoechea, then twenty years old, with whom he stayed at 5 rue Marivaux, in the Hôtel Favart. This young relation's uncle was Martín Miguel de Goicoechea, Javier's father-in-law. When Goya

Bibl. 167

Political amnesty. Goya asks for leave to visit France

Bibl. 154, docs 251-256
Bibl. 137, p. 233

Ill. p. 337

Bibl. 154, doc. 250

Bibl. 154, docs 257-262

Dromedary
Cossack or Mameluke
c.1821-26. Black chalk 14·8 × 10·5 cm. Two drawings probably made by Goya for the little Rosario Weiss whom he encouraged by giving her amusing sketches to copy.

Dromedary   [1868] c.1821-26. Black chalk. Lázaro Galdiano Museum, Madrid

Cossack [1856] Biblioteca Nacional, Madrid

Loco furioso (Raging lunatic) Album G.*3[3]* [1738] Priv. coll., Paris   *Loco picaro* (Crafty lunatic) G.*43* [1748] Nationalmuseum, Stockholm

Two drawings from a group of thirteen showing different kinds of lunatics. Whether seen by Goya in the asylum in Bordeaux or recreated from his imagination, they include some of his most disturbing images.

Stay in Paris

Bibl. 137, pp. 235-240

Bibl. 134, p. 73

Ill. p. 335

arrived in Paris he had just left for England with one of his daughters, Manuela (of whom Goya had painted a little portrait on copper in 1815 [II.846] at the time of her sister Gumersinda's marriage with Javier), and the man who was her fiancé or perhaps already her husband, José Francisco Muguiro. The year before his death, Goya painted a portrait of his brother, Juan Bautista, which is one of his finest works [1663].

Goya stayed in Paris for exactly two months, from 30 June to 31 August 1824. This brief visit to the French capital is one of the most interesting periods of his life to study and one would like to know exactly what he saw and whom he met in Paris. We now know the names of the most important Spanish *émigrés* whom he could have encountered there; in the *salon* of the famous jurist González Arnao there would have been a number of old acquaintances, the Countess of Chinchón, the Duke of San Carlos, the Marchioness of Pontejos, to evoke memories of bygone days. He was on intimate terms with Joaquín María Ferrer who appears in the police reports as a dangerous revolutionary; in spite of his miserly nature, he kept up an ostentatious style of living in Paris, with his young wife Doña Manuela and his brother-in-law. Goya painted both his portrait and that of his wife [1659, 1660] as well as a bullfighting scene [1672] handled with a verve which shows that the old *aficionado* was as keen as ever, as he himself confided to Moratín who reported his statement that 'with a sword in his hand he fears nothing'.

A drawing probably made from memory on his return to Bordeaux evokes a curious means of transport which had impressed him as he strolled about the streets. He wrote on it *Yo lo he visto en Paris* (I saw it in Paris) [1736], and as far as we know this is the only tir he wrote the name Paris in his own hand. The police reports record that 'he only goes out to visit the monuments and walk about in public places'. It is therefore probable that he visited the Louvre and the Luxembourg where he would have discovered the works of David, Girodet, Horace Vernet, Gérard, Fragonard and the two great 'modern' painters, Ingres and Delacroix whose *Dante and Virgil* had been acquired by the State at the Salon of 1822.

Bibl. 137, p. 235

The most important artistic event of the year occurred five days before Goya left for Bordeaux, with the opening of the Salon exhibition. Of all the Salons of that period, it was surely the most outstanding in that it saw the confrontation between Ingres with his *Vow of Louis XIII* and Delacroix whose *Massacre of Chios* heralded the advent of the new Romantic school. Beside them hung a number of pictures by English artists – Constable, Lawrence and Bonington – in which the French, tired of the cold, classical style of the school of David, discovered a new approach to painting. Goya almost certainly visited

Woman in white fallen to the ground. Album H.*18* [*1781*] 1824-28

Woman in white fallen to the ground
Black chalk 18·8 × 15 cm.
Private collection, Paris
The second series of drawings executed in Bordeaux, most of them without titles but signed, includes this design which achieves a strikingly beautiful plastic effect through the strong contrasts of black and white. The enigma of the scene adds to the emotive power of the drawing. Who is this white Ophelia – fallen? fainting? dead? – who is watched over or waited for by a massive, almost faceless figure behind the broken stump of a tree? Of what drama is she the victim? Each must invent his own answer.

340

the Salon before his return to Bordeaux on 1 September and one would like to know which works particularly caught his eye. It is impossible to speculate and one should not even attempt to attribute to him preferences which might seem self-evident. The only French artist to whom he ever referred, mentioning him in one of his letters, is the mysterious but, according to him, 'incomparable Monsieur Martin', possibly identifiable with one of two deaf-mute miniature painters of the period whose work is now unknown. This identification would be of great significance since Goya was probably already interested in miniature painting and in a review of the 1824 Salon the critic Etienne Delécluze wrote 'I do not believe that miniature painting has ever been handled with such freedom'. However, Goya may have been following the Spanish custom of referring to people by their Christian name rather than their surname, in which case his 'Monsieur Martin' could be Michel Martin Drolling, a pupil of David who won the Prix de Rome in 1810 and was a regular exhibitor at the Salon where he was awarded a first-class medal in 1819.

Bibl. 137, pp. 242-243; 149, pp. 12-13

Soldier with a drinking companion. Album H.51 [1810] 1824-28

Soldier with a drinking companion
Black chalk 19·1 × 14·7 cm.
Private collection, Paris
This is another drawing from the album without titles but it comes after the signed drawings of which number 38 is the last in the series. Like all the drawings in the two 'albums' made in Bordeaux, it is executed with a greasy crayon similar to that used in lithography. Here the drinking scene is an amusing pretext which enables Goya to set a very light figure – an innocent victim? – against a dark background peopled by suspicious and disturbing characters.

It has also been suggested that Goya travelled to Paris for the express purpose of finding out for himself about the new lithographic processes used by the French and especially by Carle and Horace Vernet who had acquired an international reputation and whom his 'friend Cardano', who had printed his first lithographs in Madrid in 1819, had known since 1817. The visit to Paris would thus lie behind the important works which he subsequently executed in Bordeaux: the group of miniatures painted during his first winter there [1676-1697], the four lithographs known as the *Bulls of Bordeaux* [1707-1710] and the two last albums of drawings executed almost entirely with a soft, greasy crayon, handled in a way which makes them look very much like lithographs [1711-1822]. *See pp. 308, 346*

It would also be interesting to know whether Goya had the opportunity during his two months in Paris of meeting some of the young French romantic writers or artists for whom Spain, more than any other country, seemed to symbolize the dark and violent passions which filled so many of their works. It is tempting to imagine a meeting between Goya and Victor Hugo, perhaps at the home of Nodier who had just opened his Salon de l'Arsenal. The young poet would have recalled memories of Spain, the College of Nobles in Madrid, the Masserano palace where he lived with his mother and two brothers, only a short distance from Goya's house, their playfellow Victor Guye who had posed for the old master in the dress of a page to King Joseph [III.884] and above all his father, General Hugo, the companion-in-arms of General Guye [III.883]. And yet such an encounter appears unthinkable when one remembers the political views of the young romantics in 1824. In spite of his youth, Hugo was already the leader of the new school and he was an unreserved admirer of Chateaubriand and his policies. In 1823 he wrote an *Ode à la Guerre d'Espagne* and on 7 June 1824 another ode to Chateaubriand after the latter's dismissal from the Ministry of Foreign Affairs, while in the spring of 1825 he was awarded the Cross of the Legion of Honour for having supported 'the sacred cause of the Altar and the Throne'. As far as Goya, a liberal *émigré*, was concerned, this same 'sacred cause' had led the 'Cent Mille Fils de Saint Louis' to the walls of Trocadero and brought about the downfall of his country. He and Hugo stood in opposite camps. *Ill. pp. 208, 209*

As far as other artists were concerned, Goya could not have met David who remained in exile in Brussels after the Restoration, and Géricault had died just before his arrival. He does not seem to have known Delacroix and was thus unaware that the painter of the *Massacre of Chios* had already studied the copy of the *Caprichos* belonging to the Guillemardet *See p. 134*

Man picking fleas from a little dog   [1683]

Woman with clothes blowing in the wind   [1690]

Goya wrote to his friend Joaquín Ferrer on 20 December 1825, telling him that he had painted some forty miniatures on ivory the previous winter, in an original technique which was 'more like the brushwork of Velázquez than of Mengs'. His biographer Matheron described this revolutionary technique: '. . . he blackened the sliver of ivory and let a drop of water fall onto it, which, as it spread, lifted off part of the black ground, tracing chance highlights. Goya took advantage of these lines and always got something original and unexpected out of them.'

* Bibl. 60, p. 131

Nude reclining against rocks   [1688]

Majo and maja seated   [1689]

family, had made copies from most of the plates, and dreamed of making 'caricatures in the manner of Goya'*. He was also unaware that the publishing firm of Motte, under the artistic direction of the young Achille Devéria, was preparing a little album of ten lithographs entitled *Caricatures espagnoles, Ni plus ni moins, par Goya* which was ready for sale early in 1825. These poor copies of some of the *Caprichos* prints and a few volumes of the original edition were soon to make him famous in Paris and throughout the whole of Europe. The men who later acclaimed him as one of the great precursors of modern art never suspected that they may have passed him as he walked about the streets of Paris, a completely unknown, deaf, old man, much more interested to see what was going on in the streets rather than in the fashionable *salons*.

Return to Bordeaux

Goya went back to Bordeaux with Don Martín Miguel de Goicoechea and his daughter Manuela and son-in-law José Francisco Muguiro. He settled there in a pleasant house at 24 Cours de Tourny and a few days later Leocadia Weiss arrived from Spain with her two children Guillermo and Rosario. It is curious, and highly significant, that she should have declared to the authorities in Bayonne that she was going to Bordeaux 'where she is to join her husband'. Don Isidoro Weiss never went to France and was still living in Madrid at that time. However, her statement was only a half-lie for she and Goya soon fell into the sort of conjugal routine to which they were clearly already accustomed and which included, according to Moratín, its share of family quarrels.

Bibl. 137, pp. 256-257

Bibl. 134, p. 22

Bordeaux at that time was full of Spanish refugees who formed a colourful community in which writers, businessmen, bankers, politicians and aristocrats all rubbed shoulders. They met in the house of Braulio Poc, an Aragonese liberal and former defender of Saragossa, to dream of their country, discuss the news, talk a great deal and hope even more as they waited for better days and drank the thick, dark chocolate which only the Spanish know how to prepare.

Ill. p. 334

Ill. p. 135

The miniatures

However, the closest friends of Goya and Leocadia were still Manuel Silvela and Moratín. Towards the end of 1824, Goya made a portrait of Moratín [1661] which is a moving image of his loyal old companion, painted twenty-five years after the portrait in the Academy of San Fernando [II.685]. Painting, however, occupied much less of his time and apart from a few portraits of friends or relations he devoted himself with an astonishingly youthful energy to new techniques which he handled with prophetic originality. During the winter of 1824-25 he painted about forty miniatures which in fact have little in common with traditional miniature painting. At the age of nearly eighty he invented a charac-

343

teristically original method which resulted in a kind of wash on ivory, 'things which look more like the brushwork of Velázquez than of Mengs', as he proudly explained. They are again *caprichos*, but transposed now into the same key as the 'black paintings' and the *Disparates* prints, with a boldness of handling which makes them some of Goya's most modern works [1676-1697]. One can understand his surprise when Ferrer wrote to him from Paris to say that a new edition of the *Caprichos* would be easy to sell (no doubt after the success of Motte's poor copies); for Goya the days of the *Caprichos* were already long past and though Paris was only discovering them twenty-five years later, he himself was now creating the miniatures, the *Bulls of Bordeaux* and the drawings of the last two albums, and was far ahead of all the other artists of his day.

Bibl. 72, p. 55; 172, pp. 113-114

See p. 346

Conscious of how little time he had left, Goya was preoccupied by financial worries during his stay in Bordeaux. It was not that he in fact lacked money but he was afraid that his salary as Court Painter would be stopped and took great care to get his leave of absence regularly renewed, waiting anxiously for the king's decision. He was even more concerned, however, about what to do with his savings. Javier was worried and wrote asking for specific information, since he still feared that part of the money would be set aside for Leocadia and her children. Right up to his death, Goya continued to repeat his reassurances to his son, '. . . you know very well that what we have put by with Galos belongs entirely to you'.

Bibl. 150, p. 27

Bibl. 72, p. 57

But apart from all this, his last years were brightened by the joy of having the little Rosario with him. She was ten years old when she arrived in Bordeaux and her child's affectionate nature made him forget her mother's temperamental outbursts. His love for her seems typically paternal in its blindness and he marvelled at her precocious talent, declaring to Ferrer that she was 'the greatest prodigy in the world, taking account of her age'. He resumed the art lessons which he had started giving her three years before in Madrid, and in order to perfect her drawing he dashed off endless little sketches of figures for her to copy. This explains the series of sketches, often very unskilfully drawn, which have been grouped together with some rather uninteresting but nevertheless more firmly drawn originals by Goya [1842-1870].

Artistic education of Rosario

Bibl. 72, p. 54; 172, p. 112

Ill. p. 338

At this time he made two series of drawings in black chalk and lithographic crayon, which are among his most remarkable works. At the age of eighty his hand was surer than ever and in the total of some one hundred and twenty sheets, which he possibly intended to engrave, we find a procession – as of actors running across the stage to take their final bow before the curtain falls – of all the figures, both real and imaginary, which his genius had created over a quarter of a century and more: madmen, monks, beggars, witches, horrible old women, pensive young women, flying figures, prisoners, majas [1711-1822]. Like Paul Lafond who published a large number of them, we could call them *Nouveaux Caprices de Goya* – they were his latest and also his last series of *caprichos*.

Last 'albums' of drawings

Ill. pp. 335, 336, 339-341
Bibl. 98

1824-1828. Goya is 78 to 82 years old. The four lithographs of the 'Bulls of Bordeaux' (1825). Lithography in Paris. Gaulon, printer-lithographer in Bordeaux. Last engravings. Reign of Ferdinand VII in Spain. The Restoration (Charles X) in France. At his death in 1828, Goya leaves an œuvre of 290 known engravings and lithographs.

The lithographs which Goya made in Bordeaux in the last years of his life were among the first masterpieces in this new medium, and will stand for all time as some of the finest lithographs ever made. After his tentative experiments in Madrid a few years before, Goya quickly mastered the technique and evolved his own very personal methods of work.

Portrait of Gaulon
This lively and sympathetic portrait was Goya's tribute to the man who helped him fully to express his genius in the art of lithography. Gaulon had opened a lithographic printing works in Bordeaux six years before Goya settled in the town, and since he printed all Goya's lithographs, including the edition of the *Bulls of Bordeaux* [1707-1710], he undoubtedly advised the old master who was virtually a beginner in this new field. Providing him with perfectly prepared stones and using a matchless printing technique when Goya had completed his work, Gaulon captured on paper all the impetuosity, all the strength and sensitivity of the old man's hand and heart. The young Spanish painter, Antonio Brugada, who was a companion of Goya in Bordeaux, described how this portrait was made, and one marvels at the record of his tirelessly inventive and original methods. Through them he created the masterpieces which the skill and understanding of Gaulon have preserved in all too rare impressions.

Portrait of Gaulon   [1703] 1824-25. Lithograph. Davison Art Center, Middletown (Conn.)

By comparison with the series of etchings made during the quarter century between the elaboration of the *Caprichos* and his departure for France, Goya's lithographs are few in number. Only thirteen are attributable to the Bordeaux period [1698-1710], but they include a series of four lithographs – the famous *Bulls of Bordeaux* [1707-1710] – of such remarkable vigour and technical brilliance that they are as richly rewarding as the far longer series of etchings.

On 6 December 1825, Goya wrote to Joaquín Ferrer in Paris saying that he had sent him 'a lithographic proof representing a fight with young bulls so that you and friend Cardano might see it and if you thought it saleable I would send as many as you would like; this note I put with the print, and having heard nothing, I pray you again to let me know because I have three more ready of the same size and subject of bulls'. The proof which Goya sent to Ferrer was no doubt the *Diberslón de España* (Spanish entertainment) [1709]. How astonished Cardano must have been when he saw this large and powerfully handled composition, drawn directly on the stone with the greatest freedom and assurance, and remembered the none too successful attempts at transfer lithography which he had printed for Goya in Madrid a few years before [IV.1643-1650]. In fact his response may well have been one of incomprehension in the presence of a work which was so far in advance of its time. Perhaps his reaction and advice influenced Ferrer's reply which can be deduced from another of Goya's awkwardly phrased letters, written on 20 December: 'I have learnt and agree with what you tell me about the prints of bulls, but as I rather thought that they would be seen by art connoisseurs who abound in that great capital, and also of the large number of people who would have seen them, without counting the Spaniards, I thought that it would be easy to have given them to a print seller without mentioning my name, and to have done it at a low price.' Ferrer had apparently suggested instead that Goya would do better to issue another edition of the *Caprichos*. In his reply, Goya said that this was impossible since the plates were now in the royal chalcography in Madrid, and he added that he would not copy them 'because today I have better ideas for things which would sell to greater effect'. There is something at once pathetic and moving in the old exile's suggestion that these last masterpieces could be sold cheaply and anonymously in the French capital, and in his proud refusal to copy the *Caprichos*. As mentioned in the previous chapter, the year 1825 saw the publication in Paris of a little booklet of ten very poor lithographic copies after plates from the *Caprichos*, and the fact is that at the moment when the old master was producing the *Bulls of Bordeaux* he was only beginning to be known and appreciated in France for this early series of satirical prints.

There has been much speculation concerning Goya's stay in Paris during the summer of 1824, and if there was a practical purpose to his visit it may well have been to find out what was being done there in the field of lithography. When José Cardano was studying this new technique in Paris, he undoubtedly met the man who had established lithography in France with a highly successful studio and printing works opened in 1816: Charles de Lasteyrie was a most active, liberal aristocrat who had travelled in Spain between 1797 and 1799, gathering material for a treatise on sheep-farming, a subject which was dear to the heart of Jovellanos (it was one of the mainstays of his plans for economic reform) and which also interested the French government of the day. His treatise was written in Spain in 1798, the year in which Goya painted his portraits of Jovellanos [II.675] and of the French Ambassador, Guillemardet [II.677], and it is tempting to suppose that he may have met Lasteyrie at this time. Lasteyrie turned his interest to lithography in 1804, and between 1816 and 1825 he was the inspiration of a group of French artists who explored the possibilities and perfected the technique of lithography. They included Charlet, Achille Devéria (who may have been responsible for the unsigned lithographic copies after the *Caprichos*) and Carle and Horace Vernet, the father and son, whom Goya seems certainly to have known and visited in Paris. Many writers have contributed evidence

The 'Bulls of Bordeaux'

Bibl. 72, pp. 54-55; 173, p. 113
Ill. p. 347

See p. 308

Bibl. 72, p. 55; 173, pp. 113-114

Bibl. 137, p. 271; 88, I, pp. 12-13
Bibl. 60

Lithography in Paris

Dibersion de España (Spanish entertainment)   [1709] 1825. Lithograph 30×41 cm.

This was the lithograph which Goya sent to Ferrer in Paris in December 1825. It shows the most popular aspect of the bullfight in Spain, the loosing of young bulls into the ring or a village square, where they run wild and are taken on by the crowd. With the swirling composition and lively crayon technique, Goya expresses the exuberant mixture of carnival and carnage which characterizes this uniquely 'Spanish entertainment'.

* *Bibl. 61; 132; 137, p. 240; 145*

The printer-lithographer Gaulon

Bibl. 40; 88, I, p. 220

which tends to suggest that there were numerous links connecting Goya with those most interested in lithography in Paris in 1824, where for the first time the Salon devoted a special section to this technique*.

However, if his actual activities and contacts in Paris remain the subject of speculation, there is no mystery about the way in which his lithographs were made and published in Bordeaux. He himself paid tribute to the man who helped him to achieve technical mastery and who printed the edition of the *Bulls* and the rare proofs of all the other lithographs: Goya's portrait of Gaulon is one of the finest of his lithographs and the only portrait known by him in this medium [1703]. Cyprien-Charles-Marie-Nicolas Gaulon, to give him his full name, was a professional calligrapher. In 1818 he received his printer-lithographer's licence and opened a lithographic printing works which was very successful. In 1825, between 17 November and 23 December, Gaulon registered the edition of one hundred copies of Goya's four lithographs which he described as *Courses de Taureaux* (Bullfights). Two of the four have titles, in Spanish only, suggesting that although Goya was hoping

Modern duel [1702]. Lithograph. British Museum, London   El vito [1701] 1824-25. Lithograph 18×18 cm. British Museum, London

to dispose of them in Paris, he may have intended to send part of the edition to Madrid and probably expected to sell most of it to the numerous Spanish refugees in Bordeaux. The sale of the lithographs was apparently handled by Jacques Galos [1662] who looked after Goya's affairs in Bordeaux and to whom the edition of the *Bulls of Bordeaux* was entrusted.

Ill. p. 352
Bibl. 124, n. 10, p. [104]

    Not only is the manner of their printing known, but one of the early biographies of Goya gives an extraordinarily vivid account of his method of work. Laurent Matheron's description of Goya's last years in Bordeaux was based on the first-hand accounts of the young painter Brugada who spent much time with the old man, and of his lithographs he wrote: 'The artist worked at his lithographs on his easel, the stone placed like a canvas. He manipulated his crayons like brushes and never sharpened them. He remained standing, walking backwards and forwards every other minute to judge his effects. Usually he covered the whole stone with a uniform grey tone and then removed with the scraper those parts which were to appear light: here a head, a figure; there a horse, a bull. Next the crayon was again employed to strengthen the shadows, the accents, or to indicate the figures and give them movement. In this way, using the point of a razor and without any retouching, he once made a curious portrait emerge from the dark ground tone. (The portrait of M. Gaulon [who] printed all Goya's lithographic designs.) You would perhaps laugh if I said that all Goya's lithographs were executed under a magnifying glass. In fact, it was not in order to do very detailed work but because his eyesight was going.' The range of tones in the lithographs is wide and subtle, the use of 'scratching' gives vitality to the shaded areas, and the velvety blacks are slashed with scraped highlights whose vigour and dramatic sweep are matched only in the lithographs of Daumier.

Bibl. 124, ch. XI, pp. [95-96]

    Goya did not entirely abandon the etching technique in these years, but it is not surprising that very few plates are known. The process of biting a copperplate and pulling proofs is a long and delicate one, and for an impatient old man with failing sight it would

Last engravings

348

Modern duel   El vito (Andalusian dance)
These two lithographs could be interpreted as a variation on the theme of life and death which Goya first evoked in his earliest albums of drawings. Here the drama of the fatal sword-thrust is set beside the unquenchable vitality of the Andalusian dance.

Ill. p. 48

Goya's engraved and lithographic œuvre

be difficult even with assistance from an artist friend. He made etchings on both sides of three little copperplates – three pairs of figures, with and without aquatint: majas and old people swinging and an old man with a gun, which failed in the aquatint version [1823-1828]. The three, repeated figures are taken from one of his late sketchbooks – album H, pages *22, 31* and *58* [1785, 1793, 1816] – and it may be that he intended to publish his late drawings as a new series of engraved *caprichos* but abandoned the attempt because of the technical difficulties. The last engraving in the catalogue shows a *Blind singer* plucking his guitar [1829] and recalls the print etched nearly fifty years before, after one of Goya's early tapestry cartoons [I.87]. The whole course of his art is summed up in the contrast between the gay and spacious eighteenth-century composition with its different 'types' and costumes and the stocky, solitary figure, alone with his instrument in a dark and claustrophobic setting, where the rough, expressive handling suggests a mingled sense of vitality and tragedy.

When he died, Goya left an œuvre of two hundred and ninety known etchings and lithographs and about as many preparatory drawings. Most of these drawings are in the Prado Museum. The etchings, printed and reprinted from the original copperplates (the great majority of them kept in the chalcography of the Royal Academy of San Fernando) were the first of his works to become widely known outside Spain and are now scattered throughout the world in public and private collections. Popular, accessible, Goya's prints reflect every aspect of this extraordinary man – the vigour, the rough humour and biting satire, the dreams and obsessions, the pessimism and compassion, and the basic, unquenchable optimism and vitality which committed him throughout his life to the observation, description, castigation and encouragement of his fellow-men. His prints stand beside those of the greatest artist-engravers: Dürer, Rembrandt, Daumier, Toulouse-Lautrec, Picasso. But his profound humanity and emotional power bring him closest to Rembrandt whom he acknowledged as one of his masters, together with Velázquez and Nature. Goya's prints are public statements about his most deeply felt concerns, and are one of the most moving and passionately interesting parts of his artistic legacy.

Old man and *Old woman(?) on a swing*
1825-27. Etchings 18·5×12 cm. (the 'Old man' with the addition of aquatint)
Three little pairs of etchings and a single figure are the only known engravings by Goya from the years in Bordeaux. The prints illustrated were based on a drawing in album H – number *58* [1816] – and were etched on the front and back of a small copperplate. The pure etching plate contrasts with the coarsely aquatinted one, and the dynamic, laughing figures, swinging furiously on their cords, seem to express the sense of freedom and renewed vitality which Goya experienced at the end of his life in France.

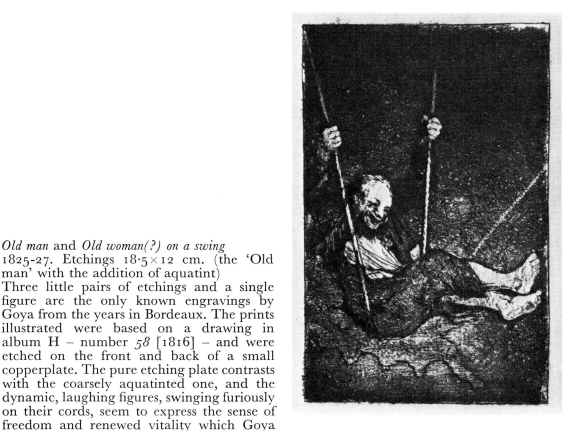

Old man on a swing   [1825]

Old woman(?) on a swing   [1826]

We have already seen the precautions which Goya took to prepare his departure for France and his success, with the help of kind supporters, in obtaining official leave of absence for six months under the pretext of going to take the waters at Plombières. A few days before the six months were up (without his ever having been to Plombières), he asked his son Javier to request a renewal of his leave for a second period of six months, still on the grounds of his poor state of health and the necessity of going this time to take the waters at Bagnères. Ferdinand VII gave his consent on 13 January 1825. For the time being Goya's position was secure and his worries at an end, for his greatest fear was that he might lose his salary. It would have meant a final break with his country and with his past and this he did not want. He wrote to Javier that if this happened he 'would set out [for Madrid] whatever the weather conditions' and he added that 'although this place [Bordeaux] is agreeable it is not sufficient to leave one's homeland'. In spite of everything, he remained faithful to Spain, the country in which he had spent his formative years and achieved fame and fortune, the country which remains for ever inseparable from all the emotion and feeling which is expressed in his work.

In the spring of 1825 Goya fell seriously ill. The doctors diagnosed paralysis of the bladder as well as a large tumour on one of the bones in his leg, which at his great age was regarded as incurable. He was unable to move and the worst was feared. After the second six-month period of leave had expired, Javier asked for a renewal for one year which would enable the artist to be cared for in France. On 4 July, having considered a report which gave little hope of Goya's survival, Ferdinand gave his assent once again.

And yet it was this old man, burdened by illness and infirmity, who drew directly on the stone, as if it were the easiest thing in the world, the four remarkable lithographs known as the *Bulls of Bordeaux* [1707-1710]. He had completed them by 6 December of the same year and wrote to Ferrer in a much quoted letter, dated 20 December, that he had 'neither sight, nor strength, nor pen, nor inkwell, I lack everything and only my will remains'. But this will carried him to greater and greater heights. There was no question of copying the *Caprichos*. At the age of nearly eighty he was inventing a new art which was younger and more modern than that which was considered revolutionary in Paris. The youthful, creative vigour which remained with the old artist till the end is symbolized by the two words of the title on one of his drawings: *Aun aprendo* (I am still learning) [1758].

On 30 March 1826 Goya was eighty years old. Proud of his age and the sureness of his brushwork, he signed and dated the portrait of Jacques Galos [1662], the governor of the Bank of Bordeaux and an ardent liberal to whom he had entrusted the administration of his property. His third period of leave was now running out and it was time to think of retirement. As he had written to Javier, it was possible that he would 'live like Titian until the age of ninety-nine'. He therefore had to obtain the most difficult favour of all from the king, his permission to retire on full pay from his post as Court Painter. It was important that he should succeed because everything he owned had already been divided among his inheritors, no doubt at the urgent request of Javier and perhaps also of Martin Miguel de Goicoechea before his death in Bordeaux on 30 June 1825. Thus he had only his salary on which to live in France with Leocadia and her children.

On 30 May 1826, two years to the day after he had obtained his first leave of absence, he appeared in Madrid to present his request to retire in person, emphasizing that he had served under three reigns since the day when 'Mengs called me back from Rome'. Ferdi-

1825-1828. Goya is 79 to 82 years old. Journey to Madrid to obtain his retirement (1826). Last paintings, including the 'Milkmaid of Bordeaux'. Death on 16 April 1828. Reign of Ferdinand VII in Spain. The Restoration (Charles X) in France.

Bibl. 154, docs 257-262

Bibl. 72, p. 57

Bibl. 154, docs 263-268

Bibl. 72, p. 55; 173, p. 114

Ill. p. 354

Ill. p. 352

Bibl. 72, p. 56

Journey to Madrid. His request for retirement on full pay is granted

Nun

In spite of this traditional title, the languid charm of the face and the meaningful look suggest that this may be a portrait of a young woman enveloped in a cape. An inscription on the back of the canvas gives the date 1827. Goya was eighty-one and one is struck by the astounding freedom with which he executed this painting. The modernism of its technique shows the extent to which this old man was constantly renewing his style, searching for new solutions, without ever contenting himself with the repetition of tried and tested formulas.

Nun   [1668] 1827. 38·7×24 cm. Private collection, England

Bibl. 154, docs 269-274   nand VII gave his assent on 17 June, and Goya received the fifty thousand reales due to him annually until his death two years later. While he was in Madrid, the most fashionable artist of the day, Vicente López, painted his portrait; a faithful representation, down to the last minute details, it is a perfect example of academic painting. Goya it seems, like Stendhal, created only for posterity. There was no successor to follow him, no one to try to live up to his example, nothing but a great void.

Ill. p. 353   It was generally believed that after this journey Goya stayed in Bordeaux until his death, though there were difficulties in determining where he had painted the portrait of Mariano [1664], which before relining bore the date 1827, given that his grandson did not go to France before 1828. However, it is now known that Goya made a second journey to Madrid during the summer of 1827. The reason for the journey is not known but one marvels at the incredible vitality of the eighty-one year old traveller. And in the last year before his death this extraordinary artist painted the vigorous portrait of *Juan Bautista Muguiro* [1663], the prophetically expressionist *Monk* and *Nun* [1668, 1669] and above all the *Milkmaid of Bordeaux* [1667] whose mysteriously melting charm is graced with all the magic qualities of his palette and expresses his last farewell to colour, to beauty and to the light which here divides the tones some fifty years before Renoir.

Second and last journey to Madrid (1827)
Bibl. 137, p. 258

The 'Milkmaid of Bordeaux'   *Ill. p. 25*

On 28 March 1828, Javier's wife and Mariano arrived in Bordeaux, alarmed by the state of Goya's health which must suddenly have deteriorated. On 2 April he awoke to find himself paralysed down his right side and after thirteen days hovering between life and death he finally breathed his last on 16 April at two o'clock in the morning. At his bedside were the young artist Brugada and his friend Pío de Molina, whose portrait he had not

Death of Goya on 16 April 1828

Jacques Galos   [1662] 1826. 55×46 cm. Barnes Foundation, Merion (Pa)

Jacques Galos   Mariano Goya
During the last four years of his life, Goya painted relatively few portraits, devoting himself almost exclusively to his drawings, miniatures and lithographs. He only took up his brushes for a few friends and for his grandson Mariano, and these portraits are usually signed, often with a dedication where he gives the date and his age.

The portrait of Jacques Galos is connected with the money problems about which the old artist frequently writes in his letters to Javier. He had handed over the management of his affairs, including the sale of the *Bulls of Bordeaux* lithographs, to Galos who was Governor of the Bank of Bordeaux, and was fifty years old in 1826. Galos was French, not Spanish as was often thought even in his own day. He was born at Arance, near Pau, and lived for several years in Pamplona before settling in Bordeaux in 1804. Businessman, then banker, he found the Caisse d'Epargne de Bordeaux in 1819 and in 1827 was elected to the Chamber of Commerce. This energetic man, with a fiery look in his eyes, was one of the most active liberals in the town. With the Revolution of 1830 he became a town councillor and a deputy, but his political career was soon cut short by his death on 30 December of the same year.

The portrait of Mariano is the third which Goya painted of his grandson, proof of the special affection which he always felt for the boy who was the family's only male heir. The earlier portraits show him as a small child [III.885, 1553] (see p. 247). Here, he is twenty-one years old and the portrait must have been painted at the time of Goya's last visit to Madrid, during the summer of 1827. Mariano arrived in Bordeaux with his mother on 28 March 1828, a few days before the death of his grandfather of which he gave official notification to the Spanish Consulate.

Mariano Goya   [1664] 1827. 52×41·2 cm. George A. Embiricos, Lausanne

Aun aprendo (I am still learning) Album G.*54* [1758] 1824-28. Black chalk. Prado, Madrid

Aun aprendo
This drawing is generally regarded as the most splendid and moving testimony to the vitality of Goya in his old age. In one of his letters to Javier, written in Bordeaux, he wondered whether he would live to the age of ninety-nine, like Titian, but old age and his physical infirmities were not enough to slow down the forward movement of his art. Always interested in everything new, he was constantly learning and turning to his own account the latest technical processes of the day, such as aquatint and lithography, and at an age when most people have already decided to rest on their laurels, he was still concerned with new ideas, using his brush and crayon to spread them abroad, and acquired through his reading a much broader general culture than has usually been admitted. Although this drawing cannot strictly be regarded as a self-portrait, it nevertheless represents the personal *credo* of the artist who in his eighties created this symbolic old man as an expression of his eternal youth.

been able to complete [1666]. Leocadia had not had the strength to stay with him to the end, but she wrote a moving letter to Moratín describing his death: '. . . on April 2, his saint's day, he woke at five o'clock unable to speak, though this soon came back, and paralysed on one side. He remained like this for thirteen days, recognizing us all until three hours before his death and able to see his hand but as if in a stupor . . . he died between the fifteenth and sixteenth at two in the morning . . . it was as if he just fell asleep and even the doctor was amazed at his courage and said that he did not suffer, but I am not sure about this.'

Goya was buried beside Martín Miguel de Goicoechea in Bordeaux and his mortal remains stayed there until 1901 when they were taken to Madrid. Finally, in 1919, they were transferred to the hermitage of San Antonio de la Florida where his own angels had been waiting for him for more than a century.

Bibl. 36 (1928), p. 89, n. 2

CATALOGUE V 1824-1828

INTRODUCTION

PAINTINGS   Apart from the drawings, prints and miniatures in this last part of the catalogue, Goya created barely twenty oil paintings between 1824 and 1828, and among them only eight portraits. His increasing preference, from the early years of the century, for intimate, experimental works rather than official commissions was reinforced, during these last four years, by the isolation of his life in Bordeaux and by the evident decline of his physical strength.

Among the paintings is a group of bullfight scenes which are particularly difficult to catalogue. Apart from the one which was painted by Goya in Paris and is authenticated and dated by his friend Ferrer's inscription [1672], it seems that a group of paintings which had previously been attributed to Lucas should now be reconsidered, since they show a striking and complex relationship to some of the prints from the *Tauromaquia* and to the lithographs of the *Bulls of Bordeaux* (see notes to [1672-1675]).

Matheron recorded, on the evidence of Antonio Brugada, that in Bordeaux Goya made use of any piece of panel, card or paper that came to hand, often painting over what the had done the day before, and that he abandoned his brushes entirely, using the palette-knife, a rag or any other means. He mentioned in this context not only a number of bullfight scenes but also a great many still-lifes which Goya painted after visits to the market, 'in a trice, between two cigarettes'. These paintings are apparently lost or unidentified, since virtually all the known still-lifes were included in the 1812 inventory [III.903-912] (see p. 251).

Matheron also referred to the portraits which Goya painted for his friends, commenting that with double-lens spectacles on his nose and in front of the sitter he found his touch again and citing the portrait of Galos [1662] as the finest example.

MINIATURES   It is only recently that the miniatures on ivory, painted during Goya's first winter in Bordeaux in 1824-25, have been grouped together. In 1966 an 'essai de catalogue' by Eleanor Sayre opened the way to further research, for only ten miniatures have so far been localized, while a dozen others are known from sale catalogues. In his letter to Ferrer, dated 25 December 1825, Goya referred to 'a collection of about 40' miniatures. However, Matheron's text, quoted below, suggests that the artist himself effaced a great many of his compositions. Matheron's text, which is based on the souvenirs of Antonio Brugada, reads as follows: 'His miniatures in no way resembled, and one has no difficulty in believing it, the delicate Italian miniatures or even those of Isabey. Goya had never been able to imitate anyone and he was too old to start. He blackened the sliver of ivory and let a drop of water fall onto it, which, as it spread, lifted off part of the black ground, tracing chance highlights. Goya took advantage of these lines and always got something original and unexpected out of them. These little productions still belonged to the family of the *Caprichos*; they would be much sought after today if the old man, in order to economize on the ivory, had not effaced a large number of them. Those which remained at his death were, I believe,

taken to Madrid by his son.' The description of his revolutionary technique has been confirmed by laboratory tests made at the Boston Museum of Fine Arts.

DRAWINGS   These make up the most important part of Goya's œuvre in Bordeaux. Of the 150 known drawings, 114 come from the albums G and H. Whereas the other albums of drawings constituted by Goya between 1796 and 1823 were all executed with the brush and wash (in Indian and/or sepia inks), those in Bordeaux are the only ones where he used a technique of black chalk and lithographic crayon [1711-1822]. In 1947, Pierre Gassier demonstrated for the first time that this whole group of drawings included two distinct series (see catalogue). The two albums are drawn on the same paper and the drawings in album H, up to number *38*, are all signed – a unique case in Goya's albums.

Among the other drawings, we would draw attention to the two in the Diocesan Museum in Gerona, which were published by Lafuente Ferrari and attributed by López-Rey to Rosario Weiss [1832-1833]. They were studied by Pierre Gassier who found that they were drawn in two autograph albums which belonged to Matilda O'Doyle and her sister Aglaë, Countess of Norona. The albums contain drawings, inscriptions and poems, some of them dated in Paris or Brussels in 1824, and Goya's drawings were probably improvised in a Paris *salon* where he met the two young women.

The problem of the drawings copied by the little Rosario Weiss from models given to her by Goya is still far from clear [1842-1870]. Although the clumsiest drawings are undoubtedly by the child – whose talent was less extraordinary than the doting old artist maintained – others are undoubtedly partially by Goya, though the part played by him varies considerably. Further study of the album of seventy drawings in the Hispanic Society of America may help to clarify this problem. On a more general plane, a better knowledge of the copies made by Rosario Weiss after Goya's works, including paintings, where we know that she was rather too expert (Bibl. 102, pp. 337-338), would probably help to settle several doubtful attributions.

ENGRAVINGS AND LITHOGRAPHS   Goya's print-making activity during his years in Bordeaux was almost exclusively concerned with lithography. He settled in Bordeaux in September 1824, and in December of the following year wrote to Ferrer in Paris, saying that he had made four lithographs of bullfights. Since the so-called *Bulls of Bordeaux* [1707-1710] represent the crowning achievement of his lithographic œuvre, it is probable that all the thirteen lithographs catalogued here had been executed by this date, and that Goya set to work with Gaulon immediately after his return from Paris. His first attempts at working directly on the stone may be represented by the lithographs of the *Monk* [1698] (which is sometimes placed together with the lithographs made in Madrid [IV.1643-1650]) and the *Bull attacked by dogs*

[1704]. The *Woman reading* [1699] represents a considerable advance, and the immediate preparation for the series of the *Bulls* is the lithograph known from a unique proof [1706], which he probably abandoned on account of the lack of clarity and firmness in both composition and technique. The *Bulls of Bordeaux* as well as the two lithographs of a *Duel* [1702] and an *Andalusian dance* [1701] are handled with remarkable vigour and assurance if, as Matheron recorded, they were indeed done with the help of a magnifying glass. Goya made much use of the scraper, to alter passages of the design, to lighten areas of tone by means of delicate scratching and to add sudden accents or define a contour with a deeply scraped highlight in an area of velvety black. The figures in these lithographs have the same solid, dumpy shapes as those in the late albums of drawings [1711-1822], and the themes represent the same mixture of observation from life and of dream and fantasy.

It seems almost certain that Goya had some hopes of publishing his late drawings in the form of lithographs or etchings. Seven little etchings are known from the years in Bordeaux [1823-1829] and, as already mentioned, six are based on three drawings from the album without titles [1785, 1793, 1816]. Carderera recorded having seen a number of badly damaged copperplates which had never been printed. They represented 'des scènes de majos ou des sujets de genre, des *Rêves* ou des *Proverbes*', and he added that they must date from Goya's last period 'car les hommes et les femmes sont courts et n'ont plus cette svelte souplesse des personnages des *Caprices*' (Bibl. 45, [III], pp. 247-248). It may be that the seven etchings catalogued here are all that have survived from a series which Goya abandoned.

Of the total of 290 known prints by Goya – engravings and lithographs – 20 (13 lithographs and 7 engravings) are catalogued within this fifth and last period of his career.

NOTES TO CATALOGUE V   [1658-1870]

1658-1666 Matheron, relying on the testimony of Antonio Brugada, referred to the portraits which the old and infirm Goya painted of his friends in Bordeaux: 'Là encore, en présence de la nature, et lorsqu'il avait chargé son nez d'un double binocle, il se retrouvait un instant' (Bibl. 124, ch. XI, p. [92]).

1658 Said to have been drawn in Paris in 1824 for Ferrer [1659]. Cp. the profile portrait in the *Caprichos* [II.451]. Copy in the Fundación Lázaro, Madrid.

1659 Núñez de Arenas discussed Ferrer's life and character, and referred to his activities as a publisher of books (including a miniature *Don Quixote*) in Paris (Bibl. 137, pp. 238-240). Exhibited, together with [1660], in 1951 (Bibl. 17, nos 57, 58). Goya's letters to Ferrer have been published in Bibl. 72, pp. 54-55, and, with an English translation, in Bibl. 173, pp. 112-114. Lafond gave them in a French translation in Bibl. 99.

1661 Signed on the papers. The date is inferred from Moratín's letter to Melón [IV.1637], dated 20 September 1824 and saying that he had just returned from the country to find Goya installed with Leocadia and the children: 'Quiere retratarme, y de ahí inferirás lo bonito que soy, cuando un diestro pinceles aspiran á multiplicar mis copias' (Bibl. 134, p. 18). Cp. the earlier portrait [II.685]. Moratín's correspondance with Melón appears in Bibl. 134 and was partially quoted by Beruete (Bibl. 36, I, pp. 86-88) and in translation by Lafond (Bibl. 99).

1662 Inscribed at lower left *D.ⁿ Santiago Galos / pintado por Goya de / edad de 80 años / en 1826*. See Núñez de Arenas (Bibl. 137, pp. 249-250) and Trapier (Bibl. 188, p. 46). Galos looked after Goya's financial affairs in Bordeaux, and Matheron (who considered this the most remarkable of Goya's late portraits) recorded that the whole edition of the *Bulls of Bordeaux* lithographs was handed over to him (Bibl. 124, p. [104], n. 10). See note to [1707-1710].

1663 Inscribed at lower right *D.ⁿ Juan de Muguiro, por / su amigo Goya á los / 81. años, en Burdeos, / Mayo de 1827*. The brother of José Francisco Muguiro who married Manuela Goicoechea, the elder sister of Goya's daughter-in-law. He became a friend of Goya in Bordeaux and acquired the painting of the *Milkmaid* [V.1667] from Leocadia Weiss after Goya's death. For biographical information, see Núñez de Arenas (Bibl. 137, pp. 253-254).

1664 Inscribed on verso before relining *Goya á su / nieto en. 1827, / á / los 81 de su / edad*. See Diego Angulo Iñiguez, 'Un retrato de Mariano de Goya, por su abuelo', *Archivo Español de Arte*, XXI, 1948, pp. 305-307. On Mariano's life and character, see Lafuente (Bibl. 102, pp. 295-300). Angulo referred to the passage concerning his violent character and his frequent recourse to duelling

and fights which had left his body full of scars (Lafuente, *op. cit.* p. 296, n. 3), and suggested that the curious mark on the left side of his jaw in the portrait was perhaps the result of a wound. Exhibited 1970 (Bibl. 30, no. 58). Cp. the earlier portraits [III.885, 1553].

1665 This portrait has generally been thought to represent Victoria Silvela, the daughter of Manuel Silvela (cp. [III.891]) who had established a college in Bordeaux and moved to Paris in the autumn of 1827 (cp. Bibl. 166, p. 126). However, Núñez de Arenas considered this identification unlikely and tentatively suggested that the sitter was a Madame Pons, a leading member of Bordeaux society, of whom it is recorded that Goya painted a portrait (Bibl. 137, pp. 254-255). The portrait, which was in the Schleier collection, has not been seen since it was exhibited for several years in the Alte Pinakothek, Munich.

1666 This portrait is generally considered to have been Goya's last work, left incomplete at his death.

1667 The painting remained in Leocadia's possession and she disposed of it to Juan Bautista de Muguiro [1663], saying in a letter written on 9 December 1829 that Goya had told her not to let it go for less than an ounce of gold (Bibl. 164, p. 62). See also Bibl. 102, pp. 293-294.

1668 and 1669 The inscriptions were not written by Goya. The monogram of the Infante D. Sebastián Gabriel (initials S.G. surmounted by a crown) is also visible on the back of the canvases. The pair was exhibited in 1928 (Bibl. 10, nos 90, 91) from the collection of D. Alfonso de Borbón. They were in England by 1938 (when the *Monk* was shown in the exhibition *From Greco to Goya*, The Spanish Art Gallery, London, no. 24, ill.). They remained unseen for many years and were examined by Juliet Wilson in preparation for the 1970 exhibition (Bibl. 30, nos 54/56, 55/57). The *Nun* was apparently first painted as a *maja* – traces of a black mantilla are visible around the face and there are signs of considerable alteration and repainting.
    Deceptive copies of both paintings, purporting to be the originals, were being offered for sale (together with a copy of [I.198]) at the time of writing.

1670 and 1671 These paintings are known only from Moreno photographs (see Bibl. 72, nos 218, 219). They were exhibited together in 1900, among the supplementary pictures, as no. 165 *Dos brujas* (see Bibl. 182, p. 200, n. 1; 57, I, p. 51, n. 3).

1672-1675 The Brugada inventory of 1828 listed *Ocho bocetos (como de una vara) corridas de toros* among the paintings in the Quinta del Sordo (Bibl. 57, I, p. 53, n. 1; see Appendix II, no. 4). No such paintings, 'of about [83.5 cm.]', have been identified among the works painted before Goya left for France. (The eight early paintings on tin [II.317-324] were in the Chopinot collection before 1805).

Lafuente referred to a complete collection of small paintings on tin, reproducing all the *Tauromaquia* compositions and therefore made after 1815, but he had not seen them to check the attribution (Bibl. 101, p. 187, n. 4; 102, p. 230, n. 2). Only one bullfight picture is certainly known to have been painted in France [1672], although Matheron recorded that in Bordeaux, where he gave up the use of brushes and painted with the knife, a rag, or any other means, Goya 'redid' several bullfight scenes (Bibl. 124, ch. XI, p. [91]). A number of bullfights have been attributed to Goya or Eugenio Lucas or his son Lucas Villaamil or even to Rosario Weiss (cp. Mayer, Bibl. 128, p. 74; Trapier, Bibl. 186, pp. 57-59; Lafuente, Bibl. 102, pp. 230-231, 234-235; López-Rey, Bibl. 117, p. 32). Xavier de Salas, 'A Group of Bullfighting Scenes by Goya', *Burlington Magazine*, CVI, 1964, pp. 37-38, reattributed to Goya three paintings previously given to Lucas, and these are tentatively included here [1673-1675] (although the attribution would not seem to be supported by the Brugada inventory or the testimony of Father López who, in the passage quoted by Salas, was not referring exclusively to bullfight scenes – see note to [III.951-957]).
    Matheron's text reads 'Il refit. . .quelques courses de taureaux, comme pour rajeunir son cœur; quelques-uns de ses *Caprices*. . .', and the conjunction of the two subjects suggests that if he 'redid' the *Caprichos* prints as paintings, the bullfights were also based on the prints of the *Tauromaquia*. This seems to be borne out by the compositions of the paintings listed here, as indicated in the individual notes (and it is certainly true of the lithographs of bullfights [1704-1710]).
    A pair of paintings, much more calligraphic than those already referred to and which almost exactly copy two of the lithographs from the *Bulls of Bordeaux* series, was mentioned by Mayer who gave the provenance of one of them as the de Lacy collection in Bordeaux. The two were in the Edwards sale in Paris in 1905 (Bibl. 57, II, p. 270) and Trapier (Bibl. 186, pp. 57-58), Lafuente (Bibl. 102, p. 230) and Gaya Nuño (*Eugenio Lucas*, Barcelona, 1948, p. 33) attributed them to the elder Lucas:
        Copy of [1708]   63×93 cm.   Toledo (Ohio), Mus.(29.139)   G.757.
        Copy of [1707]   60×90 cm.   Lima, Mújica Gallo M.666a, Gaya Nuño 1121 (Bibl. 65), G. 756 (incorrectly listed as at Winterthur)   Published by the owner in the Madrid Sunday newspaper *ABC* on 23 March 1969 (incorrectly identified as the missing picture referred to by Salas – the pair to [1673]).
    Two extravagantly 'goyesque' paintings were attributed by Mayer (after some hesitation) to the master, but were definitely ascribed to Lucas by Lafuente (*op. cit.* p. 230). They appear closely related in style and technique to a third picture which José Lázaro, for whom the painter worked for many years, identified as by Lucas Villaamil, the son (cp. Trapier, *op. cit.* p. 66 and Lafuente, *op. cit.* pp. 234-235), and this attribution should perhaps apply to all three.

356

The Lucas Villaamil in the Berlin N.G. was reproduced by Lafuente (pl. 50); the other paintings, a pair, are in Washington, N.G. (1350), and Winterthur, Reinhart Coll. (These two were very tentatively ascribed to the hand, at least in part, of Rosario Weiss by López-Rey – see Bibl. 117, p. 282). Trapier gave both of them to Lucas senior, basing the attribution on a signed tempera sketch which was no doubt used for the Washington picture (Bibl. 186, p. 48, pl. XXXII-XXXIV), but the hectic technique of the two pictures appears to differ markedly from that of all the other Lucas bullfight paintings discussed by her.

1672 Inscribed on verso by Ferrer *Pintado en Paris en Julio de 1824. / Por / D.n Fran.co Goya. / JMF* (inscription reproduced by Salas, *op. cit.* in note to [1672-1675], fig. 30). Painted for Ferrer during Goya's visit to Paris, together with the two portraits [1659, 1660]. Cp. the earlier bullfight scene [III.969], *Tauromaquia* plates 22 and 27 [III.1194, 1204], and the lithographs made in Bordeaux [1705, 1706].

1673 Given to the Prado in 1962 and officially catalogued in Bibl. 2, p. 28. A pendant sold with this picture in 1924, together with [1674, 1675], is unknown (see Salas, *op. cit.* in note to [1672-1675], p. 38, n. 9). Cp. *Tauromaquia* plates 10, 11 and 22 [III.1167, 1171, 1194].

1674 and 1675 Sold in 1924 as by Eugenio Lucas, together with [1673], all three were attributed to Goya by Salas (*op. cit.* in note to [1672-1675]). Although very close to two of the *Bulls of Bordeaux* lithographs, the compositions are inverted which, as Salas pointed out, suggests that the lithographs were made from the paintings rather than vice versa. They were attributed to Lucas by Trapier (Bibl. 186, pp. 58-59, pl. XLIV, XLV). Exhibited 1963-64 (Bibl. 27, nos 133, 134).
1674 The main group with the bull is very close to *Tauromaquia* 33 [1217], and the swirling disposition of the figures, intensified in the lithograph [1709], recalls the crowd in album F.42 [III.1467].
1675 Closer in details to parts of *Tauromaquia* 30 and 31 [III.1210, 1212] (e.g. the figure confronting the bull with raised banderillas) than to the lithograph [1710]. Cp. also the large earlier painting [III.953].

1676-1697 In his letter to Ferrer Goya wrote 'Es cierto q.e el invierno pasado pinte sobre marfil y tengo una colección de cerca de 40 ensayos pero es miniatura original que yo jamas he visto por que no esta hecha a puntos y cosas q.e mas se parecen a los pinceles de Velazquez que a los de Mens' [sic] (Bibl. 72, p. 55). Matheron described Goya's technique, from the first-hand account of Antonio Brugada: 'Ses miniatures ne ressemblaient guère . . . aux fines miniatures italiennes, ni même à celles d'Isabey: Goya n'avait jamais su imiter personne; il était trop vieux pour commencer. Il noircissait la plaque d'ivoire et y laissait tomber une goutte d'eau, qui, en se répandant, enlevait une partie du fond et traçait des clairs capricieux. Goya tirait parti de ces sillons et en faisait toujours sortir quelque chose d'original et d'inattendu. Ces petites productions étaient encore de la famille des *Caprices*; elles seraient aujourd'hui très recherchées si le bonhomme, pour faire des économies d'ivoire, n'en eût pas effacé un grand nombre.' The text adds, 'Celles qui restaient à sa mort furent, je crois, emportées par son fils à Madrid.' (Bibl. 124, ch. XI, p. [93].) The miniatures have been discussed and analysed by Sayre and tentatively catalogued (giving previous references) according to the chronological order of the exhibitions or sales in which they first appeared (Bibl. 173), and this order has been followed here except in the case of four miniatures of which no reproduction is known [1694-1697]. Sayre has pointed out the similarities between some of the miniatures and other works by Goya, and such indications are given in the individual notes.

1676 Exhibited 1970 (Bibl. 30b, no. 20).

1686 Cp. the drawing [1854].

1687 Cp. the lithograph [1699].

1689 Cp. the watercolour drawing [1841].

1690 . . . in the wind. Owned by Mr and Mrs Kirk Askew.

1693 Exhibited 1970 (Bibl. 30b, no. 19).

1698-1710 Goya's lithographic technique was described from a firsthand source by Matheron: 'L'artiste éxécutait ses lithographies sur son chevalet, la pierre posée comme une toile. Il maniait ses crayons comme des pinceaux, sans jamais les tailler. Il restait debout, s'éloignant ou se rapprochant à chaque minute pour juger ses effets. Il couvrait d'habitude toute la pierre d'une teinte grise, uniforme, et enlevait ensuite au grattoir les parties à éclairer: ici une tête, une figure; là un cheval, un taureau. Le crayon revenait ensuite pour renforcer les ombres, les vigueurs, ou pour indiquer les figures et leur donner le mouvement. . . . [L]es lithographies de Goya ont toutes été exécutées à la loupe. Ce n'était pas en effet pour faire fin; mais ses yeux s'en allaient.' (Bibl. 124, ch. XI, pp. [95-96].)

1698 Catalogued by Harris among the ink lithographs made in Madrid. Further examination suggests that this was probably one of Goya's first attempts with the crayon. It may have been made in Madrid.

1699 Possibly retouched with ink in the shadows behind the woman. Sayre has pointed out the affinity between the two children listening and those in the miniature [1687] (Bibl. 173, p. 106). Cp. the similar composition in reverse in the small painting attributed to Goya [IV.1657a]. A proof unknown to Harris, in a German private collection, was exhibited in 1970 (Bibl. 30b, no. 78).

1701 Andalusian song and dance.

1703 The description of Goya's lithographic technique by Matheron (quoted in the note to [1698-1710]) was specifically applied by him to this portrait in the following terms: 'Il fit ainsi sortir une fois de la teinte noire du fond, à la pointe du rasoir et sans aucune retouche, un curieux portrait. C'est le portrait de M. Gaulon, lithographe. . . . M. Gaulon a imprimé tous les dessins lithographiques de Goya.' (*op. cit.* p. [96] and n. 11, p. [105].) It should be pointed out, as Sayre has done (Bibl. 173, p. 106), that Matheron's description of Goya's technique is not to be taken too literally: this portrait appears mainly to have been drawn with the crayon and then scraped.

1704-1706 These lithographs, which must have preceded the *Bulls of Bordeaux* series [1707-1710], were based on the *Tauromaquia* prints which Goya no doubt took with him to France and which he probably used for the paintings [1672-1675].

1704 The design is taken from *Tauromaquia* plates 25 and C [III.1200, 1223]. Two proofs unknown to Harris are in private collections in Germany and the U.S.A.

1705 The design is very close to *Tauromaquia* plate 1 [III.1149] for the landscape setting and plate 27 [III.1204] for the picador and bull. Cp. also the painting made for Ferrer [1672].

1706 The confused design includes elements from *Tauromaquia* plates 32, E and F [III.1214, 1227, 1229]. This unique proof, identified in 1946, is the same size as the *Bulls of Bordeaux* and was listed together with them by Matheron as 'Cinq courses de taureaux'. He described this scene in detail, apparently unaware that it was unique (Bibl. 124, ch. XI, pp. [94-95]). The lithograph was no doubt a first attempt at the large compositions which Goya published in 1825, and the signature, place and date inscribed on the stone recall his characteristic habit of signing and dating the first copperplates whenever he embarked on a new series of prints (cp. also his first lithographs [IV.1643, 1644]). Reproduced in Bibl. 80, final plate. Exhibited 1970-71 (Bibl. 30a, no. 157, ill.).

1707-1710 Goya's letters to Ferrer are printed in Bibl. 72, pp. 54-55 and reprinted by Sayre, with English translations, in Bibl. 173, Appendix I, pp. 112-114. They were also quoted in a French translation by Lafond (Bibl. 99, p. 242). The lithographs were printed by Gaulon, and Delteil reproduced in facsimile the registration of the edition made by him in the archives of the Gironde Préfecture (Bibl. 55, II, preceding nos 286-289). Matheron recorded that the whole edition (which he erroneously thought was of 300 proofs) was handed over to Jacques Galos [1662], the banker friend who looked after Goya's financial affairs in Bordeaux and who no doubt kept the accounts of the sale of the prints (Bibl. 124, note 10, p. [104]).
Two of the lithographs have Spanish titles, and Harris has described the set in the Biblioteca Nacional, Madrid, with pencilled numbers on the proofs and a long inscription below the first lithograph [1707], which were no doubt designed to be printed on the proofs of a projected Spanish edition (Bibl. 88, I, p. 220).

1707 (The famous American, Mariano Ceballos). The lithograph is based on *Tauromaquia* plates 24 and [J] [III.1198, 1237]. See notes to [III.1196, 1198].
A copy in oils by Lucas is mentioned in the note to [1672-1675].

1708 Based on *Tauromaquia* plates 26 and [F] [III.1202, 1229]. The picador on the left is similar to that in the painting [1672]; cp. also [1673].
A copy in oils by Lucas is mentioned in the note to [1672-1675].

1709 Probably derived from the painting [1674], in its turn partially based on *Tauromaquia* plate 33 [III.1217].

1710 Probably derived from the painting [1675], based on *Tauromaquia* plates 30 and 31 [III.1210, 1212], but also reminiscent of the bull and matador in the unpublished plate [I] [III.1235].

1711-1822 The two albums were first identified and partially reconstructed by Gassier (Bibl. 122, cat. IV. A and B), and their technical characteristics were defined by Sayre (Bibl. 171, Appendix I, p. 133, 'Journal-albums G and H'). An attempt has been made to give previous references for drawings in private collections.
The 31 lost drawings which were in the Gerstenberg collection are known from Moreno photographs and from Lafond's facsimiles (Bibl. 98). These drawings disappeared in Berlin during the last war and are presumed to have been destroyed.

1711-1764 The Prado and Gerstenberg drawings were listed with the album numbers by Gassier (Bibl. 122, pl. 183-195, cat. IV. B).

1711 This drawing and [1744] were acquired by Federico de Madrazo from Javier Goya, according to the identical inscriptions by C. Gasc on the verso of both sheets. Unseen since the 1922 exhibition, it is reproduced from the catalogue (Bibl. 9, no. 197).
Copy: 18·4×14·3 cm. Berlin-Dahlem, K.K. (4390) Mentioned by Mayer (Bibl. 127, p. 376).
Forged copies are also known of [1744] and [1785]. All the originals were in the C. Gasc collection and bear his mark (Lugt 542). If the originals of [1774] and [1814] are rediscovered, they may prove to have come from the same collection.

1712 Cp. album C.71 [III.1308], and see note. Both drawings are reproduced in Bibl. 187a, pl. 12a, 12b.

1713 Cp. the additional *Disparates* drawing [IV.1611].

1716 (. . . hunchbacked dancer). The phrase *El cojo y* was added afterwards by Goya.

1717 The second phrase is almost effaced. Cp. the earlier drawings on this theme [II.654-656].

1719 (. . . and on horseback). Reproduced by Mayer (Bibl. 127, p. 379).

1721 Sánchez Cantón noted an almost illegible inscription *B.1825* – for Bordeaux?

1722 (Mid-Lent. Cutting the old woman in two). The first title is written over the almost illegible second one. Cp. the same subject in the early album B.60? [II.420] and see note for bibliographical references.

1723 . . . *Muger la Otra / Dulce Union* (Sure and natural union. Man one Half, Woman the Other. Sweet Union). The second title is written, almost illegibly, above the final one, beneath which a third is almost completely obscured. Inscribed *Goya* on verso. See Carlos van Hasselt, 'Three drawings by Francisco Goya (1746-1828) in the Fitzwilliam Museum, Cambridge', *Apollo*, LXV, 1957, pp. 87-89 (v. [1756, 1770]). Exhibited 1963-64 (Bibl. 27, no. 191). Cp. *Caprichos* plate 75 [II.602] and *Proverbios* plate 7 [IV.1581].

1724 (He appeared like this, mutilated, in Saragossa, in the early 1700's). Reproduced by Mayer (Bibl. 127, p. 379).

1725 The first word is written over the second. Exhibited 1963-64 (Bibl. 27, no. 192).

1726 (He says he was born with them and keeps them on for life).

1727   Probably one of the acts seen by Goya at the fair or circus in Bordeaux (cp. [1768, 1801, 1802, 1806, 1813]).

1728   From the collection of E. Calando (Lugt 837).

1730   . . . // A la comedia / No 89 (New stage-coaches or shoulder chairs) written over an illegible inscription; (To the theatre. No. 89) written on the door of the sedan chair. Reproduced by Mayer (Bibl. 130, pl. 23). Exhibited 1963-64 (Bibl. 27, no. 193). Pierre Gassier points out that Goya stayed at 5 rue Marivaux in Paris, almost next to the Théâtre des Italiens (now the Opéra-Comique); see Bibl. 137, p. 235.

1732   Reproduced by Mayer (Bibl. 130, pl. 24).

1733   (. . . Not for hire). The second phrase is crossed out. Reproduced by Mayer (Bibl. 127, p. 383).

1734   (Beggars who get about on their own in Bordeaux). Reproduced by Mayer (Bibl. 127, p. 382).

1736   Reproduced by Mayer (Bibl. 130, pl. 21).

1737   Exhibited 1963-64 (Bibl. 27, no. 194).

1738   Reproduced by Mayer (Bibl. 127, p. 383; 130, pl. 22).

1740   Reproduced by Mayer (Bibl. 127, p. 381).

1743   Inscription written twice, at the top and bottom of the sheet.

1744   See note to [1711]. Exhibited 1922 (Bibl. 9, no. 198). Reproduced from the catalogue.
Copy: 18·1×14·3 cm.   Berlin-Dahlem, K.K. (4392) Mentioned by Mayer (Bibl. 127, p. 376). See note to [1711].

1745   Reproduced by Mayer (Bibl. 127, p. 377). Exhibited 1963-64 (Bibl. 27, no. 195).

1746   From the collection of E. Calando (Lugt 837). Exhibited 1970 (Bibl. 30b, no. 14).

1747   Inscription almost illegible. Reproduced by Mayer (Bibl. 127, p. 377).

1748   (Crafty lunatic). Reproduced by Mayer (Bibl. 127 p. 381).

1749   The inscription is written at the top, and López-Rey has deciphered an almost illegible word written within the composition as santo; he also suggested that errar was Goya's mis-spelling of herrar and that the title should be translated as 'Crazy enough for branding' (Bibl. 118, p. 366). Exhibited in 1963-64 (Bibl. 27, no. 196).

1750   . . . Libertad / Alegria / Gusto (Mad woman who sells delights. Health Sleep Liberty Joy Pleasure). Carderera recorded the title with the additional phrase 'She is French' (Bibl. 45, [II], p. 227).

1751   Published by Crispolti (Bibl. 52, pl. LIV, fig. 10). Exhibited 1969 at Colnaghi's in London, at the Uffizi in Florence and at the Louvre in Paris (European Drawings from the National Gallery of Canada, Ottawa, London, 1969, no. 67, ill., with a discussion of the meaning of this drawing).

1755   See Tancred Borenius and Rudolf Wittkower, Catalogue of the collection of drawings by the Old Masters formed by Sir Robert Mond, London, [n.d.], no. 282. It proved impossible to obtain a photograph of this drawing which is not known to have been reproduced.

1756   Exhibited 1963-64 (Bibl. 27, no. 198). See van Hasselt, op. cit. in note to [1723].

1757   (They fly, they fly) and above, fainter (Fiesta in the air) and beneath this (The butterfly bull). Cp. the additional Disparates plate [IV.1604]. Exhibited 1963-64 (Bibl. 27, no. 200), and discussed by López-Rey (Bibl. 118, p. 368). See also the note to [III.956].

1761   (Holy week in Spain in times past). Cp. album B.80 [II.438] and the paintings [III.966, 974]. Exhibited 1963-64 (Bibl. 27, no. 201) and 1969 (see note to [1751], cat. no. 68, ill.).

1764   . . . / aun muerto le vitupera, / mas el hombre liberal / todos sienten q.e se muera (One can expect no

good from a miser and even after his death everyone speaks ill of him, whereas everyone regrets the death of a generous man).

1765-1822   The Prado and Gerstenberg drawings were listed with the album numbers by Gassier (Bibl. 122, plates 156-182, catalogue IV.A). All the Gerstenberg drawings disappeared during the last war with the exception of number 32 [1794] — see note.

1770   Inscribed Goya on verso. See van Hasselt, op. cit. in note to [1723]. Exhibited 1963-64 (Bibl. 27, no. 202).

1771   Cp. album C.25 [III.1263].

1773   Cp. album D.18 and [f] [III.1375, 1383].

1774   A forged copy of an unknown drawing, in the same style as that of album H.22 [1785]. Both copies came from the collection of Philippe Burty. See note to [1711].

1782   Exhibited 1963-64 (Bibl. 27, no. 203) and 1969 (see note to [1751], cat. no. 69, ill.). The young girl, whose little wings on her slippers make her a witch, is neither skipping nor swinging as has previously been suggested. The rope end hangs loose over her right hand and the curve of the rope follows her skirt and does not support her body nor is she skipping over it; as an accomplished witch, she is doing a rope trick. Cp. Caprichos plate 61 [II.573], showing the Duchess of Alba flying away on a group of witches.

1785   Used for the etching [1824]. Published by A. L. Mayer, 'A Goya drawing', Burlington Magazine, LVI, 1930, pl. 270.
Copy: 18·4×13 cm.   London, B.M. (1876.5.10. 375) See notes to [1774] and [1711].

1786   Copies:
Black chalk 17·5×14·5 cm.   Paris, priv. coll.   (The woman is caressing only one little dog).
Brush and sepia wash 24·8×16·7 cm.   With a 'dark border', and numbered 52 with the brush at top centre (the 2 altered to 4 in pencil)   Pencil inscription below: el ternura [sic] (tenderness)   Sold at Sotheby's, London, 10 May 1961, lot 73.

1788   Reproduced by Mayer (Bibl. 127, p. 381). Cp. the lithograph [1700].

1790   The first numeral 1 was altered to 2.

1793   Used for the engravings [1827, 1828]. Cp. also the drawing [1838].

1794   This drawing was given to a friend of the Gerstenberg family in Madrid and was seen there by Pierre Gassier in 1955, together with the additional drawing Lafond pl. C. These are the only two Gerstenberg-Beruete drawings known to have survived. See note to [III.1531].

1797   The numeral 5 was first written as 7.

1798   Reproduced by Mayer (Bibl. 127, p. 381).

1801   (Serpent 4 varas long in Bordeaux), i.e. nearly four yards. See note to [1727].

1804   Published by Trapier (Bibl. 187a, p. 20, n. 16, pl. 18).

1806   . . . / Llamado el Esquelete vibiente / en Bordeaux año 1826 (C. . . A. . . S. . . Known as the Living Skeleton in Bordeaux the year 1826). Núñez de Arenas mentioned a lithograph of the same subject by the Bordeaux artist Louis Burgade (Bibl. 137, p. 250). See note to [1727].

1807   Drawing first studied and published by Gassier (Bibl. 62a). Exhibited 1970 (Bibl. 30b, no. 15).

1810   Reproduced by Mayer (Bibl. 127, p. 383).

1811   The Prado title 'Pleading demon' suggests the figure is on his knees, whereas he is flying like the figure in [1817], and is apparently witnessing the fall of the distant figure. Cp. the flying dog and men in album G.5 [1715] and Disparates plate 13 [IV.1591].

1812   The identity of the man is not known. Exhibited 1963-64 (Bibl. 27, no. 199).

1813   See note to [1727].

1814   This drawing may be a copy of a lost original. See note to [1711].

1816   Used for the etching [1826]. Published by Trapier (Bibl. 187a, p. 20, n. 17, pl. 19).

1818   Cp. Disparates plate 4 [IV.1576].

1821   Trace of a signature at lower right. No trace of a number.

1822   Number illegible.

1824   Engraved on the verso of the copperplate; masking hides the stamp JUERY. R. St. Jacques 43.
This etching was the one copied from the album drawing (and so appears in the reverse).
Another drawing was described by Boix as the basis for this print but it is of doubtful authenticity (see Bibl. 9, no. 194 – not known in reproduction).

1826   This etching was the one copied from the album drawing, and the description 'old woman' is no doubt incorrect.

1827   A technically unsuccessful plate where most of the coarse dark aquatint has been scraped away. No contemporary proofs are known. The few modern impressions show the stamp described in [1824].

1828   This etching was the one copied from the album drawing. It has been suggested that the bull, which does not appear in the drawing or the aquatinted version of the print, was added by another hand, perhaps Rosario Weiss.

1829   No drawing is known which corresponds with this plate.

1830-1841   López-Rey, in an article which attempted to distinguish the drawings of Rosario Weiss from those of her teacher Goya (Bibl. 117), attributed to the little girl some drawings which are listed here as probably by Goya. It should be remembered that Rosario was copying from original drawings by Goya who no doubt adapted his style to make them easier for her to follow. (See [1842-1867].) In spite of some awkwardness and even crudeness of handling, the strength of the drawings listed here [1830-1833] and the brio of their signatures, including the significant date on [1830] which was apparently unknown to López-Rey, suggest that they form a group whose style is characteristic of the lost drawings which were copied by Rosario.
It is also significant that a number of them have been found in autograph albums. From the time when he made paintings and drawings of the friends who had aided him in Madrid [IV.1633-1635], Goya evidently continued throughout his years in France to thank those who helped him by giving them his works or painting their portraits. A letter, dated 30 November 1824 and addressed to the Duquesa de San Fernando in Paris was catalogued and reproduced in facsimile by Kornfeld and Klipstein, Ausstellung von Graphik Francisco de Goya, Berne, 1968/69; transcribed and discussed by Xavier de Salas, 'Una carta de Goya y varios comentarios a la misma', Arte Español, XXVI, 1, 1968-69, pp. 27-28. In it Goya mentioned three dwarfs, seen at the fair in Bordeaux two months previously, and which he was sending (no doubt in the form of a drawing) as a gift. This drawing is unknown, as is a full-length portrait of the Duquesa (the younger sister of the Condesa de Chinchón), which was listed by Carderera (Bibl. 148, no. 39).

1830   Inscribed El 6 de Julio del año 1824. Franco de Goya. Goya was in Paris from 30 June to 1 September. The drawing, which was in the collection of the Marqués de la Scala in 1922, was described by Boix as in Indian ink but he is not always reliable (cp. note to [1835]). Its present whereabouts is unknown.

1831   . . . watched by a seated woman. Exhibited together with [1830] — see note.

1832 and 1833   These two signed drawings, published by Lafuente (Bibl. 102, p. 39, figs 9, 10), were examined by Pierre Gassier some years ago. One is drawn in each of the autograph albums which belonged to two sisters, Aglaë and Matilda O'Doyle (who was Countess of Noroña). In the two albums, the pages immediately preceding and following these drawings include inscriptions, poems and drawings, some of which are dated Paris or Brussels in 1824. The author of the inscription on the page following [1832] referred to Goya's drawing in which the hideous old women seemed to him so out of keeping with the beauty of the album's owner.

1833   Signed on a mirror or picture (?) above the head of the woman in white. The strong brown wash has attacked and partially eaten away the paper, especially at the top of the sheet.

1835   Described by Boix as in Indian ink. The drawing is now covered by a mount, and the dimensions are taken from the Boix catalogue (visible dimensions in mount: 14·6×14 cm.)
      Copy(?) in reverse: red chalk 18·4×15·3 cm. Seattle, Mus. (52.SP30/G7488.1).

1836   Known only from a Mas photograph (G/-6185). Cp. the Goya-Weiss drawings, particularly [1851], and album H.5 [1768].

1837   Probably made during Goya's first winter in Bordeaux in 1824-25. Described by Lafond as in Indian ink. Cp. album H.28 [1790] and the earlier F.30 [III.1456]. For a note on the Gerstenberg collection, and the relevant abbreviations, see p. 364 and the note to [1711-1822].

1838   Very similar to the figure in album H.31 [1793], and possibly a copy.

1839   From the collections of Madrazo and E. Calando. Cp. *Tauromaquia* plates 18 and 29 [III.1186, 1208]. Exhibited 1961-62 (Bibl. 24, no. 177) and 1970 (Bibl. 30b, no. 16).
      A drawing similar to this and [1840] was in a private collection in Madrid in 1955. See note to [1794]. This drawing from the Gerstenberg collection did not come from Beruete.

1840   Cp. *Tauromaquia* plate 27 [III.1204] and the lithograph [1705]. The attribution of this drawing has been questioned.

1841   Cp. the miniature [1689]. The signature at right is not authentic.
      Carderera said that he had only seen three watercolours by Goya, and that they represented *toreros* seated on the promenade and talking with *manolas* in mantillas. His description exactly applies to this drawing (Bibl. 45, [II], p. 227).
      Sánchez Cantón recorded a note he had made of a watercolour drawing of a 'Bald old man wearing a cloak or coat', with an inscription on the verso 'Collection de Mme la Duchesse de Montellano offert par Goya à Mme la Duchesse à Bordeaux'. He had seen the drawing in 1938 among works stored by the Junta del Tesoro Artístico (Bibl. 168, I, Introduction, p. [21]).

1842-1870   The biography of Rosario Weiss (published in *Semanario Pintoresco Español*, 26 November 1843, and reprinted in Bibl. 102, pp. 337-338) described the drawing lessons which Goya gave her from the age of seven (1821), making sketches and caricatures which she copied with the pen, and added that when he went to Bordeaux in 1823 (sic), leaving Rosario in the care of Tiburcio Pérez (see [IV.1630]), she began to use the shading stump and Indian ink (wash?) and during that summer would copy three or even four of Goya's *caprichos* in a day. He must have left a collection of drawings to keep her occupied during his absence, and no doubt continued the lessons when she rejoined him in Bordeaux in September 1824. Very few of the original drawings copied by 'la Mariquita'

are known, and those which have been attributed to Goya (from the group in the Biblioteca Nacional, Madrid) were no doubt made when he was working beside the child, in Madrid or in Bordeaux.
The drawings of Rosario Weiss were discussed by López-Rey (Bibl. 117) who attempted to distinguish those made by Goya and reworked by Rosario, those where Rosario was copying from a known or unknown Goya original, and those were she redrew and improved on her earlier attempts and copied in a more skilful and fluent style. He suggested that the Hispanic Society album was probably later than the mixed group of drawing in the Biblioteca Nacional, and he published a signed drawing by Mariquita Rosario [1858]. He also attributed to Rosario a number of drawings which are attributed in this catalogue to Goya (see note to [1830-1843]).
All the drawings in the Hispanic Society album were reproduced by Starkweather (Bibl. 181), and those which are copies of drawings catalogued here are referred to in the individual notes. The drawings in the Biblioteca Nacional were published by María Elena Gómez-Moreno (Bibl. 67a), and her order is followed here. For additional information on Rosario Weiss see Lafuente (Bibl. 102, pp. 156-159) and Sayre (Bibl. 173, p. 87, 108 and nn. 11, 36, with an English translation of part of *Semanario* article). Mayer reproduced a circular bust portrait of Goya, drawn in pencil and signed *M. del Rosario Weiss*, which was in the Lázaro collection (Bibl. 129, pl. 134).

1842   (Oh ah how tired I am). López-Rey no. I, fig. 1, as by Goya and Weiss. On the verso of this sheet is a version of [1843] – see note.
      There is a poor version on the verso of [1843], reproduced by López-Rey fig. 2.
      Another version in the Hispanic Society (A.713), Starkweather pl. II, López-Rey fig. 3.

1843   López-Rey no. II, fig. 4, as by Goya and Weiss. On the verso of this sheet is a version of [1842] – see note.
      There is an incomplete copy of the verso of [1842], reproduced by López-Rey fig. 5.
      Another version in the Hispanic Society (A.759), Starkweather pl. XLIII, López-Rey fig. 6.

1844   López-Rey no. III, fig. 7, as by Goya and Weiss. On the verso of this sheet is a small sketch of a woman's head, reproduced by López-Rey fig. 22.
      Another version in the Hispanic Society (A.752), Starkweather pl. XXXV, López-Rey fig. 8.

1845   López-Rey no. IV, fig. 9, as by Goya and Weiss.
      Another version in the Hispanic Society (A.754), Starkweather pl. LXVI, López-Rey fig. 10.

1846   López-Rey no. V, fig. 12, as by Goya (and Weiss?).
      Another version in the Hispanic Society (A.710), Starkweather pl. XXXIII, López-Rey fig. 11.

1847   López-Rey no. VII, fig. 20, as by Goya and Weiss. He suggested that the words *Goya* and *Paris* could be deciphered in the ripples of the water (*op. cit.* pp. 14-15).

1848   López-Rey fig. 21.

1849   This and the drawing on the other side of the sheet should properly have their recto and verso descriptions reversed: the chalk drawing on [1850] was spoiled when the wash drawing was added on the other side. López-Rey fig. 17, as by Goya and Weiss. Cp. the similar figure in [1863].

1850   López-Rey no. VI, fig. 18; the top figure as by Goya, the lower figure by Weiss. Cp. [1861] for another version of this design.

1851   Certainly by Goya, this drawing was not apparently copied by Rosario. On the verso is a crude pen and ink sketch, scribled through, of a woman with a fan – reproduced by López-Rey fig. 24.

1852   Published by Sayre as by Goya (Bibl. 173, p. 87, fig. 6). It was drawn after the sheet was torn in half – see [1853] – and is strictly speaking on the verso of that cut drawing.

1853   See note to [IV.1621] for a portrait by Rosario Weiss of her mother.

1854   Possibly by Goya. On the verso are some black chalk scribbles.

1855   Probably by Goya. On the verso are pen and Indian ink scribbles and repetitions of the monogram *MR* (Mariquita Rosario).

1856   A fine drawing, by Goya. Cp. *Desastres* plate 31 [III.1046]. On the verso is an insignificant pencil profile of a woman by Rosario.

1857   On paper with the watermark *AÑO DE 1821* (the 2 is illegible). López-Rey no. VIII, fig. 23, as by Weiss.

1858   First published by López-Rey, *op. cit.* p. 12, fig. 16, as by Weiss.
      Another version in the Hispanic Society (A.690), Starkweather pl. XXXIV, López-Rey fig. 14.

1859   López-Rey fig. 15. Possibly a sketch of her mother, Leocadia.

1860   Exhibited in 1937 (Bibl. 14, no. 39, ill.). Attributed to Rosario by Sayre (Bibl. 173, p. 109, n. 11). On the verso (or more properly the recto of the torn half sheet) is the back half of an animal similar to the *Panther cub* [1870], also drawn in black chalk.
      Another version in the Hispanic Society (A.705), Starkweather pl. XLIV, López-Rey fig. 13.

1861   Attributed to Rosario Weiss by Sayre (Bibl. 173, p. 109, n. 11). Cp. the similar subject in [1850].
      Another version, without the signature, in the Hispanic Society (A.707), Starkweather pl. LXX, López-Rey fig. 19.

1862   Attributed to Rosario Weiss by Sayre (Bibl. 173, p. 109, n. 11).
      Another version in the Hispanic Society (A.697), Starkweather pl. XIII.

1863   Another version in the Hispanic Society (A.741), Starkweather pl. X. Cp. the similar subject in [1849].

1865   López-Rey fig. 31, as by Weiss. The Prado title 'They take off his fetters' is no doubt incorrect, since the drawing recalls those in the albums where monks and priests are 'comforting' prisoners (cp. [III.1289, V.1805]).
      This drawing is closely connected with another made for or from the etching [III.986] and attributed by López-Rey to Weiss – see note to [III.987].

1867 and 1868   A Moreno photograph (519) shows that these two drawings were once on a single sheet with a central fold, the *Fox* 'above' the *Dromedary*.

TABLE OF WORKS IN CATALOGUE V   1824-1828

ABBREVIATIONS AND SIGNS

[ ]   Numbers within square brackets refer to the works listed in the catalogue. The number is preceded by a roman numeral (I-V) referring to the section of the book in which the work appears. (This is omitted if the reference is to a work within the same section.)

TITLE
Goya's autograph titles are given in *italics*. Where there is no room for the whole title or its translation in the catalogue legend, it is continued in the note.

DATE
Examples:
	1797	dated by Goya
	1797	certain date
	1797?	probable date
	c.1797	about 1797
	1797-99	executed during the period indicated

d.   Dated
Doc.   Date indicated by a document

SIGNATURE
s.   Signed

INSCRIPTION
italics   Title or inscription by Goya
Inscr.   Inscription
/   Change of line in an inscription
MS.   Manuscript

TECHNIQUE
All works are in oil on canvas unless otherwise specified
Aq.   Aquatint
L.   Lithograph

DIMENSIONS
cm.   Centimetres
approx.   Approximately
vis.   Visible dimensions (e.g. where work is partly covered by a mount or frame)
diam.   Diameter

Dimensions of the drawings are those of the sheet of paper.
Dimensions of the engravings are those of the copperplate.

COLLECTION
A.I.   Art Institute
B.M.   British Museum, London
B.N.   Biblioteca Nacional / Bibliothèque Nationale
C.   Calcografía Nacional, Madrid (see Bibl. 5)
Fund. Lázaro   Fundación Lázaro Galdiano, Madrid (the indication M = Museum, B = Biblioteca)
Gal.   Galerie / Gallery
Inst.   Institut / Institute / Instituto
Hispanic Soc.   Hispanic Society of America, New York
K.K.   Kupferstichkabinett (Print room)
Min.   Ministère / Ministerio / Ministry
Mus.   Musée / Museo / Museum (of Fine Arts, unless otherwise indicated)
M.F.A.   Museum of Fine Arts, Boston
M.M.A.   Metropolitan Museum of Art, New York
N.G.   National Gallery
Patr. Nac.   Patrimonio Nacional, Madrid
R.A.   Real Academia / Royal Academy
P. Palais   Petit Palais (Musée des Beaux-Arts de la Ville de Paris)
Rhode Is. S. D. Mus.   Museum of the School of Design, Providence (Rhode Island)

V. and A.   Victoria and Albert Museum, London
coll.   Collection (a capital C indicates a public collection, e.g. Frick Coll., New York)
priv.   Private
destr.   Destroyed

Acquisition or inventory numbers are given in brackets after the name of the collection. See Index of Collections, page 394.

BIBLIOGRAPHICAL REFERENCES
Bibl.   See the numbered Bibliography, page 386. The most frequently used abbreviations are:
B.   Barcia, *Catálogo de la Colección de Dibujos Originales de la Biblioteca Nacional* (Bibl. 3)
D.   Delteil, 'Francisco Goya', *Le Peintre graveur illustré* (Bibl. 55)
DF.   Desparmet Fitz-Gerald, *L'Œuvre peint de Goya* (Bibl. 57)
G.   Gudiol, *Goya* (catalogue raisonné) (Bibl. 85)
H.   Harris, *Goya. Engravings and lithographs* (Bibl. 88)
M.   Mayer, *Francisco de Goya* (Bibl. 128)
S.   Sambricio, *Tapices de Goya* (Bibl. 154)
SC.   Sánchez Cantón, *Museo del Prado: Los dibujos de Goya* (Bibl. 168)

ILLUSTRATION
Ill. p. (or p.)   See the reproduction in the text at the page indicated.

NOTE
*   Reference to a note on the pages preceding the illustrated catalogue.

CATALOGUE V
1824-1828

[1658-1870]

PORTRAITS 1824-1828

In spite of his years, Goya's hand retained its cunning and he proudly added his age beside many of the signatures on the late portraits. With his eyesight failing, his style became less and less 'finished' and he used a very restricted palette based on black. The broad, almost tremulous handling creates a moving intensity of expression, especially in the portraits of the year before his death.

[1658-1666]   *

1658

Self-portrait (age 78) 1824.
Pen and sepia ink 7×8·1 cm.
Madrid, Prado (483)   SC.466
Ill. p. 333   *

1659

Joaquín María Ferrer   s.d.
Goya Paris 1824.   73×59 cm.
Rome, Marquesa de la Gándara
M.259, DF.516, G.735   *

1660

Manuela Alvárez Coiñas de Ferrer
s.d. *Goya 1824*.   73×60 cm.
Rome, Marquesa de la Gándara
M.260, DF.518, G.736

1661

Leandro Fernández de Moratín
1824. s. *Goya* 54×47 cm.
Bilbao, Mus. M.539, DF.523,
G.737 Ill. p. 334   *

1662

Jacques Galos s.d. *1826*
with inscr. 55×46 cm.
Merion (Pa.), Barnes Foundation
M.269, DF.525, G.761 p. 352 *

1663

Juan Bautista de Muguiro s.d.
1827 with inscr. 102×85 cm.
Madrid, Prado (2898)
M.361, DF.526, G.762   *

1664

Mariano Goya   1827.   [Inscr.]
52×41·2 cm.
Lausanne, Georges A. Embiricos
M.313a, G.765 Ill. p. 353   *

1665

Portrait of a young woman
c.1826-27.   59·6×48·5 cm.
Collection unknown
M.422, G.766   *

1666

José Pio de Molina   c.1827-28.
70×50 cm.
Winterthur, Reinhart Coll. (80)
M.387, DF.527, G.768   *

VARIOUS FIGURES 1824-1828

The *Milkmaid of Bordeaux* is one of Goya's most sensitive and moving works and is remarkable for its advanced handling of bright, clear colours laid on in broken, juxtaposed touches.
Studies from life or creations of Goya's imagination, the figures of a *Monk* and a *Nun* have the same emotional intensity as the late portraits. The last two paintings are known only from photographs, and may have been executed before Goya left Madrid.

[1667-1671]

1667

The milkmaid of Bordeaux
1825-27. s. *Goya* 74×68 cm.
Madrid, Prado (2899)
M.647, DF.277, G.767   p. 25 *

1668

Nun   Inscr. *Por Goya 1827*
on verso   38·7×24 cm.
England, priv. coll.
M.523, DF.515, G.763   p. 351 *

1669

Monk   Inscr. *Por Goya 1827*
on verso   40×32·5 cm.
England, priv. coll.
M.485, DF.522, G.764   *

1670

Old man in ecstasy   c.1819-27.
56×43 cm. Formerly Madrid,
Marqués de la Torrecilla
DF.519   *

1671

Monk holding a crucifix
c.1819-27. 56×43 cm. Formerly
Madrid, Marqués de la Torrecilla
M.541, DF.520, G.727   *

BULLFIGHTS 1824-1825

In July 1824 Goya painted a bullfight scene [1672] for his friend Ferrer [1659] during his visit to Paris.
Recently, X. de Salas has suggested that three further paintings should be added to the documented one. Two of these [1674, 1675] have usually been attributed to Eugenio Lucas, mainly on the grounds that they are very close to the *Bulls of Bordeaux* lithographs of 1825 [1707-1710]. In fact these paintings are as close to some of the prints from the *Tauromaquia* series [III.1149-1243] (which Goya no doubt took with him to Bordeaux) as to the lithographs, and may represent an intermediate group of works made before Goya started on the lithographs.
The whereabouts of a further painting, sold in 1924 as a pair to [1672], is unknown.
See notes for a discussion of other bullfight scenes not here accepted as by Goya.

[1672-1675]   *

1672

Bullfight - Suerte de vara   1824.
Inscr. on verso   50×61 cm.
Rome, Marquesa de la Gándara
M.664, DF.274, G.734   *

1673

Bullfight - Suerte de varas
1824-25.   23×40 cm.
Madrid, Prado (3047)
G.760   *

1674

Spanish entertainment
1824-25.   44×57 cm.
Oxford, Ashmolean Mus. (252)
G.758   *

1675

The divided ring
1824-25.   46×58 cm.
Oxford, Ashmolean Mus. (253)
G.759   *

MINIATURES   1824-1825

In a letter to his friend Ferrer
[1659] who was in Paris, written
on 20 December 1825, Goya
mentioned a collection of some
forty miniature paintings on ivory
which he had made the previous
winter, emphasizing the originality
of his technique and concluding
with pride that they were
'things which look more like
the brushwork of Velázquez than
of Mengs'.
Some twenty-two of these
miniatures have been identified
from catalogues. Only ten are
known at present, in various
public and private collections,
as well as a further eight from
reproductions.

Abbreviations and signs, see p. 3
ES = Eleanor Sayre, Bibl. 173
MS = Martin Soria, Bibl. 179

[1676-1697]

1676

Maja and a celestina   1824-25.
Ivory 5·4×5·4 cm.
London, Lord Clark
ES.3, MS.17; G.747   *

1677

Three men drinking   1824-25.
Ivory 5·5×5·5 cm. (vis.)
Collection unknown
ES.4, MS.15; M.674, G.752

1678

Man smoking a cigar   1824-25.
Ivory 5·5×5·5 cm. (vis.)
Collection unknown
ES.5, MS.16; M.647a, G.754

1679

Man looking for fleas in his shirt
1824-25.   Ivory 6×5·9 cm.
Los Angeles, Mr and Mrs Vincent
Price   ES.6, MS.6; G.750

1680

Six madmen(?)   1824-25.
Ivory 9×9 cm. (vis.)
Collection unknown
ES.8, MS.14; M.623a, G.743

1681

Judith beheading Holofernes(?)
1824-25.   Ivory 8·7×8·5 cm.
Collection unknown
ES.9, MS.1; M.17a, G.741

1682

Susannah and the elders(?)
1824-25.   Ivory 5·5×5·5 cm.
London, S. Sebba
ES.10, MS.2; M.16a, G.746

1683

Man picking fleas from a little dog
1824-25.   Ivory 8·8×8·6 cm.
Dresden, K.K. (1899.40)   ES.11,
MS.3; M.646a, G.740   p. 342

1684

Bust of an old man begging
1824-25.   Ivory 5·5×5·5 cm.
Collection unknown
ES.12, MS.4; M.623b, G.751

1685

Monk talking with an old woman
1824-25.   Ivory 5·5×5·5 cm.
Collection unknown
ES.13, MS.5; M.542, G.748

1686

Man eating leeks   1824-25.
Ivory 6·2×5·6 cm.
Dresden, K.K. (1899.41)
ES.14; G.753   *

1687

Two children looking at a book
1824-25.   Ivory 5×5 cm.
Providence, Rhode Is. S.D. Mus.
(21.129) ES.15, MS.10; G.749 *

1688

Nude reclining against rocks
1824-25.   Ivory 8·8×8·6 cm.
Boston, M.F.A. (63.1081)
ES.18, MS.8; G.739   Ill. p. 343

1689

Majo and maja seated   1824-25.
Ivory 8·8×8·3 cm.   Stockholm,
Nationalmuseum (NMB 1879)
ES.19, MS.9; G.738   p. 343   *

1690

Woman with clothes blowing..
1824-25.   Ivory 9×9·5 cm.
New York, R. Kirk Askew, Jr
ES.20, MS.7; G.742   p.342

91

ung woman kneeling in the dark
24-25.   Ivory 8·7×7·8 cm.
llection unknown
.21, MS.12; G.744

1692

Two Moors   1824-25.
Ivory 8·5×8 cm.
Collection unknown
ES.22, MS.11; G.745

1693

Boy frightened by a man(?)
1824-25.   Ivory 5·9×6 cm.
England, priv. coll.
ES.23, MS.13; G.755   *

Four miniatures listed from
references but unknown in
reproduction. Their attribution to
Goya is therefore uncertain.

1694-1697

1694
Bullfight
ES.1, MS.19; M.668

1695
Bullfight
ES.2, MS.20; M.669

1696
Monk preaching
Ivory 9×9 cm. (vis.)
ES.7 MS.18

1697
Prisoner lying on the ground
Ivory 6×5·5 cm.
ES.16

THOGRAPHS   1824-1825

Bordeaux Goya abandoned the
satisfactory transfer technique
ee [IV.1643-1650]) and took to
orking directly on the stone. He
oduced a number of master-
eces including the portrait of
ulon [1703], the printer-
nographer who made the
ition of the *Bulls of Bordeaux*
him. Apart from this famous
, the lithographs are known
ly from rare or unique proofs.
e four *Bulls of Bordeaux*
707-1710] are preceded by
ferent essays based on the
uromaquia prints and the group
bullfight paintings [1672-1675],
d the first of these may be one
his earliest attempts with the
yon on stone [1704].

Abbreviations and signs, see p. 360
D = Delteil, Bibl. 55
H = Harris, Bibl. 88
L = Lithograph
If not a proof from an edition:
1/1 = unique proof; 1/3 = one of
three proofs known.
Dimensions of lithographs
without a border are approximately
those of the worked area

[1698-1710]   *

1698

Monk   1819-25.
L. crayon 13×9 cm.   1/1
Berlin-Dahlem, K.K. (201-1905)
D.270, H.273   *

1699

Woman reading   1819-25.
L. crayon 11·5×12·5 cm.
1/7(?)   Madrid, B.N. (45624)
D.276, H.276   *

1700

Group with fainting woman
1824-25.   L. crayon 13×16 cm.
1/4   Madrid, Fund. Lázaro
(M.I-11611)   D.277, H.279

01

vito   1824-25.   s. *Goya*
crayon 18×18 cm.   1/7
ndon, B.M. (1876.5.10.362)
278, H.280   Ill. p. 348   *

1702

Modern duel   1824-25.   s. *Goya*
L. crayon 19×19 cm.   1/6
London, B.M. (1876.5.10.363)
D.279, H.281   Ill. p. 348

1703

Portrait of Gaulon   1824-25.
s. *Goya*   L. crayon 27×21 cm.   1/3
Middletown, Davison Art Center
D.284, H.282   Ill. p. 345   *

1704

Bull attacked by dogs   1824-25.
L. crayon and pen 16·5×12·5 cm.
1/8   New York, Hispanic Soc.
(Q7069)   D.274, H.277   *

1705

Picador and bull in open country
1824-25.   L. crayon 25×35·5 cm.
1/1   Berlin-Dahlem, K.K.
(801-1906)   D.275, H.278   *

06

llfight   s.d. *Goya Bodeaux* [sic]
25.   L. crayon 31×41·5 cm.
1   Bordeaux, Mus.   H.287   *

**THE BULLS OF BORDEAUX
1825**

Goya's lithographic masterpieces,
drawn on stone in 1825 and
printed by Gaulon in an edition
of 100 copies.
6 December 1825: Goya wrote
to Ferrer in Paris, sending him a
proof of [1709] and saying that
he had three more bullfighting
scenes ready.
On November 17 and 29 and
December 23, Gaulon registered
the printing of 100 impressions of
each lithograph.
Two of the four have Spanish
titles below the designs.

[1707-1710]   *

1707

*El famoso Americano, Mariano
Ceballos*   1825.   s. *Goya*
L. crayon 30·5×40 cm.
D.286, H.283   *

1708

Bravo toro (or The picador
caught by a bull)   1825.   s. *Goya*
L. crayon 30·5×41 cm.
D.287, H.284   *

1709

Dibersion de España (Spanish
entertainment)   1825.   s. *Goya*
L. crayon 30×41 cm.
D.288, H.285   Ill. p. 347   *

1710

TWO ALBUMS OF DRAWINGS 1824-1828

These last two albums were drawn in Bordeaux between 1824 and 1828. Their technical characteristics are identical: same paper (maximum known sheet size 19·5×15·6 cm.), same combination of lithographic crayon and black chalk. The drawings were probably intended to be etched or lithographed.

[1711-1822] *

The divided ring 1825.
s. *Goya*
L. crayon 30×41·5 cm.
D.289, H.286 *

ALBUM G

The highest page number: 60. Fifty-four drawings are known, of which thirteen belong to the Prado and sixteen were in the collection of Beruete and passed to Gerstenberg in Berlin. All the drawings have autograph titles and numbers.

Abbreviations and signs, see p. 360
B = Beruete (Moreno negative number for Beruete collection)
Bx = Boix, Bibl. 9
L = Lafond, Bibl. 98
SC = Sánchez Cantón, Bibl. 168
destr. = destroyed

[1711-1764] *

1711 G.*1*

Se hace Militar (He's turning into a soldier) 1824-28. Black chalk 19×15·5 cm. Madrid, Marqués de Castromonte Bx.197 *

1712 G.*2*

Mirar lo q.ᵉ no ben (Looking at what they can't see) 1824-28. Black chalk Berlin, Gerstenberg destr. B.248, L.7

1713 G.*3*

Gran coloso durmido (Great colossos asleep) 1824-28. Black chalk Berlin, Gerstenberg - destr. B.272, L.25 *

1714 G.*4*

Animal de letras (Literate animal) 1824-28. Black chalk 18×13 cm. Madrid, Prado (398) SC.431

1715 G.*5*

El perro volante (The flying dog) 1824-28. Black chalk 19×15 cm. Madrid, Prado (394) SC.436

1716 G.*7*

El cojo y Jorobado Bailarin (The lame and . . .) 1824-28 Black chalk 18·5×13·5 cm. Madrid, Prado (415) SC.422 *

1717 G.*8*

Ni por esas / Que tirania(?) (Nothing doing. What tyranny) 1824-28. Black chalk 19×15 cm Madrid, Prado (405) SC.425

1718 G.*9*

Gran disparate (Great folly) 1824-28.
Black chalk 19·2×15.2 cm. Madrid, Prado (382) SC.415

1719 G.*10*

Andar sentado a pie y a cavallo (To go along seated, on foot . . .) 1824-28. Black chalk 19·2×15 cm. U.S.A., priv. coll. *

1720 G.*12*

Mal sueño (Bad dream) 1824-28.
Black chalk 19×13 cm. Madrid, Prado (396) SC.430

1721 G.*13*

Mal Marido (Bad husband) 1824-28.
Black chalk 18·5×13·5 cm. Madrid, Prado (414) SC.429 *

1722 G.*14*

Mitad de cuaresma / Partir la vieja(?) 1824-28. Black chalk Berlin, Gerstenberg destr. B.244, L.3

1723 G.*15*

Segura union natural / Hombre la Mitad... 1824-28. Black chalk 19.2×15 cm. Cambridge, Fitzwilliam Mus. (2067) *

1724 G.*16*

Amanecio asi, mutilado, en/ Zaragoza, a principios/de 1700 1824-28. Black chalk 19·4×14·8 cm. Paris, priv. coll. *

1725 G.*17*

Loco / Calabozo (Madman. Cell) 1824-28.
Black chalk 19×14 cm. Buenos Aires, Z. Bruck *

1726 G.*19*

Dice q.ᵉ son de nacimiento, y pasa su/vida con ellos 1824-28. Black chalk 18×13 cm. Madrid, Prado (397) SC.438 *

1727 G.*20*

Borrico q.ᵉ anda en dos pies (A donkey on two legs) 1824-28. Black chalk 19·1×14·7 cm. Madrid, Prado (376) SC.440

'28 G.22

'ego (Fire) 1824-28.
ack chalk 19×15 cm.
aris, priv. coll. *

1729 G.23

Reza (He's saying his prayers)
1824-28. Black chalk
Berlin, Gerstenberg - destr.
B.250, L.9

Group of drawings showing
various picturesque methods of
transport which Goya actually
saw, in Paris and in Bordeaux.

1730 G.24

*Diligencias/Nuebas/o sillas de
es/paldas...* 1824-28.
Black chalk 19·1×15·2 cm.
Boston, M.F.A. (53.2378) *

1731 G.25

Coche barato/y tapado (An
economical covered carriage)
1824-28. Black chalk 19×15 cm.
Madrid, Mus. Cerralbo

'32 G.26

aseo (Promenade) 1824-28.
ack chalk
erlin, Gerstenberg - destr.
246, L.5 *

1733 G.28

De todo sirven / No se alquilan(?)
(Can be used for anything...)
1824-28. Black chalk
19·2×14·7 cm. U.S.A., priv. coll. *

1734 G.29

*Mendigos q.ᵉ se lleban solos en/
Bordeaux* 1824-28.
Black chalk 18·4×14·2 cm.
Paris, priv. coll. Ill. p. 336 *

1735 G.30

Con animales pasan su vida (They
spend their life with animals)
1824-28. Black chalk 19×14 cm.
Madrid, Prado (400) SC.410

1736 G.31

Yo lo he visto en Paris (I saw it
in Paris) 1824-28.
Black chalk 19·4×14·8 cm.
Paris, priv. coll. Ill. p. 335 *

'37 G.32

ocos patines (Mad skates)
324-28.
ack chalk 19·2×15·1 cm.
oston, M.F.A. (53.2377) *

Series of drawings portraying
lunatics of different types.
Compare the paintings of 1793-94
[II.330] and c.1812-19 [III.968].

1738 G.3[3]

Loco furioso (Raging lunatic)
1824-28.
Black chalk 19·3×14·5 cm.
Paris, priv. coll. Ill. p. 339 *

1739 G.34

Loco Africano (African lunatic)
1824-28. Black chalk
Berlin, Gerstenberg - destr.
B.255, L.12

1740 G.35

Locos (Lunatics) 1824-28.
Black chalk 18·6×14·7 cm.
Boston, M.F.A. (55.662) *

741 G.36

e la C.ᵉ(?) *M.ʳ Loco* (Lunatic
om the Calle Mayor)? 1824-28.
ack chalk Berlin, Gerstenberg -
estr. B.256, L.13

1742 G.37

Locos (Lunatics) 1824-28.
Black chalk
Berlin, Gerstenberg - destr.
B.277, L.29

1743 G.38

El hombre feliz (The happy man)
1824-28. Black chalk
Berlin, Gerstenberg - destr.
B.260, L.14 *

1744 G.39

Locos (Lunatics) 1824-28.
Black chalk 19×14·5 cm.
Formerly Madrid, Marqués de
Castromonte Bx.198 *

1745 G.40

Loco furioso (Raging lunatic)
1824-28.
Black chalk 19×14·4 cm.
Paris, priv. coll. *

1746 G.41

Loco p.r escrupulos (Mad through scruples) 1824-28.
Black chalk 18×14 cm.
Paris, priv. coll. *

1747 G.42

Se muere (He's dying) 1824-28.
Black chalk 19·4×14·8 cm.
Paris, priv. coll. *

1748 G.43

Loco picaro 1824-28.
Black chalk 19·2×15 cm.
Stockholm, Nationalmuseum
(274.1968) Ill. p. 339 *

1749 G.44

Loco p.r errar(?) (Mad through erring) 1824-28.
Black chalk 19·1×14·6 cm.
Boston, M.F.A. (53.2378) *

1750 G.45

*Loca q.e bende los placeres //
Salud / Sueño . . .* 1824-28.
Black chalk Berlin, Gerstenberg
destr. B.269, L.24

1751 G.46

Enrredos de sus vidas (Their lives'
entanglements) 1824-28.
Black chalk 19·3×15·2 cm.
Ottawa, N.G. (2997) *

1752 G.47

Sucesos campestres (Rural events)
1824-28. Black chalk
Berlin, Gerstenberg - destr.
B.275, L.28

Two drawings of the guillotine
which Goya perhaps saw in use
at Bordeaux.

1753 G.48

Castigo frances (The French
penalty) 1824-28. Black chalk
Berlin, Gerstenberg - destr.
B.267, L.20

1754 G.49

Castigo (The penalty) 1824-2
Black chalk
Berlin, Gerstenberg - destr.
B.266, L.19

1755 G.50

No reproduction available

Gimiendo y llorando (Weeping
and wailing) 1824-28.
Black chalk 19·3×15·3 cm.
London, heirs of Sir Robert Mond *

1756 G.51

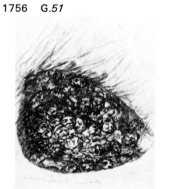

Comico descubrimiento (Comical
discovery) 1824-28. Black
chalk 19·2×14·9 cm. Cambridge,
Fitzwilliam Mus.(2066) *

1757 G.53

*Buelan buelan // fiesta en el ayre //
El toro mariposa* 1824-28.
Black chalk 19×15 cm.
London, priv. coll. *

1758 G.54

Aun aprendo (I am still learning)
1824-28. Black chalk
Madrid, Prado (416) SC.441
Ill. p. 354

1759 G.55?

Come/mucho (He eats a lot)
1824-28.
Black chalk 18·9×13·9 cm.
Madrid, Prado (384) SC.417

1760 G.56

Aqui algo/ha de aber (Here
something is bound to happen)
1824-28. Black chalk Berlin,
Gerstenberg - destr. B.274, L.27

1761 G.57

*Semana S.ta/en tiempo pasado/
en España* 1824-28.
Black chalk 19·1×14·6 cm.
Ottawa, N.G. (2999) *

1762 G.58

Quien vencera? (Who will win?)
1824-28. Black chalk
Berlin, Gerstenberg - destr.
B.273, L.26

1763 G.59

Se quieren mucho (They love
each other very much) 1824-28.
Black chalk 19×15 cm.
Madrid, Prado (392) SC.434

1764 G.60

*Del avaro no se espera/ningun
bien, y cada cual . . .* 1824-28.
Black chalk Berlin, Gerstenberg
destr. B.257, L.6

LBUM H   1824-1828

e the general note on the
o late albums, p. 364.
e highest page number: 63.
f the fifty-eight known drawings,
enty-nine belong to the Prado
d fifteen were in the collections
 Beruete and then of Gerstenberg
 Berlin.
ost of the drawings have no
le, but all are numbered and
ost in the first half of the album
e signed. Three of the drawings
ere used for engravings - see
823-1828].

obreviations and signs, see p. 364.

765-1822]   *

1765   H.2

Childish rage   1824-28.   s. *Goya*
Black chalk 19·1×15·6 cm.
Madrid, Prado (318)   SC.400

1766   H.*3*

Guitar-playing monk   1824-28.
s. *Goya*
Black chalk 18·3×13·6 cm.
Madrid, Prado (364)   SC.401

1767   H.*4*

Good counsel   1824-28.
s. *Goya*   Black chalk 19×14 cm.
Madrid, Prado (402)   SC.412

1768   H.*5*

The performing wolf   1824-28.
s. *Goya*   Black chalk 19×15·4 cm.
Madrid, Prado (375)   SC.424   *

---

769   H.*6*

nding or burying treasure
824-28.   s. *Goya*
ack chalk 19×15·5 cm.
adrid, Prado (406)   SC.426

1770   H.*7*

The pen is mightier than the
sword   1824-28.   Black chalk
19·2×15·6 cm.   Cambridge,
Fitzwilliam Mus. (2068)   *

1771   H.*8*

Pensive shepherdess   1824-28.
s. *Goya*
Black chalk 18·5×13·5 cm.
Madrid, Prado (320)   SC.406   *

1772   H.*9*

Nightmare   1824-28.   s. *Goya*
Black chalk 19×15·5 cm.
Madrid, Prado (404)   SC.414

1773   H.*10*

Devout woman   1824-28.
s. *Goya*
Black chalk 19·1×15·4 cm.
Madrid, Prado (322)   SC.402   *

---

774   H.[11]

OPY - Man mocked by demons
824-28.   s. *Goya*
ack chalk 18·9×15 cm.
ondon, B.M. (1876.5.10.376)   *

1775   H.*12*

Priest and monks singing
1824-28.   s. *Goya*
Black chalk 19×14 cm.
Madrid, Prado (381)   SC.427

1776   H.*13*

Procession of monks   1824-28.
s. *Goya*   Black chalk 19×14 cm.
Madrid, Prado (380)   SC.428

1777   H.*14*

Prisoner by the roadside
1824-28.   s. *Goya*
Black chalk 19·1×15·4 cm.
Madrid, Prado (321)   SC.403

1778   H.*15*

Allegory - War or Evil(?)
1824-28.   s. *Goya*
Black chalk 19×15 cm.
Madrid, Prado (391)   SC.432

---

779   H.*16*

aja and cloaked man   1824-28.
Goya   Black chalk
erlin, Gerstenberg - destr.
263, L.17

1780   H.*17*

Medical examination   1824-28.
s. *Goya*   Black chalk 19×14 cm.
Madrid, Prado (401)   SC.411

1781   H.*18*

Woman in white fallen to the
ground   1824-28.   s. *Goya*
Black chalk 18·8×15 cm.
Paris, priv. coll.   Ill. p. 340

1782   H.*19*

Young witch flying with a rope
1824-28.   s. *Goya*
Black chalk 19·2×15·5 cm.
Ottawa, N.G. (2996)   *

1783   H.*20*

Man pulling on a rope   1824-28.
s. *Goya*   Black chalk
Berlin, Gerstenberg - destr.
B.264, L.18

367

1784   H.*21*

Kneeling man with hands bound
1824-28.   s. *Goya*
Black chalk 19·1×14·8 cm.
Madrid, Prado (323)   SC.404

1785   H.*22*

Maja   1824-28.   s. *Goya*
Black chalk 19·1×14·6 cm.
Buenos Aires, A. Santamarina   *

1786   H.*23*

Woman with puppies   1824-28.
Black chalk
Berlin, Gerstenberg - destr.
B.262, L.16   *

1787   H.*24*

Woman helping a sick person drink
1824-28.   Black chalk
Berlin, Gerstenberg - destr.
B.254, L.11

1788   H.*25*

Young woman fainting,
surrounded by witches(?)
1824-28.   Black chalk
18·9×15 cm.   Paris, priv. coll.

1789   H.*27*

Travelling witch   1824-28.
s. *Goya*   Black chalk 19×15 cm.
Madrid, Prado (390)   SC.433

1790   H.*28(18)*

Lay brother on skates
1824-28.   s. *Goya*
Black chalk 19×14 cm.
Madrid, Prado (379)   SC.300   *

1791   H.*29*

Man holding a musket(?)
1824-28.
Black chalk 19·1×15·2 cm.
Berlin-Dahlem, K.K. (14.716)

1792   H.*30*

Half-naked prisoner   1824-28.
s. *Goya*   Black chalk
Berlin, Gerstenberg - destr.
B.242, L.1

1793   H.*31*

'Embozado' (cloaked man) with
a gun   1824-28.   s. *Goya*
Black chalk 19·2×15·2 cm.
Madrid, Prado (319)   SC.405

1794   H.*32*

Monk floating in the air
1824-28.   s. *Goya*   Black chalk
Madrid, priv. coll. (ex-Gerstenberg)
B.261, L.15   *

1795   H.*33*

Old woman with a mirror
1824-28.   s. *Goya*
Black chalk 18·5×13·5 cm.
Madrid, Prado (412)   SC.420

1796   H.*34*

Man killing a monk(?)
1824-28.   s. *Goya*
Black chalk 19×15 cm.
Madrid, Prado (403)   SC.413

1797   H.*35(37)*

Two old crones dancing
1824-28.
Black chalk 18·5×13·5 cm.
Madrid, Prado (417)   SC.423   *

1798   H.*36*

Wounded soldier leaning on
a tree-trunk   1824-28.
Black chalk 19·4×15·4 cm.
Paris, priv. coll.   *

1799   H.*37(39)*

Monk drawing with a compass
1824-28.   s. *Goya*
Black chalk 19×14 cm.
Madrid, Prado (378)   SC.419

1800   H.*38(48)*

Easy victory   1824-28.   s. *Goya*
Black chalk 19×14 cm.
Madrid, Prado (399)   SC.409

1801   H.*40*

Serpiente de/4 bar$/en Bordeaux
(Serpent four yards long in B . . .)
1824-28.   Black chalk   Berlin,
Gerstenberg - destr. S.270, L.23   *

1802   H.*41*

Cocrodilo / en Bordeaux (Crocodile
in Bordeaux)   1824-28.
Black chalk   Berlin, Gerstenberg -
destr.   B.271, L.21

1803   H.*42*

The enema   1824-28.
Black chalk
Madrid, Prado (383)   SC.416

804   H.*43*

Woman with two children
1824-28.   Black chalk
19·1×14·6 cm.   New York,
Hispanic Soc. (A.3311)   *

1805   H.*44*

He's helping him to die well
1824-28.
Black chalk 18·3×13·6 cm.
Madrid, Prado (365)   SC.407

1806   H.*45*

*Claudio Ambrosio Surat/Llamado
el Esquelete vibiente* . . .   1826-28.
Black chalk   Berlin, Gerstenberg -
destr.   B.268, L.22   *

1807   H.*47*

Man brandishing a knife   1824-28.
Black chalk 19·1×15 cm.
Rotterdam, Mus. Boymans (S.15)
*

1808   H.*48*

Penitent monk   1824-28.
Black chalk
Berlin, Gerstenberg - destr.
B.243, L.2

---

809   H.*49*

Woman with a child on her lap
1824-28.   Black chalk
Berlin, Gerstenberg - destr.
B.279, L.31

1810   H.*51*

Soldier with a drinking companion
1824-28.
Black chalk 19·1×14·7 cm.
Paris, priv. coll.   Ill. p. 341   *

1811   H.*52*

Daedalus seeing Icarus fall(?)
1824-28.
Black chalk 19×15 cm.
Madrid, Prado (395)   SC.435   *

1812   H.*53(52)*

Muerte de/Anton Requena (The
death of A . . . R . . .)   1824-28.
Black chalk 19×15·2 cm.
Ottawa, N.G. (2998)   *

1813   H.*54*

Tele-/grafo (Telegraph)
1824-28.
Black chalk 19·1×15·2 cm.
Madrid, Prado (377)   SC.437   *

---

814   H.*56(55)*

COPY(?) Group of monks
beneath an arch   1824-28.
Black chalk 18·6×13·4 cm.
Berlin-Dahlem, K.K. (4293)   *

1815   H.*57(56)*

United by the devil   1824-28.
Black chalk 19×15 cm.
Madrid, Prado (393)   SC.439

1816   H.*58(57)*

Old man on a swing   1824-28.
Black chalk 19×15·1 cm.
New York, Hispanic Soc. (A.3313)
*

1817   H.*59*

Young woman floating in the air
1824-28.   Black chalk
Berlin, Gerstenberg - destr.
B.278, L.30

1818   H.*61*

Phantom dancing with castanets
1824-28.
Black chalk 18·9×13·9 cm.
Madrid, Prado (385)   SC.418   *

---

819   H.*62*

Two women in church(?)
1824-28.   Black chalk
Berlin, Gerstenberg - destr.
B.249, L.8

1820   H.*63*

Monk guzzling from a large bowl
1824-28.   Black chalk 19×14 cm.
Madrid, Prado (366)   SC.408

1821   H.*[a]*

The broken pot   1824-28.
s. *Goya*(?)   Black chalk
Berlin, Gerstenberg - destr.
B.251, L.10   *

1822   H.*[b]*

The idiot   1824-28.   Black chalk
Berlin, Gerstenberg - destr.
B.245, L.4   *

LAST ETCHINGS 1824-1826

Only seven etchings are known from Goya's last years in Bordeaux. Three are based on drawings from album H, and it seems probable that he intended to publish a new series of *caprichos*, but abandoned the technically tricky etching medium in favour of lithography.

The first six designs are etched on the front and back of three copperplates. Only one contemporary proof is known, of [1825]. A small edition was printed in Madrid in 1859, and the plates now belong to Philip Hofer of Cambridge (Mass.).

The last plate found its way to Paris and a very small edition was printed in the nineteenth century. It is most widely known from the impressions bound as the frontispiece to Delteil's catalogue, published in 1922. The plate was then in the collection of Edmond Gosselin in Paris and is now the property of Dr Zdenko Bruck in Buenos Aires.

Abbreviations and signs, see p. 360
D = Delteil, Bibl. 55
H = Harris, Bibl. 88

[1823-1829]

1823   on recto of 1824

Maja on a dark ground   1825-27. Etching and aquatint 19×12 cm. D.28, H.30

1824   on verso of 1823

Maja on a light ground   1825-27. Etching 19×12 cm. D.29, H.31   *

Album H.22 - see [1785]

1825   on recto of 1826

Old man on a swing   1825-27. Etching and aquatint 18·5×12 cm. D.25, H.32   Ill. p. 349

1826   on verso of 1825

Old woman(?) on a swing   1825-27.   Etching 18·5×12 cm. D.26, H.33   Ill. p. 349   *

Album H.58 - see [1816]

1827   on recto of 1828

'Embozado' with a gun 1825-27. Etching and aquatint 19×12 cm. H.34n.   *

1828   on verso of 1827

'Embozado' with a gun 1825-27.   Etching (bull in drypoint) 19×12 cm.   D.27, H.3

Album H.31 - see [1793]

(Reproduction inverted by mistake)

1829

The blind singer   1825-27. Etching and aquatint 19×12 cm. D.30, H.35   *

VARIOUS DRAWINGS 1824-1828

Goya marked his stay in Paris with some drawings which he made as souvenirs for friends. The superb drawing of skaters (now destroyed) is no doubt a record of his first winter in Bordeaux. Two bullfighting drawings in brush and wash recall the brio and impetuous handling of all his *tauromaquia* scenes, and the seated figures in the unique watercolour recall those in one of the miniatures [1689].

Abbreviations and signs, see p. 360
Bx = Boix, Bibl. 9
SC = Sánchez Cantón, Bibl. 168

[1830-1841]   *

1830

Beggar holding out his hat   s.d. 6 July 1824   Pen and Indian(?) ink 17·8×20·5 cm.   Madrid, Marqués de la Scala   Bx.195B   *

1831

Monk and cleric . . .   1824? s. *Goya*   Pen and Indian(?) ink 17·8×20·5 cm.   Madrid, Marqués de la Scala   Bx.195A

1832

Two old people   1824.   s. *Goya* Pen and sepia ink with wash Gerona, Mus. Diocesano   *

1833

Two women by a window   1824. s. *Goya* Pen and sepia ink with wash Gerona, Mus. Diocesano   *

1834

Seated man with a hat   1824? Pen and sepia ink 14·6×17·5 cm. Madrid, Fund. Lázaro (Mus. I-10, 657)

1835

Blind beggar with dog   1824? Pen and Indian(?) ink with wash 15·1×14 cm.   Madrid, Fund. Lázaro (Mus.I-4045)   Bx.202   *

1836

Beggar with a crutch   1824-28. Black chalk Madrid, priv. coll.   *

1837

The skaters   1824-26.
Pen and Indian(?) ink
Berlin, Gerstenberg - destr.
B.253, L.32   *

1838

'Embozado' with a gun
1824-27.
Sepia ink wash 25×18 cm.
Paris, priv. coll.   *

1839

Matador drawing the bull with
a hat   1824-27.
Indian ink wash 17·5×29 cm.
Paris, priv. coll.   *

1840

Bulls and garrochistas in the open
1824-27.
Indian ink wash 20×31 cm.
Ottawa, N.G. (3000)   *

1841

Majos on the paseo   1824-27.
Watercolour 10·3×26 cm.
Madrid, Prado (331)   SC.A   *

THE GOYA/WEISS DRAWINGS c.1821-1826

María del Rosario Weiss was born on 2 October 1814, and it is recorded that from the age of seven Goya encouraged her to draw, giving her sketches and caricatures to copy.
One complete sketchbook of seventy drawings by Rosario Weiss, presumably after lost originals by Goya, is in the Hispanic Society in New York; a group of thirteen drawings in various media is in the Biblioteca Nacional, Madrid (some certainly by Goya); further drawings have been identified in the museums in Baltimore and Boston, and some drawings in the Prado Museum are here tentatively included

among the Goya/Weiss drawings. Four small sketches of animals in the Lázaro Museum are here classified as drawings, having been wrongly described as lithographs in the Goya print catalogues [1867-1870]. Although it was not considered justifiable to reproduce the whole of the Hispanic Society album, the other known drawings have been included as an indication of the lost Goya material.

Abbreviations and signs, see p. 360
GM = Gómez-Moreno, Bibl. 167a
SC = Sánchez Cantón, Bibl. 168

[1842-1870]   *

1842

Clown   Inscr. *Hay ay q.e me canso.*
c.1821-26.   Pen and sepia
ink with wash 14·4×10·3 cm.
Madrid, B.N. (GM.1 r.)   *

1843

Children with a cart   c.1821-26.
Pen and sepia ink with wash
14·5×10·3 cm.
Madrid, B.N. (GM.2 r.)   *

1844

French soldier   c.1821-26.
Pen and sepia ink with wash
14·5×10·3 cm.
Madrid, B.N. (GM.3 r.)   *

1845

Monk   c.1821-26.
Pen and sepia ink 14·8×10·4 cm.
Madrid. B.N. (GM.4)   *

1846

Cripple on crutches   c.1821-26.
Pen and sepia ink with wash
14·6×10·7 cm.
Madrid, B.N. (GM.5)   *

1847   recto of 1848

Washerwomen   c.1821-26.
Pen and sepia ink 10·7×14 cm.
Madrid, B.N. (GM.6 r.)   *

1848   verso of 1847

Mannequin   Pen and sepia ink
with wash 14×10·7 cm.
See [1847].   B.N. (GM.6 v.)   *

1849   recto of 1850

Seated figure   c.1821-26.
Brush and sepia wash over slight
black chalk 14·9×10·3 cm.
Madrid, B.N. (GM.7 r.)   *

1850   verso of 1849

Dead monk holding a crucifix
(repeated twice)
Black chalk 14·9×10·3 cm.
See [1849].   B.N. (GM.7 v.)   *

1851

Man dressed in skins and carrying
serpents   c.1821-26.
Black chalk 14·8×10·3 cm.
Madrid, B.N. (GM.8 r.)   *

1852   recto of 1853

Head of a man   c.1821-26.
Black chalk 8·2×10·9 cm.
Madrid, B.N. (GM.9 r.)   *

1853   verso of 1852

Head of a woman (Leocadia
Weiss?)
Black chalk 10·9×8·2 cm.
See [1854].   B.N. (GM.9 v.)   *

1854

Two men's heads   c.1821-26.
Black chalk 8·3×10·8 cm.
Madrid, B.N. (GM.10)   *

1855

Two heads of witches(?)
c.1821-26.
Red chalk 14·9×10·6 cm.
Madrid, B.N. (GM.11) *

1856

Cossack or Mameluke with fur hat
c.1821-26.
Black chalk 14·8×10·5 cm.
Madrid, B.N. (GM.12 r.) p. 338 *

1857

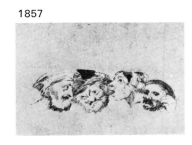

Four heads c.1821-26.
Pen and Indian ink 9·9×14·4 cm.
Madrid, B.N. (GM.13) *

1858 recto of 1859

Boy with a sling c.1821-26.
Indian ink wash 15×10 cm.
Paris, priv. coll. *

1859 verso of 1858

Woman on a bed
s. *Mariquita Rosario*
Indian ink·wash 10×15 cm.
See [1858]. *

1860

Man with a mattock c.1821-26.
Brush and sepia wash
14·5×10·3 cm.
Boston, M.F.A. (AL 1022) *

1861

Dead monk holding a crucifix
s. *Goya* c.1821-26. Pen and
brush with sepia ink 10·2×14·1 cm.
Baltimore, Mus. (55.30.15) *

1862

Crippled, legless beggar
c.1821-26. Pen and brush
with sepia ink 12·4×9·3 cm.
Baltimore, Mus. (55.30.14) *

1863

Seated figure reading a book
c.1821-26.
Sepia wash 14·5×10·2 cm.
Paris, priv. coll. *

1864

Study of a young man (with
sketches of heads) c.1821-26.
Sepia wash 20·5×15 cm.
Madrid, Prado (6) SC.463

1865

Monk and kneeling figure
c.1821-26. Pen and sepia ink
with wash 11×8 cm.
Madrid, Prado (386) SC.334 *

1866

Head of an old man asleep
c.1821-26.
Indian ink wash 11×7·4 cm.
Madrid, Prado (5) SC.462

1867

Fox c.1821-26.
Black chalk Madrid,
Fund. Lázaro (M.I-11,579)
D.283, H.291 *

1868

Dromedary c.1821-26.
Black chalk Madrid,
Fund. Lázaro (M.I-11,578)
D.280, H.288 Ill. p. 338 *

1869

Dog c.1821-26.
Black chalk Madrid,
Fund. Lázaro (M.I-11,577)
D.283, H.289

1870

Panther cub c.1821-26.
Black chalk Madrid,
Fund. Lázaro (M.I-11,580)
D.282, H.290

OTES TO CATALOGUE I - IV CONTINUED

ATALOGUE I   [279-316]

79-288   Charles IV and María Luisa were proclaimed ng and queen on 17 January 1789, and in the ensuing onths Goya was commissioned to provide many portraits the royal couple for the coronation festivities on September 23. Three such pairs were documented in a comporary account (Bibl. 36, II, p. 148; 156, p. 88) and a rther pair (now lost, or unidentified among those in the rado collection) was painted for the Duke and Duchess Osuna to whom Goya presented his account for 000 reales on 27 February 1790 (Bibl. 174, p. 198; 109, 161; cp. Appendix V).
ambricio suggested that all these portraits were derived Goya and/or assistants from a lost pair painted for the oyal Palace between 9 January and 20 March 1789 Bibl. 156, pp. 86-87, citing documents from Bibl. 154, ocs 124, 125, and see note to [279, 280]). Of the existing airs of portraits, that in the Real Academia de la Historia generally regarded as the finest [281, 282]. Sambricio's nportant study (Bibl. 156) has opened the way to an etailed analysis of all the known portraits, of which the nief examples are listed here, together with a pair repre- enting a variation in design which may not have originated Goya's studio [287, 288].

79 and 280   Sambricio showed that these were no doubt e two full-length portraits for which materials were listed accounts presented on 30 June 1789 (Bibl. 156, pp. 86, 3; 154, docs 124, 125). It is clear from the accounts that e half-length portraits were sent to the Royal Palace in ladrid (see note to [279-288]) and that this full-length air went in the larger crate to Aranjuez. The portrait of the ng was deposited by the Prado with the Ministerio after s acquisition in 1847 with [280], and does not appear in ny of the Prado catalogues.
30   Listed by Carderera (Bibl. 148, no. 8). Until Sam- ricio's article, it was often thought that this portrait of the ueen, wearing a 'tontillo' (hoop skirt), was painted onsiderably later, but he pointed out, in addition to the ocuments already mentioned, that she is not wearing the signia of her Order which was instituted in 1792 (Bibl. 56, p. 88). See Held for dating on grounds of style (Bibl. 89, . 47).

31 and 282   The Real Academia de la Historia commis- oned Jovellanos, on 20 March 1789, to order portraits of e king and queen. They were completed and hanging y 11 September, when Goya signed and dated his account r 6,000 reales (Bibl. 162, pp. 9-10). First exhibited 1961 3ibl. 23, nos XXXII, XXXIII).
Replicas (apart from [283-286]) include:
Charles IV   126×94 cm.   Madrid, Prado (740a) 1.123, DF.339   See Held (Bibl. 89, p. 187).
Charles IV   Doc. 6 March 1790 (Goya's receipt for 000 reales: Luis Benavente, 'Un retrato y un autógrafo de oya', *ABC*, Madrid, July 1934)   Santiago de Compostela, lus. Municipal   G.289.
María Luisa   125×94 cm.   Paris, Spanish Embassy xhibited 1961-62 (Bibl. 24, no. 46).

33 and 284   The king in a blue costume. Probably painted y assistants. For a later copy of the king's portrait, see note [II.781].

35 and 286   Commissioned by the Casa de la Moneda. he royal order for payment of 4,000 reales for these *tratos de medio cuerpo* was published by Sambricio when e pictures were exhibited in 1961 (Bibl. 23, nos LXXIV, XXV).

37 and 288   Another and less formal version of the royal ortraits, probably painted by an assistant.
Replicas:
Charles IV   Madrid, priv. coll.   Exhibited 1961 3ibl. 23, hors catalogue)   The sash of the Order of harles III partially over-painted following its modification June 1792.
María Luisa   113×79 cm.(?) Dimensions given by layer: 111×76 cm., and by Gudiol: 113×90 cm.   Paris, riv. coll.   M.139, DF.337, G.307   Exhibited 1961-62 3ibl. 24, no. 41).

These two portraits were in the Boadilla del Monte collection (nos 215, 218); they were catalogued by Viñaza (Bibl. 190, pp. 220-221, nos XXII, XXIII) and mentioned by Tormo (Bibl. 182, p. 206, n. 1).

289   Inscribed *CARLOS IV*. The drawing is published here for the first time, by kind permission of the present owner. The engraving by Carmona, 15·3×10·8 cm., is lettered *CARLOS IIII. / Goya pinx. Carmona sculp.t* It was used as the frontispiece to all editions of the *Kalendario Manual y Guia de Forasteros en Madrid* for the years 1791 to 1795 (the sash being altered after 1792). The portrait was re-engraved, in an oval, for the *Kalendario* for the years 1796-98 and 1801. This information was confirmed by the complete set of the *Kalendario* in the British Museum. Cp. Castañeda (Bibl. 46, nos II-XIII) and Bibl. 4 (nos 1712-40 to 48).

290   Inscribed on the paper (as if his friend were reading one of his many letters) *Mi Amigo Mart.n / Zapater. Con el/ mayor trabajo/te a hecho el/Retrato/Goya/1790* (My friend Martín Zapater. I have painted your portrait with the greatest difficulty (or, with the greatest care).) Goya was in Saragossa from 9 October to 4 November 1790 (Bibl. 166, p. 45). Exhibited in 1963-64 (Bibl. 27, no. 69). Cp. the later portrait [II.668].

291   Probably painted to commemorate Pignatelli's rôle in the completion of the Canal de Aragón in 1790. Viñaza noted that the original, which belonged to the Pignatelli family, the Condes de Fuentes, had probably been sold in Italy. He listed three copies, including this one, signed and dated by Narciso Lalana in 1821 (Bibl. 190, pp. 240-241, no. LXXII).
Reduction: Saragossa, Hilarian Gimeno (photo Mora 2158).

292   A 'copy of the bust' of [291] was mentioned by Viñaza in the Zapater collection in Saragossa, and is recorded in the 1961 exhibition catalogue as a copy of this study (Bibl. 23, no. XVIII).

293   Inscribed *D. LUIS MARIA DE CISTUE Y MARTI- NEZ. A- LOS / DOS AÑOS Y OCHO MESES DE SU ED[AD]*. The son of the Barón de la Menglana [294], he was born on 23 July 1788. See Sánchez Cantón (Bibl. 166, pp. 46-47).

294   It is not certain whether the original portrait is this one or another, half-length version where the sitter holds a sheet instead of a roll of paper in his hand:
Inscribed on paper *El YII.mo S.r / D.n Joseph / Cistue* 120×80 cm.   Saragossa, Mus. (173, deposit of José Cistué).
Neither portrait has previously been catalogued, and their attribution lacks documentary evidence.

295-299   The commissioning of this series of cartoons in January 1789 and Goya's refusal to begin work until May 1791 were documented by Sambricio (Bibl. 154, pp. 163-168, docs 127-144). Although Goya claimed for painting materials acquired between January and December 1791 and allegedly used for his work on the tapestry cartoons (docs 145-147, 150-152), the account for canvases and stretchers for the sketches and cartoons was not presented and paid until 26 June 1792 (*op. cit*. pp. 169-170, docs 153, 154). It may be that in spite of his letter to Bayeu, dated 3 June 1791 and referring to the 'nearly completed' sketch for the largest cartoon i.e. *La boda* (doc. 142), Goya did not in fact paint the sketches until the end of the year. Sambricio suggested that they were presented to the king shortly before Christmas, citing one of Goya's letters to Zapater (*op. cit*. pp. 168-169).

295   (Women water-carriers). Sambricio noted the changes in composition between sketch and cartoon [300], and an examination of the cartoon shows that the woman on the left of the sketch was included and then painted over. A large *X.13* on the verso of the sketch suggests that it may have been included among the paintings listed in the

inventory of 1812 – see note to [III.963]. It was probably one of the *diez y seis bocetos pequeños de los tapices* listed in the Brugada inventory of 1824 (Bibl. 57, I, p. 53, n. 1). See Appendix I, no. 13, and II, no. 1. It was acquired as well as [III.958], by Francisco Acebal de Arratia. Exhibited 1928 (Bibl. 10, no. 10).

296   Published by Juan Lafora García, 'Goya: Estudio biográfico crítico', *Arte Español*, IX, 1928-29, p. 361, fig. 2. Attribution doubted by Sambricio. Reproduced in colour in *Connaissance des Arts*, no. 243, Sept. 1970, p. 84.

297   From the Contini-Bonacossi collection (Bibl. 110, no. 25). A repetition, with minor variations, of [296]. Considered very doubtful by Sambricio.
Further examination of the cartoon may help to prove or disprove the attribution of these sketches.

298   Probably the final sketch for the cartoon, it may or may not have been 'nearly completed' in June 1791 (see note to [295-299]). The 'stretcher with its fine, primed canvas', the largest for the group of sketches, was probably the one listed individually at 14 reales in the carpenter's account (Bibl. 154, doc. 154). According to Sambricio, the sketch was acquired by Luis de Madrazo, but there seems to be some confusion with a later 'Scene beneath a bridge' – see [III.948]. If the provenance from Madrazo is correct, it may have been acquired, along with other paintings, from the collection inventoried in the Quinta del Sordo (see note to [295]). Published in colour by the Jockey Club in 1928, *Tres cuadros de Goya*.

299   Published by José Gudiol, 'Bocetos inéditos de los cartones de Goya', *Coloquio*, 49, 1968, pp. 8-9. The painting is so close to the cartoon that it suggests a reduction rather than a sketch.
Another painting, described by Sambricio as a 'first sketch, although of uncertain attribution', has figures almost identical with those in the cartoon (closer than those in [298]), but an open background with trees: Madrid, Marqués de Bermejillo   S.59a, pl. CLXXXV.

300-306   See note to [295-299]. Goya's account, which included six months wages for his colour grinder, from January to June 1792 (Bibl. 154, docs 153-156), suggests that the stretchers and canvases were supplied not much more than six months previously, and he probably began work on the cartoons early in the new year.

300   (Women water-carriers). See note to [295] concerning changes in the composition.

304   One of the cartoons stolen from the Royal Palace in 1870 – see note to [129] and Bibl. 154 (doc. 280, no. . . . .37). Exhibited 1970 (Bibl. 30, no. 12).

306   (The see-saw). One of the cartoons stolen from the Royal Palace in 1870 – see note to [129] and Bibl. 154 (doc. 280, no. . . . .41). The cartoon has never reappeared.

307 and 308   Sometimes described as cartoons for tapestries which were never executed (cp. Sambricio, Bibl. 154, p. 173). Possibly painted as over-doors for Sebastián Martínez in Cadiz. The Conde de Maule mentioned the existence of three over-doors painted by Goya (Bibl. 126, XIII, p. 340), and Trapier suggested that these pictures might be two of them (Bibl. 188, pp. 8-9). Gudiol suggests [II.746] as the third.
307   Exhibited 1970 (Bibl. 30, no. 3/4).

309   This painting, known only from a photograph and of uncertain authenticity, recalls the facial types in the tapestry cartoons of 1791-92 [300, 301] and also those in a painting of 1784 [198].

310 and 311   For Goya's visit to Valencia, see Sánchez Cantón (Bibl. 166, p. 44) and Sambricio (Bibl. 154, p. 165, doc. 136). Drawings published by August L. Mayer, *150 Handzeichnungen spanischer Meister*, Leipzig, 1920, nos 133, 134, and González Martí (Bibl. 69, ill. pp. 435, 437).

312 Engraving, 33·8×23·5 cm., inscribed on book *Metodo de/Estudios de/S.ⁿ Ysi-/dro el/Real, en/1770*, on plinth *A D.ⁿ Manuel de Villafañe/el amor filial.*, and below *F. Goya pinx.* and *F. Hubert Esculp, anno 1791*. Nothing is known about the sitter. Catalogued by the Biblioteca Nacional (Bibl. 4, no. 9812).

313 Engraving, 18·2×12·5 cm. (design), inscribed *El Ex.ᵐᵒ S.ᵒʳ D.ⁿ Miguel de Muzquiz, / primer Conde de Gausa*, and below *Fr.ᶜᵒ Goya lo dibujó* and *Fer.ᵈᵒ Selma lo grabó*. Published as the frontispiece to the *Elogio del Excmo. Señor Conde de Gausa que ... leyó ... don Francisco de Cabarrús...*, Madrid, 1786. Catalogued by Castañeda (Bibl. 46, no. XVIII) and the Biblioteca Nacional (Bibl. 4, no. 6399).

Mayer listed the original pencil drawing in the collection of Mrs Jay, Frankfurt-am-Main (1925) M.684. Cp. the painting [215].

314 Engraving, 16·4×9 cm. (cut); inscribed on plinth *EL EXCMO SEÑOR / MARQUÉS DE BAXA-MAR.* and below *F. Goya pinx.* and *J. Asensio sculp.ᵗ*. Published as the frontispiece to the Spanish translation of James Harris, *Historia literaria de la Edad Media*, Madrid, 1791. Catalogued by Castañeda (Bibl. 46, no. XX) and the Biblioteca Nacional (Bibl. 4, no. 7408).

A painting was attributed by Soria to Agustín Esteve (though with some doubts) and may be a copy after Goya's lost original: inscribed *Exmo. S. D.ⁿ Antonio/ Aniceto de Porlier 1.ᵉʳ/Marques de Bajamar/Ministro de G. y J. y Conse/gero de Estado de Carlos 3.ᵒ* 101×80 cm. Madrid, Marqués de Bajamar M.207, Soria 14 (Bibl. 180).

315 Engraving, 20·6×14·1 cm. (design); inscribed on banner *NOREBUZNARON EN / BALDE EL UNO [Y EL OTRO] ALCALDE* (They brayed not in vain, the bailiffs twain), and below *Francisco Goya la inv. y dibujó*. and *J. Joaquin Fabregat la gravó*. Lafuente suggested that this engraving was a project for the illustrations to the magnificent edition of *Don Quixote* published by the Real Academia Española in 1780 (Bibl. 106, pp. IV-V). The engraving is exactly the same size as those by Antonio Carnicero and other artists included in the four volumes and since the composition is very successful it is not clear why it should have been rejected. It illustrates an incident which occurs in the 1780 edition in volume III, pp. 239-24 (with the verse inscribed on the banner printed on p. 242) The proof illustrated is in the Biblioteca Nacional (33144). The engraving was referred to, in relation to the much later drawing of *Don Quixote* [III.1475], by Rodríguez-Moñino (*op. cit.* in the note).

316 Engraving, 16·5×10·4 cm. (design); inscribed on th monument, below the portrait of Lemaur (a French engineer) *SCRIPTIS CESTIS. / ANIMO. SANCTITATE. CLARISSIMO VIRO. / CAROLO. LEMAUR.*, and below *Goya invenit* and *P. Choffard, sculpsit Parisiis 1788*. The mourner leans over Lemaur's maps and plans for roads an canals in Spain. The existence of this engraving was noted by Lafuente (Bibl. 106, p. V) and the proof illustrated is in the Biblioteca Nacional (Retratos franceses, caja 41).

CATALOGUE II   [836-873a]

I, p. 53, n. 1) may represent Lorenza Correa. See Appendix II, no. 25. Cp. note to [III.890].

836 Isidro Máiquez, the actor-manager [858], was frustrated in his attempt to engage Lorenza Correa for his company in 1803, and she left for Italy and France (see Emilio Cotarelo y Mori, *Isidro Máiquez y el Teatro de su Tiempo*, Madrid, 1902, p. 163). The portrait was probably painted shortly before her departure.

837 A singer and composer (1775-1832), he is not to be confused with Manuel García de la Prada [819]. Loga recorded an inscription *D. Fr. Goya 1815*, and was echoed by Mayer (who said that he had not seen it) and by Sánchez Cantón. It does not appear to exist, and if the portrait is a pendant to [836] it was probably executed about the same time and in any case before García left Spain for good in 1808. See above, and also Cotarelo, *op. cit.* p. 267.

838 Reproduced in *The Antiquarian*, March 1931, p. 30, as belonging to Mrs Daniel Guggenheim.

840-852 The four portrait drawings were included in the 1922 exhibition (Bibl. 9) and the copper miniatures were published by Soria (Bibl. 179). On the Goicoechea family, see Lafuente (Bibl. 102, p. 290) and Saltillo (Bibl. 153, family tree facing p. 38).

840 Dated at top left; inscribed on verso *Doña Josefa Bayeu, por Goya, en el año 1805* (according to Boix, from whom the dimensions are also taken). See note to [686].

841 Black chalk with pen and Indian ink. Dated at top right; inscribed below in pen and ink *Dª Juana Galarza*. Cp. [849] and [III.886].

842 Dated at top right; inscribed at lower right *Gumersinda Goicoechea*. Said to have been destroyed; reproduced from the 1922 catalogue. Cp. [845] and [851].

843 Inscribed below *Xavier Goya*. It is worth pointing out that the form of the *X* is very close to that in the inventory mark of 1812 (see text p. 246), and it seems very likely that it was Goya himself who marked the pictures which were allotted to his son. In his letters, he spells the name with an X or a J.

844 This portrait of Javier and its companion [845] are published here for the first time. Both came originally from the Salas Bosch collection in Barcelona and passed to the Goupil family in France, together with [847] and [848]. Exhibited with [845] in 1970 (Bibl. 30b, nos 17, 18).

845 Before the appearance of this miniature, the following one was identified as Gumersinda. However, there seems to be a closer resemblance between this miniature and the drawing [842] and full-length painting [851]. The pose of the girl, who would naturally be turned towards her husband, serves to confirm the identification. See note to [844].

846 Here tentatively identified as the oldest of the Goicoechea sisters: in 1805 she was twenty, Gumersinda was seventeen. See Saltillo (Bibl. 153, facing p. 38). The miniature was first published by Lafuente (Bibl. 102, p. 38, ill.) but identified as Gumersinda and dated c.1826.

847 Inscribed on verso *1805 / a los 15 años / Geronima / por/Goya*.

848 Inscribed on verso *1806 / Goya / a los 12 años / la Cesarea*.

849 and 850 Exhibited in 1900 (Bibl. 8, nos 64, 65), the miniatures were published by Lafuente in 1947 (Bibl. 102, pp. 37, 38, ill. and p. 347) with a reference to their having left Spain some years before. He identified them as Javier and Gumersinda; Soria tentatively identified them as the Goicoechea parents (Bibl. 179, p. 4 [12]).

851 Listed in the Brugada inventory of 1828 as *Dª Gumersinda, tamaño natural* (Bibl. 57, I, p. 53). See Appendix II, no. 12. Listed by Carderera (Bibl. 148, nos 25, 64).

852 Listed in the Brugada inventory as *Retrato de Dn Javier con un perro. Tamaño natural*. See note to [851] and Appendix II, no. 8. Listed by Carderera (Bibl. 148, nos 25, 64).

853 Inscribed on back of sofa *D.ª Fran.ᶜᵃ Vicenta Chollet y/Cavallero/Por Goya. año 1806*.

854 Inscribed in lower left corner *D.ⁿ Tadeo Bravo de/ Rivero por su am.º Goya/1806*. See Trapier (Bibl. 188, pp. 30-31).

A small version of this portrait, with variants, has recently come to light: panel 22×12 cm. Inscribed along right edge *Borron de Dn. Tadeo Bravo ... Goya* Madrid, priv. coll.

855 Inscribed at upper left *D. Antonio Porcel por su amigo Goya 1806*. Destroyed in the fire at the Jockey Club, the picture is known from photographs and from a colour reproduction published by the Jockey Club in 1928, *Tres cuadros de Goya*. Compare the portrait of his wife [817].

856 and 857 It is known that Goya designed and painted the shield which adorned the façade of the Pestalozzi Institute in Madrid, founded by Godoy in 1806 — see [873a]. There is, however, no actual record of his having painted a version of the large composition known from the painting in New York [856] (attributed by Soria to Esteve, Bibl. 180, no. 106), a fragment in Dallas [857] (which corresponds with the composition of [856]), and another version:

250×132 cm. Madrid, R.A. San Fernando (698) Attributed by Gudiol to Carnicero and by Soria to Esteve (*op. cit.* no. 105).
See José Milicua, 'Un cuadro perdido de Goya: el Escudo del Real Instituto Militar Pestalozzi', *Goya*, 35, 1960, pp. 332-334.

858 Inscribed on sofa at right edge. Exhibited at the Academy of San Fernando in 1808 (Bibl. 177).

Replica: 82·3×63·3 cm. Chicago, A.I. (1933.1077)
Copy by Esteve(?): 92×70 cm. Madrid, Marqué de Casa Torres Soria 116 (Bibl. 180). Ill. Bibl. 72, pl. 9

859 Inscribed on paper *D.ⁿ Ysidro/Gonzalez/P.ʳ Goya 1801*. Both Sánchez Cantón (Bibl. 166, p. 170) an Catton Rich (Bibl. 16, no. 77) suggested that restoration might have altered the more likely 7 to a 1. However, the replica also bears the date 1801, and unless this is a copy made after an early restoration, it will be necessary to change the date of the picture. See Lafuente on the sitter (in *Archivo Español de Arte*, IX, 1933, pp. 68-71) and Trapier (Bibl. 188, p. 22).

Replica or copy: 102×79 cm. Inscr. *D. Isidro Gon zález. Por Goya. En 1801* Madrid, Generoso González Exhibited 1932 (Bibl. 102, p. 355, no. 1).

860 Inscribed on the paper *Ex.ᵐᵃ S.ʳᵃ Mar[quesa]/d Caballero/Goya. 1807*. Formerly Madrid, Marqués d Corvera. See Trapier (Bibl. 188, pp. 33-34). Reproduced in *Agnew's 1817-1967*, London, 1967, no. 3.

Replica: 105×84 cm. Inscribed *Ex.ᵐᵃ S.ʳᵃ Marq./d Caballero/Por Goya/1807* Formerly Madrid, Montero d Espinosa M.218, G.543 Exhibited 1928 (Bibl. 10, no. 22)

861 Inscribed on the papers *Ex.ᵐᵒ S.ᵒʳ / Marques de, Caballero / Ministro de / Gracia y Justicia / & & and Po Goya/1807*. Exhibited 1970 (Bibl. 30, no. 39).
Replicas:
153×84·3 cm. Inscribed *Ex.ᵐᵒ S.ᵒʳ / Marques de, Caballero / Min.ᵗʳᵒ de / Gr.ª y Jus / & and Goya / 180* Jacksonville, Cummer Gallery (loaned by Cintas Foundation Inc., New York) M.217a, DF.459, G.544n.
100×79 cm. Unfinished Houston, Mus. (54.26 Gaya Nuño 1038 (Bibl. 65). Authenticity disputed by Soria (*op. cit.* in note to [III.1546], p. 162, n. 1).

862 Born 1749, assassinated 1809, he was the founde of a cast-iron works in a remote province of Spain, which kept the Spanish forces supplied when the others had been destroyed or occupied by the French. He was killed for his close association with Godoy. The painting is ver heavily restored.

863 Traditionally called Lola Jiménez, Sánchez Cantón and Beroqui tentatively identified the sitter as the 'wife o D. José Folch' whose portrait was exhibited at the Academy of San Fernando in 1808 (see Bibl. 166, pp. 86, 171; 177) It was formerly in the collection of S. Oppenheimer, Paris

864-871 For the inventory of 1812 see Bibl. 161 and 147, and the note to [III.914-984], also Appendix I.

864-869 Listed in the 1812 inventory as *seis quadros de Maragato señalados con el numero ocho* (Bibl. 161, p. 106 Appendix I, no. 8). The inventory numbers had apparently already been removed when the pictures were photographed in Madrid by E. Otero in the collection of Lafitte (Bibl. 147, p. 109 – not mentioning these photographs).

For an account of the actual incident and Goya's sources see Font (Bibl. 62).

864 ...at Friar Pedro de Zaldivia. Exhibited 1970 (Bibl. 0, no.33).

865 ...El Maragato's gun.

866 ...from El Maragato.

868 Exhibited 1970 (Bibl. 30, no.34).

870 Tentatively identified by Sánchez Cantón as a painting in the 1812 inventory: *Unas ylanderas con el numero quince* (Bibl. 161, pp. 88, 106; Appendix I, no. 15). The painting, which was described by Mayer and dated 1810 (Bibl. 128, p. 61), has not been seen for many years. Cantón listed it in a private collection in Switzerland; an Alinari photograph (21177) gives the collection as Trieste, Casa Francesco Basilio.

871 Inscribed *MEDIC* or *MEDIO* in white on the ground between the figures. Sánchez Cantón suggested that this was the painting listed in the 1812 inventory as *Unos borrachos con el n.º veinte y dos* (Bibl. 161, pp. 87, 106; see Appendix I, no. 22). Beruete, describing the picture as 'really very odd' (in relation to Goya's œuvre), said that it had first been described as Dutch school, then attributed to Velázquez. He, however, supported the attribution to Goya (Bibl. 36, II, p. 98).

872 Engraving inscribed with the name and titles of the Condesa-Duquesa and below *Fran.co Goya le dibuxó. Año de 1794. Fern.do Selma le grabó*. Used as the frontispiece to Pierre le Moyne, *Galería de mujeres fuertes*, Madrid, 1794. This Spanish translation was dedicated to the leader of Spanish intellectual society. The countess-duchess wears the Order of María Luisa, awarded to her on 17 December 1792. Engraving published by Castañeda (Bibl. 46, no. XIX) and catalogued in Bibl. 4, no. 298-1. See also Bibl. 135 (ill. p. 120). Cp. the portrait of 1785 [I.220].

873 Lithograph inscribed beneath the oval *Goya lo pinto* and *J. Oton lo litog.o*, and below *RAMON CABRERA*. This lithograph was published with the posthumous edition of Cabrera's *Diccionario de Etimología de la Lengua Castellana*, Madrid, 1837. Catalogued by Castañeda (Bibl. 46, no. XXIV) and in Bibl. 4, no. 1457.
A portrait in oils, which appears almost identical with the lithograph, is reproduced from a Moreno photograph in Bibl. 72, pl. 110 (coll. Marqués de Santillana). A latin scholar and student of the Spanish language, Cabrera was attached to the Duchess of Alba's household, becoming her last librarian, and was named as one of her seven heirs. He held office briefly as President of the Real Academia Española in 1814. For his relationship with the Duchess of Alba, see Bibl. 58, pp. 202, 261 and 278.

873a The sign was painted by Goya for the façade of Godoy's Pestalozzi Institute in Madrid, and appears in the paintings discussed in the note to [856 and 857]. Engraving published by Castañeda (Bibl. 46, no. I). See Milicua (*op. cit.* in note to [856 and 857]).

CATALOGUE III   [1407-1570]

1407 (...Remember your age).

1408 Exhibited 1941 (Bibl. 16, no. 63, ill.). Catalogued by Sayre (Bibl. 171, p. 136, fig. 6).

1409 Exhibited 1941 (Bibl. 16, no. 64, ill.). Catalogued by Sayre (Bibl. 171, p. 136).

1410 (God deliver us from such a bitter fate).

1411 From the collection of E. Calando (Lugt 837). Exhibited 1961-62 (Bibl. 24, no. 173).

1414 (You make a mistake if you marry again).

1415 A. Beurdeley sale, Galerie Georges Petit, Paris, 2-4 June 1920, lot 172, ill.

1417 (Work is always rewarding).

1418 Cp. E.30 and verso sketch [1399, 1400].

1420 Sold at Galerie Charpentier, Paris, 9 April 1957, lot 3, ill. Published by Crispolti (Bibl. 52, fig. 3). Exhibited 1970 (Bibl. 30b, no. 8, ill.).

1422 From the collection of Paul Meurice. Published by Crispolti (Bibl. 52, fig. 7).

1423 Reproduced from a photograph in the collection of the Hispanic Society, New York, where the drawing is listed as in the collection of Robert MacDonald, North Africa. Its provenance is not known.

1424 Erroneously described in the original French edition of this book and reproduced without the black border. Exhibited 1963-64 (Bibl. 27, no. 178) and 1970 (Bibl. 30b, no. 9).

1425 Cp. sketch on the verso of E.48 [1413].

1426 Without a border, but very close to E.36 and especially the sketch on the verso [1404, 1405]. This drawing and [1427] (which have the same provenance) were probably cut within the black border by a collector (Bonnat?) who thought the borders were a later addition.

1427 See note to [1427]. Cp. the painting on tin [929] and the three etchings and drawings of prisoners [986-992].

1428 The drawing illustrated was in the Heidsieck sale at Parke-Bernet, New York, 12-13 February 1943, lot 104, ., entitled 'Beggar's repast'; no provenance was given. It is possible that it may correspond with the drawing entitled *Ceux qui fuient le travail finissent ainsi'* from the Doria collection, sold at Galerie Georges Petit, Paris, 8-9 May 1899, no. 433, although the dimensions of this drawing were given as slightly larger, 26·5×17 cm.

1429 A. Beurdeley sale, Galerie Georges Petit, Paris, 2-4 June 1920, lot 174, not illustrated, but sold with five 'black border' drawings.

1430 This drawing, from the collections of Federico de Madrazo and Louis Thienon, has recently come to light. The characteristics of the paper have not yet been checked, but it is tentatively placed at the end of this album of drawings. The title is described as written with the pen.

1431-1516 The technical characteristics of this album were defined by Sayre (Bibl. 171, Appendix I, p. 133, 'Journal-album F'). The album has been reconstructed by Wehle (Bibl. 192, pp. 14-16, illustrating all the Metropolitan Museum drawings), and partially by Gassier for the Prado drawings (Bibl. 122, pl. 134-155, catalogue III). The titles given by Sánchez Cantón to the Prado drawings have in the main been used here.

1431-1447 Pierre Gassier points out that all the sheets used for drawings 1 to 19 have a circular seal attached to the paper near the top.

1434 Pierre Gassier points out that the seal at the top of the sheet (see note above) became detached, leaving a white circle which has been interpreted as a full moon. This of course was not a feature of the original drawing.

1440 Used for one of Goya's earliest lithographs [IV. 1644], made in 1819.

1444 The authenticity of the pen and ink inscription is uncertain.

1445 Cp. the etching showing fleeing refugees in the *Desastres*, plate 45 [1066].

1449 Similar to some of the famine scenes in the *Desastres*, plates 48-64 [1070-1103].

1450 Cp. *Desastres* plate 49 [1072].

1451 Cp. *Desastres* plates 52 and 53 [1078, 1080].

1455 The shaded arch covers an inscription, not by Goya, which begins *En el dia 1.o de Junio de 1799* and is almost illegible. The catalogue of the Oppenheimer sale, Christie's, London, 10-14 July 1936, lot 449, described it as a record of transactions relating to a government loan.

1462 Inscribed *En voyage* in another hand. Exhibited 1961-62 (Bibl. 24, no. 171) and 1966 (Bibl. 28, no. 13), incorrectly identified and dated. Reproduced here for the first time.

1463 ...*y el religioso quedo muy / maltratado del caballo y la Borrica* (This incident occurred in Aragon when I was a boy, and the monk was very ill-treated by the horse and so

was the donkey). Inscription in pencil(?) across the top of the sheet. From the collection of E. Calando (Lugt 837). Reproduced here for the first time(?).

1468 The number is very much cut. From the J. P. Heseltine collection. Reproduced here for the first time(?).

1470 Cp. *Desastres* plates 79 and 80 [1132, 1134].

1472 Drawing used for the figures in *The forge* [965].

1475 This drawing was the subject of an article by José López-Rey, 'Una cospirazione del gusto – Un falso Goya', *Critica d'Arte*, 1957, no. 20, pp. 143-159. The author stated that the drawing was not by Goya but was a copy of an etching by Félix Bracquemond after a lost original by Goya. The etching was published in the *Gazette des Beaux-Arts*, VII, 1860, facing p. 244, and accompanied an article by Carderera on Goya's drawings (Bibl. 45); it was republished in Bibl. 97, facing p. 84.
However, the drawing, with its autograph number, corresponds with all the characteristics of album F as described by Sayre in 1958 (Bibl. 171, p. 132). In particular, the sheet shows part of the watermark (kindly traced by the museum restorer). The signature, which provides López-Rey with one of the essential elements of his thesis (it also appears in the Bracquemond etching), was probably added by Carderera. Cp. the almost identical signatures on other drawings, e.g. [898, 899]. It was Goya's drawing which Bracquemond took as his model, copying every detail including the supposed signature of the artist (but excluding the number which would have been of no significance to him).
Two works by Goya on the theme of Don Quixote are known. On the one hand, a lost drawing, known from the engraving executed as a project for the *Don Quixote* published by the Spanish Academy in 1780 [I.315]; on the other hand, the drawing catalogued here. Antonio Rodríguez-Moñino referred to both drawings in *Goya y Gallardo. Noticias sobre su amistad*, Madrid, 1954, where he cited an article by Gallardo, a contemporary of Goya, alluding to a series of *caprichos* to which the artist had given the title *Visions of Don Quixote*. The drawing catalogued here bears a striking resemblance to *Caprichos* plate 43, which Goya originally designed as the frontispiece to the series of prints [II.536, 537]. Both compositions show the protagonist assailed by the creatures of his dreams and visions. This drawing may recall Goya's frontispiece for the *Don Quixote* series mentioned by Gallardo, if it is not the actual design itself.

1477 First published by Trapier (Bibl. 187a, p. 20, n. 13, pl. 16). It represents the torture of the rack. Cp. the drawings in album C.97 and 99 [1333, 1335].

1478 Number cut. For a discussion of the subject see Bibl. 27, no. 183, and also the note to [922-925].

1479 Exhibited 1941 (Bibl. 16, no. 127, ill.).

1481   Exhibited 1961-62 (Bibl. 24, no. 176) and 1970 (Bibl. 30b, no. 10). From the collection of E. Calando (Lugt 837). Reproduced here for the first time(?).

1482   Published by Mayer (Bibl. 130, pl. 27).

1483   With a long, illegible inscription on the dark arch, as in F.29 [1455]. Published by Lafond (Bibl. 98, p. 12, pl. D). Moreno photograph: Beruete collection 265. Although Lafond gave no dimensions and described the technique as Indian ink, the drawing shows such strong similarities with others in this album — cp. F.19 and 21 [1447, 1449] and F.29 mentioned above — that it is tentatively included here.

1485   Exhibited 1963-64 (Bibl. 27, no. 184).

1491   Published by Trapier (Bibl. 187a, p. 20, n. 15, pl. 17).

1492   Published by Valerio Mariani (Bibl. 123, fig. 5).

1493   Discussed by Gassier (Bibl. 62a, fig. 18).

1497   The subject could be a scene in a madhouse, or sick and starving men as in Desastres plates 54, 57 and 58 [1082, 1088, 1090].

1499   From the collection of E. Calando (Lugt 837). Exhibited 1961-62 (Bibl. 24, no. 174). Reproduced here for the first time.

1500   The 'interfering man' is a constable, as in F.81 [1499].

1501   From the collection of E. Calando (Lugt 837). Exhibited 1970 (Bibl. 30b, no. 11).

1502   ...por per / seguidor de estudiantes, y mugeres de fortuna, / las q.e le hecharon una labatiba con cal viva (Death of Constable Lampiños because he persecuted students and women of the town who gave him a douche of quicklime). Inscription in pen and ink. The number is half cut at the top.

1504   From the collection of E. Calando (Lugt 837). Exhibited 1961-62 (Bibl. 24, no. 175).

1507   Inscribed in pencil by another hand Le portefaix. From the collection of E. Calando (Lugt 837). Reproduced here for the first time.

1509   From the collection of E. Calando (Lugt 837). Reproduced here for the first time.

1510   Discussed by Gassier (Bibl. 62a, fig. 17).

1512   From the collection of E. Calando (Lugt 837). Reproduced here for the first time. Exhibited 1970 (Bibl. 30b, no. 12).

1513   From the collection of Mariano Fortuny y Madrazo (see note to [1401]). This drawing has recently come to light and is reproduced here for the first time from a photograph kindly made available by the owner. Exhibited 1970 (Bibl. 30b, no. 13).

1516   Published by Valerio Mariani (Bibl. 123, fig. 6).

1518   Inscribed in pencil by another hand Le chasseur à l'affût. From the collection of E. Calando (Lugt 837). Reproduced here for the first time.

1519   Signed along the upper left edge of the cushions on which the 'sultan' is seated. From an autograph album which belonged to the Duquesa de Hijar whose husband, as Sumiller de Corps in the Royal Palace, was concerned with Goya's various requests for leave of absence to go to or continue to remain in France (cp. Bibl. 154, docs 251-274). Exhibited 1961-62 (Bibl. 24, no. 172). Published by Xavière Desparmet Fitz-Gerald, 'Deux dessins inédits de Francisco Goya', Pantheon, XXIII, 1965, pp. 111-115. See note to [V.1830-1841].

1520   Very similar to many of the preparatory drawings for the Desastres and Tauromaquia prints (cp. [1156-1164]) and clearly related to [1519]. The title is Sánchez Cantón's.

1521a-e   A group of eight drawings was included in the 1922 exhibition catalogue (nos 192 A-H) and described as part of an album. Two of them had inscriptions: Pobre trabajador, cuanto sostiene (192A) and Qué bien bailan (192D). Four were illustrated in the catalogue, and a fifth is known from a photograph.

1521a   Cp. album F.7 and 79 [1435, 1497].

1521b   Cp. album C.25 [1263]. The title given in the Boix catalogue indicates a girl from the Pas valley and such young women were well known as wet-nurses.

1521c   Cp. Desastres plate 82 [1138] and album C.25 [1263].

1521e   Known from a photograph kindly made available by Enriqueta Frankfort Harris.

1522   This drawing is very similar to album F.7 and 75 [1435, 1494] and may in fact belong in the album.

1523 and 1524   Dimensions from the Boix catalogue; the drawings now have an overlapping mount. Cp. album D.18 and [f] [1375, 1383].

1525   (Indissoluble bonds). Inscribed in pencil. This drawing with a black border has been connected with album E — see the 1963-64 exhibition catalogue (Bibl. 27, no. 179).

1526 and 1527   The drawings recall the famine scenes in the Desastres series [1070-1103], and [1526] is very close in style and technique to the preparatory drawing for one of the early lithographs of c.1819 [IV.1649].

1528   Published by Lafond (Bibl. 98, p. 12, pl. E). Moreno photograph: Beruete collection 276. The authenticity of this drawing, known only from a photograph, is uncertain.

1529   The authenticity of this drawing, known only from the reproduction in the Boix catalogue, is uncertain.

1530   The inscription is of uncertain authenticity. The technique is most unusual but the subject — women weeping over a dead or dying man in prison(?) — recalls many of the drawings in the albums.

1531   Three small drawings were published by Lafond (Bibl. 98, p. 12, plates A-C). He described them as 'au crayon' but the Moreno photographs show that all three were drawn with the brush. The Monk, catalogued here, recalls the subject of one of Goya's lithographs [V.1698]. The two others represented a Kneeling man (A) and a Prisoner in irons (C). Of these three drawings, only the last is still known. See note to [V.1794].

1532   Used for one of the Disparates prints [IV.1603]. Although the etching shows only one elephant (the one on the left of the drawing, copied, and therefore reversed, in the print), traces of the second elephant are clearly visible on the left of the print. Cp. the flying elephant in the painting at Agen, discussed in the note to [956].

1534   In May 1815, Goya's friend Munárriz gave up his post as secretary of the Royal Academy of San Fernando to become director of the Royal Company of the Philippines, and the commission for this painting may have originated with him. In the same year Goya painted Munárriz's portrait, perhaps as part of an official series for the company — cp. [1545-1547]. The identification of the scene, which has been a matter of doubt (cp. Bibl. 166, pp. 108-109), is confirmed by the title shown on a Laurent photograph of about 1870. See Bibl. 25, no. 125.

1536-1541   The Brugada inventory of 1828 listed a Retrato del Rey Fernando VII, busto which must have been made by Goya either from the life in 1808 or, with the help of earlier studies such as [877], as the basis for the numerous portraits commissioned in 1814. The portrait study [1537] may be identifiable with the inventory picture (see Appendix II, no. 26).
       A portrait now in the Thyssen collection is said to have come from a great-granddaughter of Goya. It shows the king wearing an ermine cape over which hangs the chain and decoration of the Golden Fleece. A similarly described portrait was sold in 1866 from the Eustaquio López collection, together with [947-950] and [1558], all as from the collection of Mariano Goya. Another, very similar version (without the Order of the Fleece and showing the king holding a baton) is also known. Their style and technique are entirely different from the portraits listed here, and they are not included in this catalogue. Their details are given for reference purposes:
       85×63 cm. Lugano, Baron Thyssen Bornemisza (158)   M.166, DF.462n, G.626   See Pantheon, IX, 1932 p. 113.
       Formerly Eustaquio López (Bibl. 57, II, pp. 260 261, no. 7, described as with the Golden Fleece).
       83×67 cm.   Signed FG   São Paulo, Mus. (175 M.167, DF.462, G.627   Without the Fleece; but repro duced in Calleja (Bibl. 72, pl. 35) as from the Eustaqui López collection.

1536   Inscribed FERNANDO III DE NAVARRA / Y VII D CASTILLA. Commissioned June 1814 and paid for o 12 July. See J. R. Castro, 'El Goya de la Diputación d Navarra', Príncipe de Viana, III, 1942, pp. 37-39. Exhibite 1951 (Bibl. 17, no. 39; Goya's receipt exhibited, and tex quoted, Documents I, p. 77).

1537   Known only from a photograph (Moreno 426 Reproduced in Bibl. 72, pl. 36 (Vizconde de Val de Err collection). See note to [1536-1541]. Sambricio suggeste that it was the study made from life in 1808 (Bibl. 23, no. X but Sánchez Cantón did not believe that it was done fro life (Bibl. 166, p. 104). Possibly the portrait included in th inventory of 1828 (see Appendix II, no. 26).

1538   Dimensions checked at the time of the Hague ex hibition in 1970. The entire iconographical scheme wa dictated by the Town Council of Santander, and Goy estimated that he could paint it in not less than a fortnigh He signed the receipt for 8,000 reales on 1 December 1814 See E. Ortiz de la Torre, 'Un retrato de Fernando VII pc Goya', Boletín de la Biblioteca Menéndez y Pelayo, (San tander, 1919, I, pp. 26-30, and the exhibition catalogues fc 1961 (Bibl. 23, no. X), 1963-64 (Bibl. 27, no. 107) an 1970 (Bibl. 30, no. 45).

1539   Once belonged to Francisco Javier Mariátegui, th father-in-law of Mariano Goya and an architect connecte with the Department of Civil Engineering (cp. Prado cata logue and Lafuente, Bibl. 102, p. 296).
       Replica with variants: Madrid, Museo del Ejércit M.160, DF.502n, G.628   Discussed in detail by Beruet (Bibl. 36, I, p. 131). Unseen by the authors.

1540   Came to the Prado from the Ministerio de la Gober nación (Interior). Considered by Held a replica of [1541 (Bibl. 89, p. 190).

1541   Signature (apocryphal?) at lower left F.co Goya Commissioned by the Canal Imperial de Aragón, togethe with [1542], on 20 September 1814; paid for on 15 Jul 1815. See F. Olivan Baile, 'Breve historia de dos Goyas Seminario de Arte Aragonés, IV, 1952, pp. 93-98. Bot paintings are on deposit in the museum from the Junta of the Canal Imperial.

1542   Inscribed at lower left El Ex.mo S.or Duque de S. Carlos / por Goya año 1815. See note to [1541]. Listed b Carderera (Bibl. 148, no. 53).

1545   Inscribed D. Jose Munarriz / P.r Goya 1815 on boo cover, and Comp. / DE / BLAIR on the spine. In May 181 Munárriz became director of the Royal Company of th Philippines, and he possibly commissioned the great pictur of the Junta [1534] and a series of portraits of the director who appear at the high table with the king — his own an those of two ministers of the Council of the Indies [154é 1547]. See Bibl. 25, no. 125. For Munárriz's interest i Hugh Blair, whose lectures on esthetics he translated i 1798, see López-Rey (Bibl. 113, p. 146).

1546   Inscribed on paper Fluctibus Reipublicae / expulsus Pintado p.r Goya. 1815. (Expelled through the vicissitude of the State). For the correct identification of the sitte (previously known as Francisco Espoz y Mina), see Marti Soria, 'Goya's Portrait of Miguel de Lardizábal', Burlingto Magazine, LII, 1960, pp. 161-162. He was Minister of the Indies from May 1814 to September 1815. See note t [1545]. Exhibited 1970 (Bibl. 30, no. 46).

1547   Inscribed on papers YLmo Sor Dn Ygnacio Omulryan y Rourera Mino / del Consejo y Camara de Yndias / Por Goya. 1815. He was Minister of the Indies i 1815. See note to [1545].

1548   Inscribed along lower edge El Yllmō Señor D. Fr. Miguel Fernandez Obispo de Marcopolis, Administrado Apostolico de Quito. P.r Goya año 1815. The bishop wa consecrated on 17 September 1815; he never went t Ecuador. See Trapier (Bibl. 188, pp. 40-41), giving previou references.

1549   Inscribed at lower right *Quixano. Compositor / de / Música. p.r Goya 1815*. He was the director of the Teatro de la Cruz in Madrid from 1814. See Sánchez Cantón, *La Colección Cambó*, Barcelona, 1955, pp. 88-90.

1550   Inscribed on copperplate *D.n Rafael Esteve. P.r Goya. â 1815*. Esteve was an expert engraver and copperplate printer who may have printed the editions of the *Caprichos* in 1798-99 and the *Tauromaquia* in 1815-16. See Harris (Bibl. 88, I, pp. 107-108).

1551   Listed in the Brugada inventory of 1828 as *Retrato de Goya firmado 1815, busto* (Bibl. 57, I, p. 53, n. 1; see Appendix II, no. 27) and given to the Academy by Javier Goya in 1829 when the final (and much reduced) payment was made to him for the equestrian portrait which Goya had painted in 1808 [875]. See Sánchez Cantón (Bibl. 157, 18).

1552   Inscription on left. Held suggested that this portrait, less forceful and assured than [1551], was the earlier version (Bibl. 89, p. 189).
    A portrait of doubtful authenticity combines features of both [1551] and [1552]: 66×50 cm.   Northampton (Mass.), Smith College   M.304, DF.491, G.639.
    Yriarte and Lafond thought that all three versions were studies for [IV.1630] (Bibl. 193, p. 150; 97, pp. 128-29, nos 122-124). Cp. Yriarte (*op. cit.* p. 133).

1553   Inscribed on verso *Goya a su nieto*. The boy appears to be about nine or ten years old. Cp. the earlier portrait [885]. Exhibited 1963-64 (Bibl. 27, no. 112).
    A portrait of a little girl, known as Nona, who holds a sheet of music very similar to that in [1553], has been attributed to Goya: Oklahoma City, Frank Buttram (according to Frick Art Reference Library). Cp. the portrait of Manuel Alcázar, reproduced by Lafuente (Bibl. 102, 276, fig. 80).

1554   Inscribed on paper *ADn Fra.co del Mazo / Calle ANTAN / DER* [in red] / *Madrid*. Dating discussed in the 1963 exhibition catalogue (Bibl. 25, no. 124). Held maintains the later date of c.1820 (Bibl. 89, no. 125). Exhibited 1970 (Bibl. 30, no. 47).

1555   Catalogued by Sánchez Cantón (Bibl. 162, pp. 19-22), discussing the possible date which he considered to be not later than 1800. Held dated the portrait c.1807 (Bibl. 89, no. 108), but a date of c.1815 has generally been accepted. Helman showed that Fray Fernández may have died in 1817 (not 1819 as has always been repeated) and discussed Goya's relationship with the sitter (Bibl. 95). Cp. the drawing of the friar on his deathbed [1562]. Exhibited 1963-64 (Bibl. 27, no. 110).

1556   This portrait was described in detail by Beruete (Bibl. 36, I, p. 128) and is reproduced in Bibl. 159, pl. 58. A Moreno photograph (278) appears to show a replica of the bust; see Bibl. 72, pl. 138.

1557   Inscribed on ground below rock (according to Beruete, Bibl. 36, I, p. 136) *El Duque de Osuna por Goya 1816*. The museum says that the inscription is no longer visible. Painted in August 1816, according to Goya's letter to the duke, written on 17 November 1816 and asking for the recompense which had been promised: 'Despues de aver tenido la satisfaccion de llenar los deseos de V.E. con su retrato de cuerpo entero, que tube el gusto de hacer este Agosto ultimo, V.E. me preguntó por escrito cuanto devia enviarme por el referido retrato, a lo que contesté que jamás habia tasado mis producciones, pero que en visto del vibo deseo que tenía V.E. en corresponder con mis areas, las creia recompensadas con haverle servido, y al mismo tiempo con diez mil rvn.' Letter quoted in full by Sentenach who recorded that the duke assented the following day and that Goya was paid on 28 March 1817 (Bibl. 175; see Appendix V).
    Listed by Carderera (Bibl. 148, no. 19). Osuna sale 1896 (Bibl. 32, no. 91). Cp. the portrait of the duke as a small boy in [I.278], and the 1816 portrait of his sister [1560].

This portrait and the sketch and drawing [1557-1559] are illustrated together in Bibl. 166, figs 40-42.

1558   The model for both the sketch and drawing [1559] is supposed to have been Javier Goya. The sketch first appeared in the Eustaquio López sale of 1866, incorrectly identified (as the Marquis de Sandinos), but with a provenance from Mariano Goya (Bibl. 57, II, pp. 260-261, no. 8). Its authenticity was doubted by Desparmet and Loga. In view of its provenance, it is possible that this is the *Retrato de un joven, boceto* listed in the Brugada inventory of 1828 (Bibl. 57, I, p. 53, n. 1; see Appendix II, no. 23). Cp. the 1808 sketch of Ferdinand VII [876] and the note. The picture was lost during the last war.

1559   Inscribed below (probably by Carderera) *Idea p.a el retrato q.e pinto Goya del Duque de / Osuna y existe en el Palacio del act.l Duque su hijo*. Listed by Carderera (Bibl. 148, no. 19).

1560   Inscribed on sheet of music *D.na Manuela Giron y Pimentel / Duq.sa de Abrantes. // P.r Goya. 1816*. She was the sister of the Xth Duke of Osuna [1557], born in 1794 (after the execution of the family portrait [I.278]). Goya was paid 4,000 reales for this portrait on 30 April 1816, according to the Osuna accounts. Exhibited, and documents quoted, in 1961 (Bibl. 23, no. XXXI). See also Bibl. 157 and Appendix V.

1561   Inscribed at lower left *D.n Juan Ant.o / Cuerbo. / Direct.r de la R.l / Academia de S.n Fern.ando. / Por su Amigo Goya / año 1819*. Listed by Carderera (Bibl. 148, no. 16). Discussed by Trapier (Bibl. 188, pp. 41-42). Exhibited 1970 (Bibl. 30, no. 50).

1562   Drawn on the verso of the portrait of Wellington [898]. Inscribed at upper edge *Al espirar Fray Juan Fernandez Agustino . . . [?]* (At the death of Friar Juan Fernández Augustinian). The drawing of Wellington was listed by Mariano Goya, with a note which says that together with other works it was stored away in a cupboard for the whole of the year 1818 (see Appendix VII). Helman published a reference to the 'exemplary death' of the friar at San Felipe el Real in Madrid in 1817, but concluded that this did not certainly disprove the generally accepted date of death in 1819 (Bibl. 95, pp. 1, 11). Cp. note to [1555]. The inscription on the drawing is certainly in Goya's hand, but does not prove that the drawing was made at the actual time of the friar's death, either in 1817 or 1819. There may be a connection between this drawing, sketched with an unusual lack of firmness, and the serious illness which Goya himself suffered at the end of 1819 and recorded in the painting where he shows himself half-dying in the arms of his doctor [IV.1629]. See also the note to [IV.1638].

1563   The signature and date are written vertically along the left edge (the date was read by Mayer and Sánchez Cantón as 1813). Exhibited 1961 (Bibl. 23, no. XLIV). The identity of the sitter and the early provenance of this picture have not been established but it may be identifiable with the painting listed in the 1828 Brugada inventory as *Una maja vestida echada (mas de una vara)* (Bibl. 57, I, p. 53, n. 1; see Appendix II, no. 7). See notes to [1566] and [II.744].

1564   Incorrectly described by Desparmet and Gudiol as on panel. Exhibited in 1963-64 (Bibl. 27, no. 117).

1565   Apparently the portrait included among the works listed by Mariano Goya (see Appendix VII) as *Un retrato de la Rita-Luna actriz del tiempo de Moratín*. It was acquired by Carderera who listed it as *Retrato de la célebre actriz retratada de bastante edad. Busto solo* (Bibl. 148, no. 66). Viñaza specified that it was painted at El Pardo where the retired actress was living (Bibl. 190, p. 239, no. LXIX). The note by Mariano Goya means that the picture was executed before 1818. Both the 1928 exhibition catalogue (Bibl. 10, no. 83) and Edith Helman ('Goya y Moratín', *Insula*, XV,

1960, pp. 1, 10, 14) referred to another portrait of the actress by Goya. Exhibited 1951 (Bibl. 17, no. 40). See note to [IV.1625].
    Viñaza catalogued a bust portrait of an unknown actor or playwright which he said was painted by Goya, who pasted the canvas onto a panel, as a pair to the portrait of Rita Luna: 38×39 cm.   Formerly Madrid, Valentín Carderera (no. 230 of his *Catálogo de retratos*)   Viñaza CVII (Bibl. 190, p. 259).

1566   Salas has tentatively identified the sitter as Leocadia Weiss (Bibl. 169, p. 85, fig. 131), but the *Leocadia* of the Quinta del Sordo [IV.1622], painted when she was just over thirty, is a much comelier figure than this mature and heavy-featured matron. See notes to [1563] and [IV.1622]. Exhibited 1963-64 (Bibl. 27, no. 111).

1567   With a pencil inscription on the stretcher *Se colocó esta pintura el día 13 de junio de 1812. . . . La hizo Dn. Francisco Goya, Pintor de Cámara de S.M. el Sr. D. Fernando VII*. Catalogued (but not exhibited) in 1961 (Bibl. 23, no. LXXVIII, giving previous references).

1568   Six grisaille paintings, by Goya and other artists, made to decorate one of the rooms, in the Royal Palace in Madrid, prepared for the second wife of Ferdinand VII, Isabel de Braganza. On 20 April 1817, José Aparicio requested an extension of the six months' pension he had received in order to paint his heroic composition *Las Glorias de España* (cp. note to [982-984]) because the work had been delayed 'con el haber empleado el tiempo en pintar el cuadro de claro obscuro que se le mando hacer para Palacio'.
    At the death of Ferdinand VII in 1835, these paintings were listed in an inventory made by Vicente López: *Pieza tocador, no. 13. 6 sobrepuertas pintadas al temple, claro-obscuro, dos por López, una por Goya, otra por Zacarías Velázquez, otra por Aparicio y otra por Camarón. Sucesos de varias personas Reales, de siete pies en cuadro, vale cada una con su marco, a siete mil quinientos reales y las seis 45.000.* The subjects were historical events or persons symbolically connected with the king and his new wife. The paintings were recently discovered in the palace store-rooms and were published with the documents by Paulina Junquera, 'Un lienzo inédito de Goya en el Palacio de Oriente', *Archivo Español de Arte*, XXXII, 1959, pp. 185-192. Exhibited 1970 (Bibl. 30, no. 48). Cp. Goya's sketch for an earlier painting of the same subject [II.738], and see the remarks of Paul Guinard, 'Goya et la tradition religieuse au siècle d'or', *Revue du Louvre*, 1970, nos 4-5, pp. 265-270.

1569   Inscribed on paper at lower left *Francisco de Goya y Lucientes. Cesar- / augustano y primer Pintor de camara / del Rey. Madrid año de 1817* (Cesaraugustano is the latin form of Saragossan). According to the Prado catalogue entry for [1570], the painting was sketched in by 27 September 1817 and was hanging by 14 January 1818. Ceán Bermúdez was responsible for commissioning the picture on behalf of the Cathedral Chapter, and he published an anonymous article in its praise in the *Crónica científica y literaria*, no. 73, 9 December 1817 (reprinted in facsimile, from a pamphlet published the same year, in Bibl. 70).
    The altarpiece was apparently painted in Madrid, but Ceán described the careful preparatory studies which Goya made in the cathedral at Seville before beginning work. In spite of Ceán's article and the enthusiastic contemporary sonnets written in praise of the painting (MSS. in the British Museum, reprinted by Loga, Bibl. 109, p. 170, n. 231), this has generally been considered one of Goya's least successful religious paintings. Cp. Viñaza (Bibl. 190, p. 206, no. XVIII; references to sonnets on p. 6, n. 5 contd.). See also Sánchez Cantón (Bibl. 166, pp. 113-114); Klingender (*op. cit.* in note to [IV.1638]), illustrating Murillo's painting of the same subject which may have been the source of Goya's composition and mentioning another possible source; and Guinard (*op. cit.* in note to [1568]).

1570   Ceán Bermúdez asked Goya to make three or four sketches, and this was no doubt the one chosen.

CATALOGUE IV   [1636-1657d]

further details, and it was not included in the 1922 exhibition catalogued by Boix. (Sánchez Cantón, in Bibl. 167, suggested that the drawing was in fact the portrait of Goya's son [1636] included in that exhibition.) If the drawing described by Beruete was executed, it would be one more in the series of portraits of the close friends who helped Goya in the difficult months before he left for France.

1636 The inscription is written twice, the second time more legibly. Sánchez Cantón suggested that it was made by Goya to take with him to France (Bibl. 166, p. 124). Exhibited in 1922 (Bibl. 9, no. 187) and published by Crispolti (Bibl. 52, fig. 12).

1637 The existence of this print after a lost drawing by Goya was indicated to Pierre Gassier by Jean Adhémar, Conservateur en Chef of the Cabinet des Estampes in the Bibliothèque Nationale, Paris. The drawing was no doubt made at the same time as [1634], [1636] and that referred to in the note to [1635]. The Abbé Melón was an intimate friend of Goya and Moratín, and Moratín's letters to him from Bordeaux are a major source of information about Goya's activities in France. See note to [V.1661]. For a mention of Melón by Godoy, see Bibl. 58, p. 226, n.1.
The lithograph, lettered *Goya del.* and *Gilliaug Lith.*, has the inscription *D.n JUAN ANTONIO MELON, / Docto Erudito y digno Español, / Consejero de Hacienda: / Murió el 17 de Abril de 1843, / Llorado por sus numerosos amigos.* Proof in Paris, B.N. (Portraits gravés N.2/779). Catalogued in Bibl. 4, no. 5774.

1638 . . . of Saint Joseph of Calasanz. Inscribed at lower left *Fran.co Goya. / Año 1819*. Commissioned in May 1819 by the fathers of the Escuelas Pías in Madrid. Goya was to receive 16,000 reales for this large painting which was completed by the saint's day, August 27 (see Bibl. 166, p. 116).
Two letters by Goya to the rector, Father Pío Peña, were published by Joaquín Tello, 'Dos Goyas poco conocidos', *Boletín de la Sociedad Española de Excursiones*, XXXVI, 1928, pp. 66-67. In the first, Goya wrote to return all but 1,200 of the first instalment of 8,000 reales which he had received when the work was half-completed, saying 'Devuelvo esto al encargado de pagar, o al rector, y dígale

que algo ha de hacer D. Francisco Goya en obsequio a su paisano el Santo José de Calasanz'. A few days later he wrote again, sending the small *Christ on the Mount of Olives* [1640] as an additional gift. Goya's relationship with the Escuelas Pías, and the founding and development of the teaching order of Saint Joseph were discussed by F. D. Klingender, 'Notes on Goya's *Agony in the Garden*', *Burlington Magazine*, LXXVII, 1940, pp. 4-14 (incorporated in Bibl. 96, pp. 181-188). Sánchez Cantón illustrated a possible source in Crespi's *Communion* (Bibl. 163, figs 18, 19; 166, figs 49, 50), and Guinard suggested the influence of Jerónimo de Espinosa (*op. cit.* in note to [III.1568]). Cp. the head of the saint with the drawing of Fray Fernández de Rojas on his deathbed [III.1562], and that of the father behind the officiating priest with the later head of a *Monk* [V.1669].

1639 The sketch appears listed in the 1828 inventory of the contents of the Quinta as *San José de Calasanz, boceto* (Bibl. 57, I, p. 53, n. 1; see Appendix II, no. 2), and it was seen in Javier's house by Father Tomás López (Bibl. 190, p. 463). The sketch was in the collection of Paul de Saint-Victor. Its authenticity has been doubted by Held (Bibl. 89, p. 186).
Desparmet noted a 'replica' on canvas in the Stchoukine collection in Paris.

1640 Inscribed at lower left *Goya. fecit. año. 1819*. Goya sent this small painting to the rector of the Escuelas Pías in Madrid with a covering letter saying 'Aquí le entregó a usted este cuadro que dejo para la comunidad, y será lo último que haré yo en Madrid' (Tello, *op. cit.* in note to [1638]).
Another version of this subject is not attributed in this catalogue to Goya: 43·2×34·3 cm.   Sold at Sotheby's, London, 26 March 1969, lot 74   M.20a, G.695 Reproduced in Bibl. 166, p. 117, fig. 48.   Exhibited 1951 (Bibl. 17, no. 54).

1641 and 1642 Probably painted as a pair. Their early provenance is not known. Exhibited together in 1970 (Bibl. 30, nos 56/54, 57/55).
1642 was published in *Museum*, V, 1917, p. 97, and by

A. L. Mayer in *Burlington Magazine*, LXXI, 1937, p. 1[?]
Exhibited Toledo (Ohio), Museum, in 1941 (no. 103, il[?]

1643-1650 For an account of Goya's technique see Ha[?] (Bibl. 88, I, p. 215).

1644 A proof with the inscription *Madrid Marzo 18[?]* was in the collection of Paul Lefort and is known from facsimile. The lithograph is very close to one of the duel[?] scenes from album F, no. 12 [III.1440].

1645 The lower part of the drawing [1646] failed [?] transfer and does not print in the lithograph.

1647 This drawing is so similar to the preceding one th[?] it was probably made in preparation for a lithograph.

1648 (Expression of double force). Goya's title is writt[?] on the proof in New York, Public Library (Bibl. 88, I, [?] p. 217).

1649 Exhibited 1963-64 (Bibl. 27, no. 152). Cp. a ve[?] similar drawing [III.1526].

1651-1656 The rejection of the paintings in the Muni[?] catalogue was influenced by the opinion of Lafuente. Th[?] were exhibited in 1963-64 (Bibl. 27, nos 118-121) a[?] opinion was divided concerning their authenticity. A furth[?] painting in the series is said by Salas to be in a private co[?] lection in Madrid.

1653 Cp. the lithograph of a duel [V.1702].

1656 Published by Juan Lafora, 'Goya – Estudio Bi[?] gráfico Critico', *Arte Español*, IX, 1928, pl. V, fig. 22.

1657a Cp. the lithograph of the same subject [V.169[?] Exhibited, with 1657d, en 1970 in Paris (Bibl. 30, A[?] pendice, 53 bis, ter).

1657b Cp. album F.62 [III.1483].

1657c Cp. the miniature [V.1680].

1657d Cp. the small panel [1654]. See note to [1657a[?]

Appendices Bibliography Indices

APPENDICES

APPENDIX I   INVENTORY OF 1812

List of the paintings in Goya's house in the Calle de Valverde, which were made over to 'Don Francisco Xavier de Goya', the artist's son, in October 1812.
(Document published by F. J. Sánchez Cantón, 'Como vivía Goya', *Archivo Español de Arte*, XIX, 1946, p. 105)

A total of 78 paintings were listed in thirty entries in the inventory. Although some were not by Goya (the tenth entry listed 'Two pictures by Tiepolo'), many have been identified, either at the time by Sánchez Cantón or later by Xavier de Salas (Bibl. 147) and José Gudiol (Bibl. 84). The inventory list is republished here together with an indication of all the pictures so far identified, with their catalogue numbers which also refer to the notes where they are discussed in greater detail. The inventory mark (X followed by a number, in white paint in the lower left or right corner of the canvas) is given where it is still visible on the picture and appears in square brackets where it has been removed. Tentative identifications are preceded by a question mark.

Original text of the document   Value in reales

1 *Quatro quadros iguales con el numero primero en*   1.800
   X.1   The maypole. Madrid, Duque de Tamames [III.951]
   X.1   Procession in Valencia. Zurich, Bührle Collection [III.952]
   [X.1] Bullfight in a divided ring. New York, Metropolitan Museum [III.953]
   ?   Carnival scene. Formerly Budapest, Baron Herzog [III.954]

2 *Dos bocetos con el n.º segundo en*   80

3 *Dos con el n.º tercero en*   40

4 *La filosofía y S. Gerónimo con el número quatro en*   300

5 *Una cabeza con el número quinto en*   15

6 *Dos cuadros pequeños con el n.º seis en*   50

7 *Id. Un San Antonio con el n.º siete en*   40

8 *Seis quadros del Maragato señalados con el número ocho en*   700
   [X.8] The capture of the bandit El Maragato (6 panels). Chicago, Art Institute [II.864-869]

9 *Otros seis de varios asuntos con el nueve en*   800
   X.9   Scene of rape and murder. Frankfurt, Städelsches Kunstinstitut

X.9   Women attacked by soldiers. Frankfurt, Städelsches Kunstinstitut
X.9   The hanged monk. Chicago, Art Institute
X.9   Prison scene. Guadalupe (Estremadura), Monastery
X.9   Procession. Oslo, National Gallery
Group of five panels, all with the inventory mark; a sixth is known from a description [III.930-935]

10 *Dos de Tiepolo con el numero diez en*   200

11 *Doce bodegones con el n.º once en*   1.200
   X.11   Sheep's head and joints. Paris, Louvre
   [X.11] Dead turkey. Madrid, Prado
   [X.11] Dead birds. Madrid, Prado
   [X.11] Plucked turkey and frying pan. Munich, Pinakothek
   X.11   Golden bream. Paris, David-Weill
   [X.11] Duck. Zurich, Mme Anda-Bührle
   [X.11] Hares. New York, private coll.
   [X.11] Woodcocks. New York, private coll.
   [X.11] Salmon steaks. Winterthur, Reinhart Coll.
   [X.11] Still-life with bottles, fruit, bread. Winterthur, Reinhart Collection
   Group of ten still-lifes of identical dimensions, two of which are known to have the inventory mark. [III.903-912]

12 *Otros doce de los Horrores de la Guerra con el número doce en*   2.000
   ?   The eight paintings in the collection of the Marqueses de la Romana [III.914-921] were tentatively identified by Sánchez Cantón as part of this group. Cp. also the group [III.936-944].

13 *Una aguadora y su compañero con el número trece en*   300
   [X.13] The water-carrier. Budapest, Art Museum [III.963]
   [X.13] The knife-grinder. Budapest, Art Museum [III.964]
   (See the discussion of these pictures in the notes)

14 *Un retrato de la de Alva con el número catorce en*   400
   [X.14] The Duchess of Alba. New York, Hispanic Society [II.355]

15 *Unas ylanderas con el número quince en*   100
   ?   Women spinning. Formerly Trieste, Francesco Basilio [II.870]

16 *El congreso de los Dioses con el n.º diez y seis en*   200

17 *El retrato de Velazquez y su Compañero con el número quince, digo diez y siete, en*   400

18 *Un gigante con el n.º diez y ocho en*   90
   [X.18] The colossus. Madrid, Prado [III.946]

19 *El retrato de Perico Romero con el n.º diez y nueve*   100
   [X.19] Pedro Romero. ? Fort Worth, Kimbell Foundation [II.671] ? Geneva, priv. coll. [II.671 replica]

20 *Un San Juan con el n.º veinte en*   150

21 *Un San Pedro con el n.º veinte y uno en*   80

22 *Unos borrachos con el n.º veinte y dos en*   100
   ?   The topers. Rahleigh, North Carolina Museum [II.871]

23 *El tiempo con el n.º veinte y tres en*   150
   X.23   'Les vieilles' – Time and the old women. Lille Museum [III.961]

24 *Dos quadros de unas jóvenes al balcon con el n.º veinte y quatro en*   400
   [X.24] Maja and celestina. Madrid, Bartolomé March [III.958]
   X.24   Majas on a balcony. Private collection [III.959]

25 *El lazarillo de Tormes con el n.º veinte y cinco en*   100
   X.25   El Lazarillo de Tormes. Madrid, Marañon [III.957]

26 *Un boceto de un ginete con el n.º veinte y seis en*   30
   ?   A mounted picador. Madrid, Prado [I.255]
   ?   Equestrian sketch of Manuel Godoy(?) Dallas, Meadows Museum [II.344]
   ?   Equestrian sketch of Ferdinand VII. Agen, Museum [III.876]

27 *Otros quatro de las Artes con el n.º veinte y siete en*   80
   ?   This item may refer to the sketches for the four allegories painted for Godoy [II.690-692], of which only one possible example is known [II.693]

28 *Quatro de otros asuntos con el n.º veinte y ocho en*   60
   X.28   Village on fire. Buenos Aires, Museum [III.947]
   This painting was identified by Gudiol together with two others, without the inventory mark, in the same museum. A fourth of the same dimensions was in the Jockey Club in Buenos Aires. See notes to [III.947-950], where the identification is discussed.

29 *Unos pájaros con el n.º veinte y nueve en*   25

30 *Una Concepción con el n.º treinta en*   95
   See note to [I.188-191].

APPENDIX II   INVENTORY OF 1828

List of the paintings by Goya inventoried by Antonio Brugada in the Quinta del Sordo after Goya's death in Bordeaux in April 1828.
(Document published by X. Desparmet Fitz-Gerald, *L'Œuvre peint de Goya*, Paris, 1928-50, vol. I, p. 53, n. 1.)

In principle, none of the works listed in the inventory of 1812 should appear in this later list, since they already belonged to Goya's son and were not a part of the father's estate.
   The very summary descriptions make it difficult to identify more than a few paintings with any degree of certainty. The list of the 'black paintings' on the walls of the Quinta is given in Appendix VI.

The inventory also included the following items concerning Goya's prints and drawings:
Dos cajas de grabados y dibujos, aquatinta, caprichos, etc.
Tres libros de dibujos originales inéditos.
Quatro cartones de grabados, caprichos. Siete cajas de objetos y cobres.

1 *Diez y seis bocetos pequeños de los tapices*
   See note to [I.295]

2 *San José de Calasanz, boceto*
   Sketch for the *Last Communion of St Joseph of Calasanz*. Bayonne, Musée Bonnat [IV.1639]

3 *Diez cuadritos, horrores de la guerra*
   ?   Madrid, Marqueses de la Romana [III.914-921] Cp. Appendix I, no. 12
   ?   Ten paintings formerly in the Stchoukine collection [III.931, 932], see notes, and others in the group [III.936-944]

4 *Ocho bocetos (como de una vara) corridas de toros*
   ?   Eight bullfight scenes on tinplate [II.317-324]. These pictures were apparently already in the Chopinot collection by 1805. In any case, the indication *como de una vara* (1 vara = 83·5 cm.) would make the inventory pictures at least twice as large as the series on tinplate

5 *Quatro cuadritos fiestas y costumbres*
   ?   Four panels in the Academy of San Fernando in Madrid [III.966-969]. They were acquired by Manuel García de la Prada (after Goya's death?) Cp. no. 18.

6 *Retrato de Goya, busto*
   ?   Self-portrait. Agen Museum [I.201]. Acquired by Federico de Madrazo. Cp. nos 20, 31.

7 *Una maja vestida echada (mas de una vara)*
   ?   Condesa de Baena(?) Zumaya (Guipúzcoa), Zuloaga Coll. [III.1563]
   ?   See note to [II.744]

8 *Retrato de Dn Javier con un perro. Tamaño natural*
   Javier Goya 'L'Homme en gris'. Paris, heirs of the Comtesse de Noailles [II.852]

9 *Retrato de señora con una rosa. Medio cuerpo*

10 *Retrato de D.ª Catalina Viola con un abanico. Medio cuerpo*
? Young woman with a fan. Paris, Louvre [III.890]

11 *Retrato de D.ª Juana Galarza*
? Madrid, Marquesa Viuda de Casa Riera [III.886]
? Portrait drawing. Madrid, Marqués de Casa Torres [II.841] Cp. no. 13.

12 *Retrato de D.ª Gumersinda, tamaño natural*
Gumersinda Goicoechea. Paris, heirs of the Comtesse de Noailles [II.851]

13 *Retrato de D.ª Gracia Lucientes (Lapiz) busto*

14 *Retrato de D.ª Josefa, medio cuerpo*
? Josefa Goya y Bayeu(?) Madrid, Prado [II.686]
? Portrait drawing. Madrid, Marqués de Casa Torres [II.840] Cp. nos 11, 13.

15 *Dos caprichos, bocetos*

16 *Siete caprichos (bocetos de la casa de campo)*
Sketches for the 'black paintings' in the Quinta. See [IV.1628a-d].

17 *Reo en capilla; boceto*
Unknown; formerly in the collection of Louis-Philippe. See Bibl. 6 (no. 98) and 31 (no. 351).

18 *Baile de mascaras (de una vara)*
? The burial of the sardine. Madrid, Academy of San Fernando [III.970] Cp. no. 5.
? Carnival scene. Formerly Budapest, Baron Herzog [III.954] Cp. Appendix I, no. 1.

19 *Una procession (de una vara y media)*
? Procession in Valencia. Zurich, Bührle Collection [III.952] Cp. Appendix I, no. 1.

20 *Un globo*
? The balloon. Agen Museum [III.956] Acquired by Federico de Madrazo. Cp. nos 6, 31.

21 *Un Entierro*
Unknown; formerly in the collection of Louis-Philippe. See Bibl. 6 (no. 97) and 31 (no. 375).

22 *Incendio de un pueblo (una vara)*
? Village on fire. Buenos Aires, Museum [III.947] Cp. Appendix I, no. 28

23 *Retrato de un joven, boceto*
? Sketch for the portrait of the Xth Duque de Osuna. Formerly Bremen, Kunsthalle [III.1558]

24 *Retrato de señora desconocida, medio cuerpo*

25 *Retrato de señora con abanico, medio cuerpo*
? Lorenza Correa. Paris, heirs of the Comtesse de Noailles [II.836]

26 *Retrato del Rey Fernando VII, busto*
? Ferdinand VII. Formerly Madrid, Duque de Tamames [III.1537]

27 *Retrato de Goya, firmado 1815, busto*
Self-portrait. Madrid, Academy of San Fernando [III.1551]

28 *Dos escenas de bandoleros, bocetos*
See note to [III.948]

29 *Un baile, cuadro*
? Fiesta. Buenos Aires, Museum [III.949] Cp Appendix I, no. 28
? Carnival scene. Formerly Budapest, Baron Herzog [III.954] Cp. Appendices I, no. 1, and II, no. 18.

30 *Dos corridas de toros, cuadro*
? Bullfight in a divided ring. New York, Metropolitan Museum [III.953] Cp. Appendix I, no. 1.

31 *La misa de parida, cuadro*
? Agen Museum [III.975] Acquired by Federico de Madrazo. Cp. nos 6, 20.

APPENDIX III   THE PARMA COMPETITION OF 1771: LETTER FROM GOYA AND VERDICT OF THE JURY

Letter addressed by Goya to Count Carlo della Torre Rezzonico, perpetual Secretary of the Royal Academy of Fine Arts in Parma, and dated 20 April 1771, concerning the painting which he had sent for the Academy's competition.

III.ᵐᵒ Sig.ʳᵉ Sig.ʳᵉ Prōne Collend.ᵐᵒ
Il Sig.ʳᵉ Conte Rezzonico Segretario
Perpetuo della Reale Accad.ª delle tre
belle Arti di   Parma

III.ᵐᵒ Sig.ʳᵉ e Prōne [Padrone] Collend.ᵐᵒ
Doppo di avere preventivamᵗᵉ avvisato a V. II.ᵐᵃ
del cuadro che io faccevo pʳ il concorso di codesta Reale
Accad.ª & sono ora pʳ di nuovo dargli avviso di
aver consegnato il mio cuadro alla Posta pʳ che
egli sia giunto alle sue mani. Il moto con cui jo
lo ho contradistinto secondo l'ordine della med.ᵐᵃ

Accad.ª è un verso delle Eneide di Virgilio al lib.
sesto che dice Jam tandem Italiæ fugientis pren-
dimus oras.
Spero che il cuadro possa giungere a tempo del con-
corso e che le mie deboli forze siano compatite,
mentre spero quella risposta che la Accad.ª giudicarà
convenᵗᵉ intanto che pieno di ossequio e di rasegna
zione mi dico di V.S.III.ᵐᵃ

Roma li 20 Aprile 1771.   Vᵐᵒ e Devot.ᵐᵒ Sere.ʳᵉ
Fran.ᶜᵒ Goja

Letter published by Giovanni Copertini, 'Note sul Goya', Parma, 1928, with a facsimile reproduction of the text. Reprinted by Sánchez Cantón (Bibl. 160) and Sambricio (Bibl. 154, p. 21).

Extract from the manuscript 'Acts of the Royal Academy of Painting, Sculpture and Architecture' in Parma, concerning the *Distribuzione de' Premj* celebrated on 27 June 1771.

Il Quadro contrassegnato dal verso di Virgilio = Iam tandem Italiæ fugientis prendimus oras = à riportato sei Voci. Vi si è osservato con piacere un maneggio facile di pennello, una calda espressione nel votto, e nell'attitudine d'Annibale un carattere grandioso, e se più al vero s'accostassero le sue tinte, e la composizione all'argomento, avrebbe messa in dubbio la palma riportata dal primo.
L'Autore n'è il Sig. Francesco Goja Romano, e scolare del Signor Francesco Vajeu Pittore di Camera di S. M. Cattolica.

Both texts are here transcribed from photographs of the original documents kindly made available by the Academy of Fine Arts in Parma.

APPENDIX IV   THREE LETTERS FROM GOYA TO BERNARDO DE IRIARTE IN 1794

Three letters sent by Goya to Don Bernardo de Iriarte, Vice-Protector of the Royal Academy of San Fernando, on 4, 7 and 9 January 1794. The first two are entirely autograph, the third is written by an amanuensis and signed by Goya. They are transcribed from the original documents in the Department of Manuscripts at the British Museum. See the reproductions in the text, pp. 108 and 110.

Letter of 4 January 1794   MS. Egerton 585, folio 74
recto

YII.ᵐᵒ S.ʳ
Para ocupar la imaginaci.ⁿ
mortificada en la consideracᵒⁿ
de mis males, y para resarcir
en parte los grandes dispend-
dios q.ᵉ me an ocasionado,
me dedique a pintar un jue-
go de quadros de gabinete, en
q.ᵉ he logrado hacer observacio.ˢ
a q.ᵉ regularmente no dan lu-
gar las obras encargadas, y en
que el capricho y la invencion
no tienen ensanches. He pen-
sado remitirlos a la Academia
para todos los fines q.ᵉ VS.Y. co-
noce q.ᵉ yo puedo prometerme
en exponer esta obra a la cen-
sura de los profesores; pero para
asegurarme en estos mismos —

verso
fines he tenido por conveni-
ente, remitir antes a VS.Y. los
quadros p.ᵃ q.ᵉ los bea y por el res
peto con q.ᵉ los ara mirar esta
circunstancia por la autoridad
y por la singular inteligencia

de VS.Y. no tenga lugar la emu-
lacion. Protejalos VS.Y. y proteja-
me ami en la situacion q.ᵉ mas
necesito el fabor q.ᵉ siempre me
ha dispensado. Dios gûe a VS.Y.
m.ˢ a.ˢ Madrid 4 de Enero de
1794
YII.ᵐᵒ S.ʳ
B.L.M. de VSY. su
mas atento serv.ʳ Fran.ᶜᵒ de Goya

YII.ᵐᵒ S.ʳ
D.ⁿ Bernardo de Yriarte

Letter of 7 January 1794   MS. Egerton 585, folio 75
recto

YII.ᵐᵒ S.ᵒʳ
Si pudiera yo espresar
á VS.Y. mi agradecimiento
de tantos fabores q.ᵉ le me-
reccol quedaria tan conten-
to, como de el âprecio, q.ᵉ he
merecido á los S.ʳᵉˢ y profe-
sores de la Academia de S.ⁿ
Fernando: tanto del cuida-
do de mi salud! como de la
benignidad con q.ᵉ ân mira
do mis producciones; pero —
quedo nuebamente inflama
do haplicandome con mu-
cho animo, segun mis espe
ranzas á presentar cosas
q.ᵉ sean mas dignas de tan
respetable cuerpo. Tengo —

verso
ygual satisf.ⁿ de q.ᵉ queden
los Quadros en casa de VS.Y.

todo el tiempo q.ᵉ guste, y
en concluir el q.ᵉ tengo empe
zado: q.ᵉ reprs.ᵗᵃ un corral de
locos, y dos q.ᵉ estan luchan
do desnudos con el q.ᵉ los cui-
da cascandoles, y otros con los
sacos; (es asumto q.ᵉ he pre-
senciado en Zaragoza). lo em
biare a VS.Y. p.ᵃ q.ᵉ este com-
pleta la óbra.
No se fatigue VS.Y.
en apresurar su destino, q.ᵉ
me ago cargo las dificulta-
des del asumto. Dios gûe á
VS.Y. m.ˢ a.ˢ Madrid a 7 del Ene
ro de 1794
YII.ᵐᵒ S.ʳ
B.L.M. de VS.Y.
su mas at.ᵗᵒ serv.ʳ Franᶜᵒ de Goya

YII.ᵐᵒ S.ʳ D.ⁿ Bernardo de
Yriarte

Letter of 9 January 1794   MS. Egerton 585, folio 76
recto, verso

Muy Sr. mio, y de todo mi respeto, despues de dar a VS.Y.
las mas debidas gracias por lo que me honra y se interesa
en mi bien, tengo que hacerle la suplica de que permita
que los quadros se lleben de [?] mi parte a casa del
Sr. Marques de Villaverde, porque sé que la Señorita como
tan inteligente en el dibuxo tendra gusto de verlos, y en todo
caso es un obsequio muy debido; quando VS.Y. disponga
los podra llevar el mismo criado que seria portador de esta.
Disimule VS.Y. mis molestias y mandeme mientras ruego á
Dios que su vida m.ˢ a.ˢ
Madrid a 9 de Enero de 1794   Franᶜᵒ de Goya

APPENDIX V GOYA AND THE OSUNA FAMILY. DOCUMENTS

Texts of the various documents, compiled from the publications in which they have appeared[1], concerning the commissions which Goya executed for the Osunas between 1785 and 1816. The catalogue numbers are given after the titles of the various works.

1785 16 July

Order of payment (4,800 reales) for the two portraits of the IXth Duke and the Countess-Duchess of Benavente [1.219, 220].

Ma^d, 16 de Julio de 1785. D. Manuel de Cubas. Para que se despache un libramiento de orden de S.E. à favor de D. Francisco Goya pintor de 4800 R^s de Vⁿ por los dos retratos que ha hecho de sus Ex.^{as}

Loga, Bibl. 109, p. 109, n. 125

1787 22 April

Note concerning the transport of paintings — probably [I.248-255] — from Goya's house to the Alameda.

*Recibo de los mozos de cordel de 100 R^s por haber conducido à la Alameda pinturas de la casa de Dⁿ Juan de la casa de S.E. á d^a villa al respecto de 25 R.^s.
Madrid, 22 de Abril de 1787.   Joachin Gomez*

Loga, Bibl. 109, p. 160, n. 128

12 May

Goya's account for a small picture with the portraits of the three Osuna children (lost) and for the seven decorative paintings for the Alameda [I.248-255]

*Cuenta de los cuadros que he pintado por orden de la Excma. Señora Condesa de Peñafiel:
Primeramente un quadro en pequeño de los retratos de los tres señoritos, de cuerpo entero, al oleo; su valor   3.000
Id. Para la Alameda, siete cuadros todos de composicion, asuntos de campo; el primero representa un apartado de toros, con varias figuras, de á caballo, y de á pié, y los toros para formar su composicion, con su pais correspondiente: su valor   4.000*

2.º Otro que representa unos ladrones que han asaltado á un coche y despues de haberse apoderado y muerto á los caleseros, y un oficial de guerra, que se hicieron fuertes, estan en ademan de atar á una muger y á un hombre, con su pais correspondiente; su valor   3.000

3.º Otro cuadro que representa unos jitanos divirtiendose, columpiando á una jitana y otras dos sentadas mirando y tocando una guitarra, con su pais correspondiente; su valor   2.500

4.º Otro cuadro que representa una procesion de una aldea, cuyas figuras principales ó de primer termino, son el Cura, Alcaldes, Regidores, Gaitero, etc. y demas acompañamiento, con su pais correspondiente; su valor   2.500

5.º Otro cuadro que representa una romeria en tierra montuosa, y una muger desmayada, por haber caido de una borrica, que la estan socorriendo un Abate y otro que la sostiene en sus brazos, y otras dos que van en borricas espresando el sentimiento con otro criado que forma el grupo principal, y otros que se atrasaron y se ven á lo lejos, y su pais correspondiente; su valor   2.500

6.º Otro cuadro que representa un Mayo, como en la plaza de un lugar con unos muchachos que van subiendo por él, á ganar un premio de pollos y roscas, que está pendiente en la punta de él, y varias gentes que estan mirando, con su campo correspondiente; su valor   2.000

7.º Otro cuadro que representa una obra grande, á la que conducen una piedra con dos pares de bueyes, y un pobre que se ha desgraciado, que llevan en una escalera, y tres carreteros que lo miran lastimados; con su pais correspondiente, que es su valor   2.500

*Importanta esta cuenta   22.000
Madrid y Mayo á 12 de 1787   Francisco de Goya*

Sentenach, Bibl. 174, p. 198; 176, p. 209, n. 1
Beruete, Bibl. 36, II, pp. 62-63

[1] To the documents cited here should be added those published by Carmen Muñoz de Figuera, Condesa de Yebes, *La Condesa-Duquesa de Benavente*, Madrid, 1955. This work was brought to the authors' attention too late to be consulted for this appendix.

7 June

Order of payment for 10,000 reales of the 22,000 in the account dated 12 May; signed by the duchess; on the verso is Goya's receipt dated 27 August.

*Un libramiento para que paguen à Goya dies mil reales por cuenta de veintidos mil reales que han importado varios cuadros que ha pintado de mi órden.
Firmado en Aranjuez a 7 de Junio de 1787.
Ca condes^a Duq.^{sa}*

On the verso

Recibi los dies mil reales que expresa el libramiento. Madrid, 27 de Agosto de 1787.   Fran^{co} de Goya.

Loga, Bibl. 109, n. 128, p. 161

1788 26 February

Order of payment for the remaining 12,000 reales owing on the account of 12 May 1787; on the verso is Goya's receipt, undated.

...que han importado los quadros que ha pintado de mi órden, el uno de ellos de mis hijos y los seis [sic] restantes para mi casa de campo de la Alameda como consta por menor de su cuenta.

Loga, Bibl. 109, n. 128, p. 161

16 October

Goya's account (12,000 reales) for the picture of the *Family of the Duke of Osuna* [I.278] — referred to in an undated note concerning a sum of money due to him.

Ha de haber el mismo D. Francisco de Goya [16.000 rv] importe de dos cuentas que ha presentado en esta contaduria con fecha 16 de Octubre de 1788, y la otra de 27 de Febrero de 1790, por los retratos de nuestros Augustos Reyes, para las funciones de su coronacion, y un cuadro de los retratos de S.S. y sus cuatro hijos, de cuerpo entero.

Sentenach, Bibl. 174, p. 198

16 October

Goya's account (30,000 reales) for the two paintings of San Francisco de Borja in the cathedral at Valencia [I.240, 243].

*Madrid 16 de Octubre de 1788.
D. Francisco de Goya. Pintor.
Su cuenta de dos cuadros que ha pintado representativos de pasages de la vida de San Fran.^{co} de Borja para la nueva Capilla que á expensas de S.E. se ha hecho en la Iglesia Catedral de Valencia.
R.^s de v.^{on} 30 dr.*

Beruete, Bibl. 36, II, p. 33

1789 22 May

Note concerning the payment of the account of 16 October 1788.

Se despachó libramiento de esta cantidad á favor del interesado, y contra Don Francisco Sanifo, Pror. Patrimonial del Estado de Gandía, en 22 de Mayo de 1789

Beruete, Bibl. 36, II, p. 33
Sentenach, however, maintained that only part of this sum was paid in May 1789 and that the balance of 6,000 reales was transferred to Goya on 18 September 1790 in Valencia, where he was staying with his wife. Bibl. 174, p. 199.

1790 27 February

Goya's account (4,000 reales) for the portraits of Charles IV and María Luisa (unidentified, cp. [I.281-286]) — referred to in an undated note concerning a sum of money due to him. See the text quoted above, 16 October 1788 (Sentenach).

Goya's receipt for the 12,000 reales paid to him for the *Family of the Duke of Osuna* [I.278], according to the account dated 16 October 1788. Cited by Sánchez Cantón, Bibl. 166, p. 44.

No date

Inventory of the works painted by Goya for the Osunas' houses in Madrid and at La Alameda.

Se han pintado por D. Francisco Goya para las casas de S.E. en esta Córte y la Alameda los cuadros siguientes.

Para Madrid	*R^s de Vⁿ*
Primeramente dos retratos de los Reyes NN.SS. en	*4.000*
Otro quadro grande que representa à SS.EE. y los quatro Señoritos de cuerpo entero	*12.000*
Otro quadro pequeño de los retratos de los tres Señoritos en	*3.000*
	19.000

Para la Alameda.
Siete quadros cuya composicion es asuntos de campo.

1. Represt^a un apartado de toros con varias figuras a caballo en	*4.000*
2. Que representa a unos Ladrones en	*3.000*
3. Que representa à una gitana columpiandose	*2.500*
4. Que representa una procesion de Aldea	*2.500*
5. Que representa una romeria en Tierra montuosa	*2.500*
6. Que representa un Mayo en	*2.000*
7. Que representa la conduccion de una piedra con dos pares de Bueyes en	*2.500*
	38.000

Loga, Bibl. 109, p. 161

1793 17 January

Letter from Goya, who was ill, asking for money to be made available to him in Seville.

*Muy estim.^{do} Sr D.ⁿ Manuel de Cubas: Le he de merecer a V^m el fabor de acer presente a su Ex.ª q.^e he estado dos meses en cama de dolores colicos, y q.^e paso a Sevilla y a Cadiz con licencia, y q.^e suplico a su Ex.ª si quiere dignarse q.^e por su recomendación ò su apoderado, pueda yo tomar algun dinero en Sevilla, se lo estimaria entrañablemente quedando siempre sumamente reconocido à los fabores q.^e siempre ha recivido el q.^e B. L. M. de V^m y ruega a Dios le gu.^e m.^s a.^s su servidor   Fran.^{co} de Goya.
Madrid 17 de Enero de 93.*

In the margin

*Se restan 10 [mil.] r.^s v.ⁿ
Se le libraron contra d.ⁿ Andres de Coca en 18 de Enero de 1793.*

Sambricio, Bibl. 154, doc. 158

1798 6 May

Goya's account (10,000 reales) for paintings for the study of the countess-duchess — referred to in an undated note concerning the sums which were due to him. The paintings, paid for on 26 April 1799, are identifiable among [I.256-261, 272-275].

Más ha de haber D. Francisco de Goya [10000 rv] importe de una cuenta que ha presentado en la contaduria con fecha 6 de Mayo de 1798, de varias pinturas que ha hecho para el gabinete de S.E. mi señora...

Sentenach, Bibl. 174, p. 199

27 June

Goya's account (6,000 reales) for the portrait of General Urrutia [II.679], paid for on 29 June.

*Madrid 27 de Junio de 1798
Don Francisco de Goya. Pintor. Su cuenta de un retrato de cuerpo entero que ha hecho para la casa de S.E. en esta Córte, que representa al Capitan Gral. D. José Urrutia, que importa — R^s de vⁿ — 6.000*

Beruete, Bibl. 36, I, pp. 72-73
A note concerning the sum due to the artist for this portrait is cited by Sentenach, following the note referring to the account dated 6 May. His text gives the same date for the account quoted here, but this is no doubt an error.

27 June

Goya's account (6,000 reales) for the six scenes of witchcraft painted for the Alameda [II. 659-664].

*Cuenta de seis quadros de conposición de asuntos de Brujas, que están en la Lameda seis mil r.^s v.ⁿ
Madrid 27 de Junio de 1798   Francisco de Goya
60 r.^s v.ⁿ*

Miguel Herrero, 'Un autógrafo de Goya', *Archivo Español de Arte*, XLIII, 1941, pp. 176-177

29 June
Order of payment for the witchcraft scenes in the account of 27 June.

...para abonar á D.F.º de Goya seis mil reales importe de seis quadros cuya composicion es de asuntos de Brujas que ha hecho para mi casa de campo de la Alameda.

Loga, Bibl. 109, p. 166, n. 183

Note concerning the payment of the sum on the same day.

Madrid 27 Junio 1798
Don Francisco de Goya, Pintor.
Dentro su cuenta del importe de seis cuadros que ha hecho para la Casa de S.E. en la Alameda (asuntos de brujas) que importan reales de vellón, 6000. Se despachó libramiento de esta cantidad a favor del expresado Goya, en 29 de Junio citado.

Miguel Herrero, *op. cit.* with reference to the account of 27 June

29 June
Order of payment (6,000 reales) for the portrait of General Urrutia in the account of 27 June, with Goya's receipt on the verso.

Libramiento para que el cajero abone á Goya seis mil reales importe de un retrato de cuerpo entero que ha hecho para mi casa en esta Corte y representa al Capitán General D. Josef Urrutia, como consta de cuenta que ha presentado y queda en mi contaduria en la que se tomará razon.
Madrid, 29 de Junio de 1798.

Loga, Bibl. 109, p. 166, n. 182

1799 17 January
Order of payment (1,500 reales) for four copies of the edition of the *Caprichos* [II.451-613].

Sr. D. Josef Serrano. El Duque mi señor manda se despache un libramiento de un mil quinientos reales vellón á favor de D. Francisco de Goya por importe de unas estampas que ha tomado S.E. de su casa. Lo que prevengo á v. m. para su cumplimiento. Madrid, 17 de Enero de 1799.

Sentenach, Bibl. 174, p. 199
The same author, in Bibl. 175, mentioned Goya's receipt on the verso of the document. The full text was published by Loga:

Recivi de la Exma Sra Duquesa de Osuna joben mil y quinientos reales de vⁿ por los quatro libros de caprichos y grabados á la agua fuerte pr mi mano. Madrid 17 de Enero de 1799 Francⁿ de Goya

Loga, Bibl. 109, p. 163, n. 155

26 April
The Duke of Osuna's order of payment, with Goya's receipt, for the seven pictures (sketches for the tapestry cartoons) intended for the study of the countess-duchess and listed in the account dated 6 May 1798.

El Cagero de mi Tesor.ª D.ⁿ Miguel de Osa en vᶠd de éste y de recibo pagará á D.ⁿ Fran.co Goya, Pintor de Camara de S.M. Diez mil r.ˢ v.ⁿ en tres vales de à 150. pes.ˢ de 15. de Setᵉe, y el resto en dinero, por el importe de siete Pinturas, que representan una la Pradera de S.ⁿ Ysidro; quatro de las Estaciones del año; y dos asuntos de Campo, que hizo para el Gabin.ᵗᵉ de la Condesa Duquesa mi muger. Y de este libram.ᵗᵒ se tomarà razon en mi Contad.ª Madrid veinte y Seis de Abril de mil setez.ᵗᵒˢ nov.ᵗᵃ y nueve.
....
V.E. dá Libram.ᵗᵃ sre su Tesor.ª de 10 [mil] r.ˢ v.ⁿ á favor de d.ⁿ Franc.co Goya, Pintor imp.ᵗᵉ de Siete Quadros que hizo p.ª el Gavin.ᵗᵉ de mi Sra.

On the verso
Recivi, Fran.co de Goya.

Sambricio, Bibl. 154, doc. 192
Also quoted by Beruete, Bibl. 36, II, p. 66 and Loga, Bibl. 109, p. 167, n. 185.

1816 30 April
Note concerning the payment (4,000 reales) of the portrait of the Duchess of Abrantes [III.1560].

Son data 4.000 reales entregados al pintor D Francisco Goya de orden de S.E. en consideració al retrato que ha hecho de la Excelentísima señor. Duquesa de Abrantes, segun consta del abon no. 29.

Sentenach, Bibl. 175, and Bibl. 23, no. XXXI

17 November
Goya's letter concerning the payment (10,000 reales) for the portrait of the Xth Duke of Osuna

Excmo. señor: Despues de haver tenido la satisfac cion de llenar los deseos de V.E. con su retrato d cuerpo entero, que tube el gusto de hacer est Agosto ultimo, V.E. me preguntó en escrito cuant devia enviarme por el referido retrato, a lo que con testé que jamás habia tasado mis producciones, per que en visto del vibo deseo que tenía V.E. e corresponder con mis tareas, las creia recompensa das con haverle servido, y al mismo tiempo con die mil rvn. Distraido con mi trabajo no he llamado l atencion de V.E. sobre este asunto hasta est momento, en el que necesitando de dicha cantidad desearé se me satisfaga como es justo. Dios guard á V.E. muchos años.
Madrid 17 de Noviembre de 1816

Francisco de Goy

Sentenach, Bibl. 175. He indicated that the duke agreed on the following day and that Goya was paic on 28 March 1817.

APPENDIX VI THE 'BLACK PAINTINGS' IN THE QUINTA DEL SORDO

Shown here are the plans of the two rooms on whose walls Goya executed the 'black paintings' now exhibited in the Prado Museum.

The paintings are listed first according to the order of the catalogue [IV.1615-1627a]; then, using the same numbering as a means of identification, according to that of the inventory made by Brugada in 1828 (published by X. Desparmet

Fitz-Gerald, *L'Œuvre peint de Goya,* Paris, 1928-50, vol. I, p. 53, n. 1) and finally according to that of the catalogue by Charles Yriarte (*Goya,* Paris, 1867, pp. 140-141).

Yriarte described the Quinta in these terms: 'L'habitation est de dimension très-modeste... La maison a été construite ou du moins disposée sur les indications de Goya, qui fit réserver au rez-de-chaussée et au premier étage deux

grandes salles, dont les murs furent divisés en panneaux. Plus tard, son fils a fait élever la partie à droite de la grille... (see ill. p. 313).

The plans are based on those published by F. J. Sánchez Cantón and Xavier de Salas, *Goya and the Black Paintings,* London, 1964 (Bibl. 169); the disposition of the doors and windows is to some extent hypothetical.

FIRST-FLOOR ROOM

Yriarte wrote (p. 94): 'La disposition de la salle du premier étage est la même que celle du rez-de-chaussée, avec cette différence que les deux faces latérales, au lieu de ne présenter qu'un seul grand panneau, sont divisées en deux et séparées par une fenêtre.'

Order followed in the catalogue

1 Atropos or The Fates [1615]
2 Duel with cudgels [1616]
3 Men reading [1617]
4 Two young people laughing at a man [1618]
5 Promenade of the Holy Office [1619]
6 Asmodea [1620]
7 The dog [1621]
[7a Two witches, by Javier Goya]

Brugada (inventory of 1828)

1 *Atropos*
2 *Dos forasteros*
3 *Dos ombres*
4 *Dos mujeres*
5 *El san officio*
6 *Asmodea*
7 *Un perro*
7a *Dos brujas* (acheté depuis par le marquis de Salamanca) [Note added by Desparmet]

Yriarte (catalogue 1867, pp. 140-141)

7 *Un chien luttant contre le courant*
6 *L'Asmodée*
5 *Promenade du saint-office*

4 *Deux femmes riant à gorge déployée*
3 *Les Politiques*
2 *Les Gardeurs de bœufs*
1 *Les Parques*

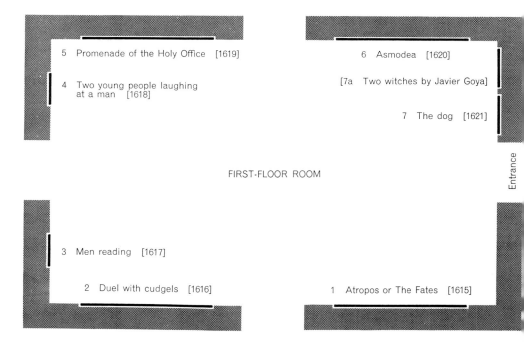

5 Promenade of the Holy Office [1619]
4 Two young people laughing at a man [1618]
6 Asmodea [1620]
[7a Two witches by Javier Goya]
7 The dog [1621]
FIRST-FLOOR ROOM
Entrance
3 Men reading [1617]
2 Duel with cudgels [1616]
1 Atropos or The Fates [1615]

7a **....** ... transportée à Vista-Alegre, propriété de M. de Salamanca. Elle ne serait pas de Goya, mais bien de son fils, selon que l'atteste la correspondance du marquis de l'Espinar. [Note by Yriarte]

GROUND-FLOOR ROOM

Yriarte wrote (p. 92): 'La salle du rez-de-chaussée contient six compositions, dont deux occupent toute la largeur des deux faces les plus étendues, celles qu'on a à sa droite et à sa gauche en entrant. De chaque côté de la porte et en face de celle-ci sont disposés deux panneaux, soit quatre sur les deux faces les plus petites.'

Order followed in the catalogue

1 La Leocadia [1622]
2 The great he-goat [1623]
3 Saturn [1624]
4 Judith and Holophernes [1625]
5 The pilgrimage of San Isidro [1626]
6 Two old men [1627]
7 Two old people eating [1627a]

Brugada (inventory of 1828)

2 El gran cabron
1 La Leocadia
7 Dos mujeres
3 Saturno
6 Dos viejos
4 Judith y Oloferno
5 La Romeria de San Isidro

Yriarte (catalogue 1867, p. 140)

6 Les Vieillards
5 La Romeria de San-Isidro
4 Judith et Holopherne
3 Saturne dévorant ses enfants
2 Le Gran Cabron
1 La Leocadia
7 Deux vieilles femmes mangeant à la gamelle

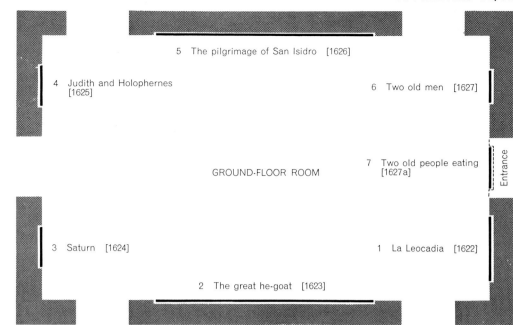

5 The pilgrimage of San Isidro [1626]

4 Judith and Holophernes [1625]

6 Two old men [1627]

GROUND-FLOOR ROOM

7 Two old people eating [1627a]

Entrance

3 Saturn [1624]

1 La Leocadia [1622]

2 The great he-goat [1623]

APPENDIX VII   WORKS BY GOYA IN THE LIST SENT BY MARIANO TO VALENTÍN CARDERERA

List of works by Goya which were stored away in 1818 and were found hidden in a cupboard by his grandson Mariano. The list was sent by Mariano to Valentín Carderera, together with a note of the prices he was asking for the prints.

All the works listed were acquired by Carderera who wrote that the proof of the *Colossus* [III.985] was first shown to him by Mariano in 1859 (Bibl. 45, [III], p. 248). The drawing of Wellington [III.898] was acquired by the British Museum in 1862, together with Mariano's note to which Carderera added a brief French translation.

The note, previously published by Helman (Bibl. 95),

is given below, with the catalogue numbers following the works mentioned. It is transcribed from the original document in the Department of Prints and Drawings (BM 1862-7-12-186).

En una lacena [sic] *tapeada de la posessor se han encontrado entre papeles mui interesantes lo sig.te*
Un retrato de la Rita-Luna, actriz del tiempo de Moratín [III. 1565]
Un dibujo hecho en Alba de Tormes despues de la batalla de Arapiles del Duque de Weelingthon por el q.e se hizo el retrato [III. 898]

Un ejemplar del cuadro de familia [I. 107]
Otro de un gigante cuyas laminas fueron rotas [III. 985]
Las Estampas qe acompañan de los toros, rotas las laminas [III. 1233-1241?]
Guardado todo el año 1818, segun los apuntes, sin saberse con q.e objeto
Goya

Valor q.e se quiere
El ejemplar de las meninas [I. 107]   1300 r.
El del gigante [III. 985]   160
Cada una de los toros [III. 1233-1241?]   120

APPENDIX VIII   GOYA'S HOUSES IN MADRID

1773 Goya married Josefa Bayeu in Madrid. It is not known whether he was already settled in Madrid or whether he returned to live in Saragossa.

1774 He was called by Mengs at the end of the year to work for the Royal Tapestry Factory, and was then living with his brother-in-law, Francisco Bayeu, at nos 7-9 Calle del Reloj. (See Sambricio, Bibl. 154, note 69, pp. 289-290.)

1777 He was living at no. 66 Carrera de San Jerónimo, on the second floor of the house known as the 'casa de Liñan', which belonged to the Marquesa de Campollano. (See Zapater y Gómez, Bibl. 72, p. 49, and Sánchez Cantón, Bibl. 161, p. 91.)

1782 He was living at no. 1 Calle del Desengaño (from 1779?) (See August L. Mayer, 'Goyas Briefe an Martin Zapater', *Beiträge zur Forschung*, I, Munich, 1913, p. 44).

His house was in the *manzana* 344. His son Francisco Javier was born there in 1784. In 1799 the *Caprichos* were offered for sale in a perfume and liquor shop at the same address. (See Saltillo, Bibl. 153, p. 13; the announcement of the *Caprichos*, ill. p. 129.)

1800 Goya sold to Godoy, through Antonio Noriega, the house in the Calle del Desengaño and bought the house at no. 15 Calle de Valverde, *manzana* 345, which forms an angle with the Calle del Desengaño. (See Saltillo, *op. cit.*)

1803 Goya bought a house at no. 7 Calle de los Reyes. It was given to his son Javier in 1806, when he and his wife left his parents' home, but he does not seem to have lived in it. He mortgaged it in 1809. (See Sánchez Cantón, Bibl. 161, pp. 75-79.)

1809 Javier was living at no. 9 Calle de la Zarza, near the Puerta del Sol. (See Demerson, Bibl. 56, p. 181.)

1812 Javier was living at no. 5 Calle de las Tres Cruces. (See Sánchez Cantón, *op. cit.* p. 79.)

In October the division of the joint property of Goya and his late wife gave the house in the Calle de Valverde to Javier, but he no doubt left the use of it to his father. Although Goya no longer legally owned a house, he probably continued to live in the Calle de Valverde until 1819. (See Sánchez Cantón, *op. cit.* pp. 77-78 and Appendix III, p. 107; Saltillo, *op. cit.*)

1819 27 February: Goya acquired the Quinta called 'del Sordo' on the outskirts of Madrid. He lived there from 1819 until 1823-24. (See Sánchez Cantón, *op. cit.* pp. 91-96 and Appendix IV, pp. 107-108; Saltillo, *op. cit.* p. 17.)

1823 17 September: Goya made over the Quinta as a gift to his grandson Mariano. (See Sánchez Cantón, *op. cit.* pp. 91-96 and Appendix V, pp. 108-109).

BIBLIOGRAPHY

This is a bibliography of works referred to in the text and catalogue and cited by means of numbered references. Additional works, cited in full in the notes to the catalogue, are indicated here by the name of the author and the phrase 'v. Note...'

After the museum catalogues, exhibition catalogues and then sale catalogues are given in chronological order. Books and articles are given in the alphabetical order of their authors.

MUSEUM CATALOGUES

The latest editions of the existing catalogues have been consulted, but they are not specifically cited as a general rule.

In the case of the Prado Museum, the 1963 catalogue has been used in conjunction with that of 1920 which lists all the paintings by Goya acquired up to that date, including many now in store or on loan to provincial museums. These catalogues are completed by the one published for the exhibition of recent acquisitions (1969). The first Prado catalogue to include modern artists, with paintings by Goya (1828), is also referred to in the text and catalogue. For the drawings by Goya in the Prado, see Bibl. 168.

1   1828   *Noticia de los Cuadros que se hallan colocados en la Galería del Museo del Rey Nuestro Señor, sito en el Prado de esta Córte,* Madrid (Paintings by Goya: nos 279, 319, 320)
2   1969   *Principales Adquisiciones de los últimos diez años (1958-1968),* Museo del Prado, Madrid
3   [Biblioteca nacional] Angel M. de Barcia, *Catálogo de la Colección de Dibujos Originales de la Biblioteca Nacional,* Madrid, 1906
4   [Biblioteca Nacional] ed. Elena Paez Ríos, *Iconografía Hispana. Catálogo de los retratos de personajes españoles de la Biblioteca Nacional,* Madrid, 1966
5   [Calcografía Nacional] Luis Alegre Núñez, *Catálogo de la Calcografía Nacional (Real Academia de Bellas Artes de San Fernando),* Madrid, 1968
    [Gijón, Instituto Jovellanos] – v. Bibl. 139

EXHIBITION CATALOGUES

6   1838   *Notice des Tableaux de la Galerie Espagnole exposés dans les Salles du Musée Royal au Louvre,* Paris, 1838 (Paintings by Goya: nos 97-104)
7   1846   *Catálogo de las obras de Pintura, Escultura y Arquitecto... ejecutadas por los profesores existentes y los que han fallecido en el presente siglo,* Licéo Artístico y Literario, Madrid (reprinted in Bibl. 102, pp. 339-346)
8   1900   *Obras de Goya,* Ministerio de Instrucción Pública y Bellas Artes, Madrid (with a supplement of 18 pictures, listed in Bibl. 57, I, p. 51, n. 3, and Bibl. 182, p. 200, n. 1)
9   1922   *Exposición de Dibujos 1750-1860,* Sociedad Española de Amigos del Arte, Madrid
10   1928   *Catálogo ilustrado de la Exposición de Pinturas de Goya,* Museo del Prado, Madrid
11   1928   *Exposición de Obras de Goya,* Zaragoza, 1928
12   1932   *Antecedentes, Coincidencias e Influencias del Arte de Goya,* Sociedad Española de Amigos del Arte, Madrid (reprinted in Bibl. 102, pp. 349-368)
13   1935   *Exposition de l'Œuvre gravé, de Peintures, de Tapisseries et de Cent dix Dessins du Musée du Prado,* Bibliothèque Nationale, Paris
14   1937   *Exhibition of Paintings, Drawings and Prints by Francisco Goya,* California Palace of the Legion of Honour, San Francisco
15   1938   *Peintures de Goya des Collections de France,* L'Orangerie du Musée du Louvre, Paris
     1938   *From Greco to Goya,* The Spanish Art Gallery, London – v. Notes II. 688, V. 1668, 1669
16   1941   *The Art of Goya. Paintings, Drawings and Prints,* Art Institute, Chicago
17   1951   *Goya,* Bordeaux
18   1953   *Goya – Gemälde, Zeichnungen, Graphik, Tapisserien,* Kunsthalle, Basel
19   1954   *Goya – Drawings, Etchings and Lithographs,* The Arts Council, London
20   1955   *Goya. Drawings and Prints from the Museo del Prado and Museo Lázaro Galdiano, Madrid, and the Rosenwald Collection, National Gallery of Art, Washington, D.C.,* circulated by the Smithsonian Institute
     Supplement: *Paintings, drawings and prints... at The Metropolitan Museum of Art,* New York, May
20a   1955   *Goya,* Palacio de Carlos V, Granada
21   1956   *De Tiepolo à Goya,* Bordeaux
22   1959-60   *Stora Spanska Mästare,* Nationalmuseum, Stockholm
23   1961   *Goya (IV Centenario de la Capitalidad),* El Casón, Madrid
24   1961-62   *Goya,* Musée Jacquemart-André, Paris
25   1963   *Trésors de la peinture espagnole — Eglises et Musées de France,* Musée des Arts Décoratifs, Paris
26   1963   *El Greco to Goya,* John Herron Museum of Art, Indianapolis, Ind.; Rhode Island School of Design, Providence, R.I.
27   1963-64   *Goya and his Times,* Royal Academy of Arts, London
28   1966   *Goya – Zeichnungen Radierungen Lithographien,* Ingelheim am Rhein
29   1966   *Spanische Zeichnungen von El Greco bis Goya,* Kunsthalle, Hamburg
30   1970   *Goya,* Mauritshuis, Den Haag; Orangerie du Musée du Louvre, Paris (1st ed. Dutch and German; revised English ed. and 2nd Dutch ed.; revised French ed.)
     Some of the catalogue numbers were changed in the French edition; in the notes to the present catalogue the later number is given immediately after the original one.
30a   1970-71   *De Grafiek van Goya,* Rijksmuseum, Amsterdam
30b   1970   *Goya – Dessins Gravures Lithographies,* [n.d.], Huguette Berès, Paris

SALE CATALOGUES

     1853-1946   'Essai d'un Relevé des Catalogues des ventes où le nom de Goya a figuré' – v. Bibl. 57, II, pp. 259-278
     (The list has been used in the notes to this catalogue as a convenient reference)
31   1853   *Catalogue of the... Pictures forming the celebrated Spanish Gallery of His Majesty the late King Louis Philippe,* Christie & Manson, London, May 13-21
32   1896   *Catálogo de los Cuadros... de la Antigua Casa Ducal de Osuna expuestos en el Palacio de la Industria y de las Artes,* Madrid (2nd ed.)

AUTHORS

Adhémar, Jean – v. Notes II. 614, 618; Bibl. 13
Alegre Núñez, Luis – v. Bibl. 5
Angulo Iñíguez, Diego – v. Notes I. 206-212, II. 342, IV. 1622-1627a, V. 1664
Araujo Sánchez, Zeferino
33   *Goya,* Madrid, [1896] (Reprinted from *La España Moderna,* 1895, pp. 20-45, 64-90, 101-134, 74-114)
Arco, Ricardo del – v. Note I. 10-16

Barcia, Angel M. de – v. Bibl. 3
Baticle, Jeannine – v. Bibl. 30
Baudelaire, Charles – v. Note II. 744
Baur, Christian – v. Note II. 717-735
Benavente, Luis – v. Note I. 281 and 282
Bentley, G. E. – v. Note II. 760-765
Beroqui, Pedro
34   'Una biografía de Goya escrita por su hijo', *Archivo Español de Arte,* III, 1927, pp. 99-100 (Translation in Bibl. 87, p. 23.) Cp. Bibl. 71
35   *El Museo del Prado (Notas para su historia) I El Museo Real (1819-1833),* Madrid, 1933 V. Note III. 1149-1243

Beruete y Moret, Aureliano de
36   *Goya pintor de retratos* (I), Madrid, 1916 *Goya, composiciones y figuras* (II), Madrid, 191? *Goya grabador* (III), Madrid, 1918 (Abridged edition 1928) [Boadilla del Monte]
37   *Catálogo de las pinturas existentes en el Palacio d? Boadilla del Monte,* n.d. (Cited by Viñaza in hi? catalogue, v. Bibl. 190)
37a   Boelcke-Astor, Catharina 'Die Drucke der Desastres de la Guerra von Francisc? Goya', *Münchner Jahrbuch der Bildenden Kuns?* III/IV. 1952/53, pp. 253-334. See also Bibl. 28
     Boix, Félix
38   'La Litografía y sus orígenes en España', *Art? Español,* VII, 1925, pp. 279-302
39   'Asensio Juliá (El Pescadoret)', *Arte Español,* X 1931, pp. 138-141
     V. Bibl. 9
     Borenius, T., and Wittkower, R. – v. Note V. 175?
     [Boston Museum Bulletin] – v. Note III. 1402
     Bouvy, Eugène
40   *L'Imprimeur Gaulon et les origines de la lithographie ? Bordeaux,* Bordeaux, 1918 (Reprinted from *L? Revue Philomathique de Bordeaux et du Sud-Ouest* XX, no. 6, 1917)
     Braham, Allan – v. Notes III. 896, 897
     Brunet, Gustave – v. Note III. 898

     [Calleja] – v. Bibl. 72
     Calvert, Albert F.
41   *Goya,* London, 1908
     Camón Aznar, José
42   *'Los Disparates' de Goya y sus dibujos preparatorios?* Barcelona, 1951
     Carderera, Valentín
43   'Biografia de D. Francisco Goya, pintor', *El Artista* II, 1835, pp. 253-255 (Reprinted in Bibl. 102 pp. 302-305 and in translation in Bibl. 87, pp.24-27?
44   'Goya', *Semanario Pintoresco,* 1838, no. 120, p? 631-633 (Reprinted in Bibl. 102, pp. 305-308?
45   'François Goya – Sa vie, ses Dessins et ses Eaux-Fortes', *Gazette des Beaux-Arts,* VI, 1860, pp. 215-227 [I Vie, II Dessins]; XV, 1863, pp. 237-249 [II? Eaux-Fortes]
     Castañeda, V.
46   'Libros con ilustraciones de Goya', *Boletín de la Real Academia de la Historia,* 1946, pp. 43-61
     Castro, J. R. – v. Note III. 1536
     Cavestany, Julio – v. Note I. 234
     Ceán Bermúdez, Juan Agustín
47   *Diccionario Histórico de los mas ilustres Profesores de las Bellas Artes en España,* Madrid, 1800
48   *Análisis de un cuadro que pintó D. Francisco Goya para la Catedral de Sevilla,* Sevilla, 1817 – v. Bibl. 70
     Cervantes Saavedra, Miguel de – v. Notes I. 315, III. 1475
     Chastenet, J.
49   *L'Espagne de Goya,* Paris, 1961
50   *Manuel Godoy,* Paris, 1961
     Chueca Goitia, Fernando – v. Note II. 758
     Cook, Walter W. S.
51   'Spanish Paintings in the National Gallery of Art. I? Portraits by Goya', *Gazette des Beaux-Arts,* XXVIII, 1945, pp. 151-162
     Cotarelo y Mori, Emilio – v. Note II. 836 and 837
     Crispolti, Enrico
52   'Disegni inediti di Goya', *Commentari,* IX, 1958? pp. 124-132
53   'Otto nuove pagine del taccuino "di Madrid" di Goya ed alcuni problemi ad esso relativi', *Commentari,* IX, 1958, pp. 181-205
     Cruz y Bahamonde – v. Maule, Conde de
     Cruzada Villaamil, Gregorio
54   *Los tapices de Goya,* Madrid, 1870

     Delteil, Loys
55   'Francisco Goya', *Le Peintre graveur illustré,* XIV, XV, Paris, 1922

Demerson, Georges

56 'Goya, en 1808, no vivía en la Puerta del Sol', *Archivo Español de Arte,* XXX, 1957, pp. 177-185
Desparmet Fitz-Gerald, X

57 *L'Œuvre peint de Goya,* Paris, 1928-50, 2 vols text, 2 vols plates (including: the Brugada inventory of 1828 in I, p. 53, n. 1 — see Appendices II and VI; the supplement to the 1900 exhibition in I, p. 53, n. 3 — cp. Bibl. 8; the will of Goya and Josefa Bayeu, with a French translation, in II, pp. 243-245; an 'Essai d'un Relevé des Catalogues des ventes où le nom de Goya a figuré' [1853-1946] in II, pp. 259-278)
Desparmet Fitz-Gerald, Xavière — v. Notes I. 19, 20, II. 330, 721, III. 1406, 1519; v. Bibl. 24
Dodgson, Campbell — v. Note I. 102
Du Gué Trapier — v. Trapier

Ezquerra del Bayo, Joaquín

58 *La Duquesa de Alba y Goya,* Madrid, 1928
59 'Las Pinturas de Goya en el Oratorio de la Santa Cueva, de Cádiz', *Arte Español,* IX, 1928, pp. 388-391

Fernández de Moratín — v. Moratín
Florisoone, Michel

60 'Comment Delacroix a-t-il connu les "Caprices" de Goya?', *Bulletin de la Société de l'Histoire de l'Art Français, 1957,* 1958, pp. 131-144
61 'La raison du voyage de Goya à Paris', *Gazette des Beaux-Arts,* LXVIII, 1966, pp. 327-332
Font, Eleanor Sherman

62 'Goya's source for the Maragato series', *Gazette des Beaux-Arts,* LII, 1958, pp. 289-304

Galindo, Pascual — v. Note I. 178, 179; Bibl. 151
Gassier, Pierre

62a 'De Goya-Tekeningen in het Museum Boymans', *Bulletin Museum Boymans, Rotterdam,* IV, 1, 1953, pp. 12-24
63 'Les dessins de Goya au Musée du Louvre', *La Revue des Arts,* 1, 1954, pp. 31-41
64 *Goya,* Genève, 1955
V. Bibl. 122
Gaya Nuño, Juan Antonio

65 *La Pintura Española fuera de España,* Madrid, 1928
V. Note V.1672-1675
Glendinning, Nigel

66 'A new view of Goya's *Tauromaquia', Journal of the Warburg and Courtauld Institutes,* XXIV, 1961, pp. 120-127
67 'Goya and England in the Nineteenth Century', *Burlington Magazine,* CVI, 1964, pp. 4-14
V. Notes II. 567, 673, 817, III. 946, 1106/1108
Gómez-Moreno, M. — v. Notes II. 798, III. 951
Gómez-Moreno, María Elena

67a 'Un cuaderno de dibujos inéditos de Goya', *Archivo Español de Arte,* XIV, 1941, pp. 155-163
González Azaola, Gregorio

68 'Sátiras de Goya', *Semanario Patriótico,* Cádiz, 27.III.1811 (v. Bibl. 86 for the Spanish text with an English translation)
González Martí, Manuel

69 'Goya y Valencia', *Museum,* III, 1913, pp. 429-450 (reprinted in *Boletín de la Sociedad Española de Excursiones,* XXXVI, 1928, pp. 41-46)
González Palencia, Angel

70 'El estudio crítico más antiguo sobre Goya', *Boletín de la Real Academia de la Historia,* 1946, pp. 75-87 (with a facsimile of Bibl. 48)
Goya y Bayeu, Francisco Javier

71 Biography of Francisco Goya: longer version published in Bibl. 34 and in translation in Bibl. 87, p. 23; shorter version, sent to the Academy of San Fernando in 1831, published in Bibl. 72, p. 60
[Goya]

72 *Colección de cuatrocientos cuarenta y nueve reproducciones de Cuadros, Dibujos y Aguafuertes de Don Francisco de Goya Precedidos de un Epistolario del gran pintor y de las Noticias Biográficas publicadas por Don Francisco Zapater y Gómez en 1860,* ed. Saturnino Calleja, Madrid, 1924
Goya y Lucientes, Francisco

73 Memorial to the Junta de Fábrica of the temple of Nuestra Señora del Pilar in Saragossa, 17 March 1781 (Published in Bibl. 190, pp. 168-173 and in an English translation in Bibl. 41, pp. 40-46)
74 Report to the Academy of San Fernando on the study of art, 14 October 1792 (Published with a German translation in Bibl. 90, and in translation in Bibl. 87, p. 28)
75 Report on the restoration of paintings addressed to

Don Pedro Cevallos (Protector of the Academy of San Fernando), 2 January 1801 (Published in Bibl. 72, p. 63, and in translation in Bibl. 87, p. 29)
76a Announcement of the publication of *Los Caprichos* in the *Diario de Madrid,* 6 February 1799 (Reprinted in Bibl. 115, I, pp. 185-186, with an English translation on pp. 78-79) V. ill. p. 129. An earlier draft of an announcement concerning the publication of 72 prints, together with commentaries on the 80 plates (v. Bibl. 76b), is said to have been copied from a MS in Goya's hand. It was described and partially published (in a French translation) by Carderera in Bibl. 45, [III], pp. 240-241. Cp. Bibl. 88, I, pp. 95, 98.
76b Commentaries on the plates of *Los Caprichos,* c.1799-1803, from the MS in the Prado Museum (Published in Bibl. 93, pp. 219-241, and Bibl. 88, II, pp. 443-446 (see reproduction in I, p. 96), with English translations in the catalogue; and with English translations in Bibl. 78 and 115, I, pp. 187-212)
77 Autobiographical notice in Bibl. 1, pp. 67-68 (Published in translation in Bibl. 87, p. 23)
78 *Los Caprichos,* New York, 1969 (Introduction by Philip Hofer)
79 *The Disasters of War,* New York, 1967 (Introduction by Philip Hofer)
80 *La Tauromaquia and The Bulls of Bordeaux,* New York, 1969 (Introduction by Philip Hofer)
81 *The Disparates or, The Proverbios,* New York, 1969 (Introduction by Philip Hofer)
V. also Bibl. 106, 189
Gudiol Ricart, José

82 'Goya and Ventura Rodríguez', *Spanska Mästare,* Stockholm, 1960, pp. 141-156 (with an English summary p. 180)
83 'Les peintures de Goya dans la Chartreuse de l'Aula Dei à Saragosse', *Gazette des Beaux-Arts,* LVII, 1961, pp. 83-94
84 'Paintings by Goya in the Buenos Aires Museum', *Burlington Magazine,* CVII, 1965, pp. 11-16
85 *Goya* [biography and catalogue raisonné of paintings] Ediciones Polígrafa, Barcelona, 1970, 4 vols
V. Notes I. 30-33, 299
Guinard, Paul — v. Note III.1568

Harris, Enriqueta

86 'A contemporary review of Goya's "Caprichos"', *Burlington Magazine,* CVI, 1964, pp. 38-43 (v. Bibl. 68)
87 *Goya,* London and New York, 1969; Köln, 1969 (with translations of early texts and documents — v. Bibl. 43, 71, 74, 75, 77)
Harris, Tomás

88 *Goya. Engravings and Lithographs,* Oxford, 1964 (I Text, II Catalogue)
Hasselt, Carlos van — v. Notes V. 1723, 1756, 1768
Held, Jutta

89 *Farbe und Licht in Goyas Malerei,* Berlin, 1964
90 'Goyas Akademiekritik', *Münchner Jahrbuch der Bildenden Kunst,* XVII, 1966, pp. 214-224 (v. Bibl. 74)
V. Note II. 697-707
Helman, Edith F.

91 'The elder Moratín and Goya', *Hispanic Review,* XXIII, 1955, pp. 219-230
92 'The younger Moratín and Goya: on *Duendes* and *Brujas', Hispanic Review,* XXVII, 1959, pp. 103-122
93 *Trasmundo de Goya,* Madrid, 1963
94 'Identity and style in Goya', *Burlington Magazine,* CVI, 1964, pp. 30-37
95 'Fray Juan Fernández de Roxas y Goya', *Homenaje a Rodríguez-Moñino,* Madrid, 1966, I, 241-252
V. Notes I. 266, II. 623
Herrero, Miguel — v. Note II. 659-664
Hofer, Philip — v. Bibl. 78-81

[Jockey Club, Buenos Aires] — v. Notes I. 298, II. 855, III. 950
Junquera, Paulina — v. Notes II. 738-740, III. 1568

[Kalendario Manual y Guia de Forasteros en Madrid] — v. Notes I. 289, II. 781
Klingender, F. D.

96 *Goya in the democratic tradition,* London, 1948; 2nd ed. 1968
Goya und die Demokratische Tradition Spaniens, Berlin, 1954
V. Note IV. 1638

Lachenal, François - v. Note III. 1241 and Bibl. 28
Lafond, Paul

97 *Goya,* Paris, 1902 (Reprinted from *La Revue de l'Art ancien et moderne,* V, 1899, pp. 133 ff.; VI, 1899, pp. 45 ff., 461 ff.; VII, 1900, p. 45 ff.; IX, 1901, pp. 20 ff., 211 ff.)
98 *Nouveaux Caprices de Goya. Suite de trente-huit dessins inédits,* Paris, 1907
99 'Les dernières années de Goya en France', *Gazette des Beaux-Arts,* XXXVII, 1907, pp. 114-131, 241-257
Lafora García, Juan — v. Notes I. 296, III. 938, IV. 1656
Lafuente Ferrari, Enrique

100 *Goya: El Dos de Mayo y los Fusilamientos,* Barcelona, 1946
101 'Ilustración y elaboración en la "Tauromaquia" de Goya', *Archivo Español de Arte,* LXXV, 1946, pp. 177-216
102 *Antecedentes, coincidencias e influencias del arte de Goya,* Madrid, 1947 (v. Bibl. 12)
103 'Miscelánea sobre grabados de Goya', *Archivo Español de Arte,* XXIV, 1951, pp. 93-111
104 *Los Desastres de la Guerra de Goya y sus dibujos preparatorios,* Barcelona, 1952
105 *Les fresques de San Antonio de la Florida à Madrid,* Genève, 1955 and 1965
The frescoes in San Antonio de la Florida in Madrid, Geneva, 1955
Die Fresken von Goya, Genf, 1955
Los frescos de San Antonio de la Florida, Ginebra, 1964
106 *Goya. Gravures et Lithographies. Œuvre complète,* Paris, 1961
Goya, Sämtliche Radierungen und Lithographien, Wien und München 1961
Goya, Complete Etchings, Aquatints and Lithographs, London, 1962
V. Notes I. 184-187, II. 721, 859, III. 1149-1243
Bibl. 10, 12, 20a
Lasso de la Vega — v. Saltillo, Marqués del
Lázaro y Galdiano, José

107 *La Colección Lázaro de Madrid,* Madrid, 1926 (I), 1927 (II)
Levitine, George

108 'Some Emblematic Sources of Goya', *Journal of the Warburg and Courtauld Institutes,* XXII, 1959, pp. 106-131
Loga, Valerian von

109 *Francisco de Goya,* Berlin, 1903
Longhi, Roberto, and Mayer, August L.

110 *Gli Antichi Pittori Spagnoli della Collezione Contini-Bonacossi,* Roma, 1938
López, Padre Don Tomás

111 *Noticias tradicionales de D. F. Goya* — v. Bibl. 190, pp. 462-465
López-Rey, José

112 'A contribution to the study of Goya's art. The San Antonio de la Florida frescoes', *Gazette des Beaux-Arts,* XXV, 1944, pp. 231-248
113 'Goya and the world around him', *Gazette des Beaux-Arts,* XXVIII, 1945, pp. 129-150
114 *Goya y el mundo a su alrededor,* Buenos Aires, 1947
115 *Goya's Caprichos. Beauty, Reason and Caricature,* Princeton, 1953 (I Text, II Plates)
116 *A cycle of Goya's drawings,* London, 1956
117 'Goya and his pupil María del Rosario Weiss', *Gazette des Beaux-Arts,* XLVII, 1956, pp. 251-284
118 'Goya at the London Royal Academy', *Gazette des Beaux-Arts,* LXIII, 1964, pp. 359-369
V. Notes II. 829, III. 875-902, 903-912, 1336, 1354-1367, 1475
[Los Angeles County Museum Bulletin] — v. Notes I. 219-220, II. 829
Lozoya, Marqués de

119 'Goya y Jovellanos', *Boletín de la Real Academia de la Historia,* 1946, pp. 95-103
120 'Algo más sobre Goya en Italia', *Archivo Español de Arte,* XXIX, 1956, pp. 59-66
V. Notes I. 175, 195
Lurie, Ann T. — v. Note II. 713

Madrazo, Pedro de

121 *Viaje Artistico,* Barcelona, 1884
Malraux, André

122 *Dessins de Goya au Musée du Prado,* Genève, 1947
Goya Drawings from the Prado, London, 1947 (with an 'essai de catalogue' by Pierre Gassier)
Mariani, Valerio

123 'Primo Centenario dalla Morte di Francesco Goya —

BIBLIOGRAPHY

Disegni Inediti, *L'Arte*, XXXI, 3, 1928, pp. 97-108

Matheron, Laurent
124 *Goya*, Paris, 1858
125 'Goya', *Artistes contemporains des pays de Guyenne, Béarn, Saintonge et Languedoc... Notices...*, Bordeaux, 1889 (Reprinted in Bibl. 145)

Maule, Nicolás de la Cruz y Bahamonde, Conde de
126 *Viage de España, Francia é Italia*, Cádiz, 1813

Mauquoy-Hendrickx, M. – v. Note II. 771

Mayer, August L.
127 'Dibujos desconocidos de Goya', *Revista Española de Arte*, XI, 1923, pp. 376-384.
128 *Francisco de Goya*, München, 1923; London, 1924; Barcelona, 1925 (The 1924 edition is the one referred to in this book)
129 'Echte und falsche Goya-Zeichnungen', *Belvedere*, 1930, I. pp. 215-217
130 'Some unknown drawings by Francisco Goya', *Old Master Drawings*, IX, 1934-35, pp. 20-21, pl. 21-27
131 'Les tableaux de Goya au Musée d'Agen', *Gazette des Beaux-Arts*, LVII, 1935, pp. 173-178
V. Notes I. 148, 310-311, II. 710, III. 911, IV. 1628a-d, 1642, V. 1785; Bibl. 110

Mélida, José Ramón – v. Note I. 204

Mellerio, André, and Nussac, Louis de
132 'La lithographie en France – Charles de Lasteyrie', *Gazette des Beaux-Arts*, XIV, 1935, pp. 106-119

Milicua, José
133 'Anotaciones al Goya joven', *Paragone*, V, 1954 (Arte), pp. 5-27
V. Notes II. 856-857, 873a

Moratín, Leandro Fernández de
134 *Obras Póstumas*, III, Madrid, 1868 (Correspondance with Juan Antonio Melón, partially reprinted by Beruete, Bibl. 36, I, p. 145, and in translation by Lafond, Bibl. 99)

Mújica Gallo – v. Note V. 1672-1675

Muller, Priscilla E. – v. Note V. 783

Múñoz y Manzano – v. Viñaza, Conde de la

McVan, Alice Jane
135 'The Alameda of the Osunas', *Notes Hispanic*, V, 1945, pp. 113-132

Nordström, Folke
136 *Goya, Saturn and Melancholy*, Stockholm, 1962
V. Notes I. 203, 219-220

Núñez de Arenas, M.
137 'Manojo de noticias – La suerte de Goya en Francia'. *Bulletin Hispanique*, 3, Bordeaux, 1950

Nussac, Louis de – v. Bibl. 132

Oertel, Richard – v. Note II. 791

Olivan Baile, F. – v. Note III. 1541

Ortiz de la Torre, E. – v. Note III. 1538

Paez Ríos, Elena – v. Bibl. 4

Pardo Canalis, Enrique – v. Note II. 738-740

Pérez de Guzman, Juan
138 'Las colecciones de cuadros del Príncipe de la Paz', *La España Moderna*, 140, 1900, pp. 95-126

Pérez Sánchez, Alfonso E.
139 *Catálogo de la Colección de Dibujos del Instituto Jovellanos de Gijón*, Madrid, 1969

Ponz, Antonio
140 *Viage de España*, Madrid, 1772-1794, XVIII vols (Reprinted by Aguilar, Madrid, 1947 – the edition cited in this book)

[Real Academia de Nobles Artes de San Fernando]
141 Preface to the first edition of *Los Desastres de la Guerra* by Goya, Madrid, 1863 (Reprinted in facsimile, with an English translation, in Bibl. 79)

Rodríguez-Moñino, Antonio – v. Note III. 1475

Saint-Paulien
142 *Goya Son Temps Ses Personnages*, Paris, 1965

Salas, Xavier de
143 *Goya: La Familia de Carlos IV*, Barcelona, 1944
144 'Miscelánea Goyesca', *Archivo Español de Arte*, XXIII, 1950, pp. 335-346 ('Goya, pretendiente', pp. 335-337, publishing British Museum MS Egerton 586 on p. 337, n. 6, but taking the reference to the death of Francisco Bayeu (1795) for one to

Ramón (1793); 'Goya y los Vernet: Notas á unos naufragios', pp. 337-346)
145 'El segundo texto de Matheron', *Archivo Español de Arte*, XXXVI, 1963, pp. 297-305 (v. Bibl. 125)
146 'Sobre un autorretrato de Goya y dos cartas inéditas sobre el pintor', *Archivo Español de Arte*, XXXVII, 1964, pp. 317-320
147 'Sur les tableaux de Goya qui appartinrent à son fils', *Gazette des Beaux-Arts*, LXIII, 1964, pp. 99-110
148 'Inventario de las pinturas de la colección de Don Valentín Carderera', *Archivo Español de Arte*, XXXVIII, 1965, pp. 207-227
149 'Precisiones sobre pinturas de Goya: *El Entierro de la Sardina*, la serie de obras de gabinete de 1793-1794 y otras notas', *Archivo Español de Arte*, XLI, 1968, pp.1-16
150 'Una carta de Goya y varios comentarios a la misma', *Arte Español*, XXVI, 1 fasc., 1968-69, pp. 27-28
151 'Inventario. Pinturas elegidas para el Príncipe de la Paz, entre las dejadas por la viuda Chopinot', *Arte Español*, XXVI, 1 fasc., 1968-69, pp. 29-33 (Partially published by Pascual Galindo, 'Goya pintando en el Pilar', *Aragón*, IV, 31, 1928, pp. 152-158, from which it appears that the inventory must date from c.1805)
152 'Sur cinq dessins de Goya au Musée du Prado', *Gazette des Beaux-Arts*, LXXV, 1970, pp. 29-42
V. Notes I. 246, II. 697-707, III. 894, 1196, V. 1830-1841; Bibl. 169

Saltillo, Marqués del
153 *Goya en Madrid: su familia y allegados (1746-1856)*, (Miscelánea Madrileña, Histórica y Artistica. Primer serie), Madrid, 1952
V. Note I. 188-191

Sambricio, Valentín de
154 *Tapices de Goya*, Madrid, 1946
155 *Francisco Bayeu*, Madrid, 1955
156 'Los retratos de Carlos IV y María Luisa, por Goya', *Archivo Español de Arte*, XXX, 1957, pp. 85-113
V. Notes I. 10-16, II. 784-788; Bibl. 23

Sánchez Cantón, F. J.
157 'Goya en la Academia', *Real Academia de Bellas Artes de San Fernando, Primer Centenario de Goya. Discursos...*, Madrid, 1928, pp. 11-23
158 *Los dibujos del viaje a Sanlúcar*, Madrid, 1928
159 *Goya*, Paris, 1930
160 'La estancia de Goya en Italia', *Archivo Español de Arte*, VII, 1931, pp. 182-184
161 'Como vivía Goya', *Archivo Español de Arte*, XIX, 1946, pp. 73-109
162 'Los cuadros de Goya en la Real Academia de la Historia', *Boletín de la Real Academia de la Historia*, 1946, pp. 7-27
163 'Goya, Pintor religioso', *Revista de Ideas Estéticas*, IV, 1946, pp. 277-306
164 'De la estancia bordelesa de Goya', *Archivo Español de Arte*, XX, 1947, pp. 60-63
165 *Los Caprichos de Goya y sus dibujos preparatorios*, Barcelona, 1949
166 *Vida y obras de Goya*, Madrid, 1951
The Life and Works of Goya, Madrid, 1964 (no in-text illustrations; revised chronological list of works)
167 'Goya, refugiado', *Goya*, 3, 1954, pp. 130-135
168 *Museo del Prado: Los dibujos de Goya*, Madrid, 1954 (I Estudios para Los Caprichos, Los Desastres, La Tauromaquia. Caprichos no grabados. II Dibujos para los Disparates. Dibujos no grabados. Estudios para pinturas y varias)
169 *Le Pitture Nere di Goya alla Quinta del Sordo*, Milano, 1963
Goya y sus pinturas negras de la 'Quinta del Sordo', Barcelona, 1963
Goya et ses Peintures Noires à la Quinta del Sordo, Milan et Paris, 1963
Goya and the Black Paintings, London, 1964
V. Notes I. 143-159, II. 690-696, 745, 770, III. 959, 1122, 1549

Sarrailh, Jean
170 *L'Espagne éclairée de la seconde moitié du XVIIIe siècle*, Paris, 1954

Sayre, Eleanor A.
171 'An Old Man Writing – A Study of Goya's Albums'. *Boston Museum Bulletin*, LVI, 1958, pp. 116-136

172 'Eight books of drawings by Goya – I', *Burlington Magazine*, CVI, 1964, pp. 19-30
173 'Goya's Bordeaux miniatures', *Boston Museum Bulletin*, LXIV, 1966, pp. 84-123

Seilern, Count Antoine – v. Note III. 1369

Sentenach, Narciso
174 'Nuevos datos sobre Goya y sus obras', *Historia Arte*, I, 1895, pp. 196-199
175 'Notas sobre la Exposición de Goya', *La España Moderna*, 138, 1900, pp. 34-53
176 *La Pintura en Madrid*, Madrid, 1907 ('Goya', ch XVIII, pp. 203-218; ch. XIX, pp. 219-232)
177 'Goya, Académico', *Boletín de la Real Academia de Bellas Artes de San Fernando*, 1923, vol. 17 p. 170 ff.
V. Notes I. 176, III. 875; Bibl. 32

Sherman Font – v. Font, Eleanor Sherman

Soria, Martin S.
178 'Agustín Esteve and Goya', *Art Bulletin*, XXV, 1943 pp. 239-266.
179 'Las miniaturas y retratos-miniaturas de Goya', *Cobalto*, fasc. 2, 1949, pp. 1-4
180 *Agustín Esteve y Goya*, Valencia, 1957
V. Notes II. 690-696, III. 1546

Starkweather, William E. B.
181 *Paintings and drawings by Francisco Goya in the collection of the Hispanic Society of America*, New York, 1916

Stolz, Ramón
'Goya's fresco technique' – v. Bibl. 105, pp. 135-14

Taylor, René – v. Note II. 708-712

Tello, Joaquín – v. Note IV. 1638

[Time-Life Library of Art]
The World of Goya – v. Note I. 208

Tormo, Elías
182 'Las Pinturas de Goya y su clasificación cronológica', *Varios Estudios de Arte y Letras*, I, nos 1, 2 1902, pp. 200-233 (Reprinted from the *Revista de la Asociación Artístico-Arqueológico Barcelonesa*, 1900)
183 'La Pintura aragonesa cuatrocentista y la Retrospectiva de la Exposición de Zaragoza en general *Boletín de la Sociedad Española de Excursiones*, XVII, 1909, pp. 227-285
184 'Los Goyas del Museo de Agen', *Boletín de Sociedad Española de Excursiones*, XXXVI, 1928 pp. 3-9
185 'El Paraninfo de la Central, antes Templo de Noviciado, Y los muy Nobles Retablo y Sepultur. subsistentes', *Boletín de la Sociedad Española d Excursiones*, XLIX, 1945, pp. 81-135, 171-250
V. Note I. 218

Trapier, Elizabeth du Gué
186 *Eugenio Lucas y Padilla*, New York, 1940
187 *Goya. A study of his portraits 1797-99*, New York 1955
187a 'Unpublished drawings by Goya in the Hispanic Society of America', *Master Drawings*, I, 1963 pp. 11-20, pl. 8-19
188 *Goya and his sitters*, New York, 1964
V. Notes II. 834, III. 1395

Valdeavellano, L. G. – v. Note I. 223-228

Velasco y Aguirre, Miguel
189 *Grabados y Litografías de Goya*, Madrid, [1928]

Viñaza, C. Muñoz y Manzano, Conde de la
190 *Goya: su tiempo, su vida, sus obras*, Madrid, 1887

Weissberger, Herbert
191 'Goya and his handwriting', *Gazette des Beaux-Arts*, XXVIII, 1945, pp. 181-192

Wehle, Harry B.
192 'Fifty Drawings by Francisco Goya', *The Metropolitan Museum of Art. Papers*, no. 7, New York, 1938

Yriarte, Charles
193 *Goya. Sa biographie, les fresques, les toiles, le tapisseries, les eaux-fortes et le catalogue de l'œuvre* Paris, 1867

Zapater y Gómez, Francisco
194 *Goya. Noticias biográficas*, Zaragoza, 1868 (Reprinted in Bibl. 72, pp. 17-49; all references in thi book are to the reprint)

ANALYTICAL INDEX OF WORKS

This index is divided into Paintings, Drawings and Prints.
It groups the works as they appear in the catalogue, with
their corresponding numbers. For the portraits, religious
subjects, historical, mythological and allegorical subjects
and genre scenes, see also the Alphabetical index of works.

For the series of drawings and prints, whose individual
titles do not appear in the Alphabetical index, this index
includes a summary of the technical characteristics by
which they can be identified.

The catalogue numbers are followed by references to
the illustrations and to the relevant pages of text.

PAINTINGS

A total of 688 works in the illustrated catalogue. 82 replicas
cited in the notes.

Portraits

1771-1775	[I.25-28]	
1780-1788	[I.199-233]	Don Luis de Borbón and Osuna families, Bank of Spain, etc.
1789-1792	[I.277-294]	Charles IV and María Luisa
1792-1797	[II.331-355]	The Duchess of Alba, etc.
1797-1799	[II.665-689]	The ilustrados
1799-1808	[II.853-863]	Royal family, Goya's family, bourgeois portraits
1808-1814	[III.875-902]	Afrancesados, Wellington, etc.
1814-1819	[III.1536-1566]	Ferdinand VII, Goya, etc.
1820-1824	[IV.1629-1637]	
1824-1828	[V.1659-1666]	

Ill. pp. 19, 29, 31, 34, 35, 42, 58-65, 103, 104, 107, 109,
114, 115, 123, 133-135, 146, 149-151, 154, 155, 158, 205,
208, 209, 214, 222, 224-226, 229, 246, 247, 301, 304, 307,
334, 337, 352, 353
Text pp. 58, 73, 132, 154, 210, 223, 251, 321, 355 and
passim
Cp. also [III.874, 1534, 1535] and the engravings after
lost portraits [I.312, 314, II.873]
See the Alphabetical index of works: Portraits (in particular
the self-portraits, under Goya y Lucientes, Francisco)

Religious paintings

1763-1771	[I.1-16]	Sobradiel
1772-1775	[I.30-48]	Saragossa, El Pilar (coreto), Aula Dei, etc.
1775-1785	[I.160-195]	Saragossa, El Pilar (cupola); Madrid, San Francisco el Grande, etc.
1785-1788	[I.234-247]	Valladolid, Valencia, etc.
1792-1801	[II.708-740]	Cadiz, Santa Cueva; Madrid, San Antonio de la Florida
1812-1817	[III.1567-1570]	
1819-1824	[IV.1638-1642]	

Ill. pp. 32, 39-41, 52-57, 112, 113, 140-145, 147, 305, 306,
Text pp. 38, 51, 73, 139, 159, 305, 321
See Alphabetical index of works: Religious subjects

History, mythology, allegory

1768-1771	[I.17-24]	
1775-1785	[I.198]	See also [I.167, 169]
1797-1800	[II.690-696]	
1800-1805	[II.745]	
1810-1814	[III.874, 946, 980-984]	

Ill. pp. 20, 37, 136-138, 206, 207, 213, 215
See Alphabetical index of works

Tapestry cartoons

1775-1778	[I.57-69]	Hunting
1776-1778	[I.70-85]	Popular amusements
1778-1780	[I.124-142]	Popular amusements, etc.
1786-1788	[I.256-271]	The Seasons
1788-1789	[I.276]	Blind man's buff
1791-1792	[I.295-306]	Rural subjects

Ill. pp. 15, 43, 44, 46, 47, 66, 69, 70
Text pp. 43-47, 69-71, 73

Genre, figures, various

1775-1785	[I.118-120, 143-159a]	Paintings after Velázquez, children's games, etc.
1786-1787	[I.248-255]	Paintings for La Alameda
1780-1792	[I.307-309]	

1793-1794	[II.317-330]	Cabinet pictures
1795	[II.352-354]	
1797-1798	[II.659-664]	Witchcraft scenes
1797-1810	[II.742-746]	The Majas
1806-1812	[II.864-871]	The Maragato series
1808-1814	[III.914-979]	Still-lifes, pictures in the 1812 inventory, etc., panels in the Academy of San Fernando
c.1815	[III.1534 1535]	Session of the Royal Philippines Company
1820-1824	[IV.1651-1657d]	
1824-1828	[V.1667-1671]	

Cp. also the engraving after a lost work [II.873a]
Ill. frontispiece, pp. 25, 110, 111, 122, 153, 156, 157, 211,
224, 225, 243-245, 248-250, 351
Text pp. 105, 159, 210, 240, 251, 321, 355
See Alphabetical index of works: Genre scenes
See Appendices I and II for the pictures inventoried in
Goya's home in 1812 and 1828

The 'black paintings'

1820-1823 [IV.1615-1627a]
Ill. pp. 23, 314, 316-320. Text p. 313, 321. Appendix VI

Miniatures on copper

1805-1806 [II.844-850] The Goya and Goicoechea
families
Ill. p. 154. Text pp. 154, 156

Miniatures on ivory

1824-1825 [V.1676-1697]
Ill. pp. 342, 343. Text pp. 341, 343, 355

DRAWINGS

A total of 904 works in the illustrated catalogue

Drawings belonging to the 'albums'

Album A (known as the Sanlúcar album)
1796-1797 [II.356-376]
21 known drawings (including 3 or 5 copies). Brush and
Indian ink wash. Maximum sheet size 17·2×10·1 cm.
Drawings recto-verso. No numbers or titles.
Ill. p. 117. Text pp. 117, 160

Album B (known as the Madrid album)
1796-1797 [II.377-450]
74 known drawings. Brush and Indian ink wash (sometimes retouched with the pen and sepia ink). Maximum
sheet size 23·7×14·8 cm. Drawings recto-verso. Numbered
with the brush at the top, to the right (recto) or left (verso).
Highest number: 94. Titles from number 55 on, written with
the brush or pen below or sometimes above the design.
Ill. pp. 118-121, 127. Text pp. 118, 160

Album C
c.1814-1823 [III.1244-1367]
124 known drawings. Brush and Indian ink or sepia wash.
Maximum sheet size 20·8×14·4 cm. Drawings recto only.
Numbered with the brush at top right. Highest number: 133.
Titles in pen and ink or black chalk, usually below the
drawing.
Ill. pp. 237, 239, 301, 302. Text pp. 230, 234-238, 251

Album D
c.1801-1803 [III.1368-1384]
17 known drawings. Brush and Indian ink wash. Maximum
sheet size 23·7×14·7 cm. Drawings recto only. Numbered
with the brush at top centre. Highest number: 22. Titles in
black chalk below.
Ill. p. 231. Text pp. 230, 231, 251
Cp. also [III.1523, 1524]

Album E ('dark border' album)
c.1806-1812 [III.1385-1430]
38 known drawings, plus 3 possible drawings and 5 sketches.
Brush and Indian ink wash. Maximum sheet size 27×19 cm.
Drawings recto only (sometimes with a sketch on the verso).
Numbered with the brush or with pen and sepia ink at top
centre. Highest number: 52. Titles in black chalk below,
usually under the dark border. Single or double border ruled
with the brush and Indian ink (occasionally in sepia).
Ill. pp. 21, 232, 233. Text pp. 230-234, 251
Cp. also [III.1525]

Album F
c.1812-1823 [III.1431-1518]
88 known drawings. Brush and sepia wash. Maximum
sheet size 21×15 cm. Drawings recto only. Numbered with
the brush or pen at top right. Highest number: 106. No titles
(except nos 16, 38, 86?).
Ill. pp. 234-236, 241, 303. Text pp. 230, 238, 251
Cp. also [III.1522]

Album G
1824-1828 [V.1711-1764]
54 known drawings. Black chalk and lithographic crayon.
Maximum sheet size 19·3×15·3 cm. Drawings recto only.
Numbered at top right. Highest number: 60. Titles below.
Ill. pp. 335, 336, 339, 354. Text pp. 339, 344, 355

Album H
1824-1828 [V.1765-1822]
58 known drawings. Black chalk and lithographic crayon.
Maximum sheet size 19·5×15·6 cm. Drawings recto only.
Numbered at top right. Highest number: 63. No titles
(except nos 40, 41, 45, 53, 54) but almost all signed.
Ill. pp. 340, 341. Text pp. 344, 355

Preparatory drawings for the engravings and lithographs

Drawings for the Copies after Velázquez
1778 [I.88-113]
13 known drawings. Various techniques.
Ill. p. 50. Text pp. 48-50, 73

Drawings for Los Caprichos
1797-1798 [II.451-621]
82 known drawings for 85 plates. Pen and sepia ink,
sometimes with Indian ink wash, or red chalk or sanguine
wash.
Ill. p. 127. Text pp. 125-131, 160

Drawings for the Caprichos which were not engraved and
drawings connected with the Caprichos
1797-1798 [II.622-647] and [II.648-658]
38 drawings. The same techniques as the drawings for
Los Caprichos

Drawings for Los Desastres de la Guerra and additional
drawings
1810-1823 [III.993-1148]
73 known drawings. Red chalk (except for a few drawn
with the pen or brush in sepia ink).
Text p. 252

Drawings for La Tauromaquia
1815-1816 [III.1149-1243]
50 known drawings. Red chalk (4 with the addition of
sanguine wash).
Text p. 252

Drawings for Los Disparates or Los Proverbios and
additional drawings
1815-1824 [IV.1571-1613]
20 known drawings. Brush and sanguine wash over red
chalk
Ill. p. 311. Text p. 322. Cp. also [III.1532]

Drawings for various engravings
Religious subjects [I.54, 56] Ill. p. 42
The garrotted man [I.123]
Landscapes [II.749, 751]
Dios se lo pague a usted [II.773]
Prisoners [III.987, 989, 991, 992]
Cp. also [V.1785, 1793, 1816]

ALPHABETICAL INDEX OF WORKS

Drawings for lithographs
1819   [IV.1646, 1647, 1649]
Text p. 322. Cp. also [III.1526]

Other drawings

Drawings for the tapestry cartoons
1775   [I.62, 64, 65, 67]
1776-1778   [I.71-73, 75, 86]
III. p. 46. Text p. 73

Drawings for paintings
Portraits   [III.898, 899, 1559]
Religious subjects   [I.32, 33, 193, 242, 245, 247]
History, allegory, genre, etc.   [I.196, 197, II.642, 643, III.971]   III. p. 136. Cp. also [III.1314, 1472]

Drawings for the *Dictionary* of Ceán Bermúdez
1798-1799   [II.697-707]
11 known drawings. Red chalk. Inscriptions by Goya in red chalk, sometimes traced over in pen and ink.
III. p. 136

Drawings after Flaxman
c.1800-1808   [II.760-765]
6 known drawings. Brush and Indian ink. Sheet size approx. 19·5×27 cm.

Various portraits
[I.289]
[II.769-771, 779, 780, 806, 840-843]
[III.898, 899, 1559, 1562]
[IV.1634, 1635 note, 1636]
[V.1658]
III. pp. 154, 246, 333
Cp. also the portraits for the *Dictionary* of Ceán Bermúdez (see above) and the lost drawings (see below). Cp. also the Alphabetical index of works: Portraits.

Various drawings
Studies from the model   [I.310, 311]
Symbolic drawings, physiognomic studies   [II.648-658, IV.1613]
Landscapes, balloons, architecture, various   [II.752-759, 766-768]

Drawings connected with albums C to F   [III.1519-1532]
Various 1824-1828   [V.1830-1841]
Drawings by Goya and/or Rosario Weiss
c.1821-1826   [V.1842-1870]
III. p. 338. Text p. 355

Lost drawings (known from prints)
[I.313, 315, 316, II.872, IV.1637]
Cp. also the copies by Weiss after drawings by Goya (see above)

ENGRAVINGS AND LITHOGRAPHS

A total of 290 prints – 272 engravings and 18 lithographs – in the illustrated catalogue. The preparatory drawings (see under DRAWINGS) are reproduced after the respective prints. The copperplates of the five series and a few of the single prints are in the Calcografía Nacional, Madrid.

Copies after Velázquez
1778-1779   [I.88-112]
13 engravings published in 1778-79 (and 4 which were not published). 4 editions of the equestrian portraits and 3 of the other subjects printed between 1778 and 1930. Etching with or without aquatint. Maximum plate size 38×31 cm. (equestrian portraits) or 30·5×22 cm. (for the other portraits). Titles engraved below the design.
III. pp. 49, 50. Text pp. 48-50, 73

Los Caprichos
1797-1799   [II.451-621]
80 engravings published in 1799 (and 5 which were not published). 12 editions printed between 1799 and 1937. Etching and aquatint (plates *32* and *39* in aquatint only). Plate size approx. 21·5×15 cm.
Engraved numbers and titles
III. pp. 17, 125, 127, 128, 130, 131. Text pp. 125-131, 160

Los Desastres de la Guerra
1810-1823   [III.993-1148]
82 engravings, of which 80 were published in 1863. 7 editions printed between 1863 and 1937. Etching and aquatint or lavis. Maximum plate size 17·5×22 cm. Engraved numbers

and titles (first number at lower left, final number at top left)
III. pp. 216, 218-221. Text pp. 217-221, 252

La Tauromaquia
1815-1816   [III.1149-1243]
33 engravings published in 1816. 7 additional engraving first published in 1876 (A-G). 5 engravings remaine unpublished [H-L]. 7 editions printed between 1816 an 1937. Etching and aquatint or lavis. Plate size approx 25×35 cm. Numbers engraved by Goya; letters A-C engraved by Loizelet. Titles of plates *1* to *33* according t the list published with the first edition; of plates A-C according to the French titles published with Loizelet edition.
III. pp. 123, 228, 229. Text pp. 227-229, 252

Los Disparates or *Los Proverbios*
1815-1824   [IV.1571-1604]
22 engravings of which 18 were published in 186 (9 editions between 1864 and 1937) and 4 were publishe in the French periodical *L'Art* in 1877. Etching and aquatin 24·5×35 cm. Numbers engraved on the 18 plates for th second edition. Titles engraved on the 4 plates for th *L'Art* edition.
III. pp. 309, 311, 312. Text pp. 309-312, 321

Various engravings
Religious subjects   [I.52, 53, 55]
The blind guitarist   [I.87]   III. p. 48
The garrotted man   [I.122]
Arms of Jovellanos   [II.747]   III. p. 132
Landscapes   [II.748, 750]   III. p. 216
Dios se lo pague a usted   [II.772]
The colossus   [III.985]
Prisoners   [III.986, 988, 990]
Engravings from album H   [V.1823-1828]   III. p. 349
The blind singer   [V.1829]

Lithographs
1819   [IV.1643-1645, 1648, 1650]
III. p. 308. Text pp. 308, 322
1824-1825   [V.1698-1710]
III. pp. 345, 347, 348. Text pp. 345-349, 355

ALPHABETICAL INDEX OF WORKS AND SUBJECT INDEX

PORTRAITS, RELIGIOUS SUBJECTS, HISTORICAL, MYTHOLOGICAL AND ALLEGORICAL SUBJECTS, GENRE SCENES

The index includes all the works in these categories which are cited in the catalogue and the notes (references to the notes are preceded by the letter 'N'). The article before a common noun is omitted in the titles. The numbers in italics indicate drawings and prints.

PORTRAITS

Abrantes, Duquesa de   [III.1560]   III. p. 64
Acedo, Diego de   [I.*105, 106*]
Alba, Duque de   [II.349, 350]
Alba, Duquesa de   [II.351, 352, 355, *356, 358, 360, 372, 374, 759*]   III. pp. 115, 117   V. also [II.*573, 619, 620*]
Altamira, Conde de   [I.225]   III. p. 61
Altamira, Condesa de (and her daughter María Agustina) [I.232]
Altamirano   [II.667]
Álvarez Coiñas de Ferrer, Manuela   [V.1660]   V. also Ferrer, Joaquín María (her husband)
Arbasia, Cesar   [II.698]
Arias de Enríquez, Tadea   [II.336]
Arias de Saavedra, Juan José   [II.347]
Arrieta   [IV.1629]   III. p. 307
Asensio – v. Juliá
Azara, Félix de   [II.826]
Baena, Condesa de   [III.1563]
Bailó, wife of Antonio   N.[II.835]
Bajamar, Marqués de   [I.314]
Baltasar Carlos, prince   [I.*95, 117*]   III. p. 49
Barañana de Goicoechea, Narcisa   [III.889]   V. also Goicoechea, Juan Bautista (her husband)
Baruso Valdés, María Vicenta   [II.830]   V. also Valdés de Baruso (her mother)
Bayeu, Francisco   [I.199, 229, II.345]   III. p. 42
Bayeu de Goya, Josefa   [II.686(?), *840*]   III. p. 246   V. also Goya y Lucientes (her husband)
Benavente – v. Osuna

Berganza, Luis   [II.353]
Bonaparte, Joseph (I of Spain) – v.[III.874]
Bondad Real, Marqués de   [II.683]
Bonells de Costa, Fernanda   [III.894]   V. also Costa y Bonells (her son)
BORBÓN (family of Charles IV)   III. pp. 149, 150-151
Carlos María Isidro   [II.783, 784]
María Josefa   [II.783, 785]
Francisco de Paula Antonio   [II.783, 786]
Antonio Pascual   [II.783, 787]
Luis, prince of Parma   [II.783, 788]
Ferdinand, prince of Asturias   [II.783, 791]   V. also Ferdinand VII
María Isabel   [II.783, 792]
V. also Charles IV, María Luisa
Borbón, Infante Don Luis Antonio de   [I.206, 208, 212, 213]; N. [206-212]   III. p. 60.   V. also Vallabriga (his wife)
Borbón y Vallabriga, Luis María de (Cardinal)   [I.208, 209, II.794, 795]   III. p. 60
Borbón y Vallabriga, María Teresa de (Condesa de Chinchón)   [I.208, 210, II.793]   III. pp. 19, 59, 60.
Borgia or Borja – v. RELIGIOUS: St Francis Borgia
Bravo de Rivero, Tadeo   [II.854]
Caballero, José Antonio, Marqués de   [II.861]
Caballero, Marquesa de   [II.860]
Cabarrús, Conde de   [I.228]   III. p. 61
Cabrera, Ramón   [II.873]
Candado, Joaquina   [II.809]
Cano, Alonso   [II.*699*]
Carlos, Infante Don   [I.*116*]
Carpio – v. Solana
Casti, J. B.   [II.770]
Castilla Portugal de Garcini, Josefa   [II.821]   V. also Garcini (her husband)
Castro – v. Pérez de Castro
Castrofuerte, Marqués de   [II.823]
Castrofuerte, Marquesa de   [II.822]
Cayetano Soler, Miguel   [II.806]
Ceán Bermúdez, Juan Agustín   [I.222, II.334, *697*]   III. p. 136

Ceán Bermúdez, wife of (?)   [II.335]
Céspedes, Pablo de   [II.*700*]
Charles III   [I.18, 224, 230]   III. p. 31   V. also [I.18
Charles IV   [I.279, 281, 283, 285, 287, *289*, II.774, 776, 779, 780, 782, 783, 789]   III. pp. 104, 149, 150-151   V also *Borbón*, María Luisa
Chinchón, Condesa de   [II.793]   III. p. 19   V. als Borbón y Vallabriga
Chollet y Caballero, Francisca Vicenta   [II.853]
Cistué, José, Barón de la Menglana   [I.294]
Cistué, Luis María de   [I.293]
Cobos de Porcel – v. Porcel
Colón de Larriategui, Félix   [II.339]
Company, Archbishop Joaquín   [II.798-800]; N.[II.794]
Correa, Lorenza   [II.836]
Costa y Bonells, Pepito   [III.895]   III. p. 208   V. als Bonells de Costa (his mother)
Cuervo, Juan Antonio   [III.1561]
Cuervo – v. Pérez y Cuervo, Tiburcio
Duaso y Latre, José   [IV.1633]
Erasmus of Rotterdam   [II.*771*]
Espoz y Mina, Francisco   N.[III.1546]
Esteve, Rafael   [III.1550]   III. p. 229
Felipe – v. Philip
Ferdinand VII   [II.783, 791, III.875, 876, *877*, 1536-1541 V. also [III.1534]   III. pp. 222, 224, 225   V. also Ferdi nand, prince of Asturias under *Borbón*
Fernán Núñez, Conde de   [II.808]
Fernán Núñez, Condesa de   [II.807]
Fernández, Luis   [II.*701*]
Fernández, María del Rosario ('La Tirana')   [II.340, 684
Fernández de Moratín, Leandro   [II.685, V.1661]   II pp. 135, 334
Fernández de Rojas, Friar Juan   [III.1555, *1562*]
Fernández Flores, Friar Miguel   [III.1548]
Fernando, Infante Don   [I. *97, 98*]   III. p. 50
Fernando – v. Ferdinand
Ferrer, Joaquín María de   [V.1659]   V. also Alváre Coiñas de Ferrer (his wife)
Ferrer, Mariano   [I.216]
Flores – v. Fernández Flores

Strolling players [II.325] III. p. 110 V. also [III.1435, 1487] and Fair
Sueño (Dream) [II.426, 477, 536-538, 572, 578, 582, 584, 588, 590, 592, 593, 619, 620, 625, 627, III.1297, 1374, 1378, V.1720] III. pp. 125, 131, 231 V. also Nightmare, Visions
Swing [I.131, 249, II.391, 640, V.1816, 1825, 1826] III. p. 349 V. also [V.1782]
Teacher [II.522, 584, 587, III.1389] V. also School-master
Telescope – v. Spy-glass
Tobacco guard [I.147, II.446, 472, 473]
Torture [I.122, 123, III.1047-1050, 1270, 1321-1339, 1477, V.1753, 1754] III. pp. 237, 239, 303

Transport – v. [V.1719] and Animals: Donkeys, Horses, Ram; Balloons, Carriages, Flying figures
Transporting a stone [I.252]
Vendor – v. Seller
Village on fire [III.947]
Visions [III.1277-1285] V. also N.[III.1475]
War and violence [III.918, 921-927, 930-932, 936-946, 980-984] III. pp. 20, 211, 213, 216, 218-220 V. also Bandits, Desastres de la Guerra, Executions, Fights, Garrotting, Hanging, Kidnap, Murder, Rape
Warrior N.[IV.1601]
Washerwomen [I.132, 146, II.411, III.962, 1406, V.1847]

III. pp. 21, 243
Water-carriers [I.114, 295, 300, III.963, 1314] III. p. 245 V. also [I.85, 86, 87], ill. p. 47
Wedding – v. Marriage
Wine vendor [I.309]
Witchcraft, witches [II.416, 417, 531, 539-613 passim, 625, 626, 640-642, 659-664, III.1305-1307, 1368-1370, 1374, 1522, IV.1615, 1620, 1623, 1652, V.1782, 1788, 1789] III. pp. 23, 120, 122, 128, 231 V. also Aquelarre
Wood-cutters [I.139]
Writers and poets [II.432, 528, III.1264, 1350] III. p. 30 V. also N.[IV.1622]
Young women ('Les jeunes') [III.962) III. p. 243

INDEX OF COLLECTIONS

The names of museums, abbreviated or given in translation in the catalogue, are given here in full, in their original language. Names of private collectors, given in full in the catalogue, are cited here without their titles of nobility or the particle 'de'.

This index includes some 1750 paintings and drawings referred to in the illustrated catalogue and the notes. The roman figures indicate the five parts of the catalogue. Figures in italics indicate drawings, engravings and lithographs. The letter 'N' indicates a reference to the notes.

Where the engravings and lithographs are concerned, only the proof states mentioned in the catalogue or illustrated in the text are included in this index. For a detailed list of proof states in public collections, see Harris (Bibl. 88, II, Appendix VII, pp. 451-454).

EUROPE

AUSTRIA

Wien (Vienna)
Albertina [III.1421]
Kunsthistorisches Museum, Neue Galerie N. [III.968]
Eissler (formerly) N. [II.671, III.918]
Kaunitz (formerly) N. [III.963, 964]
Miethke (formerly) N. [III.947]

BELGIUM

Private collection [II.441/442]

CZECHOSLOVAKIA

Praha (Prague)
Národní Galerie (National Gallery) [III.1546] III. p. 226

DENMARK

København (Copenhagen)
Statens Museum for Kunst [III.913]

FRANCE

Agen
Musée d'Agen (legs Chaudordy) [I.201, III.876, 956, 975]; N. [II.354, III.956]
Bayonne
Musée Bonnat [II.681, III.1426, 1427, 1557, IV.1639]
Besançon
Musée des Beaux-Arts [III.922, 923, IV.1657a-d]
Bordeaux
Musée des Beaux-Arts [V.1706]
Castres
Musée Goya [II.680, III.1534, 1554]; N. [III.950] III. p. 225
Lille
Musée des Beaux-Arts [III.961, 962] III. p. 243
Private collection [II.425/426] III. p. 118
Paris
Bibliothèque Nationale, Cabinet des Estampes [II.614, 618, III.985]; N. [IV.1637]
Musée des Beaux-Arts de la Ville de Paris (Coll. Dutuit), Petit Palais [III.1233, 1237, 1241]
Musée du Louvre (and Cabinet des Dessins) [II.341, 419/420, 421/422, 677, 707, 815, III.890, 903, 1368, 1375, 1379, 1396]; N. [II.678, III.978] III. pp. 121, 134, 136, 248
Fondation Custodia (Coll. F. Lugt), Institut Néerlandais [III.1424/1425]
Galerie espagnole du Louvre — v. Louis-Philippe
Ambassade d'Espagne N. [I.282, III.967]
Barroilhet (formerly) N. [III.932]

Beurdeley, A. (formerly) [III.1428]; N. [III.1415, 1429, IV.1583]
Bismarck [II.853] V. also New York, Metropolitan Mus.
Burty, Philippe (formerly) N. [V.1774, 1785]
Calando, E. (formerly) N. [III.1412, 1463, 1481, 1499, 1501, 1504, 1507, 1509, 1512, 1518, V.1728, 1746, 1839]
Candamo (formerly) N. [II.317, 322]
Caumartin (or Comartin, formerly) N. [III.957]
David-Weill [II.678, III.907]; N. [II.726]
Demotte (formerly) N. [I.78]
Doria (formerly; sold in Paris 1899) N. [III.1428]
Durand-Ruel (formerly) N. [II.668, III.959]
Edwards (formerly; sold in Paris 1905) N. [V.1672-1675]
Flers [III.893]
Ganay (formerly) N. [III.880]
Gasc (formerly) N. [V.1711, 1744]
Goupil et Cie (formerly) N. [I.258, II.844]
Groult (formerly) N. [III.959, 960, 976, 977]
Gunzburg [III.1420] III. p. 232
Heseltine, J. P. (formerly) N. [III.1468]
Kann, Alphonse N. [IV.1628a-d]
Kleinberger (formerly) [II.712]
Lafond, Paul (formerly) N. [I.32]
Leeb, Nat N. [III.930]
Lefèvre-Bougon (formerly) N. [II.326]
Lefort, Paul (formerly) N. [II.322, III.1233, IV.1644]
Le Garrec (heirs) V. text to catalogue [IV.1601-1604]
Louis-Philippe (formerly) N. [I.230, II.355, III.957-965, 959, 961, 962, 965]
Meurice, Paul (formerly) N. [III.1422]
Neumans, G. N. [II.809]
Niarchos, Stavros S. N. [II.809]
Noailles (heirs) [II.836, 851, 852]
Oppenheimer, S. (formerly) N. [II.863]
Sachs, Arthur (formerly) [II.682] III. p. 146
Saint-Victor, Paul (formely) N. [IV.1639]
Stchoukine (formerly) N. [III.931, 936-944, 941, IV.1639]
Thierry-Delanoue N. [II.317]
Yriarte, Charles (formerly) [III.1158]
Private collections [I.7, 8, 17-20, 24, 149, 213, II.317, 368-371, 415/416, 439/440, 658, 764, 767, 832, 833, 844, 845, III.880, 1386, 1387, 1398, 1406, 1411-1413, 1422, 1468, 1481, 1482, 1499, 1501, 1504, 1507, 1509, 1512, 1514, 1519, IV.1628a, V.1724, 1728, 1734, 1736, 1738, 1745-1747, 1781, 1788, 1798, 1810, 1838, 1839, 1858/1859, 1863]; N.[I.287, 288] III. pp. 119, 120, 154, 235, 241, 335, 336, 339, 340, 341
Strasbourg
Musée des Beaux-Arts [II.669] III. p. 109
Private collections [III.937, 941, 1391]; N. [III.931, 944, 970, V.1786] III. p. 232

GERMANY

Bayern (Bavaria)
Private collection [II.860]
Berlin
Kaiser Friedrich Museum [III.1556 destroyed]
Staatliche Museen Preussischer Kulturbesitz (DBR), Kupferstichkabinett [I.111, III.1374, 1380, 1392, 1407, 1416, 1469, 1497, 1506, 1535, IV.1650, V.1698, 1814]; N. [V.1711, 1744] III. pp. 231, 233
Staatliche Museen zu Berlin (DDR), National-Galerie N. [III.951, V.1672-1675]
Gerstenberg, Otto (formerly) – works presumed destroyed [III.1483, 1528, 1531, V.1712, 1713, 1722, 1729, 1732, 1739, 1741-1743, 1750, 1752-1754, 1760, 1762, 1764, 1779, 1783, 1786, 1787, 1792, 1794, 1801, 1802, 1806, 1808, 1809, 1817, 1819, 1821, 1822, 1837]; v. also N. [V. 1711-1822, 1765-1822, 1794]

Bremen
Kunsthalle [III.1558 destroyed]
Dresden
Staatliche Kunstsammlungen, Kupferstichkabinett [V.1685, 1686] III. p. 342
Frankfurt am Main
Städelsches Kunstinstitut [III.930, 931]
Jay (formerly) N. [I.313]
Hamburg
Kunsthalle [I.98, 100, 110, 113-117, II.377/378, 405/406, 755, 804, III.899, 1207, 1215, 1228, 1240] III. p. 5
Karlsruhe
Staatliche Kunsthalle [III.888]
Kassel
Kleinschmidt (formerly) N. [III.976]
Köln (Cologne)
Lempertz N. [II.710]
Böhler, Julius (formerly) N. [III.930, 931, 934]
München (Munich)
Alte Pinakothek [I.211] (Bayerische Hypotheken und Wechsel-Bank Coll.), [II.802, III.906, IV.1651-1654]; v. also [V.1665]
Private coll. (DBR) [I.52]; N. [II.748, 750, V.1699, 1704]

GREAT BRITAIN

Banbury
Upton House (Bearsted Coll.) N. [I.229]
Barnard Castle (Co. Durham)
Bowes Museum [II.670, III.929]; N. [II.317-330] III. p. 135
Cambridge
Fitzwilliam Museum [V.1723, 1756, 1770]
Edinburgh
National Gallery [I.142]
Glasgow
Pollok House, Stirling Maxwell Coll. [I.154, 155]
London
British Museum
Department of Prints and Drawings [I.107, 123, II.779, III.898, 1324, 1475, 1563, IV.1646, V.1701, 1702, 1774]; N. [V.1785] III. p. 348
Department of Manuscripts Egerton 585, folios 74-7? Appendix IV III. pp. 108, 110. N. [III.1569]
Library N. [I.289]
Courtauld Institute Galleries [II.676]
National Gallery [I.274, II.663, 673, 817, III.897]; N. [II.743 and 744] III. pp. 158, 214
Victoria and Albert Museum [I.106]
Wellington Museum (Apsley House) Victoria and Albert Museum Coll. [III.896]; N. [I.114, 120]
Calmann, H. M. (formerly) [II.698]
Clark [IV.1676]
Frankfort Harris, E. [II.704]
Mond (heirs) [V.1755]
Oppenheimer (formerly) N. [III.1455]
Rudolf, C. R. [II.702, 703]
Sebba, S. [V.1682]
Seilern [III.1369]
Private collections [I.235, II.447/448, IV.1649, V.1757]
Hertfordshire
Private collection [I.261]
Luton Hoo
Wernher N. [II.351]
Oxford
Ashmolean Museum [III.1478, V.1674, 1675]
Tisbury (Wilts.)
Margadale N. [I.230]
Private collections [I.219, II.778, V.1668, 1669, 1693] III. p. 351

NDEX OF NAMES

The page numbers in italics indicate illustrations. The numbers in square brackets, preceded by the letter 'N', refer to the notes to the catalogue. The index to the notes does not include references to the authors of works cited (see Bibliography) or to the collections to which the paintings and drawings formerly belonged (see Index of collections). For a complete list of the names of Goya's sitters, see the Alphabetical index of works: Portraits.

PHOTOGRAPHERS

The photographs and ektachromes of the works reproduced in the text were made by:
Brennwasser, New York, p 342 [1690]
Cooper, London, p. 351 [1668]
Freeman, London, pp.17, 49, 50 [97], 129, 216 [1013, 1044], 218 [995, 1000], 219 [1029, 1053], 220 [996, 1084], 221 [1076, 1126], 228 [1171, 1188, 1210, 1227], 229 [1192, 1206], 312 [1585], 313
Giraudon, Paris, p 243
Hinz, Basle, pp. 119, 120 [416], 141, 142, 143, 154 [844], 235, 241 [1512, 1514] 335, 336, 339 [1738], 340, 341
Jack Photo, Castres, pp. 224, 225
Kiely, Jr, West Hartford (Conn.), p. 345
Kleinhempel, Hamburg, p. 50 [98]
Knoedler, New York, p. 209
Lindsey, San Francisco, p. 118 [438]
Magallon, Madrid, pp. 103, 117 [356], 131 [619], 132, 308, 338 [1856]

Manso, Madrid, pp. 42 [229], 43 [137], 44, 46 [75], 47, 64, 70 [266, 301], 104, 110 [325], 117 [360], 122, 127, 135 [685], 136 [642, 697], 138, 149, 205, 206, 214 [901], 222, 226 [1545], 234, 237 [1321, 1330], 239, 301 [1350], 302, 306, 318, 320, 333, 338 [1868], 354
Mas, Barcelona, pp. 31, 32, 34, 37, 40, 55, 60, 110 [319], 112, 113, 139, 144, 154 [841, 842], 211, 299 [1550], 246, 250, 305, 334
Moreno, Madrid, pp. 42 (document), 63, 110 [322], 140, 145
Nahmias, Poissy, p. 232 [1420]
Oronoz, Madrid, frontispiece, pp. 15, 19, 20, 23, 25, 29, 39, 41, 42 [54], 43 [133], 46 [74], 52, 53, 54, 56 [236], 57, 58, 61, 65, 66-67, 69, 70 [257], 133, 147, 150-151, 153, 207, 213, 215, 240, 247, 309, 311 [1592], 314, 316, 319
Photo Studios Ltd, London, pp. 56 [237], 245
Service de documentation photographique des Musées

nationaux, Versailles, pp. 121 [420], 134, 136 [707], 248
Steinkopf, Berlin, p. 233
Warburg Institute, London, pp. 125, 128, 130, 131, 349

Thanks are also due to the various museums for the photographs and ektachromes which they made available.

For the illustrations in the catalogue, the photographs were obtained mainly from the following sources: Archivo Mas in Barcelona, Archivo Moreno, Magallon, Manso and Oronoz in Madrid as well as the photographic studios attached to the various museums and institutes. Photographs were also obtained from Butler and Freeman in London, Bulloz and Giraudon in Paris, Nahmias in Poissy, Prunet in Agen, Hinz in Basle.